The Oxford Handbook of the Development of Play

OXFORD LIBRARY OF PSYCHOLOGY

OXFORD LIBRARY OF PSYCHOLOGY

Editor-in-Chief PETER E. NATHAN

The Oxford Handbook of the Development of Play

Edited by

Anthony D. Pellegrini

OXFORD
UNIVERSITY PRESS

OXFORD
UNIVERSITY PRESS

Oxford University Press is a department of the University of Oxford.
It furthers the University's objective of excellence in research, scholarship,
and education by publishing worldwide.

Oxford   New York
Auckland   Cape Town   Dar es Salaam   Hong Kong   Karachi
Kuala Lumpur   Madrid   Melbourne   Mexico City   Nairobi
New Delhi   Shanghai   Taipei   Toronto

With offices in
Argentina   Austria   Brazil   Chile   Czech Republic   France   Greece
Guatemala   Hungary   Italy   Japan   Poland   Portugal   Singapore
South Korea   Switzerland   Thailand   Turkey   Ukraine   Vietnam

Oxford is a registered trade mark of Oxford University Press
in the UK and certain other countries.

Published in the United States of America by
Oxford University Press
198 Madison Avenue, New York, NY 10016

Library of Congress Cataloging-in-Publication Data

The Oxford handbook of the development of play / edited by Anthony D. Pellegrini.
    p. cm. – (Oxford library of psychology)
  Includes bibliographical references and index.
  ISBN 978-0-19-539300-2 (hardcover); 978-0-19-024704-1 (paperback)
  1. Play–Psychological aspects–Handbooks, manuals, etc. 2. Developmental psychology–
Handbooks, manuals, etc. 3. Child psychology–Handbooks, manuals, etc.
  I. Pellegrini, Anthony D. II. Title: Handbook of the development of play.
  BF717.O94 2010
  155.4'18–dc22
                                                                      2010021514

9 8 7 6 5 4 3 2 1

Printed in the United States of America
on acid-free paper

CONTENTS

Oxford Library of Psychology   vii

About the Editor   ix

Contributors   xi

Table of Contents   xiii

Chapters   1–366

Index   367

OXFORD LIBRARY OF PSYCHOLOGY

The *Oxford Library of Psychology*, a landmark series of handbooks, is published by Oxford University Press, one of the world's oldest and most highly respected publishers, with a tradition of publishing significant books in psychology. The ambitious goal of the *Oxford Library of Psychology* is nothing less than to span a vibrant, wide-ranging field and, in so doing, to fill a clear market need.

Encompassing a comprehensive set of handbooks, organized hierarchically, the *Library* incorporates volumes at different levels, each designed to meet a distinct need. At one level are a set of handbooks designed broadly to survey the major subfields of psychology; at another are numerous handbooks that cover important current focal research and scholarly areas of psychology in depth and detail. Planned as a reflection of the dynamism of psychology, the *Library* will grow and expand as psychology itself develops, thereby highlighting significant new research that will impact on the field. Adding to its accessibility and ease of use, the *Library* will be published in print and, later on, electronically.

The *Library* surveys psychology's principal subfields with a set of handbooks that capture the current status and future prospects of those major subdisciplines. This initial set includes handbooks of social and personality psychology, clinical psychology, counseling psychology, school psychology, educational psychology, industrial and organizational psychology, cognitive psychology, cognitive neuroscience, methods and measurements, history, neuropsychology, personality assessment, developmental psychology, and more. Each handbook undertakes to review one of psychology's major subdisciplines with breadth, comprehensiveness, and exemplary scholarship. In addition to these broadly-conceived volumes, the *Library* also includes a large number of handbooks designed to explore in depth more specialized areas of scholarship and research, such as stress, health and coping, anxiety and related disorders, cognitive development, or child and adolescent assessment. In contrast to the broad coverage of the subfield handbooks, each of these latter volumes focuses on an especially productive, more highly focused line of scholarship and research. Whether at the broadest or most specific level, however, all of the *Library* handbooks offer synthetic coverage that reviews and evaluates the relevant past and present research and anticipates research in the future. Each handbook in the *Library* includes introductory and concluding chapters written by its editor to provide a roadmap to the handbook's table of contents and to offer informed anticipations of significant future developments in that field.

An undertaking of this scope calls for handbook editors and chapter authors who are established scholars in the areas about which they write. Many of the nation's and world's most productive and best-respected psychologists have agreed to edit *Library* handbooks or write authoritative chapters in their areas of expertise.

For whom has the *Oxford Library of Psychology* been written? Because of its breadth, depth, and accessibility, the *Library* serves a diverse audience, including graduate students in psychology and their faculty mentors, scholars, researchers, and practitioners in psychology and related fields. Each will find in the *Library* the information they seek on the subfield or focal area of psychology in which they work or are interested.

Befitting its commitment to accessibility, each handbook includes a comprehensive index, as well as extensive references to help guide research. And because the *Library* was designed from its inception as an online as well as a print resource, its structure and contents will be readily and rationally searchable online. Further, once the *Library* is released online, the handbooks will be regularly and thoroughly updated.

In summary, the *Oxford Library of Psychology* will grow organically to provide a thoroughly informed perspective on the field of psychology, one that reflects both psychology's dynamism and its increasing interdisciplinarity. Once published electronically, the *Library* is also destined to become a uniquely valuable interactive tool, with extended search and browsing capabilities. As you begin to consult this handbook, we sincerely hope you will share our enthusiasm for the more than 500-year tradition of Oxford University Press for excellence, innovation, and quality, as exemplified by the *Oxford Library of Psychology*.

Peter E. Nathan
Editor-in-Chief
Oxford Library of Psychology

ABOUT THE EDITOR

Anthony D. Pellegrini

Anthony D. Pellegrini, Ph.D., began the study of play over 30 years ago. During that time he explored the relatively unconnected research in ethology and developmental psychology; it quickly became clear to him that play was, in many ways, a paradigm example of developmental (both phylogenetic and ontogenetic) processes at work. To this end, he has been studying the development and functions of different forms of play in children's lives. Dr. Pellegrini is Professor Emeritus of Educational Psychology at the University of Minnesota.

CONTRIBUTORS

Daryaneh Badaly
Department of Psychology
University of Southern California
Los Angeles, CA

Ed Baines
Psychology and Human Development
 Institute of Education
University of London
London, UK

Patrick Bateson
Department of Zoology
University of Cambridge
Cambridge, UK

Laura Berk
Department of Psychology
Illinois State University
Normal, IL

David F. Bjorklund
Department of Psychology
Florida Atlantic University
Boca Raton, FL

Peter Blatchford
Psychology and Human Development
 Institute of Education
University of London
London, UK

Jill R. Brown
Department of Psychology
Creighton University
Omaha, NE

Gordon M. Burghardt
Departments of Psychology and Ecology
 & Evolutionary Biology
University of Tennessee
Knoxville, TN

Carmel Conn
Graduate School of Education
University of Bristol
Bristol, UK

Robert J. Coplan
Department of Psychology
Carleton University
Ottawa, Ontario

Howard P. Chudacoff
Department of History
Brown University
Providence, RI

Richard A. Fabes
School of Social and Family Dynamics
Arizona State University
Tempe, AZ

Robert M. Fagen
University of Alaska Southeast
Juneau, AK

Kelly Fisher
Department of Psychology
Temple University
Philadelphia, PA

Lia B. L. Freitas
Institute of Psychology
Federal University of Rio Grande do Sul
Porto Alegre, Brazil

Amy K. Gardiner
Department of Psychology
Florida Atlantic University
Boca Raton, FL

Suzanne Gaskins
Department of Psychology
Northeastern Illinois University
Chicago, IL

Jeffrey Goldstein
Research Institute for History and Culture
University of Utrecht
Utrecht, The Netherlands

Roberta M. Golinkoff
School of Education
University of Delaware
Newark, DE

Artin Göncü
Department of Educational Psychology
University of Illinois at Chicago
Chicago, IL

Laura D. Hanish
School of Social and Family Dynamics
Arizona State University
Tempe, AZ

Carollee Howes
Psychological Studies in Education
University of California at Los Angeles
Los Angeles, CA

Khalisa N. Herman
Laboratory for Comparative Ethology
National Institute of Child Health and
  Human Development
Department of Human Development
University of Maryland
College Park, MD

Kathy Hirsh-Pasek
Department of Psychology
Temple University
Philadelphia, PA

Christopher Jarrold
Department of Experimental Psychology
University of Bristol
Bristol, UK

Robert D. Kavanaugh
Department of Psychology
Williams College
Williamstown, MA

Angeline S. Lillard
Department of Psychology
University of Virginia
Charlottesville, VA

Carol Lynn Martin
School of Social and Family Dynamics
Arizona State University
Tempe, AZ

Elisabetta Palagi
Centro Interdipartimentale Museo di
  Storia Naturale e del Territorio
Università di Pisa
Pisa, Italy; and

Unit of Cognitive Primatology and
  Primate Center
Institute of Cognitive Sciences and
  Technologies CNR
Rome, Italy

Annika Paukner
Laboratory for Comparative Ethology
National Institute of Child Health and
  Human Development
Poolesville, MD

Anthony D. Pellegrini
Department of Educational Psychology
University of Minnesota
Minneapolis, MN

Sergio M. Pellis
Department of Neuroscience
University of Lethbridge
Lethbridge, Alberta

Vivien C. Pellis
Department of Neuroscience
University of Lethbridge
Lethbridge, Alberta

Jaipaul L. Roopnarine
Department of Child and Family Studies
Syracuse University
Syracuse, NY

David Schwartz
Department of Psychology
University of Southern California
Los Angeles, CA

Dorothy G. Singer
Department of Psychology
Yale University
New Haven, CT

Peter K. Smith
Department of Psychology
Goldsmiths
University of London
London, UK

Stephen J. Suomi
Laboratory for Comparative Ethology
National Institute of Child Health and
  Human Development
Poolesville, MD

Brian Sutton-Smith
Resident Scholar
Strong National Museum of Play
Rochester, NY

Jonathan R. H. Tudge
Department of Human Development and
  Family Studies
University of North Carolina–Greensboro
Greensboro, NC

CONTENTS

Part One · Introduction and Overview

1. Introduction 3
   Anthony D. Pellegrini

Part Two · Definitions

2. Defining and Recognizing Play 9
   Gordon M. Burghardt
3. Cultural Variations in Beliefs about Play, Parent–Child Play, and Children's
   Play: Meaning for Childhood Development 19
   Jaipaul L. Roopnarine

Part Three · Theories

4. Theories of Play 41
   Patrick Bateson
5. Comparing and Extending Piaget's and Vygotsky's Understandings
   of Play: Symbolic Play as Individual, Sociocultural, and
   Educational Interpretation 48
   Artin Göncü and Suzanne Gaskins
6. Gene × Environment Interactions and Social Play: Contributions
   from Rhesus Macaques 58
   Khalisa N. Herman, Annika Paukner, and Stephen J. Suomi
7. Playing at Every Age: Modalities and Potential Functions in
   Non-Human Primates 70
   Elisabetta Palagi
8. Play and Development 83
   Robert M. Fagen
9. The History of Children's Play in the United States 101
   Howard P. Chudacoff
10. The Antipathies of Play 110
    Brian Sutton-Smith

Part Four · Methods

11. The Cultural Ecology of Play: Methodological Considerations for Studying
    Play in Its Everyday Contexts 119
    Jonathan R. H. Tudge, Jill R. Brown, and Lia B. L. Freitas
12. Observational Methods in Studying Play 138
    Peter K. Smith

Part Five • Dimensions of Play

13. Object Play and Tool Use: Developmental and
    Evolutionary Perspectives   153
    David F. Bjorklund and Amy K. Gardiner

14. The Development and Function of Locomotor Play   172
    Anthony D. Pellegrini

15. Not Just "Playing Alone": Exploring Multiple Forms of Nonsocial
    Play in Childhood   185
    Robert J. Coplan

16. Internalizing and Externalizing Disorders during Childhood: Implications
    for Social Play   202
    David Schwartz and Daryaneh Badaly

17. Gender and Temperament in Young Children's Social Interactions   214
    Carol Lynn Martin, Richard A. Fabes, and Laura D. Hanish

18. Social Play of Children with Adults and Peers   231
    Carollee Howes

19. Rough-and-Tumble Play: Training and Using the Social Brain   245
    Sergio M. Pellis and Vivien C. Pellis

20. Children's Games and Playground Activities in School and Their
    Role in Development   260
    Ed Baines and Peter Blatchford

21. Mother–Child Fantasy Play   284
    Angeline S. Lillard

22. Origins and Consequences of Social Pretend Play   296
    Robert D. Kavanaugh

23. The Development of Pretend Play in Autism   308
    Christopher Jarrold and Carmel Conn

24. Technology and Play   322
    Jeffrey Goldstein

Part Six • Education

25. Playing Around in School: Implications for Learning and
    Educational Policy   341
    *Kelly Fisher, Kathy Hirsh-Pasek, Roberta M. Golinkoff, Dorothy G. Singer,
    and Laura Berk*

Part Seven • Conclusion

26. Conclusion   363
    Anthony D. Pellegrini

Index   367

PART 1

Introduction and Overview

Introduction

Anthony D. Pellegrini

Abstract

The role of play in developmental psychology has been a controversial topic of study. For example, the noted evolutionary biologist E. O. Wilson (1975) anointed play as one of the most important topics for understanding human development. It has also been researched by some of the most notable and prescient scholars in our field (Bruner, 1972; Piaget, 1962; Suomi, 2005; Sutton-Smith, 1966; Vygotsky, 1967). By contrast, play has not been a central topic of inquiry in child development, as evidenced by the appearance of only one chapter on play (Rubin, Fein, & Vandenberg, 1983) in the six editions of the *Handbook of Child Psychology*, from 1946 to present. This *Handbook* is an attempt to re-set the balance in the study of play within developmental psychology by subjecting it to an interdisciplinary onslaught by scholars from anthropology, history, education, psychology, and evolutionary biology. To this end, the *Handbook* is organized into separate sections addressing definition and theory, methodology, specific dimensions of play (locomotor, object, social and nonsocial, and pretend), and educational implications.

Key words: Definitions, theories, methods, dimensions of play, education and play

The role of play in developmental psychology has been a controversial topic of study. For example, the noted evolutionary biologist E. O. Wilson (1975) anointed play as one of the most important topics for understanding human development. Similarly, some quarters of the child development community consider it a necessary experience for children, without which serious social emotional damage will be done (e.g., Zigler & Bishop-Josef, 2006). Relatedly, it has been researched by some of the most notable and prescient scholars in our field (Bruner, 1972; Piaget, 1962; Suomi, 2005; Sutton-Smith, 1966; Vygotsky, 1967).

By contrast, play has not been a central topic of inquiry in child development, as evidenced by the appearance of only one chapter on play (Rubin, Fein, & Vandenberg, 1983) in the six editions of the *Handbook of Child Psychology*, from 1946 to present. More frequently, the study of play has been embedded in the study other topics, such as research on theory of mind (Harris, 1990). Similarly, some evolutionary biologists (e.g., Martin & Caro, 1985; Sharpe, 2005) are skeptical of the value of play.

This *Handbook* is an attempt to re-set the balance in the study of play within developmental psychology by subjecting it to an interdisciplinary onslaught by scholars from anthropology, history, education, psychology, and evolutionary biology. To this end, the *Handbook* is organized into separate sections addressing definition and theory, methodology, specific dimensions of play (locomotor, object, social and nonsocial, and pretend), and educational implications.

At one level, play seems a pretty easy construct to define, after all and as is often noted: Most people recognize it when they see it (Smith & Vollstedt, 1985). As simple as it may seem, play is indeed very difficult to define in both nonhuman and human animals. Gordon Burghardt has wrestled with play and its various definitions as part of his effort to examine play in human and nonhuman animals for many years (Burghardt, 1984; 2005). For Burghardt, a clear and explicit categorical definition of play is important in order to document the occurrence of play in the animal kingdom, and perhaps most controversially among reptiles. In his chapter in this *Handbook*, Burghardt has identified a set of five criteria, each of which needs to be satisfied in at least one respect, in order to identify a behavior as play in whatever context or species being studied. In addition, play can be viewed as operating, at a functional level, in three processes (primary, secondary, tertiary) spanning the continuum from the seemingly atavistic to the developmentally valuable if not essential. This level of conceptual clarity, he notes, is necessary for scientific progress.

In the final chapter in the definition section, Jaipaul Roopnarine defines play in terms of its larger cultural context. Based on variations in parental beliefs about play and participation in play in different cultural communities, Roopnarine offers a more inclusive definition of play is offered that focuses on framed and unframed playfulness.

In a transition chapter between definitions of play and theories of play, Pat Bateson discusses in his chapter confusion over the mistaken notion that play is a unitary construct. Instead, and as reflected in different sections in this *Handbook*, it has many dimensions (locomotor, social, object, and pretend) and correspondingly different motivations and different functions. Bateson discusses not only putative benefits of play for individuals, but how it may have evolved and also how it might impact evolutionary processes per se.

In terms of theory, Piaget and Vygotsky are perhaps the most influential play theorists for developmental psychologists. The chapter by Goncu and Gaskins not only reviews these theories, but also extends them through incorporating sociocultural theory. Acknowledging a dynamic view of play and development, Herman, Paukner, and Suomi describe how research with non-human primates is clarifying the genetic and experiential factors that impact play. Importantly, this chapter demonstrates how genes and environment operate interdependently and not as separate, additive factors. Elisabetta Palagi, another primatologist, argues that play is both ephemeral and versatile. Probably for this reason it is so difficult to study systematically. Palagi presents some recent studies on primates to show that play is a response to an immediate necessity

Continuing in theory, the evolutionary biologist Robert Fagen's chapter notes that the role of play in human development remains problematic. Based on ideas of ecology, dynamic developmental systems, intersubjectivity, and communicative musicality, his chapter offers some hypotheses about proximate causation of variation in human play and presents critical analyses of some of the problems that currently plague the field.

For the historian Howard Chudacoff, children's play is defined as non-obligatory activity. Chudacoff's chapter focuses on the "latent" period of childhood, ages six to twelve, from colonial America through the recent past. In the final chapter in the theory section, Brian Sutton-Smith argues that the history of modern play theories has been characterized largely by the notion that there are good and bad forms of play. He suggests that these dualisms are mediated primarily from the character of the primary versus secondary emotions in all forms of play.

The section on methodologies used in the study of play is especially important given the wide variety of disciplines that have studied play in human and nonhuman animals. We begin with a chapter on ethnography by Tudge, Brown, and Fresitas. They present a method, designed explicitly to fit within a contextualist paradigm, for observing play in its everyday contexts, and use data derived from a single city from each of the United States, Kenya, and Brazil to illustrate the heterogeneity of young children's experiences and cast doubt on the generality of earlier findings. Peter Smith's chapter discusses the use of observational methods in the study of play, both in humans and non-human species. In the first part, he gives a short history of observational methods, and then considers issues around types of observational methods, such as participant and non-participant observation, and alternatives to observation. He also considers some theoretical presuppositions regarding observational work, with examples from studies of play.

The individual chapters in the next section of the *Handbook* address separate dimensions of play in both human and nonhuman animals. Dave Bjorklund and Amy Gardiner's chapter takes an evolutionary developmental perspective to examine the development of and sex differences in object-oriented play and tool use, and the relationship between the two. They propose that through the experience gained in object play, children begin to understand how objects can be used as tools to achieve goals and solve problems. They also posit that the existence of tool use in other great apes suggests a common root for our basic tool-use abilities. Also taking a developmental and evolutionary tack, Pellegrini's chapter discusses the definition of locomotor play in human and nonhuman juveniles, as well as ontogenetic and sex trends. He also examines locomotor play in terms of antecedents (hormonal and socialization events) and function.

A number of chapters are dedicated to various forms of social play. Starting with a relatively unstudied construct, Rob Coplan provides an overview of theory and research related to the study of multiple forms of nonsocial play in childhood. The chapter by David Schwartz and Daryaneh Badaly takes a developmental psychopathological perspective to examine the potential impact of internalizing and externalizing disorders on children's social play, including nonsocial. They contend that the available findings provide preliminary evidence that childhood disorders can have pernicious implications for social play. Like Schwartz and Badaly, Martin, Fabes, and Hanish discuss individual differences, in the form of temperament, and social play. They present new data highlighting the importance of considering dispositional regulation as a factor influencing children's interaction with same sex peers.

In Carollee Howes' chapter, the development of social play in children in the toddler and preschool periods of development is placed within a theoretical framework that integrates theories of development with theories of cultural community, or the socio-cultural context for adult socialization of children's forms and styles of social play. From this perspective, she examines antecedents of social play, including the child capacities, relationships with adult caregivers, and the social and emotional climate of the social setting of play.

Serge and Vivien Pellis examine one specific aspect of social play, rough-and-tumble play, and argue that one of its central features is reciprocity, requiring that the competition to win be attenuated by the need to maintain cooperation. Based on experimental and comparative literature on nonhuman animals, primarily rodents, they provide a guide both for characterizing the brain mechanisms involved and for identifying the behavioral rules by which such play can be effectively deployed.

Ed Baines and Peter Blatchford's chapter examines areas relatively understudied by developmental psychologists: children's games on the school playground. They show how the school playground is a useful research site because it is one of the few occasions when children interact in a relatively safe environment, free of adult control, and when their play, games, and social relations are more their own. They argue that in order to understand children's social development we need to study how these arise out of the everyday expression and reality of children's playful activities and interactions with others in everyday contexts.

Like social play, children's fantasy, or pretend play, has been extensively studied by developmental and educational psychologists, though theorists have often ignored the role of parents in children's pretending. In Angeline Lillard's chapter, four features that distinguish mothers' pretending from children's pretending with peers are presented. She also discusses the ways in which mothers might help avert confusion in their early presentations of pretense. Robert Kavanaugh continues the discussion of fantasy play during early childhood, showing how play with peers becomes an important form of social interaction for many children. He demonstrates the similarities and differences between human and nonhuman social pretend play, how human culture impacts the frequency and type of make-believe play with others, and potential consequences of role play.

Jarrold and Conn examine pretend play from a different perspective, showing how individuals with autism tend to produce much less pretense. They argue that problems in producing creative pretend play might result from executive difficulties in the control of behavior or might reflect the fact that play behavior in autism develops in an atypical sociocultural context, a view consistent with accounts emphasizing the gradual development of pretend play skills in childhood.

The role of play in educational outcomes is both controversial and interesting. It's controversial because very often using "play" as a strategy to educate children violates some of the necessary criteria in defining play, such as a means-over-ends orientation and lack of concern with outcomes. Further, adults often introduce such strategies into the mix to facilitate education, a practice sometimes used to inhibit play, as demonstrated in the Pellis' chapter. With that said, the chapter by Fisher, Hirsh-Pasek, Golinkoff, Singer, and Berk delineates this territory by presenting the evidence that playful learning pedagogies not only promote important academic learning but also more general skills. They introduce the notion of "playful learning," a teaching approach that uses free-play and guided-play activities to promote academic, socio-emotional, and cognitive development. The chapter reviews research evidence of play in school and offers suggestions and future directions for research in the emerging playful learning domain.

Lastly, Jeff Goldstein's chapter considers how children learn to play with technology, and what they learn through that play, also utilizing "playful learning," though there is little research on whether play with technology increases children's cognitive or social skills, although some toys are designed with these goals in mind. He suggests that new media do not necessarily replace older media so much as add to the range of play options available.

In sum, this *Handbook* should re-establish the importance of play in human development as both an important area of research but also by offering guidance to policy makers who have recently been concerned with children's loss of leisure time.

References

Burghardt, G. M. (1984). On the origins of play. In P. K. Smith (Ed.), *Play in animals and humans* (pp. 5–42). London: Blackwell.

Burghardt, G. M. (2005). *The genesis of animal play: Testing the limits*. Cambridge, MA: MIT Press.

Bruner, J. (1972). The nature and uses of immaturity. *American Psychologist, 27*, 687–708.

Martin, P., & Caro, T. (1985). On the function of play and its role in behavioral development. In J. Rosenblatt, C. Beer, M-C. Bushnel, and P. Slater (Eds.). *Advances in the study of behavior, Vol. 15* (pp. 59–103). New York: Academic Press.

Piaget, J. (1962). *Play, dreams, and imitation in childhood*. (Trans. C. Gattengno & F.M. Hodgson) New York: Norton. (Original work published 1951).

Rubin, K. H., Fein, G., & Vandenberg, B. (1983). Play. In E.M. Hetherington (Ed.), *Handbook of child psychology: Vol. IV. Socialization, personality and social development*, (pp. 693–774). New York: Wiley.

Sharpe, L. L. (2006). Playfight does not affect subsequent fighting success in meerkats. *Animal Behaviour, 69*, 1023–1029.

Smith, P. K., & Vollstedt, R. (1985). On defining play: An empirical study of the relationship between play and various play criteria. *Child Development, 56*, 1042–1050.

Suomi, S. J. (2005). Genetic and environmental factors influencing the expression of impulsive aggression and serotonergic functioning in rhesus monkeys. In R. E. Tremblay, W. W. Hartup, & J. Archer (Eds.) *Developmental origins of aggression* (pp. 63–82) New York: Guilford.

Sutton-Smith, B. (1966). Piaget on play: A critique. *Psychological Review, 73*, 104–110.

Vygotsky, L. (1967). Play and its role in the mental development of the child. *Soviet Psychology, 12*, 62–76.

Wilson, E. O. (1975). *Sociobiology: The new synthesis*. Cambridge, MA: Harvard University Press.

Zigler, E. F., & Bishop-Josef, S. (2006). The cognitive child vs the whole child: Lessons from 40 years of Head Start. In D. G. Singer, R. Michnick-Golinkoff, & K. Hirsh-Pasek. (Eds.) *Play = learning: How children's play motivates and enhances children's cognitive and social-emotional growth* (pp. 15–35). New York: Oxford University Press.

PART 2

Definitions

Defining and Recognizing Play

Gordon M. Burghardt

Abstract

Characterizing behavior in any organism as play, including in humans, has often been controversial. Intuitive understandings of what constitutes 'play' are often difficult to describe in words so that other researchers can use them. This leads to problems in comparing studies, formulating and testing research hypotheses, and even in having a shared conversation. To alleviate this problem, many attempts have been made to define or identify play in all its guises. Unfortunately, these attempts have generally failed due to the narrow context in which they have been developed or the conceptual language in which they are expressed (e.g., cognitive, behavioristic, physiological). A careful perusal of these attempts has led to the identification of a set of five criteria, each of which need to be satisfied in at least one respect, in order to identify a behavior as play in whatever context or species being studied. In addition, play can be viewed as operating, at a functional level, in three processes (primary, secondary, tertiary) spanning the continuum from the seemingly atavistic to the developmentally valuable if not essential. Where specific instances of play fall along this continuum can only be answered by empirical research and not by inference from the labels we give to them. In any event, conceptual clarity appears necessary for scientific progress.

Keywords: defining play; recognizing play; animal play; children's play; comparative; play types

Introduction

> Teachers mean very different things by "play" – and often it is not play at all
>
> (*Miller and Almon*, 2009: 25)

The Knoxville Zoo had acquired a 'pair' of green mambas—large, beautiful, high-strung, and deadly African snakes. I was soon contacted by the staff to observe the remarkable and violent courtship behavior that was taking place when the snakes were put together. It turned out that the behavior was not courtship at all, but male-male fighting. The 'pair' consisted of two males! Although the behavior did not look like any previously known male-female courtship in snakes, the zoo staff was, understandably, predisposed by the assumption that the snakes were a male—female pair to interpret the behavior

they objectively observed as courtship, but not one with serious consequences in this instance, as no injuries resulted due to the fact that male-male competition in venomous snakes virtually never results in snakes using their venom on each other—which would be a lose-lose proposition!

In almost all fields of science there have been struggles with conceptualizing the phenomena that are or should be studied. Generally a field settles down to some rather agreed upon content, but there are always gray areas, borderlines, or possible mislabeling. In the realm of play in animals and children it is often the case that observers confuse play with fighting, bullying, courtship, hunting, and other behavioral categories (Burghardt, 2005; see also in this volume chapters by Pellis and Pellis & Smith). And it is also true that what is play

9

in one context may not be play in another, even if the behavior appears similar in most respects. From the perspective of applying our knowledge of play in children to school settings, the above quotation underscores another serious problem: Those charged with teaching or supervising children often have a limited understanding of what play is and how it works. This is, no doubt, partially due to deficits in their education as childhood educators and the play-averse culture of many school systems around the world. At a play conference I attended an educational researcher mentioned that it is often necessary to avoid the label 'play' when seeking to integrate playful activities into school curricula. The lay view that play is not serious, and thus not important to 'real' education, is still all too common. Is the play label becoming as toxic as evolution?

But the problem is deeper than this. There are problems with recognizing behavior as play if one applies limited or restrictive criteria to what is allowed as 'play,' or legitimate, useful, or safe play. On the other hand, as Pellegrini (2009) notes, too often in the child development literature so much is considered play that the label loses meaning and thus scientific value. In some of the child and animal research literature, play is equated with 'other social' behavior, a catchall for events that cannot be put into other categories. This later gambit, by the way, also limits the play category to social behavior, another problem. As with the snake example above, labels can influence how we interpret what we observe. For example, calling an activity a 'game' predisposes us to the label of play, but we all know that for a professional member of a sports team, much of what they do is regimented, scheduled, and done for pay; success or failure have serious consequences (See Baines & Blatchford, this volume). In schools, turning memorizing multiplication tables into a flash card game is usually not viewed as play by students. Similarly, a weekend fisherman going after trout with a fly rod in the rushing streams of my beloved Great Smoky Mountains is more likely to be playing than a crew member on a fishing trawler experiencing a wintry stormy Atlantic ocean. Context *is* important, but not the entire story either.

Types of Play

Play, the subject of this volume and numerous books and thousands of research articles, has been a field of scholarly interest for well over 100 years (cf. Groos, 1898, 1901). It has to some extent coasted on what seems to have been a rather intuitive conception of play—basically seemingly purposeless behavior that is enjoyable. Many people have described and studied play in nonhuman animals and children. Play has been central to developmental, educational, and therapeutic theories (Piaget, Freud; cf. Homeyer & Tomlinson, 2008) and to understanding history, anthropology, social rituals, and the arts (Cross, 2008; Gray, 2008; Henrichs, 2008; Huizinga, 1947; Sutton-Smith, 1997). Play is also ascribed to numerous nonhuman animals (Burghardt, 2005), or just animals from here on, unless, from the context, all species, human and nonhuman, are meant.

Given the focus of this volume on developmental trajectories and processes of play, it is appropriate to set forth the phenomena to be encompassed in early childhood, at least. The listing in a recent attempt to reinvigorate the use of play in kindergartens in the US is useful (Miller & Almon, 2009). The 12 types catalogued are large-motor play, small-motor play, mastery play, rule-based play, construction play, make-believe play, symbolic play, language play, playing with the arts, sensory play, rough-and-tumble play, and risk-taking play. This is actually a quite complete list that goes beyond some recent tendencies to restrict important 'play' to pretense or socio-dramatic categories. Essays elsewhere in this volume describe all these in detail. But this list does help focus the discussion on what are the commonalities undergirding all play types. It should be obvious that the 12 types of play are not mutually exclusive, as construction play can fall into sensory and symbolic categories, large-motor play can involve mastery and risk-taking, make-believe play can fall into language play, and so on.

In animal play research, an area that has largely developed independently of the child play literature, play is typically divided into three categories: solitary locomotor / rotational play, object play, and social play (for detailed explications and examples see Burghardt, 2005; Fagen, 1981; Graham & Burghardt, in press). These three play types, like the 12 child play types, also can be combined. Furthermore, there is evidence that all the listed types of child play can be found, at least in rudimentary form, in nonhuman animals, especially in apes and some birds (e.g., parrots, Pepperberg, Breese, & Harris, 1991; see also Kavanaugh, this volume). This highlights the fact that a means of identifying play of any kind should be able to encompass play in both animals and, at bare minimum, human children. That is the strategy I have adopted here.

Some Current Research Examples of Diversity in Characterizing Play

Elsewhere, I and others have discussed the reasons why we need useful definitions of play, the problems with many current and past attempts to characterize play, and surveys of definitions used in child behavior and animal behavior research (Burghardt 2005; Fagen 1981; Pellegrini 2009). I was inspired by the writings of Brian Sutton-Smith (1997; this volume), who looked at the broad sweep of what we consider play and developed seven major rhetorics of play, each with rather different phenomena and participants. Most relevant to the subject of this volume is the 'progress' rhetoric, especially relevant to child development and educational policy areas. Although full coverage of these topics is not needed here, considering some recent uses of the play category in the research literature can highlight the problems.

For convenience, some examples from the first volume of the newly established *American Journal of Play* will be briefly described. The statement of editorial policy in the first issue acknowledges that "Play is multifaceted, diverse, and complex. It resists easy definition and engages many disciplines" (Dyson, 2008: iv). The targeted communities to be served by this journal includes psychologists, historians, early childhood specialists, animal play researchers, folklorists, sociologists, play therapists, and toy and game designers. Eclecticism is certainly enriching, and it is perhaps no surprise that the included fields encompass all the seven approaches (rhetorics) of play articulated by Sutton-Smith (1997). For those interested in developing a scientific understanding of play, is it really necessary to have some common understanding across communities of what is involved in play? Could not a general eclectic conception of play suffice? Evidence seems to suggest the answers are yes and no.

Consider the first issue of the *American Journal of Play* (AJP). A popular and influential advocate of play, David Elkind, leads off with an essay on the power of play. He assumes his readers not only know what he means by play but also that

> "Most of us engaged in the study of play consider it a form of exercise for creative dispositions—for imagination, for curiosity, for fantasy"
>
> (*Elkind*, 2008:1).

Free play seems to be preferred to organized play or play meant to be educational. The latter point is somewhat perplexing given the great emphasis Elkind lays on play as the most important means of learning in childhood. Elkind proceeds to claim that there are "three basic drives that power human thought and action, three drives essential to a full, happy, and productive life" (Elkind 2008:2). These three drives are play, love, and work, which he considers to be most likely distinct dispositions that operate best together. While I don't want to criticize a most touching depiction of the value of play, I find his distinction of play and work hard to maintain and is opposed by those who claim that play is a child's work. Yet Elkind sees work as adapting to the demands of the environment a child faces whereas play is adapting the environment to the child's imagination. Piaget's assimilation versus accommodation distinction is the basis of his view, it seems, but such a restriction on the realm of play does not accommodate rough and tumble play, climbing trees, and other large motor play, for example.

In the journal's second paper, Cross (2008), in contrast, takes a historical look at play in American society and flatly states "Obviously and inevitably, play is shaped by work" (Cross, 2008:8). Here, festivals, drinking, gambling, hunting, dancing, sewing bees, fashion, gardening, and many other activities are considered play by Cross, and mightily important ones at that. In another article in this first issue, Panksepp, an eminent neuroscientist (Panksepp, 1998) primarily studying social play in rats, develops the argument that "… joyous enthusiasm to engage PLAYfully with others" is the most necessary means "for the active construction of the social brain" (Panksepp, 2008: 56). He focuses on mammalian social play and argues that ADHD is a possible consequence of decreasing amounts of unstructured, vigorous play in children. Play fighting, even with the "dark side to play" of bullying, also is a route to social and emotional knowledge such as empathy, negotiation skills, appropriate behavioral inhibition, as well a life of joy and laughter.

In his long and thoughtful article on the nature of play, the sociologist Thomas Henricks (2008) goes through some of the major figures in play including Huizinga, Piaget, Goffman, and others. Although he notes that those studying animals must rely on "external mannerisms," people can tell us how they feel. Maybe, but I often trust a smile or facial expression more than a verbal claim (I really DID like your deep fried artichoke hearts). After presenting Huizinga's play criteria (listed below) Henricks faults them for not being applicable to child play, which Huizinga does not much address. He then goes on to characterize play in so many ways that he acknowledges that the reader may be confused. This, he says is a reflection of our need to recognize the true complexity of play. At the end of his long section on defining play, in arguing against another theorist, Henricks writes:

"Huizinga's view (and mine) is that we should see play instead as what social scientists term an "ideal type," that is, a distinctive form or *model for* behavior that can be used to judge the character of real-life events. Only then can we decide whether an activity in question is "false" or "true" play, whether it is more or less "playful," or even how it is being altered by the organizations that control it"

(*Henricks*, 2008: 170).

In the same issue, Homeyer and Tomlinson (2008:213) review play therapy. For them "Children's play is a symbolic expression of their world." It certainly can be, but play therapists typically do not use physically active play and thus their conception of play is quite restrictive. On the other hand, for Gee (2008) studying video games, play is discovery as well as a transition to work by "preparation for reality." Sorama and Clements (2009) view play as important cognitive building blocks for inculcating mathematical thinking. Bergen (2009) goes farther and sees play as the building blocks for incipient scientists, engineers, and mathematicians. Bergen notes that play must first and foremost be fun (though see Bateson, this volume). Other important traits of play she lists are internal control, intrinsic motivation, and internal reality. She favorably lists five criteria posited by Lisa Barnett for play—cognitive, physical, and social spontaneity, manifest joy, and a sense of humor.

Even trying to define a special type of play has problems. Consider word play as pretend play, studied by Nwokah and Graves (2009) and defined by drawing on a number of authoritative sources.

"We define *pretend play* as a multidimensional type of play that commonly combines communication and intimacy, that uses toys or props, and that involves more than one player"

(*Nwokah & Graves*, 2009: 429).

While the authors may be comfortable with this in a limited context, it certainly is not general. Using this definition a child cannot play or talk to an imaginary friend or teddy bear in play! Their next sentence is even more problematic: "Pretend play is nonliteral, and it transforms actions, objects, persons, places, and indeed, all other aspects of the children's immediate situations." An example might be two kids imitating cops and robbers with cardboard cutout guns. But the two sentences are quite inconsistent with one another, which makes application difficult.

Sattelmair and Ratty (2009) view physical exercise, including vigorous play, as potentially important to increase cognitive performance as well as reduce obesity. Yet physical education classes are rarely considered play, at least not in the high school I went to. The authors seem to punt:

"we conceive of physical education as a forum during which students have opportunities to engage in physical activity. A good portion of that activity we consider physically strenuous play"

(*Sattelmair & Ratty*, 2009: 365).

Nowhere do they provide a means to distinguish "physical education, physical activity, and play from each other" (Sattelmair & Ratty, 2009: 365; though see Pellegrini, this volume).

As a final example, a developmental evolutionary psychologist turning an imaginative lens on anthropology and play found that he needed a more generic definition than was available and claims to have found one with five play criteria that he claims are new: These five view play as

"1) self chosen and self directed; 2) intrinsically motivated; 3) structured by mental rules; 4) imaginative; and 5) produced in an active, alert, but unstressed frame of mind"

(*Gray*, 2009: 480).

Some of these criteria overlap two or three of those that follow. While the discussion is stimulating, little guidance is provided to applying them.

By looking closely at how these recent papers conceptualize and interpret play I am not devaluing their contents in any way. They underscore the challenge of characterizing play in more general and broad terms so that comparative and interdisciplinary research can be more productively and effectively implemented.

Issues in Recognizing Play

One of the hallmarks of ethology is that naturalistic description of behavior and construction of a behavioral inventory or catalogue should precede experimental and analytical research. This is common in animal research and has been more common in infant and child behavior as compared to adolescent and adult human behavior. However, in order to properly inventory play wherever it may occur throughout the animal kingdom one cannot rely on largely intuitive or anthropomorphic assertions.

It was largely due to such unexamined and anthropocentric identification of play that over the last century play behavior in animals was confidently limited to 'intelligent' mammals such as humans, apes, monkeys, dogs, seals, and cats along with a few birds, leading to the view that play is an evolutionarily relatively recent or derived behavior. In fact, much play has its roots in the most ancient parts of the vertebrate brain (Burghardt, 2001; Panksepp, 1998; Pellis & Pellis, 2009; this volume) and thus the potential for play may be widespread.

In the child play literature, as indicated above, there are many attempts at general definitions. These include the seminal chapter by Rubin, Fein, and Vandenberg (1983) and more recent treatments by Clark and Miller (1998) and Johnson, Christie, and Yawkey (1999). The approach has been to list criteria such as non-literality, intrinsic motivation, positive affect, process flexibility, free choice, and means rather than ends oriented (Burghardt, 2005; Pellegrini, 2009). There are often many more criteria mentioned, and the same or similar criterion given different labels that may or may not be interpreted in different ways. Little guidance in applying the criteria to given instances is provided. Some criteria are also more useful in recognizing play in humans than in other species. *Positive affect* is certainly easier to gauge in a human than in a rat, let alone a lizard or fish. Additionally, positive affect is not always obvious. Consider, for example, the previously mentioned confusion by school personnel in distinguishing between playful rough and tumble fighting and serious fights or bullying. *Non-literality* also is problematic, and seems more appropriate for make-believe play (pretense, fantasy) than sensory motor or gross motor play. Thus, while these criteria provide lists of factors that may be involved in play, they do not distinguish the essential from the inessential, as they are not meant to be exhaustive, and are rarely weighted in relative importance.

In addition to the child behavior literature, lists of criteria have also been produced for animal play (described in Burghardt, 2005; Fagen, 1981). In the human literature outside of child behavior there have also been lists. Perhaps the most influential was by the 20th Century's leading humanist historian of the late medieval period, Johan Huizinga (1955), mentioned above. For Huizinga, play was *voluntary* (related to 'freedom'), *distinct from ordinary life, disinterested* (unconnected with any immediate satisfaction of biological wants or needs; not goal directed), and *dependent on societal features or rules*, as well as *transgressions* of the latter. These criteria are difficult to apply to child, let alone animal, play. Huizinga does accept as play any behavior of animals that is not 'purely physiological.' Yet physiology enters into every action and thought an organism has, and our understanding of the biological aspects of body and mind has also expanded markedly since he wrote. In any event, a means to more clearly distinguish play from other phenomena in a manner sufficiently rigorous for scientific and comparative analysis across different play types, different species, and different levels of discourse is needed.

The Identification of Five Necessary Criteria for Recognizing Play

Elsewhere in this volume, characterizations of many different kinds of play are provided. This being said, what can we do to aid in recognizing play instances not immediately comprehended as such? Can we place a check on labeling as 'play,' behavior for which some essential information is lacking? I have attempted to do so by updating and reworking the numerous criteria that have been proposed into a working set of five criteria necessary for recognizing play in any species, including humans, and in diverse settings and contexts (Burghardt, 1999; 2005). While there are some slight alterations to the wording of the criteria given below, the rationale is the same. However, as the criteria have been occasionally misinterpreted, some explanation is provided as to how they can be applied, along with some examples. Some of these explanations are taken from the extensive discussion on defining play in Burghardt (2005). The criteria are presented singly. In applying them to any given putative play event, it is important to emphasize that NO single criterion, even if satisfied, is alone sufficient to label a behavior as play; ALL FIVE must be met in at least one respect. One of the strengths of this approach is that it helps direct attention to the kinds of information needed to confirm that a behavior is play when available information addressing some of the criteria are positive, but sufficient information for evaluating the others is lacking. This was critical to the project of identifying play in animal species where play was considered not only absent but impossible to confirm. The stress is on behavior, what we can see, describe, and record using objective methods, but does not ignore motivational, emotional, and cognitive processes (e.g., intrinsic motivation, positive affect).

The first criterion for recognizing play is that the performance of the behavior is not fully functional in the form or context in which it is

expressed; that is, it includes elements, or is directed toward stimuli, that do not contribute to current survival.

The critical term here is 'not fully functional,' instead of 'purposeless,' nonadaptive, or having a 'delayed benefit.' The most common attribute of play is some variant of the view that play behavior is not serious, is not of immediate use, and is not necessary for survival. However, to show that a behavior has *some* possible immediate function or current adaptive role cannot be used to eliminate the notion that the behavior is play. A behavior or structure can be of value even if it has not evolved for that purpose. For example, the vigorous exercise involved in much play may improve the oxygen-carrying capacity of the blood. On the other hand, many behaviors that have no immediate function are certainly not play, such as self-mutilation, highly stereotyped repetitive obsessive-compulsive behavior, or bulimia. Play may indeed have some current function (arousal, physiological toning) and thus cannot be said to be entirely nonfunctional even if no delayed benefits can be identified. Another aspect of play, particularly play with objects, is that the behavior may be directed at normal stimuli (cats playing with mice), directed at stimuli that might be construed as "normal" (kitten with a ball of yarn or rubber mouse), or directed at stimuli that may have little or no reference to natural objects (monkeys playing with pegboards). In young children, making a sand fort may at one level seem designed to fight off enemies, but at another the fort is clearly not functional in any serious sense. This example helps clarify a conundrum in how to label constructive play such as building a sand fort or a block castle (Pellegrini, 2009; Rubin et al., 1983). If play is conceived of as entirely means oriented or a process, rather than being done with an end or goal, as in constructive play, then such sand and block play is not play! While this may be good strict Piagetian thinking, this is not good reasoning in trying to identify play as a general category. Criterion 1 covers both constructive and more generic object play.

Another problem with the 'no immediate function' criterion so often found in play definitions is that there may in fact be one, but we just do not recognize it. The frequent used of the phrase "no apparent function" in reference to play is a largely useless criterion. Many claimed instances of play have been tempered when more is known about the natural history of the species. However, the same could be said about vestigial organs or claims about the lack of adaptiveness of any behavior or structure.

Essentially the issue is one of probabilities. When we add other criteria to our definition, we solve this problem.

The second criterion for recognizing play is that the behavior is spontaneous, voluntary, intentional, pleasurable, rewarding, reinforcing, or autotelic ("done for its own sake").

Only ONE of these often overlapping concepts needs to apply. The idea that play must be enjoyable or fun is widespread and certainly captures a major component of play in familiar settings or with animals that it is easy to relate to anthropomorphically. Note that while this criterion accommodates any inferred subjective concomitants of play (having fun, enjoyable, positive affect), it does not make them essential for recognizing play. Play is also often characterized as something that animals seem to engage in voluntarily. Play often appears to be spontaneous or intrinsically motivated or the sensory stimulation produced by the activity is rewarding or reinforcing. All these can be assessed even when positive emotions are hard to decipher, as in a fish. Sometimes the features of play falling under this criterion are so reliable or striking that claims are made that a drive or motivation to play is play's primary characteristic and thus such play is considered instinctive or autotelic.

Although the mere performance of play actions may be stimulating, rewarding, or in some other way reinforcing to a child or an animal, many other behaviors that are not play have similar stimulus seeking, self-reinforcing, and pleasurable properties. Eating is a prime example and not just in people. Rats prefer food flavored with nonnutritive saccharine. Mating behavior and maternal care also seem to have similar intrinsic reinforcing properties. Combined with the first criterion, however, we can eliminate such phenomena (though in some contexts eating, drinking, and courtship can be viewed as play).

The third criterion for recognizing play is that it differs from strictly functional expressions of behavior structurally or temporally in at least one respect: incomplete (generally through inhibited or dropped final elements), exaggerated, awkward, precocious, or involves behavior patterns with modified form, sequencing, or targeting.

Notice that this is a structural (what the behavior looks like with careful description) and temporal (developmental period) descriptive criterion that acknowledges, but does not require, that play may be found only during a limited period early in an animal's life. Thus, play can be a stage in cognitive development as in Piaget's system.

Neither of the first two criteria informs us as to what play behavior will look like (its topographical and structural properties). If the behavior, even if spontaneous and not fully functional in obtaining a specific end, appears the same as the serious performance, we are unlikely to call it play. Thus, to be play, the behavior must have some characteristic that sets it off structurally or temporally from the serious performance. This is especially important if the play behavior is highly species or culturally typical and resembles the serious performance. Many such structural differences have been noted, and some are incorporated into the definitions cited above that were most comprehensive. These elements may include the observation that the motor patterns in play fighting, for example, while outwardly similar to serious fighting, may differ in the targets and frequency of various behaviors (Pellis & Pellis, 2009).

The behavior patterns in play may also be exaggerated in intensity or duration from their normal expression. The bow used by dogs in soliciting play from another animal or its owner is an exaggerated form of social behavior. Dancing, prancing, kids chasing and racing around, and many other behaviors appear different from their source elements. Pretend play in children also often has such aspects. In children, much play is clearly that because the behavior appears earlier in ontogeny than when seriously performed. This may be especially true of fighting, chasing, and wrestling, locomotor play, and courtship, not to say many games and pretend object play. Children often try to imitate adults using vacuum cleaners, mops, and so on. If toy implements are used, then the play aspect is more obvious, of course. It may also appear at one stage of life and not be present again later. While much play fighting in animals and children may differ both in causal mechanisms and function from adult serious fighting (Pellis & Pellis, 2009), even adult-like behavior patterns performed precociously in young animals before their deployment in serious contexts fill this criterion.

Play fights with conspecifics, parents, or littermates, also may have inhibited or no biting. Animals that play with human caregivers are often noted as learning to inhibit the roughness of their play with humans as compared to conspecifics. Similarly, adults play-wrestling with their kids inhibit their actions that could cause serious injury, an aspect of social play called self-handicapping (See Roopnarine,

this volume). Certainly, no given play example will show all these structural characteristics. However, at *least one* of these structural characteristics, or precocity, needs to be present for behavior to satisfy criterion 3.

The fourth criterion for recognizing play is that the behavior is performed repeatedly in a similar, but not rigidly stereotyped, form during at least a portion of the animal's ontogeny.

There are many reports of rarely seen behavior that is often labeled play because it does not fit anywhere else. How, in fact, do we deal with reports of abnormal, but somewhat species-characteristic behavior, seen only once or at few scattered times? We need an additional criterion to eliminate the bizarre or non-replicated anecdotal report. For play to have evolved it must have a fairly widespread currency in certain contexts, even if there is much individual variability.

As with criterion 3, this criterion explicitly counters the apparent freedom, flexibility, and versatility of play that have been so often noted. It is clear from the literature that repetition of patterns of movement is found in all play and games in human and nonhuman animals. The very concept of 'rules,' so ubiquitous in descriptions of play, mandates repetition. Repetition is also useful in distinguishing exploratory responses to novel stimuli, which typically habituate quickly, from the play actions that may follow initial exploratory behavior. Repeated actions also facilitate the use of play in learning or improving skill. An 'urge' to repeat behavior (try and try again) may be essential for play to have functional and adaptive roles in behavioral development and psychological well-being. This is related to criterion 2 as well. For infants, learning to walk is a prime example of repetition, and the motivational and emotional aspects of play.

Related to the repetition aspect is the frequent observation that play seems to take on a life of its own, as in object or locomotor play where an animal may repeat an action until it has somehow mastered it, the 'mastery play" of Piaget and others. The apparent awkwardness of many juvenile play behaviors as compared to the adult form may serve as a cue to playing animals to keep on playing until the behavior is mastered, as well as providing cues to adults to keep facilitating such behavior or keep tabs on the progress made. Again, for infants, learning to walk may be an example of this.

Repeatability is important in considering behavioral performances as play that do not obviously derive from serious instinctive patterns (with or without learned elements). Behavior patterns that may structurally satisfy some of the criteria, but are performed rarely and unreliably within or across individuals, are thus not considered firmly demonstrated play, whatever their other features.

The stipulation that repeated is not the same as being 'highly stereotyped' or compulsive raises the question of when a repeated play behavior is a stereotypy. When play becomes addictive and compulsive, as in gambling, the behavior is often marked by repetitive rigidity and resistance to changes in setting or environment. The next criterion helps out here.

The fifth criterion for recognizing play is that the behavior is initiated when an animal is adequately fed, clothed, healthy, and not under stress (e.g., from physical danger, harsh weather, illness, social instability, family dysfunction), or intense competing systems (e.g., feeding, mating, competition, fear): In other words, the animal is in a "relaxed field."

Behavior termed play is uncoerced, appears voluntary, and engages the animal's interest (criterion 2). However, we did not specify how one could really know this. The last criterion not only helps in doing this job but also is in itself a critical point.

One of the prime characteristics of play is that the animal is not strongly motivated to perform other behaviors: The animal is not starving (nor even very hungry), it is not, at the moment, preoccupied with mating, setting up territories, exploring, or otherwise competing for essential resources or escaping predators. It has long been recognized that animals that are well-fed and free from environmental stresses play more than animals that are hungry, too hot or too cold, sick, or endangered by predators. In schools this is recognized by the value of providing breakfasts and lunches for children from families with limited means or poor parental care. Recent work on using play in schools to stimulate creativity and problem solving has found that it is most effective when children are very comfortable in their surroundings and with the adults present; in short they have *psychological safety* (Tegano, Sawyers, & Moran, 1989).

This criterion may underlie the finding that play is often much more common in well-maintained captive animals than in their wild counterparts. Not every behavior seen when the animal is in the relaxed field will be play, and sometimes such a state, particularly in captivity, may be hard to ascertain completely. Stereotyped behaviors, such as pacing in captive animals, may occur because of overly small cages that do not adequately accommodate the behavioral needs of the animals, especially active ones, or cages that, while spacious, are barren and sterile. The occurrence of stereotyped behavior is not a response to a relaxed field.

The Process Classification

Assessing the possible functions of play is a major goal of researchers on both animal and childhood play. One of the conceptual difficulties in this area, along with the myriad methodological ones, is that there is no single or even general answer to the value of play or how such benefits should recognized (see also Bateson, this volume). Different types of play have diverse underlying mechanisms and consequences, and these may be developmentally and contextually specific. This contrasts with the more circumscribed values one can posit for eating, drinking, reading, and so on.

It is useful, then, to characterize the putative role of play, across this variation, into three groups or processes (Burghardt, 2005). First is *primary process play*, which is results from non-play factors such as lack of stimulation (boredom), low behavioral thresholds, immature behavior, excess metabolic energy, impulsivity, and curiosity. Such play may not have immediate or long-term benefits and does not result, in the first instance, from any intrinsic play motivational mechanisms. This is probably the original basal stage in the evolution of play and may be the play process most often found in invertebrates and "lower" vertebrates, but is also seen in many of the most playful species as well. Next is *secondary process play*. Here primary process play has assumed an important role in helping to maintain the condition of the animal physiologically, behaviorally, and perceptually. For example, physical exercise accompanying play behavior may help to maintain cardiovascular and muscle functioning (see Pellegrini, this volume). In older adult humans, dancing may deter the deterioration of locomotor flexibility. Note that play does not necessarily need to be the sole or even primary means of maintaining or supporting proper development, though it may be an especially intrinsically motivated system for doing so. The final stage is *tertiary process play*. Here engaging in certain kinds of play may be useful, if not actually crucial, for reaching specific developmental milestones, cognitive accomplishments, social skills, and physical abilities. At this point we do not yet know which play in human or nonhuman animals rightfully falls under which process, as we still know little about the consequences of different kinds of play. Even within a specific type of play, such as play fighting and competitive games, there is disagreement on both the adaptive and evolutionary consequences of such behavior in terms of aggression, learning rule following, or acquiring a sense of fairness and morality. Individual differences in play propensity and skills are found in many species, including in humans, however, and such differences can provide the variation needed for selection to operate and lead to evolutionary and cultural change.

Tertiary process play may be particularly involved in the types of play that may occur in the absence of typical overt behavior. A hallmark of human cognition is the ability to play with ideas or imagine scenarios and creative outcomes without actual behavioral performance. Behavioral play could have been the essential precursor to such 'mental' play and thus a major force in the evolution of human cognitive and emotional complexity. It is possible that primary process play that initially had no adaptive consequences became useful to the individual and was transformed via selection to serve both secondary and tertiary functions in development and reproductive fitness as well as providing variation from which novel and complex behavior was rapidly facilitated. The role of gestures and facial expressions when people communicate with others as well as try to solve problems or develop, for themselves at least, new accomplishments or novel ideas, may be a result of such tertiary play processes. The play criteria presented here should be helpful in identifying such more covert behavioral processes as well as more overt behavioral play.

Conclusion

Since I first advanced the five criteria approach (Burghardt, 1999; 2005) it has been found to be useful (e.g. Pellegrini, 2009; Pellis & Pellis, 2009) and I am aware of no example of generally recognized play that is not covered by them. The criteria do help us recognize as play behavior that has not been recognized as such in contexts or in animals that have been excluded from the play pantheon. Indeed, that was the major motivation behind their formulation, as with them I could evaluate claims for play that were not acceptable due to classification blinders similar to the herpetological zookeepers or the inattentive teachers mentioned above. Thus, using the criteria has allowed identification of play in lizards, turtles, bony fishes, stingrays, and octopus (Burghardt, 2005). They were even applied recently to identifying what appears to be social play in wasps (Dapporto, Turrillazzi, & Palagi, 2006).

The description of the five criteria has been deliberately couched in the realm of non-human animal play, this being my major area of interest and expertise. Nonetheless, besides their possible use in identifying human play, they are meant to help all students of play realize that play is not only highly diverse, but shares several basic universal properties resulting from ancient evolutionary processes we are only beginning to understand. Briefly, these criteria state: Play [1] is incompletely functional in the context in which it appears; [2] is spontaneous, pleasurable, rewarding, or voluntary; [3] differs from other more serious behaviors in form (e.g., exaggerated) or timing (e.g., occurring early in life before the more serious version is needed); [4] is repeated, but not in abnormal and unvarying stereotypic form (e.g. distressed rocking, pacing); and [5] is initiated in the absence of acute or chronic stress. The claim made here is that such a scheme is more useful than any available alternative, since if all five criteria are met, we can confidently identify play in any species or context.

References

Bergen, D. (2009). Play as the learning medium for future scientists, mathematicians, and engineers. *American Journal of Play, 1,* 413–428.

Burghardt, G. M. (1999). Conceptions of play and the evolution of animal minds. *Evolution and Cognition, 5,* 115–123.

Burghardt, G. M. (2001). Play: Attributes and neural substrates. In E. M. Blass (ed.), *Handbook of behavioral neurobiology:* Vol. 13: *Developmental psychobiology* (pp. 327–366). New York: Plenum.

Burghardt, G. M. (2005). *The genesis of animal play: Testing the limits.* Cambridge, MA: MIT Press.

Clark, C. D. & Miller, P. J. (1998). Play. In H. Friedman (ed.), *Encyclopedia of mental health* (Vol. 3, pp. 189–197). San Diego: Academic Press.

Cross, G. (2008). Play in America from pilgrims and patriots to kid jocks and joystick jockeys: Or how play mirrors social change. *American Journal of Play, 1,* 7–46.

Dapporto, L., Turrillazzi, S., & Palagi, E. (2006). Dominance interactions in young adult paper wasp (*Polistes dominulus*) foundresses: A playlike behavior? *Journal of Comparative Psychology, 120,* 394–400.

Dyson, J.-P. (2008). Editorial policy. *American Journal of Play, 1,* iv.

Elkind, D. (2008). The power of play: Learning what comes naturally. *American Journal of Play, 1,* 1–6.

Fagen, R. M. (1981). *Animal play behavior.* Oxford: Oxford University Press.

Gee, J. P. (2008). Cats and portals: Video games, learning, and play. *American Journal of Play, 1,* 229–245.

Gray, P. (2009). Play as a foundation for hunter-gather social existence. *American Journal of Play, 1,* 476–522.

Groos, K. (1898). *The play of animals* (E. L. Baldwin, trans.). New York: Appleton.

Groos, (1901). *The play of man* (E. L. Baldwin, trans.). New York: Appleton.

Henricks, T. (2008). The nature of play: An overview. *American Journal of Play, 1,* 157–180.

Homeyer & Tomlinson (2008). Play therapy: Practice, issues, and trends. *American Journal of Play, 1,* 210–228.

Huizinga, J. (1955). *Homo ludens: A study of the play element in culture* (R. F. C. Hull, trans.). Boston: Beacon.

Johnson, J. E., Christie, J. F., & Yawkey, T. D. (1999). *Play and early childhood development.* New York: Longman.

Graham, K. L. & Burghardt, G. M. (in press). Current perspectives on the biological study of play: Signs of progress. *The Quarterly Review of Biology.*

Miller, E. & Almon, J. (2009). *Crisis in the kindergarten: Why children need to play in school.* College Park, MD: Alliance for Childhood.

Nwokah, E. P. & Graves, K. N. (2009). Word play: The creation and function of novel words in the pretend play of two siblings. *American Journal of Play, 1,* 429–450.

Panksepp, J. (1998). *Affective neuroscience: The foundations of human and animal emotions.* New York: Oxford University Press.

Panksepp, J. (2008). Play, ADHD, and the construction of the social brain: Should the first class of each day be recess? *American Journal of Play, 1,* 55–79.

Pellis, S. & Pellis, V. (2009). *The playful brain: Venturing to the limits of neuroscience.* Oxford: Oneworld Publications.

Pellegrini, A. D. (2009). *The role of play in human development.* New York: Oxford University Press.

Pepperberg, I. M., Breese, K. J., & Harris, B. J. (1991). Solitary sound play during acquisition of English vocalizations by an African Grey Parrot (*Psittacus erithacus*): Possible parallels with children's monologue speech. *Applied Psycholinguistics, 12,* 151–178.

Rubin, K. H., Fein, G., & Vandenberg, B. (1983). Play. In E. M. Hetherington (ed.), *Handbook of child psychology:* Vol. 4: *Socialization, personality and social development* (pp. 693–774). New York: Wiley.

Sarama, J. & Clements, D. H. (2009). Building blocks and cognitive building blocks: playing to know the world mathematically. *American Journal of Play, 1,* 313–337.

Sattelmair, J. & Ratty, J. J. (2009). Physically active play and cognition: An academic matter? *American Journal of Play, 1,* 365–374.

Sutton-Smith, B. (1997). *The ambiguity of play.* Cambridge, MA: Harvard University Press.

Tegano, D. W., Sawyers, J. K., & Moran, J. D. III. (1989). Problem-finding and solving in play: The teacher's role. *Childhood Education, 66,* 92–97.

Cultural Variations in Beliefs about Play, Parent–Child Play, and Children's Play: Meaning for Childhood Development

Jaipaul L. Roopnarine

Abstract

This review considers variations in parental beliefs about play and participation in play in different cultural communities. A more inclusive definition of play is offered that focuses on framed and unframed playfulness. Parents in western technologically developed societies were more likely to embrace play as important for children's cognitive and social development and to see themselves as play partners to children, whereas families in more traditional societies saw play as incidental to childhood development. These belief systems are congruent with culture specific socialization practices and goals in different developmental niches. Rough play was more characteristic of the activities of parents and children in European American than in Asian or hunting-gathering societies. Cultural variations also existed in early parent–child framed and unframed playful interactions. Sibling play was more prevalent than mother–child play in some societies, calling into question dyadic models of early play interactions. Children's play activities were considered in the context of the replication of adult activities, work and play and differential opportunities for play, and physical settings. It is proposed that play serves a scholastic function in technologically developed societies, whereas it assists in the reproduction of culture-specific tasks and behaviors in agricultural and hunting-gathering societies.

Key words: Beliefs, play, culture, fathers, siblings, scholastic, enculturation, agency

Play is an integral part of everyday childhood activities in most cultural communities around the world (Bock, this volume; Tudge et al., this volume). Among young children, play is readily observed in such diverse settings as the beaches of the Marquesan Islands (Martini, 1994), urban areas of New Delhi, India (Roopnarine, Hooper, Ahmeduzzaman, & Pollack, 1994), the communities of the Yucatan Peninsula (Gaskins & Miller, in press), the villages of the Amazon region of Brazil (Gosso, Morias, Otta, 2007), Gypsy communities in Europe (Levinson, 2005), and in the forests of Central Africa (Kamei, 2005). Play routines and activities are also evident during adult-child and sibling social encounters in different settings (Farver & Wimbarti, 1995; Haight & Miller, 1993; Roopnarine, Talukder, Joshi, & Srivastav, 1992; Singer, Singer, D'Agostino, & DeLong, 2009), though some have argued that parent–child play is a product of modernization in Western societies and is relatively absent in many communities (Lancy, 2007). Despite its ubiquity and the increasing appeal of child-centered, play-based learning across some societies (see Clarke-Stewart, Lee, Allhusen, Kim, & McDowell, 2006; Roopnarine & Metindogan, 2006; Singer et al., 2009), our understanding of the underlying connections between play and culture is far from complete. Studies of play are largely driven by conceptions of childhood and child development in western technological societies (Lancy, 1996, 2007, 2008).

In Western and other technologically developed societies, play is embraced as central in enhancing the growth of specific cognitive and social skills in young children. Parents provide numerous objects to promote opportunities for play, encourage early peer contacts, and actively engage in play stimulation activities with children throughout infancy and the early childhood years (Johnson, Christie & Wardle, 2009).

Within a "socialization model," parents who are good play partners (e.g., cheerful, affectionate, conversant, helpful, instructive) to children and those who permit children to freely explore the social and object world are applauded for investing in the long-term intellectual and personality development of their children (Grossman & Grossman, 1992; Singer et al., 2009). Mistakenly, the privileged position play holds for the development of childhood skills in European and European-heritage cultures is accepted as the universal norm. This view appears at odds with the diverse beliefs and cultural practices implemented by other groups in the care and education of children (see Lancy, 2007, for a detailed discussion of these issues), and with variability in the amount of time that children engage in play in diverse cultures (Singer et al., 2009)

A fundamental problem with universal claims about play is that they basically ignore the contrasting realities of childhood experiences and the cultural forces that may help shape caregivers' ideas about play and early learning, and children's role in their own play. Across human societies, even under difficult social and economic circumstances, cultural beliefs and practices, family structural arrangements, and modes of production have a tremendous influence on the expression of play, the determination of play partners, the settings in which play occurs, time allocated to play and work, and the links between play and everyday cognitive and social-cultural skills. In other words, play is culturally situated in the familial and social experiences of young children, often reflecting what is valued within cultural communities (Gaskins, 2006; Gaskins, Haight, & Lancy, 2006; Tudge et al., this volume). It is likely that play in all of its varied forms has culture-specific functions that have evolved over time and have been shaped by diverse forces (e.g., resources, modes of production) within particular developmental niches (see Greenfield, Keller, Fuligni, & Maynard, 2003, for a discussion of cultural pathways).

In this chapter, I provide an overview of cultural variations in adults' beliefs about play, parent–child play, and children's play. To this end, the meaning of different play activities within specific developmental niches during the early childhood years is braided into the discussion that follows. Play is broadly conceived herein to permit greater latitude to consider the range of cultural activities (e.g., among foragers and agricultural communities) that do not fit neatly into the traditional spectrum of cognitive and social modes of play activities commonly observed in technologically developed societies. Accordingly, play is defined as both culturally framed and unframed activities that are subsumed under the umbrella of "playfulness." As distinguished from conventional definitions of play, playfulness is a more universal phenomenon and includes childhood and parent–child unframed play activities that co-occur during caregiving and in children's encounters with different individuals and objects within specific developmental niches. This wider definition provides room for the inclusion of playful activities in cultural settings with simple social codes and collectivistic childrearing orientations (see Gosso et al., 2006). Taking note that the different chapters in this handbook cover much of the research on the nature and complexity of children's play in North America and Europe, I discuss play from a more global perspective with particular attention devoted to the role of cultural beliefs and practices in defining shared meaning about the manifestation of play in different settings. A point worth mentioning is that the studies considered in this overview span several decades. A lot has changed over the last few decades in family structural arrangements, familial roles, access to formal schooling, early childhood education practices, play materials, and technological access to the global community across societies. These changes are likely to influence contemporary views on how play is embraced and expressed in different cultural settings that are not yet fully captured by researchers.

Conceptual Issues

In a previous paper, my colleague and I argued that

> "cross-cultural generalizations about children's play continue to be hampered by issues of conceptualization, operationalization, measurement, and theoretical propositions that tend to ignore the cultural properties of childrearing and childhood experiences"
>
> (*Roopnarine & Krishnakumar*, 2006).

With some exceptions (Gosso et al., 2007; Kamei, 2005), the study of children's play across cultures is narrowly situated within theoretical frameworks and models that are steeped in European and European-heritage cultures that emphasize framed scholastic socialization goals and activities In most cases, play is viewed within a set of criteria (e.g., nonliterality) that may have limited application in developmental niches outside of the technologically developed world (see Gaskins & Miller, in press). The same can be said of older ethnographic studies that are often interpreted in static terms as representative of children's play today. A more productive understanding of children's play in diverse cultures would be greatly enhanced by:

(a) Theoretical frameworks and models that build on socialization beliefs, goals, and practices and the cultural pathways through which play and work activities are expressed in young children. There are multiple pathways to the acquisition of cognitive and social skills in different cultural groups other than through direct stimulation and instruction (e.g., observation/paying attention, performing tasks). Greenfield et al. (2003) proposed that while developmental psychological theories focus on universalistic principles in behavioral and cognitive development, clarifying culture-specific developmental pathways to human development should include considerations of cultural values (cultural values approach), ecological conditions (eco-cultural approach), and socialization practices (sociohistorical approach).

(b) Focusing on acculturation status and changes in ethnotheories about play as a potential tool for learning and development in immigrant and migrant families. The world is witnessing unprecedented population movements, and ethno-theories about play and learning may be modified as parents and other caregivers come face to face with childrearing and socialization beliefs and practices that emphasize modern schooling. The burgeoning body of research on acculturation and family and childhood development can be instructive in this regard.

(c) Defining more fully the relationships between work and play and their meaning for learning culture-specific skills in both boys and girls in traditional societies. Bock's work and theorizing are exemplary in this regard (Bock, 2002; Bock, this volume), but it is still not clear whether children's entry into work early in life in agricultural and hunting-gathering societies becomes a major vehicle for learning culture-specific knowledge and skills, thereby diminishing the potential that play has for learning as in technologically developed societies.

(d) Broadening definitions of play to include the wide range of playful activities, framed and unframed, that parents and children in agricultural and hunting-gathering societies pursue. As noted above, the field seems to be stuck on play activities that fall into a few general categories—mainly cognitive and social. Certain childhood and parent–child cultural activities in different developmental niches may not fit into conventional definitions of playful activities and could be misinterpreted as a lack of parental social and cognitive engagement with children.

(e) Building causal models that examine the associations between play and childhood outcomes over time. Correlational data are specious and do not consider moderating and mediating factors in determining childhood outcomes as a function of play participation or stimulation. With respect to ethnographic studies, multiple case studies undertaken in several cultural communities may aid in determining the effects of play and work on childhood development (Chick, 2010).

Beliefs about Play Across Cultures

Whether they pertain to expectations about when specific developmental milestones are reacheed (see Cote & Bornstein, 2003; Pachter & Dworkin, 1997), the use of everyday activities to teach cultural norms of behaviors (Fung, 1994), or adults' ideas about what constitutes childhood social and cognitive competence (Dubrow, 1999), parental ethno-theories about childrearing and the education of young children embody powerful cultural scripts. Psycho-cultural theorists (e.g., Super & Harkness, 1997) propose that ethno-theories or belief systems govern childrearing and the structuring and management of childhood activities. Some belief systems are passed down from one generation to the next (Greenfield et al., 2003; Schweder, 1982); others are constructed and revised relative to the demands of the cultural milieu (McGillicuddy-Delisi, 1982; Sigel & McGillicuddy-DeLisi, 2002) or remain relatively unchanged when cultural groups migrate from one society to another (Berry, 1990; Cote & Bornstein, 2003). Belief systems vary by ethnicity, cultural group membership, and socioeconomic status. For example, Lebanese-Australians have later expectations of when children acquire common developmental tasks (e.g., count from 1 to 10, know surname) compared with Anglo-Australians (Goodnow, Cahmore, Cotton, & Knight, 1984). In a similar vein, middle-income families in the United States believe in and engage in the practice of "concerted cultivation" during socialization (constantly coaching, creating opportunities) compared with low-income families who believe that children naturally acquire certain skills (Lareau, 2003). Not surprisingly, variability also exists in the value parents/adults place on conventional definitions of play for early childhood development and learning in different cultural communities.

From a limited group of studies conducted mostly in the technologically developed societies, it appears that adults from European and European-heritage cultural groups strongly endorse the belief that play assumes a significant role in children's intellectual and social development (Haight, Parke, & Black, 1997; Johnson, 1986; van der Kooj & Slatts-van den Hurk, 1991). For instance, Dutch mothers believed that play influences children's cognitive, social, personality, and socio-emotional development, and their creativity (van der Kooj & Slatts-van den Hurk, 1991), Midwestern European American mothers and fathers reported that pretend play activities contributed to children's creativity and cognitive development (Haight, Parke, & Black, 1997), and European American mothers in the northeast saw play as important for cognitive and individual development (Parmer, Super, & Harkness, 2005). These belief systems align well with the acceptance of play as an important commodity for systematic early stimulation of young children, fits within the ethos of current cultural constructions of modern childhood in North America and Europe (Lancy, 2007), and meshes well with the recent push in the United States for child-centered developmentally appropriate practices of which play is a key tenet (Bredekamp & Copple, 1997).

This enthusiasm for play is not fully embraced by all cultural groups in the technologically developed societies, however. As in the United States, Canadian, European, and Australian societies are becoming increasingly diverse and views about the value of play may vary quite a bit across ethnic groups. In some ethnic groups, such as African Americans and Hispanic Americans, childrearing cultural scripts and expectations of young children (e.g. multiple adult caregivers, sociocentric views on childrearing, respect for older members) (Harwood, Miller, Carlson, & Leyendecker, 1992), and economic and neighborhood characteristics may influence perceptions about play in preparing children for early schooling. According to Ogbu (1981), parents in underrepresented groups (e.g., involuntary migrants) make adjustments to childrearing strategies relative to the demands of the ecological niche. Likewise, because internal working models about early care and education remain tacit in immigrant groups (Roopnarine, Krishnakumar, & Li, 2009), beliefs regarding more structured early academic training may take precedence over play-based activities or at the very least present a bicultural paradox to immigrant parents. It is reasonable to expect, then, that within underrepresented and immigrant

groups in the technologically developed world, the ecological niches of children, embedded and contemporary socialization goals, and expectations of children may help define attitudes toward the benefits of play for early childhood development.

I would speculate that in foraging and agricultural developmental niches in which economic pressures are great, resources are scare, children are called upon to contribute to the household economy, and childhood mortality rates are high, parents are more likely to see play as incidental to the development of specific childhood skills. These conditions force parents into patterns of caregiving that maximize the chances for adequate nutrition and childhood survival (see LeVine, 1974). By comparison, in technologically developed ecological niches in which children are privileged economically and schooling is emphasized, there is likely to be more variability in views about the role of play in childhood development, with marginalized groups and those from non-European-heritage cultures having the least favorable attitudes toward play. More economically privileged European and European American groups are better positioned and have the luxury to invest in the longterm growth and development of children for economic and social mobility later on. Hence, stimulation of cognitive and social skills through play participation becomes one vehicle for laying the foundation for delayed educational returns. For marginalized groups in the technologically developed world, economic and social pressures may lead parents to choose didactic approaches over play in early education in order to minimize the risks attendant to school failure later on.

In an effort to further understand maternal cognitions about early care and education, Holloway, Rambaud, Fuller, and Eggers-Pieorla (1995) interviewed low-income black, Latina, and white mothers in the Boston area about early learning and education. These mothers preferred didactic lessons and did not see a relationship between play and learning. Related views about play were seen in Puerto Rican mothers in the northeastern United States. Low-income migrant Puerto Rican mothers expressed confidence in the benefits of convergent and divergent play, but emphasized learning content skills during the early childhood years (Soto & Negron, 1994). Ambiguity about the role of play in early childhood development was also found in a psychometric analysis of the beliefs of low-income African American mothers whose children were enrolled in Head Start centers (Fogle & Mendez, 2006). Although mothers thought that play assisted children to sharpen cognitive skills and prepare them for entry into school (e.g., "Play can help my child develop better thinking abilities that emerged" and "Playing at home will help my child get ready for kindergarten"), they indicated an academic focus as well (e.g., "I do not think my child learns important skills by playing" and "Reading to my child is more worthwhile than playing with him or her") (mean item response of 4.13 versus 2.18 on a five-point scale, respectively). There was a positive relationship between play support and parental education, and an inverse relationship between parental education and academic focus, suggesting that parents with higher levels of educational attainment were more likely to endorse play as a means for learning early cognitive and social skills than those with lower levels of educational attainment. Play beliefs did not differ significantly by marital or employment status or by gender of child.

Why might low-income Latina, Puerto Rican, and African American mothers have such mixed views about play? African Americans and other historically oppressed ethnic groups are well aware of the unequal access to educational opportunities, the disparities in school readiness and achievement between more privileged, middle-class children and low-income children in the United States (Suarez-Orozco, 2001). Armed with this information, they probably believe that exposure to early academic training may lay the foundation for later school success (Bowman, 1992). Stated differently, these parents may fully understand the "social value" of play but want to "prime" their children for school readiness and school success through early academic training—not through the "frivolity" of play. Indeed, the "No Child Left Behind" efforts at educating young children in the United States were premised on early achievement as measured by standardized instruments.

Uncertainty about the role of play in early childhood development is not limited to Latina and African American mothers. In a comparative study, Parmar, Harkness, and Super (2005) interviewed Asian (Korean, Chinese, East Indian, and Pakistani) and European American parents of preschool-aged children residing in the northeastern United States about the importance of play, learning, and their own role in early development. Consistent with the emphasis on early academic training that involves skills and drills in the natal culture (Clarke-Stewart, et al., 2006), Asian American parents placed more emphasis on the importance of learning. European American parents attributed greater value to play for childhood development in general, for cognitive development, and for individual development, and emphasized the role of parents as play partners and as a resource to their children than Asian American parents did. Asian American parents thought that play was far more important for the development of physical and social skills than did European American parents. Similar beliefs about play were offered by middle-class Korean-Americans, where 47% of mothers thought that play was for amusement and to relieve boredom (Farver, Kim, & Lee, 1995).

In India, Thailand, and Indonesia, alloparenting and co-sleeping are practiced, interdependence is valued, mothers are indulgent, and parents expect obedience from young children. It could be reasoned that in these societies parents would have more relaxed attitudes toward academic training for children early in their lives and see play as important for the development of social relationships and interpersonal ties. But this is hardly the case. East Indian mothers viewed play as a pleasurable activity and as incidental to childhood development (Roopnarine et al., 1994)—an activity that is a part of the culture of childhood (Goncu et al., 2000). Thai mothers had less favorable attitudes toward play-related activities (make-believe, painting, play with clay or blocks, playing with puzzles and games, singing and dancing) as compared to work-related activities (counting, learning Thai alphabet, learning color and shape names, learning the English alphabet, and moral and social conduct training) (Bloch & Wichaidat, 1986). Those who were better educated had more positive views about play than those who were less well educated. In an Indonesia sample, 69% of mothers believed that play was somewhat important for children: 39% thought that play contributed to the development of intelligence and creativity; 32% thought that play kept children happy, occupied, and not fussy; and 29% thought that play contributed to the development of social skills (Farver & Wimbarti, 1995). The last three views were present among Chinese mothers in Hong Kong as well (Holmes, 2001).

Perhaps some of the strongest evidence that parental beliefs about play are related to characteristics within the developmental niche comes from studies conducted in agricultural and hunting-gathering communities. Among the Yucatec Maya, economic activities are shared by familial members who live in close proximity to each other. Children spend most of their time around others and thus have frequent interactions with relatives. They are expected to engage in adult work. This phenomenon is not unusual in a number of other cultures (see Larson & Verma, 1999; Morelli, Rogoff, & Angelillo, 2003), and children have been observed to engage in a mixture of work and play (Chick, 2008; Lancy 1996). Amid these cultural practices and social ties, Yucatec Mayans do not see play as a central part of childhood socialization. In fact, they reported viewing play as an indication that children are healthy and as preventing them from interfering with adult work (Gaskins, 2001). Mothers in another Mayan community in Guatemala saw play as perfunctory to childhood development and laughed at the suggestion of engaging in play with young children (Goncu et al., 2000). Similarly, Kipsigis mothers in a rural African community did not see themselves as adequate playmates to children (Harkness & Super, 1985), and the Baining of the Gazelle Peninsula of East New Britain (Papua, New Guinea) believed that children learn through work and not play (Fajans, 1997). It is doubtful, too, that foraging groups have the same regard for play as their counterparts in the technologically developed world. Factors such as high child mortality rates, high fertility rates, and childrearing practices that demand a lot of physical care may lessen the importance ascribed to play as a developmental activity in foraging groups (see Lancy, 2007 for a review).

Taken together, the aforementioned studies have been conducted in cultural communities with different familial structural and social arrangements, diverse modes of economic production where economic resources flow from parent to child and child to parent, emphasis on different childrearing practices, and variable infant and childhood mortality rates. So much of what we know about parental belief systems and play is held against norms in what Morelli et al. (2003) described as middle-class communities (European or European American) in which children have considerable access to one-on-one conversations with adults, engage in child-centered activities such as adult-child play and directed speech that focus on educational activities, and have very little exposure to adult work. With this in mind, maternal beliefs about play seem to fall along a continuum—from views about play as active or concerted practices to play as peripheral to childhood development (Gaskins, Haight, & Lancy, 2007). At the moment, among the different cultural groups in Western technological societies, mothers from European and European-heritage cultures have the most positive views about the role of play in childhood development. Underrepresented ethnic groups and some immigrant groups in the United States are less inclined to make such a favorable endorsement and prefer the use of more direct, didactic approaches with children in the early learning process.

In agricultural and hunting-gathering cultural communities with closely knit, interdependent social ties, and in which childrearing values place far less emphasis on formal learning routines, parents are not impressed with the possibility of play as a mechanism for the development of early childhood skills. Parents in these cultural groups are of the opinion that play is a behavioral activity that is internally driven—something that is naturally of intrinsic interest to young children and something children engage in independent of adult guidance (see Edwards, 2000) or that it simply keeps children busy (Grantham-McGregor, Landman, & Desai, 1983). At either end of the continuum, through their ethno-theories about play—prohibitive, indifferent, or encouraging—parents are conveying to children the social and cognitive transactions that are important for the acquisition of instrumental competence within their specific developmental niches. These assertions are made cautiously, however, knowing that few studies have assessed beliefs about play in fathers, allomothers or alloparents, and siblings, who are quite involved in the care and education of young children in many cultural communities. Further, little is known about children's views about play in their own development.

Three Modes of Parent–Child Play
It was intimated that positive beliefs about play are likely to invite more detailed participation in play stimulation activities with high levels of proto-conversations between parents and young children. In Western technologically developed societies, parent–child play activities contain more language and gesture-oriented routines than peer play (Turkheimer, Bakeman, & Adams, 1989), and thus may contribute in unique ways to language and cognitive development. In particular, joint coordinated activities between parents and children in the area of object use—showing, pointing—have been linked to complex language skills (Zukow-Goldring, 1996), and fantasy play is correlated with early cognition, creativity, and a number of social skills (see Johnson et al., 2005; Smith, 2010 for review of correlational studies). These skills bode well for meeting the demands of the modern school culture and for promoting school success.

Deliberate attempts at stimulating children during parent–child play are not as pervasive in cultural groups outside the technologically developed world (Lancy, 2007). The concept of parents as "play-partners" to young children is more endemic to technologically developed than to traditional societies. Mothers in the United States acted as "playmates" to toddlers 47% of the time during planned episodes compared to 7% of the time in Guatemala, and 24% of the time in India (Rogoff et al., 1993). In many cultures, play partners routinely include non-parental figures: grandparents, cousins, siblings, aunts, uncles, and other people in the "yard" or compound (Farver & Wimbarti, 1995; Maynard, 2004). Thus, it is not uncommon for the care of young children to be distributed among several individuals. For example, Hadza mothers interacted with infants 78%, fathers 18%, sisters 18%, brothers 8%, grandmothers 9%, and others 29% of the time observed (Marlowe, 2005), and Baka child-caregivers (older siblings and maternal relatives) were within proximity of infants 19.1% of the time compared with fathers (7.7%) and grandmothers (7.5%). Maternal physical closeness with infants was very pronounced in both these cultures, suggesting other modes of early maternal stimulation (e.g., kissing, soothing, grooming, gentle rocking) (Hirasawa, 2005). Depending on the health and nutritional status of children, the focus on play stimulation would seem secondary in poorer societies as adult caregivers are forced to be practical—routinely focusing their attention on solutions regarding the immediate needs and health of young children (Keller, et al., 2004; LeVine, 2004).

In view of the questions raised about the prevalence of parent–child play across cultures and their implications for a universal understanding of play (Lancy, 2007), the focus here is on three modes of play between parents and children that, arguably, have received the most attention across cultural groups: parent–child physical play, parent–child playful stimulation activities and object use, and parent–child fantasy play. Rough stimulating play was chosen because several theses have been advanced about its importance for father-child relationships (Paquette, 2004) and because of the minimal attention devoted to father-child play across cultures. Parent–child games and fantasy play were included due to their professed significance for the development of cognitive skills (see Harris, 2000; Johnson et al., 2005; Singer & Singer, 1990; Smith, 2010).

Parent–child physical play

In prior decades, researchers have discovered that during infancy and through the preschool years,

rough play (bouncing tossing, tickling, rough-and-tumble) occurred frequently during bouts of father-child interactions among European Americans (Lamb, 1977; Macdonald & Parke, 1986; Pellegrini, this volume). In other technologically developed societies, such as Israel and Sweden, rough play between fathers and children occurred about once per hour (Lamb, Frodi, Frodi, & Hwang, 1982; Sagi, Lamb, Shoham, Dvir, & Lewkowicz, 1985). Much has changed since Lamb's (1977) initial work on early parent–infant interactions that led him to suggest that children form attachments to fathers through rough, physically arousing activities. Today, mothers and fathers assume multiple roles (e.g., moral socialization, teaching, nurturance, companion, economic provider, etc.) which may affect levels of investment in caring for and in playing with children (Tamis-LeMonda, 2004). A study conducted within the last decade on Canadian (Quebecois) families with infants indicated similarity in maternal and paternal interaction and play patterns (Laflamme, Pomerleau, & Malcuit, 2002). Might such a shift be occurring in parent–child play in cultures that are more traditional?

Our observational work in India, Thailand, and Taiwan—societies in which father work demands are high but childrearing tendencies are more relaxed than in Western technologically developed societies—assessed rough play between fathers and infants and fathers and preschoolers in the home environment. These Asian societies have all been influenced by filial piety and fathers have traditionally been viewed as distant or austere, increasing the chances that investment in playful interactions with young children may be minimal or relegated to mothers. On different levels, all three societies are still driven by collectivistic tendencies and social and religious doctrines that speak to equanimity, interpersonal ties, and group harmony (see Kakar & Kakar, 2007; Shwalb et al, 2004), society-wide forces that may discourage attempts at rough activities with young children in place of more gentle touching and physical affection.

In New Delhi, India, father-infant minor and major physical play occurred on average less than once per hour of observation and only in a small percentage of two-parent, middle-income families. The display of affection and object-mediated play by fathers was observed at higher frequencies than either minor or major rough play (Roopnarine, Talukder, Jain, Joshi, & Srivastav, 1991). Similarly, in two-parent middle-income families residing in urban and peri-urban areas of Taiwan, father-infant rough play occurred at low frequencies and far below the display of affection toward children (Sun & Roopnarine, 1996). Observations of preschool-aged children and their parents in Chaing Mai Province in northern Thailand indicated that rough play between mothers and children and fathers and children was virtually nonexistent (Tulananda & Roopnarine, 2001), and in an interview study of child-drearing practices in Malaysian families in Kuching, Sarawak, neither mother nor father reported engaging in rough play broadly defined (Roopnarine, Lu, & Ahmeduzzaman, 1989). In India, Thailand, and Taiwan, rough play between mothers and infants was exceedingly low. Nevertheless, fathers in India and Taiwan engaged in more rough play than did mothers. There were no gender of child differences in paternal participation in rough play in India, Thailand, or Taiwan, which is somewhat surprising given the traditional division of roles in most Asian societies and the strong preference for sons in some (e.g., India and China) (Kakar & Kakar, 2007; Shwalb et al., 2004).

So far it appears that physical play is more prevalent among European American and Quebecois fathers and children than between fathers and children in some Asian societies. But what about the occurrence of physical play in foraging societies, where alloparenting is practiced, and group effort and sharing are valued? The AKA foragers of the Central African Republic exemplify these practices. Extensive ethnographic work conducted on the AKA foragers indicate that major (e.g., rough-housing) and minor physical play (tickling, poking) were observed at less than one incident per hour or reported to be absent from social exchanges with young children (Hewlett, 1987). AKA mothers engaged in three bouts and fathers did not engage in any rough play in over 264 hours of observations (Hewlett, 1987). Equally striking was the fact that AKA fathers exceeded mothers in the display of affection and in soothing infants. On the rare occasions when rough play did occur, siblings were more likely than other familial members to participate in it. Likewise, among the Baka, another foraging group in the Republic of Cameroon, rough play was rarely observed between parents and children (Hirawasa, 2005).

From these data, it is highly doubtful that parent–child rough play is a primary avenue for the development of attachment relationships to fathers across cultures. Nor is it clear that, during infancy and middle-childhood, fathers are "playmates" to children more so than mothers—a point made repeatedly in the fathering literature. In North America, where much of the debate occurs about the differential roles of mothers and fathers and the development of attachment relationships (see Paquette, 2004; Tamis-LeMonda, 2004), it has been estimated from a national representative US sample that time engagement in play/companionship failed to show gender of parent differences (Yeung, Sandberg, Davis-Kean, & Hofferth, 2001), and Quebecois mothers and fathers engaged in similar levels of rough play with infants. A comparable trend was determined for Brazilian families (Benetti & Roopnarine, 2006), and in other cultural groups such as the Kadazan (Hossain, Roopnarine, Ismail, Hashmi, & Sombuling, 2008) and rural Malay Muslim families, both of Malaysia (Hossain et al., 2005). In fact, mothers in the Malaysian families spent significantly more time in play than fathers did.

Unlike the findings of differential parental interactions with boys and girls in North American families (see Lamb, 2002), mothers and fathers in cultural communities in India, Taiwan, and Thailand did not engage in more physically stimulating activities with boys than girls (Roopnarine et al., 1990; Tulananda & Roopnarine, 2001; Sun & Roopnarine, 1996). Time spent with children in Brazil and Malaysia did not show gender of child effects either. Unfortunately, the studies conducted among the Kadazan, Malay, and southern Brazilian families focused on single age groups and overall time engagement in play without determining the modes of play mothers and fathers participated in with children. As a result, it is difficult to gauge whether mothers and fathers in these historically traditional societies are consistently playing with boys and girls more equitably in different activities or that more gender-specific interactions with children begin later in societies with prolonged, indulgent childhood periods.

What purpose might parent–child physical play serve in the human species? Two recent theses have been formulated on father-child rough play: (a) work demands on fathers in industrialized, western cultures leave little time for sustained interactions with young children, so fathers participate in activities that have immediate appeal to children (Hewlett, 2004), and (b) fathers are "activators" who arouse their children during rough bouts of play which then, creates openness to social experiences thereby promoting social competence (Paquette, 2004; Tamis-LeMonda, 2004). Cross-cultural evidence for both propositions is rather sketchy because rough play is relatively absent or occurs at such low frequencies in many cultural communities even in societies where paternal work commitments are demanding (Roopnarine et al., 1992; Sun & Roopnarine, 1996). By the same token, the relative absence of parent–child rough play in many societies begs the question about an underlying biological function in humans (See Pellegrini, this volume).

If children form attachments to fathers across cultures, then what cultural practices might facilitate the development of such a bond assuming a biological underpinning? No credible scientific evidence exists that children form attachments to fathers across cultural settings, especially in those in which father availability and investment is low or in which alloparenting is a cultural norm. A safe bet is that father-child rough play may have added importance in cultures where dyadic interactions characterize family socialization patterns and in which there is overarching cultural acceptance of rough, competitive activities. In this sense, father-child play is culturally meaningful and provides access to fathers. By contrast, in societies where there are multiple caregivers, child mortality rates are high, and social cooperation is emphasized, adult-child rough play is expected to have less currency.

Early parent–child play stimulation activities

Parent–child co-playing in the form of stimulation activities not only assists in the transmission of cultural information; the properties of these activities themselves may give a boost to cognitive and social functioning, particularly for children in the technologically developed world (see Bruner, 1972; Lancy, 2007; Vygotsky, 1978). Because of the lack of information on parent–child play across societies, the implications of these associations are less defined for many cultural communities. Nevertheless, the different features of the playful activities consist of language use, turn-taking, repetition, and temporal regularities (Roopnarine et al., 1993; Stern, 1974), and offer opportunities for children to receive tactile, visual, and auditory stimulation and engage in limb or body movements (Johnson et al., 2005).

As with other areas of parent–child activities across cultures, variability exists with respect to the nature, frequency, and quality of early parent–child stimulation activities. For example, face-to-face play that is commonly observed in the social exchanges of parents and children in Western industrialized societies (e.g., North America, Europe) (see Roopnarine, Fouts, Lamb, & Lewis-Elligan, 2005) is rarely witnessed in Kaluli (Ochs & Schieffelin,

1984) or Marquesan mother-infant play (Martini & Kirkpatrick, 1992). Mothers and fathers in technologically developed societies vigorously pursue face-to-face encounters that are frequently accompanied by language use, smiling, and laughter. Again, these stimulation exercises fall within the socialization model that emphasizes the development of agency in children. By contrast, in the Kaluli, direct eye contact is avoided because it is associated with witchcraft, and the Marquesans engage in the practice of holding the infant outward so that it is open to interactions with others, reflecting early socialization emphasis on social ties and social cooperation. A drawback is that considerations of dyadic interactions between mother and infant basically ignore the role of other socialization agents. When sibling caregiving was taken into account, Kenyan and American children received about the same amount of en face (Whaley, Bekwith, Cohen, & Espinosa, 2000), suggesting different cultural pathways to the display of the same behaviors.

Other differences have been observed in the early playful interactions of mothers and infants across cultures. Japanese mothers loomed in and out, used tapping to attract visual attention, and held and touched infants, whereas European American mothers were more likely to use their voice and respond to vocalizations during face-to-face interactions (Fogel, Nwokak, & Karnes, 1993). In the technologically developed societies, parent–child playful activities are more likely to co-occur with objects and to involve labeling, gesture, and motion than in more traditional societies (Goncu et al., 2000). Analysis of early parent–child playful activities among East Indians indicated that there were high levels of tactile and verbal stimulation (songs, lullabies, poetry, and rhymes). For instance, in 87% of them the child was held close to the body or massaged, in 21% the mother sang to the baby, and 52% involved face-to-face social engagement. Another study (Rogoff et al., 1993) showed that East Indian mothers tickled, cooed, and played peek-a-boo with their toddlers to express affection, but also teased children, and scared them by growling. Games of touching, patting, hugging, kissing, and dancing were recorded in India, Turkey, Guatemala, and the United States (Goncu et al, 2000). These modes of interactions are the sine qua non of early patterns of caregiving in foraging and agricultural societies, and subtle play activities may be a part of them (see Eibl-Eibesfeldt, 1983).

A game that has generated more diverse interest among parents involves different versions of "hide-and-seek" or disappearance and emergence of the adult face. Peek-a-boo has been observed in the play of parents and infants in South Africa, Japan, Malaysia, Iran, Brazil, Russia, India, Turkey, and Korea; other cultures may have parallel forms of the game. The game's obvious gleeful qualities and surprise element recruit quite a bit of attention in infants in most cultural groups. Language use during the game is also noticeable. However, important distinctions are recognized in mother–child involvement in the game across cultures. Indian mothers used their "ghunghat" (sari to hide the face) and Turkish mothers used a doily to cover the face during peek-a-boo (Goncu et al., 2000). Among South Africans, the acoustics had a rough and gravely quality, and among Tamil and Portuguese-speaking Brazilian parents the exchanges involved use of words beyond nonsense syllables (Fernald & O'Neill, 1993). Although these attempts at "verbal stimulation" may seem casual in some cultural communities, their significance for the development of language cannot be overlooked.

Parent–child pretend play

Quite a few studies have charted the developmental progression of pretense, the documentation of different modes of pretense, and their presumed functions and benefits (see Howes, Kavanaugh, and Lillard chapters in this volume). In spite of such widespread attention, only a handful of researchers have explored the complexities of parent–child pretend play in cultures that stand apart from the Western technologically developed world. And fewer yet have concentrated on child-initiated pretend play with parents, mothers or fathers. This is rather surprising because of the universal presence of pretend play in children's groups across societies, the importance accorded pretend play in childhood development (see Haight et al., 1999; Smith, 2010), and the weight given to parents in the transmission of cultural knowledge and the reproduction of culture (Hirschfeld, 2002).

The thin body of work on parental involvement in pretend play across cultures is mostly based on mother–child dyadic interactions (e.g., Bornstein, Haynes, Pascual, Painter, & Galperin, 1999; Farver et al., 1995; Suizzo & Bornstein, 2006; Tamis-LeMonda, Bornstein, Cyphers, Toda, & Ogino, 1992). Typically, in the technologically developed societies, mother-initiated pretend play involves objects and the mother assumes an active role in initiating pretend play, sometimes entering pretend play as an actor. As an example, dyadic play with an adult partner was more frequent in Utah and Turkey than in India or Guatemala (Goncu et al., 2000). This is in direct contrast to agricultural and technologically developing communities where siblings and other relatives are playmates to young children and older siblings organize pretend play for children. In a few communities, pretend play is inseparable from sibling caregiving activities (Gaskins & Miller, in press).

A reasonable question is: Do adults initiate more fantasy play than children across cultures? A carefully designed longitudinal study of child-initiated and adult-initiated pretend play in Chinese families in Taiwan and Irish American families may aid in providing a partial answer to this question (Haight et al., 1999). Of the 14 hours of pretend play (5 hours occurring in Taiwanese homes and 9 hours occurring in Irish American homes in Chicago) out of 168 hours of home observations, all children engaged in pretend play at 30, 36, and 48 months and in pretend play with their caregivers at each age level. Child-initiated pretend play was significantly greater in Irish American than Chinese children. Correspondingly, the mean proportion of caregiver-initiated pretend play that was coded as play only was observed at higher frequencies and contained more fantasy themes in Irish American than Chinese families. No comparisons were made between child-initiated and adult-initiated pretend play, but pretend initiations were higher for caregivers at 30 months and higher for children at 48 months for both groups of families. Irish American caregiver-child pretend play was more likely to involve caretaking, whereas Chinese caregiver pretend play was more likely to involve social interactions with non-kinship adults, apparently to teach appropriate conduct. These findings suggest the decreased role of parents in pretend play as children become more immersed in the peer group. Haight et al. (1999) suggested that in technologically developed societies, European American parents may initially act as facilitators of young children's pretend play, a role that appears to be defined more by the need for scholastic training than spontaneity. At the same time, through pretend play childrearing goals are likely introduced by way of fantasy themes.

Two other observational studies may be of interest because, in addition to mothers, they focused on fathers and siblings as potential playmates during pretend episodes in Asian communities with somewhat similar childrearing expectations and practices. First, we (Tulananda & Roopnarine, 2001) observed play interactions along with a range of social activities between mothers and fathers and preschool-aged children in and around the home in Chaing Mai Province in northern Thailand. Thai parents value obedience, interpersonal ties, and respect for elders, and nurture the development of these behaviors during an indulgent childhood period. During two-hour observation periods conducted on each family during the day, it was found that Thai mothers and fathers engaged in low levels of constructive, pretend, and rough play, and in games with rules with children. Mothers and fathers engaged in less than one incident of pretend play with children during the two-hour observations. Could it be that these parents used other cultural practices for playful interactions, such as, teasing, joking, and telling stories—all of which are more centrally located in Thai socialization practices? Given Thai parents' beliefs about play versus early academic and moral training, we can only speculate that these other socialization mechanisms are probably used by parents during everyday socialization to supplant play as a primary parent–child activity in conveying socially and culturally relevant information to children. Lancy's (1996) work on the Kpelle in Liberia supports these alternate routes (e.g., story-telling as another play form) to achieving socialization goals.

The second study, conducted in Indonesia, was more structured in that toys were offered for mothers and children to play with during videotaping sessions (Farver & Wimbarti, 1995). Families were selected in which children (18, 24, and 36-month-olds) had older siblings (4.5–6 years of age). Like Thai society, the Javanese believe in maintaining interpersonal harmony and children are expected to be obedient, respectful, and empathetic toward others. Sibling caregiving is in place early in children's lives and older children manage the social contacts younger children have with others outside of the home with great efficiency (see Farver & Wimbarti, 1995 for a discussion of these issues). The semi-structured situation, in which parents and children were "encouraged to play with objects," elicited a good deal of pretend play by mothers and siblings. Interestingly, older siblings joined play, and made comments and suggestions for pretend play more frequently than mothers did. Sibling play interactions were more positively attuned than mother–child play interactions. Mother–child play contained more family role themes, whereas sibling play contained more danger in the environment themes. These data are in accord with the perspective that sibling caregivers are viable socialization

agents in several societies and may use play activities to buttresses the learning of cultural and other skills whose development may not be fully supported during parent–child interactions (Edwards, 2000; Maynard, 2004).

To summarize: The cross-cultural literature suggests that parent–child play may be more prevalent across cultures than some have argued (e.g., Lancy, 2007). The alleged lack of mother–child play interactions in other cultural communities around the world could be due to what we are not observing, a point made by Hirschfeld (2002) and Bird-David (2005) about the limited ethnographic focus on children. It is nonetheless true that the socialization model, wherein adults engage in a systematic, sustained process of play stimulation activities with children from infancy onward, is more a part of Western technologically developed than traditional societies. This does not mean, though, that parents and other caregivers in agricultural and hunting-gathering societies do not engage in early stimulation activities that encompass close physical contact, teasing, rough joking, narratives, and the like. It is in these activities that we may see hidden forms of play.

An interesting aspect of adult co-playing in games and participation in physical and social play activities with young children is that in some cultural communities parents may become less visible playmates to children toward the middle childhood years or even earlier. As indicated above, Javanese mothers and siblings engaged in almost equivalent play episodes (676 versus 663) and in some instances siblings made more suggestions for play than mothers (Farver & Wimbarti, 1995; see Gaskins & Miller, in press). As children increase their social contacts with other children outside of the home, sibling play is bound to increase, augmenting parent–child interactions in a complementary manner. A slightly different developmental process emerges for children in foraging cultures (e.g., Hadza, Efe). As is shown later, young children in a number of societies are exposed to and engage in work early in their lives, and child-focused activities and adult play with children are far below those of their counterparts in communities in the technologically developed societies (Morelli et al., 2003). The chances of co-playing with adults may decrease appreciably as work demands on children to produce resources increase between five and seven years in traditional cultural communities (see Kaplan & Bock, 2001; Gaskins & Miller, in press).

Conversely, it seems likely that in certain cultural communities, parent–child play is likely to increase in the future due to the demands of schooling in a contemporary world, increased exposure and encouragement of child-centered approaches to childrearing and early education, migration that brings people in contact with contemporary internal working models about the value of early stimulation for childhood development, and the proliferation of objects for play across societies. Changes in the play behaviors of mothers and children can already be seen in families who migrate from societies in which beliefs about play were viewed as less important for early learning (Clarke-Stewart et al., 2006). Korean-American mothers with an "assimilated" acculturation style showed greater acceptance of play and creativity and reported more play with children compared with mothers who had a marginal, integrated, or separated acculturation style (Farver & Lee-Shinn, 2000). Similarly, Cote and Bornstein (2005) in a study of Japanese and South American immigrants in the United States concluded that parenting behaviors among immigrant families may change ahead of beliefs about childrearing.

Children's Play in Different Settings

Unlike parent–child play, there are rich descriptions of children's play in many cultural settings (see Chick, 2010; Gosso, 2010; Lancy, 2007, 2010): Kpelle children in Liberia (Lancy, 1996), Xavante boys in the Brazilian rainforest (Gosso et al., 2005; Nunes, 2005), Xhosa children (Wilkins, 2002), Mbuti and Baka in the central African rainforests (Kamei, 2005; Turnbull, 1962), Igbo of Nigeria (Ottenberg, 1989), and several other groups around the world (Lancy, 2007). Distinctions and similarities have been identified in children's play in technologically developed and more traditional societies. Three findings appear more consistently across cultures and have been discussed in detail elsewhere: object use—self-constructed or manufactured objects; fantasy play; and gender-differentiated involvement in play (see Gosso, 2010; Gosso et al., 2007; Haight et al., 1999; Smith, 2010). Rather than restate these well-known findings, in this section I focus on three issues that may add to our understanding of how children play and the meaning of play in diverse cultural communities: play as a reflection of cultural skills within the immediate developmental niche, work/play combination and differential opportunities for play, and the physical settings in which play occurs. Studies that are more culturally grounded are considered.

Play as a reflection of adult cultural activities

It is not difficult to see that the play activities of young children contain both tradition-oriented and contemporary themes related to activities performed by adults. An ethnographic account of the Baka foragers of the Republic of the Cameroon (Kamei, 2005) revealed that young children engaged in 85 different types of play that involved (a) foraging activities, such as hunting (e.g., making a trap, attacking animals with stones, mouse-hunting with bows or spears), gathering (e.g., termite gathering, insect collecting), and fishing (e.g., fishing with fishing rods, fishing with baskets); (b) playing house that consisted of hut, food and cooking (e.g., making a hut, play cooking with inedible materials), clothes (e.g., making eyeglasses out of vines, washing a sash), and housework and tools (e.g., playing with fire, doll, umbrella); and (c) songs, dances and music that included traditional songs and dances (e.g. mimicking forest spirits, dancing), and instruments (grass flute, bursting leaves). Hunting and gathering and songs, dance, and music were categorized as tradition-oriented play, occupying about 48% of children's play activities. Modern play forms were observed in children using chairs to mimic car drivers, in activities with miniature airplanes made out of the stem of a papaya, and in competitive games (e.g., playing "songo," an African board game, with stones). These modern types of play constituted 21% of children's play activities and perhaps indicate the transformations that are occurring in play that could be a result of the introduction of manufactured toys and changes in the ethos of childhood. These different modes of play that children engaged in incorporate different aspects of adult activities but not in totality. Seemingly, children chose activities to mimic or imitate those that were of interest to them (Kamei, 2005).

Young children's imitation or partial replication of adult modes of behavior is also seen in detailed observations of play activities carried out in other agricultural and hunting-gathering societies. Among the Kung San! of the Kalahari (Konner, 1972), children used sticks and pebbles as huts and to tend to animals, Marquesan children spent 24% of their time in scripted fantasy (e.g., fishing, hunting) (Martini, 1994), and children of the Okavango Delta, Botswana, pretended to pound grain in a hole in the ground or in a small vessel, an important subsistence activity (Bock, 2002). Fantasy play that included a range of adult activities has been recorded in Hadza children of Tanzania (e.g., predators) (Blurton-Jones, 1993), in the Parakana Indian and seashore children of Brazil (e.g., girls using a pestle to prepare manioc flour and boys playing with bows and arrows for target and non-target shooting) (Gosso, et al., 2007), the Kpelle of Liberia (e.g., Blacksmith) (Lancy, 1996), the Xavante of Brazil (e.g., Gosso et al., 2007), and Gikuyu of Kenya (e.g., boys making axes and girls making pottery [Leacock, 1978]). In the Six Culture study, role play, constructive play, and games with rules were noticed in all of the communities for both boys and girls, and fantasy play occurred in the United States (e.g., playing sheriff and deputies, riding horses using a ruler), India, the Philippines (e.g., card playing with leaves, playing horse, sword fighting), Kenya, and Japan (e.g., sword fight, playing house).

Having established that adult activities are represented in children's play across many cultures, is there evidence that participation in them enhances the mastery of skills necessary for life within cultural communities? Put differently, do children develop a sense of agency by enacting adult roles and activities during play? Answers to this deceptively simple question can add muscle to the importance of play versus direct instruction or observation in the development of adult modes of behaviors and competencies across societies—the so-called enculturation function. A general argument is that the early apprenticeship in adult-type activities through play eventually leads to competence in them. A more immediate connection between adult practices and childhood play behaviors is seen in the Arapesh (Mead, 1935) and the Marquesans (Martini, 1994), who exemplify the cooperative spirit. In both groups, children rarely engage in competitive play. In fact, up to 93% of Marquesan children's play is of a cooperative nature. More direct evidence of the association between enacting adult activities in early childhood and later skills can be found in at least two sets of observations. The play pounding indicated for children in Botswana switches to actual pounding around 8–9 years of age when girls are called upon by mothers to assist with this activity (Bock, 2002). Around this time, there is an inverse relationship between real pounding and play pounding. Nunes' (2005) account of the "coal dust game" in the Xavante of Brazil provides yet another example of the process of enculturation. Xavante children employed a historically adult method of shaming to arouse their peers out of bed for school. That is, they would visit the homes of

children who were not up for school and rub coal dust on their faces. What is different in this case is that children restored an old Xavante adult practice that spoke to responsibility among men to provide for their families. Essentially, children transferred this sense of responsibility to the school context.

No doubt children learn culturally appropriate behaviors such as cooperation and sharing through play. This does not rule out the possibility that children in more traditional societies may learn adult modes of behaviors through observation and mimicry. Indeed, in quite a few cultural communities, children observe and then imitate adult activities in their play (see Lancy, 2007, 2008). The task ahead is to demonstrate more persuasively how children's play behaviors are connected to learning culture-specific skills in societies outside of the technologically developed world (see Gaskins & Miller, in press for a discussion of the socialization of emotions in the Yucatec Maya). As Gosso et al. (2007) suggested in their work on different groups of children in Brazil, "The structure and value transmission of these worlds have to be investigated more to base cross-cultural comparisons on a better understanding of the social representations and messages that are transmitted to the children concerning their present and their expectancies about the future" (p. 155).

Work/play combination and differential opportunities for play

Earlier it was suggested that children in traditional societies have more opportunities to observe work-related activities and that their play included more work-associated themes than children in technologically developed societies (Morelli et al., 2003). In the Six Cultures study conducted in Kenya, Mexico, Philippines, Okinawa, India, and the United States, children between 3–11 years of age were observed in play during 273 observations, in work during 85, in learning 39, and in social interactions 198. Wenger (1989), in her study of the Kaloleni in rural Kenya, reported that work activities for children showed a linear increase with age: 1% for 2–3 year-olds, 8% for 4–5 year-olds, 18% for 6–7 year-olds, and 38% for 8–11 year-olds. And assessments of the work activities of children between 3–9 years of age in the Lagoli of Kenya, the Garifuna of Belize, the Newars of Nepal, and American Samoa indicated that by the time children are 3 they spent about 10% of their time doing chores, and by age 9 they spent one-third of their nonschool time working (Munroe, Munroe, & Shimmin, 1984). Parakana Indian children enter work earlier, too (e.g., washing clothes, cooking, caring for siblings) in comparison to more privileged urban children in Brazil (Gosso et al., 2007). Other data from a wide range of societies support the early assumption of work responsibilities by young children (see Larson & Verma, 1999 for an extensive review).

Several theoretical frameworks have been proposed on children's work and play. One of them, embodied capital theory (Kaplan, 1997; Kaplan & Bock, 2001), seems pertinent to the present discussion because it addresses time devoted to work, play, and learning. Basically, there are two aspects of embodied capital: growth-based (e.g., body size, balance, strength) and experience-based (e.g., memory, cognitive functioning, task-specific skills, etc.). Within a life history framework, it can be determined how much time is distributed to work, play, and learning taking into account age, gender, household economy and subsistence strategy, and family demographics (Bock, 2002, 2005, this volume). As far as time allocated to work and play is concerned, the goal for parents is to achieve a balance between immediate returns and future gains. Parents must weigh the benefits and costs associated with growth-based and experience-based capital relative to contributions to the household economy over time (Bock, 2002, 2005). In some cases, children may spend more time in productive tasks in which they are competent, while at other times they may spend time in the development of skills that may serve them well in the future. As can be deduced, the trade-offs between allocating time to play and work is rather complex (see Kaplan, 1997, and Chick, 2010, for a more detailed discussion of embodied capital).

Although engagement in work early in life can limit opportunities for play, there are many examples of children integrating work into play. Nyansongo, Xavante, Kpelle, and children in the Kaloleni community have all been observed to mix play with domestic and other subsistence tasks (see Edwards, 2000; Fajans, 1997; Gosso et al., 2007; Lancy 1996; Wenger, 1989). For instance, children "may play marbles on their way to the grocery, or chase birds when they go out to search for water" (Gosso, 2010, p. 85). A robust finding is that across cultural communities boys have more time for play than girls. Turning to the Six Culture study once more, boys (4–5 years of age) in all of the communities spent more time in play, and with the exception

of the United States where boys and girls did not engage in any work, girls engaged in more work (e.g., housework, gardening, childcare) than boys. In Brazil, Parakana Indian boys spent about roughly 60% of their waking hours in play compared to 48% for girls (Gosso, 2010) and among children in Kaloleni, Kenya, girls worked 51% of the time and boys only 26 % of the time observed (Wenger, 1989).

Beyond inferences about the preparation for gender-specific adult roles, the meaning of these discrepancies in opportunities for play between boys and girls is not well understood (see Gosso et al., 2007; Wenger, 1989). It is obvious from the ethnographic data that young girls are involved in more caregiving and domestic tasks and are more likely to remain within or near their households and compounds than are boys (Chick, 2010; Edwards, 2000). The gendered participation in work-related childcare and household activities may be a product of the traditional division of childcare and household labor in most societies. Hence, girls carry a heavier burden of assuming these tasks, presumably to prepare them for these roles later on (see Wegner, 1989). In trying to determine the benefits children accrue from early work and play in traditional societies, one could very well argue that the admixture may have less potential for learning educational skills than it does for learning household chores, caring for young children, and engaging in subsistence type activities. Heavy involvement in work early may mean that young children do not need to practice desired cultural skills through play (Edwards, 2005; Gosso et al., 2007). By definition, household and subsistence tasks require the display of nurturance, caring, empathy, cooperation, and responsibility, all of which could be acquired and refined during work and not necessarily through play (see Chick, 2010).

Physical settings
The physical settings and familial contexts within which children reside may present opportunities and impediments to play. In hunting-gathering and agricultural societies, children's play activities receive less supervision and children explore varied activities with relative ease. In many societies, boys are given more latitude to play in open spaces, farther away from home, and play in larger groups (Edwards, 2000), whereas girls play in smaller, internal spaces nearer to home, and in smaller groups (Edwards, 2000; Smith, 2005). In the Kaloleni community, during work boys were outside of the extended family dwelling 82% and girls 54% of the time,

suggesting that girls may receive more supervision than boys (Wenger, 1989), and Kpelle children played in a public area on "the mother ground," where they engaged in "adult-guided" activities while within reach of adults. By contrast, Parakana children in Brazil, children from the Marquesas, and children in hunting-gathering societies play in hazardous places with sharp objects without much adult monitoring or guidance (Gosso, 2005; Hewlett, personal communication; Martini, 1994). Remarkably, children rarely get hurt and seem to avoid danger under most circumstances. In recording the play of the Parakana Indians, Gosso (2010) notes that

> "there are no records of accidents involving sharp objects. Somehow there must be some informal instruction, perhaps from older peers, which efficiently transmits information on how to deal with the dangers of the environment, and how to properly use dangerous objects" (p. 96).

Of course, different settings in which play occurs may lead to variable levels of playful interactions and object use and present different challenges to children. By observing Parakana Indians, Seashore children, and three groups of urban children from low-, middle-, and high SES backgrounds in Brazil, Gosso et al. (2007) implied that socialization goals and practices within the developmental niches influenced frequencies of different types of play. They suggested that the lower levels of fantasy play in Parakana Indian and Seashore children were probably due to the demanding and challenging environments in which these children lived. In settings in which there are multiple opportunities to engage in physical exercise play (climbing, bathing in rivers) or natural activities, there may be less of a need to enact sociodramatic themes. That is, as long as children can concretely engage in activities while navigating their immediate environments, the use of pretense may decline proportionately. Under these circumstances, internal representations of culture-specific skills may be accomplished through the act of repeatedly engaging and building on everyday activities to the point where children become proficient at them. Likewise, high levels of participation in contingency play among Parakana Indians is testimony to the need to develop and maintain social ties in a community that is based on collectivistic principles and simple social codes (Gosso, et al., 2007).

An aspect of the physical setting that deserves greater attention entails family and community composition. As stated throughout this chapter, children in traditional societies have multiple caregivers and have social ties to extended family members who are present in their social environments. Proximity to multiple individuals in traditional societies does not indicate assurance of their availability as play partners or attempts on their part to organize play activities for children. This is patently obvious among the Yuctaec Maya (Gaskins, 2006), Kispsigis (Harkness & Super, 1986), and the Baining (Fajans, 1997), who by virtue of their beliefs about play steer clear of playful interactions with children or encourage learning through work. In such cases, it is highly likely that play or work and play happens during sibling and peer social exchanges. The roles of individual members in the extended family system in guiding learning through play and other means may hinge on resources and density within families, demographic factors, fertility rates, and demands on caregiving (see Bock, 2001).

Divergent pathways and potential benefits

To conclude, I return to the importance of play for childhood development in cultural contexts. Using different methodological and analytical approaches, researchers from diverse disciplines (e.g., child development, early childhood education, psychology, and anthropology) have tried to place a developmental value on play. Multiple attempts have been made to establish associations between different modes of play and cognitive and social skills during the childhood years largely in the Western technologically developed societies (see Smith, 2010, for a critical analysis). Based on Smith's analysis, the correlation coefficients for the relationships between different play forms, fantasy play more specifically, and different social and cognitive measures are rather small. This aside, I would argue that in Western technologically developed societies, play has a general scholastic function wherein through organized, systematic attempts by adults in different settings children are prepared to meet the demands of early modern schooling. Thus, play stimulation is implemented at home and in early childhood settings to achieve precisely these goals. Paradoxically, in North America, play ceases to assume a central position in educational settings beyond the early childhood years.

In agricultural and hunting-gathering societies, play has an often overlooked function: that is, the reproduction of cultural practices and skills. Of course, this is not a novel proposition; it has been made by several individuals about various aspects of childhood development and in some cases about different modes of play itself (Corsaro, 1992; Gosso et al., 2007; Hirschfeld, 2002; Lancy, 1996, 2007). Given parental beliefs about play and the myriad of play activities expressed by children in agricultural and hunting-gathering societies, it is far from clear whether children are simply imitating the activities around them or they employ play activities to acquire culturally necessary cognitive and social skills. Among the Yucatec Maya, children rarely invent fantasy themes and those that are suggested by older siblings remain relatively unchanged over time (Gaskins & Miller, in press). Yet, in many other hunting-gathering and agricultural cultural communities, elaborate fantasy play is enacted with regularity. And what about children's early entry into work in traditional societies? Children appear to learn subsistence skills and domestic tasks through early participation in these activities via a combination of play and work (Chick, 2010). A challenge for cross-cultural researchers is to assess which behavioral and cognitive skills share more variance with play compared to early work, observation learning, and more direct guidance over time. No doubt, such studies would bring us closer to understanding the value of play and work in learning and the cultural pathways through which such learning is realized.

Author's note

The author was supported by Funds from the Jack Reilly Institute of Early Childhood and Provider Education in the College of Human Ecology at Syracuse University during the preparation of this manuscript. This support is gratefully acknowledged. Maria Connava provided invaluable assistance in conducting electronic searches for studies on culture and play. Professor James E. Johnson of The Pennsylvania State University graciously shared pre-published manuscripts from the Play and Culture series with me.

References

Benetti, S. P. & Roopnarine, J. L. (2006). Paternal involvement with school-aged children in Brazilian families: Association with childhood competence. *Sex Roles, 55,* 669–678.

Berry, J. (1997). Immigration, acculturation, and adaptation. *Applied Psychology: An International Review, 46,* 5–34.

Bird-David, N. (2005). Studying children in "hunter-gatherer" societies: Reflections from a Nayaka perspective. In B. S. Hewlett & M. E. Lamb (Eds.), *Hunter-gatherer childhoods: Evolutionary, developmental, and cultural perspectives* (pp. 92–101). New Jersey: Aldine Transaction Publishers.

Bloch, M, & Wichaidat, W. (1986). Play and school work in the kindergarten curriculum: Attitudes of parents and teachers in Thailand. *Early Child Development and Care, 24,* 197–218.

Blurton-Jones, N. (1993). The lives of hunter-gatherer children: Effects of parental behavior and parental reproduction strategy. In M. E. Pereira & L. A. Fairbanks (Eds.), *Juvenile primates* (pp. 405–426). Oxford: Oxford University Press.

Bock, J. (2005). Farming, foraging, and children's in the Okavanga Delta, Botswana. In A. Pellegrini & P. K. Smith (Eds.), *The nature of play: Great Apes and humans* (pp. 251–281). New York: Guilford.

Bock, J. (2002). Evolutionary demography and intrahousehold time allocation in the Okavango Delta, Botswana. *American Journal of Human Biology, 14,* 206–221.

Bornstein, M. H., Haynes, O. M., Pascual, L. Painter, K. M., & Galperin, C. (1999). Play in two societies: Pervasiveness of process, specificity of structure. *Child Development, 70,* 317–331.

Bowman, B. (1992). Reaching potentials of minority children through developmentally and culturally appropriate programs. In S. Bredekamp & R. Rosengrant (Eds.), *Reaching potentials: Appropriate curriculum and assessment for young children* (pp. 128–136). Washington, DC: NAEYC.

Bredekamp, S. & Copple, C. (1997). (Eds.). *Developmentally appropriate practice and early childhood programs* (rev. Ed.). Washington, DC: NAEYC.

Bruner, J. (1972). Nature and uses of immaturity. *American Psychologist, 27,* 687–708.

Carsaro, W. (1992). Interpretative reproduction in children's peer cultures. *Social Psychology Quarterly, 55,* 160–177.

Chick, G. (2010). Play, work and learning. In D. F. Lancy, J. Bock, & S. Gaskins, (Eds.), *Anthropological perspectives on learning in childhood.* (pp. 119–143). Rowan & Littlefield.

Clarke-Stewart, K. A., Lee, Y., Allhusen, V. D., Kim, M. S., McDowell, D. J. (2006). Observed differences between early childhood programs in the U. S. and Korea: Reflections of "developmentally appropriate practices" in two cultural contexts. *Journal of Applied Developmental Psychology, 27,* 427–443.

Cote, L. R., & Bornstein, M. H. (2005). Child and mother play in cultures of origin, acculturating cultures, and cultures of destination. *International Journal of Behavioral Development, 29,* 479–488.

Cote, L. R., & Bornstein, M. H. (2003). Cultural and parenting cognitions in acculturating cultures 1: Cultural comparisons and developmental continuity and stability. *Journal of Cross-Cultural Psychology, 34,* 323–349.

Durbrow, E. H. (1999). Cultural processes in child competence: How rural Caribbean parents evaluate their children. In A. S. Masten (Ed.), *Cultural processes in child development: The Minnesota symposia on child psychology.* Vol. 29 (pp. 97–121). Mahwah, NJ: Erlbaum.

Edwards, C. P. (2000). Children's play in cross-cultural perspective: A new look at the six cultures study. *Cross-Cultural Research, 34,* 318–338.

Eibl-Eibesfeldt, I. (1983). Patterns of parent–child interactions in a cross-cultural perspective. In A. Oliverio (Ed.), *The behavior of human infants.* (pp. 177–217). New York: Plenum Press.

Fajans, J. (1997). *They make themselves: Work and play among the Baining of Papua New Guinea.* Chicago: University of Chicago Press.

Farver, J. M., & Lee-Shin, Y. (2000). Acculturation and Korean-American children's social and play behaviors. *Social Development, 9,* 316–336.

Farver, J. A. M., & Shin, Y. L. (1997). Social pretend play in Korean- and Anglo-American preschoolers. *Child Development, 68*, 3, 544–556.

Farver, J. A., & Wimbarti, S. (1995). Indonesian children's play with their mothers. *Child Development, 66*, 1493–1503.

Farver, J. A. M., Kim, Y. K., & Lee, Y. (1995). Cultural difference in Korean- and Anglo-American preschoolers' social interaction and play behaviors. *Child Development, 66*, 1088–1099.

Fernald, A., & O'Neill, D. (1993). Peek-a-boo across cultures. In K. Macdonald (Ed.), *Parent–child play* (pp. 259–285). Albany: State University of New York Press.

Fogel, A., Nwokah, E., & Karns, J. (1993). Parent–infant games as dynamic social systems. In K. Macdonald (Ed.), *Parent–child play* (pp. 43–70). Albany: State University of New York Press.

Fogle, L. M., & Mendez, J. L. (2006). Assessing the play beliefs of African American mothers with preschool children. *Early Childhood Research Quarterly, 21*, 507–518.

Fung, H. H. (1994). *The socialization of shame in young Chinese children*. Unpublished doctoral dissertation, University of Chicago.

Gaskins, S., & Miller, P. J. (in press). The cultural roles of emotions in play. In J. Johnson (Ed.). Play and culture series. Baltimore, MD: University Press of America.

Gaskins, S. (2006). Cultural perspectives on infant-caregiver interaction. In J. Enfeld & S. C. Levinson (Eds.), *Roots of human sociality: Culture, cognition, and interaction* (pp. 279–298). Oxford, England: Berg.

Gaskins, S., Haight, W., & Lancy, D. F. (2006). The cultural construction of play. In A. Goncu & S. Gaskins (Eds.), *Play and development: Evolutionary, sociocultural, and functional perspectives* (pp. 179–202). Mahwah, NJ: Lawrence Erlbaum Publishers.

Gielen, G. & Roopnarine, G. (2004). (Eds.), *Childhood and adolescence: Cross-cultural perspectives and applications*. Westport, CT: Praeger.

Goodnow, J. J., Cashmore, J. A., Cotton, S., & Knight, R. (1984). Mothers' developmental timetables in two cultural groups. *International Journal of Psychology, 19*, 193–205.

Goncu, A., Mistry, J. & Mosier, C. (2000). Cultural variations in the play of toddlers. *International Journal of Behavioral Development, 24*, 321–329.

Gosso, M. (2010). Play in different cultures (Chapter 5). In P. Smith. *Children and play*. Chichester, UK: Wiley-Blackwell.

Gosso, M., Morais, M. D. L. S. E., & Otta, E. (2007). Pretend play of Brazilian children: A window into different cultural worlds. *Journal of Cross-Cultural Psychology, 38*, 539–588.

Grantham-McGregor, S., Landman, J. & Desai, P. (1983). Child rearing in poor urban Jamaica. *Child: Care, Health and Development, 9*, 57–71.

Greenfield, P. M., Keller, H., Fuligni, A., Maynard, A. (2003). Cultural pathways through universal development. *Annual Review of Psychology, 54*, 461–490.

Grossman, K., & Grossman, K. E. (2000). Parents and toddlers at play: Evidence for separate qualitative functioning of the play and the attachment system. In P. M. Crittenden & A. H. Claussen (Eds.), *The organization of attachment relationships: maturation, culture, and context* (pp. 13-37). New York: Cambridge University Press.

Haight, W., Wang, X-L, Fung, H. H., Williams, K., & Mintz, J. (1999). Universal, developmental, and variable aspects of young children's play: A cross-cultural comparison of pretending at home. *Child Development, 70*, 1477–1488.

Haight, W., & Miller, P. J. (1993). *Pretending at home: Early development in a socio-cultural context*. Albany: State University of New York Press.

Haight, W., Parke, R., & Black, J. (1997). Mothers' and fathers' beliefs about and spontaneous participation in toddlers' play. *Merrill-Palmer Quarterly, 43*, 271–290.

Harkness, S. & Super, C. M. (1986). The cultural structuring of children's play in a rural African community. In K. Blanchard (Ed.), *The many faces of play.* (pp. 96–103). Champaigh, Il: Huamn Kinetics.

Harris, P. L. (2000). *The work of the imagination*. Oxford, UK: Blackwell.

Harwood, R L.; Miller, A. M.; Carlson, V. J.; Leyendecker, B. (1992). Child-rearing and practices during feeding among middle class Puerto Rican and Anglo mother-infant pairs. In J. M. Contreras, K. A. Kerns, & A. M. Neal-Barnett (Eds.),. *Latino children and families in the United States: Current research and future directions*. Westport, CT: Praeger.

Hewlett, B. S. (2004). Fathers in forager, farmer, and pastoral cultures. In M. E. Lamb (Ed.), *The role of the father in child development*. (4th ed. pp. 182–195). New York: Wiley & Sons.

Hewlett, B. (1987). Patterns of parental holding among AKA pygmies. In M. Lamb (Ed.), *The father's role: Cross-cultural perspectives*. Hillsdale, NJ: Erlbaum.

Hirasawa, A. (2005). Infant care among the sedentarized Baka Hunter-Gatherers in southeastern Cameroon. In B. S. Hewlett & M. E. Lamb (Eds.), *Hunter-gatherer childhoods: Evolutionary, developmental, and cultural perspectives* (pp. 365–384). New Jersey: Aldine Transaction Publishers.

Hirschfeld, L. A. (2002). Why don't anthropologists like children? *American Anthropologist, 104*, 611–627.

Holloway, S., Rambaud, M. F., Fuller, B., Eggers-Pierola, C. (1995). What is "appropriate practice" at home and in child care?: Low-income mothers' views on preparing their children for school. *Early Childhood Research Quarterly, 10*, 451–473.

Holmes, R. (2001). Parental notions about their children's playfulness and children's notions of play in the United States and Hong Kong. In S. Reifel (Ed.), *Theory in context and out: Play and Culture Studies*, Vol. 3. (pp. 291–314). Westport, CT: Ablex.

Hossain, Z., Roopnarine, J. L., Isamel, R., Menon, S., Sombuling, A. (2008). Fathers' and mothers' reports of involvement in caring for infants in Kadazan families in Sabah, Malaysia. *Fathering, 5*, 58–78.

Hossain, Z., Roopnarine, J. L., Masud, J., Muhamed, A. A., Baharudin, R., Abdullah, R., & Jahur, R. (2005). Mothers' and fathers' childcare involvement with young children in rural families in Malaysia. *International Journal of Psychology, 40*, 385–394.

Johnson, J. E., Christie, J., & Wardle, F. (2005). *Play development and early education*. Boston, MA: Allyn & Bacon.

Johnson, J. E. (1985). Attitudes toward play and beliefs about development. In M. Mergen (Ed.), *Cultural dimensions of play, games, and sport*. The Association for the Study of Play, Volume 10, (pp. 98–102). Champaign, Il: Human Kinetic Publishers.

Kakar, S. & Kakar, K. (2007). *The Indians: Portrait of a people*. New Delhi: Viking.

Kamei, N. (2005). Play among Baka children in Cameroon. In B. S. Hewlett & M. E. Lamb (Eds.), *Hunter-gatherer childhoods: Evolutionary, developmental, and cultural perspectives* (pp. 343–349). New Jersey: Aldine Transaction Publishers.

Kaplan, H. (1994). Evolutionary and wealth flows theories of fertility: Empirical tests and new models. *Population and Developmental Review, 20*, 753–791.

Kaplan, H., & Bock, J. (2001). Fertility theory: The embodied capital theory of human life history evolution. In N. J. Smelser & P. B. Bakes (Eds.), *The international encyclopedia of the social and behavioral sciences* (pp. 5561–5568). Oxford: Elsevier Science.

Keller, H., Lohaus, A., Kuensemueller, P., Abels, M., Yovsi, R., Vorlker, S., et al (2004). The bio-cultural of parenting: Evidence from five cultural communities. *Parenting: Science and Practice, 4*, 25–50.

Konner, M. (1972). Aspects of the developmental ethology of a foraging people. In J. S. Bruner, A. Jolly, & K. Sylva (Eds.), *Play Its role in development and evolution* Hammondsworth: Penguin.

Laflamme, D., Pomerleau, A., & Malcuit, G. (2002). A comparison of fathers' and mothers' involvement in childcare and stimulation behaviors during free-play with their infants at 9 and 15 months. *Sex Roles, 47*, 507–518.

Lamb, M. E. (2002). Infant-father attachments and their impact on child development. In C. S. Tamis-LeMonda & N. Cabrera (Eds.), *Handbook on father involvement: Multidisciplinary perspectives* (pp. 93–117). Mawah, NJ: Earlbaum.

Lamb, M. E. (1977). The development of paternal preferences in the first two years of life. *Sex Roles, 3*, 495–497.

Lamb, M. E., Frodi, A. M., Frodi, M., Hwang, C. P. (1982). Characteristics of maternal and paternal behavior in traditional and nontraditional Swedish families. *International Journal of Behavioral Development, 5*, 131–141.

Lancy, D. F. (2008). *The anthropology of childhood: Cherubs, chattel and changelings*. Cambridge: Cambridge University Press.

Lancy, D. (2007). Accounting for variability in mother–child play. *American Anthropologist, 109*, 273–284.

Lancy, D. F. (1996). *Playing on the mother-ground: Cultural routines for children's development*. New York: The Guilford Press.

Lareau, A. (2003). *Unequal childhoods: Class, race, and family life*. Berkeley, CA: University of California Press.

Larson, R., & Verma, S. (1999). How children and adolescents spend time across the world: work, play, and developmental opportunities. *Psychological Bulletin, 125*, 701–736.

Leacock, E. (1978). At play in African villages. In J. S. Bruener, A. Jolly, & K. Sylva (Eds.), *Play Its role in development and evolution* (pp. 466–473). Hammondsworth: Penguin.

LeVine, R. A. (2004). Challenging expert knowledge: Findings from an African study of infant care and development. U. Gielen & J. Roopnarine (Eds.), Childhood and adolescence: Cross-cultural perspectives and applications. (pp. 149–165). Westport, CT: Praeger.

LeVine, R. A. (1974). Parental goals: A cross-cultural view. *Teachers College Record, 76*, 226–239.

Levinson, M. P. (2005). The role of play in the formation and maintenance of cultural identity: Gypsy children in home and school contexts. *Journal of Contemporary Ethnography, 34*, 499–532.

MacDonald, K., & Parke, R. D. (1986). Parent–child physical play: The effects of sex and age of children and parents. *Sex Roles, 15*, 367–378.

Marlowe, F. (2005). Who tends Hadza children. In B. S. Hewlett & M. E. Lamb (Eds.), *Hunter-gatherer childhoods: Evolutionary, developmental, and cultural perspectives* (pp. 175–213). New Jersey: Aldine Transaction Publishers.

Maynard, A. (2004). Sibling interactions. In U. Gielen & J. Roopnarine (Eds.), *Childhood and adolescence: Cross-cultural perspectives and applications*. (pp. 229–252). Westport, CT: Praeger.

Martini, M. (1994). Peer interactions in Polynesia: A view from the Marquesas. In J. Roopnarine, J. Johnson, & F. Hooper (Eds.), *Children's play in diverse cultures*. (pp. 73–103) Albany: SUNY Press.

Martini, M., & Kirkpatrick, J. (1992). Parenting in Polynesia: A view from the Marquesas. In J. L. Roopnarine & B. Carter (Eds.), *Parent–child socialization in diverse cultures* (pp. 199–222). Norwood, NJ: Ablex.

McGillicuddy-DeLisi, A. V. (1982). Parental beliefs about developmental processes. *Human Development, 25*, 192–200.

Mead, M. (1935). *Sex and temperament in three primitive societies*. New York: Morrow.

Morelli, G. A., Rogoff, B., & Angelillo, C. (2003). Cultural variation in young children's access to work or involvement in specialized child-focused activities. *International Journal of Behavioral Development, 27*, 264–274.

Munroe, R. H., Munroe, R. L., & Shimmin, H. S. (1984). Children's work in four cultures: Determinants and consequences. *American Anthropologist, 86*, 369–379.

Nunes, A. (2005). Childhood dynamics in a changing culture: Examples from the Xavante in central Brazil. In Knorr (Ed.), Childhood and migration: From experience to agency. (pp. 207–226). Bielefeld, Transkript.

Ochs, E. & Schieffelin, B. (1984). Language acquisition and socialization: Three developmental stories and their implications. In R. Shweder & R. LeVine (Eds.), *Culture and its acquisition* (pp. 276–320). Chicago: University of Chicago Press.

Ogbu, J. (1981). Origins of human competence: A cultural ecological perspective. *Child Development, 52*, 413–429.

Ottenberg, S. (1989). *Beyond rituals in an African society: An interpretation*. Seattle, WA: University of Washington Press.

Paquette, D. (2004). Dichotomizing paternal and maternal functions as a means to better understand their primary contributions. *Human Development, 47*, 237–238.

Parmar, P. & Harkness, S., Super, C. (2004). Asian and European American parents' ethnotheories of play and learning: Effects on preschool children's home routines and social behavior. *International Journal of Behavioral Development, 28*, 97–104.

Patcher, L. M. & Dworkin, P. H. (1997). Maternal expectations about normal child development in 4 cultural groups. *Archives of Pediatric and Adolescent Medicine, 151*, 1144–1150.

Rogoff, B., Goncu, A., Mistry, J. & Mosier, C. (1993). Guided participation in cultural activity by toddlers and caregivers. *Monographs of the Society for Research in Child Development*. Serial No. 236 Vol. 58, No. 8.

Roopnarine, J. L., Krishnakumar, A., & Xu, Yi-Li (2009). Beliefs about mothers' and fathers' roles and the division of childcare and household labor in Indo Caribbean immigrants with young children. *Cultural Diversity and Ethnic Minority Psychology*, 15, 173–182.

Roopnarine, J. L. & Metindogan, A. (2006). Cross-national early childhood education research. In B. Spodek & O. Saracho (Eds.), *Handbook of research on the education of young children*. Mahwah, NJ: Erlbaum.

Roopnarine, J. L. & Krishnakumar, A. (2006). Parent–child and child-child play in diverse cultural contexts. In D. Fromberg & D. Bergen (Eds.), *Children's play from birth to age 12*. (2nd Ed.). New York: Routledge.

Roopnarine, J. L., Fouts, H. N., Lamb, M. E., & Lewis, T. E. (2005). Mother-infant and father-infant interactions in low-, middle-, and upper-SES African American families. *Developmental Psychology.*

Roopnarine, J. L. Johnson, J. E., Hooper, F. H. (1994) (Eds.). *Children's play in diverse cultures.* Albany, NY: State University of New York Press.

Roopnarine, J., Hossain, Z., Gill, P., & Brophy, H. (1994). Play in the East Indian context. In J Roopnarine, J. Johnson, & F. Hooper (Eds.), *Children's play in diverse cultures.* (pp. 9–30). Albany, New York: SUNY Press.

Roopnarine, J. L., Hopper, F. H., Ahmeduzzaman, M., & Pollack, B. (1993). Gentle play partners: Mother–child and father-child play in New Delhi, India. In K. MacDonald (Ed.), *Parents and children playing* (pp. 287–304). Albany, NY: SUNY Press.

Roopnarine, J.L., Talukder, E., Jain, D., Joshi, P., & Srivastav, P. (1992). Personal well-being, kinship tie and mother-infant and father-infant interactions in single-wage and dual-wage families in New Delhi, India. *Journal of Marriage and the Family, 54,* 293-301.

Roopnarine, J. L., Talukder, E., Jain, D., Joshi, P., & Srivastav, P. (1990). Characteristics of holding, patterns of play and social behaviors between parents and infants in New Delhi, India. *Developmental Psychology, 26,* 667–673.

Roopnarine, J. L., Lu, M., & Ahmeduzzaman, M. (1989). Parental reports of early patterns of caregiving in India and Malaysia. *Early Child Development and Care, 50,* 109–120.

Sagi, A., Lamb, M. E., Shoham, R. Dvir, R. & Lewkowicz, K. S. (1985). Parent–infant interaction on Israeli kibuttizm. *International Journal of Behavioral Development, 8,* 273–284.

Shwalb, D. W., Nakazawa, J., Yamamoto, T., & Hyun, J-H. (2004). Fathering in Japanese, Chinese, and Korean cultures. In M. E. Lamb (Ed.), *The role of the father in child development.* (pp. 146–181). New York: Wiley & Sons.

Shweder, R. (1982). Beyond self-constructed knowledge: The study of culture and morality. *Merrill-Palmer Quarterly, 28,* 41–69.

Sigel, I., & McGillicuddy-De Lisi, A. (2002). Parental beliefs as cognitions: The dynamic belief systems mode. In M. Bornstein (Ed.), *Handbook of parenting* (vol. 3). (2nd. Edition). Mahwah, NJ: Erlbaum.

Singer, D. G., & Singer, J. L. (1990). *The house of make-believe: Play and the developing imagination.* Cambridge, MA: Harvard University Press.

Singer, D. G., Singer, J. L., D'Agistino, H., & DeLong, R. (2009). Children's pastimes and play in sixteen cultures: Is free play declining? *American Journal of Play,* Winter, 283–312.

Smith, P. K. (2010). *Children and play.* Sussex, UK: Wiley-Blackwell.

Soto, L. D., & Negron, L. (1994). Mainland Puerto Rican children. In J. Roopnarine, J. Johnson, & F. Hooper (Eds.), *Children's play in diverse cultures.* (pp. 104–122) Albany: SUNY Press.

Stern, D. (1974). Mother and infant play: The dyadic interaction involving facial, vocal, and gait behaviors. In M. Lewis & L. Rosenblum (Eds.), *The effect of the infant on its caregiver* (pp. 187–213). New York: Wiley.

Suarez-Orozco, M. (2001). Globalization, immigration, and education: The research agenda. *Harvard Educational Review, 71,* 345–365.

Suizzo, M-A., & Bornstein, M. H. (2006). French and European American child-mother play: Culture and gender considerations. *International Journal of Behavioral Development, 30,* 498–508.

Super, C. & Harkness, S. (1997). The cultural structuring of child development. In J. Berry, P. Dasen, & T. S. Saraswathi, (Eds.), *Handbook of cross-cultural psychology: Basic processes and human development* (pp. 1–39). Needham, MA: Allyn & Bacon.

Sun, L. C., & Roopnarine, J. L. (1996). Mother-infant and father-infant interaction and involvement in childcare and household labor in Taiwanese families. *Infant Behavior and Development, 19,* 121–129.

Tamis-Lemonda, C. S. (2004). Conceptaulizing fathers' role: Playmates and more. *Human Development, 47,* 220–227.

Tamis-Lemonda, C. S., Bornstein, M. H., Cyphers, L., Toda, S., & Ogino, M. (1992). Language and play at one year: A comparison of toddlers and mothers in the United States and Japan. *International Journal of Behavioral Development, 15.*

Tulananda, O., & Roopnarine, J. L. (2001). Mothers' and fathers' interactions with preschoolers in the home in Northern Thailand: Relationships to teachers' assessments of children's social skills. *Journal of Family Psychology, 14,* 676–687.

Turkheimer, E., Bakeman, R., & Adamson, L. B. (1989). Do mothers support and peers inhibit skilled object play in infancy. *Infant Behavior and Development, 12,* 37–44.

Turnbull, C. (1962). *The forest people: A study of the Pygmies of the Congo.* New York: Simon & Schuster.

Van Der Kooj, R., & Slaats-van den Hurk, W. (1991). Relations between parental opinions and attitudes about play and childrearing. *Play and Culture, 4,* 108–123.

Vygotsky, L. (1978). *Mind in society.* Cambridge, MA: Harvard University Press.

Wenger, M. (1989). Work, play, and social relationships among children in a Giriama community. In D. Belle (Ed.), *Children's social networks and social support.* (pp. 91–115). New York: Wiley.

Whaley, S. E., Sigman, M., Beckwith, L. Cohen, S., & Espinosa, M. P. (2000). Cultural differences in caregiving in Kenya and the United States: The importance of multiple caregivers and adequate comparison groups. Unpublished manuscript, University of California, Los Angeles.

Yeung, W. J., Sandberg, J. F., Davis-Kean, P. E., & Hofferth, S. L. (2001). Children's time with fathers in intact families. *Journal of Marriage and Family, 63,* 136–154.

Zukow-Goldring, P. (1996). Sensitive caregiving fosters the comprehension of speech: When gestures speak louder than words. *Early Development and Parenting, 5,* 195–211.

Theories

chapter 4

Theories of Play

Patrick Bateson

Abstract

As a category of behavior, play can be readily recognized and measured in mammals at least. However, it is easy to project onto children and other animals adult human notions of what is going on. It is also easy for everybody to suppose that the category called play is unitary. Solitary play and social play, imaginary play and object play are not the same and are motivated in different ways. It is far from obvious that play is always enjoyable. Many different explanations are offered for the current utilities or biological functions that increase the chances of the individual surviving and reproducing. These include the acquisition and honing of physical skills needed at once or later in life, improving problem-solving abilities, cementing social relationships and tuning the musculature and the nervous system. In principle the functions can be tested by experiment but the results are often ambiguous. How and why play evolved cannot be tested directly but may well have depended on the individual having enough resources to devote to the active promotion of its development. Once evolved, play may have acted as a driver of evolutionary change, opening up possibilities that did not previously exist. In terms of public policy, the steady reduction in children's time for play is cause for serious concern, but recommendations for reversing that trend must be based on hard thought and good evidence.

Keywords: play, development, policy factors, play theory

The Naming Problem

While I was thinking about this chapter, four young European magpies that had hatched out in a nest at the top of a tall ash tree earlier in the summer were chasing each other round a deck chair outside my window. Then one of them flew up onto the top of the deck chair and slid down the sloping surface. Others were busily picking up pebbles and dropping them. Why were these young magpies behaving like this? The same question arises every year when one of our cats, a beautiful Egyptian Mau, has kittens. After she has given birth, we watch her kittens as they develop. Around three weeks of age, the kittens become much more active and start to pat and mouth each other. Arching, pouncing, and wrestling follow. At seven weeks they start to pat inanimate objects with their forepaws. If the object is furry, they will pounce on it and, having grabbed

it, rake the object with their back legs. They spend about a tenth of each day engaged in these seemingly pointless activities.

If I called what the young magpies and kittens do "Xinging," I can readily point to the animals' activities and get students to agree with each other when they see more examples of Xinging. It might seem pedantic not to call the activities of the young animals "play" without further ado, but the neutral label does draw attention to how readily we project into other animals the experiences we have of ourselves and our fellow human beings. Also if we avoid such projections, we are less likely to confuse patting social companions with patting objects which, in the cat at least, have very different developmental trajectories and presumed functions (see Barrett & Bateson, 1977).

It is worth pursuing the issue of projection a little further. Some years ago a beautifully illustrated book called "Why Cats Paint" caused a flurry of interest among art critics (Busch & Silver, 1994). The paintings by cats, like those by some well-known captive chimpanzees, were seen as "joyous and full of life." The cats were not simply creating abstract pictures; they were playful while doing so. The cats' aesthetic activity might also reflect their developmental history. One cat, Charlie, described as a "peripheral realist" and whose work was illustrated, had been accidentally shut in a refrigerator for five hours. The experience transformed him into a prolific artist. The authors explain that: "Many human artists have attributed the sudden urge to express themselves artistically to an emotionally shattering experience in their early lives." The book attracted serious reviews in major newspapers. However, the reviewers had failed to read the list of references at the back of the book. Here are three of the entries in the bibliography:

Ball, H. (1992). *Paws for Thought. The Magic & Meaning of Litter Tray Relief Patterns.* Slive & Seymour. Cambridge.

Lord-osis, J. (1991). Pawnography. Paw marking as a mode of sexual communication among domestic cats in Sweden. *J Appl Aesthetics*, Vol VI.

Mutt, R. (1991). Decorative retromingency: Urinary embellishment as a major problem in the curation of feline art. *J Non-primate Art*, Vol XV

The book was a brilliantly conceived and beautifully illustrated spoof – an extended joke. It demonstrated (playfully) how easily humans fall into the trap of supposing that animals are like us. Of course, I am not for a second denying the great body of evidence that most, if not all, vertebrates are sentient and so too are some invertebrates like octopus. I do suggest, though, that we should be thoughtful about the names we give to our categories of behavior. Establishing such categories of behavior provides the basis for measurement, which is a crucial part of behavioral biology. In the case of play, a sceptical question about this category (or I would argue, these categories) is often shrugged off because, it is claimed, everybody recognizes play when they see an individual doing it. However, recognition is not the same as agreement. When a kitten plays, observers will readily agree about the occurrences of a variety of different components of its activities; their quantified measurements correlate strongly with each other. When a fish does something that might be called playful, however, how many scientists will state confidently what it is doing? What is the basis for the classification of behavior as play or non-play? Gordon Burghardt's (2005) discussion of this issue is especially thoughtful. If play is not a unitary category, and I think it is not, the problems identified by Burghardt are magnified.

I suspect that a major element in the naming of behavioral categories is the extent to which the animal's behavior corresponds to what humans do when playing—a not uncommon problem in the classification of many categories of animal behavior. Once classified, it is easy to provide an ostensive definition, pointing to the behavior patterns in question and saying: "That's what I mean by 'play.'" In modern ethology, such definitions are accompanied by clear verbal descriptions, drawings, and videos. That much is fine, but the subtle attributions that accompany such categories of animal behavior have to be watched carefully. This care may need to be extended to the way that the behavior of children is categorized by adult humans. By using a term like play for what a child does may imply an understanding of the child's motivation that goes way beyond the evidence.

Theories of Motivation

Despite all the naming problems, play as agreed by independent observers is typically something that children and young animals do (Burghardt, 2005; Pellis & Pellis, 2009; Pellegrini, 2009). Adults play too, of course, but generally have less time for it and less inclination. Human play comes in many different forms: solitary, imaginary, symbolic, verbal, social, constructional, rough-and-tumble, manipulative, and so forth. The play of a four-year-old boy wrestling with another four-year-old is descriptively quite different from that of, say, a solitary ten-year-old staring into space whilst indulging in some private fantasy about being a pop star or a doctor.

Play has been described in a wide variety of young animals—most mammals, some bird species, such as parrots and ravens, and is probably much more widespread in other groups than is commonly believed (Fagen, 1981; Burghardt, 2005). It may occupy a substantial proportion of their time as well (Martin & Caro, 1985). At the stage in its life when an individual does it most, play can account for around 10% of its time—not as much, perhaps, as a child's, but still a lot. Playful behavior often resembles 'real' behavior. The young animal plays at fighting or catching imaginary prey, but it is usually obvious that the animal *is* playing rather than merely being incompetent. In social play, for instance, the roles of the play partners are frequently reversed and sexual components are often incorporated long before the animal is sexually mature. During play involving running, jumping, and other rapid movements, the movement patterns tend to be exaggerated in form, jumbled in sequence, and often repeated. In some species, specific social signals are used to denote that what follows is playful rather than serious. Dogs, for example, signal their readiness to play by dropping down on their forelegs and wagging their tails, while chimpanzees have a special 'play face' which precedes a bout of social play. In the solitary manipulations of object play, the prey-catching or food-getting repertoires of adults are frequently used long before they bring in any real food. Play is also exquisitely sensitive to prevailing conditions, and is usually the first thing to go when all is not well. It is a sensitive barometer of the individual's psychological and physical well-being. For instance, young vervet monkeys in East Africa do not play in dry years, when food is scarce (Lee, 1984). Play happens only when basic short-term needs have been satisfied and the individual is relaxed. It is therefore the first activity to disappear if the individual is stressed, anxious, hungry, or ill.

One way, then, is to characterize the motivation that lies behind various facets of play as being without a serious short-term objective. Moreover, what the individual is doing is "fun." Are we justified, however, in supposing that play is invariably enjoyable, even in humans? On reflection, I think an affirmative answer is far too superficial (even though I have been guilty of such superficiality myself) and the answer doesn't address the profound matter of benefit to which I shall return later. On the matter of motivation, I'm far from clear that all behavior that we classify as play is enjoyable. Absorbing, perhaps, when engaged in imaginative play, but by no means always light-hearted. I certainly remember from when I was a child how frightening rough-and-tumble play could be and the vivid humiliation of being pinned to the ground by a bigger boy. Much later in my life when studying social play in cats, I noticed how tense kittens were just before launching themselves at a sibling. They would arch and swish their tails. If they were grabbed by me from behind at just that preparatory phase of play, they would scream, apparently in fright. Back at my desk, trying to write, the supposedly playful acts of creation are frequently agonizing.

I don't deny that many aspects of play are subjectively enjoyable. When they are, the objective evidence would be that an individual is prepared to work in order to be given the opportunity to engage in that facet of play. The opportunity would act as a reward, reinforcing the activity that provided the individual with the chance to play. Moreover, the more the individual had been deprived of the play, the more readily it would work for the opportunity and, once provided, the more it would play. Whatever is said about the motivational underpinning of play, the issue of benefit is quite different. By benefit I mean the utility in promoting survival and reproductive success.

The Utility of Play

In principle, the utility to an individual of having a characteristic that enhances its chances of surviving and reproducing is testable. Play has real biological costs. Animals expend more energy and expose themselves to greater risks of injury and predation when they are playing than when they are resting. Play makes them more conspicuous and less vigilant. For example, young southern fur seals are much more likely to be killed by sea lions when they are playing than at other times (Harcourt, 1991). Such enhanced risks of predation may explain why Golden tamarin parents are more vigilant when their offspring are playing (de Olliveira et al., 2002). Caro (1995) has carefully documented the risks to cheetah cubs when they are playing. The costs of play must presumably be outweighed by its benefits, otherwise animals that played would be at a disadvantage compared with those that did not and play behavior would be of no benefit. What then are the biological functions of play in the sense that these activities increase the individual's chances of surviving and reproducing?

I certainly wish to argue that active engagement with the environment has great benefits, because the world is examined from different angles—and the world rarely looks the same from different angles. Such engagement helps to construct a working knowledge of the environment: the recognition of objects, understanding what leads to what, discovering that things are found when stones are turned over and the world is rearranged, learning what can and cannot be done with others. All these discoveries are real benefits for the individual.

The precise nature of the benefits of play remains, nonetheless, a matter of dispute, with little hard evidence to distinguish between the possibilities. The list of putative benefits includes the acquisition and honing of physical skills needed later in life, improving problem-solving abilities, cementing social relationships and tuning the musculature and the nervous system (Martin & Caro, 1985). A notable feature of the mammalian nervous system is the superabundance of connections between neurons at the start of development. As the individual develops, many of these connections are lost and many cells die. Those neural connections that remain active are retained and the unused ones are lost. This sculpting of the nervous system reflects the steadily improving efficiency of the body's classification, command, and control systems. These internal changes are reflected in behavior. When young animals playfully practice the stereotyped movements they will use in earnest later in life, they improve the coordination and effectiveness of these behavior patterns. The short dashes and jumps of young gazelle when they are playing bring benefits that may be almost immediate, as they face the threat of predation from cheetah or other carnivores intent on a quick meal, and need considerable skill when escaping (Gomendio, 1988). The cheetah's own young also need to acquire running and jumping skills rapidly in order to evade capture by lions and hyenas (Caro, 1995). Even though the benefits may be immediate in such cases, they may also persist into adult life, not being lost in the behavioral metamorphosis that sometimes occurs during development.

Young animals may also familiarize themselves with the topography of their local terrain as a result of playing in it. Simply knowing the locations of important physical features will not guarantee rapid, safe passage around obstacles when escaping from predators or chasing prey. They need to practice. In keeping with this hypothesis, rats in a new area will typically first explore it in a cautious manner. Gradually, the speed of movement increases until the animals are running rapidly around the area along what become established pathways. The seemingly playful galloping ensures that, when fast movement becomes serious, the animal will be able to negotiate, efficiently and automatically, all the obstacles that clutter its familiar environment (Stamps, 1995). As it does so, it will be able to monitor the positions of predators, prey, or hostile members of its own species.

The argument continues that play allows the young animal to simulate, in a relatively safe context, potentially dangerous situations that will arise in its adult life (Smith, 1982). They learn from their mistakes, but do so in relative safety. On this view, play exerts its most important developmental effects on risky adult behavior such as fighting, mating in the face of serious competition, catching dangerous prey, and avoiding becoming someone else's prey. Indeed, the behavior patterns of fighting and prey-catching are especially obvious in the play of cats and other predators, whereas safe activities such as grooming, defecating, and urinating have no playful counterparts.

If play is beneficial, then it follows that depriving the young animal of opportunities for play should have harmful effects on the outcome of its development. This is, indeed, the case. For instance, the lack of play experience shows clearly in the way the animal responds to social competition. In one experiment, young rats were reared in isolation with or without an hour of daily play-fighting experience. About a month later they were put in the cage of another rat, where they were almost invariably attacked as an intruder. The defensive behavior of the play-deprived rats was abnormal. They spent significantly more time immobile than did animals that had played earlier in their lives. Other aspects of their defensive behavior were not affected, so the effects of play deprivation appeared to be specific (Einon, 1991). It seems clear that such deprivation in early life would have adversely affected the individual's capacity to cope in a competitive world. The same argument may be mounted for play-fighting in children. Through play, they learn how to cope with aggression and violence—their own and other people's.

Distinguishing between the various hypotheses advanced to explain the current utility of play is difficult because the presumed benefits are usually thought to be delayed, appearing later in life, and developmental systems tend to be highly redundant, so that if an end-point is not achieved by one route, it is achieved by another (Bateson & Martin, 1999). Playing when young is not the only way to acquire knowledge and skills. The individual can delay acquisition until it is an adult. However, when such experience is gathered without play, the process may be much more costly and difficult, even if it is not impossible. Play has features that make it especially suitable for finding the best way forward. In acquiring skills, individuals are in danger of finding suboptimal solutions to the many problems that confront them. In deliberately moving away from what might look like the final resting point, each individual may get somewhere that is better. Play may, therefore, fulfill an important probing role that enables the individual to escape from false end-points—what engineers call local optima.

Evolution of Play

Evolution is a fact. No serious biologist disputes that organisms have changed over time or that many continue to change. Other organisms have become extinct, many of them in recent times. What requires explanation is the way in which the changes take place. Darwin observed that members of a species differ from each other and that some were more likely to survive and reproduce than others, and finally that the characteristics of the fitter individuals would generally inherited by their offspring. So, by the process he termed "natural selection," lineages would evolve. What can we say about the evolution of play?

In writing about the biology of art, Desmond Morris (1962) suggested that artistic expression became possible when animals evolved to the point where they had surplus energy. Gordon Burghardt (2005) developed this idea in relation to play. Play would have evolved, he suggested, when animals had the resources that would enable them to devote themselves to such activity. Once that happened, play almost certainly evolved because its various facets conferred more than one benefit on individuals. Some aspects of play were probably concerned with honing the development of the nervous system and musculature. Some were concerned with an understanding of future social competitors and, if it came to it, with the martial arts that would be needed to cope with them. Some forms of play were involved with perfecting the predatory skills needed to catch prey without being injured, and some with developing efficient movement around a familiar environment to escape from predators or outwit competitors.

Play was clearly not a *necessary* way for young animals to learn to recognize members of their social group, acquire knowledge of local culture, or become accustomed to their local environment. Animals are patently able to acquire these forms of experience without playing. Nevertheless, these outcomes might still have been beneficial consequences of play when it evolved. They were not central to the evolution of play but, once it had evolved, any additional benefit was a bonus. The young animal was able to acquire, with no extra cost, information of crucial importance to it, such as recognizing close kin, in the course of playing for other reasons.

While the benefits of play are almost certainly heterogeneous, the overarching theme of the evolutionary argument is that the experience, skills, and knowledge needed for serious purposes later were acquired actively through playful engagement with the environment. Human play has undoubtedly acquired yet more complex cognitive functions during the course of its evolution, rearranging the world in ways that ultimately help understanding.

Creativity and innovation are all about breaking away from established patterns. Creative people perceive the relations between thoughts, or things, or forms of expression that may seem utterly different, and to be able to combine them into some new forms—the power to connect the seemingly unconnected. Play is an effective mechanism, therefore, for facilitating innovation and encouraging creativity. Playfully rearranging disparate thoughts and ideas into novel combinations—most of which will turn out to be useless—is used as a powerful means of gaining new insights and opening up possibilities that had not previously been recognized. Play, in other words, extends to pure thought. It involves doing novel things without regard to whether they may be justified by a specified payoff.

In his excellent book, Tony Pellegrini (2009) was being generous when he commented favorably on my ideas about the role of play in driving evolution (Bateson, 2005). I had been thinking for some years beforehand about the active role of behavior in evolution (Bateson, 1982, 1988, 2004). One of the spurs to the thinking of many biologists and psychologists had been the simultaneous publication of proposals about what was originally termed "organic selection" by Baldwin (1896), Lloyd Morgan (1896), and Osborn (1896). In essence their idea was that through plasticity individuals were able to meet a challenge from the environment and then by degrees some individuals were able to meet the challenge more quickly and with less effort by genetic reorganization and without recourse to plastic processes. Baldwin (1902) continued to develop his thinking and the hypothetical process became known as the "Baldwin effect." It subsequently transpired that a brilliant biologist called Douglas Spalding (1873) had published the same idea many years before Baldwin, Lloyd Morgan, and Osborn. Rather than attempting to rename the process the Spalding effect, I suggested that it would be preferable to use a descriptive term. I coined the term "adaptability driver" (Bateson, 2007).

Play is a form of plasticity, if by the experience an individual is able to acquire skills and understanding of the environment. However, in my earlier essay I did not offer a precise way in which it might impact on evolution. The time has come to remedy that shortcoming in my argument. The first step in the evolutionary process was as I described it before. Those aspects of play that were creative in solving a local problem or breaking out of local optima were beneficial to the individual. Such improvements in what could be readily perceived as cognitive ability would not have occurred by genetic recombination or mutation since the probability of the simultaneous occurrence of all the rare necessary events for the change would have been small. The next step, which I did not specify before, could occur in one of two ways. First, the discovery made through play by one individual could have spread by social learning. Second, a challenge set by the environment could have been met through play by many individuals, all of which benefited in the same way. Then, as was originally postulated in the adaptability driver hypothesis, those individuals that were able to express the beneficial trait spontaneously at lower cost were able to compete more successfully. In this way, playful activities could affect the evolution of the individual's descendants.

Play and Public Policy

The belief that children's play has a serious purpose—that of acquiring skills and experience needed in adulthood—has been a central feature in thinking about the nature of play behavior throughout history. It is commonly thought that play builds adult behavior (Smith, 1982). However, likening the development of behavior to the assembly of buildings is only partly successful as an image, because half-assembled animals, unlike half-assembled buildings, have to survive and find for themselves the materials they need for further construction. Nevertheless, one building metaphor—the use of scaffolding—is helpful in understanding the nature of development. Scaffolding is required for the building process but is usually removed once the job is complete. Play is, on the commonest view of its function, developmental scaffolding. Once this job is done, it largely falls away. Not entirely though, because, as every musician knows, continued practice maintains perfect.

Public concern has been growing about the ways in which children are being deprived of their childhood. The perceived changes have occurred for a number of reasons. Parents have become more risk averse, frightened that their children are in danger if they play outside or walk to school. Ambitious parents also want to ensure that their children do well academically and arrange for them to be coached at times when they might otherwise have been playing. Schools and educational authorities connive in these ambitions, start formal education at ever earlier ages, reduce time for recesses (or "breaks" as we call them in the UK) and abandon organized sport. Many local authorities see opportunities for financial gain by selling off their playing fields to developers.

The combined effects of all these changes are thought to damage the well-being of the new generation in the long run. Some of the dire predictions are already being seen in rising levels of obesity in children and young adults.

My own intuition, which I share with Tony Pellegrini (2009), is that play does specifically enhance physical fitness, mental well-being, and creativity. Nevertheless, any attempt to reverse current trends must be hard-headed. When opportunities for children to play are reduced, many other limitations on experience occur at the same time and, when long-term effects of lacking opportunities for play are found, these other forms of deprivation may have been the cause. Public policy advice must also take account of the remarkable ability of humans (like many other animals) to arrive at the same endpoint by many different routes. Recommendations must be clearly focused to enable parents and policy makers to plan sensibly for the future of children.

References

Baldwin, J.M. (1896). A new factor in evolution. *American Naturalist, 30*: 441–451, 536–553.

Baldwin, J.M. (1902). *Development and evolution*. London: Macmillan.

Barrett, P., & Bateson, P. (1977). The development of play in cats. *Behaviour, 66*, 106–120.

Bateson, P. (1982). Behavioural development and evolutionary processes. In: King's College Sociobiology Group (eds.) *Current problems in sociobiology* (pp 133–151). Cambridge: Cambridge University Press.

Bateson, P. (1988). The active role of behaviour in evolution. In Ho, M.-W. & Fox, S. (eds.) *Process and metaphors in evolution* (pp.191–207). Chichester: Wiley.

Bateson, P. (2004). The active role of behaviour in evolution. *Biology and Philosophy, 19*, 283–298.

Bateson, P. (2005). The role of play in the evolution of great apes and humans. In Pellegrini, A.D. & Smith, P.K. (eds.) *The nature of play: Great apes and humans* (pp. 13–24). New York: Guilford.

Bateson, P. (2006). The adaptability driver: links between behaviour and evolution. *Biological Theory: Integrating Development, Evolution, and Cognition, 1*, 342–345.

Bateson, P., & Martin, P. (1999). *Design for a life: How behaviour develops*. London: Jonathan Cape.

Busch, H., & Silver, B. (1994). *Why cats paint: A theory of feline aesthetics*. London: Weidenfeld & Nicolson.

Burghardt, G.M. (2005). *The genesis of animal play: Testing the limits*. Cambridge, Mass: MIT Press.

Caro, T.M. (1995). Short-term costs and correlates of play in cheetahs. *Animal Behaviour, 49*, 333–345.

de Oliveira, C.R., Ruiz-Miranda, C.R., Kleiman, D.G., & Beck, B.B. (2003). Play behavior in juvenile golden lion tamarins (Callitrichidae: Primates): Organization in relation to costs. *Ethology, 109*, 593–612.

Einon, D., & Potegal, M. (1991). Enhanced defense in adult-rats deprived of playfighting experience as juveniles. *Aggressive Behaviour, 17*, 27–40.

Fagen, R. (1981). *Animal play behavior*. New York: Oxford University Press.

Gomendio, M. (1988). The development of different types of play in gazelles: implications for the nature and functions of play. *Animal Behaviour, 36*, 825–836.

Harcourt, R. (1991). Survivorship costs of play in the South American fur seal. *Animal Behaviour, 42*, 509–511.

Lee, P.C. (1984). Ecological constraints on the social development of vervet monkeys. *Behaviour, 91*, 245–262.

Lloyd Morgan C. (1896). On modification and variation. *Science, 4*, 733–740.

Martin, P., & Caro, T.M. (1985). On the functions of play and its role in behavioral development. *Advances in the Study of Behaviour, 15*, 59–103.

Morris, D. (1962). *The biology of art: a study of the picture-making behaviour of the great apes and its relationship to human art.* London: Methuen.

Osborn, H.F. (1896). Ontogenic and phylogenic variation. *Science, 4*, 786–789.

Pellegrini, A.D. (2009). *The role of play in human development.* Oxford: Oxford University Press.

Pellis, S., & Pellis, V. (2009). *The playful brain: Venturing to the limits of neuroscience.* Oxford: Oneworld.

Smith, P.K. (1982). Does play matter functional and evolutionary aspects of animal and human play. *Behavioral and Brain Sciences, 5*, 139–155.

Spalding D. (1873). Instinct with original observations on young animals. *Macmillan's Magazine, 27*, 282–293.

Stamps, J. (1995). Motor learning and the value of familiar space. *American Naturalist, 146*, 41–58.

Comparing and Extending Piaget's and Vygotsky's Understandings of Play: Symbolic Play as Individual, Sociocultural, and Educational Interpretation

Artin Göncü *and* Suzanne Gaskins

Abstract

This chapter presents a comparison of Piaget's and Vygotsky's theories of symbolic play and provides an extension of them. By comparing these theories on the basis of their conceptualizations of symbolic play with regard to its origins, immediate functions, and future outcomes, we reach the conclusion that symbolic play is an activity of interpretation. We then provide an extension of their theories of play by indicating a blind spot shared by both Piaget and Vygotsky: both theorists considered symbolic play as primarily individual rather than fundamentally social and cultural activity. Going beyond Piaget (1945) and Vygotsky (1967), we argue that symbolic play's developmental origins, functions, and consequences are structured by children's social and cultural lives as well as by individual children themselves, and that a sociocultural approach is necessary to understand children's play fully. We conclude with some educational implications of this proposed view that integrates personal, social, and cultural engagement.

Keywords: Symbolic play, Piaget, Vygotsky, intersubjectivity, cultural differences in play, educational significance of play

There has been a long and active interest in exploring the degree of commensurability between the theories of Piaget and Vygotsky (e.g., Duncan, 1995; Glassman, 1994; LCHC, 1988). Such efforts focused on different aspects of children's development such as language and thought (e.g., Lucy, 1988) and learning and education (e.g., DeVries, 2000; Vianna & Stetsenko, 2006). However, there has been a paucity of work on whether or how a comparison of Piaget's and Vygotsky's views on play would enhance the study of children's play. This is surprising in view of the fact that both men offered important insights about play although neither of them considered it as his focus. Their ideas have guided much work on the development of play, its correlates, its developmental benefits, and its role in the education and psychological well-being of young children.

In view of these observations, the present chapter aims to provide a comparative account of Piaget and Vygotsky's theories of play based on our previous work (Gaskins & Göncü, 1988; 1992), including an analysis of how their theories, and their assumptions, have shaped the subsequent study of play. Since both theorists particularly stressed the significance of symbolic play in child development, providing parallel substantive information conducive to a comparison that would continue to reveal points of similarities and differences between them, we also limit our discussion to symbolic play.

Consistent with the theorists themselves, we define symbolic play as the kind of play in which children use one thing, such as an object or language, to serve as a "signifier" (e.g., a stick), to represent the meaning of another entity, the "signified" (e.g., a horse). What is represented can be any aspect of children's lived or imagined experiences such as social roles, situations, activities, or objects. Although recent work made important distinctions among different kinds of representational play according to the degree of abstraction involved in them and offered different labels for them (e.g., Mitchell, 2007), those distinctions are beyond the scope of the present paper.

The current effort is undertaken with the purpose of illustrating that Piaget and Vygotsky's theories are complementary in that they jointly lead to a novel conceptualization of "play-as-interpretation" defined as children's efforts to test their understanding of experiences in which they participate in non-playful contexts (Göncü, Abel, Boshans, in press; Göncü, Tuermer, Jain, & Johnson, 1999; Göncü, Jain, & Tuermer, 2007). As a background to this conceptualization, we present a comparison of Piaget and Vygotsky by remaining loyal to their presupposition that play is a universal and intrinsically motivated activity of the child. Moreover, consistent with previous work (e.g., Fein, 1979; Gaskins & Göncü, 1988), we constrain our comparison to what both men addressed, namely, the developmental origins, immediate functions, and future outcomes of symbolic play.

In addition, however, we explore the degree of commensurability between Piaget and Vygotsky by stepping outside of what was addressed by either of these theories. We argue that considering play as interpretation based solely on its psychological aspects, as both theorists did, provides an incomplete portrayal of this curious activity.[1] Play also needs to be described by recourse to those social and cultural features that define it as an integral activity of children's culturally organized everyday lives. Only by doing so can we provide a fully accurate and complete picture of play (see also Howes and Tudge et al., this volume). Our chapter ends with a look at the practical implications for education of what Piaget's and Vygotsky's theories explain and fail to take account of regarding symbolic play.

A Comparison and Integration of Piaget and Vygotsky

Both Piaget and Vygotsky offered important insights with regard to the developmental origins, immediate functions, and future outcomes of symbolic play that provide a background for the current proposal that play is an activity of interpretation of experience. We take up each issue in turn. As for developmental origins, Piaget (1945) conceptualized play as a predominance of assimilation over accommodation in his theory of adaptation. He stated that play emerges from the desire to make sense of lived experiences. Once the child goes through an experience

of adaptation, she puts the experience under her own voluntary control with the purpose of re-living it. As such, for Piaget symbolic play is a form of representational assimilation. For example, when a child pretends to be a doctor she is trying to re-interpret a past experience having to do with going to a doctor.

For Vygotsky though, the act of representation is more future-oriented although it derives from the past experience. Vygotsky (1967) claimed that the child is guided to the world of symbolic play by her tendencies that cannot be realized in the world of non-play. Also, he explicitly stated that the child moves into the world of play motivated by past experiences. So, consistent with Piaget, Vygotsky acknowledges that a past experience with a doctor leads the child to the symbolic world of "playing doctor," except that Vygotsky takes a step further in arguing that a child who is pretending to be a doctor is constructing something specific about her future in relation to this role. As we discuss below, for Vygotsky, play provides an arena of internalizing societal roles in the Zone of Proximal Development.

However, Vygotsky does not explain why children develop unrealizable tendencies during preschool years. In our view, Piaget's account of symbolic play as representational assimilation provides a more adequate explanation for the developmental origins of unrealizable tendencies, and thus of symbolic play itself. It is plausible that when a child is able to maintain symbols independently of their actual material contexts, the range of her desires increases to include unrealizable as well as realizable tendencies, since what the child would like to accomplish in play does not actually have to be present or even exist.

With regard to the immediate developmental functions—what the child gets from symbolic play at the moment of playing—both theorists underlined that children get comfort out of the effort to represent the experience without the constraints normally imposed in the real world. Piaget (1945) stated that symbolic play empowers children by enabling them to consolidate past experiences in terms of recapturing them, especially on their own terms, as illustrated by his own daughter pretending to be a dead duck after having been previously exposed to it in the family kitchen. When a child re-enacts an experience in this manner, she both tests her mastery of understanding and transforms it to be more in sync with her own motivations and wishes, thus experiencing pleasure. Consistent with Piaget, Vygotsky (1967) also explicitly stated that pretend play leads to generalized tension reduction and wish fulfillment. When a child pretends to be a doctor or a dead duck, she temporarily addresses and resolves immediate issues of affective significance having to do with these experiences and anticipates future experiences of similar sorts with greater strength. Both theories, then, center the immediate developmental function of symbolic play on the pleasure derived from the expression of mastery and control that is often missing in reality.

With regard to deferred developmental outcomes—that is, the future consequences of symbolic play—according to Piaget (1945), symbolic play provides action-based support for mental functions that are not yet completely separated from their material context. In addition, children consolidate past schemas in the imaginary world of symbolic play, and when the familiar schemes are combined under the child's own control, children recognize novel ways of making sense of their experiences. For Piaget, then, symbolic play is one activity where children begin to use their developing representations in making personal sense of the experiences in which they participate. Vygotsky attributed greater significance to the developmental outcomes of play than did Piaget. Vygotsky (1967) considered play as the leading activity of early childhood. This is so, he argued, because it is most prominent during early childhood, and it gives way to other activities. In symbolic play, the child functions in the cognitive realm, relying on her own tendencies and motives without the support of the external world. Thus, symbolic play serves as a zone of proximal development, where the child is able to function beyond her actual developmental level. The child, when enacting specific roles in play, abstracts social rules that she cannot yet formulate outside of play. Vygotsky's own example of two sisters pretending to be sisters in their play is the best example of this process: The two girls articulate the role of sisterhood in the world of play to an extent that they cannot yet easily to do in the real world.

It needs to be emphasized that for Vygotsky, play is a zone of proximal development because the imagined situation provides support for and guides the child's activities. For example, when children pretend to be "doctor," their previous experience based on this role guides their imaginations, enabling them to perform their understanding of this role including the possibilities of how to transform this role as each child sees fit. As such, this kind of guidance is different from what is more commonly known in the developmental literature

as guidance provided in the zone of proximal development by an adult or a more competent peer in a problem-solving situation such as solving a math problem. Clearly, play does not preclude this kind of instructional guidance by a more competent partner from occurring either.

There are two mechanisms by which play functions as a zone of proximal development. First, symbolic play is guided by the rules of the phenomenon imagined by the child. For example, when children pretend to be "doctor" or "sister," they strive to abide by the rules (as they understand them) that govern these roles. Through their enactment, then, children become conscious of the rules that have to do with these roles when, in fact, in day to day living they are not yet fully consciously aware of them, and certainly are not able to articulate them. In turn, their increased awareness of roles from play provides children the understanding and skills that they then can use in their everyday life.

The second mechanism Vygotsky refers to is the separation of meaning from objects and actions, which happens earlier in the child's life than the exploration of role relations. For young children, according to Vygotsky, objects, actions, and meanings are fused, that is, meanings exist only in relation to concrete objects and roles. However, play allows children to separate meaning from objects and actions. Thus, to use Vygotsky's example, when children use objects symbolically (for example "mounting" a stick and acting "as-if" riding a horse), they are disentangling the animal itself from the way one refers to it. The consequence of this is the development of an understanding of "word-meaning" that is necessary for language acquisition. Children come to recognize, as they use one object to represent the meaning of another object, that they can also use arbitrary symbols like words to represent the meaning of objects.

Vygotsky's view is consistent with Piaget's in that he too states that the act of representation is accomplished through abstraction enabled by symbolic play. However, Vygotsky emphasizes more strongly than Piaget that play is a leading edge of development, and he identifies two specific developmental consequences of play that go beyond the general claim he shares with Piaget: understanding of social roles and the development of word-meaning. It is interesting to note while the separation of meaning from objects and actions is also identified by Piaget as critical for a child to move from preoperational to the concrete operational stage (much later than Vygotsky discusses it happening in the formation of word-meaning), Piaget does not acknowledge it as taking place in symbolic play. Rather, he interprets symbolic play as being primarily an assimilative and expressive mechanism. In agreement with Sutton-Smith (1966), we argue that play is not only an expression of feeling and motivations through symbols but that the act of constructing those symbols is a fertile activity that develops conceptual understanding.

To sum up, there are important similarities and differences between Piaget and Vygotsky's theories that can be developed in future work. Presently, we build on their shared conviction that symbolic play is an interpretive activity. For both men, symbolic play is an activity in which children begin to detach their affectively significant experiences from their ordinary contexts and put them under their own control. This process begins with decontextualizations of lived experiences during infancy and becomes increasingly complex and abstract both with regard to the sources of experiences that are represented and the means by which such representations occur. In so doing, children make sense of their experiences. Put differently, interpretations of symbolic play enable development of consciousness.

Taken together, the theories of Piaget and Vygotsky helps make clear that the act of interpretation occurs in a seamless manner along a time continuum that builds on the past, takes place in the present, and influences the future. That is, interpretive activity may be primarily guided by the past experiences and serve for novel ways of making sense of them, as Piaget claimed. Complementarily, interpretations of the past may provide a ground for the anticipation of future experiences, as Vygotsky claimed. And in the present, as both theorists claimed, play can serve to bring pleasure and reduce frustration. Indeed, studies of children's uses of symbolic play illustrate how interpretations of past experiences endow children to cope with present circumstances and face future experiences of similar kind in a more effective manner (e.g., Clark, 2007).

Extending Piaget's and Vygotsky's Theories: Play as Sociocultural Activity

Comparing Piaget and Vygotsky on their claims about developmental origins, immediate functions, and eventual outcomes of symbolic play is only part of any interpretation of the two theorists. Not only did they hold many common ideas about symbolic play, but they also shared a common blind spot. Neither Piaget nor Vygotsky provided a description of how young children jointly construct symbolic play activities with other children or adults nor considered the theoretical implications of conceptualizing symbolic play as fundamentally a social activity. In the case of Piaget, this was due to his proposition that symbolic play is the idiosyncratic activity of the individual, pre-operational child. He stated that regardless of whether children are playing alone or with others, symbolic play was nothing more than an egocentric expression of their personal interests through assimilation (Piaget, 1945). To emphasize this, Piaget referred to children's language during play, even in the presence of others, as egocentric speech and collective monologues. Like Piaget, Vygotsky also did not directly address the developmental relevance of social symbolic play. While Vygotsky *did* conceptualize symbolic play as a social activity in the sense that the particular motivations of play emerge from children's experiences in the social world (1967), he emphasized the individual child's motivations in determining the specific content of symbolic play and did not emphasize how play is also co-constructed when it is taking place in a social group. In view of the fact that symbolic play is described as often taking place with others, we feel that the social nature of play deserves more attention than was given by either of these two theorists.

Largely because of this omission by Piaget and Vygotsky, there is a prevailing tendency among play researchers to conceptualize symbolic play as primarily an intrinsically motivated activity, even when it is experienced as a socially shared activity. While we agree with Piaget, Vygotsky, and many others that individual children often express in their symbolic play their personal interpretation of their own previous experiences (which often can be social in nature but not shared with their current playmates), we argue that this view of symbolic play is too narrow. We offer here an alternative proposal that play may be best conceptualized as being both individually and socially motivated activity (often simultaneously) and formed in significant part by the sociocultural structure of children's relationships, as well as community values and support (Gaskins, Haight, & Lancy, 2007; Gaskins & Miller, 2009; Göncü & Perone, 2009). Placing the source of the motivation to play at the level of the individual as done by Rubin, Fein, and Vandenberg (1983) fails to acknowledge the role of children's sociocultural context in shaping children's play. The attribution of responsibility of engagement to individuals, as supposedly autonomous players, has led not only to misconceptions of Western children's play but also, by extension, has precluded the accurate understanding of cultural differences in children's play (see also Howes & Tudge et al., this volume). Without a model of play as socially constructed activity, many scholars have provided context-free descriptions of Western children's play as if their social, cultural, and economic context had no impact on their play activities, and they have assumed that their descriptions are universal.

There are three distinct ways that symbolic play can be social. The first was recognized implicitly by both Piaget and Vygotsky, but was not developed by either. Both theorists argued that affectively significant experiences of children involving others lead children to the world of symbolic play in order to find a way to interpret what meaning the child attaches to them. For example, children pretend to be doctors not because of individual children's isolated desires, but rather because of emotionally meaningful experiences co-constructed with others. In this sense, neither the motivation nor the content of play comes from the individual alone. Taking this experiential feature of children's play seriously suggests that the affective antecedents of children's symbolic play stem from interactions with others accumulated across time and are culturally situated.

The second way that symbolic play can be social is found in the choice of play objects and their use in representation. Children's homes and communities obviously influence what objects (and how many) are available for use in symbolic play and how they should be used. Winnicott (1971) and Clark (2007) cogently made this point with reference to the symbolic transitional objects that provide the meaning for the child when their attachment figure is not present. For example, that a security blanket may provide comfort and safety for a child is probably the product of a particular child-caregiver relationship. Therefore, it is plausible to argue that how children attach meaning to particular play objects in symbolic play may vary across social and cultural contexts.

Finally and most directly, symbolic play is social when the ideas that children represent in their symbolic play are negotiated during that play with their partners, who unlike in other zone of proximal development environments, do not require that one player be more competent than the others nor any player intending to structure the situation for the other players. Each play partner's own values, knowledge, experiences, time, and affective needs figure into deciding what to represent, but there is also a shared social commitment with particular players to co-construct this activity through social symbolic play. The social commitment shapes (and in some cases, limits) the potential for individual expression. For example, adults, peers, or siblings as play partners each affect the enactment of play bouts in different ways. In short, we claim that symbolic play, while it may appear objectively or subjectively as intrinsically motivated, also has a significant social component that results from children's collaborations in their partnerships with others, and in turn, those collaborations are culturally organized.

Below, we will briefly illustrate some of the theoretical limitations introduced by Piaget's and Vygotsky's shared assumption that the individual child is the appropriate primary unit of analysis for understanding the developmental origins, immediate functions, and eventual outcomes of play, first by looking at how Western children's symbolic play is co-constructed, and then by looking at how Yucatec Maya children's symbolic play is culturally organized.

Symbolic Play as Intersubjective Interpretive Experience

To begin with, there is fairly consistent evidence that middle class Western parents value and make provisions to engage in symbolic play with their children (see Howe and Lillard, both, this volume). Also, there is evidence that low-income parents from different ethnic/racial communities support young children's social symbolic play in like manner (Göncü et al., 2007; Howes, this volume). Often, such engagement takes the form of acknowledging young children's motivations and initiations as well as co-constructing meaning, or intersubjectivity. Adults' construction of intersubjectivity or shared understandings with children is accomplished in multiple ways, including role playing either as co-actors or directors, building on children's affects in a manner that is sensitive to children's needs (e.g., supporting children's desires to be mothers), and facilitating children's communication in the form of extending children's play utterances (see also Fagen, this volume; Göncü et al, in press). Thus, it is safe to conclude that Western caregivers try to interpret and extend children's symbolic play (e.g., Göncü, Mistry, & Mosier, 2000; Miller & Garvey, 1984; Haight & Miller, 1993).

Playing with peers presents a different picture. In the absence of parental benevolence, children negotiate with one another the affective source, (meta) communication, and representations (Göncü, 1993).

Evidence indicates that intersubjectivity or shared understanding is required on all three grounds. Any proposal that is not accepted or is ignored (or is successfully negotiated) by the play group is given up (Corsaro, 1983; see also Howes, this volume). With regard to the actual experiences that are interpreted in social symbolic play, issues may include both traumatic themes, such as death and loss, as independently examined by Erikson, Freud, and Piaget (cf., Göncü et al., in press), and ordinary, everyday experiences, such as preparing a meal. (For reviews see Göncü, 1993; Göncü et al., in press.)

With regard to play communication with peers, there is strong evidence that Western (and non-Western as well, see Howes, Tudge, and Bock, all this volume) children have well-established notions of how to establish and maintain meta-communicative frames for their social symbolic play. Consistent with G. Bateson's view (1955/1972), children construct intersubjectivity about the meaning of their activity by exchanging messages that vary from an explicit remark such as "I'm Superman" to an implicit pretend gesture such as playfully walking like an adult female. Recent work shows that intersubjectivity about metacommunication emerges during infancy in the affective context of mother-child interaction (Lillard, 2007) and is marked by a number of behaviors such as smiles, which become increasingly varied and complex during preschool years (Göncü & Kessel, 1988).

With regard to the representation of meaning, children's negotiations to find a mutually acceptable play theme guides them to the co-construction of structures called scripts (Göncü, 1993). For example, when children attempt to enact getting a pretend shot, they may draw upon their past experiences, or scripts, as a way of integrating their individual understandings. Children use scripts, first learned through everyday life experiences, in social play, flexibly integrating different interpretive possibilities. As such, evolving social play scripts allow individuals to use their personal experiences to establish mutuality and collective understandings of social practice and construct shared symbolized representations of their meanings with peers. Thus, social symbolic play emerges, not only as an important window into the insights of individual children, or childhood in general, but as a source of socially negotiated insight.

To sum up, we agree with Piaget (1945) and Vygotsky's (1967) claims that symbolic play originates from children's needs to work out affectively significant experiences, and that in play, children make sense of such experiences as they test their mastery and control over them. But we also believe it is critical for a comprehensive and accurate theory of symbolic play that it be recognized as a social activity, not only with regard to its origins, but also its realization.

Social Symbolic Play as Culturally Structured Interpretive Experience

Conceptualizing the developmental importance of symbolic play through the lens of intersubjectivity adds a social complexity to play as an activity that is missing in Piaget's and Vygotsky's formulations. Concurrently, it raises another significant issue; if children's play is not structured solely on the basis of individual interpretation of experience but also from within children's actions during play which are situated in social worlds, then it is also structured by the cultural beliefs and practices that shape all children's everyday lives (Gaskins & Göncü, 1992; Gaskins, 1999; Göncü et al., 2007; Göncü, Patt, & Kouba, 2002). In this section, we illustrate some of the range of variation in play across cultures by focusing in depth on one case study, that of Yucatec Mayan children, in order to explore the consequences of such variation for the theoretical claims made about play by Piaget and Vygotsky.

We begin with their shared and central claim that symbolic play serves to interpret experience and reduce children's frustration that occurs in their daily lives. Gaskins and Miller (2009) have argued that the level of frustration in children's lives may vary significantly across cultures because of their different roles and both their own and their caregivers' expectations about children's experiences in the world. They argue that Yucatec Mayan children, from an early age, both have a significant amount of control over their own actions (and those of others directed toward them) and hold few expectations about their ability to influence the world in other ways. In this framework, while a shot received during a trip to the doctor may be painful, it is not necessarily an event that the child feels needs to be reinterpreted. Scripts such as "doctor," which for Western children seem to be reworkings of specific events in individual children's daily lives, are not often seen in Yucatec Mayan children's symbolic play. Their play is centered around more generalized themes that represent familiar, shared everyday experiences, like playing house. This still involves interpretation, but focuses more strongly on what actually occurs in daily life, rather than what the child wishes might or might not have happened.

When the interpretive role of play is expanded to include intersubjectivity, many other cultural factors come in to play. There is great variability in the social worlds of children around the world, including the most basic one of with whom children spend time and for what purpose. For some cultures, the social world of children, beginning as toddlers, exists largely outside the world of adults (Fortes, 1970 [1934]; Lancy, 1996). For others, the social world of children is inherently integrated into the world of adults, as they act as *legitimate peripheral participants* (Lave and Wenger, 1991) in household work (Gaskins, 1999, 2009a). Both of these social organizations differ dramatically from that of most Western children, where their child-centered social world is constructed by adults and consists of social interactions with either caregivers or same-age peers. To understand the profundity of these differences for children's play, we will go into more detail about the cultural organization of Yucatec Maya children's play as part of their daily lives (Gaskins, 1999). First, the social organization determines who are available and legitimate playmates. For the Yucatec Maya, adults do not play with children (Gaskins, 1996), and older children play only in the context of serving as caregivers of younger children. In this sense, play belongs to and is organized by children. Moreover, children's playmates are not their friends or other peers, but their siblings and other child relatives who live in the same compound or nearby. This one social fact has multiple consequences for the structure of children's play. Daily playmates are drawn from a very small group of children, and the group membership stays constant across time. Moreover, groups are multi-aged, with a wide range of competencies inherent in the group that must be accommodated in play. More significantly, with kin, there are nonnegotiable hierarchies of responsibility and respect that are brought to the assumptions and negotiations that occur in social play (Gaskins, 2006). For instance, older children do not suspend their caregiving role in which they must respond to real world dangers and distractions, even as they assert their right to be the primary organizers of the intersubjective play environment.

This case study illustrates that children's social symbolic play, precisely *because* it is in fact an intersubjective activity, is culturally structured. The resulting cultural differences can have profound impact on the immediate functions or long-term outcomes of symbolic play that Piaget and Vygotsky proposed in their theories. For instance, the time spent in symbolic play peaks for Yucatec Mayan children not during early childhood, as seen in Western children, but between the years of 6–8 (Gaskins, 2000). This later peak makes sense when it is recognized that what the children are doing in their play is working to interpret adult activities that they are beginning to master through legitimate participation, rather than creating alternative worlds based on their unrealized desires. Likewise, in a mixed-age group where the older children are directing a familiar script, younger children will not have the opportunity to explore their own personal interpretations of previous experiences. And to the extent that play is operating in a culture where it is not highly valued by adults, with much of the children's time channeled into household work, it cannot have the same developmental force that it has in cultures where it is highly cultivated by adults. Nor does it need to, since there are other kinds of rich experiences that support children's development.

These differences not only are interesting variations to enrich any account of play as an interpretive activity, but they also have direct relevance to theoretical claims made by Piaget and Vygotsky. The brief description here of the cultural construction of Yucatec Mayan children's play suggests that the developmental origins, immediate functions, and outcomes of symbolic play—whether a particular instance of play is organized at the individual or social level—will not always be the same as those articulated by Piaget and Vygotsky, bringing into question the universality of their theoretical claims. This claim is particularly interesting for Vygotsky's theory, since he explicitly recognizes that children, as they construct in their symbolic play scripts about social organizations and practices, come to be more aware of those social "facts." However, he does not articulate the social organization of the act of construction during play itself—what kinds of scripts are chosen, who does the organization, or how central such play is in children's lives. Vygotsky also did not address cultural influences on children's play despite his more general Marxist concern with social influences on developmental processes.

As such, when features of play as opportunities for meaning making are interpreted within the context of children's variable social and cultural daily lives, we see more clearly not only how each culture affords different opportunities for play, but also how the range of variation in this universal activity, both within and between cultures, comes to influence its meaning for individual children at play. In the end, the functions of play (in the immediate context) and the future outcomes of play that are presumed to be universal by both Piaget and Vygotsky come into question for both theorists from this viewpoint of play as an intersubjective and culturally organized activity.

The Role of Social Symbolic Play in Children's Education

As we have argued above, and consistent with Piaget (1945) and Vygotsky (1967), it is now empirically established that symbolic play is an activity of making sense about the experiences in which children participate in their non-play worlds. Further, depending on the system of social relationships, responsibilities, and cultural traditions and expectations, children's uses for symbolic play are varied. Therefore, when children engage in symbolic play, one of the things they are doing is presenting to the world around them information about their current understandings and their priorities for making sense of their experience, that is, they are informing others about their "curriculum" as they see fit. For example, while a Western preschooler may work through issues about separation from her parents in her symbolic play in the classroom, a four-year-old Yucatec child who spends much of her day working next to her mother may be happy in mastering the act of tortilla making through symbolic re-enactment of that script. As scholars of play, previous teachers of young children, and as current educators of teachers (Göncü, Main, & Abel, 2009; in press) and museum professionals (Gaskins, 2009b), we think it is important to recognize that symbolic play serves not only as recreation but actually as a window of opportunity for increasing understanding, as Piaget and, especially, Vygotsky recognized.

Although adults always mediate children's play either directly or indirectly, when adults participate in play as teachers, their mediation is often extensive and principled, with intentional provisions for physical spaces and structure of symbolic play in order to insure learning. Just as children introduce their own curricular priorities in classroom symbolic play, they also learn about the adults' curricular goals for them provided in organized play settings. In keeping with other scholars (e.g., Bodrova & Leong, 2007; Göncü et al., in press), we admit that use of play as a learning device through which children are introduced to adults' curriculum is productive. However, in such cases, when play becomes intentional *curriculum* of adults rather than the

spontaneously expressed activity of children, the agency of who acts as the director of that curriculum shifts from the child to the adult.

While adult guidance of play may be desirable as an educational tool, it may be questioned if such a practice is justified either by Piaget's or Vygotsky's theories about the role of play in development. Framing adult instruction as *playful interactions* is not a bad thing to do, but it transforms the activity—it is no longer play in the sense that Piaget and Vygotsky, or most other play theorists, meant when they talk about its developmental outcomes. In fact, Vygotsky (1967) argued that play's developmental impact grew out of children's use of play by themselves or with other children, not through adult-mediated play—that the Zone of Proximal Development was established by the inherent demands from within the play frame itself, not by the guidance of others from outside the frame of play. Similarly, Piaget (1945) was interpreted by constructivist educators as suggesting that adults' goals for children should be only tacitly available for children, that is, children meet adults in play by engaging in an activity of interest for themselves, not because it is requested by adults (cf., Göncü et al., 2009).

In addition, once children's symbolic play is recognized to be culturally organized, either kind of symbolic play in the classroom—child-initiated or teacher-initiated—requires careful consideration of the children's cultural background and family structure. We agree with other scholars who claim that symbolic play offers many developmental benefits to young children (e.g., Singer, Golinkoff, & Hirsch-Pasek, 2007). However, it is important to recognize that some of play's contributions will be culture specific, and a defense of instituting play in educational institutions should take place in relation to how play is seen by children's own communities (Göncü et al., in press). In communities where there is not a shared understanding between families and school about the educational benefits of play or the role of adults in children's play, it is the childhood educators' responsibility to become aware of their own values and practices about play and then develop an appropriate play curriculum with *all* the families and children, in order for children to participate and benefit from play in the classroom. This task is made all the more difficult because of the heavy reliance in early childhood education on the theories of Piaget and Vygotsky, who failed to take up the issue of the cultural relativity of children's symbolic play.

Conclusions

Piaget's and Vygotsky's theories can be seen as similar in their attempt to explain the developmental origins, immediate functions, and long-term outcomes of symbolic play. They are complementary in emphasis, however. While sharing a similar explanation of the immediate function of play being children's making sense of their everyday experiences (including dealing with their frustrations), Piaget focused in addition more on the developmental origins of symbolic play, while Vygotsky elaborated more on the long-term outcomes. Taken together, their combined vision of the importance of play in development is richer than either of them taken separately. Piaget and Vygotsky also shared a blind spot that has had a significant influence on subsequent conceptualizations of children's play. Neither theorist emphasized that children's symbolic play is often experienced with social partners, and that social symbolic play is an interpretive activity that is both inherently intersubjective and influenced in fundamental ways by its social context.

We have argued here that there are important consequences in characterizing play as intersubjective experience, rather than simply individual experience, including the increased capacity to conceptualize play as being culturally organized and variable. The first consequence is theoretical: The reconceptualization of symbolic play as intersubjective activity, when paired with knowledge of the variation that occurs in the cultural organization of children's social worlds, suggests that developmental origins, immediate functions, or long-term outcomes proposed by Piaget and Vygotsky are not necessarily universal, as they assumed. The second consequence is practical: In order for their theories to be comprehensive and of use in today's increasingly diverse world, Piaget's and Vygotsky's important insights about children's symbolic play that have informed the education of young children need to be expanded to include the social and cultural natures of that play. This contextualization of play is especially significant for early childhood learning environments, such as preschools and children's museums, which use play as a foundation, in order that their policies and practices more effectively support their goals of providing meaningful and effective educational experiences for *all* young children and their families.

Note

1 Despite Vygotsky's significant Marxist concern with social influences on developmental processes in general, we argue that he shared with Piaget this common "blind spot."

References

Bateson, G. A. (1972[1955]). A theory of play and fantasy. In G. A. Bateson (Ed.), *Steps to an ecology of mind* (pp. 177–193). New York: Chandler.

Bodrova, E. & Leong, D. (2007). *Tools of the Mind: the Vygotskian approach to early childhood education.* Upper Saddle River, NJ: Prentice Hall.

Clark, C. D. (2007). Therapeutic advantages of play. In A. Göncü, & S. Gaskins (Eds.), *Play and development: Evolutionary, sociocultural, and functional perspectives* (pp. 275–293). Mahwah, NJ: LEA.

Corsaro, W. (1983). Script recognition, articulation, and expansion in children's role play. *Discourse Processes, 6*, 1–19.

DeVries, R. (2000). Vygotsky, Piaget, and education: A reciprocal assimilation of theories and educational practices. *New Ideas in Psychology, 18*, 187–213.

Duncan, R. (1995). Piaget and Vygotsky revisited: Dialogue or assimilation. *Developmental Review, 15*, 458–472.

Fein, G.G. (1979). Echoes from the nursery: Piaget, Vygotsky, and the relationship between language and play. In E. Winner & H. Gardner (Eds.), *Fact, fiction, and fantasy in childhood (New Directions in Child Development,* pp. 1–14). Washington, D.C.: Jossey-Bass.

Fortes, Meyer (1970 [1934]). Social and psychological aspects of education in Taleland, in J. Middleton (Ed.), *From child to adult.* (pp. 14–74). Garden City, NY: Natural History Press.

Gaskins, S. (1996). How Mayan parental theories come into play. In S. Harkness & C. Super (Eds.,) *Parents' cultural belief systems: Their origins, expressions, and consequences* (pp. 345–363). New York, New York: Guilford Press.

Gaskins, S. (1999). Children's daily lives in a Mayan village: A case study of culturally constructed roles and activities. In A. Göncü (Ed.), *Children's engagement in the world* (pp. 25–81) Cambridge, England: Cambridge University Press.

Gaskins, S. (2000). Children's daily activities in a Mayan village: A culturally grounded description. *Journal of Cross-cultural Research, 34*, 375–389.

Gaskins, S., (2006). The cultural organization of Yucatec Mayan children's social interactions. In X. Chen, D. French, and B. Schneider (Eds.), *Peer relationships in cultural context* (pp. 283–309). Cambridge, England: Cambridge University Press.

Gaskins, S. (2009a). Work before play for Yucatec Maya children. In R.A. Shweder, T. R. Bidell, A. C. Dailey, S. D. Dixon, P. J. Miller, & J. Modell (Eds.), *The child: An encyclopedic companion* (p. 1040). Chicago: University of Chicago Press.

Gaskins, S. (2009b). The cultural meaning of play and learning in children's museums. *Hand to Hand, 22*(4), 1–2; 8–11.

Gaskins, S. & Göncü, A. (1988). Children's play as representation and imagination: The case of Piaget and Vygotsky. *The Quarterly Newsletter of the Laboratory of Comparative Human Cognition, 10*(4), 104–107.

Gaskins, S. and Göncü, A. (1992). Cultural Variation in Play: A Challenge to Piaget and Vygotsky. *The Quarterly Newsletter of the Laboratory of Comparative Human Cognition, 14*(2), 31–35.

Gaskins, S., Haight, W. and Lancy, D. (2007). The cultural construction of play. In A. Göncü and S. Gaskins (Eds.), *Play and development: Evolutionary, sociocultural and functional perspectives* (pp.179–202). Mahwah, NJ: LEA.

Gaskins, S. & Miller, P.J. (2009). The cultural roles of emotions in pretend play. In C.D. Clark (Ed.), *Transactions at play*

Play and Cultural Studies 9, (pp. 5–21). Lanham, MD: University Press of America.

Glassman, M. (1994). All things being equal: The two roads of Piaget and Vygotsky. *Developmental Review, 14*(2), 186–214.

Göncü, A. (1993). Development of intersubjectivity in the social pretend play of young children. *Human Development, 36*, 185–198.

Göncü, A., Abel, B. & Boshans, M. (in press). The role of attachment and play in young children's learning and development. In K. Littleton, C. Wood, & J. K. Staarman (Eds.). *International Handbook of Educational Psychology: New Perspectives on Learning and Teaching* Amsterdam: Elsevier.

Göncü, A. & Kessel, F.S. (1988). Preschoolers' collaborative construction in planning and maintaining imaginative play. *International Journal of Behavioral Development, 11*(3), 327–344.

Göncü, A., Jain, J., & Tuermer, U. (2007). Children's play as cultural interpretation. In A. Göncü, & S. Gaskins (Eds.). *Play and development: Evolutionary, sociocultural, and functional perspectives* (pp. 155–178). Mahwah, NJ: LEA.

Göncü, A., Main, C. & Abel, B. (2009). Fairness in Participation in Preschool. In J. Berthelsen, J. Brownlee, & E. Johansson (Eds.), *Participatory learning in the early years*, (pp. 185–202). New York: Routledge.

Göncü, A., Main, C. & Abel, B. (in press). Children's play and its educational significance. *Human Development*.

Göncü, A. Mistry, J., & Mosier, C. (2000). Cultural variations in the play of toddlers. *International Journal of Behavioral Development, 24*, 321–329.

Göncü, A., Patt, M., Kouba, E. (2002). Understanding young children's pretend play in context. In P. Smith & C. Hart (Eds.) *Handbook of social development* (pp. 418–437). London: Blackwell.

Göncü, A. & Perone, A. (2009). Commentary: Inquiries into the roles of adults in children's play. In C. D. Clark (Ed.). Transactions at play. *Play & Culture Studies* (pp. 125–127), Vol. 9. New York: University Press of America.

Göncü, A., Tuermer, U. Jain. J. & Johnson, D. (1999). Children's play as cultural activity. In A. Göncü, (Ed.). *Children's engagement in the world: Sociocultural perspectives*, (pp. 148–170). Cambridge: Cambridge University Press.

Haight, W. & Miller, P.J. (1993). *Pretending at home: Early development in a sociocultural context*. Albany: State University of New York Press.

Lancy, D. F. (1996). *Playing on the mother ground: Cultural routines for children's development*. New York: Guilford.

Lave, J. & Wenger, E. (1991). *Situated learning: Legitimate peripheral participation*. Cambridge, UK: Cambridge University Press.

Laboratory of Comparative Human Cognition (1988). *The Quarterly Newsletter of the Laboratory of Comparative Human Cognition,* 16 (4).

Lillard, A. (2007). Guided participation: How mothers structure and children understand pretend play. In A. Göncü & S. Gaskins (Eds.), *Play and development: Evolutionary, sociocultural, and functional perspectives* (pp. 131–153). Mahwah, NJ: LEA.

Lucy, J. A. (1988). The role of language in the development of representation: The case of Piaget and Vygotsky. *The Quarterly Newsletter of the Laboratory of Comparative Human Cognition, 16*(4), 99–103.

Miller, P. & Garvey, C. (1984). Mother-baby role play: Its origins in social support. In I. Bretherton (Ed.). *Symbolic play: The development of social understanding* (pp. 101–130). New York: Academic Press.

Mitchell, R. (2007). Pretense in animals: The continuing relevance of children's pretense. In A. Göncü, & S. Gaskins (Eds.), *Play and development: Evolutionary, sociocultural, and functional perspectives* (pp. 51–75). Mahwah, NJ: LEA.

Piaget, J. (1945). *Play, dreams, and imitation in childhood*. New York: Norton.

Rubin, K. Fein, G. & Vandenberg, B. (1983). Play. In P. Mussen (Series Ed.) & E. M. Hetherington (Vol. Ed.), *Handbook of child psychology*, 4th ed. (4, pp. 693–774). New York: Wiley.

Singer, D. G., Golinkoff, R. M. & Hirsh-Pasek, K. (Eds.) (2006). *Play=learning: How play motivates and enhances children's cognitive and social-emotional growth*. New York: Oxford University Press.

Sutton-Smith, B. (1966). Piaget on play: A critique. *Psychological Review, 73*(1), 104–110.

Vianna, E. & Stetsenko, A. (2006). Embracing history through transforming it: Contrasting Piagetian versus Vygotskyan (activity) theories of learning and development to expand constructivism within a dialectical view of history. *Theory and Psychology, 16*(1), 81–108.

Vygotsky, L. S. (1967). Play and its role in the mental development of the child. *Soviet Psychology, 5*(3), 6–18.

Winnicott, D. W. (1971). *Playing and reality*. New York: Basic Books.

Gene × Environment Interactions and Social Play: Contributions from Rhesus Macaques

Khalisa N. Herman, Annika Paukner, *and* Stephen J. Suomi

Abstract

This chapter reviews studies in nonhuman primates, particularly the rhesus macaque, which document a role for social play in reflecting and contributing to the development of social competence. We begin by reviewing what is known about the developmental progression of social play. Then we discuss what is known about the impact of various forms of early social deprivation, as well as acute environmental stressors, on the frequency and quality of social play. Subsequently, we review what is known about genetic influences, such as gender, temperament, and candidate genes, on rates of social play. In a penultimate section, we discuss what is known about gene-by-environment interactions involving gender and candidate genes, on social play. We conclude by exploring implications of nonhuman primate studies for understanding social play and the development of social competence in children.

Keywords: play, social play, primates, rhesus macaque, nonhuman primates, social development, genetic influences

Introduction

Many of society's greatest achievements can be traced back to individuals working together to attain common goals. Our ability to recruit help from others, work together as a team, and settle common disagreements, while at the same time maintaining our roles within a community describes the panoply of skills called social competence (Suomi, 1982). How do we develop the social skills necessary to be well-adjusted members of society? While it appears that some individuals are gifted with more advanced social skills from a very early age, it also appears that early experience can both enrich and impair the development of social skills. Recent work also suggests that social competence can be the product of interactions between genes and experience (Bakermans-Kranenburg et al., 2008; Fox et al., 2005). Therefore, we can make great strides toward understanding social competence by considering relations between endogenous (genes, neural organization, physiology) and exogenous (parenting, peers, culture) factors on development.

Social play is likely one of the main factors that both contributes to and reflects the development of social competence. The term social play is used to describe behavior that appears without immediate function, and where attention to process outweighs the creation of a product (Smith, 2004). Often social play is further characterized as flexible, and as having positive affect (Krasnor et al., 1980). While there has been much disagreement over how to define play (Power, 2000), researchers, teachers, and children have little trouble distinguishing play from related behaviors such as exploration and aggression (Fry, 2005).

Many researchers have argued that the quality and quantity of social play with peers provides a valuable index for assessing social competence (Rubin, 1982; Russ, 2004; Suomi, 1979). Play is a ubiquitous feature of childhood that has been observed across many cultures (Edwards, 2000), and it becomes both more social and more cognitively complex across childhood (Parten, 1932;

Rubin et al., 1983; Smilansky, 1968b). Studies have linked social play experience to a number of processes involved in social competence including emotion regulation, empathy and the ability to understand another person's emotions, as well as problem solving and conflict resolution skills (for a review, see Berk et al., in press; Russ, 2004). There are also studies that report positive associations between time with peers and social competence (Fabes et al., 2003; Ladd, 2005). Conversely, when play deviates from age and gender expectations, it tends to reflect deficits in social competence (Rubin, 1982). Collectively, these findings suggest that frequent peer play is related to improvements in social skills.

The design and frequency of play appears to reflect the influence of environmental factors. For instance, lower rates of play have been observed in children of low socioeconomic status (Smilansky, 1968a), and those with a history of maltreatment (Alessandri, 1991). Play variations may additionally reflect genetically influenced factors. We use this term to describe traits that are moderately to highly heritable at the population level. Many studies have found that boys exhibit more of one form of social play, rough-and-tumble play, than girls (DiPietro, 1981), a difference that is strongly influenced by androgens (Berenbaum et al., 1992), while others have found that certain individuals have more playful personalities (Polak-Toste et al., 2006; Singer et al., 1980), and are oriented more toward people than objects (Coplan et al., 1994; Shotwell et al., 1979). On a similar note, children with high cortisol levels, an marker for reactive temperament, display wary behaviors during peer play (Schmidt et al., 1997), and those with low vagal tone, an indicator of poor regulation over the sympathetic nervous system, display greater decreases in social play across time (Fox et al., 1989; Porges, 2001). Taken together, play patterns appear to be affected by a variety of genetically influenced traits.

Naturally, one might wonder how environmental and genetic factors may interact to influence rates of social play. For example, effects of social experiences on genetic predispositions can be examined by comparing behavioral outcomes from different rearing experiences (Collins et al., 2000; Saudino, 2005). One study examining gender differences in children's social play reported less pronounced gender differences in children of divorce compared to children growing up in intact families (Hetherington et al., 1979), a finding that may be due to fewer play opportunities for children and their fathers (Flanders et al., 2009; Lamb, 2003).

More recently, advances in molecular psychiatry have made it possible to test for interactions between genetic and environmental factors using candidate genes (Caspi et al., 2002; Kaufman et al., 2004). This concept of a Gene × Environment (G × E) interaction occurs when the expression of a genetically influenced factor such as the presence or absence of a particular gene polymorphism is modified by environmental input (for a review, see Rutter, 2007). Fox et al. (2005) reported higher levels of reticent behavior in a peer play setting in children with the short form of the serotonin transporter polymorphism (5-*HTT*LPR), but only in those children whose mothers also reported low levels of social support. These findings suggest that social play is well-suited for investigating interactions between environmental and genetically influenced traits during childhood.

However, there are many potential explanations for G × E effects on social play. Effects that have been attributed to environmental influences alternatively may be due to the effect of the parent or child's genes on developmental outcomes (Plomin et al., 1977; Scarr et al., 1983). Gene expression also varies across development (Casey et al., 2009), perhaps corresponding to sensitive periods for socioemotional development (Immelmann et al., 1981; Rutter, 2006). What has been ascribed to genetics may also reflect unmeasured environmental effects since children are exposed to countless environmental influences that can vary in intensity or duration. Therefore, in order to tease apart environmental and genetic contributions to rates of social play, researchers must be able to conduct carefully controlled studies. Due to ethical and practical concerns, opportunities to directly investigate the correlates and G × E effects on play are limited when studying children.

By contrast, researchers studying gene and environmental influences on social play in nonhuman animals are not faced with the same methodological and ethical limitations. One clear advantage of animal research is that environmental conditions can be tightly controlled and manipulated. Researchers have many designs at their disposal including cross-fostering (Meaney, 2001), and manipulation of environmental conditions (Andrews et al., 1994; Sackett et al., 1999). In addition, biological samples can be easily collected including measures to determine candidate genes, and structural and functional measures of the brain. To study G × E interactions involving social play, researchers can identify animal subjects possessing a particular diathesis (either from behavior or genetics), then randomly assign subjects to different rearing conditions, and study their behavior and biology across development (Barr et al., 2003).

Researchers studying social play have only begun studying G × E interactions in animal models (Barr et al., 2003). The value of such animal studies depends on how well the findings generalize back to understanding play in children. Non-human primates are valuable models because they frequently engage in social play as juveniles, and are highly reliant on social relationships throughout the lifespan (Suomi, 1982). Rhesus macaques (*Macaca mulatta*), in particular, are known to possess polymorphisms in a variety of candidate genes, and distinct temperament profiles, both of which have strong parallels in humans (Suomi, 2004b), making them particularly suitable as models of social play behavior. In this chapter, we argue that much can be learned about connections between social play and the development of social competence by studying non human primates. We begin by describing the normative sequence involved in acquiring skills for playing with peers. We then turn to discussing connections between early social experiences and social play, followed by a discussion about genetic factors such as candidate genes that are relevant to social play. We conclude by outlining what is known about interactions between early social experience and genetic variation on rates of social play, and their value for future research directions.

The Development of Social Play

Similar to humans, many non-human primates spend their lives as members of multiple complex social networks. Rhesus macaques in particular develop close relationships with caregivers, siblings, and peers, all within the context of a larger social troop (Hinde, 1988; Suomi, 1982; Suomi, 2005). Each troop ranges from several dozen to more than 100 subjects, and consists of multiple matrilines that are each organized around one female. Both between and within these matrilines, subjects are organized into a specific dominance hierarchy (Sade, 1972; Sade et al., 1988). By and large, females remain within their natal social groups for the entirety of their lives, whereas males leave their natal troop and attempt to join other troops starting around puberty.

Studies strongly suggest that social competence is of paramount importance to rhesus macaques (Suomi, 2005). Being socially competent consists of being able to identify fellow troop members and to respond appropriately given a past history with an animal (Higley et al., 1996a; Winslow et al., 2003). The ultimate test of social competence is to be able to meet survival needs and to gain opportunities to reproduce while at the same time being able to maintain social affiliations (Suomi, 1982). Indeed, research in both naturalistic and captive troops of rhesus has documented that a monkey's ability to survive depends on social skills (Higley et al., 1996b).

How do rhesus macaques develop the skills necessary to be socially competent with conspecifics? While secure attachment relationships with caregivers clearly provide individuals with the confidence for forming social relationships with other troop members (Suomi, 1999), we suggest that it is within the context of peer relationships that juveniles develop social skills that can be applied to other relationships (Harlow, 1969). Numerous peer partners are typically available for rhesus infants given that rhesus macaques are seasonal breeders (Berman, 1982). Their social networks begin increasing in size just as infants begin interacting with their peers. Taken together, it appears that peer relationships provide developing monkeys with many of the experiences necessary to improve their social skills.

When a developing monkey is learning to play, the mother is never far away. At any point, if the infant becomes over-aroused, it will often return to the mother for contact comfort. As has been described for human infants (Bowlby, 1969), infant monkeys tend to use their mothers as a 'secure base,' a behavior that decreases as the infant gets older. Mother monkeys also provide a safe haven for their infants against danger, immediately retrieving their infants and placing them close to their ventrum. Yet, the perception of danger is very much up to the mother, and may result in mothers depriving their infants of peer play opportunities. For instance, mothers low in dominance status tend to be more restrictive of their infants' activities, which results in the infant engaging in less exploration and play (Suomi, 2002). Other factors such as troop size are also associated with differences in infant restriction (Berman et al., 1997). Thus, monkey mothers play an important role in regulating their infants' activities with peers.

A fair amount is known about the normative developmental sequence of social play in monkeys (Suomi, 1979). Because social play rarely occurs between an infant and its mother, social play is characteristic of a peer affectional system (Harlow, 1969). Shortly after birth, infants begin taking note of nearby infants and begin interacting with them, first in a reflexive and then an exploratory fashion (Harlow, 1969). It is only after gaining a basic understanding of animate partners that infants start engaging in social play. As earlier reviews have described (Harlow, 1969; Suomi, 1979), infants pass through a number of developmental stages during the acquisition of social play behaviors starting with gentle rough-and-tumble play, an activity that involves grappling the body of a partner and mock biting. As development proceeds, rough-and-tumble play takes on a rougher quality and is more likely to escalate into aggression. The last type of social play to emerge is approach-withdrawal play, which is characterized by frequent alternations between chasing and fleeing a partner. Generally, social play bouts increase in length, become more complex, and involve a larger number of social partners across development. The full repertoire of social play behaviors are typically in place by eight to nine months after birth. However, rates of social play do not reach their apex until approximately two years (Gard et al., 1977; O'Neill et al., 1991).

One unique characteristic of social play is that juveniles are given the opportunity to engage in many of the behaviors necessary for later adult social life. Because of the non-serious nature of play, juveniles are able to interact with peers in a manner that is largely free from the consequences normally associated with behaviors like aggression (Suomi, 1979). Thus, social play allows developing monkeys to exercise social behaviors that will contribute to their social competence.

In summary, social play appears to be closely associated with the development of social competence in rhesus macaques. For one, social play is predominantly observed during the juvenile period. Second, it follows a proscribed sequence across development, becoming both more complex and more social as infants get older. It also provides juveniles with the opportunity to practice social behaviors—often specific to their gender—that will be highly relevant later in life.

Early Experience, Peers, and Social Play
The role of peers in rhesus macaques' developing social competence has been examined in a series of studies where infants have been deprived of peer companionship for varying lengths of time over the first year of life. One recent study examined the social skills of 13 subadult females ranging from two to five years of age reared only by their mothers against a similar number of subjects reared with both mothers and peers (Kempes et al., 2008). The study reported that peer-deprived subjects engaged in higher levels of abnormal behavior as well as increased submission toward social partners. Peer-deprived subjects also displayed higher levels of agonistic behavior when engaging in affiliative interactions such as grooming, and were more likely to respond with aggression to a partner's submissive acts. Early studies have also found that infants reared with only a mother, father, or unrelated adult display incompetent play skills, hyper-aggression, and shy away from interacting with others (Gluck, 1979; Redican, 1975). One longitudinal study found that the longer subjects were reared without peer companionship, the more pronounced were their social impairments (Alexander et al., 1965). These studies clearly demonstrate that peer companionship during early social development is far from a trivial matter.

We have reason to believe that deficits in social competence are due to social play deprivation (Harlow, 1969; Suomi, 1979). For one, a number of studies have documented that the opportunity to interact playfully with peers for short amounts of time on a daily basis can prevent subjects from becoming socially incompetent (Hansen, 1966; Rosenblum, 1961, 1971). However, continuous rearing with peers appears to impair rather than enhance social competence (Chamove et al., 1973; Harlow, 1969). Peer-reared subjects have been described as 'play deprived' because they engage in excessive clinging in lieu of play (Harlow, 1969). By attempting to meet the attachment needs of other infants, peer-reared subjects have fewer opportunities to develop competent social skills, which translates long-term into elevated levels of aggression (Higley et al., 1996c), and a reduced ability to use social support to alleviate stress (Winslow et al., 2003). Second, when subjects are deprived of social contact during the first year of life, they can still develop a normal repertoire of social skills when they receive 'therapy' sessions filled with high levels of play from younger, socially experienced monkeys (Novak et al., 1975; Suomi et al., 1972). At the outset, the young 'therapists' quickly began directing attachment and then play behaviors toward the isolate monkeys. Within a short amount of time, the isolates began reciprocating the initiations from the 'therapist monkeys,' and their social play bouts grew in both duration and complexity. When the isolates were later re-housed into a large social group with socially experienced subjects, they were behaviorally indistinguishable from other group members (Cummins et al., 1976; Novak, 1979).

Therefore, social play appears to facilitate the development of social competence and remediate social deficits in deprived animals.

Levels of social play also reflect the impact of environmental stressors on social competence. When mothers are removed from the social group, rhesus infants completely stop playing with their peers (Seay et al., 1962). Even after the infants are reunited with their mothers, it can take several weeks before they engage in peer play at rates comparable to the pre-separation period. Acute social stressors can have similar effects. For instance, when bonnet macaque infants are cared for by mothers who are subjected to an inconsistent foraging schedule, they spend more time clinging to their mothers and less time exploring and playing in a novel environment (Andrews et al., 1994; Rosenblum et al., 1984). Novak (1973) has reported similar effects on mother-infant interactions when rhesus infants are subjected to fear-inducing stimuli. These findings demonstrate that stressors impacting the mother-infant relationship can have a profound effect on the play behavior of infants.

The quality of care giving received by infant monkeys also impacts an infant's social play. For instance, infants reared by 'motherless mothers,' rhesus females with a history of early maternal deprivation, are subjected to higher rates of neglect and / or abuse (Harlow et al., 1966). Because infants are dependent on their mothers, they make repeated attempts to have their attachment needs met, and tend to engage in less play and heightened levels of aggressive behavior towards other infants (Arling et al., 1967). Others employing a cross-fostering paradigm have noted an association between high levels of maternal rejection and a greater incidence of solitary play in infant macaques. This finding was interpreted as conferring heightened vulnerability for becoming an abusive mother later in development (Maestripieri et al., 2006). Therefore, rates of infant play also reflect the impact of early social adversity, a factor that is likely to result in poor social competence later in development.

The behavioral effects of early experience on social play demonstrate that the early social environment can have a profound effect on the expression of social competencies, at least in rhesus monkeys. On the other hand, there are many instances when infants have demonstrated outcomes that are much better or worse than expected. Such findings indicate that some of the atypical social play outcomes may result from variation in genetic factors.

Social Play Reflects Genetic Influence

Rates of social play are also known to reflect considerable genetic influences. Two factors in particular, gender and temperament, are associated with differences in social play, and behavioral and biological differences that reflect genetic variation.

Multiple studies have noted gender differences in the quality and quantity of social play (Wallen, 2005). While both genders engage in social play, males tend to engage in higher rates of vigorous rough-and-tumble play (Weinstein et al., 2008), which often involves elements of aggression, dominance, and affiliation (Suomi, 1979). By contrast, females are more likely to incorporate play parenting and affiliative acts into their play (Suomi, 1979). As development proceeds, gender differences become more notable, and appear linked to gender-specific androgens. Wallen (2005) notes that upon exposure to androgens, males exhibit hyper-masculine play patterns, and females show increased rough play. By contrast, males exposed to estrogens show reduced rough social play. Gender differences in play are more likely to be obtained when subjects are exposed to hormones prenatally during late gestation, as the developing nervous system appears to be more susceptible to the effects of hormones during this time period. Taken together, these studies demonstrate that androgens and estrogens have opposing effects on gender-specific rates of play, a finding that demonstrates a strong genetic influence on play patterns.

Variations in temperament are also linked to differences in play behavior in rhesus monkeys. The concept of temperament refers to variations in reactivity and regulation that are thought to be under considerable genetic control (Kagan, 2001; Rothbart, 1981). Two temperament profiles, fear-anxiety and impulsivity, have been noted within troops of rhesus monkey living in captive and naturalistic settings (Suomi, 2004a), and are expected to impact play in contrasting ways.

High levels of fear and anxiety are expected to result in less social play, particularly when infants are in a novel environment. Fearful-anxious monkeys tend to respond more strongly to novelty and other mild stressors (Suomi, 2004). One common marker that is used as an indicator of fear and anxiety are high levels of reactivity. Along these lines, Higley (1985) found that subjects that were less reactive in a familiar setting and less distressed when separated from a familiar partner, displayed higher levels of social play. One reason fearful-anxious monkeys appear to engage in less play is that they spend more time clinging to a partner (Chamove et al., 1973; Harlow, 1969; but see Bolig et al., 1998). Over time, reactive individuals may compromise their own development by engaging in less social play. Higley (in press) has found that high reactive subjects that engage in low levels of social play tend to display exaggerated aggressive responses later in development.

Turning to the biological systems that give rise to inverse associations between fear-anxiety and social play, researchers have found that fearful-anxious temperament is associated with heightened cortisol levels, high heart rates, and right-frontal asymmetry (Kalin et al., 1998). Recently, a polymorphism in the serotonin transporter called rh5-*HTT*LPR (Lesch et al., 1997) has been identified that functions similarly to a polymorphism found in humans (Bennett et al., 2002). The *s* allele of this polymorphism is associated with reduced serotonin reuptake efficiency, and higher levels of reactive vocalizations in rhesus macaque infants (Champoux et al., 2002; but see also Rogers et al., 2008). In support of the idea that the *s* allele compromises play, researchers have found that infant monkeys that are homozygous for the *s/s* genotype engage in lower levels of play during a solitary playroom test in a novel environment filled with novel toys (Bethea et al., 2004). While more work is needed to investigate effects of the *s* allele in social contexts, considerable evidence suggests that play behavior is compromised by fearful-anxious temperament.

There are reasons to believe that impulsive temperament also compromises social play in monkeys. Impulsive temperament characterizes monkeys that react to novelty without hesitation and engage in high levels of risky behavior (Suomi, 2004b; Higley et al., 1996c; Mehlman et al., 1995). Over the years, we have observed that impulsive animals tend to have a harder time modulating social play interactions, and in particular, engage in social play that escalates more quickly into aggression (Suomi, 1997). Similar to fear-anxiety, impulsive temperament is also linked to variation in biological systems, including differences in candidate genes. Along these lines, researchers have found that impulsive monkeys are more likely to have lower levels of the serotonin metabolite, 5-hydroxy-indole acetic acid, or *5-HIAA*, and to possess the low activity variant of the rh*MAOA*-LPR polymorphism (Newman et al., 2005). Therefore, these social play deficits are thought to result from differences in genetic factors.

One important limitation to note is that temperament not only reflects genetically influenced

factors but is also impacted by experience (Champoux et al., 2002; Kraemer et al., 2008). For instance, exposure to prenatal stress leads to persistently higher levels of neuroendocrine activity, and to less exploration and social play during adolescence (Clarke et al., 1996). For this reason, some researchers prefer to use the term personality rather than temperament to describe individual differences in reactivity and regulation. We think that the term temperament should be reserved for studies that examine variations in observed behavior that are rooted in biological or genetic differences, and the term personality as the product of temperament and experiences (Kagan, 2001).

Certain components of personality are associated with differences in social play. For example, Capitanio et al. (2005) employed a survey measure of personality, and found that playfulness items were most strongly associated with sociability and confidence. When these survey ratings were compared to observations of behavior, high confidence scores were associated with longer amounts of time spent in social play. However, high equable scores, indicating a calm and collected personality, were inversely associated with social play (Weinstein et al., 2008). Using a different personality survey, Stevenson-Hinde et al. (1978) found that their most social monkeys were also the least fearful animals under study. Thus, studies have found that certain personality traits are associated with variations in social play, which may be due to experiential and/or genetically influenced factors.

Therefore, patterns of play behavior exhibited by monkeys can be used not only to assess the effects of early experience, but also to investigate differences in genetic factors. Conversely, the dual nature of social play is also a limitation to the interpretation of social play data, for genetically influenced factors may interact with the effects of early experience to influence the development of social competence.

G × E Interactions Involving Social Play

Studies with rhesus monkeys have demonstrated compelling independent effects of early experience and genetically influenced traits on social play. Yet, much of the variability in social play remains unexplained. Rather than reflecting independent influences, we find it likely that qualitative and quantitative differences in social play result from interactions between experiential and genetically influenced factors. Researchers have demonstrated compelling evidence of interactions between early experience and genetically influenced factors for a variety of behavioral (for reviews, see Herman et al., 2009; Nelson et al., 2009; Suomi, 2004b) and biological outcomes that are relevant to social play. For instance, it appears that serotonin metabolism and neuroendocrine activity are persistently altered by G × E interactions in rhesus monkeys (Barr et al., 2004; Bennett et al., 2002). We will illustrate how this approach has been used to identify G × E interactions involving social play using the example of gender as well as the rh-*5HTT*LPR polymorphism.

As mentioned earlier, gender provides researchers with an unvarying index of genetic makeup, making it possible to investigate differential effects of early experiences on rates of social play. For instance, by adding or removing subjects from a social group, researchers can investigate whether the makeup of particular rearing environments results in more or less pronounced gender differences in social play. One study by Goy and colleagues (1974) used this methodology, and reported that female social play behaviors more closely resemble male behavioral patterns when they were reared with males only, compared to a mixed-sex social group. In another study examining the impact of prenatal stress exposure, researchers found greater effects on males than on females: Prenatally-stressed males engaged in more clinging and less social play than control males, whereas no effects of prenatal stress exposure were found for females (Clarke et al., 1996). Therefore, these studies demonstrate that differences in play between males and females are the product of interactions between social experience and genetically influenced traits. By incorporating gender as a measure of genetic influence, it can help clarify the impact of early experiences on social development.

Researchers have recently investigated whether social play is affected by G × E interactions between the rh5-*HTT*LPR and rearing condition. In one study, 18 captive rhesus macaques were observed, balanced for gender, and either living with their mothers in social groups or in groups of four to five same-age and gender peers. Genetic differences in social play and aggression were found for the peer-rearing group only (Barr et al., 2003). In other words, infants with the *l/s* genotype engaged in less social play and more aggression than *l/l* infants, but only if they were peer-reared. The authors interpreted this result as an indicator of greater reticence in *l/s* infants, but these differences could also be due to peer-reared infants engaging in more impulsive play patterns that escalate into aggression more quickly (Suomi, 1991). There was no evidence of elevated social play or reduced aggression in mother-reared animals possessing the *l/s* genotype. This pattern of findings suggests that the effects of the *s* allele may be masked by nurturing maternal care. Taken together, this study demonstrates that G × E effects are relatively robust and can be identified even when large sample sizes are not available.

Research on G × E interactions using candidate genes has been strongly influenced by prior studies reporting conditional effects of early experience on temperament or gender play preferences (Suomi, 1987). While much has been learned by studying the role of temperament on social play, there are several drawbacks to using temperament as a measure of genetic influence, such as its moderate stability across development which reflects experience as well as genetically influenced factors. Thus, the major benefit to using candidate genes is that they provide an unvarying measure of genetic influence. On the other hand, one drawback to using the candidate gene approach is that most traits are probably determined by the actions of multiple genes or epistatic effects (Rutter, 2007). Nonetheless, despite their limitations, both methods have proven useful for improving the state of knowledge about G × E effects on social play.

Implications and Future Directions

The studies reviewed in this chapter indicate a central role for social play in the socialization of macaques. Young monkeys, when given the opportunity to interact with socially experienced peers, develop a flexible skill set for negotiating responses to a variety of stressful social encounters. By contrast, most monkeys deprived of socially experienced peers develop largely permanent deficits in social competence. However, not all monkeys are equally compromised by early social deprivation. Studies have demonstrated that patterns of play in developing monkeys appear to reflect a variety of individual differences that are thought to be rooted in biological predispositions for responding to both novel and threatening situations. Rather than reflecting independent effects of experiences and genetically influenced markers, social play in monkeys appears to reflect interactions between such factors. These studies indicate that early social experiences impact developing monkeys differently depending on genetically influenced factors such as gender or temperament. Furthermore, they demonstrate that genetically influenced risk factors in the rhesus monkey can be exacerbated by exposure to early adversity (Rutter, 2007).

It is clear that peer deprivation during early development leads to largely permanent social deficits, whereas providing the opportunity for deprived animals to engage in social play can lead to improvements in social outcomes. The positive impact of play on developmental outcomes can also be obtained by interacting with human caregivers: Recently, van Ijzendoorn and colleagues (2009) found that responsive caregiving that was described as playful led to improvements in socioemotional and cognitive outcomes in chimpanzee infants. Even more compelling are the behavioral differences that are supported by structural and functional differences in the brain. In many cases, the findings in monkeys echo the outcomes reported in rodent models. Both monkeys and rats deprived of early play experiences during peak play periods display overaggressive behaviors, impulsivity, and inappropriate levels of fear in different contexts (Hol et al., 1999; Suomi, 1979; Van den Berg et al., 1999). Taken together, current data suggest that social play is timed in such a way so as to provide input to neural circuits with experience-expectant plasticity during sensitive periods of development (Greenough et al., 1987), which may reduce the cost of having social skills pre-wired, and may also allow monkeys to develop social repertoires that best reflect their current environments. Social play for macaques appears to be far from incidental for social development.

Future studies are needed to investigate the role of social play on development in animals and children. In particular, we are in need of studies that identify gene polymorphisms influencing rates of social play in monkeys, as well as studies investigating G × E interactions involving peer deprivation and resulting social competence (Barr et al., 2003). For instance, given the link between the low activity allele of the rh*MAOA*-LPR polymorphism and heightened levels of aggression, rates of play might also be expected to be lower in these subjects, particularly if they have a history of early social adversity (Newman et al., 2005). Research investigating the role of temperament on social play is also needed, for these findings can often illuminate potential genetically influenced pathways involved in the regulation of social play. When designing such G × E studies in animal models, it is important to use measures of early experience that are generalizeable to the majority of children's experiences growing up (e.g., prenatal stress or variable foraging demand [Andrews et al., 1994]). In addition, Iarocci and colleagues (2007) recently suggested that we

can better understand how social competence develops by studying component processes such as face processing skills. Social-cognitive skills such as imitation of communicative gestures (Ferrari et al., 2006) may be telling precursors of social competence in rhesus monkeys. We hope that such studies in animals will continue to add to our knowledge of social play.

What are the implications for studying social play in children? Even though exciting parallels have been found in the form of homologous neural structures and gene polymorphisms, there is still a need for caution before assuming that the same functions of social play found in animals apply to children. It seems likely that social play would be only one of several routes to developing social competence in children (Burghardt, 2005; Smith, 2005). Given such cautions, studies with animals provide evidence from controlled studies supporting the idea that rates of social play reflect developmental status: When a child displays atypical patterns of cognitive and social play for his age and gender, it signals that something in development, whether it be environmental, genetically influenced, or both, is awry and in need of further investigation (Rubin, 1982). These arguments also strengthen the case for using social play as a form of therapy for children presenting with risk factors to development such as autism or ADHD (Heimann et al., 2006; Scott et al., 2003). Given the prominence of social play in developing animals, it is difficult to fathom how play would be any less important for children.

References

Alessandri, S. M. (1991). Play and social behavior in maltreated preschoolers. *Development and Psychopathology, 3*, 191–206.

Alexander, B. K., & Harlow, H. F. (1965). Social behavior of juvenile rhesus monkeys subjected to different rearing conditions during the first 6 months of lifes. *Zoologische Jahrbucher Physiologie, 60*, 167–174.

Andrews, M. W., & Rosenblum, L. A. (1994). The development of affiliative and agonistic social patterns in differentially reared monkeys. *Child Dev, 65*(5), 1398–1404.

Arling, G. L., & Harlow, H. F. (1967). Effects of social deprivation on maternal behavior of rhesus monkeys. *Journal of Comparative and Physiological Psychology, 64*, 371–377.

Bakermans- Kranenburg, M. J., van Ijzendoorn, M. H., Pijlman, F. T. A., Mesman, J., & Juffer, F. (2008). Experimental evidence for differential susceptibility: Dopamine D4 receptor polymorphism (DRD4 VNTR) moderates intervention effects on toddler's externalizing behavior in a randomized controlled trial. *Developmental Psychology, 44*(1), 293–300.

Barr, C. S., Newman, T. K., Becker, M. L., Parker, C. C., Champoux, M., Lesch, K. P., et al. (2003). The utility of the non-human primate model for studying gene by environment interactions in behavioral research. *Genes, Brain & Behavior, 2*(6), 336–340.

Barr, C. S., Newman, T. K., Shannon, C., Parker, C., Dvoskin, R. L., Becker, M. L., et al. (2004). Rearing condition and rh5-HTTLPR interact to influence limbic-hypothalamic-pituitary-adrenal axis response to stress in infant macaques. *Biological Psychiatry, 55*(7), 733–738.

Bennett, A. J., Lesch, K. P., Heils, A., Long, J. C., Lorenz, J. G., Shoaf, S. E., et al. (2002). Early experience and serotonin transporter gene variation interact to influence primate CNS function. *Molecular Psychiatry, 7*, 118–122.

Berenbaum, S. A., & Hines, M. (1992). Early androgens are related to childhood sex-typed toy preferences. *Psychological Science, 3*(3), 203–206.

Berk, L. E., Mann, T. D., & Ogan, A. T. (in press). Make-believe play: Wellspring for development of self-regulation. In D. G. Singer, R. M. Golinkoff & K. Hirsh-Pasek (Eds.), *Play=Learning: How play motivates and enhances children's cognitive and social-emotional growth*. New York: Oxford University Press.

Berman, C. M. (1982). The ontogeny of social relationships with group companions among free-ranging infant rhesus monkeys. 2. Differentiation and attractiveness. *Animal Behavior, 30*, 163–170.

Berman, C. M., Rasmussen, K. L. R., & Suomi, S. J. (1997). Group size, maternal behavior and social networks: A natural experiment with free-ranging monkeys. *Animal Behavior, 53*, 405–421.

Bethea, C. L., Streicher, J. M., Coleman, K., Pau, F. K., Moessner, R., & Cameron, J. L. (2004). Anxious behavior and fenfluramine-induced prolactin secretion in young rhesus macaques with different alleles of the serotonin reuptake transporter polymorphism (5HTTLPR). *Behav Genet, 34*(3), 295–307.

Bolig, R., Price, C. S., O'Neill-Wagner, P. L., & Suomi, S. J. (1998). Reactivity and play and exploration behaviors of young rhesus monkeys. In M. C. Duncan, G. Chick & A. Aycock (Eds.), *Diversions and divergences in fields of play* (Vol. one).

Bowlby, J. (1969). *Attachment and loss* (Vol. 1). New York: Basic Books.

Burghardt, G. M. (2005). Play and the brain in comparative perspective. In R. L. Clements & L. Fiorentino (Eds.), *The child's right to play* (pp. 293–308). Westport, CT: Praeger.

Capitanio, J. P., & Widaman, K. F. (2005). Confirmatory factor analysis of personality structure in adult male rhesus monkeys (Macaca mulatta). *Am J Primatol, 65*(3), 289–294.

Casey, B. J., Glatt, C. E., Tottenham, N., Soliman, F., Bath, K., Amso, D., et al. (2009). Brain-derived neurotrophic factor as a model system for examining gene by environment interactions across development. *Neuroscience*.

Caspi, A., McClay, J., Moffitt, T., Mill, J., Martin, J., Craig, I. W., et al. (2002). Role of genotype in the cycle of violence in maltreated children. *Science, 297*(5582), 851–854.

Chamove, A. S., Rosenblum, L. A., & Harlow, H. F. (1973). Monkeys (Macaca mulatta) raised only with peers: A pilot study. *Animal Behaviour, Vol. 21*(2), 316–325.

Champoux, M., Bennett, A., Shannon, C., Higley, J. D., Lesch, K. P., & Suomi, S. J. (2002). Serotonin transporter gene polymorphism, differential early rearing, and behavior in rhesus monkey neonates. *Molecular Psychiatry, 2002*(7), 1058–1063.

Clarke, A. S., Soto, A., Bergholz, T., & Schneider, M. L. (1996). Maternal gestational stress alters adaptive and social behavior in adolescent rhesus monkey offspring. *Infant Behavior & Development Vol 19*(4) Oct-Dec 1996, 451–461.

Collins, W. A., Maccoby, E. E., Steinberg, L., Hetherington, E. M., & Bornstein, M. H. (2000). Contemporary research on parenting: The case for nature and nurture. *American Psychologist, 55*(2), 218–232.

Coplan, R. J., Rubin, K. H., Fox, N. A., Calkins, S. D., & Stewart, S. L. (1994). Being alone, playing alone, and acting alone: Distinguishing among reticence and passive and active solitude in young children. *Child Development, 65*, 129–137.

Cummins, M. S., & Suomi, S. J. (1976). Long-term effects of social rehabilitation in rhesus monkeys. *Primates, 17*(1), 43–51.

DiPietro, J. A. (1981). Rough and tumble play: A function of gender. *Developmental Psychology, 17*(1), 50–58.

Edwards, C. P. (2000). Children's play in cross-cultural perspective: A new look at the Six Cultures study. *Cross-Cultural Research, 34*(4), 318–338.

Fabes, R. A., Hanish, L. D., & Martin, C. L. (2003). Children at play: The role of peers in understanding the effects of child care. *Child Development, 74*(4), 1039–1043.

Ferrari, P. F., Visalberghi, E., Paukner, A., Fogassi, L., Ruggiero, A., & Suomi, S. J. (2006). Neonatal imitation in rhesus macaques. *PLoS Biology, 4*(9), e302.

Flanders, J. L., Leo, V., Paquette, D., Pihl, R. O., & Seguin, J. R. (2009). Rough-and-tumble play and the regulation of aggression: An observational study of father-child play dyads. *Aggress Behav, 35*(4), 285–295.

Fox, N. A., & Field, T. (1989). Individual differences in preschool entry behavior. *Journal of Applied Developmental Psychology, 10*, 527–540.

Fox, N. A., Nichols, K. E., Henderson, H. A., Rubin, K. H., Schmidt, L. A., Hamer, D., et al. (2005). Evidence for a gene-environment interaction in predicting behavioral inhibition in middle childhood. *Psychological Science, 16*(12), 921–926.

Fry, D. (2005). Rough-and-tumble social play in humans. In A. D. Pellegrini & P. K. Smith (Eds.), *The nature of play: Great apes and humans* (pp. 54–88). New York: Guilford Press.

Gard, G. C., & Meier, G. W. (1977). Social and contextual factors of play behavior in sub-adult rhesus monkeys. *Primates, 18*(2), 367–377.

Gluck, J. P. (1979). Long-term consequences of early social isolation. In H. F. Harlow, L. A. Rosenblum & S. J. Suomi (Eds.), *Advances in the study of primate social development*. New York: Van Nostrand.

Goy, R. W., Wallen, K., & Goldfoot, D. A. (1974). Social factors affecting the development of mounting behavior in the rhesus monkey. In W. Montagna & W. Sadler (Eds.), *Reproductive behavior*. New York: Plenum Press.

Greenough, W. T., Black, J. E., & Wallace, C.S. (1987). Experience and brain development. *Child Development, 58*, 539–559.

Hansen, E. W. (1966). The development of maternal and infant behavior in the rhesus monkey. *Behaviour, 27*, 107–149.

Harlow, H. F. (1969). *Age-mate or peer affectional system*. Chicago, IL: University of Chicago.

Harlow, H. F., Harlow, M. K., & Dodsworth, D. O. (1966). Maternal behavior of rhesus monkeys deprived of mothering and peer association in infancy. *Proceedings of the American Philosophical Society, 110*(1), 58–66.

Heimann, M., Laberg, K. E., & Nordoen, B. (2006). Imitative interaction increases social interest and elicited imitation in non-verbal children with autism. *Infant and Child Development, 15*(3), 297–309.

Herman, K. N., Winslow, J. T., & Suomi, S. J. (2009). Primate models in serotonin transporter research. In A. Kalueff (Ed.), *Experimental models in serotonin transporter research*. UK: Cambridge University Press.

Hetherington, E., Cox, M., & Cox, R. (1979). Play and social interaction in children following divorce. *Journal of Social Issues, 35*(4), 26–49.

Higley, J. D. (1985). Continuity of social separation behaviors in rhesus monkeys from infancy to adolescence. Unpublished dissertation. University of Wisconsin at Madison.

Higley, J. D., King, S. T., Jr., Hasert, M. F., Champoux, M., Suomi, S. J., & Linnoila, M. (1996a). Stability of interindividual differences in serotonin function and its relationship to severe aggression and competent social behavior in rhesus macaque females. *Neuropsychopharmacology, 14*(1), 67–76.

Higley, J. D., Mehlman, P. T., Higley, S. B., Fernald, B., Vickers, J., Lindell, S. G., et al. (1996b). Excessive mortality in young free-ranging male nonhuman primates with low cerebrospinal fluid 5-hydroxyindoleacetic acid concentrations. *Arch Gen Psychiatry, 53*(6), 537–543.

Higley, J. D., & Suomi, S. J. Behavioral inhibition and aggression as personality traits in nonhuman primates. In A. Weiss, J. King & L. Murray (Eds.), *Primate personality and temperament*. New York: Springer.

Higley, J. D., Suomi, S. J., & Linnoila, M. (1996c). A nonhuman primate model of type II alcoholism? Part 2. Diminished social competence and excessive aggression correlates with low cerebrospinal fluid 5-hydroxyindoleacetic acid concentrations. *Alcohol Clin Exp Res, 20*(4), 643–650.

Hinde, R. A. (1988). *Individuals, relationships, and culture: Links between ethology and the social sciences*. UK: Cambridge University Press.

Hol, T., Van den Berg, C. L., & al., e. (1999). Isolation during the play period in infancy decreases adult social interactions in rats. *Behavioural Brain Research, 100*, 91–97.

Iarocci, G., Yager, J., & Elfers, T. (2007). What gene-environment interactions can tell us about social competence in typical and atypical populations. *Brain Cogn, 65*(1), 112–127.

Immelmann, K., & Suomi, S. J. (1981). Sensitive phases in development. *Behavioral development: The Bielefeld Interdisciplinary Project*, 395–431.

Kagan, J. (Ed.) (2001). *International encyclopedia of the social sciences*. New York: Elsevier.

Kalin, N. H., Larson, C., Shelton, S. E., & Davidson, R. J. (1998). Asymmetric frontal brain activity, cortisol, and behavior associated with fearful temperament in rhesus monkeys. *Behav Neurosci, 112*(2), 286–292.

Kaufman, J., Yang, B.-z., Douglas-Palumberi, H., Houshyar, S., Lipschitz, D., Krystal, J. H., et al. (2004). Social supports and serotonin transporter gene moderate depression in maltreated children. *Proceedings of the National Academy of Sciences, 101*(49), 17316–17321.

Kempes, M. M., Gulickx, M. M., van Daalen, H. J., Louwerse, A. L., & Sterck, E. H. (2008). Social competence is reduced in socially deprived rhesus monkeys (Macaca mulatta). *J Comp Psychol, 122*(1), 62–67.

Kraemer, G. W., Moore, C. F., Newman, T. K., Barr, C. S., & Schneider, M. L. (2008). Moderate level fetal alcohol exposure and serotonin transporter gene promoter polymorphism affect neonatal temperament and limbic-hypothalamic-pituitary-adrenal axis regulation in monkeys. *Biol Psychiatry, 63*(3), 317–324.

Krasnor, L. R., & Pepler, D. J. (1980). The study of children's play: Some suggested future directions. *New Directions for Child and Adolescent Development, 9*, 85–95.

Ladd, G. W. (2005). *Children's peer relations and social competence*. New Haven, CT: Yale University Press.

Lamb, M. E. (2003). *The role of the father in child development*. Hoboken, NJ: Wiley Publishers.

Lesch, K. P., Meyer, J., Glatz, K., Flugge, G., Hinney, A., Hebebrand, J., et al. (1997). The 5-HT transporter gene-linked polymorphic region (5-HTTLPR) in evolutionary perspective: alternative biallelic variation in rhesus monkeys. Rapid communication. *J Neural Transm, 104*(11–12), 1259–1266.

Maestripieri, D., McCormack, K., Lindell, S. G., Higley, J. D., & Sanchez, M. M. (2006). Influence of parenting style on the offspring's behaviour and CSF monoamine metabolite levels in crossfostered and noncrossfostered female rhesus macaques. *Behavioural Brain Research, 175*(1), 90–95.

Meaney, M. J. (2001). Maternal care, gene expression, and the transmission of individual differences in stress reactivity across generations. *Annu. Rev. Neurosci., 24*, 1161–1192.

Mehlman, P. T., Higley, J. D., Faucher, I., Lilly, A. A., Taub, D. M., Vickers, J., et al. (1995). Correlation of CSF 5-HIAA concentration with sociality and the timing of emigration in free-ranging primates. *Am J Psychiatry, 152*(6), 907–913.

Nelson, E. E., & Winslow, J. T. (2009). Non-human primates: Model animals for developmental psychopathology. *Neuropsychopharmacology, 34*(1), 90–105.

Newman, T. K., Syagailo, Y. V., Barr, C. S., Wendland, J. R., Champoux, M., Graessle, M., et al. (2005). Monoamine oxidase A gene promoter variation and rearing experience influences aggressive behavior in rhesus monkeys. *Biol Psychiatry, 57*(2), 167–172.

Novak, M. A. (1973). Fear-attachment relationships in infant and juvenile rhesus monkeys. Unpublished dissertation. University of Wisconsin at Madison.

Novak, M. A. (1979). Social recovery of monkeys isolated for the first year of life: II. Long-term assessment. *Developmental Psychology, 15*(1), 50–61.

Novak, M. A., & Harlow, H. F. (1975). Social recovery of monkeys isolated for the first year of life: I. Rehabilitation and therapy. *Developmental Psychology, 11*(4), 453–465.

O'Neill, P. L., & Price, C. S. (1991). Customizing an enrichment program: Rhesus monkeys. *Lab Animal, 20*(6), 29–40.

Parten, M. B. (1932). Social participation among pre-school children. *Journal of Abnormal and Social Psychology, 27*, 243–269.

Plomin, R., DeFries, J. C., & Loehlin, J. C. (1977). Genotype-environment interaction and correlation in the analysis of human behavior. *Psychol Bull, 84*(2), 309–322.

Polak-Toste, C., & Gunnar, M. R. (2006). Temperamental exuberance: Correlates and consequences. In N. A. Fox & P. J. Marshall (Eds.), *The development of social engagement*. New York: Oxford University Press.

Porges, S. W. (2001). The polyvagal theory: Phylogenetic substrates of a social nervous system. *Int J Psychophysiol, 42*(2), 123–146.

Power, T. G. (2000). *Play and exploration in children and animals.* Mahwah, N.J.: L. Erlbaum Associates.

Redican, W. K. (1975). A longitudinal study of behavioral interactions between adult male and infant rhesus monkeys (*Macaca mulatta*). Unpublished dissertation. University of California at Davis.

Rogers, J., Shelton, S. E., Shelledy, W., Garcia, R., & Kalin, N. H. (2008). Genetic influences on behavioral inhibition and anxiety in juvenile rhesus macaques. *Genes Brain Behav, 7*(4), 463–469.

Rosenblum, L. A. (1961). The development of social behavior in the rhesus monkey. Unpublished dissertation. University of Wisconsin at Madison.

Rosenblum, L. A. (1971). The ontogeny of mother-infant relations in macaques. In H. Moltz (Ed.), *The ontogeny of vertebrate behavior.* New York: Academic Press.

Rosenblum, L. A., & Paully, G. S. (1984). The effects of varying environmental demands on maternal and infant behavior. *Child Dev, 55*(1), 305–314.

Rothbart, M. K. (1981). Measurement of temperament in infancy. *Child Development, 52*(2), 569–578.

Rubin, K., Fein, G., & Vandenberg, B. (1983). Play. In E. M. Hetherington & P. H. Mussen (Eds.), *Handbook of child psychology* (Vol 4. Socialization, personality, and social behavior, pp. 693–774). New York: Wiley.

Rubin, K. H. (1982). Nonsocial play in preschoolers: Necessarily evil? *Child Development, 53*, 651–657.

Russ, S. W. (2004). *Play in child development and psychotherapy: Toward empirically supported practice.* Mahwah, NJ: Lawrence Erlbaum Associates.

Rutter, M. (2006). The psychological effects of early institutional rearing. In P. J. Marshall & N. A. Fox (Eds.), *The development of social engagement: Neurobiological perspectives.* (pp. 355–391). New York, NY, US: Oxford University Press.

Rutter, M. (2007). Gene-environment interdependence. *Dev Sci, 10*(1), 12–18.

Sackett, G. P., Novak, M. F. S. X., & Kroeker, R. (1999). Early experience effects on adaptive behavior: Theory revisited. *Mental Retardation and Developmental Disabilities Research Review, 5*, 30–40.

Sade, D. S. (1972). Sociometrics of Macaca mulatta. I. Linkages and cliques in grooming matrices. *Folia Primatol (Basel), 18*(3), 196–223.

Sade, D. S., Altmann, M., Loy, J., Hausfater, G., & Breuggeman, J. A. (1988). Sociometrics of Macaca mulatta: II. Decoupling centrality and dominance in rhesus monkey social networks. *Am J Phys Anthropol, 77*(4), 409–425.

Saudino, K. J. (2005). Behavioral genetics and child temperament. *J Dev Behav Pediatr, 26*(3), 214–223.

Scarr, S., & McCartney, K. (1983). How people make their own environments: A theory of genotype greater than environment effects. *Child Dev, 54*(2), 424–435.

Schmidt, L. A., Fox, N. A., Rubin, K. H., Sternberg, E. M., Gold, P. W., Smith, C. C., et al. (1997). Behavioral and neuroendocrine responses in shy children. *Dev Psychobiol, 30*(2), 127–140.

Scott, E., & Panksepp, J. (2003). Rough-and-tumble play in human children. *Aggressive Behavior, 29*, 539–551.

Seay, B., Hansen, E., & Harlow, H. F. (1962). Mother-infant separations in monkeys. *Journal of Child Psychology and Psychiatry, 3*, 123–132.

Shotwell, J. M., Wolf, D., & Gardner, H. (1979). Exploring early symbolization: Styles to achievement. In B. Sutton-Smith (Ed.), *Play and learning* (pp. 127–155). New York: Gardner Press.

Singer, J. L., Singer, D. G., & Sherrod, L. R. (1980). A factor analytic study of preschooler's play behavior. *Academic Psychology Bulletin, 2*(2), 143–156.

Smilansky, S. (1968a). *The effects of sociodramatic play on disadvantaged preschool children.* New York: John Wiley & Sons.

Smilansky, S. (1968b). Sociodramatic play as a type of play phenomenon. In *The effects of sociodramatic play on disadvantaged preschool children* (pp. 5–10). New York: John Wiley and Sons.

Smith, P. K. (2004). Play: Types and functions in human development. In B. Ellis & D. Bjorklund (Eds.), *Origins of the social mind: Evolutionary psychology and child development* (pp. 271–299). New York: Guilford Press.

Smith, P. K. (2005). Social and pretend play in children. In A. D. Pellegrini & P. K. Smith (Eds.), *Nature of play: Great apes and humans* (pp. 173–212). New York: Guilford Press.

Stevenson-Hinde, J., & Zunz, M. (1978). Subjective assessment of individual rhesus monkeys. *Primates* Vol 19(3) Jul 1978, 473–482.

Suomi, S. J. (1979). Peers, play, and primary prevention in primates. In M. Kent & J. Rolf (Eds.), *Primary prevention of psychopathology: Social competence in children* (pp. 127–149). Hanover, NH: Press of New England.

Suomi, S. J. (1982). The development of social competence by rhesus monkeys. *Ann Ist Super Sanita, 18*(2), 193–202.

Suomi, S. J. (1991). Early stress and adult emotional reactivity in rhesus monkeys. *Ciba Found Symp, 156*, 171–183; discussion 183–178.

Suomi, S. J. (1997). Early determinants of behaviour: Evidence from primate studies. *Br Med Bull, 53*(1), 170–184.

Suomi, S. J. (1999). Attachment in rhesus monkeys. In P. R. Shaver & J. Cassidy (Eds.), *Handbook of attachment: Theory, research, and clinical applications* (pp. 181–197). New York: Guilford Press.

Suomi, S. J. (2002). Parents, peers, and the process of socialization in primates. In J. G. Borkowski, S. L. Ramey & M. Bristol-Power (Eds.), *Parenting and the child's world: Influences on academic, intellectual, and social-emotional development* (pp. 265–279). Mahwah, NJ: Lawrence Erlbaum Associates.

Suomi, S. J. (2004a). How gene-environment interactions influence emotional development in rhesus monkeys. In C. G. Coll, E. L. Bearer & R. M. Lerner (Eds.), *Nature and nurture: The complex interplay of genetic and environmental influences on human behavior and development.* (pp. 35–51): Lawrence: Erlbaum Associates Publishers.

Suomi, S. J. (2004b). How gene-environment interactions shape biobehavioral development: Lessons from studies with rhesus monkeys. *Research in Human Development, 1*(3), 205–222.

Suomi, S. J. (2005). Mother-infant attachment, peer relationships, and the development of social networks in rhesus monkeys. *Human Development, 48*, 67–79.

Suomi, S. J., & Harlow, H. F. (1972). Social rehabilitation of isolate-reared monkeys. *Developmental Psychology, 6*(3), 487–496.

Van den Berg, C. L., Hol, T., Van Ree, J. M., & Spruijt, B. M. (1999). Play is indispensable for an adequate development of coping with social challenges in the rat. *Developmental Psychobiology, 34*, 129–138.

van Ijzendoorn, M. H., Bard, K. A., Bakermans-Kranenburg, M. J., & Ivan, K. (2009). Enhancement of attachment and cognitive development of young nursery-reared chimpanzees in responsive versus standard care. *Developmental Psychobiology, 51*(2), 173–185.

Wallen, K. (2005). Hormonal influences on sexually differentiated behavior in nonhuman primates. *Front Neuroendocrinol, 26*(1), 7–26.

Weinstein, T. R., & Capitanio, J. P. (2008). Individual differences in infant temperament predict social relationships of yearling rhesus monkeys, *Macaca mulatta. Animal Behavior, 76*, 455–465.

Winslow, J. T., Noble, P. L., Lyons, C. K., Sterk, S. M., & Insel, T. R. (2003). Rearing effects on cerebrospinal fluid oxytocin concentration and social buffering in rhesus monkeys. *Neuropsychopharmacology, 28*(5), 910–918.

Playing at Every Age: Modalities and Potential Functions in Non-Human Primates

Elisabetta Palagi

Abstract

Play is ephemeral and versatile. Probably for this reason it is so difficult to study systematically. Results from the last two decades of research suggest that play is a multifunctional phenomenon that varies according to different factors such as the species, age, sex, relationship quality of the players, etc. Accordingly, animal play needs to be studied in a comparative framework in order to rigorously assess the relative weight of various functions and contexts. Play is mainly an immature matter; however, in many mammalian species social play continues through adulthood. Therefore, a complete understanding of play can be reached by taking into account its occurrence during each phase of life. Here, I present some recent studies on primates to show that play is a response to an immediate necessity. But if so, why should it be surprising to see two adults playing together?

Key words: Social play, cognition, competence, fine-tuning, *Lemur catta*, *Theropithecus gelada*, *Gorilla gorilla*, *Pan* spp.

We don't stop playing because we get old;
we get old because we stop playing.
—*George Bernard Shaw*

Introduction

There are many definitions of play (e.g., Burghardt, this volume). The fact that play is not described by distinctive characteristics makes it difficult to define. Play can be only defined via litotes (from the Greek word λιτότης—a figure of speech achieved by using negation with a term in place of using an antonym of that term). As play lacks certain characteristics which are typical of so-called "serious" behaviors, play has been defined as a *non*-functional behavior with *no* obvious immediate benefits (Bekoff & Allen, 1998; Martin & Caro, 1985). As a matter of fact, compared to other behaviors, whose modalities and functions are easier to define and detect, play remains an intriguing challenge for a number of researchers interested in the study of this ephemeral and controversial phenomenon.

What then is play? Play includes activity that appears to an observer to have no obvious immediate benefits for the performer, but which involves motor patterns typical of serious functional contexts, such as agonistic, antipredatory, and mating behavior (Bekoff, 2001; Martin & Caro, 1985; Pellis & Pellis, 1996). Playful and serious contexts do not differ in the actual behavioral patterns performed, but in the modality they are performed (Bekoff & Allen, 1998). During a play session, motor patterns strongly vary in their sequence compared to those of other functional contexts (fragmentation or disordering), the movements are emphasized and repeated more often compared to serious interactions (absence of inhibition). Moreover, motor and social play sequences may lack some components found in other contexts and may be relatively incomplete (e.g., a movement may be started, but not finished) or interrupted by higher priority and/or maintenance behaviors (i.e., antipredatory behavior) (Fagen, 1981). Obviously, the looseness of the definition implies caution when dealing with studies on play behavior. Consequently, we have always to keep in mind that many of the things we think we know about play strictly depend on how play has been previously defined.

Play challenges psychologists to discover its consequences on behavioral development, anthropologists to identify its role in the evolution of social and cognitive skills, and evolutionary biologists to search for the functions of an apparently nonfunctional behavior (Burghardt, 2005). Even though we are far from a satisfactory knowledge level on play, in the last two decades many efforts have been made to better understand and clarify some aspects of this behavior, both in animals and humans. Indeed, most of these efforts were especially centered on the potential meaning of play behavior. The emergent scenario tells us that play is a multifunctional phenomenon because its roles may vary according to a number of different factors such as species, age, sex, and relationship quality of the players. For this reason, a comparative approach in the study of animal play is needed to rigorously assess the relative importance of different functions of play for different species (Fagen, 1981).

Does Play Activity Stop at Puberty? It Depends

Social play is a common feature of all primates from prosimians to apes and, as it also occurs in other non-primate species, play is a typical feature of immature phase of life (Fagen, 1993). Primate play activity begins to increase at the end of infancy, reaches peak values in the middle of juvenility, and tends to decrease at the end of the juvenile period, thus showing a typical bell-shape distribution curve (Pellegrini, 2009; Pellis & Pellis, 2009). Behavioral ecology theory (Krebs & Davies, 1997) predicts that individuals behave in a strategic way to maximize access to resources while minimizing the costs to obtain them (Wilson & Wrangham, 2003). However, since costs and benefits of a particular behavior can vary across the life span and under different ecological and social contexts, the animals' choice for specific strategies may vary accordingly.

Like any other "serious" behavior (e.g., aggression) we can assume that, even though difficult to quantify, play has costs and benefits (Burghardt, 2005; Martin, 1982). One of the possible explanations for play being so frequent in the juvenile period is that, during this period, the balance between costs and benefits tilts in favor of the latter.

As predicted by Burghardt's surplus resource theory (Burghardt, 1984; 2005), play is particularly common in those species with a long period of immaturity and, consequently, long-lasting parental care (Fagen, 1993). The safety and provisioning by parents permit juveniles to explore by playing both the social and ecological environment around them (Figure 7-1). For this reason the most sophisticated form of play (social play) is more frequent in species characterized not only by a long immaturity period but also by complex cognitive abilities (Lewis, 2000; Pellegrini, 2009). However, we have to consider that in many mammalian species social play continues through adulthood (Pellis & Iwaniuk, 1999; Pellis & Pellis, 1991). For this reason a complete understanding of the potential roles of play can be reached by taking into account its occurrence during each phase of life.

In many primate species, behavioral plasticity is an essential component to track an environment which frequently changes both from a social and an ecological point of view. Play is one of the best means to obtain and maintain such plasticity (Bateson, this volume). In several primate species characterized by a sufficient degree of freedom in social relationships, social play is maintained into adulthood as much as any so-called serious behavior.

When adults engage in social play, they most often do so with their own infants (Power, 2000). In this case, social play can be view as parental investment. During such play sessions infants can improve their own physical activity (combat practice) and cognitive ability (deriving from the necessity to manage the session). Both of these aspects may provide the appropriate skills to face the unexpected and eventually to increase survival probability (Pellegrini, Dupuis, & Smith, 2007; Špinka, Newberry, & Bekoff, 2001). Mothers can gain benefits related to fitness as parents invest resources in their offspring to maximize the likelihood of their survival and reproduction (Hamilton, 1964).

Play can also be used by animals to acquire and expand their social competence by interacting with each other. In this case, play benefits go beyond the enhancement of intrinsic abilities, being translated from the individual to the social level. Play between

A   B

Fig. 7.1 Sequences of play fighting in spider monkeys. Two unrelated immature subjects are playing in proximity of the mother of one of them.

(Photos by Tommaso Ragaini.)

unrelated conspecifics falls into this category: Play is the first behavior used by infants to interact with unrelated individuals. Play represents a main "portal" to access the social environment. When play occurs between adults and unrelated immatures, it can be used as a bridge to reach other adults (e.g. immature parents) in order to gain social support and friendship (Mancini & Palagi, 2009; Palagi, Cordoni, & Borgognini, 2004).

Play involving only unrelated adults opens new scenarios regarding the potential role of this behavior and its repercussions on social relationships. Several explanations have been put forth to justify play between unrelated adults. They involve the promotion, the establishment, and the maintenance of social bonds (Cordoni, 2009; Palagi, 2006; Palagi & Paoli, 2007). By playing, animals can get information on possible partners and/or competitors and test relationship quality (Pellis & Iwaniuk, 2000). An indepth competence of social network is the prerequisite for social manipulation, which is the ability to manage inter-individual relationships for personal benefits (Brueggeman, 1978; Palagi, 2009).

In the following paragraphs, I discuss modalities and potential roles of social play as a function of the difference ages of playmates, taking as examples several non-human primate species showing different social structures and a strong variability in cognitive skills.

Fine-tuning a play session: Immature gorillas under spotlights

Several authors considered play behavior as one of the most complex types of social communication (Burghardt, 2005; Fagen, 1981, 1993; Pellegrini, 2009; Pellis & Pellis, 2009). Social play is correlated with the proportion of the brain composed of neocortex in some primates, and this behavior might therefore be implicated in the development of cognition and social competence typical of many primate species (Lewis, 2000). As mentioned above, one commonly held view is that species with a longer juvenile period play more and do so in a more complex manner. The complexity derives from the fact that playmates have to fine-tune ongoing play sequences to maintain a playful mood and to prevent play from escalating into real aggression (Bekoff & Byers, 1998; Power, 2000). To do that, a precise detection of those stimuli that might appear ambiguous is needed (e.g., intentions of other animals). The ability to interpret such ambiguous features of social signaling could represent a central issue in the evolution of behavioral flexibility and social intelligence in animals (Bekoff, 1995; Fagen, 1981, 1993;

Pellis & Pellis, 1996). Investigating whether immature animals are able to finely modulate such activity according to the different social conditions and to the diverse playmate availability could provide information on social cognitive skills and help to develop hypotheses on the roles of social play.

Palagi, Antonacci, and Cordoni (2007) analyzed play frequency and modality in lowland gorillas, taking into account age and gender of playmates and different social contexts (e.g., space availability and food distribution) in which the playful interactions occurred. The authors found that social play sessions were common among juvenile gorillas (Figure 7-2), who invited each other to play more frequently compared to adults and infants. In a play fight it is useful to practice against a well-matched

Fig. 7.2 Social play in immature gorillas. Hand clapping to invite to play (Fig. 7.2a); Playful facial display (the mouth is opened with the upper and lower teeth exposed) to signal "it's only play!" (Fig. 7.2b); Play biting (Fig. 7.2c); Play slapping (Fig. 7.2d). (Photos by Elisabetta Palagi.)

partner and this tendency is evident in many primate species (e.g., Brueggeman, 1978 for macaques; Cheney, 1978 for baboons; Mendoza-Granados & Sommer, 1995 for chimpanzees). Symmetry characterizing play sessions among size-matched playmates may provide them with the possibility to compete, practice, and strategize in a more effective way. For juvenile gorillas, playing with infants might not be challenging enough to test and improve their strength and motor ability due to the physical asymmetry characterizing the two playmates (Power, 2000).

Partner choice in juvenile primates often means a partner of the appropriate gender (Fagen, 1981). Gender differences in play fighting vary as a function of male–female diversity in the importance of fighting for adult roles, the extent of sexual dimorphism, and reproductive strategies (Byers & Walker, 1995; Fagen, 1981, 1993). In humans, gender differences are present both in the frequency of play fighting and in its intensity, with boys showing more (and more intense) play fighting than girls (Power, 2000). The "male supremacy" in play fighting decreases in species that are sexually monomorphic (Stevenson & Poole, 1982, for young *Callithrix jacchus*; Cleveland & Snowdon, 1984, for young *Saguinus oedipus oedipus*; and Pedersen, Glickman, Frank, & Beach, 1990, for young *Crocuta crocuta*) or characterized by female dominance (Palagi, 2006, for adult *Pan paniscus*; Palagi, 2009 for *Lemur catta*).

Gorillas show strong sexual dimorphism in size and external features (Meder, 1993) and a social system based on male and female dispersal (Robbins & Robbins, 2005; Watts, 1990, 1994). Male–male relationships are characterized by strong physical competition and confrontation and the relationships among females are ephemeral, with friendly contacts and agonistic support extremely uncommon (Watts, 1996).

Palagi et al. (2007) found that play sessions among females were less frequent compared to those among males, but no difference emerged between female–female and male–female play frequency. This last finding may be explained with the peculiar relationships existing between male and female gorillas. Adult females tend to stay in spatial proximity with the dominant male, searching for his protection. Such closeness to the alpha male also implies the reduction of inter-female distances. We can say that spatial proximity is the main form of social interactions typical of gorilla females; in fact, they rarely engage in cooperative interactions with males and other females (Stoinski, Kuhar,

Lukas, & Maple, 2004). Considering gentle and rough play sessions separately, however, Palagi et al. (2007) found surprising results. The gentle sessions seemed to be uniformly distributed across all the sex-class combinations, conversely, the most striking difference was found in the rough sessions (play fighting), which showed peak levels among males. This specific play practice could be particularly fruitful in providing an immediate feedback on physical skills of developing individuals (Nunes et al., 2004). Such an immediate feedback can be used to regulate future activities. The motor training hypothesis predicts that play fighting rehearses the ability to fight seriously later with conspecifics and that the frequency of juvenile rough play increases with the degree of adult intra-specific competition in a given species (Byers & Walker, 1995). In this view, juvenile males need to assess their own fighting skills with the best training partners and by the most convenient roughness.

The investigation on environmental constraints revealed that social play among juvenile gorillas raised under condition of spatial reduction. Although this result may be also viewed as an increased interaction opportunity (reduction of inter-individual distances) (Aureli, van Panthaleon van Eck, & Veenema, 1995), it shows that juveniles are able to finely modulate their behaviors by selecting age/size-matched playmates. Under high-density conditions juveniles avoid interactions with adults. Specifically, adult avoidance fits with the 'coping-model,' which predicts that individuals stay away from risky partners, especially when escape opportunities are limited (Cordoni & Palagi, 2007; de Waal, 1989; Judge & de Waal, 1993). Under such conditions it becomes essential for individuals to avoid aggressive escalation by signaling an honest statement of purpose, making it clear what is serious and what is not (Bekoff, 1995; Bekoff & Allen, 1998; Pellis & Pellis, 1996). The use of play signals under space reduction confirmed this assumption; in fact, juvenile gorillas increased their playful facial displays during indoor play sessions, thus confirming the strategic use of fine-tuning in play communication. The function of play in the ontogeny of primate social cognition may be to recognize stimuli, which may indicate the intentions of conspecifics. The ability to encode and decode social signals could represent a central issue in the evolution of behavioral flexibility and intelligence in primates (Fairbanks 2000; Pellegrini 2009).

In conclusion, juvenile gorillas are able to fine-tune their play behavior depending on playmates, social contexts, and environmental conditions.

They are not only able to maintain a play session by using playful signals appropriately (Flack, Jeannotte & de Waal, 2004; Palagi, 2008), but they also possess the cognitive ability to "place" the session in a proper spatial/temporal context, thus evaluating a complex net of factors (e.g. play partner, play roughness, group activity, space availability).

Play and the "social bridge" hypothesis: Evidence from monkeys and apes

Research on non-human primates strongly indicates that animals are able to plan and foresee (see for an extensive review Tomasello & Call, 1997). The ability to anticipate forthcoming stressful events could confer a selective gain to those subjects capable of planning. In several mammalian species, diverse strategies have evolved to mitigate tension and prevent conflict escalation. Communicative displays, dominance relationships, and greeting gestures are common mechanisms employed in order to avoid potential dangerous conflicts (Koyama & Palagi, 2006; Palagi & Cordoni, 2009; Preuschoft & van Schaik 2000).

Sociobiologists, and more specifically primatologists, agree that social play and grooming have an important role in the cohesion of social animals (Merrick, 1977; van Lawick-Goodall 1968). During the expected situations characterized by conflict of interest, grooming may function to maintain social stability by reducing tension and providing appeasement among companions (Aureli, Cords, & van Schaik, 2002).

Adult chimpanzees seem to cope with competitive tendencies through grooming, which appears to serve the function of alleviating tension that builds up before feeding time (pre-feeding) when competition for food may occur (Koyama & Dunbar, 1996). Moreover, Palagi, Cordoni and Borgognini (2004) found that those dyads engaging in grooming sessions during the pre-feeding period showed later a higher tolerance level around food. In chimpanzees, aggressive events between adult females and unrelated juveniles are not uncommon during the pre-feeding periods and the consequences of such agonistic episodes are potentially harmful for both of them (Palagi, Paoli, Grillo, & Cordoni, 2008). Palagi et al. (2004) found that social play between adults and juveniles showed the same fluctuation recorded for grooming interactions in adults, thus suggesting that adults and juveniles interact via a different behavioral strategy (play), which may be used as a substitute for grooming to increase the likelihood of cooperative behavior at feeding time. Moreover, there was a positive correlation between the frequency of adult-unrelated immature play (pre-feeding) and the cofeeding rates between the adults involved in play activity and adults related to the immature playmate. Social play with immature subjects represents a good indirect contact point between the adults (Palagi et al., 2004). In many primate species, females interact regularly with other females' infants, making attempts to greet, sniff, inspect, and tickle them (Maestripieri, 1994; Paul & Kuester, 1996; Schino, Speranza, Ventura & Troisi, 2003; Silk, Alberts, & Altmann, 2003). These kinds of interactions, labeled "infant handling," are often performed by experienced mothers who have successfully raised their own infants. Adult chimpanzees maintain high levels of play with immature partners, and do so by initiating playful interactions. Infants, in particular, are attracted to unrelated older individuals (probably due to their different ways of playing) and seem to interact more often with their mothers' preferred social partners (van Lawick-Goodall, 1968).

In chimpanzees, the adult-immature play strategy adopted during the pre-feeding time may provide benefits both at immediate and delayed levels. At an immediate level, play may help to reduce tension around food, thus permitting a more relaxed feeding session or discouraging possible attacks by adult relatives of the immature playmates (Kuester & Paul 2000). At a more delayed level, by playing, adult players and adults related to immature playmates may strengthen and/or maintain their social bonds.

Gelada baboons (*Theropithecus gelada*) show interesting affinities with chimpanzees in the use of adult-immature play (Mancini & Palagi, 2009). Gelada social system is characterized by two main components: the individual reproductive units (one-male unit, OMU) and a cluster of units (band or herd) that share a common home-range. An OMU consists of a single adult male, his reproductive females (ranging from to two to eight) and their offspring (Dunbar & Dunbar, 1975). The social integrity of the OMU is not maintained by the aggressive herding of males, as it occurs in hamadryas baboons (Kummer, 1968), but by the strength of the social affiliation among the unit members (Dunbar & Dunbar, 1975). The relationships within the OMU involve the maintenance of power, most of which is held by adult females (Dunbar, 1984). As has been reported, in some cases, the strength of female positive bonds is sufficient to

Fig. 7.3 Sequences of play fighting in immature geladas. Head rotation and face-to-face interaction (Fig. 7.3a); play bite on the neck and playful facial display (Fig. 7.3b).
(Photos by Elisabetta Palagi.)

maintain the OMU's integrity despite the absence of the alpha male (Dunbar & Dunbar, 1975). Due to their social peculiarities, gelada were a good model species to test some predictions on the potential functions of social play both in immature and adult subjects.

The most frequent interactions between members of different OMUs consist of playful contacts between immature subjects, which form temporary playful aggregations named 'play units' (Figure 7-3). On the other hand, adults tend to play with youngsters belonging to the same OMU (Dunbar & Dunbar, 1975). However, in their recent research, Mancini and Palagi (2009) did not obtain any significant difference in the distribution of play behavior according to the unit membership, especially when the analysis was restricted to the adult females. Furthermore, adult females engaged in social play with immature partners independently from their kinship or sex.

Adult play distribution in geladas strikingly differed from that reported for other species of monkeys (Kummer, 1995; Symons, 1978). In fact, not only social play is present between adults and unrelated immature individuals, but it is also common between adults and immatures belonging to the other OMU.

As mentioned above, in primates, infant handlers might use infants to test (Manson, 1999) or manage (Maestripieri, 1994) relationships with the mothers or other group members. For example, in macaques, the affinitive interaction (huddle and lipsmacking) with an infant significantly reduces the probability of aggression between adult males (Daeg & Crook, 1971; Kuester & Paul, 2000). In adult gelada baboons, except for agonistic/competitive contacts, playful interactions between adult females and youngsters represent the only social bridge between the different OMUs. In this perspective, we can hypothesize that in geladas adult-immature inter-OMU play may have a role in increasing tolerance levels among adults and in maintaining a peaceful co-existence between the one-male units.

Playing affairs between adults: Evidence from prosimians and apes

The efforts to study play have been primarily focused on immature subjects, and theories concerning the function of play often concentrated on long term rather than immediate benefits (Byers & Walker, 1995) without very good evidence (Martin & Caro, 1985; Pellegrini, 2009). However, adult play may provide good information on immediate benefits, which include testing social relationships (Pellis & Iwaniuk, 2000) and reducing social tensions (Palagi et al., 2004; Palagi, Paoli, & Borgognini, 2006). Adult–adult play, while less frequent, was found in some primate species and may occur in both sexual and nonsexual contexts (Pellis & Iwaniuk, 2000). Courtship play was found to be especially prevalent in solitary species in which males and females are unfamiliar with one another (e.g., *Mirza*, *Daubentonia*, *Perodicticus*, and *Pongo*). Nonsexual play is more prevalent in species with a high degree of social aggregation (Pellis & Iwaniuk, 2000).

Thus, different social structures and diverse inter-individual relationships may be highly predictive of adult play features (e.g., intensity, frequency, and distribution according to the sex of the players) and functions (Pellis & Iwaniuk, 1999). To date, most of the research on animal play behavior has involved rodents, canids, and primates, and within primates the research has mostly concentrated on haplorrhines. However, data from a wider array of primate taxa are needed for a more comprehensive understanding of possible roles of play, the social conditions under which it occurs, and the cognitive skills required for it.

Lemurs, which are relatively small brained, form an independent primate radiation and represent the most primitive group-living primates (Tattersall, 1982). Yet, comparing lemurs to the best-known haplorrhines is especially useful because these two distant primate groups share basic features of natural history. *Lemur catta* is a diurnal and highly terrestrial species living in multimale/multifemale social groups characterized by strong female dominance and male dispersal (Jolly, 1966) (Figure 7-4). Ring-tailed lemurs show behavioral and physiological changes according to photoperiodic fluctuations (Evans & Goy, 1968). In the wild, ring-tailed lemurs have a seasonal reproductive cycle with a mating season restricted to April–June (dry season) and a birth season limited to September–November (late dry-early wet season) (Jolly, 1966, 1967). At northern latitudes the mating season shifts to October–December and the birth season to March–May

Fig. 7.4 Preparation to play fighting in ring-tailed lemurs. The two players are an infant male and a sub-adult female. (Photo by Daniela Antonacci.)

(van Horn, 1975). During the pre-reproductive period (September and October in the Northern Hemisphere) both sexes show an intense intra-sexual competition with important preparatory conflicts (Vick & Pereira, 1989). Such period is strategic to investigate if play fighting has a role in testing competitive abilities. If so, one should expect that play is more frequent within the same-sex dyads. Moreover, the inter-individual relationships among ring-tailed lemurs are despotic and strongly codified according to rank rules (Pereira & Kappeler, 1997). Generally, in mammalian species, well-oriented agonistic contacts may affect play distribution. Adult play fighting seems to be useful to obtain information on other individuals and establish or test dominance relationships among group members in a relatively safe context (Pellis & Pellis, this volume; Peterson & Flanders, 2005). In this view, those dyads characterized by low levels of aggressive contacts should engage in play fighting more frequently than those dyads that often fought for real. In a study performed during the pre-reproductive season in this species, Palagi (2009) found high levels of play fighting between males and the highest play frequency in those dyads of subjects characterized by low levels of aggressive encounters. The finding that during a period of high competition between males (pre-reproductive period) they were more interested in playing with other males suggests that play fighting may have a role in testing competitive abilities during adulthood. In addition, the negative correlation found between play fighting and agonistic contacts within adult lemur dyads seem to support such assumptions. Similar results have been reported in human juveniles (Pellegrini, 1988).

A further possible explanation is that animals with greater play fighting experience might be less likely to respond to physical contact with serious aggressions (the Aggression Prevention and Control Hypothesis; Power, 2000). On the contrary, play fighting does not seem to work as social cement in ring-tailed lemurs, since no correlation was found between playful contacts and grooming in the study group. This result is consistent with recent reports on meerkats by Sharpe (2005), who showed that social play does not relate to establishing or enhancing social cohesion in this cooperative mammal. As a whole, considering that social play is a good means to compete by testing physical skills of conspecifics (Pellis & Iwaniuk, 2000), the presence of adult play fighting in *Lemur catta* during the pre-reproductive period is not surprising. However, further data are needed to evaluate how kin relationships, presence of immature subjects, and seasonal variations may affect frequency and partner distribution of play fighting in this species.

Adult-adult play appears to have a diverse role when we consider species characterized by egalitarian and tolerant societies (Palagi 2006). Here, social play seems to hold the function of social cement and aggregations. A clear example of such a role of adult social play is provided by a species extremely neglected in the study of social behavior: the bonobo (*Pan paniscus*).

Bonobo society is characterized by a rich set of social dynamics in which adults, and especially females, negotiate and maintain their relationships through coalition formation, reconciliation, conflict intervention, and even conflict mediation (de Waal, 1989; Furuichi, 1997; Hohmann & Fruth, 2002; Palagi, Paoli & Borgognini, 2004; Palagi, 2006). Thus, bonobos are expected to use complex behavioral mechanisms and, consequently, it is plausible that they have considerable awareness of their social environment and of the rules that regulate it. Being able to conform to such rules, however, implies that an individual has to obtain an appropriate social competence (the understanding of the overall set of rules and network of relationships which regulate a social group) which, in turn, can be reached by engaging in many social interactions (Flack et al., 2004) (Figure 7-5).

Adult-adult play in bonobos is a very common interaction and generally it is more frequent between adult females than in any other sex-combinations (Palagi, 2006). Particularly, a striking difference appears to be in the distribution of contact play (C play) that was particularly frequent among females, whereas locomotor-rotational play rates (L-R play) did not differ according to the sex-combination of the players. Contact play implies that playmates trust each other to maintain the rules of the game (Bekoff, 2001). It has to be considered that in primates strong affinitive relationships between unrelated females are rare. When close female relationships exist, they generally are associated with grouping patterns in which females do not migrate from their natal groups, which are hence defined as "female philopatric" (Silk et al., 2003). For example, chimpanzee females do not usually form close bonds with each other (Wrangham, 1986). In contrast, bonobo females are an exception to this general trend; they migrate from their natal groups as chimpanzees do (female exogamy), but, unlike chimpanzees, they form strong coalitions and alliances with

Fig. 7.5 Social play in bonobos. An adult male, in erection, is gently biting a foot of an infant female, who is performing a playful facial display while laughing. (Photo by Elisa Demuru.)

other unrelated females (for an extensive review see Doran, Jungers, Sugiyama, Fleagle & Heesy, 2002). These social bonds have been demonstrated to have adaptive consequences for primate females and their fitness outcomes (Silk et al., 2003). One important consequence for aggregating bonobo females is to acquire dominance advantage over some males so as to obtain feeding priority (Parish, 1996). In this perspective, the high levels of C play might represent an important means for bonobo females to assess their relationships in an "egalitarian mood" (Palagi, 2006). In addition, the positive correlation found in bonobos between affinitive behaviors (grooming and socio-sexual behavior) and play distribution also supports the hypothesis that play may function to promote social cohesion by enhancing continual contact among group members (Pellis & Iwaniuk, 1999; Thompson, 1998).

In conclusion, adult bonobos are characterized by a peculiar pattern of social play, with females more often involved in contact play than males. This finding suggests a "willingness" of females to assess reciprocally, yet safely, their relationships.

It may be that bonobos, with their egalitarian society, peculiar social structure, and playful tendency represent a good starting point to test empirically many emerging hypotheses on the role of play fighting in the evolution of fairness. According to Peterson and Flanders (2005), in humans play fighting leads to the direct inhibition and regulation of aggression, thus improving social integration. The same authors, stated that

"the formal adoption of a pro-social stance toward the world, by contrast, mediated by emergent trust in the trustworthiness of self and other, culminates not so much in the capacity to obey rules and stay on track but in the willingness to voluntarily enter into complex cooperative social games with others, mediated by shared goal directed frames of reference"
(Peterson & Flanders, 2005, p.151).

In conclusion, due to the phylogenetic closeness between bonobos and humans and their shared behavioral features (e.g., socio-sexual behavior), I think that many of the findings obtained studying bonobos will help to shed light on the potential functions of adult play in human beings.

Conclusion and Future Directions

Animals are able to evaluate costs and benefits of an action and play is not an exception. Play is an intentional experience, which animals undertake when some peculiar conditions are satisfied. The necessity to exactly evaluate the appropriate timing, partners, environmental, and social conditions under which a session can take place is probably one of the most cognitive challenges for social animals. Such a challenge can be taken up at every age because, like any other kind of experience, play can be fruitful in the immediacy as much as in the future. Yet, differently from other kind of social experience (e.g., grooming, post-conflict reunion, coalitionary support) play often offers a greater amount of information to conspecifics; in fact, the potential meanings of play may vary according to many different variables (modality, place, timing, age/sex of partners, context), which are often directly selected by the playmates themselves as a function of their immediate needs (competition, social manipulation, stress reduction, etc.). But if engaging in a play session is a response to an immediate necessity, why should it be surprising to see two adults playing together?

The collection of new data on adult and immature play in other primate and non-primate species should provide a much broader perspective on the relation of this multifaceted behavior with phylogeny and social structure. Moreover, comparisons between phylogenetically close species may furnish clues on how features and potential functions of play behavior can be modified. One of the most important points is how ecological factors (e.g. food intake, predatory pressure, population density) affect play distribution and modality. Therefore, there is a necessity to expand the study of play to wild animals. Since 2006, our research group has collected standardized and quantitative data on wild lemurs (ring-tailed lemurs, *Lemur catta* and sifaka, *Propithecus verreauxi*). We want to evaluate how long-term factors (environmental conditions, seasonality, food availability) affect play distribution in these species, which are sympatric and show different habits in feeding ecology and locomotion. We are also studying how play varies according to contingency situations. Both species are diurnal, live in stable groups, and defend territories; however, they behave differently during inter-group encounters. Ring-tailed lemurs increase play fighting between group members and sifaka increase playful episodes with conspecifics belonging to the alien groups. The variability in tolerance levels of the two species may make the difference in this weird behavioral attitude. In fact, sifaka live in social units that can show temporary limited variations in group composition (especially during the mating season), while ring-tailed lemurs live in social groups completely sealed to outsiders. It seems that under particularly stressful events, like the presence of foreign subjects, the two species direct their playful motivation "outside" or "inside" their own group as a function of their different tolerance levels.

One of the most interesting fields is the intentional communication skill in the great apes. The ability to use information conveyed by visual signals (e.g. gestures, body posture, movements, and facial displays) and to respond to them discriminatively has been critical for the evolution of social communication. Facial displays can be considered as a cooperative system benefiting both signallers and receivers (van Hooff & Preuschoft, 2003). Gesture and facial displays are commonly involved in regulating many aspects of mammalian social life such as aggression, dominance-subordinate relationships, appeasement, affiliation, and play. Playful activity is an interesting field for examining the role of visual signals as communication systems. In fact, during play, animals may use patterns that are mainly adopted for other functional behaviors (i.e., predatory, anti-predatory, mating). A major question of theoretical importance has been that of how, given this overlapping in behavioral patterns, animals can discriminate between playful and nonplayful intent. The great apes, different from monkeys, use gestures (defined as communication by means of hands, feet, or limbs; Pollick & de Waal, 2007) to communicate with companions in a referential way. Consequently, it could be interesting to evaluate if gestures are involved in the regulation of play sessions and how they are combined with facial expressions and vocalizations (multimodal communication). Generally, attention-getting gestures involving tactile and auditory components are mainly used in play invitation and visual signals (facial expressions and gestures) are specifically recruited when the players are already engaging in a face-to-face interaction. Are there gestures or particular signal combinations that are more effective in convincing a group member to play? Or, on the contrary, are such combinations adjusted as a function of the different partners or context under which the invitation occurs?

If these and other issues are clarified, some very interesting comparisons with humans will be possible and this could provide new insights in the evolution of gestures and language in the subtle modulation of social play. In this view, social play and the communication capacity for regulating it can be really used as '*a window into social cognition*' (Pellis, 2002 p. 421).

Author's note

I am grateful to Anthony Pellegrini for his kind invitation to contribute to this book, Sergio Pellis and Gordon Burghardt for support and encouragement they regularly give me, and Roscoe Stanyon for his invaluable comments. This contribution is dedicated to my son Tommaso with whom I regularly engage in endless play sessions.

References

Aureli, F., Cords, M., & van Schaik, C. P. (2002). Conflict resolution following aggression in gregarious animals: A predictive framework. *Animal Behaviour, 63,* 1–19.

Aureli, F., van Panthaleon van Eck, C. J., & Veenema, H. C. (1995). Long-tailed macaques avoid conflicts during short-term crowding. *Aggressive Behavior, 21,* 113–122.

Bekoff, M. (1995). Play signals as punctuation: The structure of social play in canids. *Behaviour, 132,* 419–429.

Bekoff, M. (2001). Social play behavior. Cooperation, fairness, trust, and the evolution of morality. *Journal of Consciousness Studies, 8,* 81–90.

Bekoff, M., & Allen, C. (1998). Intentional communication and social play: How and why animals negotiate and agree to play. In M. Bekoff, & J. A. Byers (Eds.), *Animal play evolutionary, comparative, and ecological perspectives* (pp. 97–114). Cambridge: Cambridge University Press.

Bekoff, M., & Byers, J.A. (1998). *Animal Play: evolutionary, comparative and ecological perspectives.* Cambridge: Cambridge University Press.

Brueggeman, J. A. (1978). The function of adult play in free-living *Macaca mulatta.* In E. O. Smith (Ed.), *Social play in primates* (pp. 169–192). New York: Academic Press.

Burghardt, G. M. (1984). On the origins of play. In P. K. Smith (Ed.), *Play in animals and man.* Oxford, UK: Blackwell.

Burghardt, G. M. (2005). *The genesis of animal play: Testing the limits.* Cambridge, MA: MIT Press.

Byers, J. A., & Walker, C. (1995). Refining the motor training hypothesis for the evolution of play. *American Naturalist, 146,* 25–40.

Cheney, D. L. (1978). The play partners of immature baboons. *Animal Behaviour, 26,* 1038–1050.

Cleveland, J., & Snowdon, C. T. (1984). Social development during the first twenty weeks in the cotton-top tamarind (*Saguinus oedipus oedipus*). *Animal Behaviour, 32,* 432–444.

Cordoni, G. (2009). Social play in captive wolves (*Canis lupus*): Not only an immature affair. *Behaviour, 146,* 1363–1385.

Cordoni, G., & Palagi, E. (2007). Response of captive lowland gorillas (*Gorilla gorilla gorilla*) to different housing conditions: Testing the aggression/density and coping models. *Journal of Comparative Psychology, 121,* 171–180.

de Waal, F. B. M. (1989). Food sharing and reciprocal obligations among chimpanzees. *Journal of Human Evolution, 18,* 433–459.

Daeg, J. M. & Crook, J. H. (1971). Social behaviour and agonistic buffering in the wild Barbary macaque (*Macaca sylvanus*). *Folia Primatologica, 15,* 183–200.

Doran, D. M., Jungers, W. L., Sugiyama, Y., Fleagle, J. G., Heesy, C. P. (2002). Multivariate and phylogenetic approaches to understanding chimpanzee and bonobo behavioural diversity. In C. Boesch, G. Hohmann & L. F. Marchant (Eds.), *Behavioural diversity in chimpanzees and bonobos* (pp. 14–34). Cambridge, UK: Cambridge University Press.

Dunbar, R. I. M. (1984). Reproductive decisions: An economic analysis of the gelada baboon social system. Princeton, NJ: Princeton University Press.

Dunbar, R. & Dunbar, P. (1975). *Social dynamics of Gelada baboons.* Basel, Switzerland: Karger.

Evans, C. S., & Goy, R. W. (1968). Social behaviour and reproductive cycles in captive ring-tailed lemurs (*Lemur catta*). *Journal of Zoology of London, 156,* 181–197.

Fagen, R. (1981). *Animal play behavior.* New York: Oxford University Press.

Fagen, R. (1993). Primate juvenile and primate play. In M. E. Pereira & L. A. Fairbanks (Ed.), *Juvenile primates* (pp. 182–196). Oxford, U.K.: Oxford University Press.

Fairbanks, L. A. (2000). The developmental timing of primate play. A neural selection model. In: S. T. Parker, J. Langer, & M. L. McKinney (Eds.), *Biology, brains, and behavior. The evolution of human development* (pp. 211–219). Santa Fe: School of American Research Press.

Flack, J. C., Jeannotte, L. A., & de Waal, F. B. M. (2004). Play signalling and the perception of social rules by juvenile chimpanzees (*Pan troglodytes*). *Journal of Comparative Psychology, 118,* 149–159.

Furuichi, T. (1997). Agonistic interactions and matrifocal dominance rank of wild bonobos (*Pan paniscus*) at Wamba. *International Journal of Primatology, 18,* 855–875.

Hamilton, W. D. (1964). The genetical theory of social behavior. *Journal of Theoretical Biology, 7,* 1–52.

Hohmann, G. & Fruth, B (2002). Dynamics in social organisation of bonobos (*Pan paniscus*). In: C. Boesch, G. Hohmann & L. Marchant (Eds.), *Behavioural diversity in chimpanzees and bonobos* (pp. 138–150). Cambridge: Cambridge University Press.

Jolly, A. (1966). *Lemur behaviour: A Madagascar field study*. Chicago: University of Chicago Press.

Judge, P. G., & de Waal, F. B. M. (1993). Conflict avoidance among rhesus monkeys: Coping with short-term crowding. *Animal Behaviour, 46,* 221–232.

Koyama, N. F., & Dunbar, R. I. M. (1996). Anticipation of conflict by chimpanzees. *Primates, 37,* 79–86.

Koyama, N. & Palagi, E. (2006). Managing conflict: Evidence from wild and captive primates. *International Journal of Primatology, 27,* 1235–1240.

Krebs, J. R. & Davies, N. B. (Eds.). (1997). *Behavioural ecology: An evolutionary approach*. Oxford: Blackwell Science.

Kuester, J., Paul, A., (2000). The use of infants to buffer male aggression. In: F. Aureli & F. B. M. de Waal (Eds.), *Natural conflict resolution* (pp. 91–93). Berkeley, C.A.: University of California Press.

Kummer, H. (1968) *Social organization of hamadryas baboons. A field study*. Basel: Karger.

Kummer, H. (1995). *In quest of the sacred baboon. A scientist's journey*. Princeton: Princeton University Press.

Lewis, K. P. (2000). A comparative study of primate play behavior: Implications for the study of cognition. *Folia Primatologica, 71,* 417–421.

Maestripieri, D. (1994). Social structure, infant handling, and mothering styles in group-living Old World monkeys. *International Journal of Primatology, 15,* 531–553.

Mancini, G. & Palagi, E. (2009). Play and social dynamics in a captive herd of gelada baboons (*Theropithecus gelada*). *Behavioural Processes, 82,* 286–292.

Manson, J. H. (1999). Infant handling in wild *Cebus capucinus*: Testing bonds between females? *Animal Behaviour, 57,* 911–921.

Martin, P. (1982). The energy cost of play: Definition and estimation. *Animal Behaviour, 30,* 294–295.

Martin, P., & Caro, T. M. (1985). On the functions of play and its role in behavioral development. *Advances in the Study of Behavior, 15,* 59–103.

Meder, A. (1993). *Gorillas*. Ökologie und Verhalten. Heidelberg: Springer.

Mendoza-Granados, D., & Sommer, V. (1995). Play in chimpanzees of the Arnhem zoo: Self-serving compromises. *Primates, 36,* 57–68.

Merrick, N. J. (1977). Social grooming and play behavior of a captive group of chimpanzees. *Primates, 18,* 215–224.

Nunes, S., Muecke, E.-M., Lancaster, L. T., Miller, N. A., Mueller, M. A., Muelhaus, J., & Castro, L. (2004). Functions and consequences of play behavior in juvenile Belding's ground squirrels. *Animal Behaviour, 68,* 27–37.

Pedersen, J. M., Glickman, S. E., Frank, L. G., & Beach, F. A. (1990). Sex differences in the play behavior of immature spotted hyenas, *Crocuta crocuta*. *Hormones and Behavior, 24,* 403–420.

Palagi, E. (2006). Social play in bonobos (*Pan paniscus*) and chimpanzees (*Pan troglodytes*): Implications for natural social systems and interindividual relationships. *American Journal of Physical Anthropology, 129,* 418–426.

Palagi, E. (2008). Sharing the motivation to play: The use of signals in adult bonobos. *Animal Behaviour, 75,* 887–896.

Palagi, E., (2009). Adult play fighting and potential role of tail signals in ring-tailed lemurs (*Lemur catta*). *Journal of Comparative Psychology, 123,* 1–9.

Palagi, E. & Cordoni, G. (2009). Triadic post-conflict affiliation in *Canis lupus*: Do wolves share similarities with the great apes? *Animal Behaviour, 78,* 979–986.

Palagi, E., & Paoli, T. (2007). Play in adult bonobos (*Pan paniscus*): Modality and potential meaning. *American Journal of Physical Anthropology, 134,* 219–225.

Palagi, E., Antonacci, D., & Cordoni, G. (2007). Fine-tuning of social play by juvenile lowland gorillas (*Gorilla gorilla gorilla*). *Developmental Psychobiology, 49,* 433–445.

Palagi, E., Cordoni, G., & Borgognini Tarli, S. (2004). Immediate and delayed benefits of play behavior: New evidence from chimpanzees (*Pan troglodytes*). *Ethology, 110,* 949–962.

Palagi, E., Paoli T. & Borgognini Tarli, S. (2004). Reconciliation and consolation in captive bonobos (*Pan paniscus*). *American Journal of Primatology, 62,* 15–30.

Palagi, E., Paoli, T., & Borgognini Tarli, S. (2006). Short-term benefits of play behavior: Conflict prevention in captive bonobos (*Pan paniscus*). *International Journal of Primatology, 27,* 1257–1270.

Palagi, E., Paoli, T., Grillo, M., & Cordoni, G. (2008). Adult females and juvenile threats: What social effects in chimpanzees? *International Zoo News, 55,* 282–288.

Paoli, T., Palagi, E. & Borgognini Tarli, S. (2006). Re-evaluation of dominance hierarchy in bonobos (*Pan paniscus*). *American Journal Physical Anthropology, 130,* 116–122.

Parish, A. R. (1996). Female relationships in bonobos (*Pan paniscus*). *Human Nature, 7,* 61–96.

Paul, A., & Kuester, J. (1996). Infant handling by female Barbary macaques (*Macaca sylvanus*) at Affenberg Salem: Testing functional and evolutionary hypotheses. *Behavioral Ecology and Sociobiology, 39,* 133–145.

Pellegrini, A. D. (1988). Elementary school children's rough-and-rumble play and social competence. *Developmental Psychology, 24,* 802–806.

Pellegrini, A. D. (2009). *The role of play in human development*. New York: Oxford University Press.

Pellegrini, A. D., Dupuis, D., & Smith, P. K. (2007). Play in evolution and development. *Developmental Review, 27,* 261–276.

Pellis, S. M. (2002). Keeping in touch: Play fighting and social knowledge. In M. Bekoff, C. Allen, & G. M. Burghardt (Eds.), *The cognitive animal* (pp. 421–427). Cambridge, MA: MIT Press.

Pellis, S. M., & Iwaniuk, A. N. (1999). The problem of adult play-fighting: A comparative analysis of play and courtship in primates. *Ethology, 105,* 783–806.

Pellis, S. M. & Iwaniuk, A.N. (2000). Adult–adult play in primates: Comparative analyses of its origin, distribution and evolution. *Ethology, 106,* 1083–1104.

Pellis, S. M. & Pellis, V. C. (1991). Role reversal chances during the ontogeny of play-fighting in male rats: Attack vs. defense. *Aggressive Behavior, 17,* 179–189.

Pellis, S. M., & Pellis, V. C. (1996). On knowing it's only play: The role of play signals in play fighting. *Aggression and Violent Behavior, 1,* 249–268.

Pellis, S., & Pellis, V. (2009). *The playful brain: Venturing to the limits of neuroscience*. Oxford: Oneworld Publications.

Pereira, M. E., & Kappeler, P. M. (1997). Divergent systems of agonistic behaviour in lemurid primates. *Behaviour, 134,* 225–274.

Peterson, J. B., & Flanders, J. L. (2005). Play and the regulation of aggression. In R. E. Tremblay, W. W. Harturp, & J. Archer (Eds.), *Developmental origins of aggressions* (pp. 133–157). New York: Guilford Press.

Pollick, A. S. & de Waal, F. B. M. (2007). Ape gestures and language evolution. *Proceedings of the National Academy of Sciences, 104,* 8184–8189.

Power, T. G. (2000). *Play and exploration in children and animals.* Mahwah, NJ: Erlbaum.

Preuschoft, S. & van Schaik, C. P. (2000). Dominance and communication. In F. Aureli & F. B. M. de Waal (Eds.), *Natural Conflict Resolution* (pp. 77–105). Berkeley, CA: University of California Press.

Robbins, A. M., & Robbins, M. M. (2005). Fitness consequences of dispersal decisions for male mountain gorillas (*Gorillla beringei beringei*). *Behavioral Ecology and Sociobiology, 58,* 295–309.

Schino, G., Speranza, L., Ventura, R., & Troisi, A. (2003). Infant handling and maternal response in Japanese macaques. *International Journal of Primatology, 24,* 627–638.

Sharpe, L. L. (2005). Frequency of social play does not affect dispersal partnerships in wild meerkats. *Animal Behaviour, 70,* 559–569.

Silk, J.B., Alberts, S.C., & Altmann, J. (2003). Social bonds of female baboons enhance infant survival. *Science, 302,* 1231–1234.

Špinka, M., Newberry, R. C., & Bekoff, M. (2001). Mammalian play: Training for the unexpected. *The Quarterly Review of Biology, 76,* 141–167.

Symons, D. (1978). *Play and aggression: A study of rhesus monkeys.* New York: Columbia University Press.

Stevenson, M. F., & Poole, T. B. (1982). Playful interactions in family groups of the common marmoset (*Callithrix jacchus jacchus*). *Animal Behaviour, 30,* 886–900.

Stoinski, T. S., Kuhar, C. W., Lukas, K. E., & Maple, T. L. (2004). Social dynamics of captive western lowland gorillas living in all-male groups. *Behavior, 141,* 169–195.

Tattersall, I. (1982). *The primates of Madagascar.* New York: Columbia University Press.

Thompson, K. V. (1998). Self assessment in juvenile play. In M. Bekoff, & J. A. Byers (Eds.), *Animal play evolutionary,* comparative and ecological perspectives (pp. 183–204). Cambridge, MA: Cambridge University Press.

Tomasello, M. & Call, J. (1997). *Primate cognition.* New York: Oxford University Press.

van Hooff, J. A. R. A. M. & Preuschoft, S. (2003). Laughter and smiling: The intertwining of nature and culture. In F. B. M. de Waal & P. L. Tyack (Eds.) *Animal social complexity* (pp. 260–287). Cambridge, MA: Harvard University Press.

van Horn, R. N. (1975). Primate breeding season: Photoperiodic regulation in captive *Lemur catta. Folia Primatologica, 24,* 203–220.

van Lawick-Goodall, J. (1968). The behaviour of free-living chimpanzees in the Gombe Stream Reserve. *Animal Behaviour Monography, 1,* 161–311.

Vick, L. G., & Pereira, M. E. (1989). Episodic targeting aggression and the histories of *Lemur* social groups. *Behavioral Ecology and Sociobiology, 25,* 3–12.

Watts, D. P. (1990). Ecology of gorillas and its relationship to female transfer in mountain gorillas. *International Journal Primatology, 11,* 21–45.

Watts, D. P. (1994). Social relationships of immigrant and resident female mountain gorillas, II: Relatedness, residence, and relationships between females. *American Journal of Primatology, 32,* 13–30.

Watts, D. P. (1996). Comparative socioecology of mountain gorillas. In W. C. McGrew, L. F. Marchant, & T. Nishida (Eds.), *Great ape society* (pp. 16–28). Cambridge: Cambridge University Press.

Wilson, M. L., & Wrangham, R. W. (2003). Intergroup relations in chimpanzees. *Annual Review of Anthropology, 32,* 363–392.

Wrangham, R. W. (1986). Ecology and social evolution in two species of chimpanzees. In D.I. Rubenstein and R.W. Wrangham (Eds.) *Ecology and social evolution: Birds and mammals* (pp. 352–378). Princeton: Princeton University Press.

Play and Development

Robert M. Fagen

Abstract

This chapter offers biological hypotheses about proximate causation of variation in human play. Topics include the developmental role of social contingency play in middle infancy; ecological life-history analysis of play across the lifespan; rhythm-based learning; developmental rates as biological dependent variables; play in late childhood (the "bubblegum years"); and active, embodied, playful engagement with rhythms of space and time. Rhythm-based learning is primary, indeed definitive, in human nature. This novel view of human nature and human cognition has its genesis in novel insights that emerge from the study of communicative musicality and from research on children's geographies. Rhythmically-based playful interactions in space and time develop meanings, relationships, embodied minds, and intersubjectivities. Self-referential play emerges simply and inevitably from spatiotemporal play in development but further serves to transcend the bounds and veils of space-time, as William Blake long ago recognized.

Key words: biological dependent variables, bubblegum years, children's geographies, communicative musicality, developmental rates, embodied mind, intersubjectivity, life-history, musicality, rhythm, rhythm-based learning, self-reference, social contingency play, strange loop

Introduction

Nearly 400 pages into his magistral treatise on play, Thomas Power (2000) finally cuts to the chase. "What are the effects of play on development?" he asks. In the next sentence, he answers his own question: "Research allows few general conclusions to be drawn." To end the book, he underscores this point: "Considerably more research must be conducted before the many claims about the effects of play can be substantiated." The reiterated passive voice of the last sentence amounts to highly-effective metacommunication. Sober and low-key, Power's conclusions offer an instructive contrast to the rousing proclamations of developmental significance that constitute what Peter Smith (1988) has termed a "play ethos."

Nine years later comes Tony Pellegrini's (2009) turn to ask, "What's it all mean?" A rhetorical question, to be sure, but eminently fair. After all, his book is entitled *The Role of Play in Human Development*. Readers of a book built in part around the ecological idea of beneficial payoffs might well feel entitled to an answer more enlightening than (a) strength, skill and/or versatility, (b) none of the above, (c) versatility or something, or perhaps not, anyway, we need more research, (d) sorry, folks, play is developmentally useless, hate to disappoint you.

Tony meets the challenge with characteristic aplomb. "The behavioral-flexibility characteristic of play," he suggests, "is its main function." He then sums up: Play predicts a variety of beneficial outcomes supported, albeit modestly, by data. These outcomes include increased bone density, social dominance, theory of mind, and early literacy. That play's role in human development might be to impart behavioral and cognitive flexibility, is, he reminds us, still no more than speculation.

These play theorists may not lack all conviction, but their absence of passionate intensity reflects purposed caution. As Pellegrini ruefully concludes, bad evidence will surely drive out good if given a chance. He urges play advocates to "stick to realistic readings of the data."

Brian Sutton-Smith's (2005) creative "fantasy of what play might still be" adds a touch of contrasting counterpoint to the dirge from whose ground these two prudent voices rise. His fantasy seeks to put fun back into thinking about play, in ways that might lead beyond existing conclusions. In the spirit of MacLean (1990), he opposes the thinking brain to the feeling brain. He argues that it makes excellent sense to view play in the context of a functional design problem posed by the coexistence of thinking and feeling brains in the same vertebrate skull. Play does seem to have something to do with the strange loop that creates and unites the two minds. Sutton-Smith concludes that play's parodic (self-referential?) fun is "at base a kind of courage" that affords protection from emergencies and transcends dreary everyday realities.

Clearly, the heart of all play remains a profound mystery. For generations, scholars and their ilk have tugged, twisted, pushed, pulled, poked, and prodded at the topic with no demonstrable success. Sutton-Smith (1997) wryly reviews what he aptly characterizes as a century and more of silliness.

The picture fascinates even as it baffles. Behavioral innovation, in wild Bornean orangutans, arises most often in play (van Schaik, van Noordwijk, & Wich, 2006). Also in orangutans, rapid mimicry of play-faces reveals a world of relational intersubjectivity (Ross, Menzler, & Zimmermann, 2008). Results of a ten-year field study of free-ranging coastal Alaskan brown bears suggest that play *per se* contributes to pre-adult survival (Fagen & Fagen, 2004; Fagen & Fagen, 2009).

The fascination of human development, and of development generally, is that complex and novel forms can emerge from simple beginnings. Indeed, even more fascinatingly, simple and elegant forms can emerge from complex beginnings. It seems almost a miracle. (Biologists confront two nontrivial problems of just this form, often simultaneously: First, development itself, and then the emergence of complexity in the history of life, including the very knotty and as yet unsolved problem of macroevolution.) Leigh Van Valen (1973)'s celebrated maxim "Evolution is the control of development by ecology" neatly linked the two problems. Much intellectual water has flown under many interdisciplinary

bridges since Van Valen penned those words, but the mystery remains.

Astonishingly, one of the most salient properties of human development, and indeed of behavioral development across higher vertebrates, is its propensity, virtually a biological imperative, to produce unique, qualitatively-new individuals. The creative power of development, however shadowed by the past, amounts to a higher-order miracle. The development of a single multicellular organism from a single cell is amazing enough. But when we consider all the biological and psychological implications of individual uniqueness, we cannot help but be floored. That there was indeed a Mozart, but only one, is almost stranger than we can imagine. But the very same thing can be said, and for the very same reasons, about every human being who ever lived. And, when we read the work of primatologists like Jane Goodall, and of so many other students of animal behavior (the work of Cynthia Moss and Phyllis Lee on the African elephants of Amboseli National Park comes immediately to mind), it seems hard to deny the reality of individual uniqueness in species other than our own.

Approaches to human play and development can look back in time or can look ahead. A few, like Janus, attempt to do both. To look back is to emphasize past influences, however constituted, on present-day behavior and society. Forward-looking analyses emphasize flexibility and innovation. These views recognize that biological individuals, including humans, tend to optimize their fit to present circumstances while somehow mustering enough flexibility to adjust when those circumstances change. Such analyses acknowledge the empirical fact that those species that persist have typically done so in an ever-changing, capricious world. But according to Oyama (2000), nature-nurture dualisms, of which constraint/flexibility is presumably one, may be at least part of the problem. Accordingly, this chapter adopts alternative perspectives on development. For background on these perspectives, see Bateson & Martin (2000), Oyama (2000), and additional sources cited in their works. Further general theoretical and empirical bases of this chapter include G. Bateson (1972, 1978), P. Bateson (2005), Hinde (1997), Pellegrini (2009), Sander, Amadei, & Bianchi (2007), and Sutton-Smith (1997).

Clearly, any effort of this sort necessarily treads contested ground. The geographies of children's geographies, and the speculative biogeography and paleobiology of human childhood, span vast landscapes. My research for this chapter led me to two important fields of study, both new to me and both having profound implications for the study of play and human development. These fields of study are (1) communicative musicality, including rhythms of movement (e.g., Malloch & Trevarthen, 2009; King, 2004) and (2) children's geographies (e.g., Holloway & Valentine, 2000). I found much substantive research on play and human development in fields and in settings far removed from Darwinism's sphere of influence in the West. Indeed, nothing could differ more from the hardened, narrow, doctrinaire "modern synthesis" and "new synthesis" of mid-20th-century Darwinism. For nearly two centuries, highly significant research on play and human development has progressed in the Commonwealth and former Commonwealth nations, in continental Europe (e.g., Jambor & van Gils, 2007), and, since the 1860's, in Russia (Todes 1989). Thorough treatment of these important bodies of work is beyond the scope of this chapter. The fruitfulness, depth, sophistication, and richness of these intellectual traditions clearly pose a major challenge to many current views hatched within the Darwinist henhouse. Darwin might well have appreciated the irony. He might even have been pleased to see geographers, naturalists, and historians like himself rediscover and expand his original views of human nature.

I found the following simple analogies helpful to me as I sought to understand just what Oyama et al. (2002) were trying to accomplish (and as I began to sense the muffled tread of the Development Police on my front porch). Oyama, Bateson, and Martin all emphasize that genes do not determine behavior and that environments do not determine behavior, even through interaction. Bateson and Martin (2000, p. 15–16) engagingly illustrate this point with a story about a would-be chef who learns that both raw ingredients (read genes and environments) and the way they are combined (read development) are important. Some other analogies: The score of a piece of classical music, the sheet music of a popular song, or the libretto and choreography for a dance are not sufficient to determine what happens in any given performance of the work. Individual artist, setting, and more are all important as well. Performance may involve a relatively-large amount of improvisation (characteristic of jazz, but also not infrequent in Western classical music performances prior to the 20th century). Or it may simply involve moment-by-moment interpretation and real-time creation of a previously-mastered part. A classical *Nutcracker* ballet has a Clara, though she may sometimes be named Marie. Each Clara performs and

thereby constructs her personal, unique *Nutcracker*. As a metaphor, the emergence of a particular performance of a work by a particular artist based on a given script, songbook standard, set choreography, or musical score comes, I think, as close as any metaphor can to explain just how Oyama, Bateson, and Martin view development and how their view differs from previous approaches. And the fact that music and dance performance prove especially serviceable as metaphorical windows through which to view development should not escape notice.

As Stephen Jay Gould (1977, p. 409) famously remarked, "There may be nothing new under the sun, but permutation of the old within complex systems can do wonders." Gould further recognized that simple, continuous changes in underlying processes could exhibit unbounded potential. With Pellegrini (2009), I characterize human play in terms of two key, interrelated criteria: (1) primacy of means over ends, and (2) nonfunctional orientation. Behavior that meets these criteria can be developmentally important in many ways (Bateson & Martin, 2000; Fagen, 1981; Pellegrini, 2009). Currently, the possibility that play can produce behavioral flexibility (e.g., Bateson, 2005; Fagen, 1981; Pellegrini, 2009; Sutton-Smith, 1997) is attracting particular attention. It is precisely this potential openness to novelty that students of play now see as emerging in development as the result of the kinds of simple changes (in a context, to be sure, of material complexity) that define development itself.

Metaphors about development have their drawbacks (Oyama, 2000). Current views of play and development (e.g., Bateson & Martin, 2000) often analogize play to scaffolding. The context is architecture—humans building structures. The idea is that the scaffolding serves as a means for constructing nonplay behavior. The follow-through tag virtually compels us to think that once the nonplay behavior has been constructed, the scaffolding disappears entirely and without a trace. But now we are thinking in the metaphor's terms, not in terms of the behavioral domain about which the original metaphor was invoked. This kind of unexamined thought shift can enhance poetry, music, literature, and everyday discourse. But in science it can be a very bad idea. Let's try a different metaphor. Let's compare play's role in the construction of nonplay to African plains ungulates constructing a grazed and browsed ecosystem. After gazelle, wildebeest, and zebra have moved on, the grazing succession they constitute having developed the latest instance of a co-evolved grassland, the cloven hoofprints of history are all that remain. (Of course, philosopher N.R. Hanson wrote "cloven hoofprint of theory," but hoofed mammals are, after all, famously diverse.) In all of biology, history leaves traces, from the seven vertebrae in a giraffe's neck to hox genes and the rudimentary hind limb bones of whales. Why, but for entirely irrelevant metaphorical reasons, can't scaffolding recycle as girders, beams, joists, flying buttresses, and/or foundation? Then anything that play develops may retain some characteristics of play. These characteristics may be abstract or concrete, highly functional or trivial, adaptive or exaptive. Metaphors provide us just enough rope to hang ourselves.

Once we recycle the scaffolding, the study of human play reveals an alternative view that accepted practices might well obscure: the fact that temporary developmental scaffolding can become enduring behavioral structure. Human play has been controversial and confusing because the overall scope of different views of human play varies widely. Some approaches zoom in on just a few relatively-coherent target areas. Pellegrini (2009), for example, recognizes four forms of human play: social, object, locomotor, and pretend. Other students of play, following, e.g., Huizinga (1950), cast their nets far more widely. For these students, human play may also include games with rules, storytelling, the arts, spiritual and religious belief and practice, and/or further postural, gestural, and linguistic forms of human cognition and activity. These "higher" forms seem playlike and at the same time very serious. In my own mind, I have tried to resolve this apparent contradiction by supposing that essential structural and mechanistic elements of play enter and reshape the dynamics of human behavior as it develops over the lifespan. Given such an extended basis for behavior and cognition, humans have been able to produce complex forms of behavior unknown in any other species.

Metaphor also lends to confusion about constraint and flexibility. Oyama (2000) prefers not to use the word "constraint" at all because the metaphor unleashes so many unhelpful concomitants of the nature-nurture dichotomy. Gould (2002) saw constraint as actually fostering innovation and flexibility. The idea of constraint was central to Gould's view of life. Accordingly, he took great pains to explain just how constraint could produce increased biological diversity and novelty. The details of his argument are well beyond the scope of this chapter, but to me they seem to resonate with some of Oyama's (2000) philosophical concerns. Two examples, one from the literary arts and one from the performing arts, both clearly indicate that constraint and highly-original artistic production are by no means mutually exclusive. Nearly all Emily Dickinson's poems follow the metric forms of traditional Congregational Church hymns. Jazz improvisation works with popular songs, often standards from the American songbook, and with their chord changes. Tune and chart furnish a springboard for innovative, flexible flights into and around a rich musical space of very high dimensionality.

Scope

The scope of this chapter is proximate causation. What is human play, how does it develop, and how does it affect development? Prometheus' fate notwithstanding, scholars have also sought to view play through the lens of ultimate causation, but readers will not find my views on this topic in the current chapter. An overly narrow working definition of play might place restrictive limits on the current chapter's scope, but boundaries can be helpful. Although play by many definitions would seem to encompass much, even all, of human nature and human behavior, including many phenomena of undeniable interest to scholars of play and development, this chapter will emphasize proximate causation of human locomotor, object, social, and pretend play.

From infancy onward, the human behaviors here termed play express unique qualities of movement and of emotion, and perhaps of cognition as well. These voluntary enactments, viewed in their definitive context of non-immediate function, charmingly evoke joy and delight. Across the human lifespan, play takes changing forms and may serve changing functions as well. But despite much bafflement and debate, most play scholars, while urging caution, now appear to agree, albeit provisionally, on a few basics. All play forms, though multifunctional, share a common structural theme of common movement qualities. Currently, a consensus hypothesis is that play may impart flexibility, adaptability, and resilience to behavior, in keeping with the slow course of human development and the open developmental programs that characterize the human species. Pellegrini (2009) takes closer looks at four major forms of human play.

Paying the Rates

In the King's English, "rates" means (roughly) what an American would call "taxes." Rates of development and of behavior are as salient as taxes and, inevitably, death. How often per hour, per individual does play occur? What fraction of each hour of direct observations of a given individual does play occupy? How do such measured rates vary across individuals, with age, with time, and with other conditions? And once we have an adequate idea of the rates of play per hour and on their chief sources of variation, what about other measurable characteristics of play—forms, qualities, partner choice, and the like? What are the rates at which these characteristics of play occur over time, and with what factors do these rates vary?

Rates of behavior and rates of development are both important. In particular cases, they may even be linked in ways that shed light on proximate and perhaps on ultimate causation. For example, vestibular stimulation (Clark, Kreutzberg, & Chee, 1977) stimulates motor development in human infants. Few things could be more typical of active play, including primate play, than vestibular stimulation. Falling, body or body part rotation, somersaults, and pirouettes are a universal theme of physically active play (Fagen, 1981). These disequilibrial, balance-disturbing actions enjoy considerable potential functional significance for nonhumans (see, e.g., Spinka, Newberry, & Bekoff, 2001). In other instances, changes in play rates can accompany changes in rates of development (Bateson, Mendl, & Feaver, 1990; Smith, 1991) around the time of weaning.

Play may increase when milk availability begins to decrease. It is as if the animals in the study had a requirement for play and could anticipate an imminent decrease in the energy and nutrition needed to fuel play. Extra play occurred while there was still a chance, while a rich food source was still available. Apart from this possible example of a compensatory, functional increase in play rates, decreased energy and nutrition typically decrease play, and conversely (Fagen, 1981; Fagen, 1993; Sharpe, Clutton-Brock, Brotherton, Cameron, & Cherry, 2002).

Human access to food varies sufficiently to affect play rates over many different time scales. For example, human nutritional improvements over several centuries have been implicated in secular increases in average height and decreases in age of puberty. The best evidence for these trends comes from industrialized countries (see discussions in Bateson & Martin, 2000, pp. 109–114). We would expect that an increasing nutritional level would produce increased rates of play. These changes may have been

large-scale and, if play in fact affects development, may have had immense consequences for nearly everything that psychologists and human behavioral biologists seek to measure and explain. Chudacoff's historical account (2007) documents children's play in America from early colonial times to the present, but we will almost surely never know whether secular trends in rates, types, forms, or qualities of play accompanied nutritional improvements or the demographic transition. Some of the answers we would most wish to have about changes in human behavior, in culture and even in human biology over time may never be known because we do not know how play rates have changed. But play rates and characteristics could indeed have varied, perhaps quite drastically, over multiple time scales. These time scales include those of European colonization in America, of the demographic transition, of cycles of drought in Africa and Asia, of cycles of glaciation in high and mid-latitudes, and of the transitions from hunter-gatherer to pastoral and agricultural societies. Any aspect of human behavior that can be influenced potentially by play is at issue. Any hypothesis about change in humans over time scales that involve varying nutritional levels is on the table for discussion. And any proposed explanation must be hedged by the following strong caveat: "Yes, but the change in question could also have been due, at least in part, to nutrition-induced changes in play through the changes in development that followed in consequence."

In the sequel, I will discuss infant social contingency play (Gosso et al., 2005, p. 219), arguably a developmentally important pinnacle of human ontogeny. To frame the ensuing discussion, I suggest some ways that ideas about rates of development as biological dependent variables (Trivers, 1985) might help make the study of infant social contingency play more pluralistic as well as more scientifically productive.

Cross-cultural information on infant social contingency play is problematic. Experts differ. Would it be surprising to find no play between infants and noninfants in some human group at some time in human history/prehistory? Would it be more surprising or less surprising if such play were instead a human universal, "always and everywhere?" Findings accumulate, spinning as they drop.

Ecologically based hypotheses that address developmental rates might help. Two such hypotheses are presented here. The first hypothesis addresses presumptive changes in infant experience as preindustrial societies change into industrial and postindustrial societies. The second hypothesis focuses on presumptive changes in resource availability and quality over these and longer time scales. Both hypotheses allow variation across cultures and over time in rates, qualities and complexity of infant-noninfant play. They embrace the rich natural history of elaborate infant-mother social contingency play as described by Stern and others (see below) in industrial and postindustrial societies. Likewise, they anticipate discovery of less elegant versions of this play form, as well as cultures in which infants experience little or no social contingency play. All these cases fall on a (no doubt multidimensional) spectrum and are equally orthodox.

Details of both hypotheses may vary according to developmental specifics. For the sake of brevity and concreteness, consider the specific application to social contingency play between infants aged roughly 2–6 months and older caregivers (typically adults and often mothers). With appropriate modifications, these ideas can also apply to play in later infancy and in the second year of life. These hypotheses also serve as models for approaches that would distinguish among different age, sex, and relatedness classes of play partners for infants and/or toddlers.

Hypothesis 1. Noble Savage Redux. In industrial and postindustrial societies, I hypothesize, infant social contingency play makes up for the lack of a natural environment rich in smells, sounds (including music), tastes, textures, touch, tactile-kinesthetic experience, vestibular stimulation, and visual patterns and movements that an infant can take in. Babies in hunter-gatherer societies

> "experience intense bodily contact with their mothers, who take them wherever they go, with the help of a sling. In this way the babies begin to get familiar with the world surrounding them, as they ride along with their mothers to the field, during gathering, and during long walks through the forest" (*Gosso et al.*, 2005).

The richness of forest, garden, tundra, steppe, and preindustrial village is largely gone from contemporary cities and high-density suburbs. An infant's daily feel and sense of earth, sky, air, and water when carried by a working, dancing, or resting adult no longer exists in its historical state. As experiential givens, these rich sensorimotor, tactile-kinetic ecologies could have become facilitative or even necessary for healthy development. The mothers and other playmates of infants in Manhattan, Edinburgh, Japan, India, Sweden, Botswana, and all the other places where infant social contingency play with noninfants has been found in the last 50 years are doing a heroic thing. They are making a new world in an effort to replace the world that has been lost. They are working mightily to furnish what development needs. They are literally the infant's world. So suppose cultural variation, rather than stress, inadequate observation, or observer bias, is an adequate explanation of the still-hypothetical culture in which no infant-noninfant play can be found. Then I would predict that modern infants reared under the equivalent of preindustrial conditions, richer if perhaps less medically secure, would have less developmental need for infant-noninfant play. And I propose that something precious, even noble has been lost from the contemporary world of infants and noninfants.

Hypothesis 2. Life-History Plasticity. An optimization model for developmental rates (Charnov, 2010) distinguishes between growing and stable populations. Ecological perspectives view developmental rates, strategies, and tactics as variable, perhaps adaptively, in the face of local, regional, and/or global change, in climate for example. Such change, through its influence on resource availability and other potential limiting factors, will affect population growth and cause rearing environments to vary. Populations with more abundant resources tend to grow, whereas populations at the upper limits of what resources can sustain remain constant in size ("stable"). Of course, real and even model populations do far more interesting things than grow at roughly constant rates or maintain a constant size. The key theoretical idea here is that developmental rates should vary in ways that we can predict from information about those factors that determine rates of population growth (including the special case of stasis), since those factors work proximately through their effects on individuals in the simple models considered here.

Some of Stern's (1977) key insights helped frame the current discussion. In his formulation, one important role of social contingency play in infant development is to facilitate attachment and sense of self. Many kinds of "raw" infant experiences can contribute to these goals, but social contingency play furnishes these experiences in concentrated, effective, safe, and enjoyable form, bundled in a package that the infant could not assemble or wrap on his or her own, or in the pedestrian round of feeding, grooming, eliminating, and sleeping.

Now suppose that resources vary in ways that call for changes in the rate of infant development. (Precisely what is to develop, and from what source these calls originate, must be left as details at this point. For concreteness, say that the rate of development of the sense of a core self (Stern, 1977) is at issue, and that the decision to accelerate or retard this process rests on ecological considerations which in turn reflect whatever complications and simplifications developmental systems theory can offer in place of discarded dichotomies involving inherited tendencies, culture, and economics.)

To slow down development, play less. All the experiences required for basic maintenance will still be present in trace amounts in nonplay contexts, and development will proceed more slowly, but with a "normal" outcome of a sense of core self at a later-than-normal age. To accelerate development, play more. The "normal" outcome and sense of core self will occur at an earlier-than-normal age.

Information required in order to make this decision involves many different sorts of variables. If, for example, as in Hypothesis 1, nutrition is better, then faster development should occur in order to allow the next infant to be produced sooner. This is the conventional adaptive argument. But the opposite prediction makes equal sense. Better nutrition may allow opportunities for more learning and varied experience, perhaps so as to anticipate future change and impart flexibility and adaptability. Then, development should slow down. Play may decrease if other available sources of relational experience can produce a more versatile sense of core self. Or, if such sources are not sufficient, then each phase of social contingency play needs to be elaborated to make the experience of each day richer, rather than advancing development so that the window of current opportunity closes and subsequent forms of social contingency play are then required.

Whether the change in question is global climate change, the changes accompanying the demographic transition, cycles of glaciation and deglaciation, or cycles of rainfall and temperature and forest-savanna-grassland-scrub-desert oscillation, the path to changes in developmental rates leads through resource availability. Necessary complications and interactions result from thermoregulation, challenges to the immune system as it interacts with the nervous and endocrine systems, and the rest of a bulging package of familiar ecological and physiological variables that relate to the economics of stress and somatic flexibility (e.g., Bateson, 1963). This framework and others like it cannot, of course, be the only possible approach to historical and cultural variation in social contingency play. But it ought to improve the current level of discussion. The topic

deserves something better than a continuing squabble between those who deify infant social contingency play and those who have perforce adopted a curmudgeonly role, to the continuing delight of the media.

Waypoints

The richness, beauty, and order-in-chaos of human development have long fascinated writers, storytellers, mythmakers, humanists, and more recently, scientists. By way of illustration, I offer a personal selection of those developmental waypoints whose contemplation should forever knock off metaphorical socks. My use of the word "waypoints" is an attempt to suggest a more theory-neutral term for what are generally called "milestones" or "norms," as found, for example, in baby books that offer parents information and advice. All suggested age ranges are schematic and can be expected to vary significantly over all relevant scales of space (culture, geography) and time.

Middle infancy (2 to 5 months)

The first year or so of postnatal human development is as near as anything in nature to "something new under the sun." Rates of brain growth and development during this period resemble those found in fetal great apes. Based on simple extrapolation from great ape ontogeny, human infants should be born after 21 months in utero (Portmann, 1941; Portmann, 1945; Gould, 1977, p. 369). Prolonged immaturity is arguably the single most awesome and profound biological fact of human ontogeny. By middle infancy, forms of social contingency play emerge that make this argument for human uniqueness even more strongly.

Play of infants with adults offers keys to the role of play in early human development. Hinde (1974, p. 184) calls human infant-adult play "an almost qualitative advance over non-human forms." Subsequent perspectives justly omit the "almost."

Beginning at age 2–3 months, infants in many cultures enter dancelike, musical, game-like interactions with a caregiver, usually the mother. Unique rhythm, phrasing, and dynamics of human mother-infant play in Western societies are all characteristic of these behaviors, which involve gaze, sound, facial expression, movement, and body contact A comprehensive bibliography of human infant-adult play would exhaust the information storage capacity of most researchers, if not of their computers. Yet from its outset this work has remained vital and compelling.

Darwin (1877) was arguably the first scientist to describe play in middle infancy. Almost a century later, Daniel Stern (1971, 1974a, 1974b, 1977, 1985, 2004; Stern & Gibbon, 1979), Mary Catherine Bateson (1971, 1975, 1979), and others of like stature (e.g., Als, Brazelton, the Papoušeks, Sander, Trevarthen, Tronick, Watson) began to document one of nature's most extraordinary phenomena. Their tools included microanalysis of film and video, observational perspectives of field ethology, and the intellectual stances of psychoanalysis. Further studies, employing increased focus and analytical precision, tended to zero in on one aspect or another of the phenomenon. For a long time the result was largely-disjunct literatures of gesture, sound, and facial expression, literatures that urgently required resynthesis (Beebe, Jaffe, Feldstein, Mays, & Alson, 1985; Beebe, Stern, & Jaffe, 1979; several chapters in MacDonald, 1993; Pellegrini, 2009). What eventually emerged from these and similar resyntheses is a novel universe of discourse about infant mind and human nature, centered around expansive concepts of intersubjectivity, affect attunement, and communicative musicality (e.g., Malloch & Trevarthen, 2009). The bottom line, if one yet exists in regard to such a new and dynamic field, is not only that human nature is indeed noteworthy in a context of comparative ecological life-history analysis with particular emphasis on primate developmental rates. The big surprise is that wholly new conceptual and analytic bases are now essential for further progress. These bases take the study of human nature and of play and development far from its historical roots in philosophy, psychology, biology, general dynamic systems analysis, and cognitive science. Music and dance, viewed from a synthetic developmental dynamic systems perspective that encompasses biology, philosophical and cognitive psychology, and cognitive science, now appear to hold new answers and novel questions regarding the long-sought roots of human nature and cognition. Students and practitioners who have slaved heroically to master Smale's horseshoe, Hamilton's theory, Price's equation, Gödel's incompleteness proof, and many other intellectual dragons confronting late 20[th]Century developmental psychology may well scream in frustration to learn that what they should have been doing all along is taking dance classes and studying an instrument. Or, they may shout "Hallelujah!" Compassionately, one hopes that the latter will be the case. It's really rather fun.

Multiple revolutions shaped vertebrate phylogeny. Understandably, we may be forgiven for feeling that the emergence of humanity deserves pride of place. In no case is this distinctiveness more compelling than in the study of play in middle infancy. We have met the singularity, and it is us.

The bubblegum years (9 to 12)

Here, if anywhere, is play's terra incognita. In these years, children begin to master skills ranging from reading to storytelling and from chess to athletics, they elaborate and propagate age-group cultures and their hallmark games, they collect anything and everything that admits of exhaustive classification, they dream of dancing Clara in the *Nutcracker* and of tying the ribbons on their first pair of gleaming Ballet Pink pointe shoes. Some spin prescient webs of imagination and fantasy. Mind reveals its full diversity, engaging, alluring, rude, unsanitary, and paradoxical. Thornburg (1979) coined the term "the bubblegum years" and sought to draw deserved attention to his topic. More recently, the catchy term "tweens" has focused popular and marketing attention on these same important ages—a classic demonstration that words have power and that boundaries are countries in hiding. Manning (2006) offers a concise overview of play in late childhood and early adolescence. Major and minor literary classics—Janet Frame's *An Autobiography*, Elizabeth Knox's *The High Jump*, Brian Sutton-Smith's *Our Street*, *Smitty Does A Bunk*, and *The Cobbers*, Mark Twain's Tom-Huck duo, Kenneth Grahame's *Dream Days* and *The Golden Age*, Arthur Ransome's *Swallows and Amazons*, and Booth Tarkington's Penrod series—evoke the atmospheres of long-ago childhoods and the agonies and ecstasies of play.

Play in the bubblegum years seems almost to be taken for granted by academics, even as burdens of earlier and earlier sexual maturation (Eveleth & Tanner, 1990; Hauspie, Vercauteren, & Susanne, 1997) and, some argue, rampant commercialism threaten the very survival of this span of childhood. Whether, as many argue, this implosion of an entire developmental universe is only a temporary concomitant of the demographic transition remains to be seen. Bateson & Martin (2000, p. 112) are cautiously optimistic that pubertal precocity is leveling off throughout Europe, and that the previous trend to earlier maturation is even reversing. One only hopes that their view will ultimately prove correct.

Adulthood (25 years to whenever)

Adults develop. Adults play. The truisms of lifespan developmental psychology apply with considerable force to the study of play and development. In specific circumstances, adults may play more than commonly believed. Some forms of play may persist in new guises after being brought inside developmentally. And adults continue to play in recognizable ways with immature conspecifics, with pet dogs and cats, and with appropriate adult partners. Adult play with companion animals (e.g., domestic dogs: Mitchell & Thompson, 1986, 1990, 1991, 1993; Mitchell, 2002, 2004; Rooney, Bradshaw, & Robinson, 2000, 2001, 2002; Toth, Gacsi, Topai, & Miklosi, 2008) appears frequent, even near-ubiquitous, in some societies. To my knowledge, no one has actually measured rates of this form of adult play in terms of daily time budgets or in comparison with those of other play forms. But for some adults, play with a pet dog or cat may be the chief source of play experience. Finally, some forms of adult play reflect dark sides of human nature. Play is a recurrent theme, for example, in sexual abuse of children (see, e.g., Knox, 2000).

Might play scaffolding-brought-inside effects act definitively in human adulthood? Huizinga (1950) thought so. Creativity in the arts and in the sciences, pursuit of hobbies and interests, personal and organized spirituality, ballroom dance, Tai Chi, luxury cruises, Ultimate Frisbee, sport fishing, and indeed much of human culture, including ritual and festival, have all been interpreted at one time or another as dynamic aspects of the ongoing development of play-brought-inward.

Play in each epoch of development constructs subsequent behavior through ascending hierarchies of increasingly-elaborate and increasingly-abstract scaffolding. Once in place, play serves to generate novelty, creativity and innovation. It may shape more complex forms of behavior. Alternatively, it may carve away all that is not essential, a crucial "refine and simplify" mode of development: Less is more. The ascent continues across the human lifespan. At no age does play necessarily cease. Rather, it becomes more and more deeply embedded in the dynamo of development, so that its observable products are less and less recognizable as play. Those adults fortunate to retain sufficient quality of life in middle and old age may find that being an elder has its joys: grandchildren, hobbies, friends, creative and artistic heights that can only be reached after a lifetime of study and practice, and for some, spiritual fulfillment, even bliss.

Not everyone is so lucky. But ideally, at least in theory, even this does not terminate the phrase. We can imagine increasingly abstract levels of attainment, perhaps not yet described and perhaps even not describable. From both East and West, the playful work of accomplished artists and scholars of advanced age embodies a seemingly paradoxical juxtaposition of play and seriousness, of complexity and simplicity, best termed wisdom. Quoting Blake's *Auguries of Innocence*, Erik Erikson explored this not-so-far-off borderland in *Toys and Reasons* (1977).

The ascending hierarchy of developmental complexity and abstraction takes a paradoxical jump back into simplicity with increasing age. Hofstadter (1999) might be tempted to characterize this life-history phenomenon as a strange loop. Play seems to swim up closer and closer to the surface and seems at the same time to be descending towards unimaginable depths.

Play and development: Three hypotheses

The following three hypotheses, one null and two alternative, address developmental complexity of human play.

1. A CANONICAL NULL HYPOTHESIS: ENACTMENT

Enactment, George Eisen's felicitous term, refers to the fact that play shares common themes with overall behavior and reflects local circumstances (Fagen, 1981). This pattern, most evident in cross-species comparisons, holds with equal force over a vast range of other kinds of differences, including age, sex, population, and immediate past experience. It is fascinating and delightful, though not at all surprising, that the ground-adapted patas monkey, like other cursorial species (e.g., cheetah, pronghorn, zebra) exhibits spectacular terrestrial running and chasing games that are exceptional when compared with noncontact play of each species' close (but less cursorial) biological relatives. Play complexity and possibly frequency increase with relative brain size when appropriate comparisons are made (Fagen, 1981), but how could it be otherwise? If species X is adapted to do y, it is an empirical fact that, all other things being equal, play of species X will have y as a dominant theme. But it cannot and does not follow that play of species X functions to develop y. This same principle applies with equal force to differences within species. In particular, suppose that males of some particular species are more physically active and assertive than the species' females. We would expect male-female differences in play that parallel this sex difference. These differences in play have no necessary functional or adaptive significance. They follow directly from the empirical principle that play reflects overall biology. (I thank Martha McClintock and Stephen Jay Gould for offering this important idea.)

How does human play reflect human specializations? A list of likely characteristics ranges from the obvious (bipedalism) to the not-so-obvious (use of the hand, use of language, incorporation of musical and body movement rhythms, reflection of current situational and experiential themes in pretend play). But if the chief human specialty is in fact versatility, flexibility, and nonspecialization, then the canonical null hypothesis becomes much more subtle. We would expect human play to be itself variable and flexible, with no necessary functional implications for the development of behavioral flexibility, much less for development of innovation and creativity.

The canonical null hypothesis also empowers a more careful, thorough look at play. If close analyses show that some kinds of species-typical behavior are disproportionately included in play (or excluded from it), we know we're onto something. Human infant-adult play is one case in point. But microanalyses of any human play form ought to reveal additional cases.

2. CONVENTIONAL CONSENSUS: FLEXIBILITY AND ADAPTABILITY

Flexibility and adaptability hypotheses about the role of play in development were around long before their competitors went extinct. Rather like mammals during the Age of Dinosaurs, these hypotheses waited their turn for generations until some cataclysm removed the competition and gave them free rein to inherit the earth. What has happened in the study of play over the past half-century is not at all like the popular conception of scientific progress, or even like the Kuhnian notion of scientific revolution. Of course, this is not to say that flexibility hypotheses could not be correct in theory, do not have empirical support (e.g., in laboratory rats of the hooded strain, Pellis & Pellis, 2009), or might not even be right. In fact, the old idea that play confers flexibility, adaptability, and versatility is now spurring fascinating new research and speculation on a number of fronts (see, e.g., P. Bateson, 2005; Pellegrini, 2009; Pellis & Pellis, 2009).

Caution seems to pervade the most authoritative and credible accounts of the possible role of play in human development (e.g., Power, 2000; Pellegrini, 2009). Over the years, many scholars opined that play experience might somehow influence cognitive-behavioral flexibility, adaptability, and versatility (see, e.g., Bruner, 1972; Fagen, 1981; Sutton-Smith, 1997). Pellegrini (2009) summarizes this position, and he clearly (and correctly) identifies it as a working hypothesis. He further reviews and

summarizes the very few conclusions reached to date regarding a possible role or roles for play in human development. Though they are undeniably noteworthy, these conclusions largely remain tentative. In the light of current public and policy interest in human play, I find Pellegrini's caution eminently commendable. In discussing developmental benefits of play, it is important to continue to distinguish between speculation and scientific fact, particularly once cameras roll and reporters grub.

How can one behavior pattern characterized by means over ends and non-utilitarianism cook a different behavior, or even an entire individual, so that the resulting phenotype is more able to confront surprise, the unexpected (Spinka, Newberry, & Bekoff, 2001), and capricious change? One interesting candidate for an actual mechanism is linked to the self-referentiality of play, a characteristic first noted as definitive by Gregory Bateson. As Fein (1984) correctly noted in a generally-neglected article, we who study play should be no strangers to concepts of self-reference. And, as Fein pointed out, when Hofstadter (1999, 1st ed. 1979) linked self-referentiality to the development of consciousness, play researchers should have been ready and willing to leap in. Workers in the field of cybernetics, a constituent of the general systems theory universe that also includes information and communications theory and has since expanded to include large areas of cognitive science, have addressed these issues energetically. Self-reference is the way to bring the new into being (Guddemi, 2007). Have students of play castigated theoreticians for neglecting proximal mechanisms, or alleged that theory had nothing to offer to those interested in proximate causation, only to ignore possible mechanisms that followed immediately from some of the field's chief historical concerns?

3. SOMETHING DIFFERENT: MUSICALITY AND THE RHYTHMS OF SPACE

As students of play, we have long approached the topic from two equally meritorious but very different perspectives. One of these perspectives, very timely at the moment of this writing, constitutes nonconfrontational skepticism, the sober common sense of a Patrick Bateson or a Tony Pellegrini, a perspective grounded in good science and one that, in a fair and just world, would long ago have punctured the many intellectual and media hot air balloons that would-be pundits are forever launching from the field of play.

A place remains for novel perspectives on play, imaginative and bold as play itself. Play is still so totally mysterious and intractable that we may need a whole new (or almost new) story about the universe before we can even start to get it right. Hofstadter's attempt to craft one such story about human consciousness was, if nothing else, interdisciplinary and highly-entertaining. But, strangely indeed for such a playful writer and thinker, he never seems to have considered play *per se* in connection with his far-reaching speculations. When we do, we find ourselves launched into a universe of discourse lying far beyond tepid, timid sound bites.

The narrator of Bruce Chatwin's (1987) imaginative and influential work *The Songlines* envisions that "in theory, at least, the whole of Australia could be read as a musical score." In the discussion to follow, I argue that fundamental advances are currently resituating the study of play and development in space (children's geographies) and in time (communicative musicality). Precisely the same sort of radical conceptual expansion, a novel embedding, has transformed the science of ecology (Rosenzweig, 1995). A predictive theory of ecology finally emerged when ecologists began to study organism-environment relationships at all scales of space and time. This chapter presents overviews of relational, rhythm-based construction of space and time in development. A genuinely novel conception of development has taken shape from studies of children's geographies (e.g., Holloway & Valentine, 2000; Aitken, 2001; Aitken, Lund, & Kjørholt, 2008; Holt, in press; Hopkins, in press) and from studies of human musicality (e.g., Bråten & Trevarthen, 2009; Stern, 1977; Stern, 1985; Stern, 2004). A core sense of self situated in place and in history is the developmental outcome of rhythmic engagement with space and time. The spatiotemporal course of human life can be read not only as a musical score but also as an improvised, ongoing song performance, or perhaps more properly as dance, in the strict sense of the term "rhythm" as defined and discussed in the following paragraphs.

Embodiment, kinetic melodies and moments of awareness

When Spinoza and Leibnitz locked horns over Cartesian mind-body dualism, they inherited a long history of intellectual conflict (Stewart, 2006). Recently, embodied mind has taken center stage. With Husserl's phenomenology as their springboard, alternative views of human nature "are rapidly gaining strength" (Stern, 2004, pp. 25–27, 95–96). These views resonate with cognate studies of motor behavior (Luria, 1976, pp. 174–179),

touch (Josipovici, 1996), tactile-kinesthetic intelligence (Sheets-Johnstone, 1990, 1992, 1999, 2009; Wilson, 1998), and gesture (King, 2004). Mind and cognition are embodied in sensorimotor activity, they are in intimate relation with their immediate physical environment to such an extent that conventional mind-environment dualisms are no longer meaningful, and they are in intimate relation with other minds to such an extent that conventional self-other dualisms are invalid (Stern, 2004, p. 95). All these findings seem wholly concordant with the fundamental nonduality and essential embeddedness that characterize present day developmental systems theory (Oyama 2000; Oyama, Griffiths, & Gray, 2002).

This view of embodied cognition has further surprising consequences. Minds are "intersubjectively open" to other minds, creating the conditions for infant-adult play relationships: attunement, meshing, synchrony, and the like (e.g., Stern, 1977; Stern, 1985; Stern, 2004), and later on for empathy. Under these conditions, the basic biological and developmental roots of behavior are the very same primitives that allow humans to fashion orderly, elaborate patterns of dance and music (Bråten, 2007; Malloch & Trevarthen, 2009).

That natural rhythms of music and movement help children learn is a truism of practical pedagogy. The fact of uniquely effective learning through music and movement may perhaps even point to basic modules of human learning capacity. Indeed, children seem especially primed to grasp information and relationships embodied in music and movement. Natural readiness to learn more effectively in particular domains and/or in particular ways ("biological learning predispositions" and the like) is a much-discussed topic in psychology, education, and cognitive science because such readiness ultimately points to possible biological bases for education, and therefore to the prospect of biologically based educational policies and practices—a Holy Grail for some, anathema for others.

Academics eagerly and entrepreneurially sought to exploit this basic insight. The result: large-scale confusion, from multiple intelligences and the Mozart effect to the kind of screaming controversy among academics that never fails to delight the press. The recent Dana Consortium report's well-intended and careful effort to sort things out (Gazzaniga, Asbury, & Rich, 2008) offers a few cautious suggestions, but leaves the problem in the dust.

Previous findings and controversies on arts participation in relation to development of learning ability are such a mess because the academy was asking the wrong questions all along. The real "good stuff" relates to the hypothesis that young children learn more readily, more quickly, and with more enjoyment when the context ("the medium") for what is to be learned ("the lesson" or "the message") is rhythm, music and movement. To learn an alphabet, put it in a song and dance about it. To learn words, sing them. This is wonderful stuff, but it has little or nothing to do with babies listening to Mozart or prima ballerinas proving the Implicit Function Theorem. For once, it really matters to place a psychological and educational question in a comparative context of natural history. As humans, for what kind of learning does our biology equip us? Just what are we doing when we do what we do best in the world of learning? A look at preliterate and at preindustrial societies may provide some hints. George Burarrwanga (George Rrurrambu), the celebrated frontman of the Warumpi Band, said it best (Jarvis, 2007): "We learn through song and dance." Roots of this definitively human learning phenotype may well be found, as Malloch and Trevarthen argue, in the communicative musicality of infant-adult play's intersubjectivity, or even earlier in development, in the rhythms of caregivers' walking, heartbeat, breathing, and movement—all shaped by the earth's terrain and landscapes. Considering the potential for what may ultimately prove to be one of the very few genuine findings to date in the natural history of human directed learning, the numerous other proposals in this area seem hopeful at best. And the ways in which specifically human learning through musicality (communicative musicality with other humans, with animals and plants in landscapes, and geographically with earth, air, sky, and constructed meanings of place and space) has diverged from its roots in primate phylogeny ought to be particularly interesting to investigate. An obvious prediction is that directed learning through musicality will turn out to be one of those constructive constraints that Stephen Jay Gould loved to write about, constraints that promote diverse outcomes. For Gould (2002), constraints (interpreted as dynamic, intrinsic wavefronts rather than fixed, prior givens) are channels for change. They promote evolutionary novelty. In the case of humans, the constraint on learning represented by communicative musicality has ultimately produced a species of innovative, adaptable generalists like nothing else in nature. Human behavioral flexibility and creativity are as unique as they are extraordinary in an animal kingdom that already offers a wealth of examples of

fantastically sophisticated directed learning—examples that in each case embody the ecology of the learner.

Reasoning from the studies of human infant-adult play that he helped pioneer in the 1970s, Trevarthen and others (Malloch & Trevarthen, 2009) expansively assert that fundamental rhythms, the implicit order, of music and dance dynamically constitute human nature. Meaning as rhythm and musicality is the very stuff of embodied mind and, indeed, of the universe itself. The moving body is biology, body is mind, embodied mind is dance and music, as in Eliot's *Four Quartets* and Yeats' *Among School Children*.

Because the term "musicality" can mean very different things in different contexts, additional explanation may help. As Bradley (2009, p. 264) explains, "Babies may not be the slightest bit 'musical' in the way one might view a promising school-age pianist." But babies show early signs of a capacity to enjoy music, and they like and even enter into some rhythms but not others. Infant musicality does not necessarily mean musical talent. Nor, to clear up another possible source of confusion, does it refer to a desirable artistic quality of physical expressiveness and sympathetic responsiveness to music that many young ballet students lack, even after several years of intense, regular training. One of the most frequently-heard corrections in intermediate-level ballet class continues to be "Listen to the music!!" Young dancers' musicality can be improved by appropriate training, but sometimes musicality seems to blossom virtually overnight. A student whose dancing has been technically correct, but expresses no relationship with the music other than superficial conformity with a regular beat, seems to flower all at once one day at the barre or while going across the floor. Among the virtues of the classic Cecchetti exercises for the *port de bras* (Beaumont, 1975), especially as codified and taught by the late Margaret Craske, is that they allow students at all levels to focus most effectively on musicality.

Concepts of musicality and of rhythm are deeply and fundamentally related. Rhythm does not mean beat, meter, or time signature, though rhythms can emerge from these underpinnings. Rhythm constitutes the flow, pulse, and shape of music in time. For example, each barre exercise in classical ballet requires a different piece and style of music as accompaniment. The fundamental beat of the music defines a skeleton framework for an exercise (e.g., *ronds de jambe à terre* in ¾). Equally important, the phrasing, melodic lines and movements, and their harmonic and rhythmic underpinnings fill out and support the dynamic shape of the exercise. In *ronds de jambe à terre en dehors,* the working leg moves from front to back in a semicircle and then returns to front in a straight line through first position. The ¾ beat controls the speed of the movement. The overall rhythm and shape of the music guide the rhythm and shape of the movement. Drum accompaniment serves the same function for other dance forms. When Stern, Malloch, Trevarthen, et al. talk about rhythm, they clearly intend this far more ample characterization of the term.

As students of mind reshaped previous concepts of human nature, they found it imperative to reconsider the concept of time itself. Their familiarity with the ideas of rhythm outlined above gave them a sense of time as nested and textured, recursive, and even self-referential, almost like that intimated in Eliot's *Four Quartets* or Nabokov's *Ada.* With these insights, they revisited Husserl and proposed a *kairos*-like idea of time as lived presentness enfolding both past and future (Stern, 2004; Malloch & Trevarthen, 2009).

These developments, perhaps revolutionary, are all direct outgrowths of microbehavioral research on human infant-adult play. Stern (2004) and Malloch and Trevarthen (2009) review the history of research on infant-mother play forms that observers promptly termed "musical" or "dance-like." Like below-ground ecologies in which symbiotic mycorrhizae and root anastomoses weave individual trees together to make a coacting forest, the roots of rhythm, musicality, play, and mind all intertwine symbiotically.

Based on their integrated analyses of embodied mind and of intersubjectivity, Stern (2004) and Malloch and Trevarthen (2009) suggest that traditional concepts of the human individual are no longer satisfactory. Their concept of the extended mind has two kinds of implications. First, one body houses multiple persons both in time and at a given time—and in space as well. As Daniel Stern once remarked to Jerome Robbins (Vaill, 2006, p. 500): "You don't have to be a coherent person and have a single identity. You're a patchwork piece of reality, and the thing is to accept that."

The concept of the extended mind also means that a particular mind can extend over several different bodies. In theory, this expanding envelope has no bounds. Intersubjectivity generalizes to admit primary synergies between humans and living nonhumans, and between humans and the inanimate universe at all spatial and temporal scales. The logical conclusion of this reframing of human nature is

clearly something like David Bohm's holonomic universe and Hofstadter's strange loops, though neither formulation is sufficiently precise to generate explicit formal models. And the story does not end there. As evolving views of mind and nature began to converge with fundamental insights from the developing theology of Hans-Urs von Balthasar and others, subsequent thought refined these early prototypes in even more radical directions, yielding a view of the child that both resonated with and extended the philosophical developments of the past half-century (e.g., Marty, 2007).

The view of human nature constituted by embodiment, intersubjectivity, and musicality amounts to a lofty enterprise indeed. This view is necessarily further imbedded in geography's synthesis of space and meaning. That it emerged largely from studies of human infant-adult play clearly suggests that play is intrinsically involved with this mode of thinking about and of doing behavioral biology, and in fundamental ways. Legitimately, we may ask what these insights might tell us that we do not know already about play, and about a possible role for play in human development.

Generally, play serves these new visionaries as a window on human nature. They seldom address the basic questions "What are the effects of play experience and the role of play in human development?" Clearly Stern, and to some extent Malloch and Bråten, seem to consider play important. Stern (1977, pp. 70ff.) identifies a sense of core self and core others as a primary developmental project of infants aged 2–6 months. He sees a key role for infant-mother social contingency play in this project.

Because human infants aged 2–6 months are still at a uniquely early stage of development compared to nonhuman primate infants, infant-mother social contingency play arguably has unique roles in human development. It is natural to look for immediate nonplay outcomes of this form of play at this age, outcomes that can then be demonstrated in general behavior of slightly older infants. The emerging sense of core self and core others would be one such example. But a very different kind of outcome is theoretically possible for play that occurs in a phase of early human development comparable to that of a fetal great ape. Specifically, infant-mother contingency play at 2–6 months, for all its rich, elaborate structure, may have one key role in development—to allow play itself to develop so that it can emerge, ready to function in ways parallel to its functions in infant great apes, at a developmentally appropriate later age that corresponds to the stage(s) of infancy in infant great apes at which play yields take-home outcomes that stretch beyond play itself. Then, infant-mother contingency play at 2–6 months would constitute an ontogenetic adaptation, behavior for developing behavior. In this case, play itself (in its differentiated forms in older infants and young toddlers) would be the behavior developed by ontogenetically earlier play. The role of the mother (or other adult) in framing, shaping, and modulating her very competent infant's social contingency play at this age has all the hallmarks of ontogenetic adaptation: Something extraordinary is needed to produce the necessary result, something that only an adult can provide to an infant whose charm, allure, and humor make her almost irresistible. Something, well, musical. This observation underscores the tragedy of depressed mothers' inability to enter into social contingency play with their infants.

This hypothesis has further implications. Perhaps core sense of self and other are both exaptive consequences of infant-mother contingency play at 2–6 months. Generalizing this thought, I suggest that core sense of self and other, and perhaps many more equally fundamental and equally essential aspects of human nature, mind, and cognition, are accidental (though undeniably important) byproducts of a functional need to have play emerge in earlier ontogeny, in ways that serve functionally to develop play itself. This argument might sound like a biologist's cavalier attempt at curmudgeonly debunking of a cognitive-developmental magic kingdom, but I argue that even if my suggestion proves to be correct, every bit of the old magic will still be there, and perhaps even some new magic as well. Tinker Bell lives.

These speculations notwithstanding, the current consensus undeniably offers considerable intuitive appeal. Play's creative spark brings the new into being. "The new" can consist of more complex and more elaborate play in later infancy and in early childhood. "The new" can also consist of intersubjectivity and a core sense of self and other. The early stage of development at which infant-mother contingency play emerges suggests pervasive reshaping and redirection of ontogeny, in effect a new creation. From this cradle, human nature itself emerges in ways long familiar to developmental systems theorists. Intersubjectivity affords relationships with other bodies in shared personhood, relationships with the other persons or selves occupying a given body, and in the relationships that Gregory Bateson envisaged with the ecological world (for older infants and toddlers, a world necessarily and importantly including inanimate objects) and with the other leaves (roots, blossoms, bole) of the tree of life. Play leaps beyond the given and innovatively reenacts the developmental past—a fictionalized autobiography—in each and all possible arenas of human activity, over the entire lifespan. This view of play seems to hold that the dance of play, like the dance (rās līlā) of Krishna with the gopis (Handelman, 1992; Hawley, 1981) and the mystery of the Trinity (Hart, 2003; Hunt, 1977), is the embodied mind's relational, reciprocal, self-referential, musical creation of itself and its intersubjective universe. In its sheer audacity, this global perspective goes far beyond Huizinga. Though questions of mechanism and possible equifinality remain in each arena of interest, the overall picture is very clear in general outline and represents a legitimate challenge to conventional ways of thinking about play and human development.

Conclusion

The chapter offers five major conclusions (numbered) and five important corollaries (indexed by lower-case letters).

1. Play can regulate developmental rates.
   a. Rates of social contingency play in middle infancy are expected to vary across cultures and within cultures over time.
2. Ecological resources affect play. By doing so, they affect development.
3. Rhythm's formative role in human development has ecological bases. From infancy, the structure and qualities of play embody these rhythmic primitives, which constitute a uniquely human style of learning and reveal human predispositions to learn particular kinds of things in particular ways.
   a. Musicality and its underlying rhythms are primitive functions for development of embodied mind and intersubjectivity through self-reference in play, with Hofstadter's strange loops as one possible mechanism.
   b. Musicality and its underlying rhythms construct children's geographies and histories, in part through play.
   c. Learning is strongly efficacious when music and movement are its vehicles. This uniquely human predisposition is most evident in early and middle childhood.

d. Extrapolation of these learning contexts to very different sorts of domains and ages is, however, highly problematic, as indicated by prolonged and acrimonious debates about a possible educational role for the arts.

4. Recycling of play's developmental scaffolding into developmental structures leaves enduring marks, specific and intrinsic to play, on later behavior.

5. Equifinality works both ways. Constraint promotes novelty. Mind is embodied and extended.

6. Fruitful study of the role of play in human development requires both sober caution and bold speculation.

Defining developmental consequences (effects, outcomes, sequelae, etc.) of play is difficult. Assigning proximate benefits and/or costs, of whatever sort, to these consequences is far more difficult. Whether such findings are possible in theory will depend on the specific theory chosen. Whether they are possible in practice depends on the outcomes of negotiated, historically contingent and discipline-dependent standards for scientific evidence and for scientific proof. We can expect profound disagreement between practitioners of experimental and of historical sciences regarding these standards—and developmental psychology is, famously, both an experimental and a historical science.

That play has important roles in human development seems an inescapable conclusion, but convincing evidence remains elusive. Developmental arenas in which play seems to matter range from sense of self, theory of mind, and intersubjectivity to forging armor that helps humanity survive drastic, unexpected change. By far the amplest conception of play is that of a creative force that shapes embodied, extended minds and their domains of discourse from the very small to the very large.

This chapter echoes with many voices of play and of play research. Purposed caution and bold speculation weave a web of polyphony and polysemy that alternates now abruptly, now indistinguishably with cacophony. Enharmonic changes lead into unexpected keys. Promises of resolution take tentative shape, then fade into new and contradictory progressions. The music repeats, but it is never the same.

Future Directions

The power of the comparative method in biology stems precisely from its ability to address both phylogenetic and ecological similarity/difference. Our science would be weak and ineffective in the absence of one or of the other. Correct use of the comparative method will surely yield improved perspectives on human play and development. Nonhuman species other than higher primates offer informative comparative baselines and suggest dimensions along which factors other than recent phlogeny are likely to vary. For example, to compare human play and development with that of bottle-nosed dolphins, elephants, ravens, carnivores, and other intelligent species would offer different kinds of perspectives from those afforded by comparisons involving great apes. And studies of human (including adult human) play with companion animals could offer novel perspectives on roles of play across the human lifespan.

Empirical directions include expanded ethological studies that measure rates of play and play characteristics. Other studies might seek to determine how play varies with nutrition, especially in transitional societies experiencing rapid economic development.

The study of play and development is pluralistic and diverse. British psychology is not American psychology. Continental psychology differs vastly from both. Meritorious research, past and present, of scholars worldwide deserves a fair hearing. Awareness of applicable advances in other disciplines demands further breadth and depth of understanding. Advances in the study of children's geographies and of infants' communicative musicality are two compelling cases in point. *Lector, si monumentum requiris, circumspice* ("Reader, if you seek a monument, look around you.").

Geography and musicology are now irreversibly polynational. Nigel Osborne (2009), for example, cites uniquely important work in music theory from the former East Bloc countries. These studies, he correctly remarks, are still virtually unknown in the West. Likewise, the exceptional depth, vigor, and originality of Russian evolutionary and geographical research remained largely unknown in the West until relatively recently, though informed Western scholars gleaned early intimations of this richness from pre-Revolutionary sources (e.g., Beketov, Kessler, Przhevalsky, Grum-Grzhimailo, Potanin, Potanina) and from Vladimir Nabokov's writings. Exploring new directions in the study of play and human development demands global perspectives.

Another future need is science media reform and responsible reporting in psychology, especially at its interfaces with biology and with brain science. Need I say more?

New theoretical directions can reshape the study of human play and development. Scaffolding recycles. Equifinality works both ways: Other behaviors may compensate for lack of play, but play may likewise compensate for lack of other behaviors. And the current fuss about embodied mind and communicative musicality may well be worth taking seriously. Suppose dancelike rhythmicity and musicality truly are primary sources of human nature. Suppose early infant-adult play is in fact the royal road to understanding early development. Suppose persons are indeed distributed across and within bodies, over time and over space. In this scenario, the study of all play and of all development takes on an entirely new shape. And what of play, self-reference, and consciousness?

An empirical smoking gun or two would make the claim of an ongoing revolution in the study of play and development far more credible. Arguably, microanalyses of human infant-adult play, with its shared, face-to-face delight, might in fact correspond to the gazes through telescopes and microscopes that ultimately brought forth the Copernican Revolution and the Enlightenment. The latest flood of potential changes feels overwhelming because so much is simultaneously involved—embodied minds, self-reference, strange loops, the deep rhythms and impulses of something primal and human that is clearly almost, but not quite like dance and music—intersubjectivity, persons that are more than individuals—the list goes on and on. No one could be blamed for feeling dizzy. It is all just too much, too fast, and perhaps too soon.

But a fundamentally new worldview may well define future directions in the study of play and development. In a possible future metaphysics, meaning, relationship, and play may be the primary factors from which all else necessarily follows. Contemporary perspectives are already taking this route. That information is more fundamental than matter and energy as a key governing principle for mind and the universe has already gained some currency. The idea that interaction is pervasive is no longer surprising. And some sort of creative, symmetry-breaking process, whether we call it play, ideas, or fashion and frivolity, has long been felt necessary to complete the picture of what would otherwise be a lifelessly static universe populated by inert minds.

If the concept of information is not sufficient, then meaning must be essential, as many have already argued. Likewise, interaction will not suffice. Rather, relationship is the key to understanding phenomena like intersubjectivity. Play is the inevitable, necessary third pillar of a worldview whose other two pillars are meaning and relationship,

Author's note

I thank Rebecca Salsman for pointing out the effectiveness of musical and movement rhythms for children's learning, and Whitney Harding for introducing me to the scholarly discipline of children's geographies.

References

Aitken, S. C. (2001). *Geographies of young people*. London: Routledge.

Aitken, S. C., Lund, R., & Kjørholt, A. T. (Eds.). (2008). *Global childhoods: Globalization, development and young people*. London: Routledge.

Bateson, G. (1963). The role of somatic change in evolution. *Evolution, 17*, 529–539.

Bateson, G. (1972). *Steps to an ecology of mind*. New York: Ballantine Books.

Bateson, G. (1978). *Mind and nature*. New York: Dutton.

Bateson, M. C. (1971). The interpersonal context of infant vocalization. *Quarterly Research Report of the Research Laboratory of Electronics, MIT, 100*, 170–176.

Bateson, M. C. (1975). Mother-infant exchange: The epigenesis of conversational interaction. *Annals of the New York Academy of Sciences, 263*, 101–113.

Bateson, M. C. (1979). The epigenesis of conversational interaction: A personal account of research development. In M. Bullowa (Ed.), *Before speech* (pp. 63–77). Cambridge: Cambridge University Press.

Bateson, P. (2005). The role of play in the evolution of great apes and humans. In A.D. Pellegrini & P.K. Smith (Eds.), *The nature of play* (pp. 13–24). New York: Guilford.

Bateson, P., & Martin, P. (2000). *Design for a life*. New York: Simon and Schuster.

Bateson, P., Mendl, M., & Feaver, J. (1990). Play in the domestic cat is enhanced by rationing the mother during lactation. *Animal Behaviour, 40*, 514–525.

Beaumont, C. W. & Idzikowski, S. (1975). *A manual of the theory and practice of classical theatrical dancing*. New York: Dover Publications.

Beebe, B., Jaffe, J., Feldstein, S., Mays, K., & Alson, D. (1985). The application of an adult dialogue model to mother-infant vocal and kinesic interactions. In F. M. Field & N. Fox (Eds.), *Social perception in infants* (pp. 217–247). Norwood, NJ: Ablex.

Beebe, B., Stern, D.N., & Jaffe, J. (1979). The kinesic rhythm of mother-infant interactions. In A. W. Siegman & S. Feldstein (Eds.), *Of speech and time: Temporal speech patterns in interpersonal contexts* (pp. 23–34). Hillsdale, NJ: Erlbaum.

Bradley, B. S. (2009). Early trios: Patterns of sound and movement in the genesis of meaning between infants. In S. Malloch & C. Trevarthen (Eds.), *Communicative musicality* (pp. 263–280). Oxford: Oxford University Press.

Bråten, S. (Ed.). (2007). *On being moved*. Amsterdam, Netherlands and Philadelphia, PA: John Benjamins Pub.

Bruner, J. S. (1972). Nature and uses of immaturity. *American Psychologist, 27*, 687–708.

Charnov, E. L. (2010). Optimal (plastic) life histories in growing versus stable populations. *Evolutionary Ecology Research,* in press.

Chatwin, B. (1987). *The songlines.* New York: Viking.

Chudacoff, H. P. (2007). *Children at play.* New York: New York University Press.

Clark, S. L., Kreutzberg, J. R., & Chee, F. K. W. (1977). Vestibular stimulation influence on motor development in infants. *Science, 196,* 1228–1229.

Darwin, C. R. (1877). A biographical sketch of an infant. *Mind, 2,* 285–294.

Erikson, E. H. (1977). *Toys and reasons.* New York: Norton.

Eveleth, P. B., & Tanner, J. M. (1990). *Worldwide variation in human growth.* 2nd ed. Cambridge: Cambridge University Press.

Fagen, R. (1981). *Animal play behavior.* New York and London: Oxford University Press.

Fagen, R. (1993). Primate juveniles and primate play. In M. Pereira & L. Fairbanks (Eds.), *Juvenile primates* (pp. 182–196). New York: Oxford University Press.

Fagen, R., & Fagen, J. (2004). Juvenile survival and benefits of play behaviour in brown bears, *Ursus arctos. Evolutionary Ecology Research, 6,* 89–102.

Fagen, R., & Fagen, J. (2009). Play behaviour and multi-year juvenile survival in free-ranging brown bears, *Ursus arctos. Evolutionary Ecology Research, 11,* 1053–1067.

Fein, G. (1984). New wine in old bottles. *New Directions in Child Development, 25,* 71–84.

Gazzaniga, M., Asbury, C., & Rich, B. (2008). *Learning, arts, and the brain. The Dana Consortium report on arts and cognition.* New York and Washington: Dana Press.

Gosso, Y., Otta, E., Salum e Morais, M., Ribiero, F. L., & Bussab, V. S. R. (2005). Play in hunter-gatherer society. In A. D. Pellegrini & P. K. Smith (Eds.), *The nature of play* (pp. 213–253). New York: Guilford Press.

Gould, S. J. (1977). *Ontogeny and phylogeny.* Cambridge, MA: Belknap Press of Harvard University Press.

Gould, S. J. (2002). *The structure of evolutionary theory.* Cambridge, MA: Belknap Press of Harvard University Press.

Guddemi, P. (2007). Foreword: bringing the new into being. *Cybernetics and Human Knowing, 14,* 5–7.

Handelman, D. (1992). Passages to play: Paradox and process. *Play & Culture, 5,* 1–19.

Hart, D. B. (2003). *The beauty of the infinite.* Grand Rapids, MI: Eerdmans.

Hauspie, R. C., Vercauteren, M., & Susanne, C. (1997). Secular changes in growth and maturation: An update. *Acta Paediatrica, Supplement, 423,* 20–27.

Hawley, J. S. (1981). *At play with Krishna.* Princeton, NJ: Princeton University Press.

Hinde, R.A. (1974). *Biological bases of human social behaviour.* New York: McGraw-Hill.

Hinde, R. A. (1997). *Relationships: A dialectical perspective.* Hove, East Sussex: Psychology Press.

Hofstadter, D. (1999). *Gödel, Escher, Bach: an eternal golden braid.* 20th anniversary ed. New York: Basic Books.

Hofstadter, D. (2007). *I am a strange loop.* New York: Basic Books.

Holloway, S. L. & G. Valentine (Eds.). (2000). *Children's geographies: Playing, living, learning.* London: Routledge.

Holt, L. (Ed.). (2010). *Geographies of children, youth and families.* London: Routledge.

Hopkins, P. E. (2010). *Young people, place and identity.* London: Routledge.

Huizinga, J. (1950). *Homo ludens.* Boston, MA: Beacon Press.

Hunt, A. (1997). *The Trinity and the Paschal mystery.* Collegeville, MN: Liturgical Press.

Jambor, T. & J. van Gils (Eds.). (2007). *Several perspectives on children's play.* Antwerp-Apeldoorn: Garant.

Jarvis, M. W. B. (2007). Music, dance, & culture – Building bridges and opening doors. Retrieved September 6, 2009 from Australian Council of State School Organisations (ACSSO) Web site: http://www.acsso.org.au/natconf07/jarvis.pdf

Josipovici, G. (1996). *Touch.* New Haven, CT: Yale University Press.

King, B. (2004). *The dynamic dance.* Cambridge, MA: Harvard University Press.

Knox, E. (2000). *The high jump.* Wellington, N.Z.: Victoria University Press.

Luria, A. R. (1976). *The working brain.* New York: Basic Books.

MacDonald, K. (ed.). (1993). *Parent–child play.* Albany, NY: State University of New York Press.

MacLean, P. D. (1990). *The triune brain in evolution.* New York: Plenum.

Malloch, S., & Trevarthen, C. (Eds.). (2009). *Communicative musicality.* Oxford: Oxford University Press.

Manning, M. L. (2006). Play development from ages eight to twelve. In D. P. Fromberg & D. Bergen (Eds.), *Play from birth to twelve,* 2nd ed. New York: Routledge.

Marty, M. E. (2007). *The mystery of the child.* Grand Rapids, MI: Eerdmans.

Mitchell, R. W. (Ed.). (2002). *Pretending and imagination in animals and children.* Cambridge: Cambridge University Press.

Mitchell, R. W. (2004). Controlling the dog, pretending to have a conversation, or just being friendly? *Interaction Studies, 5,* 99–129.

Mitchell, R. W. & Thompson, N. S. (1986). Deception in play between dogs and people. In R. W. Mitchell & N. S. Thompson (Eds.), *Deception: Perspectives on human and non-human deceit* (pp. 193–204). Albany, NY: State University of New York Press.

Mitchell, R. W. & Thompson, N. S. (1990). The effects of familiarity on dog-human play. *Anthrozoös, 4,* 24–43.

Mitchell, R. W. & Thompson, N. S. (1991). Projects, routines, and enticements in dog-human play. *Perspectives in Ethology, 9,* 189–216.

Mitchell, R. W. & Thompson, N. S. (1993). Familiarity and the rarity of deception: Two theories and their relevance to play between dogs (*Canis familiaris*) and humans (*Homo sapiens*). *Journal of Comparative Psychology, 107,* 291–300.

Osborne, N. (2009). Towards a chronobiology of musical rhythm. In S. Malloch & C. Trevarthen (Eds.), *Communicative musicality* (pp. 545–564). Oxford: Oxford University Press.

Oyama, S. (2000). *The ontogeny of information.* 2nd ed. Durham, NC: Duke University Press.

Oyama, S., Griffiths, P. E., & Gray, R.D. (Eds.). (2002). *Cycles of contingency* . Cambridge, MA: MIT Press.

Papoušek, M., & Papoušek, H. (1981). Musical elements in the infant's vocalization: their significance for communication, cognition, and creativity. *Advances in Infancy Research, 1,* 163–224.

Pellegrini, A. (2009). *The role of play in human development.* New York: Oxford University Press.

Pellis, S.M., & Pellis, V.C. (2009). *The playful brain.* Oxford: Oneworld Publications.

Portmann, A. (1941). Die Tragzeiten der Primaten und die Dauer der Schwangerschaft beim Menschen: ein Problem der vergleichen Biologie. *Revue Suisse de Zoologie, 48*, 511–518.

Portmann, A. (1945). Die Ontogenese des Menschen als Problem der Evolutionsforschung. *Verhandlungen der Schweizeschen Naturforschenden Gesellschaft, 125*, 44–53.

Power, T. G. (2000). Play and exploration in children and animals. Mahwah, NJ: Erlbaum.

Rooney, N. J., Bradshaw, J. W. S., & Robinson, I. H. (2000). A comparison of dog-dog and dog-human play behaviour. *Applied Animal Behaviour Science, 66*, 235–248.

Rooney, N. J., Bradshaw, J. W. S., & Robinson, I. H. (2001). Do dogs respond to play signals given by humans? *Animal Behaviour, 61*, 715–722.

Rooney, N. J., Bradshaw, J. W. S., & Robinson, I. H. (2002). An experimental study of the effects of play upon the dog-human relationship. *Applied Animal Behaviour Science, 75*, 161–176.

Rosenzweig, M. L. (1995). *Species diversity in space and time.* New York: Cambridge Univ. Press.

Ross, M.D., Menzler, S., & Zimmermann, E. (2008). Rapid facial mimicry in orangutan play. *Biology Letters, 4*, 27–30.

Sacks, O. (2007). *Musicophilia.* New York: Random House and London: Picador.

Sander, L. W., Amadei, G., & Bianchi, I. (2008). *Living systems, evolving consciousness, and the emerging person.* New York: Analytic Press.

Sharpe, L.L., Clutton-Brock, T.H., Brotherton, P.N.M., Cameron, E.Z., and Cherry, M.I. (2002). Experimental provisioning increases play in free-ranging meerkats. *Animal Behaviour, 64*, 113–121.

Sheets-Johnstone, M. (1990). *The roots of thinking.* Philadelphia, PA: Temple University Press.

Sheets-Johnstone, M. (1992). *Giving the body its due.* Albany, NY: State University of New York Press.

Sheets-Johnstone, M. (1999). *The primacy of movement.* Amsterdam, Netherlands and Philadelphia, PA: John Benjamins Pub.

Sheets-Johnstone, M. (2009). *The corporeal turn.* Bramford Speke, Exeter, UK and Charlottesville, VA: Imprint Academic.

Smith, E.F.S. (1991). Early social development in hooded rats (*Rattus norvegicus*): A link between weaning and play. *Animal Behaviour, 41*, 513–524.

Smith, P. K. (1988). Children's play and its role in early development: A re-evaluation of the "play ethos." In A. D. Pellegrini (Ed.), *Psychological bases for early education* (pp. 207–226). New York: Wiley.

Spinka, M., Newberry, R.C., & Bekoff, M. (2001). Mammalian play: Training for the unexpected. *Quarterly Review of Biology, 76*, 141–168.

Stern, D. N. (1971). A micro-analysis of mother-infant interaction: Behaviors regulating social contact between a mother and her 3½-month-old twins. *Journal of the American Academy of Child Psychiatry, 10*, 501–517.

Stern, D.N. (1974a). The goal and structure of mother-infant play. *Journal of the American Academy of Child Psychiatry, 13*, 402–421.

Stern, D.N. (1974b). Mother and infant at play: the dyadic interaction involving facial, vocal and gaze behaviors. In M. Lewis & L. Rosenblum (Eds.), *The effect of the infant on its caregiver* (pp. 187–213). New York: Wiley.

Stern, D. N. (1977). *The first relationship.* Cambridge, MA: Harvard University Press.

Stern, D. N. (1985). *The interpersonal world of the infant.* New York: Basic Books.

Stern, D. N. (2004). The present moment in psychotherapy and everyday life. New York: Norton.

Stern, D. N., & Gibbon, J. (1979). Temporal expectancies of social behaviors in mother-infant play. In E. B. Thoman (Ed.), *Origins of the infant's social responsiveness* (pp. 409–429). Hillsdale, NJ: Erlbaum.

Stewart, M. (2006). *The courtier and the heretic.* New York: Norton.

Sutton-Smith, B. (1997). *The ambiguity of play.* Cambridge, MA: Harvard University Press.

Sutton-Smith, B. (2005). Play as a fantasy of emergency. In J. E. Johnson, J. F. Christie, & F. Wardle, *Play, development, and early education* (pp. xiii–xv). Boston, MA: Pearson Education.

Thornburg, H. (1979). *The bubblegum years.* Tucson, AZ: H.E.L.P. Books.

Todes, D. P. (1989). Darwin without Malthus: The struggle for existence in Russian evolutionary thought. New York and Oxford: Oxford University Press.

Toth, L., Gacsi, M., Topai, J., & Miklosi, A. (2008). Playing styles and possible causative factors in dogs' behaviour when playing with humans. *Applied Animal Behaviour Science, 114*, 473–484.

Trivers, R. (1985). *Social evolution.* Menlo Park, CA: Benjamin/Cummings.

van Schaik, C. P., van Noordwijk, M., & Wich, S.A. (2006). Innovation in wild Bornean orangutans (*Pongo pygmaeus wurmbii*). *Behaviour, 143*, 839–876.

Van Valen, L. (1973). Festschrift. *Science, 180*, 488.

Wilson, F. (1998). *The hand.* New York: Pantheon.

The History of Children's Play in the United States

Howard P. Chudacoff

Abstract

Children's play, defined as non-obligatory activity, has often been a contested endeavor between adults, who, in their capacity as teachers and protectors, have tried to guide children toward productive pastimes and the younger generation who, in their quest for autonomy, have tried to fashion their own ways of amusement. This essay focuses on the "latent" period of childhood, ages six to twelve, when play is often regarded as the special "work" of children. Four contexts of play—environment, materials, playmates, and risk-freedom—are examined over five chronological periods—colonial America, early nineteenth century, late nineteenth century, early twentieth century, the most recent past. Changes and continuities have characterized all contexts and all periods, but the general trend has been toward increased adult control of children's activities and diminished opportunities for unstructured, independent play.

Key words: play, play site, toys and playthings, playmates, autonomy, appropriation, incorporation, transformation

Introduction

Early in the nineteenth century, Catherine Elizabeth Havens, nine-year-old daughter of a New York merchant, wrote in her diary, "I don't think grownup people understand what children like." Catherine liked to play, to amuse herself in her own way, but it seemed to her that adults were always interfering (Havens, in Berger & Berger, 1966, p. 219). Maria Kraus-Bolte, however, the nineteenth century educator and founder of the kindergarten movement in the United States, expressed a different view, the kind of outlook that provoked Catherine's complaint. "American children," she declared, "must be taught *how to play*" (Kraus-Bolte, in Mergen, 1982, p. 57) (emphasis hers). To Kraus-Bolte, play was too important to be left to children's own designs; adult intervention was necessary. These two points of view represent a generational tension that has characterized the history of children's play in the

United States from colonial times to the present, a history characterized by change as well as continuity.

For over a century, experts have believed children's play to be serious business, often identifying it not only as the one activity common to all children but also as essential to a variety of developmental qualities of physical, social, and emotional growth and maturity. Consequently, adults—parents, teachers, clergy, psychologists, and others—have consistently tried to direct children's play toward what they, the adults, believed to be positive outcomes. But even the older generation has admitted that self-structured play can define the main joy of childhood, a means whereby, under the right conditions, youngsters independently learn and adapt through self-expression, risk-taking, and interaction. Play, as Johan Huizinga pointed out, is not ordinary; it is in many ways an expression of freedom (Huizinga, 1955, pp. 8–9). And the quest for freedom, the longing for autonomy, has characterized children's behavior throughout American history.

This essay will be less concerned with a formal definition of play than with its role in children's lives and the contested definitions that arose between generations—the differences between Catherine Havens and Maria Kraus-Bolte. Certainly play consists of amusing activities that provide behavioral, social, intellectual, and physical rewards. But also there is a particular non-obligatory quality of play best expressed when Mark Twain has Tom Sawyer explain near the beginning of *The Adventures of Tom Sawyer* that "Work consists of whatever a body is *obliged* to do. Play consists of whatever a body is not obliged to do" (Twain, 1875, p. 33). The following examination, which utilizes diaries and autobiographies as well as standard primary and secondary sources, focuses on children of a certain age cohort, that of years six through twelve, the period that Freud labeled "latency" and that Erikson identified as characterized by a crisis of competency and transition from the world of home to the world of peers (Erikson, 1950, p. 72). It is, and has been, a time in which gender and age structure a child's life and a time in which play takes on special meaning as the "work" of childhood.

Any analysis of children's play in American history—in fact, in all of human history—must take into account the reality that until very recently most youngsters in the age group six-to-twelve worked. Some may have been employed, but the great majority engaged in activities that contributed to the family economy by working in the fields, in the home, and in the streets. Moreover, variations have existed, not only across time periods but also according to various categories such as region, socioeconomic status, race, ethnicity, and, especially, gender. Nevertheless, children also have played in similar ways, not just in a distinct "play time" but also on stolen times in which they intermingled games, songs, and other amusements into their labor. These common activities have occurred within four contexts: the play site; the materials (toys and playthings); the playmates (including solitary play); and the tension between self-constructed and adult-structured play. Though the environments, the things, the playmates, and the scale of freedom have changed over the course of American history, kids have always been kids: sometimes angelic, sometimes devilish, and always wondrous in the unexpected and creative ways they do things, especially the ways they play.

Though, unlike political or economic history, the history of play does not fall into neatly defined chronological periods, the societal context of childhood and its relationship to play can be divided into five eras: the pre-modern period before 1800; the transformational period between about 1800 and 1850; the beginnings of a child-centered society of 1850-1900; the rise of a commercialized childhood between 1900 and 1950; and the modern era of a media-centered and adult structured childhood since 1950. In each period, uninvited intrusions of poverty, disease, injury, abuse, and bondage tempered the carefree existence of many children, and over time the adult impulse for protecting and enriching childhood resulted in ever-expanding management of children's play time. Yet kids of all types in all places never abandon their search for autonomy, and a "dance of generations" (Graff, 1995, p. 11) survived social and economic shifts both inside and outside the family.

Play in Early America

High birthrates, high rates of mortality, and low life expectancy comprised the context of childhood in pre-1800 America. Most colonies were tri-racial, consisting of free and indentured whites, enslaved Africans and African Americans, and native Indians. In spite of frequent infant deaths, most white families had numerous offspring, in part resulting from women's early age at first marriage. Slave women also married formally and informally at young ages, and bore many children. Indians may have had somewhat lower birthrates than whites because native women tended to nurse longer, and numbers of Indian children may have been relatively smaller because Indians suffered high death rates from illness and white violence.

These demographic contexts affected children's lives in several ways. The high death rates meant that even though young people might have lived in large families, they experienced loss of siblings as a fact of life. The death of a parent also was common, while remarriage of a widowed father could add stepsiblings to a child's household. Also, with numerous births occurring across a mother's childbearing years, generational boundaries blurred as older children often helped to rear younger siblings. Within black and white families, private life blended with public supervision, and children worked with adults in the household and in the fields. Obedience to parents, to God, and, for slave and indentured children, to masters and mistresses dictated youngsters' behavior. Indian attitudes toward authority were less severe, allowing native children more independence.

Except in the wealthiest families, most children in all parts of American colonial society were contributors to the household economy, meaning that play, when it happened, often occurred on borrowed or stolen time. To the strictest adults, such as New England Puritans, pure play meant "idling," a nonproductive activity that occurred in "the devil's workshop" (Ilick, 2002, p. 30; Mergen, 1982, pp. 6–8; Calvert, 1992, p. 50). Yet, there was some recognition of orderly, functional play; that is, play that suited adult needs and interests for cultivating reverence and cooperation. Moreover, what might have appeared as idling to the older generation could mean true enjoyment to youngsters. "Rambling" in forests, swimming and fishing in ponds and streams, sledding down hillsides, rolling hoops across meadows, and many more outdoor activities were common ways that children appropriated natural play sites for their own amusement. Slave children blended singing games and informal competitions into their labor, and Indian boys practiced hunting on inanimate targets. Indoors, children made up games and played with cards and dolls,

Playthings in these unstructured pastimes were mostly improvised. A few toys, often imported, such as dolls, doll furniture, miniatures, wagons, and puzzles could be found in wealthier households; but objects that children created or appropriated for themselves constituted the most common materials of play. Sticks carved into fishing poles and game pieces, dolls made from corn cobs, pieces of discarded wood utilized to make forts and cabins, and household utensils became play implements. Samuel Goodrich, growing up in Ridgefield, Connecticut, recalled making constant use of his penknife as "a source of great amusement and even recreation" because he could fashion so many playthings with it (Goodrich, 1856, vol. 1, pp. 92–93).

In this early period, play involved interaction with siblings and other family members more than with unrelated peers. There was not much consciousness about what types of play were appropriate for different age groups, and sometimes parents and children amused themselves by playing together. Games such as blindman's bluff and find-the-bean, along with card games and puzzles could occupy an entire family, and joint activities such as reading and singing occurred as well. Invariably, play among children was usually sex-segregated, both by choice and by social prescription. Girls' entertainment with dolls and miniature household items was intended to prepare them for skills they would need as women; boys hunted, raced, and roamed together in their male-only world.

The commonly acknowledged inferior status of children meant that adults accepted a basic responsibility to guide the young toward a moral and obedient adulthood, but children could and did seek to find their own place in the world by engaging in independent play even when retribution loomed. New Englander John Barnard wrote that "I was beaten for my play, and my little roguish tricks," but he indulged in such activity anyway (Barnard quoted in Axtell, 1974, p. 196). Whether roaming through woods, creating fantasies and games with self-fashioned playthings, or idling with others, young people managed to fashion their own play and in a world of hardship and toil endeavored to follow their own inclinations.

Thus, play in these early years occurred within a context of family and community. For all but the wealthiest, children participated in a requisite home economy in which they were less miniature adults than adults-in-training. Yet they were at times able to create their own play culture of games, improvised toys, engaging with siblings, and interacting with nature. Always reminded of their obligations to obey parents and God, they also found ways to follow their own inclinations.

Play in the Early Nineteenth Century

Many of the factors that characterized the social context of childhood before 1800 remained in place in the first half of the nineteenth century. Birth rates and mortality rates remained high, and the family's need for children's labor, both slave and free, restricted time for amusement. Yet, the expansion of market economies in preindustrial America effected changes that began to impinge on youngsters' lives in important ways. As new labor patterns began to separate place of work from place of residence, the household became the sanctuary of women. Mothers assumed greater responsibilities for protecting children's innocence, and school attendance, though not yet compulsory, increasingly occupied children's daily lives. Slave children, trapped between the embrace of their biological family and the authority of their owners, still lived under difficult conditions. But in society at large, influences from the Enlightenment about the innocence and wholesomeness of children helped to spread new attitudes about the need for sheltering the young in ways that included a greater tolerance for play and toys.

As they had done in previous generations, children continued to appropriate the home and the outdoors as their sites for self-amusement. New domestic architectural features such as attics, cellars, and, among families with means, children's own bedrooms, offered play spaces that were removed from parental monitoring. But more than household spaces, youngsters utilized places beyond the home: barns, yards, fields, and woods, both for active entertainment and private reverie. Henry Wright, raised on the New York frontier, loved to roam the woods with his dog and "feel myself shrouded in forest darkness" (Wright, in Jones, 1965, p. 107). Slave children as well as free found enjoyment in nature. William Flannagan recalled that in his boyhood on a plantation in Simpson County, Mississippi, "All us had to amuse us wuz what us found in de woods, wid de trees, streams, an' de hillsides" (Flannagan, vol. 6, pp. 222–24). As increasing numbers of youths grew up in cities, they discovered new environments for play: stoops, sheds, docks, and stables where they ventured without regard for trespass.

Formal toys remained scarce, so children applied inventiveness to their play objects. Sometimes, they made facsimiles of conventional toys that their families could not afford: hoops, sleds, hobbyhorses, boats, and dolls fashioned from a wide variety of resources. Discarded home implements and clothing offered particular appeal. Jeannette Leonard Gilder, forced by family poverty to grow up in the household of an aunt in New Jersey, found joy in such objects as a broken cookstove, an unused bureau, and a discarded doll. "These were my greatest treasures," she announced, "because I could really use them" (Gilder, 1901, p. 96). Mary Crosby recalled from her childhood in New York City, "My mother had preserved various bonnets of different fashions from the extremely large to the extremely small... these always created great amusement" (Crosby in Dargan and Zeitlin, 1990, p. 122).

Though some wealthier youngsters were herded into formal groupings such as literary societies and lyceums, the most accessible play partners remained siblings and other relatives, and the vast majority of play activities remained sex-segregated. Considerable evidence exists, mostly from the narratives collected from former slaves by the Works Progress Administration during the 1930s, that in the South, white and black kids played together, at least up to a certain age, usually around ten. Generally, the unstructured, informal quality of play groups meant that there was consistency in playmates. Environments might change, but youngsters usually played with the same people: siblings, cousins, neighbors.

Notions that children entered the world with innate wickedness were fading from their eighteenth century prevalence, but adults were no less attentive to steering the younger generation away from idleness. And youngsters were, if anything, more intent on loosening the reins on their activities. An upsurge in prescriptive literature advised parents to guide their offspring into games, hobbies, and other activities that cultivated "habits of order and arrangement." Harvey Newcomb, a widely read author of advice manuals, allowed that there was "no more harm in the play of children than in the skipping of lambs." Yet, he prescribed sixteen rules for play behavior and advocated that play promote "Christian duty" (Newcomb, 1847, pp. 10–11, 182–83). Such habits included mimicking adult activity in domestic and breadwinning functions. But alternatives, even defiance, were not far away, even when consequences might be unwelcome. Maine native Brown Thurston filled his journal with references to independent efforts at amusement: He attended the circus against his father's wishes, escaped his aunt's supervision to learn how to chew tobacco, and nearly drowned while playing with a friend on a homemade raft. Future naturalist John Muir mused in reflection, "No punishment, however sure and severe, was of any avail against attractions of the fields and woods" (Thurston, n.d., n.p.; Muir, 1913, p. 48). Risk and autonomy were as much a part of childhood as obedience and restraints.

By 1850, the playful rather than the sinful quality of childhood was winning acceptance, so that children's self-structured play was receiving a more widespread stamp of approval—so long as such play respected adult prerogatives for controlling the younger generation. As production of goods moved increasingly out of the home, the domestic environment offered more opportunities for play, and children like Jeanette Gilder, Brown Thurston, and John Muir were quick to seize them.

Play in the Late Nineteenth Century
Between 1850 and 1900, demographic and economic transition altered American childhood. Birth rates dropped; place of work separated from place of residence; a consumer society emerged, a new middle class arose, school attendance began to become compulsory, and age-based peer cultures became common. Professional experts in fields of education and psychology began urging intervention in children's lives not only to ensure appropriate learning and character development but also to shield youngsters from supposedly harmful influences of urban-industrial society. Sheltering kids in schools and playgrounds became a widespread goal,

reflecting both the experts' protective motives and their lack of trust in parents' abilities. Thus a New York reformer could declare,

> "That which parents do not or cannot control in the private sphere of the home, the city must control in the public spheres of park, playground, schools, and recreation centers"
> (*Frost & Woods*, 1998, pp. 232–33).

More than before, happiness came to be accepted as a particular quality of childhood, with the result that play as well as education and protection became desired goals. The availability of mass-produced toys, games, dolls, and books increased dramatically after the Civil War, transforming commercialized playthings from instruments of instruction to items to produce joy.

Play environments shifted as the urban-built environment offered new sites and material. Nature still gave youngsters sites for "roaming," and domestic spaces still could be appropriated for games and fantasies. But now, paved streets, better lighting, telephone poles, fire hydrants, and fences increased hazards but also provided opportunities for playful inventiveness. As future editor and critic Henry Seidel Canby recalled, the yards and streets of his native Wilmington, Delaware, offered a "series of city states to play in," and vacant lots could be transformed into a "true frontier…" Anthropologist Stewart Culin observed how city kids utilized lampposts and trees for their invented games (Canby, 1934, p. 35; Culin, 1891, p. 230).

The sheltered-child model increasingly included commercial toys as a means of occupying time. In an appeal to parents as toy providers, manufacturers used bright colors and patriotic themes for games, tops, and miniature vehicles. In an age of fascination with technology, doll manufacturers fashioned their products with mechanical movements, though some female manufacturers such as Martha Jenks Chase of the M.J. Chase Doll Company created more realistic dolls that were soft and flexible. However, though children played with new dolls and achieved expanded mobility with newly minted bicycles, they continued to improvise playthings from objects appropriated from nature, the household, and the streets. John Albee, for example, used "all movable objects" as toys, including his mother's knitting needles which, as a sword, could "slay a thousand foes at one stroke…"(Albee, 1910, pp. 42–43).

Increasingly, children played in same-sex peer groups, usually defined by associations at school and in neighborhoods. Such patterns of play not only grouped together youngsters of the same age but also fomented peer-influenced socialization that widened the gulf between generations. Thus Ethel Spencer, raised in Pittsburgh in the late nineteenth century, observed that her adult relatives were less important to her childhood than were "friends of our own age with whom we played every day" (Spencer in Weber & Stearns, 1983, p. 58). Some girls expressed resentment at being excluded from play with boys; Californian Loretta Berner wrote later in her life that "At the age of nine, I was sorry I was a girl because [like boys] I too wanted to be roam the world free as a bird" (Berner, 1970, p. 2). But most children seemed content to involve themselves with their own gender. In addition, however, the proliferation of commercial games and other toys made playing alone more appealing to many kids.

Like their predecessors, children of this era tried to express their autonomy by eluding adult supervision. Adults split on how, whether, and how much to tolerate this independent behavior. Some educators and psychologists subscribed to a view that children's judgment was too undeveloped to allow leeway to what they did, while others cautioned that a child's "play instinct" was a healthy characteristic that should be cultivated by the child herself or himself. Psychologist T. R. Crosswell was one of several social scientists who undertook detailed study of unstructured play by preadolescents and concluded that such activity had beneficial effects. To the surprise of many, Crosswell discovered that these youngsters preferred games and toys that they created themselves to the playgrounds and toys created for them by adults (Crosswell, 1899, p. 6). On their part, children used self-structured play to explore their environment and learn from others and from their own experiments. At times this behavior included risk-taking and misbehavior, especially among boys but occasionally among girls as well. Kids climbed trees, dove into ponds, grabbed free rides on streetcars, and played pranks, most of which was harmless, though occasionally resulted in property damage or injury. Though parents undertook efforts to safeguard young people, there were as yet few institutional measures such as consumer protection laws and police efforts to stifle risky behavior; children's amusement often was left to their own devices.

As the nineteenth century closed, adults exhibited increasing ambivalence about how much freedom children should have in their expanding unstructured time. Guidance toward productive behavior remained pervasive and a sheltered model of childhood became more pervasive, but new attitudes reflected indulgence and appreciation for the skills and self-regulation that youngsters might accomplish when adults backed off from strict supervision and the notion of fun as an entitlement for children acquired new credence. Never far removed, however, adults were poised to enter the child's world in new ways after the new century began.

A Golden Age of Play?

The history of American children's play in the early twentieth century is bounded by two important phenomena: the onset of child-saving during the Progressive Era just after 1900 and the appropriation of children's culture by television in the mid-1950s. During these years, adults made powerful incursions into play life, yet, paradoxically, children made successful assertions of play independence. Attitudes about the social roles of young people reflected full flower of the sheltered model of childhood, in which the state and its institutions, as well as parents, set apart children by age and status and channeled them toward a protected physical, intellectual, and emotional development. American society became more child centered, removing children from work responsibilities, passing laws to make sure they attended and stayed in school, and giving them more time and opportunities for play. At the same time, professional child study and child saving promoted the idea that youngsters should not lose their"play instinct." Indulgence was not the result; children's activities needed to tailored to the demands of living in a consumer-oriented, technological society. Still, youngsters conspired alternative modes of action, using new freedoms and new playthings for their own purposes.

Heightened concern with protecting children from harmful influences resulted in imposed limitations on play sites. Playgrounds became the major tool for removing kids from city streets, but children did not accept playgrounds with the enthusiasm that reformers expected. Surveys revealed that kids visited playgrounds once or twice, then, voting with their feet against unwanted supervision, returned to their informal play environments. As one eleven-year-old testified, "I can't go to the playgrounds now. They get on my nerves with so many men and women around telling you what to do" (Rosenzweig, 1983, p. 151). Similar rebellions occurred around the expanding toy box. A few toys became highly popular: scientific and construction toys for boys; realistic baby dolls and fashion-oriented paper dolls for girls. But instead of adopting these "educational" and preparation-for-adult playthings, youngsters frequently expressed greater desire for fantasy toys and dolls inspired by radio, comics, and movies involving characters such as Shirley Temple, Mickey Mouse, and Dick Tracy. Moreover, especially among youngsters from low-income households but also among those more advantaged, improvised playthings, more than commercial toys, absorbed play time. Thus humorist Sam Levenson, who grew up in an urban immigrant family, recalled,

> "ashcan covers were converted into Roman shields, oatmeal boxes into telephones, combs covered with tissue paper into kazoos… candlesticks into trumpets, orange crates into store counters…"

and many more ways of appropriation and transformation (Levenson, 1967, p. 83).

In these years, sex-segregated play became an especially prominent factor in the lives of preteens of all socioeconomic ranks. Boy culture flourished in an independent, alternative world where values of loyalty and competitiveness prevailed. Sports were especially predominant in their physical games and in board games also. Girls, for their part, predictably engaged in gender-prescribed activities, dressing up, playing with dolls, and engaging in singing games. But unstructured active play was also characteristic; riding bicycles, playing tag games, and skating were common for both girls and boys. The rhyming jump-rope game of double dutch, fostered among urban African American girls, was especially popular. Importantly, the independent, mutual play of peers among both boys and girls fortified the elements of a separate pre-teen children's culture and widened the gap between generations.

As in previous eras, youngsters used unstructured play in their quest for autonomy. Steeped more than ever in peer culture and able to escape into a variety of environments at home and in their neighborhoods, children dodged adult control to a greater extent than those of previous generations. Most of the time, they were "good," but they could also be devious. Future Texas Congresswoman and African American feminist Barbara Jordan lived with strict grandparents but admitted that sometimes "I would sneak around—I mean literally sneak out" to play with friends (Jordan & Hearon, 1979, p.122). Such behavior involved risks and misbehavior: petty thievery, swimming and skating in unsafe ponds, exploring storm sewers and abandoned buildings. Such secret activities formed a cherished part of modern childhood. As writer Robert Paul Smith reflected,

> "When we were kids, we had the sense to keep these things to ourselves. We didn't go around asking grownups questions about them. They obviously didn't know"
> (*Smith*, 1957, pp. 40–41).

There can be no doubt that events beyond their control intruded on children's lives and affected their play. Two world wars sandwiched around extended years of economic hardship imposed limitations on the things and time that many children had available to them for play. Yet diaries, journals, and autobiographies of children who grew up in those times suggest that kids in all socioeconomic categories had just as much, perhaps even more, opportunity to just be kids than their counterparts of previous generations. Their independent play, combined with the expanded opportunities for appropriating play sites, the new cornucopia of commercial toys, and the creative ways of improvising playthings arguably made the first half of the twentieth century a golden age of play. This scene would soon change dramatically.

Commercialization and Co-optation of Children's Play

The debut of *The Mickey Mouse Club* television show in 1955 was a landmark event not only because it was the first television show aimed directly at preadolescent children but also because one of its sponsors was the Mattel Toy Company. Previously, toy manufacturers advertised their products mainly at Christmas time if at all. Now, however, Mattel marketed its products—first a ping-pong-ball-shooting "burp gun" and later Barbie dolls and other classic playthings—every weekday. Moreover, by advertising on *The Mickey Mouse Club*, Mattel aimed its pitch directly at children, cultivating their demand for its products. As one analyst later defined the goal for Mattel and subsequent other toy companies, "The trend is for children to get more decision making authority and exercise that authority at younger and younger ages" (Rancese, 1985, p. 121).

Mattel and its counterparts knew what they was doing because in the two decades after World War II, a Baby Boom markedly increased the American population of youngsters, marching a huge generation of consumers into the market. By 1960, there were more than 33 million Americans ages five to fourteen, an increase of 37 percent in ten years and constituting 18 percent of the nation's total population. Some kids could afford more than others, but everywhere play became associated with toys. Also, more than ever, peer-oriented activity consumed children's time. Numbers of preteens dropped somewhat in the 1970s and 1980s as the Baby Boom subsided, but by then a new factor affected children's lives: mothers entered the workforce in increasing numbers. By 1999, 78 percent of mothers of kids ages six to thirteen were employed. The result was that direct, at virtually all socioeconomic levels, parental supervision of play diminished, replaced by adult-structured, out-of-the-home activities such as sports leagues, non-academic lessons, and youth clubs.

Two goals—some would say obsessions—have thus characterized adult control of children's play in the past several decades: protections and enrichment. Terrified by the polio epidemic of the early 1950s, parents kept offspring away from swimming pools, summer camps, and even from playmates. Subsequently, childcare experts and journalists fixated on protecting youngsters from every possible threat and hazard, and the Consumer Product Safety Commission, created in 1972, increasingly focused on safeguarding children from "unsafe" playground equipment, toys, and clothing. Moreover, sensationalized media publicity of child deaths and abuse frightened parents into preventing activities such as unsupervised neighborhood play and even confining youngsters to the house where they could amuse themselves in front of a TV set or computer screen. Beyond shielding children from a threatening environment, middle-class parents also added an impulse for equipping their offspring for success in postmodern society. They wanted the younger generation to be better than average in all things and tried to provide them with professionally run out-of-school pursuits and materials that would expand children's minds, tone their bodies, develop physical skills, and enhance self-esteem.

These trends effected a major shift in the play environment. The disappearance of open space in cities, coupled with safety concerns in suburbs and cities, constricted the number of play sites for preteens, often increasing indoor play even in good weather. Tightened adult control of play gave rise to indoor, air-conditioned "pay-for-play" sites and "child entertainment centers" for those who could afford the price of admission. Computer games and Internet play also expanded the hours of indoor play. Aided by marketing directed at kids, indoor toys and games became part of a larger complex that combined toys, movies, TV programs, and books symbiotically. Such media phenomena as Harry Potter, "Transformers," Spiderman, and Barbie spawned back stories that accompanied new toys. Youngsters from low-income families might not have been able to afford these toys—or at least not as many of them—yet manufacturers made cheaper, knock-off versions.

The shifting environment and new play activities have altered the composition of play groups. As residential areas—suburban neighborhoods as well as urban apartment complexes—became more impersonal, the importance of neighborhood "gangs" (units of playmates) diminished, replaced by more fluid assemblages. A nine-year-old now might be involved with one set of kids on a soccer team, another in an art class, and another on a school bus. Informal play is more likely to occur in a group of two or three rather than the choosing-up of sides for an impromptu game. As well, indoor, media-related play has increased time spent in solitary, sedentary play. As in the past, however, most play groups remain sex-segregated, especially in later preteen years.

Though increasingly herded into structured activities, children still find ways to conspire independent ways of playing. When beyond watchful eyes, they sometimes take risks, testing physical abilities that may result in newfound confidence but also lead to skinned knees or bruises. Tree-climbing, balancing on a ledge, running up a slide instead of gliding down, playing games in prohibited areas, just "goofing around," and many more acts of defiance continue to define children's guerilla tactics for seizing their own play. Occasionally, more serious consequences occur, especially when youngsters get access to power tools, medications, or firearms. Parents and teachers thus face a quandary in determining how much supervision and risk aversion they should assume.

By the beginning of the twenty-first century, the swift and pervasive rise of electronic media dominated fantasy play and gave children of all socioeconomic statuses the contexts for much of their play. At the same time, however, adults leaned more toward control than toward freedom, intervening in children's lives to structure their time away from school in adult-supervised activities, especially sports. While children of the present have had more influence over their own consumer choices than earlier generations

of youngsters, adults now dictate children's play activities more extensively than in the past.

Conclusion

The history of children's play in America features both change and continuity. Environments have shifted from the informal and natural to the formal and supervised. Toys have become ever more elaborate, especially as electrification and software have come to characterize many playthings. The composition of play groups was altered by the rising importance of peer groups. And adult-structured activity has diminished opportunities for free, unstructured play. Yet continuities persist. Kids still find ways to appropriate their own play sites, incorporate and transform a multitude of objects into playthings, and conspire ways to elude adult management. Most of all, they learn how to adapt through their play to two different worlds, the one created by adults and the one they inhabit by themselves. Author and critic William Dean Howells perhaps said it best when recollecting his childhood in small-town Ohio in the 1840s. In one part of that childhood, Howells earnestly engaged with his parents, sharing with them his "world of foolish dreams." But he also played in another half, in which he "swam and fished, and hunted, and ran races, and played tops and marbles, and squabbled and scuffled in the Boy's Town" (Howells, 1890, p. 177). More recently, Kate Simon, daughter of immigrant parents living in New York City, recalled how she climbed and fell off ledges but never told her parents, and her confession in her autobiography illuminates much about children's culture when she wrote, "I was... practiced in the hypocrisies of being a good girl" (Simon, 1982, pp. 4–5). That ability to find fun in a "town" of boys or girls, exclusive of adults, is and has been what is wondrous about children's play.

Future Directions

– How, if at all, has socioeconomic status influenced environments, playthings, playmates and freedom of children's play?

– To what extent has race been an influencing factor?

– Will efforts to restore more outdoor and free play for children be successful?

– Have current computer-oriented games made American children more sedentary and contributed to childhood obesity?

– Was there ever a "golden age" of children's play in America?

Author's note

Material for this essay has been drawn from Howard P. Chudacoff, *Children at Play: An American History* (New York: New York University Press, 2007).

References

Albee, J. (1910). *Confessions of boyhood*. Boston: Richard G. Badger.

Axtell, J. (1974). *The school upon a hill: Education and society in colonial New England*. New Haven: Yale University Press.

Berner, B. (1970). Sketches from 'way back,' *Los Fierros, 7*.

Calvert, K. (1992). *Children in the house: The material culture of early childhood, 1600–1900*. Boston: Northeastern University Press.

Canby, H. S. (1934). *The age of confidence: Life in the nineties*. New York: Farrar and Rinehart.

Chudacoff, H. (2007). *Children at play: An American history*. New York, NY: New York University Press.

Crosby, M. (1990). Quoted in A. Dargan & S. Zeitlin, *City play*, New Brunswick, NJ: Rutgers University Press.

Cross, G. (1997). *Kids' stuff: Toys and the changing world of American childhood*. Cambridge, MA: Harvard University Press.

Crosswell, T. R. (1899). Amusements of Worcester schoolchildren, *Pedagogical Seminary, 6*.

Culin, S. (1891). Street games of boys in Brooklyn, *Journal of American Folklore, 4*.

Dargan, A. & Zeitlin, S. (1990). *City play*. New Brunswick, NJ: Rutgers University Press.

Erikson, E. (1950). *Childhood and society*. New York: Norton.

Flannagan, W. William Flannagan, in Rawick, Suppl. 1, *Mississippi Narratives*, vol. 6

Formanek-Brunell, M. (1993). *Made to play house: Dolls and the commercialization of American girlhood, 1830–1930*. New Haven, CT: Yale University Press.

Fromberg, D. & Bergen, D., eds. (1998). *Play from birth to twelve and beyond*. New York, NY: Garland.

Frost, J. L. and Woods, I. C. (1998). Perspectives on play in playgrounds," in D. P. Fromberg & D. Bergen, eds., *Play from birth to twelve and beyond*, New York: Garland, 1998.

Gilder, J. L. (1901). *The autobiography of a tomboy*. New York: Doubleday Page.

Goodrich, S. (1856). *Recollections of a lifetime*, 2 vols. New York: Miller, Orton, and Mulligan.

Graff, H. (1995). *Conflicting paths: Growing up in America*. Cambridge, MA: Harvard University Press.

Havens, C. (1966). When I am old and in a remembering mood..., in J. Berger & D. Berger, eds., *Small voices*. New York: Paul S. Eriksson.

Howells, W. D. (1890). *A boy's town*. New York: Harper and Brothers.

Huizinga, J. (1955). *Homo Ludens*. Boston: Beacon Press.

Ilick, J. (2002). *American childhood*. Philadelphia: University of Pennsylvania Press.

Jones, L. C. Ed. (1965). *Growing up in Cooper country: Boyhood recollections of the New York frontier*. Syracuse, NY: Syracuse University Press.

Jordan, B. & Hearon, S. (1979). *Barbara Jordan: A self-portrait*. Garden City, NY: Doubleday.

Kraus-Bolte, M. (1982). In B. Mergen, *Play and playthings: A reference guide*. Westport, CT: Greenwood Press.

Levenson, S. (1967). *Everything but money*. New York: Pocket Books.

Mergen, B. (1982). *Play and playthings: A reference guide*. Westport, CT: Greenwood Press.

Mintz, S. (2004). *Huck's raft: A history of American childhood*. Cambridge, MA: Belknap Press of Harvard University Press.

Muir, J. (1913). *The story of my boyhood and youth*. Boston: Houghton Mifflin Company.

Newcomb, H. (1847). *How to be a man: A book for boys*. Boston: Gould, Kendall, and Lincoln.

Rancese, P. (1983). *American demographic: Trends and opportunities in the children's market*. Ithaca, NY: Cornell University Press.

Rosenzweig, R. (1983). *Eight hours for what we will: Workers and leisure in an industrial city, 1870–1920*. (Cambridge: Cambridge University Press.

Simon, K. (1982). *Bronx Primitive: Portraits in a Childhood*. New York: Vintage.

Smith, R. P. (1957). *"Where did you go?" "Out." "What did you do?" "Nothing"*. New York: W. W. Norton.

Sutton-Smith, B. (1997). *The ambiguity of play*. Cambridge, MA: Harvard University Press.

Sutton-Smith, B. (1979). The play of girls," in C. B. Kopp, Ed. *Becoming female: Perspectives on development*. New York, NY: Plenum Press.

Sutton-Smith, B. (1986). *Toys as culture*. New York, NY: Gardner Press.

Thurston, B. (n.d.) Journal, '834–'893, manuscript collection of the American Antiquarian Society, Worcester, Massachusetts.

Twain, M. (1875). *The adventures of Tom Sawyer*. New York: Harper and Brothers.

Weber, M. P. & Stearns, P. N. (1983). *The Spencers of Amberson Avenue*. Pittsburgh: University of Pittsburgh Press.

West, E. & Petrik P., Eds. (1992). *Small world: Children and adolescents in America, 1850–1900*. Lawrence, KS: University of Kansas Press.

Wright, H. C. (1965). Human life, in L. C. Jones, Ed., *Growing up in Cooper country: Boyhood recollections of the New York frontier*. Syracuse, NY: Syracuse University Press.

The Antipathies of Play

Brian Sutton-Smith

Abstract

This paper argues that history has treated play as a special kind of antipathetic existential duality, characterized often by the notion that play contains both good (fun) and bad (waste of time) elements. So widespread are these antipathetical play dualities in play theories that there is reason to think of all types of play as basically territories for existential affective ambiguities, an approach developed in my prior book *The Ambiguity of Play* (1997). There it is contended that these play dualities (from Kant to Goffman) are functional transcendents beyond the "work ethic" using formulae as positive as those of Huizinga (1944) or as negative as those of Freud (1938). The hypothesis here, therefore, is that these play dualisms, although they are inherently pleasurable, also have an adaptive function mediated primarily by the underlying character of the primary versus secondary emotions in all forms of play as this is inferred from the biology of Damasio (1994,1999, 2030) and the neurology of Fredrickson (1998). In our present account play is seen to balance the antipathetical negative emotional effects of sadness, shock, fear, anger, disgust, and apathy, by regulation through the positive secondary emotions: of pride, empathy, embarrassment, guilt, and shame, all of which become sociological and biological representations underlying the various basic kinds of existential evolutionary struggles for survival presented in this article. It will be shown that this duality of the emotions and their ludic management become the mediators for evolutionary struggles and presumably underlie the issues of reproduction, social power, and territoriality as in Darwin's evolutionary interpretations (1872).

Key words: play, history, emotion, adaptation

Introduction

Let us begin with the impressive fact that in a recent soccer World Cup final, one billion human beings witnessed this football game on television. This presumably may have been more people perceptually engaged at the same time in a common interest than has ever occurred before in human history. Does this mean that such vicarious activity, which I treat as "play," by the audiences is the most important thing in their lives as human beings? Perhaps not, but it certainly means we should attempt to understand why so many humans beings are so universally engaged with such phenomena. Play can hardly be trivial or only for fun if it can be so

engaging to so many people. Particularly as the immediate stadium audiences are often quite "emotional" in their yelling, screaming, and even singing, let alone playing their drums, listening to bands, and watching beatific cheerleaders. I had a U. Penn female student once who told me that the one reason she liked watching University basketball games was that it was the only time she ever really allowed herself to scream and yell. We would say that this was possible for her because these playful expressions were representations (or pretences or semblances) of emotion rather than more direct real life enactments. Play, it seems, is based on representing emotional expressions but only within systems of regulation such as rules, rituals or referees, although these restrictions sometimes break down under the force of the original emotion. This is the latent antipathy which is the focus of this chapter. Considering that some play theorists have said that play is also a very elementary form of civilization (many mammals play) these play antipathies between emotional representations and direct emotional expressions take on considerable importance. We might even say that the issue of what civilization is all about hangs emotionally in the balance.

In *The Ambiguity of Play* (Sutton-Smith, 1997), I listed 130 or so concepts that modern play theorists have seen as connoting the character of play. From this list we can conclude that play is both extremely diverse and often extremely complex. On closer examination, it becomes apparent that the concepts offered about the meanings of play depend in part at least on whether you are a biologist (which means that play is explained as genetically disposed or composed of neurological adaptations or even neurological plasticity), a sociologist (describing play as social skills and gamesmanship), a psychologist (offering multi-functional skill usages), a philosopher (framing play realities as in deterministic, chaotic, existentialist, or as a form of desire), or, finally a folklorist (giving us play as ancient or traditional).

Burghardt, in his notable work, *The Genesis of Animal Play* (2005), tried to integrate these variations into a statement that play is not functional (in the real world), but is typically voluntary, nonserious, repetitive, and relaxed. The problem, however, with all of these connotations, valid as they all are with some kinds of play, is that we can nearly always point to play exceptions of a contrary character. For example, strong-armed baseball and cricket players being very skillful at throwing hand grenades when they are involved in a war. But more problematic is that this concept of play as nonfunctional reflects the older work ethic notion of the term functional (meaning being tied to work). But how can anyone say from today's research that our dreams, or our theater or the arts or the entertainments, or our religion, or even play therapy are not very importantly "functional" in our lives especially when they all typically make us feel so much better about being alive?

It is also clear that what some consider "play" is not completely voluntary, as is the case with coached sports, and that it can also be quite serious, as in major carnivals and hazings. All of which means that it has always been difficult to know how to take the first explanatory step with these theoretical play variegations of many kinds. This has led me to attempt to define play in evolutionary terms as a ferment of adaptive variability which provides a basis at all times for what we might call adaptive potentiation, by which we mean that some forms of play variability are potentially useful in so-called real life. More currently interesting, however, is that throughout play's theoretical history of the past 200 years, many thinkers have seen play as a kind of antipathetical duality of one sort or another. For example, they have often contrasted what they saw as good play with what they saw as bad play, which leads us to examine these various kinds of duality (or antipathy) that has governed theory in the field of play

Good versus Bad Play

In the post-1800 period, the growth of play theories has largely been an unwittingly negative response to prevailing Puritan and industrialist antagonisms towards the uncontrollability of various forms of play, in particular as these were found in adult carnivals, festivals, or childhood nonsense. The origins of these antagonisms has been described most comprehensibly by Barbara Ehrenreich in her book *Dancing in the Streets* (2006), which is the first historical work to provide us with the vivid adult play contexts within which the most exciting engagements with play have been unconsciously embraced during the past several thousand years. She makes us realize that the first quasi-modern context of adult play was represented in the religious battles over the character of group communal festivals which had been features of European life from the Middle Ages. These festivals could be described as events involving shameless dancing with wild abandon and drunken licentiousness, also with painted bodies and faces and grotesque behavior, as well as with shouting and stamping of feet. Such "irrational" festivals were also originally found even within church parodies of conventional respectable life as in "The King of Fools," "The Lord of misrule," and "The Feast of Fools" amazing church customs (Strutt, 1801).

These mass communal and religious trances can even be traced back at least as far as the times of early Christianity as is shown by Baigent (2006). In some interpretations it has been suggested that these ancient mass celebratory trance-like occasions were originally of an empathic social and religious character ultimately derived from the propensity of humans to be able to act as a unified crowd in their own predations or defenses against dangerous other groups of humans or animals. It is said that when primates became terrestrial these needs were the best primate and ultimately human defense. In our more recent ages, however, the development of priestly, business, military, and social class elites has led to ever-developing criticisms of these wild trance-like pursuits, particularly when located within churches.

When festivals were cancelled within churches, they were increasingly left to be occupied by the lower economic level populations outside of churches. And indeed many times as a result of such neglect from the 1600s onwards, these festivals became a political disguise for realistic revolts against higher status elites or even foreign governors. In the 1800s these issues were further encased in the debates over evolution and progress. As a result, it is not surprising that from roughly 1800 onwards many of the major modern European advocates of play have implicitly conceded the existence of a negative "work ethic" by making discriminations between "good" and "bad" play. This implicit if unwitting strategy was perhaps designed to gain some general approval of what many saw as "serious" play by showing that selected forms of play were in fact quite positive, particularly those advocated for children. In the 1800s, to give one example, Froebel with his advocacy of children's kindergarten play as involving variously designed arrangements of blocks, gave great support to the successful notion that children should go to preschool to gain these play forms of progress.

The Antipathetical Roles of Emotions

These seemingly contradictory descriptions can be framed as a potential duality but the most fundamental form of this duality, we will contend, is in terms of the emotional antipathies within play. The reason for this approach is as follows. After a lifetime of authoring or editing a multiplicity of books on play, I was one day struck by the fact that the best empirical collection of all the different possible kinds of traditional child play that I had seen was that compiled by folklorists Iona and Peter Opie in *Lore and Language of School Children*. It was derived from their sources throughout the British Isles. Their book came out in the year 1959, the same year as my own, *The Games of New Zealand Children*, saw the light of day. They covered many more folklorist play topics than I did, for example, with their seeing play: just for fun, wit and repartee, guile, riddles, parody, impropriety, topical rhymes, codes of oral legislation, nicknames and epithets, jeers and torments, half beliefs, children's calendar, occasional

custom as authority and pranks. After some time it occurred to me that I might reduce these and other folklore examples of play to the specific variety of key emotions that were implicit diversely within all of them. I was lead towards an attempt to understand these plays in terms of basic human emotions because it has become clear from recent neuropsychological research that emotions are key neural instruments behind all kinds of behavioral motivation (Ledoux, 1992).

Damage to those areas of the brain in which specific emotions are quartered can leave an individual without any feelings for them at all. Consequently, psychological researchers are now more attentive to the essentially distinctive role of emotional motivations in everyday life, as opposed to the ancient view that emotions are always just something that must be controlled (Wierzbicka, 1999). This led me to the view that it might be useful to see what different roles the emotions might have in these various forms of folk play following the work of the neurologist Antonio Damasio (1994, 1999, 2003). Damasio pointed out and labeled what he calls the primary emotions which he saw as universal forms of human adaptation. These emotions were sadness, shock, fear, anger, disgust, and also happiness. All of these emotions, except happiness, are clearly stress-inducing, so we have added apathy as if it provides the stress to which happiness can be the answer. It is particularly relevant inversely to the form called play "as peak experience," which is a subjective or even narcissistic positive focus on the experiential self. Happiness in general, however, is meant to be an outcome for all of these forms of play.

Most of these basic human emotions, then, are initially stress inducing and relatively uncontrollable. But Damasio also introduces the notion of what he calls secondary emotions, which are those of pride, empathy, embarrassment, guilt, and shame, and they are meant to modulate or regulate the presentations of the primary emotional expressions. Clearly this formulation of the two kinds of emotion describes play as inherently an antipathetical (emotional) phenomenon. The comparative psychological data to support Damasio on the universal presence of these two kinds of basic emotions is to be found in Table 10-1.

Darwin was the first early modern scientist to attempt an identification of these human group emotions. In his book, *The Expression of the Emotions in Man* (1872), Darwin describes these emotions as collective social possessions. The specific emotions that he names include, among others, Damasio's six

Table 10.1 Damasio's Primary and Secondary Emotions

PRIMARY EMOTIONS (Damasio)
Shock, anger, fear, disgust, sadness, and happiness

SECONDARY EMOTIONS
Empathy, pride, envy, embarrassment, guilt, and shame

primary ones. It is also notable that in Ekman's (1992) cross-cultural studies of different peoples' ability to interpret emotions from photos of facial expressions, the emotions said to be most universally perceived are indeed anger, sadness, fear, surprise, disgust, contempt, and happiness, thus validating Damasio. (In the present work, I include Ekman's "contempt" item as a subset of anger.) Further evidence comes from Plutchik (2003). But the primary evidence for the possible value of focusing on these emotions as central for each of my own six play types was the close parallel I found between these six emotions and in what I have called the "rhetorics of play" (Sutton-Smith, 1997). Those rhetorics I had classified: as Surprise, Identity, Fate, Power, Deviance, and Self. While the cultural parallels were not perfect, they were sufficient to suggest that these play types may not be as universal as are the emotions.

My earlier work suggests that cultural play rhetorics and these primary emotions go together along with some additional supplementary US folk items (Bronner, 1988). What is important is that the parallels suggest that the enjoyments or happiness which characterizes each of these kinds of folk play also provide a transcendence over the very stressful emotions on which they are based. As psychologist Erikson (1950) might have put it, the players typically respond to the basic stress of these emotions (loneliness, shock, fear, anger, disgust, and apathy) with their own play-made masteries. Thus, loneliness is overcome by the antics of group membership in festivals, etc. In turn, the shocks of harassments in initiation-like ceremonies are transcended by the resilience in the responses of the chosen players. The fears of risk taking of the physical or economic kinds are comforted by courage. The anger of attacks is modified by defense against it. Disgust as profane can be modulated by hilarity, and finally, happiness covers all these cases but is also provided most directly in overcoming apathy by the joys, or flow, of peak experiences. We also suppose that these peak experiences are themselves to be contrasted with the alternative of apathy—a relation only implicit in Damasio's conceptions.

Note, in summary, that all of these primary emotions engender behavioral disequilibria which are then countered and equilibrated by these transcending play behaviors. It is not difficult to say that the excitements of play are always there because of this essential antipathetical coupling of imagined threats with the ludic representations of secure responses. Without this latter promised transcendence it would not be play. But what also seems implied by the primary emotions seen in loneliness, shock, fear, anger, disgust, and apathy is that if they should in fact be the major emotional menu of group lives throughout primate history they would have been describing a fairly dangerous and miserable existence. In these terms play may not just have been an emotional mastery or respite from these dangers; it might also have been a desperate mastery.

And one then wonders whether that is still the driving force that leads millions of people, cross-culturally, to represent anger in their own "desperate sports." And on the child level, play, which we normally take lightly as a matter of fun, may also have a similar kernel of desperation in those pressured representations within which they must perform. The anthropologist John M. Roberts showed that cross-cultural data correlated the presence of strategy games (e.g., chess, etc.) with being found in more complex societies. But more importantly for us is that he and I, in further research, found that there was also greater obedience training underlying the socialization of persons living in societies with these more complex games (Roberts & Sutton-Smith, 1962). Furthermore, we found that more achievement training pressures in socialization across cultures led also to the presence of more highly competitive forms of play. Given these data, it is possible to hypothesize that all of these disequilibrating emotional occasions (fear, anger, etc.) are key factors in a range of significant basic life-preserving motivations. Their linkage to the traditional types of play is in effect the evidence that in regular socialization such emotional dangers have to be modulated to become socialized.

It is this background of negative socialization emotions and their related negative behaviors which are meant to show the need by players to guard against such facts as that loneliness is depressing, shock immobilizes action, etc. These outcomes suggest that play has been and continues to be an immensely important evolutionary exercise of relatively civic behavior rules that muffle these antipathetical emotional threats in the games foreground. The data on children's play and stories (Sutton-Smith, 2001) shows even more clearly how the very young seize the pressures of the worlds they live in and partially circumvent them with their own self-originated narrative representations. Thus, all of these types of play are about mimicking the emotional struggles for life by providing a pantomimed behavioral representation of the antipathies which are evoked by the primary disequilibrium.

All play, in these terms, is basically an emotional exercise in mock ludic struggles, suggesting that these emotions can be equilibrated (with rules). At the same time, however, we must underline that experiencing these primary emotions in play makes the players somewhat more comfortable with their dangerous character. Think, for example, of multiple chasing or tagging games where many children accustom themselves to fear, by running away or by hiding, which they continue throughout much of their childhood. That play is giving them a semi-protected cognizance of fear that they might not have access to otherwise. It follows that play provides a learned cognizance for all the primary emotions.

Conclusion: The Good, the Bad, and the In Between

Clearly, the theorists of the Play-as-Positive group are more accepting of play's dualistic nature than were the proponents of the prior good and bad perspectives. But what most of these theorists have in common is that they treat play as something of a dualistic puzzle. Nearly all of the above approaches see play as some combination of positive and negative qualities. Considering that play behaviors probably emerged millions of years ago, we may indeed seek to use an evolutionary framework to account for the long-term functioning of these varied dualistic qualities in contemporary play. That is, we can ask the question whether we can analyze play as if it is some kind of antipathetical dualism: As if play is a Darwinian-like "struggle for survival" phenomena as often suggested in biology, neurology, sociology, and psychology. Indeed, the antipathetical dualities might be conceived as occurring because play is involved in representing dire fateful contestive and unconventional events, yet typically nobody gets killed, loses their shirt, or is deeply embarrassed. Of course, at the adult level, these dire events in play sometimes happen and players can get killed and injured or can lose their gambled money. But more importantly, perhaps, than the dualistic theatric play usage (i.e., play seems real but is not real) is perhaps the recent view that the fundamental underlying duality involved here is between evolutionary phenomena on the one hand and modern cultural cognitive learning influences on the other. It can be suggested for example that there is an evolutionary cooperation between these dual parallel influences in making play occur. Thus, Peter Coming (2005) says

> "Curiously, these two sets of nondeliberate, nonconscious reactions—those innate and those learned—may well be interrelated in the bottom pit of our unconscious. One is tempted to say that their possible nonconscious interplay signifies the intersection of two intellectual legacies, that of Darwin and Freud, two thinkers who dedicated their work to studying the diverse influences of the innate and the acquired from below stairs" (p. 48).

We need to remind ourselves, however, that there is an even more complex issue within evolutionary science itself as to whether, for example, play has been "naturally" selected or whether it is a mutation of some of the other "innate" and learning elements as discussed by Corning.

In conclusion, I would like to emphasize not just that play is an antithetical exercise of reality and representation, or riots and regulations, but that being able to express these emotions is also a cue to the skilful importance that the experience and control of these emotions have for all of us. They are the realities with which we live at all times and give us feelings that we are more truly alive. Being at play is generally being more alive than usual in the world in which we all live. Play, as such, is a kind of personal emotional survival. All of which is to show that these emotions mediate the struggles for survival that they represent. Darwin suggested, for example, that our struggle for survival depended on our ability to command reproduction, social power, and territorial possessions. What I would claim is that whatever such object needs for survival in the modern or any other world, they are all necessarily mediated by the same disequilibrial primary emotions described here as the struggling antipathies of play. The basic struggle is actually personified by these very angers and fears, and so forth, giving the players models of the power to be had by their representational overcoming.

References

Baigent, M. (2006). *The Jesus papers.* San Francisco: Harper.

Bateson, G. (1972). *Steps to an ecology of mind.* New York: Macy.

Bronner, S. (1988). *American children's folklore.* Little Rock, Arkansas: August House.

Burghardt, G.M. (2005). *The genesis of animal play: testing the limits*. Cambridge, MA: MIT. Press.

Caillois, R. (1961). *Man, play and games*. Glencoe, IL: Free Press.

Carse, P. J. (1986). *Finite and infinite: Vision of life as play and possibility*. New York: The Free Press.

Corning, P.A. (2005). *Holistic Darwinism: Synergy, cybernetics, and the bioeconomics of evolution*. Chicago: University of Chicago Press.

Damasio, A.R. (1994). *Descartes error: Emotion, reason and the human brain*. New York: Putnam.

Damasio, A.R. (1999). *The feeling of what happens*. New York: Harcourt.

Damasio, A.R. (2003). *Looking for Spinoza*. New York: Harcourt.

Darwin, C. (1965/1872). *The expression of the emotions in man and animals*. Chicago: University of Chicago Press.

Ehrenreich, B. (1997). *Blood rites*. New York: H. Holt.

Ehrenreich, B. (2007). *Dancing in the streets*. New York: H. Holt

Ekman, P. (1992). Are there basic emotions? *Psychological Review, 99*, 550–553.

Erikson, E. (1950). Childhood and society. New York: Norton.

Frederickson, B.L. (1998). *What good are positive emotions? Review of General Psychology, 2*, 3, p. 300–319.

Freud, S. (1938). *The basic writings of Sigmund Freud*. New York: Modern Library.

Freud, S. (1955). *Beyond the pleasure principle*. London: Strachey.

Froebel. F. (1987). *The education of man*. New York: Appleton.

Henricks, T. S. (2006). *Play reconsidered*. Urbana, IL: University of Illinois.

Huizinga, J. (1949), (1944). *Homo Ludens: A study of the play element in culture*. London: Routledge & Kegan Paul.

Jamison, K. R. (2004). *Exuberance: The passion for life*. New York: Vintage Books, Random House.

Jones, W.T. (1975). *Kant and the nineteenth century*. NY: Harcourt Brace.

Jones, W.T. (2000). *Handbook of emotions*. NY: Guilford Press. pp. 137–156.

Kant, I. (1783/1982). *The critique of pure reason*. New York: Cambridge University Press.

Ledoux, J. (1998). *The emotional brain*. New York: Simon & Schuster.

Lewis, M. & J.M. Haviland-Jones (2000). (Eds.) *Handbook of 2000. High school hazing*. New York: Grolier O'Brien.

Mithin, S (2009). *Freedom through cooking*. New York Review of Books. Pp. 44–46.

Opie, I. & P. (1959). *The lore and language of schoolchildren*. Oxford: Clarendon Press.

Piaget, J. (1951). *Play, imitations and dreams in childhood*. New York: Norton.

Plutchik, R. (2003). *Emotions and life*. Washington: DC: American Psychological Association.

Roberts & Sutton-Smith, B. (1962). Child training and game involvement. *Ethnology, 1*, (2): pp. 166–185.

Salen, K. & Zimmerman, E. (2006). *The game design reader*. Cambridge, MA: M.I.T Press.

Schiller, T.C. (1795). *On the esthetic education of man*. NY: F. Ungar.

Schechner, R. (2002). *Performance studies*. NY: Routledge.

Spariosu M. (1989). *Dionysus reborn: Play and the aesthetic dimension in modern philosophical and scientific discourse*. New York: Cornell University Press.

Spencer, H. (1896). *Principles of psychology*. New York: Appleton.

Spinka, M., Newberry, R.C., & Bekoff, M. (2001). Mammalian play: Training for the unexpected. *The Quarterly Review of Biology, 76*, 2 pp. 141–168.

Strutt. J. (1801). *The sports and pastimes of the people of England*. London: Methuen.

Sutton-Smith, B. (1960). Shut up and keep digging, *Jl. of Mid Western Folklore, 10*, pp. 11–27

Sutton-Smith, B. (1959). *The games of New Zealand children*. Berkeley, University of California Folklore Studies, #12.

Sutton-Smith, B. (1966). Piaget on play: A critique. *Psychological Review, 73*, 17–30.

Sutton-Smith, B. (1983) Piaget, play and cognition revisited. In Overton W.F. (Ed). *The relationship between social and cognitive development*. NJ: Erlbaum, pp. 229–250.

Sutton-Smith, B. (1974). *The anthropology of play*. Association for the Anthropological Study of Play. pp. 227–258.

Sutton-Smith, B. (1975). *Play as adaptive potentiation. Sportswissenschaft, 5*, 103–118.

Sutton-Smith, B. (1978). *Die Dialektic des Spiels*. Schorndorf: Germany, Hofmann.

Sutton-Smith, B. (1981). *A history of children's play*. Philadelphia: University of Pennsylvania.

Sutton-Smith, B. (1981). *The folkstories of children*. Philadelphia: University of Pennsylvania.

Sutton-Smith, B. (1986). *Toys as culture*. New York: Gardiner Press.

Sutton-Smith, B. (1997). *The ambiguity of play*. Cambridge: Harvard: University Press.

Sutton-Smith, B. (2001a). Reframing the variability of players. In S. Reifel (Ed.) *Play and Culture Studies, 3*, pp. 27–50.

Sutton-Smith, B. (2001b). Play as the tertiary emotion. In J.L. Roopnarine (Ed.) *Play and Culture, 4*.

Sutton-Smith, B. (2001c). Emotional breaches in play and narrative. In A. Goncu & E.L. Klein. *Children in play, story and school*. New York: Guilford Press. Pp. 161–176.

Sutton-Smith, B. & J. Roberts (1963). Game involvements in adults. *J of Social Psychology, 60*, pp. 15–30.

Sutton-Smith, B & S. (1974). *How to play with children and when not to*. New York: Hawthorne.

Sutton-Smith, B., Mechling, J., Johnson, T.W., & McMahon, F.F., (Eds.) (1999). *Children's folklore*. Logan, Utah: Utah State University Press.

Turner, V. (1982). *Celebration: Studies in festivity and ritual*. Smithsonian, Washington, D.C.

Wierzbicka, A. (1999). *Emotions across languages and cultures: Diversity and universals*. New York: Cambridge University Press.

Winnicott. D.W. (1971). *Playing and reality*. NY: Basic Books.

PART 4

Methods

The Cultural Ecology of Play: Methodological Considerations for Studying Play in Its Everyday Contexts[1]

Jonathan R. H. Tudge, Jill R. Brown, *and* Lia B. L. Freitas

Abstract

Children's play in industrialized societies such as the United States tends to be observed either under controlled conditions, in a laboratory or studied via closed-choice questionnaires, or under semi-controlled conditions in the home or child-care center. By contrast, studies of play in the majority world tend to be conducted by ethnographers who observe in any of the typical settings in which children are found. There are both disciplinary and paradigmatic reasons for this. However, even those methods that are intended to assess children's naturally occurring play in their everyday contexts may misrepresent the extent to which children play, their types of play, and their typical partners in play. Misrepresentation may occur by examining play in limited settings or by relying on parental reports (in the industrialized world) or by ignoring the heterogeneity of contexts in rapidly changing parts of the majority world. We present a method, designed explicitly to fit within a contextualist paradigm, for observing play in its everyday contexts, and use data derived from a single city from each of the United States, Kenya, and Brazil to illustrate the heterogeneity of young children's experiences and cast doubt on the generality of earlier findings.

Key words: play; culture; ecology; ethnography; paradigms; contextualism; methods; United States; Kenya; Brazil; children; parents; everyday lives

Introduction

Play is ubiquitous. For some, play is hanging upside down; for others it is twirling around until that feeling rises in your stomach and carries an infectious smile up to your mouth; for some it is a daydream that folds upon itself several times while walking home. In its most basic form it proceeds without a complex intellectual framework and is preconscious and preverbal, arising out of ancient biological structures that existed before our consciousness and our ability to speak (Brown, 2009). A common definition of play is a form of juvenile behavior resembling functional behavior but in a more exaggerated form, seemingly less serious, with individual components arranged in unusual sequences (Burghardt, this volume; Pellegrini & Bjorklund, 2004). From this point of view, means are more important than ends and play probably has little

cost or benefit. Others, however, have focused on the adaptive and preparatory nature of play, holding that some forms of play demand heavy costs in terms of energy and risk. Traditionally, play has been described as preparing males for hunting roles and females for mothering roles (Smith, 1982). Payoffs, in this case, may also be large but deferred, in terms of developmental benefits (Bjorklund & Pellegrini, 2002; Bock, this volume; Bock & Johnson, 2004).

Given the variety of experiences that can be described as play and the difficulties of definition, it is not surprising that those who have been interested in studying it have used different methods. Ethnographers and ethologists (see Bateson, Burghardt, and Smith, all this volume) have studied it in its natural settings, trying to change those settings as little as possible. Others, typically psychologists, have either observed for less time than most ethnographers, and more often in a restricted setting (home or child-care center or during free play at school) or have gathered information from parents about their children's play, either keeping a time diary or being asked directly about the children's time spent in play. The use of different methods is in part because of the different paradigms within which scholars work. However, it is also the case that ethnographers have typically gathered their data in parts of the "majority world" (Kağitçibaşi, 1996, 2007), whereas those with a background in psychology generally collect data in parts of the industrialized world. Some scholars with an interest in cultural variations have used one method when gathering data within their own culture and a different method in a different culture (see, for example, Bloch, 1989; Harkness & Super, 1992).

One problem with the use of different methods is that it may give a false impression of the extent to which play occurs in different cultural contexts. Our goal in this chapter is thus to describe one particular method that has been used to study play in its typically occurring everyday contexts. The method is one that can be applied in many different cultures, so long as observers are highly familiar with the culture being studied or, preferably, a member of the cultural group. The goal is to show that cultures vary in the extent to which they encourage their children's involvement in different types of activities (including play) and that older members serve differentially as children's partners in play.

We will illustrate these issues with data from three different societies—Kenya, Brazil, and the United States. Kenya was chosen because, thanks in part to the Six Cultures studies (Whiting, 1963; Whiting & Edwards, 1988), a number of scholars have observed children's play in different Kenyan tribes. Almost exclusively, however, the data have been gathered from rural areas, featuring parents who have been minimally schooled at best. Only Weisner (1979, 1989) examined child rearing in an urban environment. However, Kenya, like all societies, is changing, and increasing numbers of the population live in cities and have access to education. The major focus on rural and minimally schooled groups has led commentators to make generalizations about "Kenyan" practices that ignore possible within-society heterogeneity (see, for example, Bornstein, 2006). For this reason, we will discuss data about children's play in a Kenyan city, examining families from both middle- and working-class

backgrounds, to assess similarities to and differences from the data from rural regions of that country.

In the case of Brazil there is an extensive literature on children's play conducted by Brazilian scholars. However, like in the case of the United States, most of this work examines children's play in specific settings, primarily in child-care centers (for example, Carvalho & Pedrosa, 2002; Lordelo & Carvalho, 2006; Pedrosa & Carvalho, 2006; Sager & Sperb, 1998) and sometimes under controlled or experimental conditions (see, for example, Domeniconi, Costa, Souza, & Rose, 2007; Gil & Almeida, 2000; Sperb & Conti, 1998) or "toy libraries" (Kishimoto & Ono, 2008; Macarini & Vieira, 2006; Wanderlind, 2006). By contrast, the majority of the work on parents and children that is known in the United States focuses on street children (Hecht, 1998) and their everyday mathematics (Guberman, 1996; Nunes, Schliemann, & Carraher, 1993; Saxe, 1991; Schliemann, Carraher, & Ceci, 1997), on indigenous children (Gosso, Morais, Rebeiro, & Bussab, 2005), or on parents living in poverty (Scheper-Hughes, 1985, 1990, 1992). To what extent do these data give a false impression of what children's lives are like in Brazil more generally? Again, to prevent us from treating data from some types of children in a given society as synonymous with children in the society at large, the data that we report in this chapter come from city-dwellers, but not those who are living in poverty.

There is also a good deal of research on play in the United States (see, for example, Göncü & Gaskins, 2006; Pellegrini, 2009; Pellegrini & Smith, 2005). Most of this research takes place in controlled or semi-controlled settings and does not attempt to assess children's play in their everyday contexts, but some researchers try to assess children's naturally occurring play (Bloch, 1989; Göncü, Jain, & Tuermer, 2006; Haight, 1999; Haight & Miller, 1993; Hofferth & Sandberg, 2001; Parmar, Harkness, & Super, 2004; Pellegrini, 2006; Pellegrini & Smith, 1998; Timmer, Eccles, & O'Brien, 1989). The methods used by these scholars, however, rely on observations in one or two of the many settings in which children find themselves or on parent reports of the activities, including play, in which their children engage (see Smith, this volume). What is not done in the United States is to follow children around for lengthy periods, observing their typically occurring play, alone and with others, in the various settings in which they find themselves. In this chapter, we therefore report on young children's play in a single U.S. city, using the same method as used to gather data in the Kenyan and Brazilian cities. As with those cities, we examine some heterogeneity of context by choosing African American and European American families, half of whom were middle class and half working class.

The reasoning behind the use of the same methods to study in three different societies is clearly to allow comparisons among the different groups. This is an approach fraught with danger. There is a large cross-cultural literature devoted to comparative research, from observational methods to the application of scales, developed in one society, back-translated and used in many other societies. In some cases the researchers appear to be using a single measuring stick (for a critique, see LeVine, 1989) in which those who score higher on the scale or who are observed doing more of one or other activity are treated as better than others who are viewed as having a deficit. Other scholars, however, are more interested in understanding the reasons for the difference in patterns observed or are not at all interested in making comparisons. The two approaches are related to different views of the world, and their related ontologies, epistemologies, and related methodologies.

Paradigms and Related Methods in the Study of Human Development

Although methods can be applied well or poorly, the quality of a method cannot be discussed in the abstract; instead, our belief is that methods need to be clearly tied to the theoretical foundation or paradigm to which they are linked, whether explicitly or implicitly. As Guba and Lincoln wrote, a paradigm can best be thought of as a "basic belief system or worldview that guides the investigator, not only in choices of method but in ontologically and epistemologically fundamental ways" (1994, p. 105). Pepper (1942) made essentially the same argument when writing about four "world views" (mechanism, organicism, contextualism, and formism). In this chapter we will focus on the two most relevant to the study of play—mechanism, a neo-positivist paradigm, and contextualism, one that is non-positivist. From an ontological point of view, neo-positivists believe that although reality as such is not directly knowable, one can use methods that allow incorrect views of reality to be disproved by subjecting different claims of reality to careful and critical examination. Epistemologically, this requires establishing clear separation between the investigator and the participants in the study so that the ideas, values, beliefs, and practices of the investigator do not influence those of the people being studied.

Neo-positivists (mechanists) have therefore designed methods to bring about that separation; great care is taken to ensure that participants are treated as similarly as possible. This is most easily accomplished by bringing participants to a university laboratory. If the researcher is interested in studying mother–child play, for example, use of the lab means that the setting is necessarily always the same, extraneous interruptions can be avoided, and identical play materials can be provided to all participants. Observations may take place in the home, but investigators working within the mechanist paradigm try carefully to control that setting—observing within each home at the same time of day, asking the mother to be available to play with her child (as opposed to engaging in any of the other tasks which might otherwise occupy her time), not engaging with the dyad as mother and child play, and so on.

Alternative methods, though equally positivistic, involve mothers responding to questionnaires about their beliefs about the value of children's play, or about its extent; mothers might also be asked to complete time diaries to show what sort of play their children were involved in and for how long. The questionnaires most likely allow forced-choice responses or, if open-ended responses are allowed, are controlled to the extent to which the questions are always identical for each participant and always appear in the identical order. Even when mothers are interviewed about their children's play, control is kept by ensuring that even the follow-up prompts are carefully scripted in advance. The goal is to discover the mothers' views about their children's play with the absolute minimum influence of the investigator (or at least an influence that is as similar as possible for all participants).

By contrast, the contextualist worldview, a non-positivist paradigm, involves completely different ontological and epistemological positions and, not surprisingly, methods that are unlike those used by neo-positivist investigators. In terms of ontology, contextualists hold that multiple realities exist, at least to the extent that "people's perceptions of reality are necessarily constrained and shaped by their specific circumstances" (Tudge, 2008, p. 59). This holds as true for people living during different historical periods as for people in different cultural groups, whether those cultural groups are viewed as separate societies or different groups found within a single society.

The contextualist paradigm's epistemology is also different from that of mechanism; contextualists hold that creating a clear separation between investigator and participant is not only a chimera, but also prevents understanding the participants' reality from their perspective. The methods that they use are lengthy observations in context, participant observation, or open-ended interviews. Their focus of attention is activities and interactions as they happen within the settings in which the participants are typically situated. If they are interested in mother–child play, for example, they might observe in and around the child's home, to see whether the mother actually is involved in that play and, if so, the extent to which she is. In other words, the very assumption that mothers play with their children is open to assessment. Mothers might be interviewed about their beliefs about children's play, their roles in that play, and so on, or they might be shown pictures of film of their children in play, and be asked to explain what is happening. In none of these situations would there be any control of the precise questions, or their order—what would be asked would be in part a response to what the participant has earlier said. The investigator, in other words, is expected to be a part of the context, changing it necessarily simply by being there, and not separate from it, as neo-positivist scholars would require.

It is worth mentioning that Pepper (1942) used different metaphors for the world views he described. The metaphor for mechanism is that of the machine, emphasizing cause–effect relations. Contextualism's metaphor is the "historical event," although this metaphor is misleading, as can be seen from Pepper's description: "By historic event, however, the contextualist means…the event alive in its present… literally the incidents of life" (Pepper, 1942, pp. 232–233). On the one hand, then, contextualism focuses on everyday practices, but it is also clear from Pepper's writing that for contextualists there can be no simple cause–effect relations, as individuals, the people with whom they interact, and the contexts in which they are situated, are necessarily interconnected. Moreover, the cultural relativism that is inherent in contextualism means that "optimal" development can only be judged in terms of the prevailing practices and values within a given cultural group; there can be no "single measuring stick" to evaluate competence.

To a large extent, mechanist methods are used within psychology, whereas cultural anthropologists are likely to use contextualist methods, particularly ethnography. Psychologists have been interested in testing the universality of their findings by using randomly selected samples observed in standardized settings or, if this is not possible, short-term observations under relatively controlled conditions, or questionnaires. By contrast, anthropologists have typically used ethnographic methods to describe the culturally relevant nature of their findings (see Bock, this volume; LeVine, 1989, 2007).

An ethnographic approach to studying play is a descriptive account, drawn from observations of (as well as interviews about) the daily activities, experiences, and lives of children in a particular time and place, and of the cultural, social, economic, and institutional contexts that need to be understood to make sense of children's and their partners' behavior in that moment (LeVine, 2007). LeVine argues, as do many other ethnographers, that if childhood experiences, and play in particular, were uniform across human populations and historical period, ethnographic accounts would not be needed. Ethnographic methods to study play, emerging from the contextualist worldview, are based on the assumption that the conditions that shape play vary from one population to the next and are not fully comprehensible without intimate knowledge of the contexts, both social and cultural, that give them meaning.

Not surprisingly, given these different approaches, one can see the tension between mainstream mechanistic psychology and contextualist cultural anthropology, a tension that dates back to Freud. Levine (2007) points out that this tension began with Malinowski (1927) challenging Freud's oedipal complex in the matrilineal society of the Trobriand Islands and Mead (1928/1961) arguing that the adolescent turmoil that Hall proposed as universal did not exist in Samoa. This trend has been found more recently with the universality of Piaget's stages of cognitive development questioned by Greenfield (1976) and others, Kohlberg's views of moral development critiqued by Shweder et al. (1990), and Bowlby's ideas of attachment re-assessed by Harwood et al. (1995).

We do not wish to imply that the crucial difference is between psychology and anthropology; that would be too simplistic. There are anthropological approaches that fit nicely into the mechanist paradigm just as there are researchers using contextualist ideas within psychology. Even among psychologists who are interested in culture, one can see a split between cross-cultural psychologists, whose paradigm is mechanism, and those who term themselves cultural psychologists, who fit within contextualism (see, for example, Adamopoulos & Lonner, 2001; Shweder, 1990; Tudge, 2008). Göncü and his colleagues noted the division within the field of play, critiquing the view that norms "based on the play of middle-income children provide absolute universal criteria against which the play of children from diverse cultures should be judged" (Göncü, Tuermer, Jain, & Johnson, 1999, p. 152). Instead, they argued, "the development of play characterized in Western theories is only one of many possible cultural models of children's play" (loc cit). Nonetheless, despite these divergent positions, psychology, almost from its inception, has positioned itself within a neo-positivist or mechanist paradigm rather than a contextualist paradigm. It did not have to be this way. Wilhelm Wundt, during the late nineteenth century, actually proposed a dual approach to psychology—one approach that involved highly controlled methods and the other, that he termed "folk psychology," that did not (Cole, 1996; Miller, Hengst, & Wang, 2003). Examples of research that could be considered folk psychology (those that have taken a contextualist or ecological approach to development) have consistently been found within psychology over the past century, but they have always been peripheral to the field, and mechanist (neo-positivist) theories and methods have been clearly at the forefront (Tudge, Gray, & Hogan, 1997).

We will now focus on studies of play in their natural settings (rather than in those that are experimental or controlled), comparing what is known about the extent to which young children engage in play and, where possible, the type of play in which they engage.

Assessments of Children's Play in the United States

Göncü et al. (2006) studied low-income black and white children, observing them both in free play in child care and in one other setting in which each child was typically found, as well as interviewing their teachers and parents. They discussed the types of play in which the children engaged (including pretend, physical, language, and "sound and rhythm" play), but provided no information on the extent to which they engaged in the different types of play. Other scholars have focused their observations on a specific type of play. For example, Pellegrini and his colleagues studied rough-and-tumble play, observing extensively during children's play time outside (see, for example, Pellegrini, 2006, 2009; Pellegrini & Smith, 1998) and found that American 4-year-old children spend about 4% of their time engaging in this type of play. Haight (1999; Haight & Miller, 1993) observed

children's pretend play in a different setting—at home with their mothers and found that when the children were three to four years of age they spent between 8 and 12 minutes every hour engaging in pretend play (the sole focus of this longitudinal research). When they were three, their mother was their primary partner in this play (70% of the time) and at age four she was still the most common partner.

Bloch (1989), by contrast, assessed the extent to which children engaged in different types of activities, including play, but did so not by observing directly but by phoning parents and asking them to report on what their preschool-aged children were doing. This had the advantage of allowing her to assess the extent to which the children were involved in numerous activities, including play, but only from the parents' perspective. Interestingly, Bloch (1989; Bloch & Adler, 1994) also examined play in Senegal, as we will discuss later, but in this African context (as is typical) relied on observations of the children's activities rather than parental reports. Harkness and Super (1992) did the same thing in their study of father involvement with young children, relying on observations in Kokwet, Kenya, but interviews (primarily with the children's mothers) to assess the extent to which the fathers served as their children's partners in their play and other activities. Other scholars, too, rely on parent reports for their assessments of children's play in the United States, whether in small-scale (Parmar et al., 2004) or nationally representative studies (Hofferth & Sandberg, 2001; Timmer et al., 1989).

Limitations with these types of studies

The studies described above attempt, in different ways, to assess children's play in their natural settings. Some rely on observations, others on parent reports, and some use both methods. The observational studies that focus on a specific type of play (pretend or rough-and-tumble) are very useful, but the authors, as they sometimes acknowledge, may well be over-estimating the prevalence of such play by studying it in those settings where it is most likely to be found (playing at home with the mother, in the case of pretend play, and playing outside during free play at preschool or school). Relying on parent reports may minimize this problem, but parents can only report what they see, and so are unable to provide information when their children are out of sight, whether in another area of the home or in a different setting, such as child care. Moreover, even when the respondent (typically the mother) is within ear- or eyeshot of the child, she may have been occupied with other tasks around the home rather than observing carefully what her child is doing. There have been attempts to assess the accuracy of parental reports by comparing parents' reports of television-watching with data gathered more directly (Anderson, Field, Colllins, Lorch, & Nathan, 1985; Robinson, 1985; Robinson & Godbey, 1997). However, given that television programs are of an easily calculable length, accuracy in assessing this activity may not generalize to others.

The final problem of either focusing on a single type of play or looking more broadly at play but using parental reports occurs when people make comparisons with children's play in other parts of the world, with data collected in more ethnographic fashion. Bloch (1989) and Harkness and Super (1992), for example, assume that the data that they collected from Senegal and Kenya, observationally, can be directly compared to those collected via parent reports, which seems something of a stretch.

Assessments of Children's Play in Parts of Africa and Brazil

Ethnographic approaches to childhood and play in the majority world can be traced back to the 1920s (Malinowski, 1927; Mead, 1928/1961), and a number of cultural anthropologists, most involved with the Six Cultures original study and follow-up studies (see Whiting & Edwards, 1988), have written extensively about children's experiences, including their play, in different parts of Kenya. They reported the absence of parents, or other adults, from their children's play (play occurs primarily among siblings and peers), and often goes on while the children are engaged in work (Harkness & Super, 1985; LeVine et al., 1994; LeVine & LeVine, 1963; Wenger, 1989; Whiting & Edwards, 1988; Whiting & Whiting, 1975).

As noted above, Bloch (1989; Bloch & Adler, 1994) observed extensively in a rural community of Senegal, and found that two- to four-year-olds were often involved in a mixture of play and work. Similarly, Lancy (1996) found this to be true for Kpelle girls aged five and older, although boys were not expected to be involved much in work until they were aged seven or eight, and Bock (2002, 2005; Bock & Johnson, 2004) also noted this connection between play and work in northern Botswana. Bloch (1989) noted that Senegalese two- to four-year-olds engaged in play about 25% of the time and Boch (2005) noted that four- to six-year-olds in Botswana played between 25% and 30% of the time.

Very little Brazilian research on play involves ethnographic observations, and almost none of what exists, as is true of the situation in Kenya, involves city-dwellers or, if it does, focuses on children living in poverty. Alves (2004), for example, studied the everyday activities of "street children" (i.e., those found mostly, if not entirely, on the streets of a large southern city). She noted that children and adolescents played a good deal of the time that they were on the street; not surprisingly, much of their play involved singing and using their own bodies as instruments (tapping rhythmically on their arms, for example). By contrast, Gosso and her colleagues focused their attention on the play of children in forager groups living in remote areas of the country (Gosso et al., 2005). These authors explicitly noted the differences between rural African young children's lives, which commonly involve work, and Brazilian Indian children, who spend large amounts of their time in play, and are never involved in work. Gosso and her colleagues reported that the four- to six-year-old children they studied in the Amazon rain forest spent about 60% of their time in play in the case of boys, and 52% in the case of girls.

However, Gosso and her colleagues (Gosso, Morais, & Otta, 2007) also compared these children's play with those from other groups—children in a small seashore village and three groups from São Paulo (low, high, and mixed SES). Unfortunately, it is impossible to tell the proportion of time that these children spent in play in comparison to other activities, as play was the sole focus of attention. It is also noteworthy that the observations of all but the Indian group took place during free play at preschool; the Indian children were observed playing in various parts of the village.

Limitations with these types of studies

Although these studies do a far more comprehensive job of assessing the extent to which children play, and the types of play that occupy their time, than those focusing on children in the United States, it seems to us to be a major flaw that almost all of the work conducted on children's play in Africa features children living in rural areas with parents who are non- or minimally schooled. This seems a particular problem with countries such as Kenya developing rapidly, and increasing proportions of the population living in large cities and large majorities of young children in school (Tudge & Odero-Wanga, 2009).

Moreover, given that schooling has been a priority since Kenyan independence, many parents have had education to college-level and beyond, and are likely to treat their children quite differently than do those parents with little or no education. Moreover, once girls aged six and over are in school, they clearly are no longer available to look after younger siblings, and boys who are in school are not able to spend their time looking after the family's animals, as used to be the case. As Serpell (2008) has expressed the situation: "Despite the existence of real problems, to portray the general population… as characterized by pervasive poverty, disease, or corruption… is to commit the synecdochal error of representing the whole by one of its parts." It is only because so much attention has been focused on rural families' child-rearing styles that Bornstein can state that Kenyan mothers, among others, "eschew play with children… [and] do not believe that it is important or appropriate to play with their children" (2006, p. 115) or Lancy (2007) can argue that mother–child play does not exist in Liberia specifically, and in the ethnographic record more generally.

It is also a problem that when children from rural and urban areas are compared, whether within Brazil as in Gosso et al.'s (2007) research, or across majority and industrialized societies, as with Bloch (1989) or Harkness and Super (1992), if different methods are used to gather data but comparisons are made without taking into account methodological differences.

It would be helpful if scholars interested in children's naturally occurring play in the typical settings in which play occurs used the same methods with families living in different types of societies and, within those societies, with families living in different types of circumstances. Given what we wrote earlier about paradigms, it is clear that one's choice of method must relate to the paradigm within which the research is being conducted. As several scholars have argued, the value of a method can only be ascertained by reference to the theory and paradigm within which it fits (Eckensberger, 2002; Goldhaber, 2000; Kuczynski & Daly, 2003; Tudge, 2008; Winegar, 1997). We will therefore describe an explicitly contextualist theory and show how methods that fit within that paradigm and theory can be used to study play in its everyday contexts.

Contextualist Theories

The two most prominent examples of contextualist theories are those of Vygotsky and Bronfenbrenner; both treat development as an interaction among activities, individual characteristics, and the changing contexts within which those activities occur

(Bronfenbrenner & Morris, 2006; Göncü & Gaskins, this volume; Tudge, 2008; Vygotsky, 1934/1987). A strength of Vygotsky's theory is his highlighting the idea that all practices, including interactions, can only be understood within their cultural and historical context (see also Bateson, this volume; Cole, 1996, 2005; Tudge & Scrimsher, 2003; Valsiner & Winegar, 1992). Bronfenbrenner, by contrast, put regularly occurring everyday interactions, that become progressively more complex over time ("proximal processes") at the center of his theory, and argued that they are modified simultaneously by individual characteristics, by the context in which the activity is taking place, and by historical time (Bronfenbrenner & Morris, 2006).

However, there are some clear weaknesses in both theories from a contextualist point of view. Vygotsky, because of the ideology paramount in the Soviet Union when he was writing during the 1920s and early 1930s, could hardly do other than view development in terms of a progression toward a single optimal goal. It would have been impossible for him to argue that competence within capitalist societies would not only be different from but equal to the type of competence that would be appropriate for a communist society. Vygotsky, moreover, paid little attention to the role of the individual in changing his or her own context. Bronfenbrenner was far clearer about the ways in which individuals change proximal processes but focused relatively little on the role of culture. In a single chapter (Bronfenbrenner, 1993) he provided an account of what he termed "sub-cultural" differences within a single society. However, with the first appearance of the "process-person-context-time" (PPCT) model of development (Bronfenbrenner, 1994) and its subsequent elaborations (see, for example, Bronfenbrenner, 1995, 1999, 2001/2005; Bronfenbrenner & Morris, 2006) the richer discussion of culture disappeared. Instead, what he termed "good" proximal processes were those that are clearly related to what is considered desirable in contemporary white North American middle-class values, beliefs, and practices. Another weakness, from a contextualist point of view, stems from the missing link in the writings of both theorists—that between theory and methods; neither theorist wrote explicitly about the methods that should be used to gather data in keeping with the contextualist nature of the theory.

Cultural–ecological theory

Cultural–ecological theory, by contrast, was designed explicitly as a contextualist theory and the methods were intended to fit the theory. As the first author has discussed at length elsewhere (Tudge, 2008), this theory is based largely on Vygotsky's and Bronfenbrenner's theories. However, unlike these theories, it incorporates a richer conceptualization of culture, and takes seriously the contextualist position that not only do multiple realities exist, both across and within societies, but also that different cultural groups have different conceptions of children's competence.

Central to the theory is the idea that development occurs in large part through the typically occurring everyday activities and interactions involving developing individuals and their social partners. It is in the course of engaging in these regularly occurring activities that children come to fit into their cultural world. They learn what is expected of them, the types of activities considered appropriate or inappropriate for them, how they are expected to engage in these activities, the ways other people will deal with them, and how they are expected to deal with others. Children often initiate activities themselves, and try to draw others into those activities, and it is in the course of these activities that they try out different roles and observe the roles of others, both with regard to themselves and with others.

The culture within which these activities and interactions take place clearly plays a central role in influencing the types of activities and interactions that are available to the young of that culture, and influences which of them the children are encouraged to participate in (or discouraged from). The group's values and beliefs about raising children, the practices they consider normative or appropriate, the resources and settings available to them, and so on, clearly are implicated in the children's typically occurring activities and interactions. As Tom Weisner (1996) wrote, if you want to know how children will develop, the most important single thing to know is the cultural group of which they are a part.

Culture has been defined (see Tudge, 2008) as consisting of a group that shares a general set of values, beliefs, practices, institutions, and access to resources. The group may have a sense of shared identity, or the recognition that people are in some way connected and feel themselves to be part of the group, and the adults of the group should attempt to pass on to the young of the group the same values, beliefs, practices, and so on. Members of different countries or societies clearly constitute different cultural groups. But the same can be said of groups within any given country or society, to the extent to which their members share values, beliefs, practices, institutions, resources, etc., feel a sense of identity with other members of that group and try to pass on those shared values, beliefs, practices, and resources to their young. Rather than think about people being part of just one culture, it thus makes more sense to think of them being part of several cultures: their society, their ethnicity, their social class, perhaps their geographic region, and so on. The cultural group with which a person identifies at any one time is likely to be dependent on a relevant comparison group; someone who has grown up in Rio Grande do Sul is Brazilian when talking with a group of Europeans, a Gaucho when talking with people from other areas of Brazil, of Italian descent when talking with Gauchos of German descent, or a middle-class descendent of Italians when meeting working-class people from the same ethnic background.

However, even if culture is hugely important in influencing children's development, so are the children's own characteristics. In any cultural group there are children who are differentially inclined or motivated to learn some skills, ideas, practices than are others. Children themselves change the nature of the activities and interactions in which they engage simply because of their own unique natures. The same is true, of course, of the other people (children and adults) with whom they are interacting. The young of the cultural group thus do not simply imitate or internalize the practices of those who are more competent in the ways of the culture but recreate those practices in the course of engaging in them. There is thus always the possibility that those practices will change over time. The same is true for values and beliefs about raising children. Although the older generation may try hard to transmit those same values and beliefs to their young, it is not always the case that members of the younger generation accept their parents' ideas. In cultures in which tradition is considered highly important there is greater pressure on children to accept their parents' ways; in other cultures, however, in which creativity and independence are more valued, one should expect to find faster change. Cultural groups are thus themselves developing under the influence of the new generation while at the same time they are helping that new generation become competent in the ways of the group. In other words, cultural–ecological theory treats development as a complex interplay among cultural context, individual variability, and change over time, with the key aspect being activities and interactions, where context and individual variability intersect.

Cultural–ecological methods

What, then, are the methods that should be used with such a theory? Ethnographic methods seem most applicable when the goal is to understand the types of everyday activities and interactions that occur in the everyday lives of the people being studied, particularly when the focus is on play. Play, after all, is an activity that one often does in interaction with others and, even when a solitary activity, is not one that is typically kept hidden from others. It therefore lends itself to observation. Ethnography takes many different forms (Atkinson, Coffey, Delamont, Lofland, & Lofland, 2001); nonetheless, its primary focus is on "the study of people in naturally occurring settings…by means of methods which capture their social meanings and ordinary activities" (Brewer, 2000, p. 10). As such, ethnographic methods fit well with contextualist theories.

The specific ethnographic method[2] used by the first author (Tudge, 2008) does not require long-term immersion in the field, as is often the case with ethnographic research, but is a time-sampling observational approach that can best be done by someone from the culture of interest, trained in its use. The method requires observation of activities and interactions, occurring in natural settings, over the equivalent of one complete day in the life of each participant. Data are gathered in blocks of 2 or 4 hours, such that one observational session starts prior to the child waking in the morning, another at the end of the day, and other blocks distributed over the entire day. Data are gathered for a total of 18 hours for each participant, in three blocks of 2 hours and three blocks of 4 hours, and a further 2 hours are videotaped.

In Tudge's Cultural Ecology of Young Children project (Tudge, 2008), the developing individuals of interest were three-year-olds from a variety of cultural groups. The main activities of interest included *lessons* (or explicit attempts to give or receive information) in four domains (school-relevant activities, appropriate behavior, about why and how things work, and religion), *work* (14 sub-categories), *conversations* (defined as talking about things from the past or future, rather than a part of on-going activities, sub-divided into three categories), and *play*. Play, which included exploration and entertainment, was divided into 15 different sub-categories, including two types of pretend play, three types of play with school-relevant objects, play with objects intended to be played with by children ("toys"), play with objects from the adult world, whether discarded or not, play with no object at all (for example, rough and tumble, chase, or play with one's own body or singing), and being entertained (six sub-categories, including watching television, listening to the radio or to music, etc.).

Each child carried a wireless mike, to enable the observer to hear what was being said by or to the child without having to be too close, and the observer also listened to an endless-loop tape that marked the passage of time. Observations were live and continuous (or as close to continuous as possible), but coding only took place immediately after a 30-second "window" that occurred every six minutes. During these windows, the observer noted the following: Any of the above-mentioned sub-categories occurring in the child's vicinity; all activities in which the child was involved, either as an active participant or an observer; who started each of the activities (the child, another person, or the child in conjunction with someone else); who was responsible for the child becoming involved in each of the activities (the child, another person, or the child in conjunction with someone else); who else (if anyone) was involved in each activity; the roles each participant (including the child) played in each activity.

This approach captures children's activities in an ecologically appropriate way (children are not separated from context) and it does so over enough time to give, we believe, a reasonable sense of the types of activities that typically occur in these children's lives. The approach also allows us to examine the types of activities that are going on in which the children do not participate, or those in which they would like to participate but are discouraged from so doing.

Given the nature of the theory on which this method is based, it is also important that the observations also allow us to examine what the children themselves do to start activities, involve others in those activities, and try to get out of activities that those around them would like them to engage in. In other words, children play a highly active role. They are involved in activities not simply because others get them involved; they initiate activities themselves, and try to recruit others to be their social partners. They initiate lessons (asking questions about words, numbers, or how things work), conversations, and even work—asking to help and not simply being asked to help. Most commonly, given the nature of the activity, children are most likely to initiate the play in which they are engaged. They also, on occasion, work hard to get other people involved in their play.

Context is necessarily implicated when examining children's activities in the locations in which they are situated. We therefore observe in any of the settings in which the children are situated, and observe any of the social partners with whom the children interact. This means that we observe in the home, child-care center if a child goes to one, with friends or relatives, at the park, in the streets, or at the shops if the child goes there. The data are gathered in any setting in which the child spends time because we believe that it is important to know more than what goes on in the home or child-care center, the most usual locations where observational data are gathered by researchers working in North America. We therefore not only follow the child wherever he or she goes during the observational session, but also find out where the child is scheduled to be for the next session, so as to be in that place at the appointed time.

These observations allow us to view more than the activities in which children are involved and the settings in which these activities take place. We also are able to see the roles played by the children and their partners in these activities, revealing both the interactions and the expectations for interactions that the children (and their typical partners) have developed. In most instances, we would expect children to be *participating* in play, but on occasion they try to *manage or direct* the play in which they are engaged (actively trying to make it occur in a certain way), trying to *resist or stop* the play (for example, if partners in play are doing things they do not like, or if they have become bored with it), and *observing* the play of others. We also include as a role *eavesdropping*, similar to observing but from a greater distance and with no assumption that the person being watched is aware of being watched. Through these codes we create a chronicle of the actions and responses of children and their social partners. The chronicle contains the details of the ongoing adjustment and negotiation of relationships that forms the fabric of children's everyday experiences.

The context of play clearly involves more than the immediate setting, however, but also the broader socio-cultural context. It is at this level that we can see culture-relevant differences in the types of play (and all other activities) in which children engage, differences in the extent to which children are encouraged to and discouraged from participating in different activities and in initiation of those activities.

How do we instantiate culture using this methodology? In part this depends on the definition of culture; as mentioned earlier, we define culture as any group that can be differentiated on the basis of its values, beliefs, and practices, its social institutions, its access to resources, its sense of identity, and its desire to pass on those values, practices, etc., to the young of the group. Data were initially collected in the United States, where the first author works. Because of his experience in the former Soviet Union, it made sense to gather comparative data in Russia and Estonia, two distinct cultures in which the parents had been raised in a single society. We also were able to gather data in Finland, culturally and linguistically similar to Estonia but without the Soviet experience, and in South Korea, Kenya, and Brazil. In each case, the first author trained members of the respective countries to collect these data. These societies, of course, vary on many dimensions. Our goal was therefore to choose a single city in each society, of medium size by the standards of that society, with a range of cultural, educational, and professional possibilities.

Culture and society are clearly not synonymous, and within any society can be found a variety of different cultural groups, given our definition of culture. Different ethnic groups may therefore constitute separate cultural group, and so may members of different social classes. In this study we examined, in every city, children from two groups—those who were defined as either working class or middle class on the basis of their parents' education and occupation. In the city in the United States, in addition, we examined children from black and white families, equally divided by social class.

If one wishes to study development, one has to study individuals over time. In this research we gather the types of observational data discussed above when the children are of preschool age, and then gather follow-up data once the children have entered school. We are interested in examining the relations, if any, between three-year-old children's initiation of and engagement in different types of activities and their parents' and teachers' perceptions of them during the early years of school (Tudge, Odero, Hogan, & Etz, 2003). However, as noted earlier, it is important to situate research participants not simply in their physical context (whether considered as the immediate setting or as the cultural group) but also in their temporal context. The way in which even young children experience their environments depends in part on what is happening, in historical time, in the culture of which those children are a part. This is true for children in a society that is rapidly industrializing, in an industrialized society in the midst of recession or boom, or, as in the case of our research, in societies struggling to adapt to the changes wrought by the collapse of the Soviet Union.

Observations of Children's Play in Greensboro (the United States), Kisumu (Kenya), and Porto Alegre (Brazil)

In this chapter we report data from a single city from three different societies: the United States, Kenya, and Brazil. The North American families were from Greensboro, NC, and half were African American and half European American, equally divided by social class. The Kenyan families were from Kisumu, a city on the shores of Lake Victoria, and were ethnically Luo. The Brazilian families were from Porto Alegre, the capital of the southernmost state in Brazil, and were of primarily European (Italian, German, and Portuguese) descent (although in this city, as elsewhere in Brazil, people are ethnically and racially diverse). In Kisumu and Porto Alegre, as in Greensboro, the families were equally divided by social class, as determined by education and occupation criteria. Families that we called "middle class" were those in which both parents had a college degree or higher and, if they worked outside the home, had a professional occupation. Members of "working-class" families, by contrast, did not have a college degree and, if they worked outside the home, had a non-professional occupation. We excluded from the study families in which one parent was middle class and the other was working class.

Because of the way in which the data were collected, we noted when play (including entertainment) was occurring in the same setting as the child was situated and whether the child was involved in that play. In each of the cities, play was available to the children from 60% to 70% of the time we observed, and children were actually involved in it, in each city, just under 60% of the time. Clearly it was the activity in which these three-year-olds were most involved. What sort of play were the children involved in? In this chapter we discuss eight broad categories of play: pretend play, in which children were observed to be taking on the role of someone or something else; play with toys (play objects designed or created to be played with by children); play with school-related objects (books, objects intended to help children with numbers or letters, mathematical shapes, and so on); play with objects from the adult world (whether discarded or not); play with objects from the natural world (sticks, sand, mud, etc.); play with no objects (running, chase, play with one's own body, and so on); watching television (generally not considered part of play, though included here as an activity engaged in purely for its entertainment value); and other types of relatively passive entertainment, such as listening to the radio or to music, which occurred far less frequently than did watching television.

Obviously there could be overlap across these different categories. Children could be using objects in their pretend play, or could be chasing after one another to kick a ball, or could be playing with toys in the sand. In these cases, however, we coded what appeared to be the children's overarching goal— pretend play, in the first case, ball play in the second, and playing with toys in the third. Equally, there would be times during which children were combining their play with a different type of activity— engaged in some type of lesson, for example, or working, or carrying on a conversation. In each of these cases we coded both the play and the other activity or activities that were going on at the same time. For example, while a father is reading with his daughter (play with a school-related object) he asks her how many ducks are in the picture, and after he has counted them with her (a school-related lesson) she reminds him of when they saw ducks in the park at the weekend (a conversation). In this chapter, however, we will focus just on the children's play.

As can be seen in Table 11.1, in Greensboro, in each of the four communities (divided by race/ethnicity and class) the children were most often observed playing with toys, from about 18% of their observations in the case of the white middle-class children to more than 27% of observations in the case of the white working-class children. In the black communities, middle-class children were more likely to be observed playing with toys than were their working-class counterparts. The type of play that was next most often observed was watching television; in both the white and black communities working-class children were more likely to do this than were middle-class children. Almost all of the programs that the children watched were those designed for children, although occasionally they observed programs that their parents were more interested in, whether news programming or wrestling. Other types of entertainment (listening to music or the radio) were very rarely observed, as noted above.

Children from the black communities in Greensboro were more likely than those from the white communities to play with objects from the

Table 11.1 Means and Standard Deviations for Children's Engagement in Types of Play in Greensboro (percent of observations)

Types of Play	White MC (n=11)	White WC (n=9)	Black MC (n=9)	Black WC (n=10)
Pretend	3.71 (3.1)	3.20 (3.0)	1.86 (2.4)	1.33 (1.6)
School-related	5.26 (3.9)	4.33 (4.5)	4.21 (4.1)	3.69 (4.4)
Child-related obj.	18.06 (9.4)	27.82 (9.7)	25.29 (13.1)	19.94 (8.2)
Adult-related obj.	3.04 (1.8)	6.62 (3.6)	7.81 (4.3)	8.87 (5.8)
Natural obj.	2.35 (1.5)	3.27 (2.1)	3.27 (3.1)	3.12 (2.2)
No obj.	3.59 (1.7)	3.85 (2.3)	7.32 (3.7)	9.38 (2.8)
TV	8.32 (5.0)	13.11 (8.1)	10.99 (8.8)	14.84 (10.7)
Entertainment	1.09 (1.6)	0.37 (0.7)	1.44 (1.6)	0.66 (0.7)
All play	45.52 (11.4)	62.64 (12.7)	62.21 (12.7)	61.83 (10.5)

adult world, with the middle-class white children observed least often playing with those types of objects. The black children were also twice as likely to play with no object at all as were the white children. We observed the other types of play equally rarely; white children were more likely to be observed in pretend play than were black children, and middle-class children (whether from white or black families) were more likely to be observed playing with school-related objects than were children from working-class families.

Our data, collected ethnographically, differ in some interesting ways from data gathered either in a restricted locale (observing on the playground, for example, or in the home) or provided by parents asked to report on their children's daily activities. Haight and Miller (1993) observed American children at home with their mothers, and found that when the children were of a similar age to those in Tudge's (2008) study they spent between 8 and 12 minutes every hour engaging in pretend play. Regardless of the fact that American mothers who are at home with their young children might encourage their children's pretend play, by observing only in the home under these conditions Haight and Miller might well have overestimated the extent to which children engage in pretend play. Similarly, by focusing on children at play in school playgrounds, Pellegrini (1988, 1995) is likely to have overestimated how much time children actually spend in rough-and-tumble play.

By contrast, those who have relied on parental reports may well have underestimated the extent to which children are engaged in some types of activities, including their play. Two nationally representative studies (Hofferth & Sandberg, 2001; Timmer et al., 1989) and one study conducted partly in Wisconsin (Bloch, 1989) revealed that three- to five-year-old children spent from between 18–30% of their time in play, and 10–14% of their time watching television. Parmar and her colleagues (2004) used parental reports and reported that both European- and Asian-American children spent about 16 hours per week in play, and between four and five hours a week watching television. Interestingly, our data were very similar for TV-watching (12% across our four groups from Greensboro) but the nationally representative data, and those from the other two studies, reported far less play than we did (on average, 48%, excluding time spent watching television). Our data were also very close to the nationally representative data in terms of time spent in child care (16%). Parents thus seem well able to assess the amount of time their children spend doing something with clearly delineated time boundaries (television programs and child care), but (not surprisingly) less able to tell how much time their children spend in other types of activities, including their play.

The situation in Kisumu looked very different from what we have just described in Greensboro. The Luo children, from both middle- and working-class families, were far less likely to play with toys than were any other group, but were more likely to play with objects from the adult world. They were also more likely to play with objects from the

Table 11.2 Means and Standard Deviations for Children's Engagement in Types of Play in Kisumu, Kenya, and Porto Alegre, Brazil (percent of observations)

Types of Play	KIS MC (n=10)	KIS WC (n=10)	POA MC (n=9)	POA WC (n=10)
Pretend	4.17 (4.2)	2.0 (2.8)	3.52 (2.9)	3.67 (4.9)
School-related	6.67 (3.1)	3.33 (3.9)	3.64 (3.4)	0.33 (0.7)
Child-related obj.	12.28 (4.3)	13.11 (8.8)	25.93 (7.9)	30.0 (12.9)
Adult-related obj.	14.33 (5.0)	17.67 (6.6)	5.56 (2.1)	8.89 (4.9)
Natural obj.	9.11 (7.4)	7.44 (3.1)	1.48 (1.2)	1.83 (2.1)
No obj.	9.44 (2.7)	8.44 (3.8)	5.37 (3.0)	3.67 (2.2)
TV	2.94 (3.1)	2.05 (3.4)	8.70 (6.1)	12.72 (8.1)
Entertainment	0.28 (0.9)	0.61 (1.4)	1.91 (2.1)	1.39 (2.2)
All play	59.28 (8.2)	55.44 (12.4)	56.11 (9.8)	62.50 (12.7)

natural world and with no object at all than were children from either Greensboro or Porto Alegre. Middle-class Luo children were actually more likely to engage in both pretend play and play with school-related objects than were children in Greensboro, although their working-class Luo counterparts did so much less. Not surprisingly, children in Kisumu watched less television than did the children in the other cities, averaging less than 3% in both social-class groups.

As is clear from the data that we report here, the children from Kisumu were observed in play about twice as frequently as those reported by both Bloch (1989) and Bock (2005) in Senegal and Botswana respectively. There are three possible reasons. One is that our observational approaches are different. Bloch used spot observations, randomly selected from three large (4–5 hour) blocks of time, followed by written field notes, yielding 20 observations per child. Bock also collected approximately 20 observations of each child featured in his study, with data gathered at ten-minute intervals over three four-hour blocks of time during daylight hours. By contrast, each of our children was followed continuously in blocks of two and four hours, for a total of 180 observations per child. More important than the different methods employed, however, is the fact that we gathered our data from city-dwellers, rather than from the rural areas that feature so often in anthropological studies. As Weisner (1979) pointed out, in one of the few studies that compared family experiences in both rural and urban areas of Kenya, city-dwelling children have different options than

do their counterparts in rural areas, and it is not surprising that the latter are far more likely to be involved in work than the former.

The ecologies, then, are different, but so are the parents' experiences, which links to the third reason for possible differences. Kenyan society, as is true of both Senegal and Botswana, has changed rapidly over the past 50 years; not only do many more people live in urban areas, but schooling has become of increasing importance. All of the parents in our families had at least some education, and those from middle-class families had a college education. More than half of our middle-class children in Kisumu attended a formal child-care center, as did one of the working-class children, and their experiences there included a good deal of play with school-related materials.

In Porto Alegre, children engaged in types of play similarly to those in Greensboro, in that they were most likely to be observed playing with toys in both the middle-class (26% of observations) and working-class community (30%). These children were also as likely as those in Greensboro to watch television and did so in 8% (middle class) and 12% (working class) of our observations. On the other hand, although the Brazilian children were as likely as their white counterparts in Greensboro to engage in pretend play (over 3% of our observations in both social-class groups) and with school-related objects among middle-class children (3.5%), the working-class children were almost never observed in this type of play (less than 0.5% of our observations). By contrast, they were more likely to play with objects from the adult world (6% and 8% of observations, for the middle- and working-class children) and with no object at all (5% and 4% respectively).

Thus, even within a single city one can see that children from different social classes engaged to different extents in various types of play; heterogeneity of experience is clearly not found only when comparing the majority and industrialized world or even rural and urban contexts within a single society. One must be extremely cautious about allowing any one group to "represent" an entire country.

Who were the children's partners in play? Much of the literature on young children's play in the United States and Britain focuses on the involvement of parents and siblings, with mothers featuring prominently as their children's primary partner (Dunn, 1988, 2005; Fischer & Fischer, 1963; Haight & Miller, 1993; Newson & Newson, 1968). Recently there has been greater interest in father involvement in play, with a number of scholars arguing that fathers are less involved than mothers with their children primarily because fathers spend less time in the same setting as their children; fathers are equally, or more, involved, however, in proportion to their presence in the child's environment (Lamb, 1997; Parke, 2000; Pleck, 1997). The literature on Kenya, however, paints a different picture—one in which neither mother nor father are involved in children's play, which is the domain of siblings and peers (Edwards & Whiting, 1993; Harkness & Super, 1985; LeVine & LeVine, 1963; Wenger, 1989; Whiting & Edwards, 1988).

In our data, we found that in Greensboro, Kisumu, and Porto Alegre, children were actually more likely to play by themselves than to play with their mother, and that their most likely play partners were other children (whether siblings or not). In Greensboro, in the working-class black community, grandmothers and the children's child-care teachers were almost as likely as mothers to be involved in the children's play. The same was found in Porto Alegre, in both the middle- and working-class communities. In Kisumu, however, as past scholars have noted, mothers and fathers were only minimally involved in their children's play—in a little over 5% of our observations. In that Kenyan city, the children were playing with other children in about half of our observations of their play, but in about 40% of our observations of their play they were playing alone, which does not fit well with previous data.

As far as the father's role is concerned, we always noted whether the mother or father (defined as a social category, rather than necessarily biological) was in the same setting as the child while coding the children's participation in their various activities and interactions. We thus can answer those who say that fathers, proportionally, are as involved as mothers in their young children's play. In all of the groups from whom we collected data, mothers were always more likely to be found in the children's setting than were fathers, and so clearly had the opportunity to act as their children's partners in any of the activities in which the latter were involved. Indeed, they were far more likely to be engaged with the children than were fathers in all of the children's activities.

To what extent were fathers more engaged in play with their children than mothers when taking into account their lesser availability to the children? In Greensboro they were not; mothers were one and a half times more likely than were fathers to be observed playing with their children when expressed as a proportion of their availability. However, there were some types of play in which fathers were as likely or a little more likely than mothers to feature as partners. Middle-class fathers, both white and black, were more likely to play with their children using objects from the adult world and natural world, and white working-class fathers were proportionally more involved than were mothers in their children's pretend play, play with school-related objects and play with no objects at all (rough and tumble, running, singing, and so on). Black fathers from working-class families were also more likely, proportional to their availability, to play with their children using objects from the natural world. But for all other types of play mothers were more likely to be their children's partners, both in fact and when expressed as a proportion of their availability.

In Kisumu, as mentioned earlier, mothers were far less likely to be engaged in play with their children than were mothers in other groups, but although fathers were not often observed in play or entertainment with their children, they did not look strikingly different from fathers in other cities. However, taking into account their more limited availability, in the middle-class community fathers were more involved than were the mothers, primarily because they were three or more times as likely to be engaged with their children in play with objects from the natural world, play with no object at all, and watching television. In the working-class community in Kisumu, similarly, neither mothers nor fathers were often observed playing with their children. However, fathers and mothers were similarly involved, both actually and proportionally to their availability.

In Porto Alegre, the situation also clearly varied by social class. In the middle-class community fathers were only slightly less likely to play with their children than were mothers and, expressed proportionally to availability, actually did so slightly more than did mothers. Of the seven different categories of play and entertainment, middle-class fathers were more involved with their children in four (school-related play, play with toys, play with no objects, and watching television) and were only slightly less likely to play with their children with objects from the adult world. By contrast, working-class fathers there were both less likely to be involved actually and proportionally, although they were proportionally more likely than were mothers to engage with their children in the course of their play with objects from the adult world, the natural world, and with no objects.

Conclusion

Different methods, from the experimental to the ethnographic, have been used to study play. To some extent, the choice of methods depends on one's disciplinary training. Scholars trained within psychology or human development are more likely to have learned to use methods that involve some degree of control, by observing play within controlled or semi-controlled settings or relying on scripted interviews or questionnaires. Scholars trained within anthropology are more likely to have learned to use ethnographic methods that require them to observe and interact relatively freely with their participants.

However, extending beyond disciplinary boundaries are the paradigms or worldviews into which our theories about play fit; their different ontological and epistemological positions are necessarily linked to methods that are viewed as acceptable. Those whose theories are mechanist (a neo-positivist paradigm) clearly look for methods that involve control as a way to predict and generalize, whereas those whose theories are contextualist (a non-positivist paradigm) hold that the conditions that shape play (and any other human activity) can only be understood by becoming immersed in them.

Those who study play as it occurs in its everyday contexts, the focus of this chapter, are clearly more likely to fit within the contextualist paradigm. Nonetheless, as we have shown, the methods are far from identical. Scholars conducting their research within the United States have either observed in a restricted number of the settings in which young children spend their time (home, or child-care center, or during free play at school) or have questioned parents about the extent of their children's involvement in different types of play. By contrast, those who do their research in the majority world have been far more likely to observe the children at play in any of the settings in which they would commonly be found.

This use of different methods to study play in different parts of the world is problematic, for example when we note that children in one group often play while working but when gathering data on children in another group do so only at times or under conditions in which they are unlikely to be found involved in work. Similarly, can one really compare data gathered from parents about their children's play in one group with data gathered observationally in another group? Some ethnographers might respond that the purpose is not to compare one group to another, but to understand a group solely in its own terms. The problem is that this approach implicitly leaves it up to the readers of the published research to make the comparison between this group's practices and those of their own.

It is also troubling that so much of the ethnographic research on children's play that we described above, whether collected in Kenya, Botswana, Liberia, Senegal, or Brazil, was conducted in rural areas, with parents who had little or no formal education, with little attention paid to the passage of time and the impact of urbanization and education in these societies. Children's play in these countries also occurs in middle-class homes, and in child-care centers, as well as on the streets or tending cattle. These countries cannot be simply represented as exemplifying one type of community, whether it is an isolated village or a gang of street children, but as diverse heterogeneous contexts in which children are developing.

We have therefore described in this chapter a specifically contextualist theory and methods that were designed explicitly to fit with the theory. The methods are such that they can be used in a wide variety of contexts, although so far they have only been used in urban settings, given the relative lack of such data. Here we presented data only from three cities, one from the southern United States, one from the western part of Kenya, and one from the south of Brazil. Families from middle- and working-class homes were included, simply to give a taste to the heterogeneity that exists within each city.

These data on children's play reveal things that previous research has not. For example, these city-dwelling children spent a far greater proportion of their time in play than has been noted in previous literature, and the middle-class children from Kisumu engaged in more school-related play than did the children in Greensboro. Although Kisumu parents played less with their children than was the case in the other two cities, our data call into question the idea that "Kenyan" parents do not consider it acceptable to play with their children. Our data also cast doubt on the position that "American" fathers play with their children more than do mothers, once their limited availability is taken into account or that mothers are the primary partner in play. In fact, it was only in Porto Alegre that fathers were as involved as much as were mothers in their children's play; in Greensboro, other children were more likely than was the mother to be the partner in play, and in the black community in Greensboro grandmothers and the children's childcare teachers were as likely to play with the children as were their mothers.

Lancy noted that "quantitative studies of mother–child play that would yield a metric we might use in comparing incidence cross-culturally are rare" (2007, p. 275). The method we have described here should aid in this endeavor. Quantitative metrics are dangerous tools, however; too often they can be treated as a single measuring stick, with groups falling lower on the metric viewed as at a deficit or disadvantage compared to those at the top. A contextualist approach, however, eschews such a position. Instead, what we need to understand are the cultural values and beliefs that account for the different patterns of activities and interactions that are found in different groups, or in the same group over time.

Future Directions

• Given that different paradigms involve different ontologies, epistemologies, and methods, one can argue that it is impossible to do "mixed-methods" research in which the methods stem from different paradigms.

• Alternatively, a pragmatic position (see Creswell, 2003) holds that quantitative and qualitative methods are compatible and enhance the understanding of a research problem. Is a pragmatic approach to studying play inevitable given the diversity of methods?

• Given that to understand any aspect of human development, including the extent, types, and functions of play, requires insights from multiple disciplines, including history, anthropology, sociology, and psychology, what can be done to encourage multidisciplinarity in universities dominated by disciplinary boundaries?

• Can the methods described here be used in any settings, and with adolescents or adults rather than with children? Young children quickly become accustomed to the presence of an observer and seem to behave quite normally, but would more time or different methods be needed when observing those who are older?

Notes

1 We would like to thank the parents and children from Greensboro, Kisumu, and Porto Alegre, who gave so generously of their time, and Sarah Putnam, Judy Sidden, Fabienne Doucet, Nicole Talley, Dolphine Odero-Wanga, Giana Frizzo, Fernanda Marques, and Rafael Spinneli, who collected the data reported in this chapter. We are also grateful to the Spencer Foundation, CAPES (Coordenação de Aperfeiçoamento de Pessoal de Nível Superior), and the Council for the International Exchange of Scholars (Fulbright Program) for grants and awards to the first author which assisted in the gathering of the data and the writing of this chapter.

2 An early version of the method was developed in conjunction with Barbara Rogoff and Gilda Morelli.

References

Adamopoulos, J., & Lonner, W. J. (2001). Culture and psychology at a crossroad: Historical perspective and theoretical analysis. In D. Matsumoto (Ed.), *The handbook of culture and psychology* (pp. 11–34). Oxford: Oxford University Press.

Alves, P. B. (2004). O estudo sobre crianças em situação de rua na perspectiva da teoria dos sistemas ecológicos: Contribuições teóricas e metodológicas [The study of street children from a systems theory perspective: Theoretical and methodological contributions]. In S. Koller (Ed.), *Ecologia do desenvolvimento humano: Pesquisa e intervenção no Brasil* [*The ecology of human development: Research and intervention in Brazil*] (pp. 121–141). São Paulo: Casa do Psicólogo.

Atkinson, P., Coffey, A., Delamont, S., Lofland, J., & Lofland, L. (2001). (Eds.) *Handbook of ethnography*. London: Sage.

Bjorklund, D. F., & Pellegrini, A. D. (2002). *Evolutionary developmental psychology*. Washington, DC: American Psychological Association.

Bloch, M. N. (1989). Young boy's and girl's play at home and in the community: A cultural-ecological framework. In M. N. Bloch & A. D. Pellegrini (Eds.), *The ecological context of children's play* (pp. 120–154). Norwood, NJ: Ablex.

Bloch, M. N. & Adler, S. M. (1994). African children's play and the emergence of the sexual division of labor. In J. Roopnarine, J. Johnson, & F. Hooper (Eds), *Children's play in diverse cultures* (pp. 148–178). Albany: State University of New York Press.

Bock, J. (2002). Learning, life history, and productivity: Children's lives in the Okavango Delta of Botswana. *Human Nature, 13*, 161–198.

Bock, J. and Johnson, S. E. (2004). Subsistence ecology and play among the Okavango Delta peoples of Botswana. *Human Nature, 15*, 63–81.

Bock, J. and Johnson, S. E. (2005). Farming, foraging and children's play in the Okavango Delta, Botswana. In A. Pellegrini and P. K. Smith (Eds). *The nature of play: Great apes and humans* (pp. 254–281). New York: The Guilford Press.

Bornstein, M. H. (2006). On the significance of social relationships in the development of children's earliest symbolic play: An ecological perspective. In A. Göncü & S. Gaskins (Eds.), *Play and development: Evolutionary, sociocultural, and functional perspectives* (pp. 101–129). New York: Lawrence Erlbaum Associates.

Brewer, J. D. (2000). *Ethnography*. Buckingham, UK: Open University Press.

Bronfenbrenner, U. (1993). The ecology of cognitive development: Research models and fugitive findings. In R. Wozniak & K. Fischer (Eds.), *Development in context: Acting and thinking in specific environments* (pp. 3–44). Hillsdale, NJ: Erlbaum.

Bronfenbrenner, U. (1994). Ecological models of human development. In T. Husen & T. N. Postlethwaite (Eds.), *International Encyclopedia of Education* (2nd Ed., Vol. 3, pp. 1643–1647). Oxford, England: Pergamon Press.

Bronfenbrenner, U. (1995). Developmental ecology through space and time: A future perspective. In P. Moen, G. H. Elder, Jr., & K. Lüscher (Eds.), *Examining lives in context: Perspectives on the ecology of human development* (pp. 619–647). Washington, DC: American Psychological Association.

Bronfenbrenner, U. (1999). Environments in developmental perspective: Theoretical and operational models. In S. L. Friedman & T. D. Wachs (Eds.), *Measuring environment across the life span: Emerging methods and concepts* (pp. 3–28). Washington, DC: American Psychological Association Press.

Bronfenbrenner, U. (2005). The bioecological theory of human development. In U. Bronfenbrenner (Ed.), *Making human beings human: Bioecological perspectives on human development* (pp. 3–15). Thousand Oaks, CA: Sage. (Original work published 2001)

Bronfenbrenner, U., & Morris, P. A. (2006). The bioecological model of human development. In W. Damon (Series Ed.) & R. M. Lerner (Vol. Ed.), *Handbook of child psychology: Vol. 1. Theoretical models of human development* (6th ed., pp. 793–828). New York: John Wiley.

Brown, S. (2009). *Play: How it shapes the brain, opens the imagination, and invigorates the soul.* New York: Penguin.

Carvalho, A. M. A., & Pedrosa, M. I. (2002). Culture in the play group. *Estudos Psicológicos, 7*(1), 181–188.

Cole, M. (1996). *Cultural psychology: A once and future discipline.* Cambridge, MA: Harvard University Press.

Cole, M. (2005). Cultural-historical activity theory in the family of socio-cultural approaches. *International Society for the Study of Behavioural Development Newsletter, 47*(1), 1–4.

Creswell, J.W. (2003). *Research design: Qualitative, quantitative and mixed method research.* Thousand Oaks, CA: Sage.

Domeniconi, C., Costa, A. R. A., Souza, D. G., & Rose, J. C. (2007). Exclusion-responding by 2- to 3-year-old children in a play setting. *Psicologia: Reflexão e Crítica, 20*(2), 342–350.

Dunn, J. (1988). *The beginnings of social understanding.* Cambridge, MA: Harvard University Press.

Dunn, J. (2005). Naturalistic observations of children and their families. In S. M. Greene & D. M. Hogan (Eds.), *Researching children's experience: Approaches and methods* (pp. 87–101). London: Sage.

Eckensberger, L. H. (2002). Paradigms revisited: From incommensurability to respected complementarity. In H. Keller, Y. H. Poortinga, & A. Schölmerich (Eds.), *Between culture and biology: Perspectives on ontogenetic development* (pp. 341–383). Cambridge: Cambridge University Press.

Edwards, C. P., & Whiting, B. B. (1993). "Mother, older sibling, and me": The overlapping roles of caregivers and companions in the social world of two- to three-year-olds in Ngeca, Kenya. In K MacDonald (Ed.), *Parent–child play: Descriptions and implications* (pp. 305–329). Albany, NY: SUNY Press.

Fischer, J. L., & Fischer, A. (1963). The New Englanders of Orchard Town U. S. A. In B. B. Whiting (Ed.), *Six cultures: Studies of child rearing* (pp. 869–1010). New York: John Wiley.

Gil, M. S. C. A., & Almeida, N. V. F. (2000). Mother–infant interaction patterns in play situation. *Cadernos de Psicologia, 10*(1), 89–103.

Goldhaber, D.E. (2000). *Theories of human development: Integrative perspectives.* Mountain View, CA: Mayfield Publishing.

Göncü, A., & Gaskins, S. (Eds.) (2006). *Play and development: Evolutionary, sociocultural, and functional perspectives.* New York: Lawrence Erlbaum Associates.

Göncü, A., Jain, J., & Tuermer, U. (2006). Children's play as cultural interpretation. In A. Göncü & S. Gaskins (Eds.), *Play and development: Evolutionary, sociocultural, and functional perspectives* (pp. 155–178). New York: Lawrence Erlbaum Associates.

Göncü, A., Tuermer, U., Jain, J., & Johnson, D. (1999). Children's play as cultural activity. In A. Göncü (Ed.), *Children's engagement in the world: Sociocultural perspectives* (pp. 148–170). New York: Cambridge University Press.

Gosso, Y., Morais, M. L. S., & Otta, E. (2007). Pretend play of Brazilian children: A window into different cultural worlds. *Journal of Cross-Cultural Psychology, 38*(5), 539–558.

Gosso, Y., Otta, E., Morais, M. L. S., Ribeiro, F. J. L., & Bussab, V. S. R. (2005). Play in hunter-gatherer society. In A. D. Pellegrini & P. K. Smith (Eds.), *The nature of play: Great apes and humans* (pp. 213–253). New York: The Guilford Press.

Greenfield, P. M. (1976). Cross-cultural research and Piagetian theory: Paradox and progress. In K. F. Riegel & J. A. Meacham (Eds.), *The developing individual in a changing world, Vol 1: Historical and cultural issues* (pp. 322–345). Chicago: Aldine.

Guba, E. G., & Lincoln, Y. S. (1994). Competing paradigms in qualitative research. In N. K. Denzin & Y. S. Lincoln (Eds.), *Handbook of qualitative research* (pp. 105–117). Thousand Oaks, CA: Sage.

Guberman, S. R. (1996). The development of everyday mathematics in Brazilian children with limited formal education. *Child Development, 67,* 1609–1623.

Haight, W. L. (1999). The pragmatics of caregiver–child pretending at home: Understanding culturally specific socialization practices. In A. Göncü (Ed.), *Children's engagement in the world: Sociocultural perspectives* (pp. 128–147). New York: Cambridge University Press.

Haight, W. L., & Miller, P. J. (1993). *Pretending at home: Early development in a sociocultural context.* Albany: State University of New York Press.

Harkness, S., & Super, C. M. (1992). The cultural foundations of fathers' roles: Evidence from Kenya and the United States. In B. S. Hewlett (Ed.), *Father–child relations: Cultural and biosocial contexts* (pp. 191–211). New York: Aldine de Gruyter.

Harwood, R., Miller, G., & Lucca-Irizarry, N. (1995). *Culture and attachment: Perceptions of the child in context.* New York: Guilford Press.

Hecht, T. (1998). *At home in the street: Street children of Northeast Brazil.* New York: Cambridge University Press.

Hofferth, S. L., & Sandberg, J. F. (2001). How American children spend their time. *Journal of Marriage and Family, 63*(2), 295–308.

Kağitçibaşi, C. (1996). *Family and human development across cultures: A view from the other side.* Mahwah, NJ: Lawrence Erlbaum.

Kağitçibaşi, C. (2007). *Family, self, and human development across cultures: Theory and applications.* New York: Psychology Press.

Kishimoto, T. M., & Oto, A. T. (2008). Toys, gender and education in a toy library. *Pro-Prosições, 19*(3), 209–223.

Kuczynski, L., & Daly, K., (2003). Qualitative methods as inductive (theory-generating) research: Psychological and sociological approaches. In L. Kuczynski (Ed.), *Handbook of dynamics in parent–child relations* (pp. 373–392). Thousand Oaks, CA: Sage.

Lamb, M. E. (Ed.). (1997). *The role of the father in child development* (3rd ed.). New York: Wiley.

Lancy, D. F. (1996). *Playing on the mother ground: Cultural routines for children's development.* New York: Guilford Press.

Lancy, D. F. (2007). Accountability for availability in mother–child play. *American Anthropologist, 109,* 273–284.

LeVine, R. A. (1989). Cultural environments in child development. In W. Damon (Ed.), *Child development today and tomorrow* (pp. 52–68). San Francisco: Jossey-Bass.

LeVine, R. A. (2007). Ethnographic studies of childhood: A historical overview. *American Anthropologist, 109*(2), 247–260.

LeVine, R. A., Dixon, S., LeVine, S., Richman, A., Leiderman, P. H., Keefer, C. H., & Brazelton, T. B. (1994). *Child care and culture: Lessons from Africa.* New York: Cambridge University Press.

LeVine, R. A., & LeVine B. B. (1963). Nyansongo: A Gusii community in Kenya. In B. B. Whiting (Ed.), *Six cultures: Studies of child rearing* (pp. 14–202). New York: John Wiley.

Lordelo, E. R., & Carvalho, A. M. A. (2006). Patterns of social partnership and play in daycare centers. *Psicologia em Estudo, 11*(1), 99–108.

Macarini, S. M., & Vieira, M. L. (2006). The play of schoolage children in a play library. *Revista Brasileira de Crescimento de Desenvolvimento Humano, 16*(1), 49–60.

Malinowski, B. (1927). *Sex and repression in savage society.* New York: Harcourt Brace.

Mead, M. (1961). *Coming of age in Samoa.* New York: New American Library. (Original work published 1928)

Miller, P. J., Hengst, J. A., & Wang, S. (2003). Ethnographic methods: Applications from developmental cultural psychology. In P. M. Camic, J. E. Rhodes, & L. Yardley (Eds.), *Qualitative research in psychology: Expanding perspectives in methodology and design* (pp. 219–242). Washington: American Psychological Association.

Newson, J., & Newson, E. (1968). *Four years old in an urban community.* Chicago: Aldine de Gruyter.

Nunes, T., Schliemann, A.-L., & Carraher, D. (1993). *Street mathematics and school mathematics.* New York: Cambridge University Press.

Parke, R. D. (2000). Father involvement: A developmental psychological perspective. *Marriage and Family Review, 29*(2–3), 43–58.

Pedrosa, M. I., & Carvalho, A. M. A. (1995). Social interaction and the construction of play. *Cadernos de Pesquisa, 93,* 60–65.

Pellegrini, A. D. (1988). Elementary school children's rough-and-tumble play and social competence. *Developmental Psychology, 24,* 802–806.

Pellegrini, A. D. (1995). *School recess and playground behavior.* Albany, NY: State University of New York Press.

Pellegrini, A. D. (2009). *The role of play in human development.* New York: Oxford University Press.

Pellegrini, A. D., & Bjorklund, D. F. (2004). The ontogeny and phylogeny of children's object and fantasy play. *Human Nature, 15*(1), 23–43.

Pellegrini, A. D., & Smith, P. K. (1998). Physical activity play: The nature and function of a neglected aspect of play. *Child Development, 69*(3), 289–296.

Pellegrini, A. D., & Smith, P. K. (Eds.) (2009). *The nature of play: Great apes and humans.* New York: The Guilford Press.

Pepper, S. C. (1942). *World hypotheses: A study in evidence.* Berkeley: University of California Press.

Pleck, J. H. (1997). Paternal involvement: Levels, sources, and consequences. In M. E. Lamb (Ed.), *The role of the father in child development* (3rd ed., pp. 66–103). New York: Wiley.

Sager, F., & Sperb, T. M. (1998). Plays, toys and children's conflicts. *Psicologia: Reflexão e Crítica, 11*(2), 309–326.

Saxe, G. B. (1991). *Culture and cognitive development: Studies in mathematical understanding.* Hillsdale, NJ: Erlbaum.

Scheper-Hughes, N. (1985). Culture, scarcity, and maternal thinking: Maternal detachment and infant survival in a Brazilian shantytown. *Ethos, 13,* 291–317.

Scheper-Hughes, N. (1990). Mother love and child death in northeast Brazil. In J. W. Stigler, R. A. Shweder, & G. Herdt (Eds.), *Cultural psychology: Essays on comparative human development* (pp. 542–565). Cambridge: Cambridge University Press.

Scheper-Hughes, N. (1992). *Death without weeping: The violence of everyday life in Brazil.* Berkeley: University of California Press.

Schliemann, A. D., Carraher, D. W., & Ceci, S. J. (1997). Everyday cognition. In J. W. Berry, P. R. Dasen, & T. S. Sarasthwati (Eds.), *Handbook of cross-cultural psychology. Vol.2: Basic processes and human development* (pp. 177–216). Boston: Allyn and Bacon.

Shweder, R. A. (1990). Cultural psychology – what is it? In J. W. Stigler, R. A. Shweder, & G. Herdt (Eds.), *Cultural psychology: Essays on comparative human development* (pp. 1–43). New York: Cambridge University Press.

Shweder, R. A, Mahapatra, M., & Miller, J. (1990). Culture and moral development. In J. Stigler, R. Shweder, & G. Herdt (Eds.) *Cultural psychology: Essays on comparative human development* (pp. 130–204). New York: Cambridge University Press.

Smith, P. K. (1982). Does play matter? Functional and evolutionary aspects of animal and human play. *The Behavioral and Brain Sciences, 5,* 139–184.

Sperb, T. M., & Conti, L. (1998). The metarepresentative dimension of pretense. *Padéia, 8*(14–15), 75–89.

Timmer, S. G., Eccles, J., & O'Brien, K. (1985). How children use time. In F. T. Juster & F. P. Stafford (Eds.), *Time, goods, and well-being* (pp. 353–382). Ann Arbor: Survey Research Center, University of Michigan.

Tudge, J. R. H. (2008). *The everyday lives of young children: Culture, class, and child rearing in diverse societies.* New York: Cambridge University Press.

Tudge, J., Gray, J., & Hogan, D. (1997). Ecological perspectives in human development: A comparison of Gibson and

Bronfenbrenner. In J. Tudge, M. Shanahan, & J. Valsiner (Eds.), *Comparisons in human development: Understanding time and context* (pp. 72–105). New York: Cambridge University Press.

Tudge, J. R. H., & Odero-Wanga, D. (2009). A cultural–ecological perspective on early childhood among the Luo of Kisumu, Kenya. In M. Fleer, M. Hedegaard, & J. R. H. Tudge (Eds.). *The world year book of education 2009: Childhood studies and the impact of globalization: Policies and practices at global and local levels* (pp. 142–160). New York: Routledge.

Tudge, J., Odero, D., Hogan, D., & Etz, K. (2003). Relations between the everyday activities of preschoolers and their teachers' perceptions of their competence in the first years of school. *Early Childhood Research Quarterly, 18,* 42–64.

Tudge, J. R. H., & Scrimsher, S. (2003). Lev S. Vygotsky on education: A cultural-historical, interpersonal, and individual approach to development. In B. J. Zimmerman & D. H. Schunk (Eds.), *Educational psychology: A century of contributions* (pp. 207–228). Mahwah, NJ: Lawrence Erlbaum Associates.

Valsiner, J., & Winegar, L. T. (1992). Introduction: A cultural-historical context for social "context". In L. T. Winegar & J. Valsiner (Eds.), *Children's development within social context: Volume 1, Metatheory and theory* (pp. 1–14). Hillsdale, NJ: Erlbaum.

Vygotsky, L. S. (1987). *The collected works of L. S. Vygotsky: Vol. 1, Problems of general psychology* (R. W. Rieber & A. S. Carton, Eds.; N. Minick, Trans.). New York: Plenum. (Original publication, 1934, written between 1929 and 1934.)

Vygotsky, L. S. (1994). The problem of the environment. In R. Van der Veer & J. Valsiner (Eds.), *The Vygotsky reader* (pp. 338–354). Oxford: Basil Blackwell. (Original work published 1935)

Wanderlind, F. (2006). Gender differences in play of preschool and school children at a toy library. *Padéia, 16*(34), 263–273.

Weisner, T. S. (1979). Urban–rural differences in sociable and disruptive behavior of Kenya children. *Ethnology, 18*(2), 153–172.

Weisner, T. S. (1989). Cultural and universal aspects of social support for children: Evidence from the Abaluyia of Kenya. In D. Belle (Ed.), *Children's social networks and social supports* (pp. 70–90). New York: Wiley.

Weisner, T. S. (1996). Why ethnography should be the most important method in the study of human development. In R. Jessor, A. Colby, & R. A. Shweder (Eds.), *Ethnography and human development: Context and meaning in social enquiry* (pp. 305–324). Chicago: University of Chicago Press.

Wenger, M. (1989). Work, play, and social relationships among children in a Giriama community. In D. Belle (Ed.), *Children's social networks and social supports* (pp. 91–115). New York: Wiley.

Whiting, B. B. (Ed.). (1963). *Six cultures: Studies of child rearing.* Cambridge, MA: Harvard University Press.

Whiting, B. B., & Edwards C. P. (1988). *Children of different worlds: The formation of social behavior.* Cambridge, MA: Harvard University Press.

Whiting, B. B., & Whiting, J. W. M. (1975). *Children of six cultures: A psycho-cultural analysis.* Cambridge, MA: Harvard University Press.

Winegar, L. T. (1997). Developmental research and comparative perspectives: Applications to developmental science. In J. Tudge, M. Shanahan, & J. Valsiner (Eds.), *Comparisons in human development: Understanding time and context* (pp. 13–33). New York: Cambridge University Press.

Observational Methods in Studying Play

Peter K. Smith

Abstract

In this chapter I discuss the use of observational methods in the study of play, both in humans and non-human species. In the first part, I give a short history of observational methods, and then consider issues around types of observational methods, such as participant and non-participant observation, and (briefly) alternatives to observation (for human children: indirect methods based on verbal report, such as interviews and questionnaires). Intersecting with the use of observational measures is the context of observation, and in particular whether behavior is heavily constrained within the setting, and whether the environment can be considered 'natural.' The 'discovery' of rough-and-tumble play in human children provides an interesting case study of the importance of observational methods. In the second part, I consider some theoretical presuppositions regarding observational work, moving into the main technical issues: category schemes, recording techniques, measures, sampling, analysing, and reliability and validity; with some examples from studies of play.

Keywords: play, observation, categories, sampling methods, reliability, validity

History of Observational Methods

For ethologists and psychologists interested in studying behavior, observing behavior—watching what children (or older people) and animals do—is an obvious method! Ethologists studying animal behavior, including play, have basically had to rely on this; although the sophistication of using such methods has increased. But the history of observational methods in studying children's play is more varied. Observational studies of children have, in fact, occurred in two main phases during the twentieth century. The first was in the 1930s, uninfluenced by animal research. The second has been since the 1970s, in part influenced by animal ethology (Fassnacht, 1982).

The 1930s work developed many of the main aspects of observational methodology—category systems, sampling methods, and reliability checks—that are of importance to this day; see for example the review by Arrington (1943) at the end of this period.

These studies lacked a comparative and evolutionary perspective (Smith & Connolly, 1972), and did not pay much attention to rough-and-tumble play, for example. They tended to focus on teacher-led constructs. As an example, Manwell and Mengert (1934) used categories such as Group play, Independence of group, Watching others at play, Physical activity, Creative or constructive activity, Manipulative activity, Dramatic activity, Interest in stories, Interest in pictures, and Interest in music. Nevertheless, this research laid the groundwork for our knowledge of typical behavior patterns in Western children in the twentieth century. It was put to good use in the child welfare institutes and the playgroups and nursery classes starting up in the US, the UK, and other Western countries, at that period.

Despite the 1930s work, direct observational methods largely fell into disuse after the 1940s. Most research, including that on play, used questionnaires, interviews, and tests in controlled laboratory situations. In the 1950s and 1960s observational methods were quite neglected. This began to change at the end of the 1960s, and the impetus for change first came from ethology. Ethological methodology, with an emphasis on observation in natural environments, had been developed through the preceding decades, initially, at least, largely independent from psychological research on animal behavior. Lorenz and Tinbergen, the two great pioneers of modern ethology, both advocated the application of ethology to the study of human behavior. By the late 1960s, examples of such application were appearing in Britain, Germany, and other countries.

In Britain, Blurton Jones (having completed a doctorate with Tinbergen) started studying the social behavior of children in nursery school. His first published work in this area (Blurton Jones, 1967) was in a book titled *Primate Ethology*. Another pioneer of the application of ethological methods to humans was Hutt. The 1970 volume by Hutt and Hutt (1970), *Direct Observation and Measurement of Behavior*, helped to revive interest in observational methodology generally, as well as arguing the benefits of drawing on the work of animal ethologists. These and other researchers in Britain formed a lively nucleus of human ethologists who formed links with researchers in Germany (e.g., Eibl-Eibesfeldt, 1967) and soon with researchers in the United States, such as Charlesworth and Hartup. Although natural observation was only one component of the human ethology movement, it did act as a catalyst in bringing such methods back into the mainstream of psychology. Nowadays, observational methods are recognized as having their own place among a range of methods psychologists use (e.g. Hobart & Frankel, 2004; Pellegrini, 2004), and they are certainly widely used in children's play studies. There is also a considerable literature on observational methods in the behavior analysis literature (Yoder & Symons, 2010), including important work on reliability issues, although the specific content of this work does not strongly feature play behaviors.

Non-participant and Participant Observation

'Non-participant' means that the observer stands apart from the individuals being observed, interacting minimally if at all. When we are studying behavior in, say, herring gulls, or macaques, non-participant observation is a the natural method to adopt. We cannot be participant observers in the usual sense of the word, even though we may wish the animals to be familiar with our presence. Most observational studies of children's play have also been non-participant.

Nevertheless, participant observation has a place in studying children's play. A famous example is Piaget's early study of boys playing with marbles, around Neuchatel in the suburbs of Geneva in Switzerland (Piaget, 1932/1977). He was interested in how children acquired the rules of the game, where they thought the rules came from, and whether the rules could be altered. He spent time in watching children at play; but in addition he interacted with the children in various ways—he talked to the children directly ('teach me the rules'); he played with a child, pretending to be ignorant so that the child had to explain the rules; and he interviewed children about where rules came from and whether they could be changed. A large-scale follow-up was made some 50 years later by a Spanish psychologist, Linaza (1984). He used similar methods with several hundred children, in England and Spain, about marbles and other games. He confirmed and elaborated the main aspects of Piaget's sequence, although different games did vary in the age at which certain stages of reasoning were usually attained.

Anthropology too provides examples of both non-participant and participant observation (as well as non-observational approaches). In the ethnographic method, observation is combined with verbal inquiry. Like ethologists, ethnographers (see Tudge et al., this volume) may spend time getting to know the situation before trying to interpret it (see below). But ethnographers usually engage in participant observation; they see themselves as part of the social situation. They are likely to look for key informants and question them at some length about the meaning of what is going on. They compare different informants' accounts and attempt to arrive at an interpretation of the meaning of events. Examples of ethnographic studies of children's play are (by an anthropologist) Lancy's study of Kpelle children (Lancy, 1996), and (by a psychologist) Sluckin's study of children in a primary school playground in Oxfordshire (Sluckin, 1981). By contrast, ethologists working with nonverbal animal species rely on the actual behaviors (including vocal and verbal behaviors) in interpreting what is happening.

With children, verbal material can help decide whether play is pretend, or not. Takhvar and Smith (1990) combined observations of children's object or construction play with short interviews afterwards where they asked a child what they were doing. Quite often, a child making what looked like just a pile or tower of blocks would describe it in pretend terms, as for example a 'prison' or 'space tower'; in other words, what might be categorized as just construction play might be re-categorized as pretend play after these interviews were conducted.

Many studies of children's social behavior have combined observational data with other kinds of data, such as sociometric data based on interviews, or responses to video material. For example, Humphreys and Smith (1984) combined direct observation of children's rough-and-tumble play (and choice of play partners), with peer nominations for toughness or dominance, to examine age-related changes in possible functions of rough-and-tumble play in later childhood. Few, if any, current researchers would want to argue that direct observation is the only useful way of getting data on children's play, although many might wish to advocate it as the most useful way, for certain purposes.

Direct Observation and Alternatives to Observation

'Direct' observation means that no 'indirect' measures (such as tests or interviews) stand between the observer and the observed, and that records are compiled immediately, not retrospectively. Direct observation has the advantage that the investigator can record what "really" happens, rather than what someone says happens or has an impression of happening. In this sense, direct observation appears to yield more valid data, or at least data whose validity we can be more confident of, than other methods of data gathering. In particular, interview or questionnaire data may draw out socially desirable responses. It is, of course, true that the act of observing may itself induce socially desirable behavior to be produced for the observer, or socially undesirable behavior to be inhibited (an issue discussed later under *Validity*). It is also true that what a child says happens may sometimes be as interesting as what 'really' happens. Nevertheless, direct observation clearly has strong face validity in terms of studying and understanding behavior.

As alternatives to observation, children can simply be asked about their play activities (e.g. Foster, 1930). In general, interviews are more useful with older children. Nevertheless even three and four year olds can give some useful information (as in Takhvar & Smith, above). More commonly, adults involved with a child might be interviewed or

given a questionnaire—usually, a parent or teacher. For example, there are questionnaires about imaginative or pretend play disposition that a parent can fill in to indicate the extent of such play they have seen in their child (Liebermann, 1977). Also, parental attitudes to children's play (e.g. Saar & Niglas, 2001), or parental ethnotheories (beliefs about the nature and purpose of play; e.g. Parmar, Harkness & Super, 2004), may be investigated by interview or questionnaire.

There are also more indirect sources of information on play. One possibility is to make toy inventories—lists of all the toys in a child's home. In the case of past historical periods, we cannot make direct observations, but we can learn something from toys made for children in earlier times; and from records made by adults of children playing, in diaries and autobiographies, or in paintings. Hanawalt (1993) used a range of such sources from medieval times to describe how London children then "played ball and tag, ran races, played hoops, and imitated adult ceremonies such as royal entries, masses, marriages, and the giants Gog and Magog" (p.78).

Setting Constraints and the Natural Environment

Another advantage of direct observation is that, following a period of relatively unstructured watching, the investigator may come up with behavioral categories or distinctions that were not previously conceived but that turn out to be useful or have some construct validity. This will hold force, regardless of the setting of the observation; but it may be especially meaningful if observations are made in 'natural settings.' If we take a 'natural setting' to correspond broadly to the kind of environment that the species observed has evolved in, and adapted to, then we can expect to be able to ask sensible questions about the adaptive or functional significance of behaviors (including play behaviors), which we could not, for example, about behavior in a cage or confined zoo setting. Of course more constrained or contrived situations may have some advantages in terms of control. But by simplifying the environment, certain behaviors are excluded and certain hypotheses will not be generated or tested from the resulting data; in addition, contrived situations may introduce unwanted behaviors, such as responses to a novel situation, or behavior directed to the experimenter.

The use of natural settings does not necessarily exclude some experimental control. An example of a combination of observational methods with systematic experimentation is a series of studies on the play-group environment by Smith and Connolly (1980). They carried out systematic environmental variations on two preschool play groups over a three-year period and made observations of the children's behavior. They varied aspects such as space available, toys available, and numbers of children in the group, in systematic ways; but then used direct observation to assess the effects of these environmental changes. As another example, Sharpe et al. (2002) carried out experimental manipulations of food provisioning, to examine the effects of this on play behaviors in free-ranging meerkats.

Direct observation in natural settings has had a special place in the study of animal behavior, since many zoologists, from Lorenz and Tinbergen onwards, have felt that unobtrusive recording of what goes on in the animal's natural environment is an essential first step if we want to get a clear idea of the animal's behavioral repertoire, and if we want to have any reasonable chance of understanding the functional significance of such behavior. Whereas psychologists as much as ethologists have been interested in understanding the causation and development of behavior, it has been a more distinctive concern of ethologists to understand the adaptive value of behavior for the individual, and the evolutionary history of how natural selection has favored this mode of behavioral adaptation (Tinbergen, 1951).

Observational studies of children's play, in both the 1930s (e.g. Hulson, 1930; Manwell & Mengert, 1934) and 1970s (Hutt & Hutt, 1970, Smith & Connolly, 1980) phases, although sometimes done in laboratory playrooms, have often been carried out in settings such as daycare centers, play groups, schools, or homes. This has been seen as an advantage in terms of the ecological validity of the studies and hence the confidence with which results can be taken to be representative of real life, compared with studies carried out in contrived or laboratory situations. Nevertheless, arguably no setting is totally 'natural' for humans in the way that certain settings can be seen as 'natural' for particular nonhuman species in terms of the ecological niche to which that species' behavior is adapted. As cultural animals, we have changed our environment too much; it can be argued that even the home of a nuclear family, or the large peer groups of a school, are somewhat 'unnatural' in these terms. Bensel (1992) made this point explicitly about toddler play groups. Thus, it would be wrong to be too dogmatic about the naturalness of settings in studying children's behavior. But most researchers have felt reasonably comfortable considering a play group or school playground as a natural setting, at least in comparison to the setting of a typical psychological laboratory. The basic points at issue are to which range of settings the investigator wishes to be able to generalize results, and how important and feasible it is, at the current level of knowledge, to include or exclude certain hypotheses from testing.

A Case Study: Rough-and-Tumble Play and Aggression

An interesting case study of how animal research has influenced children's research on play, and on some advantages of direct observation of behavior, comes from the history of study of rough-and-tumble play in children. The general types of fighting play had been described at least as far back as Groos (1901). However, for decades this kind of play was largely neglected by psychologists and educators; for example it does not feature in the play classifications of Piaget or Smilansky (see Smith, 2009). Blurton Jones (1967), observing children in nursery school, first described explicitly the behaviors involved in the rough-and-tumble play of preschool children, taking the term rough-and-tumble from Harlow's descriptions of play fighting in rhesus monkeys. He also showed that these behaviors occurred in sequences separate from aggressive behaviors.

Subsequent observational research on rough-and-tumble play confirmed that it can be distinguished from aggressive behavior in terms of the specific behaviors present (e.g., open rather than closed hand when making beating or hitting movements; play face rather than frown and fixate), and the context (e.g., participants tend to stay together rather than separate) (Smith & Lewis, 1985; Smith, 1997). Children who are often seen in aggression are not necessarily often seen in rough-and-tumble play (Blurton Jones, 1972). Combinations of observational work with interviews and sociometric assessments have shown that through the preschool and middle school years, children tend to like their rough-and-tumble play partners (Humphreys & Smith, 1987; Smith & Lewis, 1985), and from age four onwards, can articulate the ways in which rough-and-tumble play and real fighting can be distinguished (Smith & Lewis, 1985; Costabile et al., 1991; Smith, Smees, & Pellegrini, 2004).

Nevertheless, this distinction was not always observed in traditional psychological research.

As Blurton Jones (1972) pointed out, studies of the imitation of aggression in children (e.g., Bandura, Ross, & Ross, 1961; Nelson, Gelfand, & Hartmann, 1969) confounded play fighting with aggression. Measures such as punching a doll could be, and illustrations showed sometimes were, associated with rough-and-tumble indicators such as a play face, while measures such as gun play or fantasy aggression clearly implicated rough-and-tumble. Thus, one cannot conclude from these studies that watching aggression makes children more aggressive. Studies such as Huston-Stein, Fox, Greer, Watkins, and Whitaker (1981) and Potts, Huston, and Wright (1986) included hitting an inflated clown or bobo doll as aggressive, and thus continued this confound. In a study of the effects of density on aggression, Loo (1972) did not distinguish rough-and-tumble from real fighting. In a study of children's social networks, Ladd (1983) defined rough-and-tumble as "unorganized agonistic activity with others, e.g. fights or mock-fights, wrestling, pushing/shoving" (p. 291); thus his substantive finding, that rough-and-tumble play is more frequent in sociometrically rejected than in popular or average children, may reflect the effects of aggression as much as rough-and-tumble play per se.

From the 1980s, however, the distinctiveness of rough-and-tumble play has generally been recognized (see Pellis, this volume, for a research review). But teachers also have some misconceptions about rough-and-tumble play. Although most recognize that the two forms of behavior are distinct, Schäfer and Smith (1996), in a study of 30 English infant school teachers, found evidence that teachers overestimated the relative proportion of real fighting to rough-and-tumble play, and also the likelihood that rough-and- tumble play will turn into real fighting, compared with findings from observational studies (about 1%). Possibly, teachers are basing their judgments on unsystematic observations of a small number of aggressive and sociometrically rejected children for whom this really is true (Pellegrini, 1994; Smith, 1997).

Issues in Carrying out Observational Studies

Anyone can (and everyone does!) observe behavior. But to do it systematically, and in a way which can be communicated and replicated objectively, requires some trouble and working through a number of issues. Here, we will consider (1) theoretical presuppositions, pilot work and familiarization, (2) category schemes, (3) recording techniques, (4) measures of behavior, (5) sampling methods, (6) analyzing behavior, (7) reliability, and (8) validity.

Theoretical presuppositions, pilot work, and familiarization

There are normal preliminaries to every good observational study. Given selection of a topic, it is important to do a preliminary period of observation, or pilot work. This serves two functions. The first is to acclimatize the animals or children to the researcher's presence (see also *Validity*, later). The second is to familiarize yourself with the situation you are interested in. Even in a well-worked area, one should verify that previous studies match with one's own observations. But more generally, it is important to observe the range of behavior occurring in the situations you are working with, before moving on to categorize and record. This is so that the categories used to record would reflect what is actually going on, not our own preconceptions. Of course, some researchers will have a specific hypothesis they wish to test; for example, that play fighting will be reduced when less food is available. Even so, it will be worthwhile for that researcher to see what goes on generally when food is reduced; are there other variables that should be measured, too?

There are important philosophy of science considerations here, and a tension between primacy of theory and primacy of observation. By and large, and stemming from Aristotle, an inductivist view of science held sway for many centuries; Mill is a prominent example from the 19th century (see Chalmers, 1982). In brief, this holds that science proceeds by collecting factual data through observation, and by experimentation, which serves to increase the observational data base. For example, Pearson (who developed the well-known product-moment correlation coefficient) wrote that:

> "the classification of facts and the formation of absolute judgments upon the basis of this classification… essentially sum up the *aim and method of modern science*"
> (1891, p.6; his italics).

A crucial part of this traditional view was that hypothesis follows observation.

Yet, few modern philosophers of science accept this; most would argue that hypothesis precedes observation. Popper was one of the most well known philosophers of science to attack the traditional view, and to establish an alternative, hypothetico-deductive view (Popper, 1959, 1972). Popper held that science and knowledge progress by advancing hypotheses, making deductions from them, and using observations and experiments to continually test these deductions until they are falsified; then revising or changing the hypothesis to cope with this. (Note the increased role of experiments here, to explicitly test hypotheses). Hypotheses come first, and observations follow; "observations are interpretations... in the light of theories." Thus, observation is 'theory-laden'; there are always hypotheses implicit or explicit in observation (even, ultimately, back to innate perceptual hypotheses in the newborn infant).

This hypothetico-deductive view also has a long intellectual history, and indeed Darwin is quoted in the 1860s as saying "I have an old belief that a good observer really means a good theorist" and "how odd it is that anyone should not see that all observations must be for or against some view if it is to be of any service" (quoted in Medawar, 1969, p.11). And as Medawar (1969) put it, "we cannot browse over the field of nature like cows at pasture."

However, it is worth noting that some traditions in science and in social science are not compatible with too extreme a view of the hypothetico-deductive approach, including grounded theory in the social sciences. Ethologists too have emphasised the importance of getting rid of preconceptions, when studying a species of animal. In order to enter the animals own experienced environment, or *umwelt*, one should try to discard (so far as possible) ones' anthropomorphic expectations. Ethologists acknowledge that prior hypotheses bias our perceptions, as Popper does; but unlike Popper, they would see this as a hindrance rather than an advantage. They would argue that theories should emerge later, from immersion in the data.

No study is done in a theoretical vacuum. In an observational study of play, whether in animals or humans, the researcher will be influenced by scientific conceptions of what play is (Burghardt, this volume). It is impossible to observe 'everything,' and selections must be made about which sensory modalities to focus on, what contexts to observe in, and how behavior will be categorized and recorded (see next sections). However, a considered aim of this approach is that concepts, and subsequently theories, should emerge from an (as far as possible) unbiased immersion in what the environment or setting throws up in the way of data. Hypothesis testing is not rejected, but the intention is to go some way to an induction-deduction-testing cycle rather than a straightforward deduction-testing cycle which Popper espoused.

Developing categories

Having decided on a focus of study, and having familiarized oneself with the setting and the range of behaviors seen, the normal next step in quantitative observational research is to develop a set of behavior categories. In settings where there has been much previous research, it is often useful to take a pre-existing category scheme. For example with preschool children in play groups in Western countries, one widely used list is the Play Observation Scheme (POS) devised by Rubin (see Rubin, 2001). This is based on the Piaget/Smilansky sequence of functional, constructive and dramatic play, and Parten's categories of social participation. However, for situations where there has not been much if any previous research on play, a new category scheme will need to be developed. In any event, the category scheme should be trialed out before being used. One then can use the category scheme to make systematic observations and address the problem of interest; this might be what play behaviors occur, the sequence of behaviors, comparing animals or children of different age, sex, status or personality, or comparing play in different environments.

There are a number of issues to bear in mind in developing a category scheme:

(a) Categories may be mutually exclusive [e.g., talking/not-talking] or overlapping and possibly co-occurrent [e.g., talking/smiling/touching/looking/showing].

(b) Categories may be events, of short duration such that it may be useful to count the number of occurrences [e.g., a laugh]; or states, of relatively longer duration so that it may be useful to measure how long the individual spends in that state [e.g., parallel play].

(c) Categories may be at a micro-level, defined basically in terms of muscle movements (e.g., laugh, jump, run), at an intermediate level where some additional interpretation is needed (e.g., wrestle; what components are involved in wrestling?), or at a macro-level, requiring considerable interpretation on the part of the observer (e.g., parallel play, rough-and-tumble play; for such categories, contextual aspects such as reactions of partners will be part of the definition).

Relatedly, Pellegrini (1998) distinguishes between physical descriptions, descriptions of consequence, and relational descriptions. Physical descriptions are descriptions of muscular contractions, either micro-level items such as 'open-hand beat,' or grouped together or classified in terms of their co-occurrence, such as rough-and-tumble play (e.g., smile, open-hand beat, run, jump, kick at) (e.g., Blurton Jones, 1972). Descriptions of consequence include consideration of the outcome of the behavior(s); this might be important in distinguishing playful and aggressive behaviors, for example. It may be quite difficult to determine whether a 'hit' or 'beat' is playful or aggressive, just on physical description and without taking account of other factors. Relational descriptions take fuller account of the situational and social context; the case of 'parallel play' would be an example, as the reaction of bystanders is crucial in deciding whether a child's activities should be really classed as parallel play (similar activity to those nearby, but no substantial interaction), or some kind of group play (similar activity plus interaction related to it).

(d) The number of categories will be a consideration, bearing in mind also what recording scheme is being used (see *Recording Techniques* below). There should be sufficient to cover the range of play behaviors observed, or at least the range of behaviors of interest. Some behaviors may turn out to be very infrequent, but it may be feasible to collapse categories at a later stage for purposes of analysis. More comprehensive systems are necessary if we want to look at sequences of behavior (the probability of one behavior following another); a possibility here is to use a "dustbin" category, such as Other Behavior, that accounts for less relevant behaviors (Pellegrini, 1998).

(e) Whatever categories are used, it is important that each has some definition to clarify when it is scored. For example, in a study of play in Parakanã Indian children in Brazil, Gosso, Morais and Otta (2007) defined physical exercise play as:

'play that involves various types of movements requesting gross motor coordination (e.g. running, jumping, and swimming), as well as activities that produce action-contingent effects (e.g. throwing or pushing objects).'

Definitions such as this will never solve all decisions for the observer—there are always going to be 'grey areas'—but they will greatly increase the possibility of good inter-observer agreements (see Reliability) and thus the value of the research for others.

Recording techniques

In terms of recording observations, there are a range of possibilities. Important considerations are how obtrusive the method is (does it disturb the individuals being observed?); how well it facilitates gathering all necessary information; how much training is needed; and ease of working with the data generated. Each of the following may be the best choice, depending on the circumstances and requirements of the study.

The most traditional method is 'pen and paper'; using a diary (for narrative recordings) or a checksheet (for checking off predetermined categories at regular time intervals). This is easy to do and provides instant hard copy. It is relatively unobtrusive. However, because the observer needs to keep looking at the paper or checksheet to record what is happening, s/he is likely to miss some of the ongoing behavior.

An audio recorder can be used to circumvent the latter difficulty. The observer can dictate (either a narrative account, or just occurrence of categories) while continually watching the target individual. Subsequently, the audio account will need to be transcribed or entered direct into a data file. Alternatively an event recorder can be used, recording categories by pressing keys to store information directly on a computer disc; this needs a lot of training but does speed up the process of analyzing the data.

A video recorder or film camera can also be used, again without losing any information through taking one's eyes off the target. The video record has the advantage that it can be played over and over again. This enables very precise measurements to be made, of duration for example. It also means that things not apparent at first viewing (like reactions of a third party) can be noticed and taken account of. Especially if a radio microphone can be used in combination, then excellent audio records can be obtained with the visual record. However, analyzing video records is notoriously time consuming, and the processing of the data (i.e., categorization) has not yet been started. Video recording is less obtrusive for infants; for example Cote and Bornstein (2005) made ten minute video film records of 20-month-old children with their mothers in their homes (following 20–30 minutes of acclimatization), using these to then calculate frequency and duration of eight levels of mother-infant play.

Measures of behavior

There are a number of measures that can be useful in quantitative measurements. The ones usually discussed (Martin & Bateson, 2007) are frequency, duration, latency, and intensity.

Frequency is a measure of how often a specific behavior occurs within an observational session. It will be more useful for event categories. Frequency can be expressed as a rate per unit time; for example, that play bites occur so often per minute. *Duration* will be more useful for state categories, and measures the length of time for which that state continues, from start to finish; for instance, that a play fighting bout lasts for so many seconds. Frequency and duration are to some extent complementary measures, and together can tell us about time spent in play, or types of play—how much of the 'time budget' is spent playing (cf. Martin & Caro, 1985).

Latency refers to the time from some stimulus or event, to the start of a particular behavior. For example, it might be the time interval from a play invitation by one animal, to a response; or the interval from presenting some toys to a child, to when they start exploring, and then playing, with the toys.

Intensity is a measure of the strength or amplitude of a behavior: for example, how loud a vocalization is, or how high a jump is, or how strong a bite is. This can be important, especially in distinguishing between play and aggression or examining characteristics of 'rough play.'

Sampling methods

As it is impossible to observe everything, some sampling procedure has to be used. This is so even for video film, as choices must be made about what to film, as well as what to actually extract from the film record. What has been referred to as *ad libitum* sampling (Altmann, 1974) would be an unsystematic choice, without predetermined categories, choice of target animals or time frame. This procedure would only be suitable for the earlier, pilot stages of a study (see above). For systematic work, besides determining categories, the observer needs to decide what time frame to use, and which animals or individuals to observe.

Taking the time frame issue first, some main time-sampling methods are well described in the literature (e.g., Altmann, 1974; Martin & Bateson, 2007). Two of these do not segment up the time period:

(a) Continuous sampling: here the observer does try to record measures of all the predetermined categories, such as frequency and duration, continuously over the time period. This gives the most complete record, but may be difficult in practice.

(b) Event sampling: here, the observer watches continuously, but only starts recording when some particular event happens (such as play, or a particular kind of play). Observations continue until that event (e.g., play bout) is judged to have terminated.

In other sampling procedures, the record is broken up into intervals of, say, 10 seconds, 20 seconds, or 1 minute.

(c) All-or-none or one-zero sampling: here, time is broken up into short intervals. A 10-second interval is a common example. Then, the occurrence (or other measures) of each behavior category is noted, either as present or absent (1 or 0 on the record sheet) for each interval.

(d) Frequency sampling: here, again time is broken up into intervals, but the number of times each behavior occurs in each time interval is recorded.

(e) Instantaneous or point sampling: here, rather than watching over a time period, a 'census' is made at regular points in time. For example, instead of watching through a 10-second period, the observation is made at the end of each 10-second period (perhaps signaled by an electronic bleeper). The occurrence of behavior categories (or not) is recorded at each sampling point.

In addition, the observer needs to decide whether a particular individual is the focus of observations, or a larger group. The main choices are to focus on one individual at a time (focal sampling), or census each individual at regular intervals (scan sampling). When using focal sampling, the observer generally has a list of the individuals of interest, and (either in a predetermined or random order) selects each individual in turn, to observe for a certain time period; usually this time period will be a few minutes, at least, so that the context of the behavior can be more fully appreciated. Although that individual is focused on, obviously the observations will include any interactions this individual has with others, and might include actions by others directed to the focal individual.

When using scan sampling, the observer again has a list of individuals, but only watches each individual for a short time—just long enough to ascertain what the individual is doing (probably, what categories can be checked as occurring). The observer then moves on to the next individual, and so on through this list. This is a quick and efficient way of accumulating many observations on many individuals; however, the information will lack the detail and contextual information that can be provided by focal sampling.

All of these time sampling procedures have pros and cons. In my own observations of children's play (e.g. Smith & Connolly, 1980), I have often used one-zero sampling together with pen-and-paper recording, and focal child sampling. In studies of meerkats, Sharpe (2005) used both instantaneous sampling and also one-zero sampling over 2–0-second intervals, to document play frequencies, as well as event sampling (she refers to it as *ad libitum* sampling) to collect incidents of play fights. The choice of time-sampling method will be influenced by the recording method (see above) and by factors such as the number and frequency of behaviors of interest. If play is quite infrequent, then event sampling may make sense, gathering as much detail as possible of play bouts when they do occur. If play is quite frequent, then it may make more sense to segment up the time intervals, and use one of the alternative time sampling methods.

Frequency sampling obviously gives a measure of the frequency with which categories occur—useful for event categories. Instantaneous sampling can give an estimate of duration of behavior categories, especially if the time period interval is short relative to average duration, and this is useful for state categories. One-zero sampling does not give an exact measure of either frequency or duration (Kraemer, 1979). As such it has been criticized as an inexact and therefore not useful measure (Altmann, 1974; Kraemer, 1979). Certainly, if good measures of either frequency or duration are of primary interest, one-zero sampling should not be the method of choice. However, one-zero sampling does give a good composite measure of the 'amount' of behavior happening, which may be useful, for example, in comparing play in individuals of different age or gender, or in different environments. Arguably, it is an efficient measure to use for such objectives (Rhine & Flanigon, 1978; Smith, 1985).

Whether focal or scan sampling is used, or some other variant, the process needs to then be repeated a number of times, to accumulate sufficient observational data (see Reliability, below). Depending on what is to be analyzed and what comparisons are to be made, it may be important to take account of aspects such as the time of day at which observations are made; and for children, the day of the week may be a factor. Also, the specific order in which individuals are observed should be considered (usually, either counterbalanced or randomized) so that this does not affect, or confound, comparisons to be made.

Analyzing the behavior

The most common procedures used with quantitative observational data are to compare measures of categories (often, frequencies) across individuals, or across time. For example, frequencies of different types of play may be compared across age and gender groups. Or, frequencies are compared in the same individuals across time, for example through the infancy and juvenile periods. Choice of play partners may also be compared in this way, for example whether kin or non-kin are preferred partners (perhaps as initiators, or recipients, of play invitations).

To examine the patterning of behavior, techniques such as cluster analysis and sequential analysis can be used. In cluster analysis, the co-occurrence of categories within the same short time interval is calculated. For example, Blurton Jones (1967) followed this kind of procedure in specifying components of rough-and-tumble play in human children; see also Appleton (1980). In sequential analysis, by contrast, the patterning of behaviors over time is examined (Bakeman & Gottman, 1986). For this, transition probabilities are calculated (the probability of behavior category X occurring at time 1 being followed by behavior category Y occurring at time 2). For example, Smith (1978) calculated transition probabilities between solitary play, parallel play, and group play in preschool children. This could indicate the status of parallel play as a possible transition state between solitary and group play.

Reliability

As with any other data-gathering or measurement technique, issues of reliability and validity are important for observational work. There are a number of reliability issues, well discussed in the literature.

First, it is obviously vital to get enough observational data that it is representative of the individuals and contexts being observed. Here, analysis using split-half correlations can be helpful, especially when the emphasis in analysis is on comparing individuals in some way. The records accumulated are split in half (e.g., taking alternate observational sessions, or records). Then, the individual totals for behavior categories for one-half of the data are correlated with the totals for the other half of the data. A correction can be made for attenuation, to predict the reliability of the total sample rather than the half-samples, which this calculates. The correlations should be high (at least .7) if the data is to be considered representative.

Second, how consistently were observations made over time? One possibility is observer fatigue, especially if observations are made continuously over quite a long time period, for example, an hour or more. Fatigue may lead to behaviors not being noticed. Inconsistency in the observer can also occur through the duration of a study, especially if this lasts for some weeks or even months, as is not uncommon. The observer may, quite unconsciously, modify their criteria for scoring certain behaviors as they get more familiar with what is happening. This is sometimes referred to as *behavior drift*. These inconsistencies would not be picked up by split-half reliability testing (since both halves of the data will show the same changes; or, if instead the first half of the data were compared with the second half of the data, observer changes would be confounded with what may be real changes of behavior in the individuals observed). Observer inconsistency or drift is best checked by comparing an observer's records with those of another observer, or, best of all, against some videorecording, made at the same time.

This brings us to the third, related, topic, of what is called *inter-observer reliability*. Would another observer, familiar with and using the same behavior category scheme, and observing the same individuals at the same time, record the same data? This can easily be checked, and should routinely be reported. It can serve at least three purposes. One is a check on the ease with which the behavior categories and their associated definitions (see Categories, above) can be understood and used effectively. If there is ambiguity or vagueness in the definition of a category, then high inter-observer reliability is unlikely, and the remedy is to improve the clarity of the definition. This kind of work is best done in the pilot stage of the study. However, if inter-observer agreements are also calculated at intervals through a study, this may give some measure of observer drift (not a perfect measure, as both observers may be 'drifting,' but this will be less likely if the second observer just takes part for the reliability testing). It is also possible that the actual process of checking reliability at intervals, in this way, will improve the accuracy of the main observer—a kind of 'Hawthorne effect' (Hollway, 1991). Finally, if there is not just one main observer, but several observers sharing the load of gathering data, then it is clearly essential that all the observers are trained up to a high level of agreement in the training phases before the project starts; and in addition, highly desirable to assess and report inter-observer agreements, at points through the main project and at or near the end.

There are a range of measures of inter-observer agreement; the simplest is a percentage agreement: if there are A agreements and D disagreements between two observers recording the same behavior sequences, then the inter-observer agreement or concordance (C) can be calculated as $C = A/(A+D/2)$ (this assumes that the Ds are random so only D/2 is 'real' for each observer). However, this does not take account of the frequency with which behavior categories occur, and if agreement on non-occurrence of infrequent behaviors is counted, percentage agreement can lead to misleadingly high figures. Generally preferred are calculations based on the kappa coefficient, which takes account of this; if O is the observed proportion of agreements, and C the proportion of agreements expected by chance, then kappa = $(O-C)/(1-C)$. The correlation between the two observers is another possible measure.

Validity

Quantitative observational data has obvious face validity when compared to anecdotal reports, or (for humans) indirect verbal data such as questionnaires; but even so, the presence of the observer might affect and change the behavior being observed; this is generally called *observer effects*, analogous to experimenter effects that must be guarded against in experimental studies. In the case of some non-human species, the observer might be seen as dangerous, perhaps as a possible predator (or for a few species, as a possible prey item!). In the case of human children, it is usually found that up to around five years, they do not pay a great deal of attention to an observer; but older children, for example being observed in a school playground, will often come up to enquire what the observer is doing, and perhaps 'act up' for the observer's benefit (Sluckin, 1981; Smith & Connolly, 1980). The presence of an observer can be even more obtrusive in observing children in the home environment. Besides undesirable behaviors being introduced, certain other behaviors (perhaps considered 'socially undesirable') may be inhibited by the observer's presence.

One check on the importance of observer effects is simple: assess how often the individuals being observed, themselves watch the observer. If this is seldom, it at least suggests that observer effects are likely to be small. Also, observer effects are likely to be less if the individuals are accustomed or habituated to the presence of the observer during the pilot phase of the study. Another possibility is to make observations as unobtrusive as possible, for example avoiding filming devices, or making concealed observations from a hide.

Conclusion

Observational methods provide an obvious and natural way of examining play behaviors, whether in humans or in non-human species; although for humans there are alternatives. There are important technical and procedural issues to be considered in using observational methods, many reviewed briefly in this chapter. There are many other more detailed sources to consult regarding observational methods. Martin and Bateson (2007) remain the best straightforward guide to this area, while Fassnacht (1982) provides some history as well as detailed discussion of many topics. See also Dawkins (2007) for observational work with animals, Pellegrini and Bjorklund (1998), Pellegrini (2004), and Hobart and Frankel (2004) for work with children, Yoder and Symons (2010) for a general perspective, and Bakeman and Gottman (1986) particularly for behavior sequence analysis.

Sustained observational work can be tiring and tedious, but it can also be enjoyable and rewarding. Play is generally described as a pleasurable form of behavior, and observing play can also be fun. While a lot of play is repetitive and routine, some of it is creative and exciting, and there is always the possibility of seeing something unusual that throws new light on the topic and on the species concerned, especially when observing in unconstrained settings. Mastering the techniques of good observational work is well worthwhile, and perhaps especially in the study of play.

References

Altmann, J. (1974). Observational study of behaviour: sampling methods. *Behavior, 49*, 227–267.

Appleton, P. (1980). A factor analytic study of behavior groupings in young children. *Ethology and Sociobiology, 1*, 93–97.

Arrington, R. E. (1943). Time sampling in studies of social behaviour: A critical review of techniques and results with research suggestions. *Psychological Bulletin, 40*, 81–124.

Bakeman, R., & Gottman, J. (1986). *Observing interaction: An introduction to sequential analysis*. New York and Cambridge: Cambridge University Press.

Bandura, A., Ross, D., & Ross, S. A. (1961). Transmission of aggression through imitation of aggressive models. *Journal of Abnormal and Social Psychology, 63*, 575–582.

Bensel, J. (1992). Behavior of toddlers during daily leave-taking and separation from their parents. *Ethology and Sociobiology, 13*, 229–252.

Blurton Jones, N. (1967). An ethological study of some aspects of social behaviour of children in nursery school. In D. Morris (Ed.), *Primate ethology* (pp. 347–368). London: Weidenfeld & Nicolson.

Blurton Jones, N. (1972). Categories of child-child interaction. In N. Blurton Jones (Ed.), *Ethological studies of child behaviour* (pp. 97–127). Cambridge: Cambridge University Press.

Chalmers, A. F. (1982). *What is this thing called science?*, 2nd ed. Milton Keynes: Open University Press.

Costabile, A., Smith, P. K., Matheson, L., Aston, J., Hunter, T., & Boulton, M. (1991). Cross-national comparison of how children distinguish playful and serious fighting. *Developmental Psychology, 27*, 881–887.

Cote, L. R. & Bornstein, M. H. (2005). Child and mother play in cultures of origin, acculturating cultures, and cultures of destination. *International Journal of Behavioral Development, 29*, 479–488.

Dawkins, M. S. (2007). *Observing animal behaviour: Design and analysis of quantitative data*. New York: Oxford University Press.

Eibl-Eibesfeldt, I. (1967). Concepts of ethology and their significance in the study of human behavior. In H. W. Stevenson, E. H. Hess, & H. L. Rheingold (Eds.), *Early behaviour: Comparative and developmental approaches* (pp. 127–146). New York: Wiley.

Fassnacht, G. (1982). *Theory and practice of observing behaviour*. London: Academic Press.

Foster, J. C. (1930). Play activities of children in the first six grades. *Child Development, 1*, 248–254.

Gosso, Y., Morais, M. D. L. S., & Otta, E. (2007). Pretend play of Brazilian children. *Journal of Cross-Cultural Psychology, 38*, 539–558.

Groos, K. (1901). *The play of man*. London: W. Heinemann.

Hanawalt, B. (1993). *Growing up in Medieval London*. New York & Oxford: Oxford University Press.

Hobart, C. & Frankel, J. (2004). *A practical guide to child observation and assessment* (3rd ed.). Cheltenham: Nelson Thornes.

Hollway, W. (1991). *Work psychology and organisational behaviour*. London: Sage.

Hulson, E. V. (1930). An analysis of the free play of ten four-year-old children through consecutive observations. *Journal of Juvenile Research, 14*, 188–208.

Humphreys, A. P., & Smith, P. K. (1987). Rough and tumble, friendship, and dominance in schoolchildren: Evidence for continuity and change with age. *Child Development, 58*, 201–212.

Huston-Stein, A., Fox, S., Greer, D., Watkins, B. A., & Whitaker, J. (1981). The effects of TV action and violence on children's social behavior. *Journal of Genetic Psychology, 138*, 183–191.

Hutt, S. J., & Hutt, C. (1970). *Direct observation and measurement of behavior*. Springfield, IL: C.C. Thomas.

Kraemer, H. C. (1979). One-zero sampling in the study of primate behaviour. *Primates, 20*, 237–244.

Ladd, G. W. (1983). Social networks of popular, average and rejected children in school settings. *Merrill-Palmer Quarterly, 29*, 283–307.

Lancy, D. F. (1996). *Playing on the mother ground: Cultural routines for children's development*. New York: Guilford Press.

Liebermann, J. N. (1977). *Playfulness: Its relationship to imagination and creativity*. New York: Academic Press.

Linaza, J. (1984). Piaget's marbles: the study of children's games and their knowledge of rules. *Oxford Review of Education, 10*, 271–274.

Loo, C.M. (1972). The effects of spatial density on the social behaviour of children. *Journal of Applied Social Psychology, 2*, 372–381.

Manwell, E. M. & Mengert, I. G. (1934). A study of the development of two- and three-year-old children with respect to play activities. *University of Iowa Studies in Child Welfare*, 4, 69–111.

Martin, P., & Bateson, P. (2007). *Measuring behaviour: An introductory guide* (3rd ed.). Cambridge: Cambridge University Press.

Martin, P., & Caro, T. (1985). On the function of play and its role in behavioural development. In J. Rosenblatt, C. Beer, M.-C. Bushnel, & P. Slater (Eds.), *Advances in the study of behaviour*, Vol. 15 (pp. 59–103). New York: Academic Press.

Medawar, P. (1969). *Induction and intuition in scientific thought*. London: Methuen.

Nelson, J. D., Gelfand, D. M., & Hartmann, D. P. (1969). Children's aggression following competition and exposure to an aggressive model. *Child Development*, 40, 1085–1099.

Parmar, P., Harkness, S. & Super, C. M. (2004). Asian and Euro-American parents' ethnotheories of play and learning: Effects on preschool children's home routines and school behaviour. *International Journal of Behavioral Development*, 28, 97–104.

Pearson, K. (1891). *The grammar of science*, London.

Pellegrini, A. D. (1994). The rough play of adolescent boys of differing sociometric status. *International Journal of Behavioral Development*, 17, 525–540.

Pellegrini, A. D. (1998). Observational methods in early childhood educational research. In B Spodek, O. N. Saracho & A. D. Pellegrini (eds.), *Issues in early childhood educational research* (pp. 76–92). New York: Teachers College Press.

Pellegrini, A. D. (2004). *Observing children in their natural worlds: A methodological primer*, 2nd edition. Psychology Press.

Pellegrini, A. D., & Bjorklund, D. J. (1998). *Applied child study: A developmental approach* (3rd ed.). Hillsdale, NJ: Erlbaum.

Piaget, J. (1977, orig. 1932). *The moral judgement of the child*. Harmondsworth: Penguin.

Popper, K (1959, 3rd ed. 1972). *The logic of scientific discovery*. London: Hutchinson.

Potts, R., Huston, A. C., & Wright, J. C. (1986). The effects of television form and violent content on boys' attention and social behavior. *Journal of Experimental Child Psychology*, 41, 1–17.

Rhine, R. J. & Flanigon, M. (1978). An empirical comparison of one-zero, focal animal, and instantaneous methods of sampling spontaneous primate social behavior. *Primates*, 19, 353–361.

Rubin, K. (2001). *The Play Observation Scale*. University of Maryland (available through K Rubin's website).

Saar, A. & Niglas, K. (2001). Estonian and Russian parental attitudes to childrearing and play. *Early Child Development and Care*, 168, 39–47.

Schäfer, M., & Smith, P. K. (1996). Teacher perceptions of play-fighting and real fighting in primary school. *Educational Research*, 38, 173–181.

Sharpe, L. L. (2005). Play fighting does not affect subsequent fighting success in meerkats. *Animal Behaviour*, 69, 1023–1029.

Sharpe, L. L., Clutton-Brock, T. H., Brotherton, P. N. M., Cameron, E. Z. & Cherry, M. I. (2002). Experimental provisioning increases play in free-ranging meerkats. *Animal Behaviour*, 64, 113–121.

Sluckin, A. (1981). *Growing up in the playground: The social development of children*. London: Routledge & Kegan Paul.

Smith, P.K. (1978). A longitudinal study of social participation in preschool children: Solitary and parallel play re-examined. *Developmental Psychology*, 14, 517–523.

Smith, P. K. (1985). The reliability and validity of 1/0 sampling: Misconceived criticisms and unacknowledged assumptions. *British Journal of Educational Research*, 11, 17–22.

Smith, P. K. (1997). Play fighting and real fighting: Perspectives on their relationship. In A. Schmitt, K. Atzwanger, K. Grammer, & K. Schäfer (Eds.), *New aspects of ethology* (pp. 47–66). New York: Plenum Press.

Smith, P.K. (2009). *Children and play*. Oxford: Wiley-Blackwell.

Smith, P. K., & Connolly, K. (1972). Patterns of play and social interaction in preschool children. In N. Blurton Jones (Ed.), *Ethological studies of child behaviour* (pp. 65–95). Cambridge: Cambridge University Press.

Smith, P. K., & Connolly, K. J. (1980). *The ecology of preschool behaviour*. Cambridge: Cambridge University Press.

Smith, P. K., & Lewis, K. (1985). Rough-and-tumble play, fighting and chasing in nursery school children. *Ethology and Sociology*, 6, 175–181.

Smith, P. K., Smees, R. & Pellegrini, A. D. (2004). Play fighting and real fighting: Using video playback methodology with young children. *Aggressive Behavior*, 30, 164–173.

Takhvar, M. & Smith, P. K. (1990). A review and critique of Smilansky's classification scheme and the 'nested hierarchy' of play categories. *Journal of Research in Early Childhood*, 4, 112–122.

Tinbergen, N. (1951). *The study of instinct*. London: Oxford University Press.

Yoder, P. & Symons, F. (2010). *Observational measurement of behavior*. New York: Springer.

PART 5

Dimensions of Play

Object Play and Tool Use: Developmental and Evolutionary Perspectives

David F. Bjorklund *and* Amy K. Gardiner

Abstract

We take an evolutionary developmental perspective to examine the development of and sex differences in object-oriented play and tool use and the relationship between the two. We propose that children have intuitive notions about the physical world and evolved biases to interact with objects, both of which facilitate object-oriented play. Through the experience gained in object play, children begin to understand how objects can be used as tools to achieve goals and solve problems. Although complex tool use is a distinct characteristic of humans, a wide range of other species, including many primates, engage in simpler forms of tool use. While many of these instances are probably cases of convergent evolution, the existence of tool use in other great apes suggests a common root for our basic tool-use abilities.

Key terms: Object-oriented play, tool use, sex differences, social learning, evolutionary developmental psychology, affordances, design stance

Paleoanthropologists called the earliest member of the human genus *Homo habilis* ("handy man") because of its association with stone tools. In fact, some anthropologists believed, erroneously as it turned out, that tool use and manufacture were unique characteristics of members of the *Homo* line. Since then, tool use, and to a certain degree tool construction, have been observed in a variety of nonhuman animals, from corvids to chimpanzees. But none use tools to the extent or with the versatility as modern humans, making facility with tools, in part, responsible for *Homo sapiens* ecological dominance. However, tool use did not arise fully formed in some ancient hominid ancestor, nor does it emerge fully blown in adolescence or adulthood. Rather, tool use has both a phylogenetic and onto-genetic history. Following the tenets of contemporary evolutionary psychology, children have biases, or constraints, in how they process and interpret aspects of their social and physical worlds. This includes how they interact with objects, which may

afford efficient tool use (Geary, 2005). One such bias evident early in childhood is expressed via *object-oriented play*, during which children interact with objects, discover affordances of objects, and learn to manipulate objects as tools to produce changes in the environment.

Play, in general, is difficult to define. Nonetheless, most researchers agree that play involves seemingly less serious and more exaggerated behaviors than other routine actions, with individual components often rearranged in novel ways when compared to normal routines (see Burghardt, this volume). Play is voluntary and spontaneous and has been described as a behavior in which "means are more important than ends" (Martin & Caro, 1985; Rubin, Fein, & Vandenberg 1983; Pellegrini & Bjorklund, 2004; Pellegrini et al., 2007; Power, 2000).

Object play, like play itself, is also difficult to define precisely. One reason for this is that children frequently use props in other forms of play: A stick is used as a magic wand or a shoe as a telephone in symbolic play; cups are used to drink a make-believe beverage when children play "tea party"; and rocks are piled high upon one another as children build a fort to protect themselves from an imaginary invading army. In the case of a child using a stick as a magic wand or a shoe as a telephone, the objects are used as symbols—one thing is used to represent another. The cups themselves are not the focus of play, for example, but merely props used to facilitate social play; and the children building a fort to ward off invaders are constructing something—there is a purpose to their actions, which may be an important part of their dramatic play but, because of its goal orientation, may not reflect "play" as understood by many scholars who have studied the topic (e.g., Rubin et al., 1983).

Because of the many ways children use objects in play, different researchers have defined object play differently. For example, a distinction is usually (but not always) made between exploration and object play. In exploration, children gather information about an object. In infancy this may involve mouthing it or simple manipulation, possibly with visual inspection (Belsky & Most, 1981; Hutt, 1966). Through exploration, children are essentially asking, "What can *it* do?" Such an object orientation is different from the more person-centered orientation that guides play, as traditionally defined, where children essentially ask, "What can *I* do with it?" (Hutt, 1966). However, it is not always obvious to know where exploration ends and play begins (Weisler & McCall, 1976). Similarly, should the fact that children's actions on objects produce a product (a fort made from piling rocks, for example) preclude it from being a form of play? It is accomplished in a playful setting, sometimes when alone, as when a child uses Legos® to construct buildings, people, or vehicles, and sometimes with others, as in our "making a fort" example. If you asked most children engaged in these activities what they were doing, our guess is that they would say they are "playing."

Our primary interest in object play is its possible role in helping children discover affordances of and between objects and how objects can be used as tools. Our perspective is thus a functional one, informed by evolutionary developmental theory. We propose that infants and young children have evolved biases that influence how they process (encode, categorize, remember, learn about) objects and events in their environment, and that these biases interact with experiences to shape adaptive behavior (see Bjorklund & Pellegrini, 2000, 2002; Bjorklund & Hernández Blasi, 2005; Geary, 2005;

Geary & Bjorklund, 2000). We thus define object play as the active manipulation of objects, such as banging them and throwing them, but also the use of objects to build something, sometimes referred to as *constructive play* (Smilansky, 1968).

In this chapter we examine the development of and mechanisms underlying object play and tool use, look at object play and tool use in other animals and their possible phylogenetic history, and the relation between object play and children's developing tool use. However, we first provide a brief overview of our overriding theoretical perspective, that of evolutionary developmental psychology, especially as it relates to object play and tool use.

Evolutionary Developmental Psychology and Play

There is a long history of scholars examining play through an evolutionary lens, beginning with Darwin (1859) and extending to modern times (e.g., Bateson, 2005, this volume; Bekoff & Byers, 1998; Hinde, 1974; Martin & Caro, 1995; Pellegrini, 2011; Pellegrini & Bjorklund, 2004; Pellegrini, Dupuis, & Smith, 2007; Pellegrini & Smith, 1998; Power, 2000; Smith, 1982; Špinka, Newbury, & Bekoff, 2001). Play is phylogenetically old, being observed in most mammals, many birds, and some reptiles (Burghardt, 1998). Indeed, E. O. Wilson (1975) nominated play as one of five areas of animal behavior (along with kin-selection, parent–offspring conflict, territoriality, and homosexuality) warranting a sociobiological explanation. According to some researchers, it consumes a substantial amount of an animal's time and energy (Byers & Walker, 1995; Hinde, 1974; Power, 2000; but see Martine & Caro, 1985) and therefore likely serves (or served in the past) some adaptive value. In evolutionary biology, when a function has substantial costs, it is assumed to also have substantial benefits; otherwise it would have been eliminated by natural selection. Evolutionary interpretations of play have also assumed, implicitly or explicitly, that play has a particularly important role early in the lifespan. Beginning at least with Groos (1898, 1901), play has been considered a hallmark of the juvenile period.

Evolutionary developmental psychology examines aspects of modern ontogeny from the perspective of natural selection. It assumes that natural selection has operated as strongly, or more so, during the early stages of life as in adulthood. From this perspective, we can talk about adaptations of infancy and childhood. Some of these adaptations may serve to prepare children for life as an adult, what have been referred to as *deferred adaptations* (Bjorklund, 1997; Bjorklund & Hernández Blasi, 2005). For example, during play children may learn important social skills while interacting with their peers or may acquire abilities related to fighting or childcare, for instance, which they will continue to master through play until adulthood when they will be used "for real." Play allows children and young animals to practice these skills in a relatively safe environment, where the consequences of mistakes are rarely serious. Most scholars in the past, including Piaget (1962) and Vygotsky (1978), have assumed that play's greatest benefits are deferred (See Göncü & Gaskins, this volume; Kagan, 1996).

In contrast to deferred adaptations, evolutionary developmental psychology also assumes that there are *ontogenetic adaptations*—behaviors that adapt the individual to the niche of infancy or childhood and then disappear when they are no longer needed (Bjorklund, 1997; Bjorklund & Pellegrini, 2000). Prenatal physiological adaptations, such as the umbilical cord in mammals and the egg tooth in birds, are easily appreciated ontogenetic adaptations, but such adaptations also exist for behaviors. For example, neonatal imitation (Meltzoff & Moore, 1977) is observed shortly after birth but disappears around two months of age, only to reappear late in the first year of life. Rather than reflecting an underlying symbolic ability present at birth, some have proposed that it represents an ontogenetic adaptation, providing some immediate benefit, for example, serving to foster nursing or social communication at a time when the infant cannot direct his or her own behavior effectively (Bjorklund, 1987; Jacobson, 1979; Legerstree, 1991). Similarly, the social skills children acquire during play serve to help them navigate the niche of childhood, which has its own social hierarchies and complex forms of interaction, and not just as preparation for forming adult social relationships. From this perspective, play can be considered as a specific adjustment to the context of childhood (Bateson, 1976; Bjorklund, 1997; Bjorklund & Green, 1992; Bjorklund, Periss, & Causey, 2009). For instance, rough-and-tumble play may serve as a way for boys to learn and practice social signaling (Martin & Caro, 1985), with exaggerated movements and a play face communicating playful intent. Boys also use rough-and-tumble play to establish leadership in their peer group and assess others' strength (Pellegrini & Smith, 1998), both important in dealing with one's peers in the here and now, not just in some unspecified

future. There are also some immediate nonsocial benefits to rough-and-tumble play; it provides opportunities for vigorous physical exercise that is important for skeletal and muscle development (Bruner, 1972; Dolhinow & Bishop, 1970). Similarly, children can develop a sense of mastery and self-efficacy during play when experimenting with new activities, including tool use, which can lead to subsequent practice and afford opportunities for the learning of specific skills (Bjorklund & Green, 1992).

Contemporary accounts of evolutionary developmental psychology also assume that infants are born with a small set of *skeletal competencies* specialized to process information relating to the physical, biological, and social worlds (Geary, 2005; Spelke & Kinzler, 2007). These skeletal abilities become fleshed out with time and experience, enabling children to deal efficiently with a wide range of objects, events, and relationships as they develop. Many of the experiences that serve to hone children's developing competencies in these arenas occur during play—from the peek-a-boo games that mothers and their infants engage in, to the exploration of physical properties of a new toy, to the role-playing that goes on when sitting on the floor with friends and pouring imaginary cups of tea and doing the things that grown-ups are assumed to do when having a tea party.

Our focus in this chapter is on object-oriented play and its relation to learning to use tools. Following Geary (2005), we assume that children have intuitive notions about the physical world that develop during infancy and childhood (for example, understanding the physical properties of objects such as permanency, physical causation, the need for support; see Baillargeon, 2008; Spelke & Kinzler, 2007). Children are drawn to explore objects, first discovering their properties ("What does *it* do"), and then continue to interact with objects asking, essentially, "What can *I* do with it?" In the process, they learn about the affordances of objects (functional relationships between objects and the environment) and how objects can be used to achieve certain goals; in other words, how objects can be used as tools. As we'll show in a later section, children's facility with learning how to use tools owes as much, or perhaps more, to their intuitive psychology as to their intuitive physics; nevertheless, children learn much about objects in their world and how they can be used as tools from playful activities, making it almost inevitable they will become proficient tool users.

Developmental and Sex Differences in Object Play

Before infants and children can be said to play with objects, they first explore them. In fact, nearly all of an infant's interactions with objects in the first nine months of life can likely be described as exploration (Belsky & Most, 1981). Object exploration and play begin in infancy but are limited to babies' physical abilities to grasp and inspect objects. Humans are among a small number of animals that have opposable thumbs and that develop the manual dexterity to become "handy," using both hands in a coordinated manner, permitting effective tool construction and use. But manual dexterity takes time to develop. At birth, human infants have a grasping reflex, and some infants can get their hands or fingers to their mouths and suck on them, but there is little else neonates can do other than to make a series of repetitive movements of their heads, torsos, and limbs (Vereijken, 2005). Beginning about four or five months of age, infants can reach for and grasp objects within arm's length, with most such reaching being done bimanually (Harris, 2005). Developing simultaneously with control of the arms and hands is control of the eyes. Eye-hand coordination permits infants to guide their arm and hand movements toward an object. By three months, infants can reach for and grasp an object if it is presented on the same side as the reaching hand, and six-month olds are able to reach for objects presented in front of them or on the opposite side of the reaching hand (Provine & Westerman, 1979).

Infants discover affordances of objects through their early exploration. For example, in one study six-, eight-, and ten-month-old infants interacted with surfaces and objects that produced various combinations of physical properties (Bourgeois, Khawar, Neal, & Lockman, 2005). Infants were presented with four different surfaces one at a time: liquid water, discontinuous netting, flexible sponge, and rigid wood. A soft spongy cube and a hard wooden cube were placed on each surface for infants to manipulate. Infants pressed the cubes more often on the flexible surface than the liquid and rigid surfaces, suggesting an exploration of the pliability of the flexible surface. They also banged the hard object more often on the discontinuous and rigid surfaces than the other two surfaces, presumably to test the bounciness of the discontinuous surface and to produce noise on the rigid surface. Additionally, ten-month-olds, but not the younger infants, banged the hard cube more than the soft cube, suggesting a developmental increase in the precision of this form

of object-object exploration. Similar findings were produced in a related study that presented eight- and ten-month-olds with a composite substrate that was half rigid wood and half flexible sponge, indicating that infants adaptively explore object-surface relations even when a single surface varies substantially in composition (Fontelle, Kahrs, Neal, Newton, & Lockman, 2007).

Eye-hand coordination continues to improve over the first year, as does infants' control of their hands and fingers. Infants can make a pincer grasp by 9 to 12 months, picking up objects with their thumb and a single finger (von Hofsten, 2005). Over the next year, definite handedness is observed, and toddlers' increasing ability to use their hands, especially in coordination with their vision, affords them the opportunity to use tools, such as spoons or crayons, effectively (Harris, 2005). As children's motor skills improve, they are able to explore an increasing array of objects in a variety of situations, which can have a direct effect on their cognitive development, including their use of tools (E. Gibson, 1988; Needham, 2000). Rochat (1989) provided a detailed look at changes in object exploration between two and five months of age. At the earliest ages, infants immediately take objects placed in their hands to their mouths. By four or five months many infants grasp an object and look at it before orally inspecting it (see also Ruff, Saltarelli, Capozzoli, & Dubiner, 1992). According to Jeffrey Lockman (2000, p. 137)

> "the origins of tool use in humans can be found during much of the first year of life, in the perception-action routines that infants repeatedly display as they explore their environments."

Not surprisingly, as infants gain more experience interacting with objects, their exploratory skills improve. This was shown experimentally in a study by Needham and her colleagues (Needham, Barrett, & Peterman, 2002). Three-month-old infants were given "sticky mittens" with Velcro on the palms so they could pick up special Velcro-covered toys (blocks or rings). Infants wore the gloves and interacted with the toys in their homes over a two-week period (between 9 and 14 ten-minute sessions, no more than one per day). Infants were then brought into the laboratory and given the opportunity to interact with a variety of objects, both with and without "sticky mittens." Compared to infants in a control group who had not had the "sticky-mitten" experience at home, the experimental infants explored the objects more, both manually and orally, and looked longer at the objects than infants in the control condition, demonstrating a clear demonstration of the role of experience on object exploration.

Object exploration continues over infancy and the toddler years, with boys engaging in more object exploration than girls (e.g., Bornstein, Haynes, O'Reilly, & Painter, 1996). However, most of an infant's interaction with objects from 12 months onward can better be described as play rather than exploration (Belsky & Most, 1981). Common among early object-play behaviors is producing noise, for example by banging or shaking objects (e.g., Goldberg & Lewis, 1969; Morgante & Keen, 2008). Such "perceptually contingent" play gives way to more sophisticated forms of object play, such as building things, or constructive play. Boys typically engage in such play more than girls (e.g., Caldera, O'Brien, Truglio, Alvarez, & Huston 1999; Gredlein & Bjorklund, 2005; Hutt, 1972; Pellegrini & Gustafson, 2005; Sluss, 2002; Sutton-Smith, Rosenberg, & Morgan, 1963), although sex differences are not always found (e.g., Ball & Hagen, 1978; Henderson & Moore, 1979; McLoyd & Ratner, 1983), and sometimes favor girls (e.g., Christie & Johnsen, 1987), demonstrating the importance of context in play styles of boys and girls. For example, Pellegrini and Gustafson (2005) reported that boys used objects as tools more frequently than girls, often in the context of fantasy play (see also Saltz, Dixon, & Johnson, 1977), whereas girls used objects more often than boys in more sedentary play, such as making puzzles and doing art activities. That the sex difference often found in object play has a biological origin, at least in part, is demonstrated by research showing that girls exposed to high levels of androgen prenatally (congenital adrenal hyperplasia) engage in more object-oriented play than unaffected girls (Berenbaum & Hines, 1992; Collaer & Hines, 1995).

Children's object play is influenced by the objects they have available to them and their culture. For example, preschool-age children in Western cultures are often given toys, such as blocks or Legos®, that promote constructive play, although Western children will also play with sticks, stones, and about anything else available to build something or to use as props in fantasy play (a cardboard box as a spaceship, for example). In more traditional cultures, children are often given miniature tools that adults use in their work, or construct such objects themselves to use in their play (e.g., Bock, 2005; Eibl-Eibesfeldt, 1989; Lancy, 1996; See Tudge et al., this volume). For example, among the Parakanã of the

Amazon in Brazil, fathers often give their young boys miniature bows and arrows that they use in play, while mothers give their daughters small baskets. Four- to six-year-old girls make baskets of palm leaves, much like those used by their mothers. The baskets are not strong enough to be used in gathering, although by the age of seven or eight they start to make real baskets for their mothers' or their own use (Gosso, Otto, Morais, Ribeiro, & Bussab, 2005). Among the Kpelle from Liberia, children, usually boys, often make tools during play and occasionally build models of cars or houses, but rarely of people or animals (Lancy, 1996). Most of the play of children from traditional cultures involves mimicking aspects of adult life, often using tools, consistent with the idea that, in such cultures, play may represent a deferred adaptation as it serves as preparation for adult life (Bock, 2005; Bock & Johnson, 2002).

It is difficult to get an accurate account of how much time young children devote to object play, in part because most of their play (other than rough-and-tumble play) involves the use of objects. When all play involving objects is considered, between about one-third and one-half of young children's activity during preschool can be classified as object play (McGrew, 1972; see Pellegrini & Bjorklund, 2004 and Rubin et al., 1983 for reviews). Similar estimates (30–35%) for interactions with objects have also been reported among the !Kung of Botswana (Bakeman et al. 1990) and the Embu of Kenya (Sigman, Newmann, Carter, Cattle, D'Souza, & Bwido, 1988). When more refined measures of object play are used, the amount of time devoted to such play for preschoolers is estimated to be around 10% to 15% of all behaviors (Smith & Connolly, 1980). As with other forms of play, object play displays an inverted-U pattern, with low levels observed during the early preschool years, peaking in childhood, and decreasing in early adolescence (see Pellegrini, 2011). Bock (2005) reported a similar inverted-U pattern for children from the Okavango Delta in Botswana, with boys' object play peaking earlier (4 to 6 years of age) than girls (10 to 12 years of age).

Object Play in Nonhuman Primates
Humans are not the only animals that engage in object play. Dogs and cats will bat around and "play" with a ball or other small objects, and animals in the wild will interact with natural objects in a playful manner. Object play has been observed in many mammals, some birds, and especially nonhuman

primates (see McGrew & Marchant, 1992; Power, 2000; Ramsey & McGrew, 2005; Tomasello & Call, 1997). Because our focus is on the ontogeny and phylogeny of object play and its relation to tool use in humans, we will examine here research on object play in humans' closest relatives, the great apes.

Of the four great-ape species, relatively little research has been performed on bonobos (*Pan paniscus*), gorillas (*Gorilla gorilla*) and orangutans (*Pongo pygmaeus*), with more being known about object play in common chimpanzees (*Pan troglodytes*), both in captivity and in the wild (see Ramsey & McGrew, 2005). Moreover, in many research reports, object play is not clearly differentiated from object manipulation or tool use, making any definitive statements about object play in the various great-ape species difficult. Nonetheless, some general patterns can be discerned. First, when comparing captive chimpanzees, which use tools extensively in the wild, and captive gorillas, which use tools infrequently in the wild, the former are more likely to engage in object play than the latter (see Ramsey & McGrew, 2005). Comparisons between captive chimpanzees and captive bonobos, that use tools in the wild less often than chimpanzees, produce smaller differences, with bonobos actually engaging in more object manipulation than chimpanzees (Takeshita & Walraven, 1996). Second, captive chimpanzees that are raised much like human children (enculturated chimpanzees) display object play with toys similar to that shown by preschool children. This includes not only playful manipulation of objects, but also using objects as substitutes for other things, such as treating a doll as if it were a real baby (e.g., Hayes, 1951; Tremerlin, 1975). This suggests that chimpanzees are capable of fantasy play (see Gómez & Martín-Andrade, 2005). Similar behavior possibly reflective of fantasy play was observed in a wild female chimpanzee, which carried a log and treated it much as children treat a doll (Matsuzawa, 1997). Third, similar to research with human children, object play is more frequent in juveniles than adults, both in chimpanzees and bonobos (Markus & Croft, 1996; Takeshita & Walraven, 1996; see Ramsey & McGrew, 2005 for a review).

In the wild, chimpanzees tend to use vegetation (leaves, sticks, fruit) as objects in play. Ramsey and McGrew (2005) noted that play with such objects likely benefits the development of tool use in chimpanzees, including termite fishing and especially building nests. After being weaned, chimpanzees build sleeping nests everyday of their lives (Goodall, 1962).

According to Ramsey and McGrew (2005, pp. 102, 103): the "overarching reliance on functional object manipulation for daily shelter and for occasional subsistence through extractive foraging is reflected in the object play of youngsters."

As we mentioned earlier, object play in chimpanzees is often not differentiated from other forms of object interaction, including simple object manipulation. Ramsey and McGrew (2005) used a data base of observations of object manipulation from a group of five wild juvenile chimpanzees (McGrew, 1977) and differentiated object play from object manipulation by the presence of a play face or laughing: Object manipulation with a play face or while laughing was classified as object play, whereas object manipulation without such play signals was not so coded. They reported that of a 12-hour active day, the juvenile chimpanzees spent between one and two hours involved in object play, most of which involved vegetation.

Based on the limited amount of research that is available, object play appears to be more common, at least in wild populations, among tool-using chimpanzees than among the other great apes, none of which makes or uses of tools in the wild to the extent that chimpanzees do. This is consistent with the idea that object play serves a role in subsequent tool use and was selected over the course of evolution for that purpose. Also, based on the frequency of object play observed by Ramsey and McGrew (2005) among a small sample of wild juvenile chimpanzees, the amount of time devoted to object play appears similar to that observed in human children (between 10% and 15%).

The Development of Tool Use in Children

Tools have been prevalent throughout human evolutionary history. The earliest tools in the archeological record were crafted from stone by *Homo habilis*, and stone tools became increasingly sophisticated as early humans evolved. Stone technology may have supplemented the biological capabilities of its users and allowed them to process a wider range of resources more efficiently than other hominids, and this may have given tool-yielding individuals a selective advantage. The earliest stone-tool users were probably not dependent upon their tools for survival, but as evolution proceeded, technology may have become essential for our ancestors' adaptation (Schick & Toth, 1993).

Tool knowledge has been passed on for hundreds of thousands of years as each generation learns how to make and use the tools of their respective cultures, adds their own modifications and additions (the "cultural ratchet effect"; Tomasello, 2000), and then teaches the following generation these essential skills. Tool knowledge is not genetically inherited like many human adaptations, but as an adaptation, tool use would have provided pressure for the selection of learning mechanisms specific to how to make and use tools, such as object-oriented play. Because tool-use learning begins in early childhood, we would expect these capacities to be present in at least rudimentary form in children.

In this section, we focus on the emergence of tool-use abilities in childhood, from exploratory behaviors in infancy to solving problems with tools during the preschool period. We first discuss what must be learned to successfully use tools.

Discovering affordances and causal structure

At the core of understanding how a tool can be used is the perception of its *affordances,* or the functional relationships between the tool and the environment (J. J. Gibson, 1969, 1979). For instance, cups and bowls afford containment, knives afford cutting, and spoons afford scooping. Whether children are learning on their own, by observing someone else, or by being taught, to use a tool properly they must understand the effects the tool can have in a given situation and how to manipulate it to produce these effects. Affordances describe the relationship between the tool and the environment (cups afford containment), but can also be identified in the relationships between the individual and the tool (a firm grip will afford transport of the cup), and between the individual and the environment (which hand affords gripping may depend on placement of the cup in relation to the body). In executing a tool-use task, an individual must formulate and carry out an *action plan* that facilitates affordances at all interfaces (Smitsman & Bongers, 2003; Cox & Smitsman, 2006).

Lockman (2000) discusses affordance learning from a perception-action perspective, which focuses on exploratory behavior as the primary mechanism through which children perceive affordances and subsequently learn to use objects as tools. This approach is based on classic ecological theory (E. Gibson, 1988), which asserts that perception guides action, and action then creates changes in the environment that are subsequently perceived and acted upon. Understanding of affordances becomes refined as actions create new affordances and increasing amounts of information are learned (Adolph, Eppler, & Gibson, 1993). From the perception-action perspective, tool-use learning may be understood as a continual developmental process in which children come to understand the relations between objects through the perception of affordances, facilitated by their interactions with the environment, such as through object exploration or object play (Lockman, 2000).

As we discussed earlier in this chapter, the focused exploratory behavior of infants prepares them for more advanced forms of object manipulation, including tool use, later in development, as these simpler interactions facilitate affordance learning and provide knowledge about how to exploit the physical properties of objects (Bourgeois et al., 2005; Fontelle et al., 2007). Around 9 months, infants begin to move from simple object exploration and manipulation to actions with objects that are intended achieve desired effects in the environment. Goal-directed actions with objects are facilitated by an emerging ability to reason about means and ends, or the actions that must be performed to produce a desired physical effect. Infants begin to understand how their actions produce changes in the environment and begin to differentiate between the effects they want to produce and the behavior necessary to achieve them (Tomasello, 1999).

By preschool age, children choose exploratory strategies to investigate object affordances for tool-use tasks based on the relationship between the physical properties of tools and the objects upon which the tools are used to act, and these strategies lead to accurate judgments of tool functionality. For instance, when 3- and 4-year-olds were presented with spoons of varying bowl size to transport candies and sticks of varying rigidity to stir sugar and gravel, they used a visual exploratory strategy for the spoons, for which the relevant dimension of size could be easily assessed through vision alone, and a haptic (manual) strategy for the sticks, for which the relevant dimension of rigidity had to be discovered through physical manipulation. Children's functionality judgments were accurate in terms of these dimensions: the bigger the bowl of the spoons and the more rigid the sticks, the more likely children were to judge the tools as functional (Klatzy, Lederman, & Mankinen, 2005).

Learning about affordances through exploration and object play may allow children to discover the causal structure of complex objects. While using simple tools to exact changes in the environment is an important component of tool use, many human inventions require effects to be produced indirectly.

For instance, flipping a light switch to the "on" position should cause a light bulb to illuminate: action produces an effect by putting in motion a chain of events. Causal structure in this case is not always evident because affordances may be "hidden" behind opaque materials (wiring inside of a lamp). If the causal structure of an object is opaque, children can discover which actions must be performed through exploratory play and may indeed be motivated to focus their exploration on discovering causal structure. Schulz and Bonawitz (2007) found that when it was unclear which of two levers caused a toy to pop out of a box, preschool children engaged in focused exploration of the contraption, demonstrating a motivation to explore ambiguous causal structure. While object play does not necessarily result in accurate causal understanding, children are capable of generating evidence of causality through their play that allows them to draw accurate conclusions about causal structure (Schulz, Gopnik & Glymour, 2007).

Action planning in tool use

An important component of executing successful tool use is formulating and carrying out an action plan. As mentioned earlier, proper tool use requires integration of affordances at multiple interfaces to formulate and execute an action plan that is successful in achieving a desired goal. By far the tool that has been most studied within a developmental context in relation to action planning is the spoon. In a naturalistic study that observed spoon use in 1- and 2-year-old infants, it was found that older children used a smaller assortment of grips, smoother bodily movements more consistently, their contralateral hand to hold the dish more often, and completed the entire action more quickly than younger children (Connolly & Dalgleish, 1989). The difference between younger and older infants demonstrates that a considerable amount of experience may be necessary for young children to master the proper use of even a simple tool such as a spoon.

Once infants learn that spoons need to be gripped by the handle, this may result in adopting this action plan rigidly, even if the task requires that the spoon be gripped by the bowl end. This was shown by Barrett, Davis, and Needham (2007) in a task that required 12- to 18-month-old infants to insert the handle of a spoon or novel tool with a spoon-like structure through a small hole in the side of a box to activate a light display. After observing an adult grasp these tools by the round end and use the handles to achieve the task, infants were more likely to initially grasp the round end when using the novel tool but not when using the spoon, demonstrating a flexibility for actions directed at the novel tool, but an inflexibility for actions directed at the familiar spoon. However, older infants were more likely to grasp the round end of the tools, suggesting increased flexibility with age. In a second experiment, training infants to use the novel tool by grasping the round end as a handle produced similar biases as those found for the spoon in the first study.

By the preschool years, children are competent at using spoons and can execute successful action plans despite perturbations in the spoon's affordances (Steenbergen, van der Kamp, Smitsman, & Carson, 1997).

The "design stance"

From an early age, humans readily assume that tools are designed for an intended function, something that has been called the *design stance* (Dennett, 1990). Thus, spoons are for eating, hammers for hammering, and objects that resemble spoons and hammers were likely made for eating and hammering as well. This makes selecting and using a tool for a specific task very efficient, although it sometimes results in *functional fixedness*, the tendency not to identify alternative uses for familiar objects (German & Johnson, 2002), a phenomenon that has been demonstrated even in "technologically sparse" cultures (German & Barrett, 2005). Three-year olds tend to believe that an object designed for one purpose (a spoon, for example) is indeed a spoon, even though it can be successfully used for another function (smashing crackers, for example) (Bloom & Markson, 1998; German & Johnson, 2002).

Other research has shown that young children can acquire a "tool category" for a novel object and act as if the tool were invented "for that purpose" based on a single demonstration by an adult, reflecting a primitive form of the design stance (e.g., Casler & Kelemen, 2005). According to Casler and Kelemen (2005, p. 479), "young children exhibit rapid learning for artifact function, already possessing an early foundation to some of our most remarkable capacities as tool manufacturers and users." These findings are consistent with Geary's (2005) proposal that tool use is part of children's intuitive physics. An ability to understand how objects can be used to affect other objects and change the environment underlies tool use in humans and develops as children interact with their world (see also Smitsman & Bongers, 2002).

Tool use during the preschool years

At the preschool age, tool use has been studied in a problem-solving context by presenting children with tasks that requires the use of a tool and then allowing them to select one tool from an array containing only one functional or optimal tool and a variety of other suboptimal or nonfunctional tools (e.g., Brown, 1990; Chen & Siegler, 2000; Gredlein & Bjorklund, 2005). If children can identify the functional tool, this demonstrates an ability to accurately perceive the task affordances. The most common tool-use task presented to preschoolers involves retrieving an out-of-reach toy by using a tool to drag the toy across a tabletop, similar to the lure-retrieval task originally developed by Wolfgang Köhler (1925) with chimpanzees. In Köhler's research, a chimpanzee needed to solve a problem by assembling a combination of separated sticks to attain bananas hanging out-of-reach. Köhler related that the chimpanzee played with the sticks, seemingly with no goal in mind and, serendipitously, discovered that the sticks went together and then used the extended stick to reach the bananas.

Using a variant of the lure-retrieval task, Brown (1990) presented 18- to 36-month-old children with arrays of five tools in a series of toy-retrieval tasks. At least one tool in each array was optimal for retrieving the toy (long, rigid, with an effective head), while the others were too short, too flimsy, or had an ineffective head. While children two years of age and older were able to select the optimal tool without assistance, most children below age 2 required demonstration before they were able to choose the optimal tool. After three of these "learning" trials, children were presented with new tool arrays that included new optimal tools and some nonfunctional tools that had the same superficial color pattern as the original optimal tools. Children attended to the structural features of the new tools rather than superficial features, selecting the structurally similar functional tools over the superficially similar nonfunctional tools. A second study with 2- and 3-year-olds also found that preschoolers generalize knowledge about affordances to new tool arrays. After three successful trials with a functional tool, children were presented with a series of five sets of four tools. Children chose tools based on properties that afforded pulling, with rigidity as the most important property, the effectiveness of the tool's head as moderately important, and length as least important (see also Willatts, 1985, 1999).

Chen and Siegler (2000) also found that children can transfer knowledge of tool affordances across trials, but that initial learning may require guidance. They presented 1.5- to 2.5-year-old children with five trials on each of three toy-retrieval tasks. Children had to choose from arrays of five nonfunctional and one functional tool. For the first two problems, after the first three trials some children watched a demonstration of the solution with the working tool, some children were given a hint to choose the working tool, and others were given no instruction. Without instruction, older children retrieved the toy more frequently than younger children, but the success rate of children in both age groups was very low. Children who received a demonstration or hint solved more problems after instruction than before and they transferred this knowledge to later trials. Success, particularly for older children, also increased on trials before the modeling or hint on the second problem and over trials on the third problem, indicating that children learned about the tools through their own experience.

Sex differences in tool use

Consistent with research on object play, sex differences favoring boys have been found in some tool-use studies (e.g., Barrett, et al., 2007; Bates, Carlson-Luden, & Bretherton, 1980; Chen & Siegler, 2000; Gredlein & Bjorklund, 2005) but not others (e.g., Brown, 1990). For example, Chen and Siegler (2000) found that boys were more likely than girls to choose a tool-use strategy in a toy-retrieval task, and this difference persisted even after hints or demonstrations were given. Of children who did choose to use a tool, boys chose the functional tool more often than girls before hints or demonstration. After receiving such guidance, the sex difference disappeared, with girls who chose a tool-use strategy being just as likely as boys to choose the functional tool. A similar pattern of sex differences was reported by Gredlein and Bjorklund (2005). This study will be discussed in depth in the section on the relationship between object-oriented play and tool use.

In a study described earlier in which infants' use of a familiar tool (a spoon) was compared to their use of a novel tool on a novel task (Barrett et al., 2007), both male and female infants were more likely to initially grasp the spoon by the handle, but males were less likely than females to initially grasp the *novel* tool by the handle. Subsequently, males had more success completing the task with the spoon, but there was no difference in success with the novel tool. This suggests that female infants demonstrated a flexibility in their actions and adjusted their grasp of the novel tool as needed to complete the task, but could not overcome their biases with the familiar spoon. These researchers suggested that this sex difference was due to differences in experience with spoons, a conclusion supported by a lack of sex differences in a second study in which male and female infants received training experience on the novel tool.

Tool Use in Nonhuman Primates

Although humans may excel at tool use and manufacture, we are not the only species to use and make tools. For example, New Caledonian crows construct one of two types of hooked twigs to extract insects from trees (Hunt & Gray, 2004). But of all nonhuman animals, chimpanzees (*Pan troglodytes*) make and use the largest range of tools. One of the definitions of "culture" is the transmission of non-genetic information across generations. Using this definition, "culture" has been observed in every wild chimpanzee troop studied, with at least 39 distinct behaviors being transmitted between individuals (Whiten, Goodall, McGrew, Nishida, Reynolds, Sugiyama, Tutin, Wrangham, & Boesch, 1999). Although some of these behaviors are forms of greeting and grooming, many involve the use of tools. For example, chimpanzees use leaves to clean themselves, to sponge up water, or as rain hats; stones as weapons and hammers; and sticks to throw at opponents, for personal grooming, and to forage for termites or ants (see McGrew, 1992; Tomasello & Call, 1997; Whiten et al., 1999).

Consider the well-documented task of termite "fishing" used by the chimpanzees in the Gombe National Park in Tanzania (Goodall, 1986). Chimpanzees select sticks of the appropriate size, strip off the leaves, and insert them into a termite mound. They wait until termites climb onto the stick, and they then remove the stick and eat the termites. Termite fishing and the similar "ant dipping" are complicated tasks, taking many years to attain, with infant and juvenile chimpanzees extensively practicing the skill before mastering it (e.g., Humle, Snowdon, & Matsuzawa, 2009). In fact, some individuals never master the skill. Even more complicated is the use of large branches or stones to crack hard nuts (Boesch-Achermann & Boesch, 1993). Chimpanzees select an anvil stone upon which to place the nuts, then a hammer stone (or branch) is used to strike the nut. Chimpanzees' choice of tools does not appear to be opportunistic but seems deliberate. They rarely select a branch to open particularly hard nuts but use a stone hammer, and once they have found effective stone tools they leave them by a fruiting tree to use in the future (e.g., Carvalho, Biro, McGrew, & Matsuzawa, 2009). Like termite fishing, opening nuts this way is a difficult task for chimpanzees and often takes years to master (Boesch-Achermann & Boesch, 1993; Matsuzawa & Yamakoshi, 1996).

Although many primate researchers assume that tool use in chimpanzees is fostered by object play (e.g., Ramsey & McGrew, 2005), there is some evidence that tool use is transmitted via social learning, perhaps even teaching. Although teaching is rarely observed among chimpanzees, there have been a handful of observations of mothers teaching their offspring nut cracking or termite fishing (Boesch, 1991, Greenfield, Maynard, Boehm, & Schmidtling, 2000). For instance, Boesch interpreted the exaggerated movements of mother chimpanzees while cracking nuts in the presence of their infants as teaching. Female juveniles are more attentive to their mothers' tool use during termite fishing than male juveniles (Lonsdorf, Pusey, & Eberly, 2004) and acquire termite fishing proficiency earlier than males (Lonsdorf, 2005). In other research, the amount of time mothers spent alone or with maternal family members (which is highly correlated with time spent termite fishing) was related to their offspring's skill at specific components of termite fishing (Lornsdorf, 2006). This suggests that the juveniles were indeed learning these skills from their mothers.

Bonobos, gorillas, and orangutans rarely have been observed to use tools in the wild, but use them more frequently in captivity. In fact, orangutans, that seldom use tools in the wild (van Shaik, Fox, & Sitpmpul, 1996), may be the most adept and creative great-ape tool users in captivity (Byrne, 1995). Tool use by monkeys is also rarely observed in the wild, although some, especially South American capuchin monkeys (*Cebus capucinus*), are quite skilled at tool use in laboratory settings (e.g., Visalberghi & Limongelli, 1996).

As we noted when describing the development of tool use in children, it requires a sophisticated intelligence, including an understanding of cause-and-effect relationships as they relate to the use of objects to solve problems. Human children seem to understand this at an early age. Some argue that this means that chimpanzees, and other great apes if you consider their behavior in captivity, are able to mentally represent objects and how their actions on objects can produce meaningful results (Byrne, 1995). However, apes seem not to possess the "design stance" with respect to tools as young children do.

For instance, unlike 14-month-old children, who are more likely to use a tool that a model freely chose to use to solve a task rather than a tool she was obligated to use, apes generally show no such preference (the exception is orangutans) (Buttelmann, Carpenter, Call, & Tomasello, 2008). Unlike children, they seem not to view a person's use of a specific tool as reflecting an intentional choice, and thus likely the most effective means of solving a problem. Nonetheless, chimpanzees' frequent use of tools in the wild, and the effective tool use of the other great apes in captivity, suggests that all the great apes, including humans, evolved from a common ancestor that also had the capacity for tool use, and that different ecological conditions fostered tool use for some species (chimpanzees and humans), while these abilities lied mostly dormant in others (orangutans, gorillas, and bonobos).

The Relationship between Object Play and Tool Use in Children

Children and juvenile chimpanzees seem biased to play with objects, conservatively spending between 10% and 15% of their waking day in such activities (Ramsey & McGrew, 2005; Smith & Connolly, 1980). Members of these two species, both as juveniles and as adults, also frequently use tools. This is in contrast to the other great apes that seemingly spend less time interacting with objects and seldom use tools in their natural environments. Sex differences in humans are also found in both object play and tool use, both favoring boys. (Unlike humans, female chimpanzees seem to be the more frequent and effective tool users among members of their species.) These patterns are consistent with theorizing from evolutionary developmental psychology, suggesting that children (and chimpanzees) enter the world with biases in terms of how they relate to their physical world (Geary, 2005, 2009). These biases cause children to discover affordances of objects in relation to other objects, to learn how to use objects to solve simple problems, and, in general, predispose them to see objects as potential tools. Along similar lines, Peter Smith (1982, p. 151) argued that object exploration and play may help prepare children to use tools "over and above what could be learnt through observation, imitation, and goal-directed practice." We will return to the role of social learning in tool use later in this chapter.

Beginning in the early 1970s, researchers proposed a relation between quantity and quality of object play and subsequent tool use. Many studies used variants of the lure-retrieval task described earlier. For example, in a study reported by Sylva, Bruner, and Genoa (1976), young children were given sticks and clamps and had to assemble the sticks so they could reach a box at the opposite end of a table, open a latch, and retrieve a colorful piece of chalk. In a *Play* condition children were given the opportunity to play with the objects prior to the retrieval task; in the *Observational Learning* condition children watched someone assemble the sticks and solve the problem; children in the *Control* condition received no special experience before solving the task. Sylva and her colleagues reported that children in the Play condition generated solutions that moved from simple to complex and were more goal directed than children in the other two conditions (see also Smith & Dutton, 1979). They suggested that play provides the behavioral flexibility to solve a novel problem and affords opportunities for spontaneous problem solving with minimal frustration. Other research found a relation between the complexity of object play and solution time on a lure-retrieval task for boys, with boys showing both more complex object play and faster solution times than girls (Cheyne & Rubin, 1983). Later research called some of these early findings into question, however. The experimenters who assessed children's tool use were aware of their prior experience (i.e., being in the Play, Observational Learning, or Control condition). When precautions were taken to eliminate potential experimenter biases, no significant effects of play on subsequent tool use was found (Simon & Smith, 1983, 1985; Smith & Whitney, 1987; Vandenberg, 1980). Moreover, the tools used in the experimental tasks were often the same objects used during play, which may itself have caused some bias in the findings.

More recent research examined 3-year-old children's play styles and their use of different objects as tools in a subsequent lure-retrieval task (Gredlein & Bjorklund, 2005). Children first engaged in a free-play session, where they could play with a set of objects placed in front of them on a table for up to 10 minutes. One week later they were administered a lure-retrieval task, similar to the one used by Chen and Siegler (2000), which we described in a previous section. Approximately one week after that, they were seen again in a second free-play session with a different set of toys. Note that none of the toys used in either of the free-play sessions was used as tools or lures in the lure-retrieval task. Boys were more likely to use the objects as tools than girls, although girls were nearly as effective as boys after being given a hint, indicating that girls had the competence to use the tools to solve the problem but were less inclined to spontaneously do so than boys. Concerning play styles, boys were more apt to engage in object-oriented play (defined as stacking, securing together, or connecting two or more objects) than girls (60.8% of all play behavior for boys versus 40% for girls), with girls (21.7%) having marginally higher levels of social play (giving animate characteristics to any toys, usually including vocalizations, e.g., cow and pig playing checkers, dogs having dinner) than boys (12.1%).

Of particular interest were the relations between the different play styles and scores on the tool-use task, which are presented in Table 13.1 for all participants and separately for boys and girls. As you can see, for all participants, object-oriented play was significantly and positively related to tool-use scores. Correlations between tool-use scores and social play and contact (defined as being in contact with an object, either passively, e.g., holding, or active manipulation of objects, that did not lead to object-oriented play), were significantly and negatively related. The patterns varied, however, between the sexes. None of the correlations between play styles and tool-use scores was significant for the girls. In contrast, for the boys, the correlations between tool-use scores and object-oriented play (.59) and contact (–.76) were significant. Subsequent hierarchical multiple regression analyses indicated that both sex and object-oriented play style made unique contributions to individual differences in tool-use scores.

These findings are consistent with arguments made by Geary (2005, 2009) and others (e.g., Bjorklund & Pellegrini, 2002; Pellegrini & Bjorklund, 2004) that sex differences in early

behavior interact with inherent but still developing folk-physics systems, yielding differential behavioral competencies in males and females. It is noteworthy that significant correlations with play styles were found only for boys. Gredlein and Bjorklund (2005, p. 227) suggested that "boys may be more sensitive to such environmental experiences than girls, and that some gender-related factors (e.g., prenatal hormone exposure) other than amount of object-oriented play contribute significantly to the observed differences in tool use." The negative correlation between contact and tool-use scores likely resulted because contact, as they defined it, was less sophisticated than object-oriented play (it was used mostly by the youngest children in the sample), and in fact was only coded when object manipulation did not lead to play.

Modes of Tool-Use Development

Our focus in this chapter has been on the development of object play and its relation to the development of tool use in children. However, no one would contend that object play is the only way in which children learn to use tools. In fact, humans' substantial *social-learning* abilities, in which behavior is learned from other individuals, has been touted by many as the primary method by which children become effective tool users. We saw in an earlier section on tool using in nonhuman primates that tool-use tasks such as termite fishing and nut cracking in chimpanzees are likely transmitted from mothers to offspring via social learning (e.g., Boesch-Achermann & Boesch, 1993). It would be surprising if this were not also the case in humans.

In this section we first explore briefly the development of social learning in young children,

Table 13.1 Correlations of Play Style and Tool-use Scores at Baseline (Partially out Effect of Age) for all Participants, Boys Only, and Girls Only.

Play Style	All Participants (n = 38)	Boys Only (n = 22)	Girls Only (n = 16)
Object-Oriented	.51**	.59**	.04
Social Grouping	–.35*	–.20	–.25
Social Play	–.07	–.02	.38
Imaginary Play	.22	.18	–.07
Contact	–.58**	–.76**	–.32

* p < .05
** p < .01

(Source: Gredlein, J. M., & Bjorklund, D. F. (2005). Sex differences in young children's use of tools in a problem-solving task. *Human Nature*, *16*, 211–232.)

particularly as it relates to actions on objects. We then look at research investigating the effects of both haptic experience and social learning on infants' and young children's understanding about the affordances of objects and tool use.

Social learning of actions on objects

Infants and young children are adept at learning object use via observation from both adult models (e.g., Nagell, Olguin, & Tomasello, 1993; Tomasello, Savage-Rumbaugh, & Kruger, 1993) and other children (e.g., Flynn, 2008; Horner, Whiten, Flynn, & de Waal, 2006; White & Flynn, in press). Social-learning strategies vary over development, however. Toddlers, for instance, are more apt to engage in *emulation* (or *goal emulation*), in which they perceive the affordances between actions and objects (and may or may not perceive the intention of a model), but reproduce the same effects as a model using alternate means (e.g., Call & Carpenter, 2002; Want & Harris, 2002). In contrast, children as young as 2- and 3-years of age are more apt to engage in *true imitation*, in which an observer understands the intentions of a model and takes on this perspective to replicate the model's actions and produces the same result (e.g., McGuigan & Whiten, 2009; Tomasello, Carpenter, Call, Behne, & Moll, 2005). This has been shown in several studies in which preschool children imitate all actions that are demonstrated, whether or not they are causally relevant to reaching a goal (e.g., Brugger, Lariviere, Mumm, & Bushnell, 2007; Call, Carpenter & Tomasello, 2005; Nielsen, 2006). This imitation of causally irrelevant actions has proven to be quite robust (e.g., Horner & Whiten, 2005; Lyons, Young, & Keil, 2007; McGuigan, Whiten, Flynn, & Horner, 2007), and has been documented cross-culturally (Nielsen & Tomaselli, 2009). Children may engage in true imitation in these contexts because they appropriately assume that someone would not purposefully perform unnecessary actions (Gardiner, Greif, & Bjorklund, in press; Lyons et al., 2007). Such a perspective would be an efficient strategy for learning the adaptive functions of tools.

Children may not demonstrate this highly precise, or indiscriminate, imitation if they gain particular experience with a task before watching a demonstration. For instance, children given an easy prior experience with task materials were less likely to imitate a model than children who received a difficult prior experience, presumably because children with an easy experience had discovered relevant affordances on their own, while children with a difficult prior experience were unable to do this and needed to rely on the model for assistance (Williamson, Meltzoff, & Markman, 2008). Preschool children also imitate selectively when they know the goal of a task beforehand (Williamson & Markman, 2006), or when they are exposed to information about an object's causal structure across multiple trials (Schulz, Hooppell, & Jenkins, 2008).

Comparing observational and experiential tool-use learning

While learning from others may be essential for the cultural transmission of tool use, as we detailed in our earlier sections, haptic experience also plays an important role in tool-use development. In some cases, observation and experience may assert combined effects on tool-use learning, as shown in studies, described earlier, in which children's success improved after they were given demonstrations of tool use if they had difficulty completing a task on their own (e.g., Brown, 1990; Chen & Siegler, 2000).

How do observation and haptic experience affect tool-use learning separately, and how do their combined effects compare? A study addressed these questions by giving 2- and 3-year-olds haptic experience with task materials, observation of tool-use demonstrations, both experience and observation, or neither in a series of toy-retrieval tasks. A surprising finding emerged: Children who received only observation had greater rates of success than children in the other three conditions, which did not differ from one another (Gardiner, Gray, Bjorklund, & Greif, 2009). While children knew the goal of these tasks prior to experience or observation, it is likely that children in the observation condition were able to ascertain the action plan necessary to achieve this goal, while children in the haptic-experience condition were less likely to discover the necessary means through their own brief "object play." However, it was also found that observation might guide children's exploration; in the combined observation and experience condition, for relatively difficult tasks, children who received observation before haptic experience had greater rates of success than children who received haptic experience before observation. It is possible that having observation first focused children's attention on the affordances relevant to executing the appropriate action plan, and these affordances and understanding were refined as children gained experience with the task materials through object manipulation.

A similar conclusion was reached by van Leeuwen, Smitsman, and van Leeuwen (1994), who presented 1- and 2-year-old children with a series of toy-retrieval tasks that involved pulling an object forward using a hooked cane. Children were first presented with the hook-object configuration that was theoretically most difficult to perceive, followed by easier configurations in decreasing order of difficulty. If children could not retrieve the object on their own, the solution was modeled for them. Children who were able to solve the problem after watching the demonstration for a particular configuration always succeeded on all of the following easier configurations. The authors suggested that the demonstrations brought the affordances into focus for the children, which facilitated success on the modeled task. The observation of a more difficult task and the experience children gained on this task may have contributed to success on easier tasks.

The developmental relationship between perception and action

An interesting question that arises when comparing observational and experiential learning is whether gaining personal experience is a necessary precursor to benefiting from observations of others. In other words, do children need to have actions in their own behavioral repertoire before they can appreciate and learn from these actions in others? Work with infants has addressed this question using the habituation paradigm, in which babies are first exposed to an event until they become familiar with it and their attention to it decreases (habituation phase). They are then exposed to several test events during which the amount of time they look at the new stimuli is measured (dishabituation phase). Whichever event they look at longer is judged to be more novel or surprising.

By 6 months infants perceive actions on objects as goal directed (Woodward, 1998), and Sommerville, Hildebrande, and Crane (2008) investigated the effects of experience and observation on 10-month-olds' perception of a tool-use task as goal-directed. For a toy-retrieval task that involved pulling an out-of-reach toy forward using a cane, infants received tool-use training or observed a model demonstrate the task. Then, infants were habituated to an adult performing this task using one of two differently-colored canes to retrieve one of two different toys. For the dishabituation phase, the adult either used the same cane to retrieve a different toy (same means, different goal) or a different cane to retrieve the same toy (same goal, different means). Only infants who received experience looked longer at the different goal event than the

different means events, suggesting that only infants in the training condition selectively encoded the goal and that haptic experience, but not observation, was sufficient to perceive and encode the goal of this tool-use task.

In a similar study, 3-month-olds handled two different objects with "sticky mittens" (Sommerville, Woodward, & Needham, 2005). For the habituation event, a hand reached for and grasped one of these two objects. For the dishabituation phase, the hand was shown reaching for the same object in a new location (new means event) or a new object in the same location (new goal event). Half of the children watched these events before handling the objects and half watched after object experience. While children who handled the objects second looked equally long at both events, children who handled the objects first looked longer at the new goal event than the new path event. Furthermore, the difference in looking time between the new goal and new path events was positively correlated with the amount of infants' coordinated gaze and manual contact with the objects while wearing the mittens. These findings suggest that having this prior haptic experience enabled these young infants to detect the goal-directed structure of the model's actions, a finding that without the "sticky mitten" experience was only reliably found in 5-month-olds.

Having haptic experience with tools may also be important for understanding their causal effects (Schlesinger & Langer, 1999) and for developing an expectation that the actions of others will produce the same effects as self-actions (Elsner & Aschersleben, 2003). Additional studies have found that the benefits of observation increase with age (Elsner & Aschersleben, 2003; Provasi, Dubon & Bloch, 2001), and by 12 months infants may even gain more from observation than from their own experience (Provasi et al., 2001). It has been suggested that the relationship between perception and action is bidirectional, especially toward late infancy (Sommerville & Woodward, 2005).

Experience and observation are probably both essential for tool-use learning, but the importance of each may change across very early childhood, with observation becoming increasingly relevant during the preschool years. Younger children may require demonstration to identify functional tools, while older children may be better able to independently perceive which tools afford solutions and which do not. Haptic experience may increase understanding for both younger and older preschoolers, but this effect may be more pronounced in older than younger children. Children who need help to discover and use functional tools acquire this experience after they have learned from another individual how tools may be used. This suggests that social learning and haptic experience can have combined effects on how children come to understand affordances. The most effective method of tool-use learning for preschoolers may be a combination of haptic experience and observation, but in the particular order of observation preceding experience.

Conclusion

Children are "fiddlers." When given objects or an apparatus, they do not need to be told to interact with them to see what they might do, or what they might do with them. They do this spontaneously. In the process, they discover important properties about objects and how something works. According to Geary (2009, p. 316), the relation between object play and tool use is consistent with the idea that "the early skeletal structure of folk domains is enhanced during children's self-initiated social and play activities." Moreover, also consistent with evolutionary theory, there are sex differences in some aspects of children's folk physics. As Geary (2009, p. 316) continues: "In this case, sex differences in some folk physical abilities… may be accompanied by early sex differences in sensitivity to corresponding forms of information (e.g., attending to objects and implicitly framing them as potential tools)." Note that it is not only boys who possess these biases toward object play and tool use, although, as Geary stated, they seem more sensitive to the information gleaned from object play than girls (see also Gredlein & Bjorklund, 2005).

But, as we've seen in our discussion of social learning and tool use, children's folk psychology – particularly their ability to learn through observation – also plays a critical role in learning to use tools. Although object play and manipulation were apparently characteristics shared by the common ancestor of both humans and chimpanzees, what most differentiates *Homo sapiens* from other extant primates is our ability (and propensity) to learn from others. Object play is likely an old adaptation, which proved useful not only to humans' ancestors but also to the ancestors of modern chimpanzees. Contemporary human (and chimpanzee) youngsters continue to play with objects, which facilitates their use of tools. But this is only part of the picture. Ancient humans developed new adaptations of social learning, which seemingly became integrated with older adaptations, which make modern humans' use of tools and transmission of cultural knowledge unparalleled in the animal world.

References

Adolph, K. E., Eppler, M. A., & Gibson, E. J. (1993). Development of perception of affordances. *Advances in Infancy Research, 8*, 51–98.

Baillargeon, R. (2008). Innate ideas revisited: For a principle of persistence in infants' physical reasoning. *Perspectives on Psychological Science, 3*, 2–13.

Bakeman, R., Adamson, L. B., Konner, M., & Barr, R. G. (1990).!Kung infancy: The social context of object exploration. *Child Development, 61*, 794–809.

Ball, W. A., & Hagen, J. W. (1978). Visual refinement of haptic activity. *Perceptual and Motor Skills, 46*, 1209–1210.

Barrett, T. M., Davis, E. F., & Needham, A. (2007). Learning about tools in infancy. *Developmental Psychology, 43*, 352–368.

Bates, E., Carlson-Luden, V., & Bretherton, I. (1980). Perceptual aspects of tool use in infancy. *Infant Behavior and Development, 3*, 127–140.

Bateson, P. P. (1976). Rules and reciprocity in behavioural development. *Growing points in ethology* (pp. 401–421). Oxford, England: Cambridge University Press.

Bateson, P. (2005). The role of play in the evolution of great apes and humans. In A. D. Pellegrini, & P. K. Smith (Eds.), *The nature of play: Great apes and humans* (pp. 13–24). New York: Guilford Press.

Bekoff, M., & Byers, J. A. (1992). Time, energy and play. *Animal Behaviour, 44*, 981–982.

Belsky, J., & Most, R. K. (1981). From exploration to play: A cross-sectional study of infant free play behavior. *Developmental Psychology, 17*, 630–639.

Berenbaum, S. A., & Hines, M. (1992). Early androgens are related to childhood sex-typed toy preferences. *Psychological Science, 3*, 203–206.

Bjorklund, D. F. (1987). A note on neonatal imitation. *Developmental Review, 7*, 86–92.

Bjorklund, D. F. (1997). The role immaturity in human development. *Psychological Bulletin, 122*, 153–169.

Bjorklund, D. F. & Green, B. L. (1992). The adaptive nature of cognitive immaturity. *American Psychologist, 47*, 46–54.

Bjorklund, D. F., & Hernández Blasi, C. (2005). Evolutionary developmental psychology. In D. Buss (Ed.), *Evolutionary psychology handbook* (pp. 828–850). New York: Wiley.

Bjorklund, D. F., & Pellegrini, A. D. (2000). Child development and evolutionary psychology. *Child Development, 71*, 1687–1708.

Bjorklund, D.F., & Pellegrini, A.D. (2002). *The origins of human nature: Evolutionary developmental psychology.* Washington DC: American Psychological Association.

Bjorklund, D. F., Periss, V., Causey, K. (2009). The benefits of youth. *European Journal of Developmental Psychology, 6*, 120–137.

Bloom, P., & Markson, L. (1998). Capacities underlying word learning. *Trends in Cognitive Science, 2*, 67–73.

Bock, J. (2005). Farming, foraging, and children's play in the Okavango Delta, Botswana. In A. D. Pellegrini, & P. K. Smith (Eds.), *The nature of play: Great apes and humans.* (pp. 254–281). New York: Guilford Press.

Bock, J., & Johnston, S. E. (2004). Play and subsistence ecology among the Okavango Delta Peoples of Botswana. *Human Nature, 15*, 63–81.

Boesch, C. (1991). Teaching among wild chimpanzees. *Animal Behavior, 41*, 530–532.

Boesch-Achermann, H., & Boesch, C. (1993). Tool use in wild chimpanzees: New light from dark forests. *Current Directions in Psychological Science, 2*, 18–21.

Bornstein, M. H., Haynes, O. M., O'Reilly, A. W., & Painter, K. M. (1996). Solitary and collaborative pretense play in early childhood: Sources of individual variation in the development of representational competence. *Child Development, 67*, 2910–2929.

Brown, A. L. (1990). Domain-specific principles affect learning and transfer in children. *Cognitive Science, 14*, 107–133.

Bruner, J. S. (1972). Nature and uses of immaturity. *American Psychologist, 27*, 687–708.

Burghardt, G. M. (1998). Play. In G. Greenberg and M. M. Haraway (Eds.), *Comparative psychology: A handbook* (pp. 725–733). New York: Garland.

Burghardt, G. M. (2005). *The genesis of animal play: Testing the limits.* Cambridge, MA: MIT Press.

Buttelmann, D., Carpenter, M., Call, J., & Tomasello, M. (2008). Rational tool use and tool choice in human infants and great apes. *Child Development, 79*, 609–626.

Byers, J. A., & Walker, C. (1995). Refining the motor training hypothesis for the evolution of play. *American Naturalist, 146*, 25–40.

Byrne, R. (1995). *The thinking ape: Evolutionary origins of intelligence.* New York: Oxford University Press.

Caldera, Y. M., Huston, A. C., & O'Brien, M. (1989). Social interactions and play patterns of parents and toddlers with feminine, masculine, and neutral toys. *Child Development, 60*, 70–76.

Carvalho, S., Biro, D., McGrew, W. C., & Matsuzawa, T. (2009). Tool-composite reuse in wild chimpanzees (*Pan troglodytes*): Archaeologically invisible steps in the technological evolution of early hominins? *Animal Cognition, 12*, S103–S114.

Casler, K., & Kelemen, D. (2005). Young children's rapid learning about artifacts. *Developmental Science, 8*, 472–480.

Chen, Z., & Siegler, R. S. (2000). Across the great divide: Bridging the gap between understanding of toddlers' and older children's thinking. *Monographs of the Society for Research in Child Development, 65* (Issue no. 2, Serial No. 261).

Cheyne, J. A., & Rubin, K. H. (1983). Playful precursors of problem solving in preschoolers. *Developmental Psychology, 19*, 577–584.

Christie, J. F., & Johnsen, E. P. (1987). Reconceptualizing constructive play: A review of the empirical literature. *Merrill-Palmer Quarterly, 33*, 439–452.

Collaer, M. L., & Hines, M. (1995). Human behavioral sex differences: A role for gonadal hormones during early development? *Psychological Bulletin, 118*, 55–107.

Connolly, K., & Dalgleish, M. (1989). The emergence of a tool-using skill in infancy. *Developmental Psychology, 25*, 894–912.

Cox, R., & Smitsman, A. (2006). Action planning in young children's tool use. *Developmental Science, 9*, 628–641.

Darwin, C. (1859). *On the origin of species.* New York: Modern Library.

Dennett, D. (1990). The interpretation of texts, people, and other artifacts. *Philosophy and Phenomenological Quarterly, 1* (supplement), 177–194.

Dolhinow, P. J., & Bishop, N. H. (1970). The development of motor skills and social relationships among primates through play. In J. P. Hill (Ed.), *Minnesota Symposia on Child Psychology* (pp. 180–198). Minnesota: University of Minnesota Press.

Eibl-Eibesfeldt, I. (1989). *Human ethology.* New York: de Gruyter.

Elsner, B., & Aschersleben, G. (2003). Do I get what you get? Learning about the effects of self-performed and observed actions in infancy. *Consciousness and Cognition, 12*, 732–751.

Flynn, E. (2008). Investigating children as cultural magnets: Do young children transmit redundant information along diffusion chains? *Philosophical Transactions of the Royal Society B, 363*, 3541–3551.

Flynn, E., & Whiten, A. (2008). Cultural transmission of tool use in young children: A diffusion chain study. *Social Development, 17*, 699–718.

Fontelle, S. A., Kahrs, B. A., Neal, S. A., Newton, A. T., & Lockman, J. J. (2007). Infant manual exploration of composite substrates. *Journal of Experimental Child Psychology, 98*, 153–167.

Gardiner, A. K., Greif, M. L., & Bjorklund, D. F. (in press). Guided by intention: Preschoolers' imitation reflects inferences of causation. *Journal of Cognition and Development.*

Gardiner, A. K., Gray, S. K., Greif, M. L. & Bjorklund, D. F. (October, 2009). *Two- and three-year-olds learn tool use best through observation.* Poster presented at the biennial meeting of the Cognitive Development Society, San Antonio, TX.

Geary, D. C. (2005). *The origin of mind: Evolution of brain, cognition, and general intelligence.* Washington, DC: American Psychological Association.

Geary, D. C. (2009). *Male, female: The evolution of human sex differences* (2nd ed.). Washington, DC: American Psychological Association.

Geary, D. C., & Bjorklund, D. F. (2000). Evolutionary developmental psychology. *Child Development, 71*, 57–65.

German, T. P., & Barrett, H. C. (2005). Functional fixedness in a technologically sparse culture. *Psychological Science, 16*, 1–5.

German, T. P., & Johnson, S. (2002). Function and the origins of the design stance. *Journal of Cognition and Development, 3*, 279–300.

Gibson, E. J. (1988). Exploratory behavior in the development of perceiving, acting, and the acquiring of knowledge. *Annual Review of Psychology, 39*, 1–41.

Gibson, J. J. (1966). *The senses considered as perceptual systems.* Boston: Houghton Mifflin.

Gibson, J. J. (1979). *The ecological approach to visual perception.* Boston: Houghton Mifflin.

Goldberg, S., & Lewis, M. (1969). Play behavior in the year-old infant: Early sex differences. *Child Development, 40*, 21–32.

Gómez, J-C., & Martín-Andrade, B. (2005). Fantasy play in apes. In A. D. Pellegrini, & P. K. Smith (Eds.), *The nature of play: Great apes and humans* (pp. 139–172). New York: Guilford Press.

Goodall, J. (1962). Nest building behavior in free ranging chimpanzees. *Annals of the New York Academy of Science, 102*, 455–467.

Goodall J. (1986). *The chimpanzees of Gombe.* Cambridge, MA: Belknap Press.

Gosso, Y., Otta, E., Morais, M. de L. S., Ribeiro, F. J. L., & Bussab, V. S. R. (2005). Play in hunter-gatherer society. In A. D. Pellegrini, & P. K. Smith (Eds.), *The nature of play: Great apes and humans* (pp. 213–253). New York: Guilford Press.

Greenfield, P., Maynard, A., Boehm, C., & Schmidtling, E. Y. (2000). Cultural apprenticeship and cultural change: Tool learning and imitation in chimpanzees and humans. In S. T. Parker, J. Langer, & M. L. McKinney (Eds.), *Biology, brains, and behavior: The evolution of human development* (pp. 237–277). Santa Fe, NM: School of American Research Press.

Gredlein, J. M., & Bjorklund, D. F. (2005). Sex differences in young children's use of tools in a problem-solving task. *Human Nature, 16*, 211–232.

Groos, K., (1898). *The play of animals.* New York: Appleton.

Groos, K., (1901). *The play of men.* New York: Appleton.

Harris, L. J. (2005). Handedness. In B. Hopkins (Ed.), *The Cambridge encyclopedia of child development* (pp. 321–326). New York: Cambridge University Press.

Hayes, C. (1951). *The ape in our house.* New York: Harper.

Henderson, B. B., & Moore, S. G. (1979). Measuring exploratory behavior in young children: A factor analytic study. *Developmental Psychology, 15*, 113–119.

Hinde, R. A. (1974). *Biological bases of human social behaviour.* New York: McGraw-Hill.

Horner, V., & Whiten, A. (2005). Causal knowledge and imitation/emulation switching in chimpanzees (*Pan troglodytes*) and human children (*Homo sapiens*). *Animal Cognition, 8*, 164–181.

Horner, V., Whiten, A., Flynn, E. & de Waal, F. B. M. (2006). Faithful replication of foraging techniques along cultural transmission chains by chimpanzees and children. *Proceedings of the National Academy of Sciences, 103*, 13878–13883.

Humle, T., Snowdon, C. T., & Matsuzawa, T. (2009). Social influences on ant-dipping acquisition in the wild chimpanzees (*Pan troglodytes verus*) of Bossou, Guinea, West Africa. *Animal Cognition, 12*, S37-S48.

Hunt, G. R., & Gray, R. D. (2004). Direct observations of pandanus-tool manufacture and use by a New Caledonian crow (*Corvus moneduloides*). *Animal Cognition, 7*, 114–120.

Hutt, C. (1966). Exploration and play in children. *Symposia of the Zoological Society of London, 18*, 61–81.

Hutt, C. (1972). Sex differences in human development. *Human Development, 15*, 153–170.

Jacobson, S. W. (1979). Matching behavior in the young infant. *Child Development, 50*, 425–430.

Kagan, J. (1996). Three pleasing ideas, *American Psychologist, 51*, 901–908.

Köhler, W. (1925). *The mentality of apes.* New York: Harcourt & Brace.

Lancy, D. F. (1996). *Playing on the mother-ground: Cultural routines for children's development.* New York: Guilford Press.

Legerstee, M. (1991). The role of person and object in eliciting early imitation. *Journal of Experimental Child Psychology, 51*, 423–433.

Lockman, J. J. (2000). A perception-action perspective on tool use development. *Child Development, 71*, 137–144.

Lonsdorf, E. V. (2005). Sex differences in the development of termite-fishing skills in the wild chimpanzees, *Pan troglodytes schweinfurthii*, of Gombe National Park, Tanzania. *Animal Behavior, 70*, 673–683.

Lonsdorf, E. V. (2006). The role of the mother in the acquisition of tool-use skills in wild chimpanzees. *Animal Cognition, 9*, 36–46.

Lonsdorf, E. V., Eberly, L. E., & Pusey, A. E. (2004). Sex differences in learning in chimpanzees. *Nature, 428*, 16.

Lyons, D. E., Young, A. G., & Keil, F. C. (2007). The hidden structure of overimitation. *Proceedings of the National Academy of Sciences, 104*, 19751–19756.

Markus, N., & Croft, D. B. (1995). Play behaviour and its effects on social development of common chimpanzees (*Pan troglodytes*). *Primates, 36*, 213–225.

Martin, P., & Caro, T. (1985). On the function of play and its role in behavioral development. In J. Rosenblatt, C. Beer, M.-C. Bushnel, & P. Slater (Eds.), *Advances in the study of behavior* (Vol. 15, pp 59–103). New York: New York Academic Press.

Matsuzawa, T. (1997). The death of an infant chimpanzee at Bossou, Guinea. *Pan African News, 4*, 4–6.

Matsuzawa, T., & Yamakoshi, G. (1996). Comparison of chimpanzee material culture between Bossou and Nimba, West Africa. In A. Russon, K. Bard, & S. T. Parker (Eds.), *Reaching into the thought: The minds of the great apes* (pp. 211–232). Cambridge, UK: Cambridge University Press.

McGrew, W. C. (1972). *An ethological study of children's behaviour.* London: Metheun.

McGrew, W. C. (1977). Socialization and object manipulation of wild chimpanzees. In S. Chevalier-Skolnikoff & F. F. Poirier (Eds.), *Primates bio-social development: Biological, social, and ecological determinants* (pp. 261–288). New York: Garland.

McGrew, W. C. (1992). *Chimpanzee material culture: Implications for human evolution.* Cambridge, MA: Cambridge University Press.

McGrew, W. C., & Marchant, L. F. (1992). Chimpanzees, tools, and termites: Hand preference or handedness? *Current Anthropology, 33*, 114–119.

McGuigan, N., & Whiten, A. (2009). Emulation and "overemulation" in the social learning of causally versus causally opaque tool use by 23-and 30-month-old children. *Journal of Experimental Child Psychology, 104*, 367–381.

McGuigan, N., Whiten, A., Flynn, E., & Horner, V. (2007). Imitation of causally opaque versus causally transparent tool use by 3- and 5-year-old children. *Cognitive Development, 22*, 353–364.

McLoyd, V. C., & Ratner, H. H. (1983). The effects of sex and toy characteristics on exploration in preschool children. *Journal of Genetic Psychology, 142*, 213–224.

Meltzoff, A. N., & Moore, M. K. (1977). Imitation of facial and manual gestures by human neonates. *Science, 198*, 75–78.

Morgante, J. D., & Keen, R. (2008). Vision and action: The effect of visual feedback on infants' exploratory behaviors. *Infant Behavior & Development, 31*, 729–733.

Nagell, K., Olguin, K., & Tomasello, M. (1993). Processes of social learning in the tool use of chimpanzees (*Pan troglodytes*) and human children (*Homo sapiens*). *Journal of Comparative Psychology, 107*, 174–186.

Needham, A. (2000). Improvements in object exploration skills may facilitate the development of object segregation in early infancy. *Journal of Cognition and Development, 1*, 131–156.

Needham, A., Barrett, T., & Peterman, K. (2002). A pick me up for infants' exploratory skills: Early simulated experiences reaching for objects using 'sticky' mittens enhances young infants' object exploration skills. *Infant Behavior & Development, 25*, 279–295.

Nielsen, M. (2006). Copying actions and copying outcomes: Social learning through the second year. *Developmental Psychology, 42*, 555–565.

Nielsen, M. & Tomaselli, K. (2009). Over-imitation in the Kalahari Desert and the origins of human cultural cognition. *Psychological Science, 21,* 729–736.

Pellegrini, A. D. (2011). Play. In P. Zelazo (Ed.) *Oxford handbook of developmental psychology.* New York: Oxford University Press.

Pellegrini, A. D., & Bjorklund, D. F. (2004). The ontogeny and phylogeny of children's object and fantasy play. *Human Nature, 15,* 23–43.

Pellegrini, A. D., Dupuis, D., & Smith, P. K. (2007). Play in evolution and development. *Developmental Review, 27,* 261–276.

Pellegrini, A. D., & Gustafson, K. (2005). Boys' and girls' uses of objects for exploration, play, and tools in early childhood. In A. D. Pellegrini, & P. K. Smith (Eds.), *The nature of play: Great apes and humans* (pp. 113–135). New York: Guilford Press.

Pellegrini, A. D., & Smith, P. K. (1998). Physical activity play: The nature and function of a neglected aspect of child play. *Child Development, 69,* 577–598.

Piaget, J. (1962). *Play, dreams and imitation.* New York: Norton.

Power, T. G. (2000). *Play and exploration in children and animals.* Mahwah, NJ: Erlbaum.

Provasi, J., Dubon, C. D., & Bloch, H. (2001). Do 9- and 12-month-olds learn means-ends relation by observing? *Infant Behavior & Development, 24,* 195–213.

Provine, R. R., & Westerman, J. A. (1979). Cross the midline: Limits of early eye-hand behavior. *Child Development, 50,* 437–441.

Ramsey, J. K., & McGrew, W. C. (2005) Object play in great apes: Studies in nature and captivity. In A. D. Pellegrini, & P. K. Smith (Eds.), *The nature of play: Great apes and humans.* (pp. 89–112). New York: Guilford Press.

Rochat, P. (1989). Object manipulation and exploration in 2- to 5-month-old infants. *Developmental Psychology, 25,* 871–884.

Ruff, H. A., Saltarelli, L. M., Capozzoli, M., & Dubiner, K. (1992). The differentiation of activity in infants' exploration of objects. *Developmental Psychology, 28,* 851–861.

Rubin, K. H., Fein, G., & Vandenberg, B. (1983). Play. In E. M. Hetherington (Ed.), *Handbook of child psychology: Vol. IV. Socialization, personality and social development* (pp. 693–774). New York: Wiley.

Saltz, E., Dixon, D., & Johnson, J. (1977). Training disadvantaged preschoolers on various fantasy activities: Effects on cognitive functioning and impulse control. *Child Development, 48,* 367–380.

Schick, K. D., & Toth, N. (1993). *Making silent stones speak: Human evolution and the dawn of technology.* New York: Simon and Schuster.

Schlesinger, M., & Langer, J. (1999). Infants' developing expectations of possible and impossible tool-use events between ages 8 and 12 months. *Developmental Science, 2,* 195–205.

Schulz, L. E., & Bonawitz, E. B. (2007). Serious fun: Preschoolers engage in more exploratory play when evidence is confounded. *Developmental Psychology, 43,* 1045–1050.

Schulz, L. E., Gopnik, A., & Glymour, C. (2007). Preschool children learn about causal structure from conditional interventions. *Developmental Science, 10,* 322–332.

Schulz, L. E., Hooppell, C., & Jenkins, A. C. (2008). Judicious imitation: Children differentially imitate deterministically and probabilistically effective actions. *Child Development, 79,* 395–410.

Sigman, M., Newmann, C., Carter, E., Cattle, D., D'Souza, S., & Bwido, N. (1988). Home interactions and the development of Embu toddlers in Kenya. *Child Development, 59,* 1251–1261.

Simon, T., & Smith, P. K. (1983). The study of play and problem solving in preschool children: Have experimenter effects been responsible for previous results? *British Journal of Developmental Psychology, 1,* 289–297.

Simon, T., & Smith, P. K. (1985). Play and problem solving: A paradigm questioned. *Merrill-Palmer Quarterly, 31,* 265–277.

Sluss, D. J. (2002). Block play complexity in same-sex dyads of preschool children. In J. L. Roopnarine (Ed.), *Conceptual, social-cognitive, and contextual issues in the fields of play* (pp. 77–91). Westport, CT: Ablex Publishing.

Smith, P. K. (1982). Does play matter? Functional and evolutionary aspects of animal and human play. *Behavioral and Brain Sciences, 5,* 139–184.

Smith, P. K., & Connolly, K. (1980). *The ecology of preschool behaviour.* London: Cambridge University Press.

Smith, P. K., & Dutton, S. (1979). Play training in direct and innovative problem solving. *Child Development, 50,* 830–836.

Smith, P. K., & Whitney, S. (1987). Play and associative fluency: Experimenter effects may be responsible for previous positive findings. *Developmental Psychology, 23,* 49–53.

Smitsman, A. W., & Bongers, R. M. (2003). Tool use and tool making: A developmental action perspective. In J. Valsiner and K. J. Connolly (Eds.). *Handbook of Developmental Psychology* (pp. 172–193). London: Sage Publications.

Sommerville, J. A., Hildebrand, E. A., & Crane, C. C. (2008). Experience matters: The impact of doing versus watching on infants' subsequent perception of tool-use events. *Developmental Psychology, 44,* 1249–1256.

Sommerville, J. A., & Woodward, A. L. (2005). Pulling out the intentional structure of action: The relation between action processing and action production in infancy. *Cognition, 95,* 1–30.

Sommerville, J. A., Woodward, A. L., & Needham, A. (2005). Action experience alters 3-month-old infants' perception of others' actions. *Cognition, 96,* B1-B11.

Smilansky, S. (1968). *The effects of sociodramatic play on disadvantaged preschool children.* New York: Wiley.

Spelke, E. S., & Kinzler, K. D. (2007). Core knowledge. *Developmental Science, 10,* 89–96.

Špinka, M., Newbury, R. C., & Bekoff, M. (2001). Mammalian play: Can training for the unexpected be fun? *Quarterly Review of Biology, 76,* 141–168.

Sutton-Smith, B., Rosenberg, B. G., & Morgan, E. F. (1963). Development of sex differences in play choices during preadolescence. *Child Development, 34,* 119–126.

Steenbergen, B., van der Kamp, J., Smitsman, A. W., & Carson, R. G. (1997). Spoon handling in two- to four-year-old children. *Ecological Psychology, 9,* 113–129.

Sylva, K., Bruner, J. S., & Genova, P. (1976). The role of play in the problem-solving of children 3–5 years old. In J. Bruner, A. Jolly, & K. Sylva (Eds.), *Play: Its role in development and evolution* (pp. 244–257). New York: Penguin.

Takeshita, H., & Walraven, V. (1996). A comparative study of the variety and complexity of object manipulation in captive chimpanzees (*Pan troglodytes*) and bonobos (*Pan paniscus*). *Primates, 37,* 423–441.

Tomasello, M. (1998). Emulation learning and cultural learning. *Behavioral and Brain Sciences, 21,* 703–704.

Tomasello, M. (1999). *The cultural origins of human cognition.* Cambridge, MA: Harvard University Press.

Tomasello, M. (2000). Culture and cognitive development. *Current Directions in Psychological Science, 9*, 37–40.

Tomasello, M., & Call, J. (1997). *Primate cognition.* New York: Oxford University Press.

Tomasello, M., Carpenter, M., Call, J., Behne, T., & Moll, H. (2005). Understanding and sharing intentions: The origins of cultural cognition. *Behavioral and Brain Sciences, 28*, 675–735.

Tomasello, M., Kruger, A. C., & Ratner, H. H. (1993). Cultural learning. *Behavioral and Brain Sciences, 16*, 495–552.

Tomasello, M., Savage-Rumbaugh, S., & Kruger, A. C. (1993). Imitative learning of actions on objects by children, chimpanzees, and enculturated chimpanzees. *Child Development, 64*, 1688–1705.

Tremerlin, M. K. (1975). *Lucy: Growing up human–A chimpanzee daughter in a psychotherapist's family.* Palo Alto, CA: Science and Behavior Books.

Vandenberg, B. (1980). Play, problem solving, and creativity. In K. Rubin (Ed.), *Children's play* (pp. 49–68). San Francisco: Jossey-Bass.

van Leeuwen, L., Smitsman, A., & van Leeuwen, C. (1994). Affordances, perceptual complexity, and the development of tool use. *Journal of Experimental Psychology: Human Perception and Performance, 20*, 174–191.

van Shaik, C. P., Fox, E., & Sitpmpul, A. (1996). Manufacture and use of tools in wild Sumatran orangutans. *Naturwissenschaften, 83*, 186–188.

Vereijken, B. (2005). Motor development. In B. Hopkins (Ed.), *The Cambridge encyclopedia of child development* (pp. 217–226). New York: Cambridge University Press.

Visalberghi, E., & Limongelli, L. (1996). Acting and understanding: Tool use revisited through the minds of capuchin monkeys. In A. Russon, K. Bard, & S. T. Parker (Eds.), *Reaching into the thought: The minds of the great apes* (pp. 57–79). Cambridge: Cambridge University Press.

von Hofsten, C. (2005). Prehension. In B. Hopkins (Ed.), *The Cambridge encyclopedia of child development* (pp. 348–351). New York: Cambridge University Press.

Vygotsky, L. (1978). *Mind in society.* Cambridge: Cambridge University Press.

Want, S. C., & Harris, P. L. (2002). How do children ape? Applying concepts from the study of non-human primates to the developmental study of 'imitation' in children. *Developmental Science, 5*, 1–41.

Weisler, A., & McCall, R. B. (1976). Exploration and play: Resume and redirection. *American Psychologist, 31*, 492–508.

Whiten, A., & Flynn, E. G. (in press). The transmission and evolution of experimental 'microcultures' in groups of young children. *Developmental Psychology.*

Whiten, A., Goodall, J., McGrew, W. C., Nishida, T., Reynolds, V., Sugiyama, Y., Tutin, C. E. G., Wrangham, R. W., Boesch, C. (1999). Cultures in chimpanzees. *Nature, 399*, 682–685.

Willatts, P. (1985). Adjustment of means-ends coordination and the representation of spatial relations in the production of search errors by infants. *British Journal of Developmental Psychology, 3*, 259–272.

Willatts, P. (1999). Development of means-end behavior in young infants: Pulling a support to retrieve a distant object. *Developmental Psychology, 35*, 651–667.

Williamson, R. A., & Markman, E. M. (2006). Precision of imitation as a function of preschoolers' understanding of the goal of the demonstration. *Developmental Psychology, 42*, 723–731.

Williamson, R. A., Meltzoff, A. N. & Markman, E. M. (2008). Prior experiences and perceived efficacy influence 3-year-olds' imitation. *Developmental Psychology, 44*, 275–285.

Wilson, E. O. (1975). *Sociobiology: The new synthesis.* Cambridge, MA: Harvard University Press.

Woodward, A. L. (1998). Infants selectively encode the goal object of an actor's reach. *Cognition, 69*, 1–34.

The Development and Function of Locomotor Play

Anthony D. Pellegrini

Abstract

In this chapter locomotor play is discussed. Interestingly, this form of play has received wide and deep attention from behavioral biologists (e.g., Bekoff & Byers, 1981; Fagen, 1981) and comparative psychologists (Povinelli & Cant, 1995) but very little from developmental psychologists, with the notable exception of Pellegrini and Smith (1998). For example, in the only chapter dedicated to play in a *Handbook of Child Psychology*, Rubin, Fein, and Vandenberg (1983) made no mention of it. This is an interesting state of affairs given our current state of knowledge regarding definitions and putative functions of play. Specifically, locomotor play has been clearly defined in terms of exaggerated and nonfunctional behaviors and behavioral sequences (Fagen, 1981). Further, functional attributes of locomotor play, both immediate and deferred, have been proffered by scholars from a variety of disciplines, including zoology (Byers, 1998; Byers & Walker, 1995; Stamps, 1995) and psychology (Pellegrini & Smith, 1998; Povinelli & Cant, 1995). From this position, it seems that many psychologists have ignored one of the most common forms of play, as well as some basic theoretical and definitional assumptions regarding the functions of play. In this chapter Pellegrini discusses the definition of locomotor play in human and nonhuman juveniles, as well as ontogenetic and sex trends. He also examines locomotor play in terms of antecedents (hormonal and socialization events) and function.

Keywords: locomotion, exercise play, rhythmic stereotypes, physical training, play deprivation.

In this chapter, I examine locomotor play. Interestingly, this form of play has received wide and deep attention from behavioral biologists (e.g., Bekoff & Byers, 1981; Fagen, 1981) and comparative psychologists (Povinelli & Cant, 1995) but very little from developmental psychologists, with the notable exception of Pellegrini and Smith (1998). For example, in the only chapter dedicated to play in a *Handbook of Child Psychology*, Rubin, Fein, and Vandenberg (1983) made no mention of it, and instead talked primarily about functional and pretend play, in addition to "constructive" play, which most theorists agree (e.g., Piaget, 1962) is not a form of play.

This limitation may reflect deep-seated biases towards the study of play, to the exclusion of other forms. Specifically, there is a long tradition of a cognitive bias in the study of play, perhaps due to the long lasting impact of Piaget's theory of development on the field, and the consequential study of pretend play. When Peter Smith and Ralph Vollstedt (1985) asked adults to rate critical aspects of play, fantasy was the most important defining characteristic. Correspondingly, the current resurgence in the study of play is in due part to the study of pretend play and its role in children's theory of mind (e.g., Lillard, 1993).

This is an interesting state of affairs given our current state of knowledge regarding definitions and putative functions of play. Specifically, locomotor play has been clearly defined in terms of exaggerated and nonfunctional behaviors and behavioral sequences (Fagen, 1981). Further, functional attributes of locomotor play, both immediate and deferred, have been proffered by scholars from a variety of disciplines, including zoology (Byers & Walker, 1995; Stamps, 1995) and psychology (Pellegrini & Smith, 1998; Povinelli & Cant, 1995). From this position, it seems that many psychologists have ignored one of the most common forms of play, as well as some basic theoretical and definitional assumptions regarding the functions of play.

Locomotor play has a vigorous physical component, and thus it may variously be called physical activity play (Pellegrini & Smith, 1998) or, more commonly, locomotor play (Bekoff & Byers, 1981). Indeed, much of children's physical activity can be seen as playful in the sense that it is minimally constrained by adult demands, involves novel forms and sequences of motor behaviors and routines, and is accompanied by positive affect. Adults, however, often show some ambivalence toward children's high levels of physical activity. This ambivalence is reflected in over-diagnosed cases of attention deficit, hyperactive disorder (Pellegrini & Horvat, 1995) in boys. Children who are physically active can pose challenges for care givers; one common alternative to addressing the problem is to medicate the child so as to make him less active (Pellegrini & Horvat, 1995). This bias may also be reflected in the relative paucity of research on children's physical activity generally (Pellegrini & Smith, 1993; 1998), and on locomotor play (Pellegrini & Smith, 1998), more specifically. Yet physical activity may be important, not only for physical development, but also perhaps for cognitive performance following activity, and even for aspects of social organization and social skills. Physical activity play may, in some senses, matter psychologically.

In this chapter I discuss the definition of locomotor play in human and nonhuman juveniles, as well as ontogenetic and sex trends. I will also examine locomotor play in terms of antecedents (hormonal and socialization events) and function.

What is Locomotor Play?
Both child developmentalists and ethologists agree that players, typically children or juveniles, are concerned with means over ends (e.g., Fagen, 1981; Rubin, Fein, & Vandenberg, 1983). Further, play activity appears to be "purposeless," or to occur for its own sake and, perhaps, enjoyable (Martin & Caro, 1985; Rubin et al., 1983). Locomotor play, like other forms of play, is also multi-dimensional

and may involve symbolic activity, as in the case of boys enacting a superhero theme involving running, chasing, and play fighting. The activity may also be social or solitary, but the distinguishing behavioral features are a playful context, combined with what Simons-Morton et al. (1990) describe as moderate to vigorous physical activity, such that metabolic activity is well above resting metabolic rate. Paradigm examples of locomotor play include running, climbing, chasing, and swinging.

Because of this multi-dimensionality, the way in which any form of play is classified is not always clear cut. In this chapter, unlike in my earlier work (Pellegrini & Smith, 1998), however, I no longer consider play fighting, or rough-and-tumble play (R&T), primarily a type of locomotor play. Instead R&T is treated as a form of social play, as it has been by behavioral biologists (e.g., Fagen, 1981; Martin & Caro, 1985) and anthropologists (Fry, 2005). Like most forms of play, R&T is multifaceted and can have object, locomotor, and social dimensions, yet it is primarily social. Further, I label the form of play under discussion in this chapter as "locomotor play," not physical activity, as I have in the past (Pellegrini & Smith, 1998). This re-labeling is an effort to keep labels in the human and behavioral biology literatures consistent and minimize confusion in the literature. In what follows I first describe locomotor play in terms of its ontogeny, with examples from both the human and nonhuman literature, with corresponding sex differences, because these may indicate different types of physical activity play that may have different functional significance (Byers & Walker, 1995).

Age and sex trends in locomotor play
Play, generally, follows an inverted-U developmental course, and locomotor play is no different: It begins in early infancy, peaks during childhood, then declines during adolescence, and declines rapidly in adulthood, following my definition of play (Byers & Walker, 1995; Fagen, 1981; Rubin et al., 1983). Some scholars, such as Brian Sutton-Smith (1997), would disagree, as they consider activities such as vigorous sport, play. Briefly, sports and games are not play in the sense that they are both governed, for the most part, by *a priori* rules. From this position, the trends in locomotor play in humans appear to show in two successive peaks, reflecting three types of play, probably with different functions. These are designated as (1) rhythmic stereotypies and (2) exercise play. Each is discussed in turn.

Rhythmic stereotypies

Although most studies in the infancy literature relate to the ontogeny of symbolic play with parents and sensorimotor exploration/play, there is limited evidence documenting infants' locomotor play. Most notably, the late Esther Thelen's (1979, 1980) longitudinal study of infants' "rhythmical stereotypies" during the first year of life provides basic and important descriptive information. Rhythmical stereotypic behaviors are similar to my definition of locomotor play to the extent that they are gross motor movements, "and it is difficult to ascribe goal or purpose to those movements" (Thelen, 1979, p. 699); examples include body rocking and foot kicking. The onset of these behaviors is probably controlled by general neuromuscular maturation.

Stereotypic behaviors tend to peak during the midpoint of the first year of life; at six months, some infants spend as much as 40% of a one hour observational period in stereotypic behavior (Thelen, 1980). After this point, the behaviors gradually disappear from normal children's behavioral repertoires (Thelen, 1979). Across the first year of life, infants spend 5.2% of their time in stereotypic behaviors (Thelen, 1980). Some early parent–infant interactions probably provide other locomotor play opportunities. For example, Roopnarine, Hooper, Ahmeduzzaman, and Pollack's (1993) examination of play between parents and one-year-old infants in India suggests that locomotor play, such as tossing the infant in the air and bouncing on the knee, accounted for 13% of all play, whereas object play accounted for 80%. Similarly low rates of American parent–infant locomotor play (or vestibular stimulation) were reported by Thelen (1980). Regarding sex differences, none are reported in the incidence of rhythmic stereotypies. Specifically, Thelen (1980) compared rates for ten male and ten female infants; these averaged 35.1 and 34.4 bouts per hour, respectively; a very small and nonsignificant difference.

Exercise play

By exercise play I mean gross locomotor movements in the context of play, such as swinging, jumping/climbing, and splashing and swimming. The distinguishing feature of this play is its physical vigor; it may or may not be social, but the distinctively specialized social form of R&T was discussed in the chapter on social play. Exercise play in this sense can start at the end of the first year and it can be solitary or with parents or peers. In fact, much of the research on parent–infant play does not distinguish between exercise play from R&T, but appears to be describing "rough physical play" (Carson, Burks, & Parke, 1993; Roopnarine et al., 1993). Low rates of American parent–infant physical play have been reported by Carson and colleagues (1993), with rates peaking at around four years of age. A few cases of infant exercise play without parents have been reported. Konner (1972), for example, reported that the !Kung, a one-time Botswana foraging group, encouraged infants to chase after and catch large insects. In many cultures, ranging from model industrialized societies to foragers, exercise play is often typified by positive affect and involves learning important skills, such as swimming.

As we move to the preschool period, greater incidences of exercise play are reported, though, as was the case in infancy, most of the peer play literature for this period focuses on pretend play, not physical activity play. Further, where the latter is reported, it is often in the form of R&T, which tends to co-occur with pretend during this period (Smith & Connolly, 1980). In a few studies, "gross motor" play other than R&T is reported, sometimes occurring alone, sometimes with peers (rather than with parents).

Exercise play per se increases from the toddler to preschool period and then declines during the primary school years, with a likely peak at around four to five years (e.g., Eaton & Yu, 1989). Specifically, for two-year-olds, Rosenthal (1994) reports that it accounts for about 7% of behavior observed in daycare settings. For children two to four years of age, Field (1994) reports physical activity play accounting for 10% of all daycare behavior. Similarly, Bloch's (1989) observations of children in a Senegal fishing village found that gross motor activities accounted for 11% and 13% of children's play in the home at two to four years of age and five to six years of age, respectively.

In two ethological studies in British nursery schools, using a variety of samples, McGrew (1972) and Smith and Connolly (1980) observed children's behavior at a micro-analytical level. In McGrew's sample, with a mean age of 49.2 months, approximately 20% of children's activity was physically vigorous, such as run, flee, wrestle, chase, jump, push and pull, lift, and climb. Similarly, in Smith and Connolly's (1980) sample, with a mean age of 43.3 months, vigorous activities, such as run, chase, and climb (but also including R&T), accounted for 21% of their behavior.

As children move into primary school, a decline in physical activity is witnessed, perhaps due to the fact that they are spending more time in an environment—school—which discourages, rather than encourages, physical activity. For children aged six to ten years, "exercise play" accounted for only 13% of all outdoor behavior observed during school recess periods (Pellegrini, 1990). This relative decrease in play might be underestimated, however, because the primary school observations occurred on school playgrounds, rather than in classrooms, unlike most studies of preschoolers; the relative spatial density of classrooms, compared to playgrounds, inhibits gross motor activity (Smith & Connolly, 1980).

It will be important for our later argument for the functions of locomotor play to demonstrate that during the preschool/primary school years children engage in substantial amounts of exercise play. Blatchford (1996) described the general levels of English primary school children's activity on the school playground and found that most (60% of the children) are engaged in some form of physically active play or games during their daily break times, which lasted between 65 and 75 mm.

What about physical activity outside the school context? Simons-Morton and colleagues (1990) studied children aged nine and ten years, using children's self-reported frequency of moderate to vigorous physical activity (MVPA), that includes play and nonplay forms of physical activity, over three days. Major sources of MVPA were running, walking fast, games and sports, and cycling. MVPAs generally were slightly more common before or after school (2.3/day) than during school (1.6/day). Throughout the whole day, most children engaged in one or two long (>10 mm) MVPAs / day. In general, then, exercise, and possibly exercise play, is quite common in early/middle childhood, and appears to peak in the preschool and early primary grades, although more evidence is certainly needed to clarify exactly when the age peak occurs.

Sex differences in exercise play suggest that males tend to engage in exercise play at higher rates than females. Eaton and Enns's (1986) meta-analysis of 90 studies of sex differences in motor activity level reported a significant difference in favor of males, with the effect size tending to increase from infancy to mid-adolescence. Part of this sex difference may be due to differential maturation rates. Eaton and Yu (1989) found that relative maturity (percent of estimated adult height attained) interacted with gender, being negatively related to activity level, with girls being both less active and more physically mature than boys. As will be discussed below, these differences in physical activity probably form an

important basis for the existence of segregated sex peer groups which begin during the preschool period and wane in early adolescence (Maccoby, 1998; Pellegrini, 2004; Pellegrini, Long, Roseth, Bohn, & Van Ryzin, 2007)

Summary of age and sex trends
In summary, forms of locomotor play are quite common in childhood. In primary schools, most children engage in active play during their daily break times; further, levels of physical activity play are moderate for most children when they are out of school. An analysis of age trends suggests three successive inverted-U curves describing two different forms of locomotor play. Rhythmic stereotypies peak in infancy, at around six months of age and sex differences have been observed. Exercise play peaks during the preschool years, accounting for up to 20% of observed school recess behavior, and declines during the primary school years, accounting for about 13% of observed behavior; males, more than females, engage in exercise play. I postulate that these successive age peaks reflect different forms of play with different functions.

Males exceed females in frequency of locomotor play among many other mammalian species (Meaney, Stewart, & Beatty, 1985; Smith, 1982).

Antecedents to sex differences
Hormonal influences. Sex differences appear to be absent in rhythmical stereotypies, but appreciable for exercise play. Hypotheses about the functions of play must take account of such sex differences and the causation of such differences. Hormonal influences on play have been implicated in sex differences in vigorous physical activity. Hormonal influences typically center around the effects of endogenous and exogenous androgens on neural organization and behavior (Meaney et al., 1985). Normal exposure to androgens during fetal development predisposes boys, compared to girls, toward physical activity. Excessive amounts of these male hormones are hypothesized to "masculinize" females' play (e.g., Collaer & Hines, 1995). The experimental literature involving mice, rats, hamsters, and monkeys supports the androgenization hypothesis (e.g., Collaer & Hines, 1995). For obvious ethical reasons, the effects of androgens on human behavior can only be studied through natural experiments, where fetuses receive abnormally high levels of these male hormones because of genetic defects (e.g., congenital adrenal hyperplasia [CAH]) or difficulties during pregnancy (e.g., where mothers take synthetic progestins).

Most human studies of CAH also support the androgenization hypothesis. These studies typically have used questionnaire methodology to ask parents or children about their preferences for various activities, including physically active sports. The frequently cited research of Money and colleagues (e.g., Money & Ehrhardt, 1972) has shown that androgenized girls are more "tomboyish": They prefer male activities more than do nonandrogenized girls. Using observations of toy preferences in CAH children compared to controls, Berenbaum and Snyder (1995) found that CAH girls showed greater preference for boys' toys and activities.

Socialization effects. Socialization interacts with hormonal events in the expression of behavioral sex differences (Maccoby, 1986; Meaney et al., 1985). Beginning with interactions with their parents, boys and girls are socialized into different, and often segregated, worlds that tend to reinforce these gender differences (Maccoby, 1998; Meaney et al., 1985; Pellegrini, 2004; Pellegrini et al. 2007). For example, fathers spend more time with their sons than with their daughters and when with their sons, they engage in physically vigorous play (Carson et al., 1993). That girls are more closely supervised by parents and teachers (Fagot, 1994) may further inhibit their physically vigorous behavior (Maccoby, 1986). In the section on sex segregation, I will discuss the implications of different levels of physically vigorous behavior on children's segregated peer groups.

Functions of locomotor play

The dominant view in child development (Groos, 1898) has been that play has deferred benefits. That is, during the period of extended childhood, children engage in play to learn and practice those skills necessary to be functioning adult members of society. This assumption is based on the long-held emphasis among child developmentalists on developmental continuity (Bateson, 1981). Bateson's (1981) metaphor for the deferred-benefit view of play is "scaffolding": Play functions in skill assembly, and then is disassembled when the skill is mastered.

Alternatively, play may be viewed not as an incomplete or imperfect version of adult behavior, but as having immediate benefits during childhood. This "metamorphic" (Bateson, 1981) view posits that play and its consequences are unique to the niche of childhood, and that later benefits are not necessary for its explanation (Bjorklund & Green, 1992; Pellegrini, Horvat, & Huberty, 1998). This view is consistent with recent discussions suggesting that play occurs at specific periods during which

development may be modified (Byers & Walker, 1995; Thelen, 1979). Accordingly, the previously discussed age distribution of locomotor activity play may be useful in evaluating functional hypotheses.

Different forms and dimensions of locomotor play may serve specific developmental functions (Gomendio, 1988; Smith, 1982). I discuss the function(s) of locomotor play, considering the age trends and sex differences summarized above. I also consider both the dimension of locomotor physical activity itself and the dimension of social participation that distinguishes exercise play from R&T. Although some authors list up to 30 possible functions for play (Baldwin & Baldwin, 1977), certain functions (physical training, cognitive, and social) are most commonly advanced.

As a first step in establishing the functional importance of locomotor play during childhood, we present evidence from a small number of play-deprivation studies, either natural or experimental. These suggest that a lack of opportunity to engage in physical activity play leads to compensation later, concluding that play is of functional benefit.

The use of deprivation study to determine the effects of locomotor play has a long and interesting history in the animal literature. Rather than relying on some variant of surplus energy theory, the assumption behind play deprivation studies is that immature organism will, after deprivation, attempt to compensate for lost opportunities to exercise during deprivation. Deprivation studies, and especially social play deprivation studies (Einon, Morgan, & Kibbler, 1978) are, however, often plagued with methodological confounds, such as play deprivation being confound with other sorts of deprivation. For example, trying to deprive an animal of social play also typically deprives that animal of social interaction, so we do not know what is affecting behavior—the lack of social play or the lack of more general social interaction. Locomotor play deprivation studies are, however, less prone to this problem because locomotion can be eliminated rather easily, thus we can have relative confident in these results. Most notably, Müller-Schwarze (1968) deprived deer fawns of exercise for a prolonged period and then observed their locomotor play after release. Consistent with the prediction, deer were more active after the deprivation, than before.

In Thelen's (1980) study of rhythmic stereotypies in the first year of life, infants who engaged in spontaneous physical activities frequently when given the opportunity were those observed to receive less vestibular stimulation from caregivers and those who were more often restricted in natural movements (e.g., placed in infant seats). Thelen (1980, p. 148) concluded that "deprivation of active as well as passive movement may… promote stereotypy."

Three sets of field experiments have looked at deprivation of locomotor play during childhood. Peter Smith and Theresa Hagan (1980) studied English preschool children (3–4 years old) who were deprived of vigorous exercise by varying the amount of time they remained in their classrooms engaged in sedentary seatwork. After deprivation periods, they played outdoors. On the long, compared to short, deprivation days, children's play was more vigorous in the immediate post-deprivation period.

Utilizing a similar deprivation paradigm with American primary school children (5–9 years), Pellegrini and colleagues (Pellegrini & Davis, 1993; Pellegrini, Huberty, & Jones, 1995) replicated Smith and Hagan's results: Children in long, compared to short, deprivation periods engaged in higher levels of physical activity. Deprivation, however and predictably, interacted with sex of the children; boys, compared to girls, were especially active after long deprivation. These results support the following generalization: If children are deprived of opportunities for locomotor play, they will, when given the opportunity to play, engage in more intense and sustained bouts of locomotor play than they would have done if not so deprived. This generalization, in turn, suggests that locomotor play is serving some developmental function(s) such that a lack of it leads to compensation. It may be the case that deprivation of locomotor play during the juvenile period is especially important because this is a time when the skeletal, muscular, and neural systems are developing and practice, in the form of exercise, is necessary for normal development. If individuals are deprived of that opportunity, they may over-compensate later, when given opportunity to exercise.

In the remainder of this section, I first consider physical training (and related) functions of rhythmical stereotypies and of exercise play. We then examine possible cognitive functions of exercise play. Lastly, I examine socialization effects of a dimension of exercise play, children's levels of physical activity on their segregation into same-sex peer groups.

Physical training

Both rhythmic stereotypies and exercise play seem to have physical training benefits. First, rhythmic stereotypies, such as arms waving and kicking, peak at around six months of age. The onset of these actions is probably controlled by general maturational processes, which correspond to neuromuscular maturation. Thelen (1979), in her naturalistic longitudinal study of infants' rhythmic stereotypies, suggests that this is a sensitive period in neuromuscular development, similar to the argument of Byers and Walker (1995). Her functional inferences about physical activities are based on the systematic onset of specific behaviors and their co-occurrence with milestones of motor development. Thelen found that the individual behaviors appeared during a restricted period; onset was not randomly distributed. This pattern, she argued, is indicative of neuromuscular maturation. To support this claim further, she presented significant correlations between the age of onset of stereotypic groups (e.g., legs, arms, hands and knees) and the age of passing items from the Bayley Scales of Infant Development reflecting neuromuscular, not cognitive, development. Rhythmic movements of given body systems appear to increase just before the infant achieves voluntary control of that system.

It could be postulated that infants' rhythmic stereotypies are primarily functional for the immediate benefits of improving control of specific motor patterns. The correspondence between the ages at which these movements occur and cerebral development suggests that, initially, rhythmic stereotypies may be manifestations of immature sensorimotor integration. Play may modify or eliminate irrelevant synapse formations; with maturation, these patterns are used in more goal-directed ways (Byers & Walker, 1995; Thelen, 1979). Such a hypothesis is consistent with the lack of sex differences in these behaviors, because there is no reason to suppose that control of motor patterns at this very basic level of generality is more important for boys than for girls.

With the onset of locomotion, another developmental course may begin, as evidenced by the correspondence between exercise play and muscle differentiation, strength, and endurance. Brownlee (1954) was the first to propose that animal play was related to juvenile muscle development. Fagen (1976) extended this argument by proposing deferred benefits of exercise play for motor training, specifically, muscle strength, general cardiopulmonary functioning, and metabolic capacity. He suggested that the forms of exercise play, often involving varied, interrupted, and repeated use of muscle groups, as well as whole-body activities, would be well suited to these deferred benefits. Byers and Walker (1995), in a thorough review of the animal play and motor training literatures, evaluated the issue of immediate or deferred benefits of exercise play for three aspects of motor training: endurance, strength, and skill and economy of movement. They suggest that exercise play may improve skill and economy of movement due to the effects of exercise on muscle fiber differentiation and cerebellar synaptogenesis. They present developmental data from house mice, rats, cats, and giraffes and conclude that physical activity in the juvenile period, beginning in the early postnatal period and declining at mid-lactation, is a sensitive period in the development of these functions. Exercise play during this period has a lasting effect on subsequent economy and skill of movement.

In human juveniles, exercise play may help shape the muscle fibers used in later physically vigorous activities. This could improve the economy and skill of movement along the lines suggested by Byers and Walker in other species, although we know of no direct evidence for this. However, the evidence suggests that endurance and strength may be developed through sustained exercise bouts. The age course of exercise play also corresponds to the growth of arm and leg muscles and bones during the preschool period (Tanner, 1970). Consistent with this claim, an experimental, longitudinal study of children documented the relation between one form of exercise play, jumping, and bone mineral content (Gunter et al., 2008).

Exercise play during the school years and beyond might continue to benefit muscle and bone remodeling and strength and endurance training; physiological effects have been observed into adulthood in numerous species (Byers & Walker, 1995). Byers and Walker (1995, p. 29) were skeptical that exercise play functions to support strength or endurance. They concluded that "in many species, it is unlikely that play is a form of endurance or strength training because play bouts are too brief to prompt such benefits of exercise." They suggested that children would need to engage in daily bouts of exercise play, lasting one hour, four to five days per week, to increase endurance significantly. However, based on previous data from research on preschool and primary school children's playtime and activities out of school, we postulate that children at these ages may well engage in exercise play at levels meeting these criteria. Ethological studies of preschool children discussed above show that 20% of children's behavior during free-play periods, usually lasting the whole morning, was classified as vigorous (McGrew, 1972; Smith & Connolly, 1980).

Although some primary school children's play opportunities may be more limited, due to school regimens, their recess periods, typically accounting for 20–60 mm/day in American schools and 65–75 mm/day in English primary schools (Blatchford, 1996), are also characterized by exercise play (Blatchford, 1996; Pellegrini, 1990). These activities are supplemented by activities in other contexts, as children usually engage in more than two physically vigorous activities daily outside of school (Simons-Morton et al., 1990).

Additional evidence for the role of locomotor play and endurance training comes from comparisons of athletes and non-athletes. Although we recognize the limitations of these comparisons for making functional inferences, they do provide some evidence in a very restricted literature. This evidence supports the hypothesis that children who habitually engage in vigorous games and sports show immediate benefits in terms of being fitter than children who do not. Smoll and Schutz (1985) studied 3,000 students in British Columbia aged 9, 13, and 17 years. Athletes emerged as significantly fitter than non-athletes on all physical fitness tests. This was true for both boys and girls. Differences between athletes and non-athletes were small at 9 years, but increased substantially by 13 and 17 years. This would be consistent with physical training effects of such participation, although other explanations, such as selective participation and dropout, are also possible.

Relatedly, Lussier and Buskirk (1977) examined the effects of a 12 week endurance training program (distance running) on 8- to 12-year-old boys and girls. Training decreased heart rate during submaximal workloads and increased maximum oxygen uptake. Other studies of endurance training have had positive immediate results and reviews (e.g., Simons-Morton, O'Hara, Simons-Morton, & Parcel, 1987) concur in concluding that regular, high-intensity training can improve cardio-respiratory functioning.

The evidence presented thus far suggests that children are given opportunities for exercise play that are probably adequate for endurance training; but before firm conclusions are made, even for the preschool and primary school periods, more research is needed to document the intensity and duration of exercise play. Further, we do not know, beyond the period of childhood, the extent to which vigorous physical activities are playful, per se, or not. This remains an important task for future research.

In summary, exercise play, in the preschool years especially, seems sufficiently frequent that it can serve an immediate function for endurance and strength training. It may also improve skill and economy of movement, although specific evidence for this is lacking. This hypothesized set of functions is consistent with the age curve for exercise play (Tanner, 1970). More intriguing is its relation to the sex difference observed. Strength training at least would be more important for males in the "environment of evolutionary adaptedness" for fighting and hunting skills (e.g., Boulton & Smith, 1992); however, it could also be argued that endurance training is equally or more important for females (for gathering activities). Although very speculative at present, such hypotheses could lead to more differentiated predictions concerning gender differences in types of exercise play, analogous to Silverman and Eals's (1992) differentiation of types of spatial ability in relation to gender differences.

Three other functional hypotheses regarding the physical component of exercise play can be taken from the animal literature; these are the fat-reduction hypothesis, the thermoregulation hypothesis, and foraging and escape route learning. Initial studies of physical activity play in children were theoretically framed in variants of Spencer's (1898) Surplus Energy theory, in which such play was seen as a way of dissipating energy surplus to bodily requirements. Although little logical or empirical support currently exists for this theory (Burghardt, 1984, 1988, 2005; Smith, 1982; Smith & Hagan, 1980), Barber (1991) develops a variant of the argument. He suggests that energy is not usually in short supply for young mammals, and that play prevents obesity by ensuring that "surplus" energy is not stored as unnecessary fat. In particular, some young animals may need to consume large amounts of food to get enough protein, and play can "burn off" the excess requirements. In addition, play, by generating heat, may provide defense against cold exposure.

These postulated functions could be applied to human children as well as to other young mammals. The childhood period, which involves high rates and levels of physical activity play, also corresponds negatively to gains in fat (Tanner, 1970, p. 86). That is, after nine months of age, when play involving locomotion is increasing, fat gain has a negative velocity until six to eight years of age. Although these age trends are consistent with Barber's hypothesis applied to human children, sex differences are not; there seems no reason to suppose that fat reduction should be more important for boys in the preschool years.

The vigorous dimension of exercise play may also serve an immediate function in relation to thermoregulation—the ability of individuals to regulate their body temperatures (Burghardt, 1988). According to this hypothesis, children would engage in exercise play, which expends stored caloric energy, to raise their body temperature when the ambient temperature is low (Barber, 1991). The empirical record provides some support for this claim. Studies of outdoor play have found that exercise play is increased by cool ambient temperatures for preschool (Smith & Hagan, 1980) and primary school children (Pellegrini et al., 1995), and low levels of exercise play are observed in tropical climates (Cullumbine, 1950). Whereas exercise play might be used by children to raise body temperature, non-playful physical activity is another way in which human beings of all ages (and other mammals; Barber, 1991) can raise their body temperatures in cold climates. Therefore, these benefits are not limited to childhood. In addition, this hypothesis does not explain the specific age course of exercise play, nor does it explain the sex difference found. We hypothesize that thermoregulation is an incidental benefit of exercise play, and that thermoregulation, when important, can also be achieved by other means so far as humans are concerned.

In summary, exercise play may function primarily to develop physical strength, endurance and economy of movement. There is also some evidence to support the fat-reduction theory; and thermoregulation is postulated to be an incidental benefit of exercise play. I next examine possible cognitive functions for locomotor play.

Cognitive effects of locomotor play?
Less obvious, and more equivocal, than the likely benefits of exercise play for physical development are possible effects on psychological, and especially cognitive, factors. The role of locomotor play in nonhuman animals' foraging and escape route learning has been advanced by Judith Stamps (1995). Stamps suggests that when juveniles are placed in novel environments, their rates of time and energy spent playing increases, relative to being situated in familiar contexts. The result of this investment in play seems to take the form of animals discovering and refining routes to be used to forage for food and for escape from predators. For example, in the course of playing, birds fly around their home arenas and discover the most efficient routes to escape from a pursuing predator. To my knowledge there is no evidence for the role of locomotor play on children's

knowledge of their environments. This sort of research might not only example the role of play in knowing the local landscape but also perhaps assessing the role of play in children's ability to negotiate their way through those environments. The research of human locomotor play and cognitive performance, instead, has been mostly concerned with performance on more general cognitive tasks, school as school performance. Here I review whether engaging in exercise play has proximal consequences for cognitive performance. Effects on cognitive tasks might be expected from several theoretical viewpoints; however, these theories link any cognitive benefits to outcomes one step removed from exercise play per se, namely, arousal, breaks from cognitive tasks, and sense of mastery or well-being.

First, exercise play can lead to heightened arousal, which might influence performance following the inverted-U hypothesis (Tomporowski & Ellis, 1986). That is, moderate levels of arousal lead to better performance than do higher or lower levels. Alternatively, increased arousal may lead to a narrowing of attention to core task components. Second, exercise play might, by breaking up cognitive tasks, provide spaced or distributed practice rather than massed practice (Ebinghaus, 1885/1964). In another version of this approach, stemming from the cognitive immaturity hypothesis (Bjorklund & Pellegrini, 2000), the specifically playful nature of the break could be considered important. Relatedly, effects on performance, possibly mediated by breaks and enhanced attention, might be dependent upon enhanced feelings of mastery, or of well-being, after exercise play.

Unfortunately, much of the available research on exercise and cognitive performance is on adults. Tomporowski and Ellis (1986) provided a comprehensive review of 27 such studies directly linking exercise intervention—only some of which can be defined as exercise play—to cognitive performance. They considered effects of different types of exercise (short or long duration; anaerobic or aerobic) on cognitive tasks given during and/or after the exercise.

The pattern of findings is conflicting. The only consistent trends emerged from studies of brief, high intensity anaerobic exercise (hand dynamometer, or weight-pulling); here, moderate levels of muscular exertion usually improved cognitive task performance assessed during the exercise (e.g., participants would grip a hand dynamometer in each hand and recall nonsense syllables). This generally inconclusive pattern of findings may be due both to inconsistencies across studies and to confounding factors, such as different levels of participants' motivation to participate or different initial levels of physical fitness.

Although information on children is limited, a large-scale study of the benefits of guided physical activity (physical education classes) on children's school performance was conducted by Shephard and colleagues (1983). As part of the Trois Rivieres project in Canada, entire primary school classrooms (grades 2–6) received an additional five hours of physical education per week; control classrooms received no physical education. Teachers apparently were aware of children's condition assignments, but the influence of teacher bias was minimized by the administration of independent, province-wide examinations. The academic performance of children in the experimental group was superior to that of the control children. The authors suggest that the benefits shown in this project may have been due either to arousal caused by the enhanced exercise or by shortening of class work time (and hence "spaced practice") by inserting physical education classes (Shephard, 1983).

The latter interpretation is consistent with Stevenson and Lee's interpretation (1990) of achievement in Japanese, Taiwanese, and American schools. They suggested that the frequent breaks between periods of intense work in Japanese schools (usually ten min every hour) maximize children's cognitive performance. That children's task vigilance increases when the time spent on the task is distributed, rather than massed, is a consistent finding in the animal and human learning literatures. The massed versus distributed practice literature consistently shows few differences across age from preschool to old age. Individual differences in children, such as "distractibility" or "activity" levels, may mediate the effectiveness of distributed practice regimens, however, and should be addressed in future research.

It thus remains questionable whether it is exercise play per se, rather than just a break from sustained classroom work that is responsible for any increased cognitive performance. More will be said about the cognitive implications of children's exercise play in the chapter on educational implication of play. Briefly, there I will discuss a series of experiments with primary school children, where I and my colleagues (Pellegrini et al., 1995) examined the relation between the level of physical activity in exercise play on the school playground during recess and subsequent attention to standardized classroom tasks.

Perhaps more encouraging, and an area for future research, is the experimental evidence for the role of locomotor play on the learning due to increased synaptic and neurotransmission in mice engaging in voluntary, play-like exercise, relative to controls (Van Praag, Shubert, Zhao, & Gage, 2005). Specifically, young and aged mice were housed with or without a running wheel and injected with bromoeoxyurdine or retrovirus to label newborn cells. After one month, learning was assessed and the aged, experimental mice showed faster learning and better retention than controls. Further, running enhanced fine morphology of new neurons of both young and aged mice, suggesting that locomotor play has both immediate and deferred benefits in mice. While there are obvious limitations of the application of this work to the human case, it provides some guidance. Perhaps we should be looking at the effects of locomotor play on neural organization across ontogeny, rather than its effects on only learning.

Social effects of locomotor play

Physical activity generally and locomotor play more specifically have important effects on children's social behavior, primarily by effecting the composition of their peer groups. As discussed in Chapter 6, beginning early in the preschool years (at around 2–3 years of age) sex differences in physical activity and locomotor play bias children to spend most of their time with same-sex peers, in sex segregated groups (e.g., Fagot, 1994; Maccoby, 1998; Pellegrini, 2004; Pellegrini et al., 2007). This pattern continues through the preschool and into the early adolescent years at which point it wanes, especially in contexts encouraging integration (Pellegrini & Long, 2003; 2007). Sex segregation is a robust phenomenon across non-industrialized human societies (Bock, 2005). It is in these segregated groups that children probably learn socially proscribed social roles for males and females.

Such cross-cultural, and indeed cross-vertebrate species (e.g., Ruckstuhl, 1998), findings has lead child developmentalists to acknowledge the "interactive", but unspecified, roles of biology and socialization in determining sex segregation. The level of generality in stating that segregation is due to some unspecified interaction between biology and socialization is hardly useful in generating theory-driven hypotheses. Biology and socialization certainly interact to influence children's sex segregation and behavior, but we need theory to guide us as what interacts with what in order to generate and test

specific hypotheses. Sexual selection theory (Darwin, 1871) is one such theory of sex differences in behavior which enables us to generate testable hypotheses regarding sex segregation (Pellegrini, 2004).

Early activity biases children to interact with compatible peers but socialization pressures also force boys to interact with boys and high activity girls to segregate among themselves, separate from other girls (Pellegrini, Long, et al., 2007). An extensive corpus of observational data was collected on children's physical activity and sex segregation across much of a school year with minimal sampling and observer biases. Documentation of boys' and girls' differing levels of physical activity in the behaviors characterizing males' and females' groups in naturalistic conditions was based on the work of Pellegrini and colleagues (Pellegrini et al., 1998). Specifically, Pellegrini and colleagues (1998) conducted a series of field experiments with primary school children and established the construct validity of an observational rating scale to assess physical activity/caloric expenditure by relating these behavioral ratings to concurrent assays of aggregated heart rate and actometer readings.

A number of important methodological points made in that study must be considered when examining the role of physical activity in sex role stereotypic behaviors such as locomotor play and physical activity. First, sex differences in activity need to be documented using objective, mechanical, recording devices (i.e., actometers and heart rate monitors). Objective measures such as these minimize biases associated with male and female observers scoring boys' and girls' activity. That active behavior is assumed to be more male than female may lead to observer bias. Second, extant research examining the role of physical activity in sex segregation has used Likert-like observational ratings of children's activity with limited validity. For example, Maccoby and Jacklin (1987) used a seven point scale (1–7). The metric for physical activity used in our research was derived from a measure documenting caloric expenditure (Eaton, Enns, & Pressé, 1987) and has established construct validity (Pellegrini et al., 1998). This validity insures that physical activity, in terms of a continuous measure of caloric expenditure, is actually being measured.

Third, our observations (Pellegrini et al., 1998; 2007) were conducted in multiple classrooms across relatively long time intervals and consequently are probably more representative of individuals' behavior than some earlier work on the role of physical activity in children's sex segregation. By contrast, much previous work in this area (the work Martin & Fabes, 2001 is an exception), which minimized the role of physical activity in sex segregation (summarized in Maccoby, 1998), relied on numerous observations conducted within a very limited time period. More specifically, Maccoby's observations with preschoolers were limited to six seven-minute observations, all of which were all conducted in *one* day. Further, observations of older children (6.5 years) were limited to 71 ten-second observations, also all collected in *one* day. Indeed, Maccoby and Jacklin (1987) themselves acknowledge that failure to find an effect for physical activity on segregation may have been due to these methodological limitations.

Consistent with this concern, a recent meta-analysis on sex differences in physical activity demonstrated that limited numbers of observations attenuate sex differences in activity (Campbell & Eaton, 1999). Correspondingly, aggregating multiple observations collected during one day probably resulted in inter-dependent observational data. The dependency is due to the fact that contiguous observations (i.e., observations within each seven-minute sampling interval and within one day) tend to be more interrelated, relative to separate observations each day and being collected across a number of different days (e.g., Smith, 1985), thus further limiting the generalizability of the behavioral sample. By contrast, sampling behavior across a broader time frame as in our research yields a more representative, and valid, sample of behavior. In short, much of the extant research on the role of physical activity in sex segregation has a very limited sampling base that may result in null findings for the role of physical activity in sex segregation.

Future Research and Conclusions

In light of the relative paucity of research in the area of locomotor play, directions for future research on the nature of such play and its hypothesized benefits in physical, cognitive, and social domains are recommended. There is a need for more descriptive data on the forms of locomotor activity play and their age trends through childhood and adolescence. The reviews by Byers and Walker (1995) and Pellegrini and Smith (1998) show the importance of age trends in examining functional hypotheses. Yet, for exercise play especially, data are scanty. Although one can be reasonably confident of the inverted-U curve with age, we cannot be confident that the peak is at 4–5 years as we have assumed. Also, different types of exercise play may peak at different ages, and the developmental course may be different for boys and girls. Sex differences in exercise play are more intriguing with respect to functional hypotheses. Conceivably, these differences may be more complex and differentiated than previously thought, as Silverman and Eals (1992) found in the domain of spatial ability; for example, sex differences might be different for aspects of exercise play relevant to strength as opposed to those relevant to endurance.

The benefits of exercise play for two dimensions of motor training, strength and endurance, should be immediate and occur across the life span. By immediate we mean that strength and endurance will result from repeated activity bouts, usually across the span of a number of weeks (Byers & Walker, 1995). However, we need more information on duration, frequency, and intensity of physical exercise of both the playful and nonplayful variety from infancy through adulthood, and the correspondence between these data and measures of immediate and sustained fitness. To test the hypothesis that exercise play relates to bone remodeling and physical endurance and strength, as measured by decreased heart rate during exercise or VO2max (the maximum rate of oxygen uptake during exercise), we need to measure the separate contributions of nonplayful and playful vigorous activity to physiological measures of endurance and strength.

I have suggested that locomotor play has two forms: rhythmic stereotypies and exercise play. These forms have different age distributions and possibly different functions. Exercise play probably has immediate beneficial consequences for children's motor training. This is consistent with evolutionary reasoning as well as with the evidence, and might be hypothesized to be the earliest ultimate function for exercise play in mammals. There may be additional benefits of fat reduction and thermoregulation, which we hypothesize to be incidental.

Locomotor play deserves greater attention from psychologists. In general, conclusions have been strongly tempered by the insufficiency of available evidence. What evidence there is has not infrequently come from areas such as sports science, rather than psychology, with a consequent neglect of psychological variables. There is scope for considerable conceptual rethinking in the area; in particular, the usual stress on deferred rather than immediate benefits of play deserves reevaluation.

Even if benefits of locomotor play are more immediate than deferred, they may still be important. There are public health implications for the role of locomotor play for the physical fitness of children growing up in a modern industrial society.

Children have limited opportunities for physical activity, due to shortage of play spaces, dangerous neighborhoods, and the increased demands of formal schooling. That children seem to "need" physical activity is supported by the rebound effects observed in deprivation studies. The evidence suggests that if children are deprived of locomotor play for long periods of time, their health, in terms of cardiovascular and physical fitness, may suffer.

References

Barber, N. (1991). Play and energy regulation in mammals. *Quarterly Review of Biology, 66*, 129–147.

Bateson, P. P.G. (1981). Discontinuities in development and changes in the organization of play in cats. In K. Immelmann, G. Barlow, L. Petrinovich, and M. Main (Eds.), *Behavioral development* (pp. 281–295). New York: Cambridge University Press.

Bekoff, M., & Byers, J.A. (1981). A critical re-analysis of the ontogeny and phylogeny of mammalian social and locomotor play. In K. Immelmann, G. Barlow, L. Petronovich, and M. Main (Eds.), *Behavioural development* (pp. 296–337). Cambridge: Cambridge University Press.

Berenbaum, S.A., & Snyder, E. (1995). Early hormonal influences on childhood sex-typed activity and playmate preferences: Implications for the development of sexual orientation. *Developmental Psychology, 31*, 31–42.

Bjorklund, D. F. & Green, B. L. (1992). The adaptive nature of cognitive immaturity. *American Psychologist, 47*, 46–54.

Bjorklund, D. F., & Pellegrini, A. D. (2000). Child development and evolutionary psychology. *Child Development, 71*, 1687–1708.

Blatchford, P. (1996, October). *A national survey of break time in English schools*. Paper presented at the annual meetings of the British Educational Research Association, Lancaster.

Bloch, M. N. (1989). Young boys' and girls' play in the home and in the community: A cultural ecological framework. In M. N. Bloch and A. D. Pellegrini (Eds.), *The ecological context of children's play* (pp. 120–154). Norwood, NJ: Ablex.

Bock, J. (2005). Farming, foraging, and children's play in the Okavango Delta, Botswana. In A. D. Pellegrini and P. K. Smith (Eds.), *The nature of play: Great apes and humans* (pp. 254–284). New York: Guilford.

Boulton, M.J. & Smith, P.K. (1992). The social nature of play-fighting and play chasing: Mechanisms and strategies underlying cooperation and compromise. In J.H. Barkow, L. Cosmides, and J. Tooby (Eds.), *The adapted mind* (pp. 429–444). New York: Oxford University Press.

Brownlee, A. (1954). Play in domestic cattle: An investigation into its nature. *British Veterinary Journal, 110*, 48–68.

Burghardt, G. M. (1998). Play. In G. Greenberg and M. M. Haraway (Eds.), *Comparative psychology: A handbook* (pp. 725–733). New York: Garland.

Burghardt, G. M. (2005). *The genesis of animal play: Testing the limits*. Cambridge, MA: MIT Press.

Byers, J. A., & Walker, C. (1995). Refining the motor training hypothesis for the evolution of play. *American Naturalist, 146*, 25–40.

Campbell, D. W., & Eaton, W. O. (1999). Sex differences in the activity level of infants. *Infant and Child Development, 8*, 1–17.

Carson, J., Burks, V., & Parke, R. (1993). Parent–child physical play: Determinants and consequences. In K. MacDonald (Ed.), *Parent–child play* (pp. 197–220). Albany: State University of New York Press.

Collaer, M. L., & Hines, M. (1995). Human behavioral sex differences: A role for gonadal hormones during early development. *Psychological Bulletin, 118*, 55–107.

Darwin, C. (1871). *The descent of man, and selection in relation to sex*. London: John Murray.

Eaton, W. C., & Enns, L. R. (1986). Sex differences in human motor activity level. *Psychological Bulletin, 100*, 19–28.

Eaton, W. C., & Yu, A, P. (1989). Are sex differences in child motor activity level a function of sex differences in maturational status? *Child Development, 60*, 1005–1011.

Ebinghaus, H. (1885/1964). *Memory*. New York: Teachers College Press.

Einon, D., Morgan, M., & Kibbler, C. (1978). Brief periods of socialization and later behavior in the rat. *Developmental Psychobiology, 11*, 213–224.

Fagen, R. (1976). Exercise, play, and physical training in animals. In P. Bateson & P. Klopfer (Eds.) *Growing points in ethology*, Vol 2 (pp. 189–219). London: Plenum.

Fagen, R. (1981). *Animal play behavior*. New York: Oxford University Press.

Fagot, B.I. (1994). Peer relations and the development of competence in boys and girls. In C. Leaper (Ed.). *Childhood gender segregation: Causes and consequences* (pp. 53–66). San Francisco: Jossey-Bass.

Fry, D. P. (2005). Rough-and-tumble social play in children. In A. D. Pellegrini and P. K. Smith (Eds.) *The nature of play: Great apes and humans* (pp. 54–88). New York: Guilford.

Gunter, K. B., Baxter-Jones, A. D. G., Mirwald, R. L., Almstedt, H., Fuchs, R. K., Durski, S., & Snow, C. (2008). Impact exercise increases BMC during growth: An 8-year longitudinal study. *Journal of Bone and Mineral Research, 10*, 1359.

Hines, M., & Shipley, C. (1984). Prenatal exposure to Diethylstilbestrol (DES) and the development of sexually dimorphic cognitive abilities and cerebral lateralization. *Developmental Psychology, 20*, 81–94.

Konner, M. J. (1972). Aspects of the developmental ethology of a foraging people. In N. Blurton Jones (Ed.), *Ethological studies of child behaviour* (pp. 285–304). London: Cambridge University Press.

Lillard, A. S. (1993). Young children's conceptualization of pretense: Action or mental representational state. *Child Development, 64*, 372–386.

Lussier, L. & Buskirk, R.R. (1977). Effects of an endurance training regimen on assessment of work capacity in prepubertal children. *Annals of the New York Academy of Sciences, 301*, 734–747.

Maccoby, E. E. (1998). *The two sexes: Growing up apart, coming together*. Cambridge, MA: Harvard University Press.

Maccoby, E., & Jacklin, C. (1987). Gender segregation in childhood. In H. Reese (Ed.) *Advances in child development*, Vol. 20 (pp. 239–287).

Martin, P., & Caro, T. (1985). On the function of play and its role in behavioral development. In J. Rosenblatt, C. Beer, M. Bushnel, & P. Slater (Eds.), *Advances in the study of behavior, 15*, (pp. 59–103). New York: Academic Press.

Martin, C. L., & Fabes, R.A. (2001). The stability and consequences of young children's same-sex peer interactions. *Developmental Psychology, 37*, 431–446.

McGrew, W. C. (1972). *An ethological study of children's behaviour*. London: Methuen.

Meaney, M., Stewart, J., & Beatty, W. (1985). Sex differences in social play: The socialization of sex roles. In J. Rosenblatt, C. Beer, M. C. Bushnel, & P. Slater (Eds.). *Advances in the study of behavior, Vol. 15* (pp. 2–58). New York: Academic.

Money, J., & Ehrhardt, A. (1972). *Man & woman, boy & girl*. Baltimore: Johns Hopkins.

Müller-Schwarze, D. (1968). Play deprivation in deer. *Behaviour, 31,* 144–162.

Pellegrini, A. (1990). Elementary school children's playground behavior. Implications for children's social-cognitive development. *Children's Environment Quarterly, 7*(2), 8–16.

Pellegrini, A. D. (2004). Sexual segregation in childhood: A review of evidence for two hypotheses. *Animal Behaviour, 68,* 435–443.

Pellegrini, A. & Davis, P. (1993). Relations between children's playground and recess behaviour. *British Journal of Educational Psychology, 63,* 88–95.

Pellegrini, A. D., & Horvat, M. (1995). A developmental contextual critique of Attention Deficit Hyperactivity Disorder (ADHD). *Educational Researcher, 24,* 13–20.

Pellegrini, A.D., Horvat, M., & Huberty, P.D. (1998). The relative cost of children's physical activity play. *Animal Behaviour, 55,* 1053–1061.

Pellegrini, A.D., Huberty, P.D., & Jones, I. (1995). The effects of recess timing on children's classroom and playground behavior. *American Educational Research Journal, 32,* 845–864.

Pellegrini, A. D., Long, J. D., Roseth, C., Bohn, K., & Van Ryzin, M. (2007). A short-term longitudinal study of preschool children's sex segregation: The role of physical activity, sex, and time. *Journal of Comparative Psychology.*

Pellegrini, A. D., & Smith, P. K. (1998). Physical activity play: The nature and function of a neglected aspect of play. *Child Development, 69,* 577–598.

Piaget, J. (1962). *Play, dreams, and imitation in childhood.* (Trans. C. Gattengno & F.M. Hodgson) New York: Norton. (Original work published 1951).

Povinelli, D. J., & Cant, J. G. H. (1995). Arboreal clambering and the evolution of self-conception. *Quarterly Review of Biology, 70,* 393–421.

Roopnarine, J. L., Hooper, F., Ahmeduzzaman, A., & Pollack, B. (1993). Gentle play partners: Mother–child and father-child play in New Delhi, India. In K. MacDonald (Ed.), *Parent–child play* (pp. 287–304). Albany: State University of New York Press.

Rosenthal, M. K. (1994). Social and non-social play of infants and toddlers in family day care. In E. V. Jacobs and H. Goelman (Eds.), *Children's play in child care settings* (pp. 163–192). Albany: State University of New York. Press.

Rubin, K. H., Fein, G., & Vandenberg, B. (1983). Play. In E.M. Hetherington (Ed.), *Handbook of child psychology: Vol. IV. Socialization, personality and social development,* (pp. 693–774). New York: Wiley.

Ruckstuhl, K. E. (1998). Foraging behaviour and sexual segregation in bighorn sheep. *Animal Behaviour, 56,* 99–106.

Shephard, R.J. (1983). Physical activity and the healthy mind, *Canadian Medical Association Journal. 128,* 525–530.

Silverman, I., & Eals, M. (1992). Sex differences in spatial ability: Evolutionary theory and data. In J. Barkow, L. Cosmides, & J. Tooby (Eds.) *The adapted mind* (pp. 533–549). New York: Oxford University Press.

Simons-Morton, B. C., O'Hara, N. M., Parcel, G. S., Huang, I. W., Baranowski, T., & Wilson, B. (1990). Children's frequency of participation in moderate to vigorous physical activities. *Research Quarterly for Exercise and Sport, 61,* 307–314.

Smith, P.K. (1982). Does play matter? Functional and evolutionary aspects of animal and human play. *The Behavioral and Brain Sciences, 5,* 139–184.

Smith, P. K., & Connolly, K. (1980). *The ecology of preschool behaviour.* London: Cambridge University Press.

Smith, P. K., Hagan, T. (1980). Effects of deprivation on exercise play in nursery school children. *Animal Behaviour, 28,* 922–928.

Smith, P. K., & Vollstedt, R. (1985). On defining play: An empirical study of the relationship between play and various play criteria. *Child Development, 56,* 1042–1050.

Smoll, F.L. & Schutz, R.W. (1985). Physical fitness differences between athletes and nonathletes: Do changes occur as a function age and sex? *Human Movement Science, 4,* 189–202.

Stamps. J. (1995). Motor learning and the value of familiar space. *American Naturalist, 146,* 41–58.

Stamps. J. (2003). Behavioural processes affecting development: Tinbergen's fourth question comes to age. *Animal Behaviour, 66,* 1–13.

Stevenson, H. W. & Lee, S.Y. (1990). Concepts of achievement. *Monographs for the Society for Research in Child Development* (Serial No. 221). 55(1–2).

Sutton-Smith, B. (1997). *The ambiguity of play.* Cambridge, MA: Harvard University Press.

Tanner, J.M. (1970). Physical growth. In P.H. Mussen (Ed.). *Manual of child psychology (3rd Edition). Vol 1.* (pp. 77–156). New York: Wiley.

Thelen, E. (1979). Rhythmical stereotypies in normal human infants. *Animal Behaviour, 27,* 699–715.

Thelen, E. (1980). Determinants of amounts of stereotyped behavior in normal human infants. *Ethology and Sociobiology, 1,* 141–150.

Tomporowski, P., & Ellis, N. (1988). Effects of exercise on cognitive processes. *Psychological Bulletin, 99,* 338–346.

Van Praag, H., Shubert, T., Zhao, C., & Gage, F. H. (2005). Exercise enhances learning and hippocampal neurogenesis in aged mice. *The Journal of Neuroscience, 25* (38), 1–6.

Not Just "Playing Alone": Exploring Multiple Forms of Nonsocial Play in Childhood

Robert J. Coplan

Abstract

This chapter provides an overview of theory and research related to the study of multiple forms of nonsocial play in childhood. Topics covered include: (1) concepts, definitions, and methodologies (with a primary focus on naturalistic observations); (2) theoretical and historical perspectives that have influenced the contemporary study of nonsocial play; (3) a detailed review of the empirical literature pertaining to differences in the underlying meanings and implications of different nonsocial play types; and (4) directions for future research. In particular, the implications of the well-established conceptual and empirical distinctions between different structural forms of nonsocial play are explored.

Keywords: nonsocial play; solitary behaviors; solitude; behavioral observations; social withdrawal; social isolation

Introduction

As is evident from the contents of this volume, the importance of play in young children's cognitive, linguistic, emotional, and motor development is well established. Play also provides an important and unique context for the acquisition and implementation of young children's emerging *social* skills. Indeed, play has been described as "the method by which children communicate with each other in social settings" (Coplan & Arbeau, 2008, p. 143).

Learning to 'play nicely' with others can be considered a primary goal of early childhood (Hay, Caplan, & Nash, 2006). However, whereas some children spend most of their time engaged in peer-related play and social activities, other children are more likely to remain off by themselves, playing alone. At first glance, it seems plausible to suggest that children who most frequently play with a friend or group of peers are also the most sociable and outgoing in nature. In contrast, children who most often engage in solitary activities might be labeled as the most shy and socially withdrawn. However, a closer look at children 'playing alone' during free play at preschool would likely reveal a wide range of solitary behaviors.

For example, one child might be off in the corner drawing a picture with crayons. This child might appear to be very absorbed in his activity and quite content to play alone. Another child might stand motionless against the wall, not far from a group of children playing happily together. This child might be intently watching her peers, but despite an apparent interest, only hovers nearby and make no active attempts to join in. Finally, yet another child might be walking through the playroom, loudly banging two wooden blocks together repeatedly, giggling, and talking to himself.

These brief descriptions of diverse solitary activities just presented illustrate some of the different forms of nonsocial play that have attracted increasing research attention over the last 25 years. However, children may 'play alone' under a variety of circumstances. For example, a child at home might play quietly in their room for an extended period of time. However, for the purpose of this chapter, the term **nonsocial play** specifically refers to the display of solitary activities and behaviors in the presence of other potential play partners (Coplan, 2000). Particularly noteworthy in this definition is the explicit stipulation of a social context. Thus, nonsocial play represents an engagement in solitary activities despite immediately available opportunities to initiate peer interactions and engage in group-oriented play. It should be acknowledged that this definition of play is considerably broader than most traditional conceptualizations (e.g., Burghardt, this volume; Rubin, Fein, & Vandenberg, 1983).

Most empirical studies of nonsocial play have employed observational methodologies in laboratory playrooms (e.g., Coplan et al., 1994), preschool playrooms (Coplan, Gavinsky-Molina, Lagace-Seguin, & Wichmann, 2001), or schoolyard playgrounds (Nelson, Hart, & Evans, 2008). As will be discussed in a later section, some teacher rating scales have also been developed to specifically assess types of nonsocial play (e.g., Coplan & Rubin, 1998; Hart et al., 2000). However, for the purposes of this chapter, the review of empirical research will focus primarily on observational studies.

It is now widely accepted that nonsocial play is a complex and multidimensional phenomenon. Moreover, different subtypes of solitary activities appear to have unique underlying psychological meanings and are associated with decidedly different outcomes in childhood. This chapter provides an overview of theoretical perspectives and empirical research related to the study of multiple forms of nonsocial play in childhood. In particular, the importance of distinguishing between different structural forms of nonsocial play is emphasized.

Theoretical and Historical Perspectives

Contemporary conceptualizations of children's nonsocial play draws upon a wide range of diverse, multi-disciplinary, and often contrasting theoretical perspectives. Indeed, the historical origins of the study of multiple forms of nonsocial play can be traced back to a number of relatively distinct conceptual and theoretical 'branches.' As will be described, although some of these influential viewpoints incorporate 'classic' play theorists (e.g., Piaget, 1932; Vygotsky, 1967), others are grounded in the realms of developmental and personality psychology, education, and developmental psychopathology.

Conceptual approaches stressing the importance of social interaction
BENEFITS OF PEER RELATIONS IN CHILDHOOD

At the turn of the 20th century, several theorists and researchers began promoting the idea that the peer group might be an important and unique context for children's normal and healthy development. Cooley (1902) was among the first to argue that interactions with peers made a significant contribution to children's socialization. Piaget (e.g., 1926, 1932) echoed this suggestion, with a particular emphasis on the importance of peers in the development of children's abilities to view and accept the perspective of others. For example, Piaget postulated that the peer context provided children with unique opportunities to experience interpersonal conflict among 'equals.' Being presented with multiple conflicting views and perspectives would accordingly afford children opportunities to negotiate and compromise, reduce egocentrism, and facilitate the acquisition of interpersonal perspective-taking skills.

Other early theorists also stressed the significance of peer interaction as a context for children to learn about themselves and others. For example, in his theory of symbolic interactionism, Mead (1934) suggested that the diverse nature of social exchanges among peers assists children to gain an understanding of themselves as both 'subject' and 'object.' In this regard, Mead proposed that peer interactions were not only an important factor in the acquisition of social perspective-taking skills, but also in the more general development of the self-system. This led to the notion of the 'looking glass self,' which suggests that children experienced themselves indirectly through the responses of their peers (and other important social relationships). Similarly, Sullivan (1953) emphasized the importance of 'chumships' (close dyadic peer relationships) as essential contributors to the development of equality, mutual respect, reciprocity, cooperation, and competition in childhood. Sullivan argued that as children came to recognize and value each other's personal qualities, peers became notably influential 'shapers' of children's developing personality.

The postulations of these early theorists formed the cornerstones of contemporary theory in the study of children's peer relationships (Rubin, Bukowski, & Parker, 2006). Moreover, by explicitly establishing the peer group as a significant context for children's development, these theorists also implicitly forwarded the notion that it may be similarly important to consider children who did not frequently engage in peer interactions. Indeed, children with poor peer relations are at risk for a host of negative outcomes, including social problems (e.g., peer rejection, victimization), academic difficulties (e.g., poorer academic performance, school dropout), externalizing problems (e.g., aggression, conduct disorder), and internalizing problems (e.g., anxiety, depression) (see Rubin, et al., 2006, for a recent review). As such, it is now widely accepted that children who frequently play alone may be missing out on many of the critical and unique benefits of peer interactions in childhood (Coplan & Arbeau, 2008). Moreover, this body of research provided one theoretical impetus for studying children's nonsocial play.

'COSTS' OF SOCIAL WITHDRAWAL

Social withdrawal refers to the process whereby children remove themselves from opportunities for social interactions (Coplan & Armer, 2007). Accordingly, socially withdrawn children are more likely to engage in solitary activities in the presence of peers. Despite the early writings of peer relationships researchers (who emphasized the benefits of peer interaction), clinical psychologists have typically considered social withdrawal to be of limited developmental significance, relatively unstable, and not significantly predictive of maladjustment during the adolescent and adult periods (Kohlberg, LaCrosse & Ricks, 1972; Morris, Soroker, & Burruss, 1954; Robins, 1966).

In the 1980s, empirical research results began to emerge that challenged these long held assumptions. For example, longitudinal studies initiated by Rubin and colleagues provided strong evidence that social withdrawal was relatively stable, as well as concurrently and predictively associated with negative outcomes such as lower self-worth, loneliness, depressive symptoms, internalizing problems, and peer rejection (e.g., Rubin, 1985; Rubin & Both, 1989; Rubin, Chen & Hymel, 1993; Rubin, Hymel, & Mills, 1989).

Around the same time, child temperament researchers began to highlight the genetic (i.e., heritable) and biological substrates of behavioral inhibition (i.e., wariness during exposure to novel people, things, and places) (Garcia-Coll, Kagan, & Reznick, 1984; Kagan, Reznick, Clarke, Snidman, & Garcia Coll, 1984) and shyness (i.e., wariness in the face of social novelty and/or self-conscious behavior in situations of perceived social evaluation) (Buss & Plomin, 1984; Cheek & Buss, 1981). These findings provided a conceptual mechanism to underlie

at least one reason why children might withdraw from social interaction. Moreover, drawing upon this research, clinical psychologists began to revisit their previous assumptions and began to demonstrate links between extreme shyness/inhibition in early childhood and the development of anxiety disorders in later childhood, adolescence, and adulthood (Biederman et al., 1993; Biederman et al., 1990; Hirschfeld et al., 1992; Rosenbaum, Biederman, Hirshfeld, Bolduc, & Chaloff, 1991). As such, concerns about temperamental traits that may underlie solitary behaviors and the socioemotional 'costs' of solitude have provided an additional theoretical basis for exploring children's nonsocial play.

POSITIVE ASPECTS OF SOLITUDE

From a very different historical perspective, a number of theorists have also striven to promote the more positive aspects of solitude (e.g., Bates, 1964; Burke, 1991; Larson, 1990; Maslow 1970—see Long & Averill, 2003, for a recent review). Indeed, many potential benefits of solitude have been described. For example, aside from affording privacy (Pedersen, 1979), solitude may also provide the freedom to engage in specific thoughts or actions (Hammitt, 1982) and relief from societal pressures and expectations (Larson, 1990). Solitude has also been described as a unique context for the enjoyment of leisure activities (Purcell & Keller, 1989). Being alone may also encourage the development of creativity, promote intellectual and philosophical insights, and advance efforts of self-transformation (Csikszentmihalyi, 1996; Storr, 1988). In this regard, solitude is also considered a critically important context for the growth of spirituality and for religious experiences (France, 1997; Hay & Morisey, 1978).

Most of the historical writings espousing the benefits of solitude have focused on adults. In contrast, as described in the previous sections, there has been a predominant tendency to focus on the more negative 'risks' of solitude for children. Notwithstanding, solitude may also have positive value for children (Henninger, 1994; Martlew, McLeod & Connolly, 1976; Phillips & Sellitto, 1990). For example, solitary play among young children at preschool is often goal-directed and educational in nature (Moore, Evertson & Brophy, 1974; Rubin, Maloni & Homung, 1976). In this regard, it has been argued that solitary activities that involve manipulative materials (i.e., solitary-constructive play) serve important developmental needs and tend to be approved of and reinforced by teachers (Rubin, Watson, & Jarnbor, 1978). Indeed, (although not "data-driven") the US national guidelines for developmentally appropriate practices in early childhood programs stress the importance of solitary play for toddlers (Bredekamp & Copple, 1997).

Katz and Buchholz (1999) suggest that solitary play is viewed more positively in toddlers because of the focus on mastery. In contrast, for preschool-aged children, socialization into the peer group (i.e., social play) becomes a more central goal. Interestingly, solitude appears to become increasingly 'appreciated' again over time (Marcoen, Goossens, & Caes, 1987). For example, during late (but not early) adolescence, solitude is associated with positive emotions (Larson, 1997). Thus, the adolescent period may serve as a transition into the appreciation of solitude as a potentially beneficial state.

An acknowledgment of the possible benefits of solitary activities (for both children and adults) provides an important counterpoint to the previously presented theoretical perspectives focusing on the importance of peer interaction and risks of social withdrawal. Indeed, it is these somewhat contrasting viewpoints that have served to generate the contemporary approach to the study of solitude as a more complex and potentially multi-faceted and heterogeneous construct.

Conceptual approaches classifying types of play

SOCIAL PARTICIPATION

There is a long history of developmental psychologists and educators observing and describing different levels of children's social participation during free play with peers. The degree of children's social participation can be construed as providing varying social *contexts* for play (although early researchers often used these two terms interchangeably) (Rubin et al., 1983). Early biographical studies focusing on children's 'psychic' (i.e., psychological) behaviors often included incidental references to different social (and nonsocial) behaviors with peers (e.g., Baldwin & Stecher, 1925; Cooley, 1902; Hogan, 1898; Shinn, 1893; Tracy, 1910). The later advent of more sophisticated observational methodologies prompted researchers to develop more detailed taxonomies to specifically delineate a continuum of social participation (e.g., Andrus, 1924; Bott, 1928; Verry, 1923). Of particular note, Lehman (Lehman, 1926; Lehman & Anderson, 1928) drew attention to children who frequently played alone in the presence of peers and suggested that individual

differences in solitary and social play were related to sociability and other character traits.

Parten (1932) observed preschool children during free play in a nursery school setting over a nine month period. Among her taxonomy of social participation were several nonsocial activities, including *unoccupied behavior* (marked absence of focus or intent), *onlooking* (watching peer activities without attempts to join in), and *solitary play* (playing apart from other children in terms of distance, orientation, or attention). Parten also depicted a developmental progression of social participation across early childhood from solitary activities, to parallel play (i.e., 'next to' but not 'with' other children), and then to social play.

Subsequent research has since called this developmental progression into question. For example, although young children become more social with age, nonsocial play does not disappear as children get older (Barnes, 1971; Blurton-Jones, 1972; Rubin, Maioni, & Hornung, 1976; Rubin et al., 1978; Smith, 1978). As well, as opposed to a developmental stage, parallel play appears to function more as a "transitional bridge" from solitary to group activities (e.g., Bakeman & Brownlee, 1980; Smith, 1978) and is considered a competent peer group entry strategy for children (e.g., Dodge, Schlundt, Schocken, & Delugach, 1983). Notwithstanding, many of Parten's (1932) original social participation categories are still very much 'in general use' in the contemporary study of the various forms of children's nonsocial play behaviors (e.g., Coplan, Rubin, Fox, Calkins, & Stewart, 1994; Rubin, 1982).

Parten (1932) and others provided an explicit conceptual framework for categorizing the social participatory component of children's play with peers, which addressed the question "with whom is the child playing?" A second historical approach that has informed our understanding of nonsocial play in childhood concerns the structure or content of play activities, and addresses the question "how is the child playing?" (Coplan, 2000).

STRUCTURAL COMPONENTS OF PLAY

Developmental models and delineated taxonomies of the structural forms of children's play also have a long and rich history (e.g., Spenser, 1873; Stern, 1924). For example, Buhler's (1928) description of different childhood play types included activities such as functional/sensory-motor games, games of make-believe or illusion, passive games (e.g., looking at pictures, listening to stories) and games of construction. The modern taxonomy of subtypes of nonsocial play borrows most heavily from the structural classification system derived by Piaget (1962) and Smilansky (1968), who also proposed a linear progression of children's play forms. Again, it must be noted that the term "play" is used here in a rather broad form to incorporate activities (i.e., construction, exploration) that are not typically included in the contemporary definition of play (Rubin et al., 1983).

Infants and young children were thought to primarily display *functional* play, which involves simple and repetitive motor activities. It was argued that such 'practice play' honed basic motor skills that became the building blocks for later more complex activities (Piaget, 1962). Manipulating objects during functional play may also aid young children in learning about different physical qualities and characteristics (Hutt, 1970). As well, the physical and repetitive nature of functional activities are also thought to play an important role in the development of gross and fine motor skills in early childhood (Bar-Haim & Orit Bart, 2006).

Next in the progression was *constructive* play, which consists of the manipulation of objects for the purpose of constructing or creating something, and *exploratory* activities, defined as focused examination of an object for the purposes of obtaining information. Constructive activities help young children figure out how things work (Rubin et al., 1978) and greatly contribute to various aspects of cognitive development, including the acquisition of spatial concepts and basic mathematics (e.g., Ness & Farenga, 2007). Finally, children learn to participate in *symbolic* (or *dramatic*) play, which includes elements of pretense and the production of de-contextualized behaviors. Particularly when displayed in dyadic or group contexts (i.e., sociodramatic play or shared pretense), dramatic play is related to children's development and implementation of a wide range of important cognitive, linguistic, and socio-emotional skills (Fein, 1989; Goncu, 1989; Johnson, 1976; Vygotsky, 1967).

Similar to historical models of social participation, later empirical research results have not generally supported earlier assertions regarding a strict linear developmental progression of children's play forms (Rubin et al., 1983). Notwithstanding, building upon each of these diverse theoretical perspectives, researchers began to explore more complex models and conceptualizations of young children's nonsocial play. For example, Rubin and colleagues (Rubin, 1977; Rubin & Hayvren, 1981; Rubin &

Krasnor, 1980; Rubin, Maioni, & Hornung, 1976; Rubin, Watson, & Jambor, 1978) described the play of young children using an observational taxonomy that contained aspects of Piaget's (1962) and Smilansky's (1968) structural components of young children's play childhood *nested within* Parten's (1932) social participation categories. This research initiated the contemporary study of different subtypes of children's nonsocial play.

Subtypes of Nonsocial Play

From these diverse historical perspectives, the contemporary study of children's nonsocial play emerged. The distinction between three 'subtypes' of nonsocial play is now becoming increasingly accepted in the extant literature: (1) reticent behavior; (2) solitary-active play; and (3) solitary-passive play (Coplan & Armer, 2007). In the following sections, a detailed review of the conceptualizations and empirical findings regarding these three nonsocial play forms is presented.

Reticent behavior

The term *reticent* behavior was first coined by Coplan and colleagues (1994), to describe a type of nonsocial play consisting of onlooking (e.g., watching other children without joining in) and being unoccupied (e.g., staring off into space, wondering around aimlessly). It should be noted that—strictly speaking—reticent behavior is not really a type of 'play' (as defined by traditional theorists). Rather, this term groups together a series of behavioral responses that children may display in the presence of peers.

Reticent behavior is a relatively common form of nonsocial play, particularly in early childhood. On average, young children have been observed to engage in reticent behavior about 20% of the time in novel peer contexts (Chen, DeSousa, Chen, and Wang, 2006; Coplan et al., 1994; Nelson, Rubin, & Fox, 2005; Perez-Edgar, Schmidt, Henderson, Schulkin, & Fox, 2008) and between 10–15% of the time during free play with familiar peers at preschool or kindergarten (Coplan, Gavinski-Molina, et al., 2001; Coplan, Arbeau, & Armer, 2008; Rubin, Maioni, & HorMung, 1976; Rubin, Watson, & Jambor, 1978; Spinrad et al., 2004). This form of nonsocial play has probably been the most studied, and displays the most consistent empirical results (Coplan & Arbeau, 2006).

UNDERLYING CONCEPTUALIZATION

Reticent behavior is conceptualized as a behavioral marker for social fear and wariness in peer contexts (e.g., Coplan et al., 1994). From a motivational perspective, reticent behavior is described as a behavioral manifestation of a social *approach-avoidance conflict* (Asendorpf, 1990; Coplan, Prakash, O'Neil, & Armer, 2004). This arises when a child desires to initiate a social interaction, but this social approach motivation is inhibited by the simultaneous experience of social fear and anxiety (i.e., social avoidance motivation). If the child is unable to resolve this motivational conflict, they may end up 'stuck'—displaying interest in other children (i.e., watching), but at the same time unable to actively initiate social contact (Coplan et al., 2004). Accordingly, simply stated, children who frequently engage in reticent behavior are playing alone because, despite a desire for peer affiliation, they are also quite wary of social interactions.

Of course, this characterization of reticent behavior is meant to be applied to children who most frequently display this type of nonsocial play in the presence of peers. For example, as described earlier, it has been argued that parallel play may serve as a 'bridge' for children to transition from to social activities (Bakeman & Brownlee, 1980; Smith, 1978). Results from recent research suggest that reticent behavior may also serve a role in this transitional pathway. Robinson, Anderson, Porter, Hart, and Wouden-Miller (2003) conducted extremely extensive observations of young children's play behaviors and found that preschoolers exhibited a three-step sequential play pattern—from onlooker behavior to parallel play to social interactions with peers.

Nevertheless, there has been consistent empirical support for the notion that the frequent display of reticent behavior is a marker for social wariness and anxiety. To begin with, results from several studies have demonstrated links between temperamental shyness and reticent behavior in social situations. For example, parental ratings of child shyness have been found to predict observed reticent behaviors in early childhood in the laboratory playroom among unfamiliar peers (e.g., Coplan et al., 1994; Rubin, Cheah, & Fox, 2001; Rubin, Coplan, Fox, & Calkins, 1995), on the first day of preschool (e.g., Coplan 2000), as well as several months into the school year (Coplan et al., 2004, Coplan et al., 2008; Coplan, DeBow, Schneider, & Graham, 2009; Hastings, Sullivan, McShane, Coplan, Utendale, & Vyncke, 2008; Spinrad et al., 2004). Observed reticent behavior also appears to specifically co-occur with the observed display of overt anxious behaviors such as automanipulatives (i.e., hair pulling, digit

sucking) and crying, as well as parental and teacher ratings of anxiety and internalizing problems (Coplan & Rubin, 1998; Coplan et al., 1994; Coplan et al., 2004; Coplan et al., 2008; Fox et al., 2001; Henderson, Marshall, Fox, & Rubin, 2004; Rubin et al., 2001).

There is also some evidence linking reticent behavior to a constellation of psycho-physiological variables that are thought to underlie extreme temperamental shyness and behavioral inhibition (Henderson et al., 2004). For example, Fox and colleagues (Fox et al., 1995) reported that preschoolers who displayed a high frequency of reticent behavior (and other socially wary responses) were also more likely to exhibit right-frontal EEG asymmetries (a measure of emotional dysregulation). In contrast, more sociable and outgoing children were more likely to display left-frontal EEG asymmetries under similar conditions. Reticent behavior has also been associated with elevated levels of the stress hormone cortisol (Henderson et al., 2004; Perez-Edgar, Schmidt, Henderson, Schulkin, & Fox, 2008; Schmidt, Fox, Rubin, Sternberg, Gold, Smith, & Schulkin, 1997).

Interestingly, observed reticent behavior in early childhood has also been linked with poorer motor functioning (Bar-Haim & Orit Bart, 2006). Several possible explanations for this association have been forwarded. For example, the temperamental trait of behavioral inhibition (which may conceptually underlie the frequent display of reticent behavior) is associated with increased muscle tension (Kagan, 1994), which may interfere with children's performance of physical tasks. Similarly, individuals with heightened anxiety (a correlate of reticent behavior) tend to demonstrate poor balance control (Balaban, 2002; Balaban & Thayer, 2001; Sklare, Konrad, Maser & Jacob, 2001).

Correlates and outcomes

As described above, reticent behavior has been strongly linked with anxiety and internalizing problems in early childhood. It also appears to be the case that peers tend to respond quite negatively to children who frequently display this type of nonsocial play. Reticent behavior has been consistently associated with peer rejection and exclusion, as assessed by peer sociometric nominations (Nelson et al., 2008), teacher ratings (Coplan et al., 2008), as well as in-vivo observations of peer responses (Nelson et al., 2005).

Chen et al., (2006) observed peer responses to reticent behavior in both Canada and China among quartets of unfamiliar four-year-old peers in the laboratory playroom. Among the Canadian sample, peers were more like to directly respond to reticent behavior with acts of rejection (e.g., overt refusal, disagreement) and less likely to respond with positive behaviors (e.g., approval, cooperation). Coplan, Girardi, Findlay, and Frohlick (2007) had young children respond to hypothetical vignettes of children displaying a variety of social and nonsocial behaviors. Reticent hypothetical peers were rated as being less attractive playmates by peers as compared to age mates depicted as more sociable.

Reticent behavior in early childhood has also been associated with school adjustment difficulties. For example, reticent behavior is negatively associated with indices of cognitive competence and academic achievement (Coplan et al., 1994; Coplan, Gavinski-Molina, et al., 2001; Lloyd & Howe, 2003). Also, teachers perceive children who display reticent behavior as having problems at school (Levy-Shiff & Hoffman, 1989; Rubin, 1982). Coplan and colleagues (2008) reported that reticent behavior in kindergarten was negatively associated with a constellation of variables representing school adjustment that included teacher reports of the closeness of teacher-child relationships, teacher ratings of child academic skills, as well as self-reported perceptions of academic competence and school liking. Given these associations, it is perhaps not surprising that reticent behavior is also associated with negative self-perceptions in childhood (Coplan, Findlay, & Nelson, 2004; Nelson et al., 2005; Nelson et al., 2008).

Taken together, these findings provide a fairly clear and consistent picture of reticent behavior as a 'problematic' form of nonsocial play in childhood. Indeed, this form of nonsocial play appears to fit the 'stereotype' described at the outset of this chapter of the young solitary child as being shy, anxious, and socially withdrawn. However, as described in the forthcoming sections, other forms of nonsocial play appear to reflect different underlying social motivations and have different implications for children's socio-emotional and academic functioning.

Solitary-active play

The term *solitary-active* play is used to denote the combination of two other types of solitary activities. The first is solitary-functional behavior, which is characterized by repeated simple and repetitive sensorimotor actions with or without objects (e.g., banging two wooden blocks together, filling a bucket with sand and repeatedly pouring it out)

(Rubin, 1982). Piaget (1962) suggested that children engage in functional activities for the simple enjoyment of the physical sensations that they create (Piaget, 1962). Solitary-active play also includes solitary-dramatic behavior, which involves engagement in pretense (e.g., playing make believe, dramatizing) while playing alone.

Solitary-active play occurs quite infrequently among most young children, about 2–3% of time during indoor free play with novel or familiar peers (Coplan et al., 1994; Coplan & Rubin, 1998; Coplan, Gavinski-Molina, et al., 2001; Coplan, Wichman, & Lagacé-Séguin, 2001; Rubin, 1982). However, most young children do not engage in this form of nonsocial play at all, whereas a small group of children account for the vast majority of this observed behavior (Coplan, Wichman, et al., 2001). Perhaps as a result of this low frequency of occurrence, solitary-active play has been the least studied form of nonsocial activity, with only a handful of studies specifically exploring its meaning and outcomes (Coplan & Arbeau, 2008).

UNDERLYING CONCEPTUALIZATION

Solitary-active play is characterized as a marker variable for social immaturity and poor impulse control in early childhood (Coplan et al., 1994; Rubin, 1982). There has been fairly consistent empirical support for this conceptualization—particularly with regards to the display of solitary-active play during indoor free play in early childhood. For example, young children who most frequently display solitary-active play among peers are rated by parents as being temperamentally dysregulated (i.e., high in negative emotionality, low in soothability) (Coplan, Gavinski-Molina, et al., 2001; Coplan et al., 1994) and highly active (Coplan, 2000; Coplan, Wichmann, et al., 2001). Coplan and colleagues (1994) also found that children high in solitary-active behaviors were more likely to be off-task and disruptive during ticket-sorting and toy-cleanup with peers.

The social immaturity that is thought to underlie the display of solitary-active play also appears to be reflected in the peer context. For example, solitary-active play in early childhood has been associated with poorer social skills, the more frequent display of rough play, as well as with teacher- and parent-ratings of both internalizing and externalizing problems (Coplan 2000; Coplan, Gavinsky-Molina, et al., 2001; Coplan, Wichmann, et al., 2001; Rubin, 1982). This has led to the speculation that children who most frequently engage in solitary-active play among peers might be playing alone because they are being 'actively-isolated' by the peer group (i.e., children do not want to play with them; Rubin & Mills, 1988). Accordingly, it has been argued that because they lack the abilities to competently initiate and maintain social interactions, socially isolated children may retreat to solitary-active play in response to social rebuffs from peers (Rubin, LeMare, & Lollis, 1990).

CORRELATES AND OUTCOMES

Despite being the least common form of nonsocial play in terms of frequency of occurrence, the heightened display of solitary-active play appears to be perhaps the strongest indicator of psychosocial maladaptation in early childhood. Aside from its associations with pervasive behavior problems (as described above), solitary-active play also appears to be quite negatively salient to others (Cheah et al., 2001; Coplan & Rubin, 1998). For example, Rubin (1982) reported links between the display of solitary-active play and peer-rated (sociometric) rejection, observed negative interactions with peers, and teacher ratings of adjustment problems at school. Coplan, Wichman, et al. (2001) also found that solitary-active play was associated with poorer academic skills and less positive attitudes towards school.

However, it is particularly important to emphasize the importance of *context* when considering the construct of solitary-active play—as this behavior appears to have decidedly different meanings and implications when displayed across different settings. For example, a child alone in his room engaging in dramatic play with an action figure would be considered a common and normative behavior (Coplan, Wichman, et al., 2001). Moreover, if this same child was observed to engage in frequent sociodramatic play with other peers (i.e., shared pretense in a group), this would be considered a sign of social competence, self-regulation, and advanced cognitive and linguistic skills (e.g., Dunn & Herwig, 1992; Elias & Berk, 2002; Ervin-Trip, 1991; Fein, 1989; Howes, 1992; See Kavanaugh, this volume). However, solitary-active play denotes engaging in solitary-dramatic and -functional activities *while in the presence of other peers*, which is considered to be a deviation from the social-behavioral norms, and as such has negative implications for the child.

Interestingly, some researchers have also recently suggested that the meaning and implications of solitary-active play might differ when displayed in the context of indoor playrooms versus outdoor playgrounds (Bar-Haim & Orit Bart, 2006; Nelson et al., 2008; Spinrad et al., 2004). As described earlier, solitary-active play is observed to occur about 2–3% of the time during free play in the laboratory playroom or preschool classroom (e.g., Coplan et al., 1994; Rubin, 1982). However, in the few studies that have assessed this form of nonsocial play on the outdoor playground, solitary-active play does appear to occur more frequently in this context (Bar-Haim & Bart, 2006). Indeed, Nelson et al. (2008) observed solitary-active play on the playground about 10% of the time—primarily due to higher recorded rates of solitary-functional play.

The playground may provide a unique context for promoting certain types of child-guided activities with peers (Hart, 1993). Spinrad et al. (2004) suggested that the playground setting might elicit specific solitary-functional behaviors (e.g., swinging, running, skipping, climbing) that would be considered quite normative and appropriate. There is at least some preliminary recent empirical support for this notion. Nelson and colleagues (2008) explored the correlates of solitary-functional and solitary-dramatic play as observed in the playground setting in a sample of 361 preschoolers. They found that whereas solitary-dramatic play was related to distractibility, indices of aggression, and peer exclusion, solitary-functional play was largely unrelated to indices of psychosocial maladjustment (aside from some negative relations to indices of sociability). Thus, solitary-dramatic play in the context of the playground demonstrated a similar pattern of associations to that which has been previously reported in the laboratory and preschool playroom. In contrast, solitary-functional play appears to be comparatively more 'functional' when displayed on the playground.

Solitary-passive play

The final subtype of nonsocial behaviors is labeled *solitary-passive* play. This structural form of solitude includes solitary-constructive play, which includes the manipulation of objects for the purposes of creating something (i.e., building with blocks, doing artwork, putting a puzzle together), and solitary-exploratory behavior, which involves the examination and/or manipulation of objects for the purposes of gaining information (i.e., how does this object function?) (Rubin, 1982). Solitary-passive behavior is the most common form of nonsocial play, observed to occur between 20%–45% of the time during indoor free play in early childhood (Coplan, 2000; Coplan, Gavinski-Molina, et al., 2001;

Nelson et al., 2005; Rubin et al., 1976; Rubin et al., 1978), and somewhat less frequently on the playground (Nelson et al., 2008; Spinrad et al., 2004). However, as noted in the forthcoming sections, despite this comparably high frequency of occurrence, there remains little agreement among researchers as to the meaning and implications of solitary-passive play in childhood (Coplan & Weeks, 2010a).

UNDERLYING CONCEPTUALIZATION

Rubin (1982) introduced the notion that some forms of solitary play may not necessarily be 'problematic' in early childhood. Results from this study of preschoolers indicated that the observed display of solitary-constructive play was largely unrelated to indices of socio-emotional functioning and it was concluded that this form of solitary activity was "somewhat benign" (p. 654). This led to the speculation that solitary-passive play was in fact a behavioral marker of *unsociability* (e.g., Rubin & Asendorpf, 1993). From a motivational perspective, unsociability is thought to reflect the combination of both low social approach (i.e., lack of a strong desire to engage in social interaction) and low social avoidance motivations (lack of a strong desire to refrain from social interactions) (Asendorpf, 1990). Thus, children who more frequently display solitary-passive behavior were characterized as object-oriented (Jennings, 1975) rather than people-oriented, and were described as simply preferring to play alone (Asendorpf, 1993).

Subsequent empirical results appeared to provide further support for this characterization of solitary-passive play. For example, the display of solitary-passive behavior was linked with the temperamental trait of attention, observed task persistence, and excelling at object-oriented tasks (Coplan 2000; Coplan & Rubin, 1998; Coplan et al., 1994). Rubin, Coplan, Fox, and Calkins (1995) also reported that solitary-passive behavior was the preferred play modality of preschoolers who demonstrated a low frequency of social interactions but who were also emotionally well-regulated. Coplan, Gavinski-Molina, et al. (2001) similarly found that solitary-passive play was related to temperamental indices of emotion regulation, including lower levels of negative emotionality and ease in soothing.

However, more recently some researchers have questioned the direct link between solitary-passive play and the preference for solitude. For example, Henderson et al. (2004) argued that engaging in solitary-passive play amongst peers may also serve as a strategy for shy children to cope with feelings of social unease. That is, some shy children may choose to retreat to solitary-passive play as a means of resolving their approach-avoidance conflicts (Asendorpf, 1991). As well, in two recent studies, researchers have failed to find significant associations between observed solitary-passive play and specific measures designed to assess unsociability in children via parental reports, teachers ratings, peer nominations, and self-report (Coplan et al., 2004; Spangler & Gazelle, 2009). Moreover, as described in the next section, there have also been some inconsistent results with regards to the implications and outcomes of solitary-passive play in early childhood.

CORRELATES AND OUTCOMES

Solitary-passive play has been generally considered to be a comparatively 'benign' form of solitude (Rubin, 1982). This notion was reinforced by the results of several studies that indicated that this form of nonsocial play was largely unrelated to indices of psychosocial maladjustment in early childhood (Coplan, 2000; Coplan & Rubin, 1998; Coplan et al., 1994; Rubin et al., 1995). For example, Coplan (2000) did not find significant associations between the display of solitary-passive behavior at the start of preschool and teacher-rated behavior problems (internalizing or externalizing) four months later. Rubin (1982) argued that solitary-passive play is positively reinforced by peers and teachers, as it maintains order in the early childhood classroom.

However, more recent findings have called these initial assumptions into question. For example, Coplan and Prakash (2003) reported that teachers tended to initiate social contact with young children observed to display solitary-passive play. These authors suggested that increased awareness regarding the potential negative outcomes associated with social withdrawal in childhood could have led teachers to more frequently intervene when they perceive a child playing by themselves. There is also some evidence to suggest that peers do not view solitary-passive play in a positive light. Significant associations have been reported between solitary-passive play among preschoolers and both observed (Nelson et al., 2005) and teacher-rated peer exclusion (Spinrad et al., 2004). Spinrad and colleagues (2004) also reported relations between solitary-passive play and indices of both internalizing and externalizing problems. These researchers concluded that some children may also retreat into solitary-passive play in response to being excluded by peers (Rubin & Mills, 1988).

Notwithstanding, findings from several other recent studies continue to suggest that solitary-passive play is a comparatively positive form of nonsocial play (Bar-Haim & Orit Bart, 2006; Doctoroff, Greer, & Arnold, 2006; Lloyd & Howe, 2003). For example, Nelson et al. (2008) reported that observed solitary-passive play on the playground in early childhood was largely unrelated to indices of maladjustment. Thus, results pertaining to solitary-passive play remain quite inconsistent. Accordingly, it seems clear that the interpretation of the meaning and implications of this form of nonsocial play is more complex than originally postulated. As will be discussed in the following section, it will be important for future research to include additional factors (i.e., age, social context, culture) when considering the meaning and implications of different forms of nonsocial play.

Indeed, in a recent extensive review of the literature pertaining to the construct of unsociability in childhood, Coplan and Weeks (2010a) argued that although it may be that unsociable children do indeed tend to engage in more frequent solitary-passive play in the presence of peers, it also appears to be the case that other children also may engage in this form of nonsocial play for reasons other than the preference for solitude (i.e., coping with shyness, being excluded by others). Thus, these authors argued that there is not a 'one-to-one' correspondence between solitary-passive behavior and unsociability and that an observed high frequency of solitary-passive play should *not* be employed as the sole criterion for identifying unsociable children.

Future Directions

The last 25 years have been witness to a veritable explosion of research regarding our understanding of the meanings and implications of different forms of nonsocial play. However, despite these impressive advances, there are still many issues to be addressed and a plethora of unanswered questions to explore. In this final section, a number of suggestions for future research directions are outlined.

Methodological issues

As mentioned at the outset of this chapter, most studies of nonsocial play have employed observational taxonomies to assess children's play behaviors in different social contexts. Such techniques (see Smith, this volume) involve the systematic recording of children's nonsocial (and other) play behaviors using either time sampling (e.g., Rubin, 1982), event sampling (e.g., Harrist, Zaia, Bates, Dodge & Pettit, 1997), or scan sampling techniques (e.g., Ladd & Profilet, 1996). For example, the *Play Observation Scale* (POS, Rubin, 2001) employs a time sampling methodology whereby ten-second intervals are coded for the cognitive quality of children's play (e.g., functional, constructive, dramatic) nested within different levels of social participation (e.g., solitary, parallel, group). A modified version of the POS has been extensively employed in the study of multiple forms of children's nonsocial play by several different researchers (e.g., Coplan et al., 2008; Guralnick, Hammond, & Connor, 2003; Henderson et al., 2004; Lloyd & Howe, 2003; Nelson et al., 2008; Rubin, Burgess, & Hastings, 2002).

Advantages of the use of observational techniques include face validity, a reduction in observer bias (with the use of observers 'blind' to other information regarding the children they are observing), and the ability to train coders to record very specific and detailed behaviors. However, although behavioral observations are considered the 'gold standard' in the assessment of nonsocial play, this methodology also has some disadvantages. Most noteworthy are the immense costs (in both time and personnel) of collecting observational data of this nature.

The extensive resources necessary to conduct naturalistic observations has led some researchers to develop 'alternative-source' assessments of nonsocial play. For example, teacher-ratings are comparatively quick and inexpensive. Moreover, although subject to the same biases as other outside sources of assessments (i.e., parents, peers), teachers are able to observe children at school over extended periods of time and are often relied upon to make inferences about children's behaviors. However, because they are untrained in this area, teachers may not be able to identify the fine-grained and detailed distinctions necessary to distinguish between the different subtypes of children's nonsocial play.

A few teacher ratings have been developed to specifically assess multiple forms of nonsocial play, including the *Preschool Play Behavior Scale* (Coplan & Rubin, 1998), the *Penn Interactive Peer Play Scale* (Fantuzzo, Coolahan, Mendez, McDermott, & Sutton-Smith, 1998), and the *Teacher Behavior Rating Scale* (Hart et al, 2000). These teacher-rated scales appear to have good psychometric properties and have demonstrated evidence of construct validity with regards to associations with their observed counterparts. However, despite apparently appropriate factor structures, the subscales on these measures representing the different forms of nonsocial play tend to be extremely highly inter-correlated (Hart et al., 2000). Notwithstanding, empirical results with teacher-ratings of nonsocial play have been consistent, for the most part, with the extant literature (e.g., Coplan, 2000; Coplan & Rubin, 1998; Hart et al., 2000; Fantuzzo et al., 1998; Nelson et al., 2008; Nelson, Hart, Evans, Coplan, Roper, & Robinson, 2009). Nevertheless, there remains a clear need for future researchers to continue developing and validating alternative-source assessments of children's nonsocial play.

Developmental differences

Almost everything we have learned about nonsocial play has come from research conducted with samples of preschool children (i.e., aged 3–5 years), with only a few studies having included children aged 7–8 years (e.g., Nelson et al., 2005; Spangler & Gazelle, 2009). Virtually nothing is known about the meanings and implications of the multiple forms of nonsocial play beyond this age period. Indeed, the most basic developmental questions remain unaddressed.

Do the same forms of nonsocial play even exist for older children? It has been suggested that different forms of nonsocial play might 'merge' in middle or later childhood (Asendorpf, 1991; Rubin & Asendorpf, 1993). There is clearly a pressing need for observational studies with older children. Does nonsocial play have more negative implications for older children? Children who consistently and over time engage in comparatively less social interaction with peers may come to lag behind in the acquisition of important social skills (Rubin et al., 2006). As well, from middle-childhood through to adolescence, social withdrawal also appears to become increasingly associated with peer rejection, negative self-perceptions, and psychosocial difficulties (Rubin, Coplan, & Bowker, 2009). There is also some evidence to suggest that as children age they view solitary play as being increasingly deviant from the norm and become more likely to respond to such behaviors with peer rejection (Rubin & Mills, 1988; Younger & Piccinin, 1989).

Future researchers must also explore the longer term stability and outcomes of childhood nonsocial play. Do children who display reticent behavior in preschool grow up to be more shy and introverted? Does a preference for solitary-passive play in childhood predict a greater appreciation for solitary pursuits in adulthood? There is evidence of the long-term stability of shyness from early childhood through to adulthood (Asendorpf, Denissen, & van Aken, 2008; Kagan, Snidman, Kahn, & Towsley, 2007). It remains to be seen if different forms of childhood nonsocial play carry with them differential implications in later childhood, adolescence, and adulthood.

Sex differences

There is also a need for future researchers to more closely explore potential sex differences in children's nonsocial play. Researchers have not typically reported sex differences in the relative observed frequencies of different forms of nonsocial play in early childhood (e.g., Coplan, Gavinski-Molina, et al., 2001). However, there is at least some preliminary evidence suggesting that there may be potentially important gender differences in the associates and outcomes of nonsocial play.

To begin with, results from a few studies have suggested that the physiological substrates typically associated with reticent behavior are more pronounced among boys than girls (e.g., Dettling, Gunnar, & Donzella, 1999; Henderson et al., 2001). For example, Pérez-Edgar et al. (2008) recently reported that observed reticent behavior was associated with elevated cortisol among preschool-aged boys and girls. These authors postulated that there may be unique gender-specific links between biology and behavior with regards to the development of reticent and socially wary behaviors.

There is also some indication that solitary-passive play may have different meanings and implications for boy versus girls (Nelson et al., 2005). For example, Coplan, Gavinski-Molina, et al. (2001) reported that temperamental shyness was more strongly associated with solitary-passive behavior for boys than for girls. Moreover, their results indicated that for boys, solitary-passive behavior was positively associated with internalizing problems, and negatively associated with social competence and academic achievement. In contrast, for girls, this same form of nonsocial play was negatively related to internalizing problems, positively related to academic achievement, and relatively unrelated to social competence.

Coplan, Wichmann, et al. (2001) reported some differences in the socio-emotional outcomes of boys versus girls who most frequently displayed solitary-active play. Solitary-active girls (but not boys) displayed significantly more internalizing and externalizing problems than comparison girls. Finally, peers may also respond more negatively to nonsocial play when displayed by boys as compared to girls. There is at least some preliminary evidence to suggest that both reticent behavior and solitary-passive play are more strongly related to peer rejection for boys than for girls (Nelson et al, 2005; Hart et al., 2000).

The results of a growing number of studies have indicated that shyness is a greater 'risk factor' for boys than girls (see Rubin et al., 2009 for a recent review). For example, parents tend to respond more negatively to shy behaviors when displayed by boys than by girls (e.g., Coplan et al., 2004; Simpson & Stevenson-Hinde, 1985). As well, shyness and unsociability are both more strongly related to peer exclusion and rejection for boys than for girls (Coplan et al., 2004; Coplan & Weeks, 2010b; Gazelle & Ladd, 2003; Spangler & Gazelle, 2009). Accordingly, it has been argued that shyness is less socially acceptable for boys than for girls because it violates gender norms related to male social assertion and dominance (Rubin & Coplan, 2004).

Notwithstanding, results concerning gender differences in the associates of nonsocial play are still somewhat inconsistent (Coplan & Armer, 2007). This may be due to the additional statistical power required to detect significant interaction effects that include child sex (which may also represent relatively small effect sizes). As mentioned previously, significant resources are required to undertake observational studies with larger sample sizes. Hopefully, future researchers will commit to making the investment necessary to address these issues appropriately.

Differences across contexts

Context clearly plays a critical role in the conceptualization of children's nonsocial play. Indeed, as explicitly stated at the outset of this chapter, nonsocial play (as defined herein) consists of the display of solitary activities in the presence of available play partners (i.e., in a social context—as opposed to a child playing alone in her room). Moreover, as previously alluded to, the meaning and implications of different forms of nonsocial play may also change within different social contexts. For example, solitary-functional activities may be more normative when displayed on the playground (Nelson et al., 2008) than in the preschool playroom (Coplan, Wichman, et al., 2001).

The 'familiarity' of the social context may also play an important role. Reticent behavior appears to represent social fear and wariness in both novel (Coplan et al., 1994) and familiar (Coplan et al., 2008) social settings. However, in the few studies that have explored children's behaviors across both social contexts, reticent behavior in novel settings has not been a strong predictor of children's nonsocial

and social behaviors in more familiar environments (e.g., Asendorpf, 1990; Paquette & LaFreniere, 1994). Asendorpf (1994) has argued that the relation between children's behaviors in novel and familiar settings might be mediated by peer interaction experiences and establishing social relationships, but, to date, these issues remain largely unexplored empirically.

Future researchers should also explore the nature of children's nonsocial play in social contexts beyond the preschool, school yard, or laboratory playroom. Children engage in considerable social activities outside of school, including "playdates" (Coplan, Debow, et al., 2009), more informal social gatherings in the neighborhood (Ladd & Golter, 1988), and organized peer group contexts such as sports teams and clubs (Krombholz, 2006).

As well, virtually all of the research described in this chapter was conducted in Western cultures. Results from cross-cultural research suggest that the findings do not necessarily generalize to other places in the world (see Chen, 2010, for a recent review). For example, there is some preliminary evidence to suggest that the frequency of reticent behavior (as displayed in the same social context) varies across cultures. Young children tend to display more reticent behavior in Asian cultures (i.e., China, Korea, Indonesia) as compared to their Western age mates (i.e., Canada, United Sates, Italy, Brazil, Australia) (Chen, Hastings, Rubin, Chen, Cen, & Stewart,1998; Eisenberg et al., 2001; Farver, Kim & Lee, 1995; Rubin et al., 2006).

Moreover, responses to reticent behavior also appear to vary across cultures. For example, Chen et al., (2006) observed peer responses to the display of reticent behavior in samples of Canadian and Chinese preschoolers. It was found that whereas children in the Canadian sample tended to respond to reticent behavior with peer rejection (i.e., overt refusal, disagreement), reticent behavior in the Chinese sample was more likely to elicit more positive peer responses (e.g., approval). These findings are consistent with previous research indicating that as compared to Western cultures, shyness in Asian cultures (i.e., China) is more positively valued and is associated with positive socio-emotional and academic outcomes (Chen, Cen, Li, & He, 2005; Chen, Rubin, Li, & Li, 1999).

Future researchers should also explore potential cross-cultural differences with regards to other forms of nonsocial play. Chen (2010) recently speculated that although shyness may be viewed more positively in China, social disinterest (i.e., preference for solitude) may be responded to more negatively because it is in direct contrast to collectivistic goals. As such, it is possible that solitary-passive behavior may be more strongly associated with negative outcomes in China as compared to Western cultures. However, to date it has yet to be established that different forms of nonsocial play even 'exist' in other cultures.

Real-world applications

Finally, future researchers also need to continue to explore the implication of nonsocial play in more applied settings. Aspects of children's play have long been utilized in early intervention contexts to identify target children who might benefit from ameliorative programs, as behaviors that are subject to change as a function of participating in the intervention, as well as components of the intervention itself (e.g., Dansky, 1980; Saltz, Dixon, & Johnson, 1977; Furman, Rahe, & Hartup, 1979; see Greco & Morris, 2001; Rubin et al., 1983, for reviews).

Coplan, Schneider, DeBow and Graham (2010) recently developed and implemented a social-skills-based early intervention program for extremely shy preschool children. Among their findings, it was reported that as compared to a waitlist control group, shy preschoolers who received the eight-week intervention demonstrated a significantly greater decrease in observed reticent behavior at preschool. This study provides a good example of how findings from nonsocial play research (i.e., reticent behavior as a marker for social fear and wariness) can be directly applied to intervention studies (i.e., assessing changes in reticent behavior to help evaluate the effectiveness of an intervention program designed to assist extremely shy children).

We must continue to develop our theoretical and empirical understanding of the meaning and implications of different forms of nonsocial play forms across different age periods, social contexts, and cultures. However, as a final note, it behooves nonsocial play researchers to participate in, and assist with the process of 'knowledge translation.' We are only just beginning to understand how the study of nonsocial play might have important and direct applications for parents, childcare workers, teachers, school board officials, clinicians, and government agencies, and how these applications might ultimately serve to benefit children and youth.

References

Andrus, R. (1924). *A tentative inventory of the habits of children from two to four years of age.* Columbia University, Teachers College, Contributions to Education, No. 160.

Asendorpf, J. B. (1990). Beyond social withdrawal: Shyness, unsociability and peer avoidance. *Human Development, 33,* 250–259.

Asendorpf, J.B., Denissen, J.J.A., & van Aken, M.A.G. (2008). Inhibited and aggressive preschool children at 23 years of age: Personality and social transitions into adulthood. *Developmental Psychology, 44,* 997–1011.

Bakeman, R. & Brownlee, J. R. (1980). The strategic use of parallel play: A sequential analysis. *Child Development,* 51, 873–878.

Balaban, C. D. (2002). Neural substrates linking balance control and anxiety. *Physiology and Behavior, 77,* 469–475.

Balaban, C. D. & Thayer, J. F. (2001). Neurological bases for balance–anxiety links. *Journal of Anxiety Disorders, 15,* 53–79.

Baldwin, J.N., & Stecher, L. (1925). *The psychology of the preschool child.* New York: Appleton.

Bar-Haim, Y. & Bart, O. (2006). Motor function and social participation in kindergarten children. *Social Development, 15,* 296–310.

Barnes, K. (1971). Preschool play norms. *Developmental Psychology,* 5(1), 99–108.

Bates, A.P. (1964). Privacy-A useful concept? *Social Forces, 42,* 429–434.

Biederman, J., Rosenbaum, J. F., Bolduc-Murphy, E. A., Faraone, S. V., Chaloff, J., Hirshfeld, D. R., et al. (1993). A 3-year follow-up of children with and without behavioral inhibition. *Journal of the American Academy of Child and Adolescent Psychiatry, 32,* 814–821.

Biederman, J., Rosenbaum, J. F., Hirshfeld, D. R., Faraone, S. V., Bolduc, E. A., Gersten, M., et al. (1990). Psychiatric correlates of behavioral inhibition in young children of parents with and without psychiatric disorders. *Archives of General Psychiatry, 47,* 21–26.

Blurton-Jones, N. G. (1972). Categories of child-child interaction. In N. G. Blurton-Jones (Ed.), *Ethological studies of child behavior.* Oxford, England: Cambridge University Press.

Bott, H. (1928). Observation of play activities of three- year-old children. *Genetic Psychology Monographs, Vol. 4,* 44–88.

Bredekamp, S., & Copple, C. (1997*). Developmentally appropriate practice in early childhood programs (Rev. ed.).* Washington, DC: National Association for the Education of Young Children.

Buhler, C. (1928). *Kindheit und jugend.* Leipzig: Hirzel Verlag.

Burke, N. (1991). College psychotherapy and the development of a capacity for solitude. *Journal of College Student Psychotherapy, 6,* 59–86.

Buss, A.H., & Plomin, R. (1984). *Temperament: Early developing personality traits.* Hillsdale, N.J.: Erlbaum.

Cheek, J.M., & Buss, A.H. (1981). Shyness and sociability. *Journal of Personality and Social Psychology, 41,* 330–339.

Chen, X. (2010). Shyness-inhibition in childhood and adolescence: A cross-cultural perspective. In K.H. Rubin & R.J. Coplan (Eds.), *The development of shyness and social withdrawal.* New York: Guilford.

Chen, X., Cen, G., Li, D., & He, Y. (2005). Social functioning and adjustment in Chinese children: The imprint of historical time. *Child Development, 76,* 182–195.

Chen, X., DeSouza, A., Chen, H., & Wang, L. (2006). Reticent behavior and experiences in peer interactions in Canadian and Chinese children. *Developmental Psychology, 42,* 656–665.

Chen, X., Hastings, P., Rubin, K.H., Chen, H., Cen, G., & Stewart, S.L. (1998). Childrearing attitudes and behavioral inhibition in Chinese and Canadian toddlers: A cross-cultural study. *Developmental Psychology, 34,* 677–686.

Chen, X., Rubin, K.H., Li, B., & Li. Z. (1999). Adolescent outcomes of social functioning in Chinese children. *International Journal of Behavioural Development, 23,* 199–223.

Cooley, C.H. (1902). *Human nature and the social order.* New York: Scribner.

Coplan, R. J. (2000). Assessing nonsocial play in early childhood: Conceptual and methodological approaches. In K. Gitlin-Weiner, A. Sandgrund, & C. Schaefer (Eds.), *Play diagnosis and assessment* 2nd *Edition* (pp. 563–598). New York: Wiley.

Coplan, R.J & Arbeau, K. (2008). Peer interactions and play in early childhood. In K.H. Rubin, W. Bukowski, & B. Laursen (Eds.), *Handbook of peer interactions, relationships, and groups* (pp. 143–161). New York: Guilford.

Coplan, R.J., Arbeau, K.A., & Armer, M. (2008). Don't fret, be supportive! Maternal characteristics linking child shyness to psychosocial and school adjustment in kindergarten. *Journal of Abnormal Child Psychology, 36,* 359–371.

Coplan, R.J. & Armer, M. (2007). A "multitude" of solitude: A closer look at social withdrawal and nonsocial play in early childhood. *Child Development Perspectives, 1,* 26–32.

Coplan, R.J., DeBow, A., Schneider, B.H., & Graham, A.A. (2009). The social behaviors of extremely inhibited children in and out of preschool. *British Journal of Developmental Psychology, 27,* 891–905.

Coplan, R.J., Findlay, L.C., & Nelson, L.J. (2004). Characteristics of preschoolers with lower perceived competence. *Journal of Abnormal Child Psychology, 32,* 399–408.

Coplan, R.J., Gavinski-Molina, M.H., Lagacé-Séguin, D., & Wichmann, C. (2001a). When girls versus boys play alone: Gender differences in the associates of nonsocial play in kindergarten. *Developmental Psychology, 37,* 464–474.

Coplan, R.J., Girardi, A., Findlay, L.C., & Frohlick, S.L. (2007). Understanding solitude: Young children's attitudes and responses towards hypothetical socially-withdrawn peers. *Social Development, 16,* 390–409.

Coplan, R.J. & Prakash, K. (2003). Spending time with teacher: Characteristics of preschoolers who frequently elicit versus initiate interactions with teachers. *Early Childhood Research Quarterly, 18,* 143–158.

Coplan, R.J., Prakash, K., O'Neil, K., & Armer, M. (2004). Do you "want" to play? Distinguishing between conflicted shyness and social disinterest in early childhood. *Developmental Psychology, 40,* 244–258.

Coplan, R. J., & Rubin, K. H. (1998). Exploring and assessing non-social play in the preschool: The development and validation of the Preschool Play Behavior Scale. *Social Development, 7,* 72–91.

Coplan, R. J., Rubin, K. H., Fox, N. A., Calkins, S. D., & Stewart, S. (1994). Being alone, playing alone, and acting alone: Distinguishing among reticence and passive and active solitude in young children. *Child Development, 65,* 129–137.

Coplan, R.J., Schneider, B.H., Matheson, A., & Graham, A.A. (2010). "Play skills" for shy children: Development of a social skills-facilitated play early intervention program for extremely inhibited preschoolers. *Infant and Child Development, 19,* 223-237.

Coplan, R.J. & Weeks, M. (2010a). Unsociability in childhood. In K.H. Rubin & R.J. Coplan (Eds.), *The development of shyness and social withdrawal.* New York: Guilford.

Coplan, R.J. & Weeks, M. (2010b). Unsociability in middle childhood: Conceptualization, assessment, and associations with socio-emotional functioning. *Merrill-Palmer Quarterly, 56,* 105–130.

Coplan, R.J., Wichmann, C., & Lagacé-Séguin, D. (2001b). Solitary-active play: A marker variable for maladjustment in the preschool? *Journal of Research in Childhood Education, 15,* 164–172.

Csikszentmihalyi, M. (1996). Creativity: Flow and the psychology of discovery and invention. New York: Harper-Collins.

Dettling, A. C., Gunnar, M.R., & Donzella (1999). Cortisol levels of young children in full-day childcare centers: Relationships with age and temperament. *Psychoneuroendocrinology, 24,* 519–536.

Doctoroff, G.L. Greer, J.A., & Arnold, D.H. (2006). The relationship between social behavior and emergent literacy among preschool boys and girls. *Applied Developmental Psychology, 27,* 1–13.

Dodge, K. A., Schlundt, D. C., Schocken, I.,&Delugach, J. D. (1983). Social competence and children's sociometric status: The role of peer group entry strategies. *Merrill-Palmer Quarterly, 29,* 309–336.

Dunn, L. & Herwig, J. (1992). Play behaviors and convergent and divergent thinking skills of young children attending full-day preschool. *Child Study Journal, 22,* 23–38.

Elias, C. L. & Berk, L. E. (2002). Self-regulation in young children: Is there a role for sociodramatic play. *Early Childhood Research Quarterly,* 17, 216–238.

Ervin-Tripp, S. (1991). Play in language development. In B. Scales, M. Almy, A. Nicolopoulou, & S. Ervin-Tripp (Eds.), *Play and the Social Context of Development in Early Care and Education* (pp. 84–97). New York: Teachers College Press.

Fantuzzo, J., Coolahan, K., Mendez, J., McDermott, P., & Sutton-Smith, B. (1998). Contextually-relevant validation of peer play constructs with African American Head Start children: Penn Interactive Peer Play Scale. *Early Childhood Research Quarterly, 13,* 411–431.

Farver, J.M., Kim, Y.K., & Lee, Y. (1995). Cultural differences in Korean- and Anglo-American preschoolers' social interaction and play behaviors. *Child Development, 66,* 1088–1099.

Fein, G.G (1989). Mind, meaning, and affect: Proposals for a theory of pretense. *Developmental Review, 9,* 345–363.

Fox, N.A., Rubin, K.H., Calkins, S.D., Marshall, T.R., Coplan, R.J., Porges, S.W., & Long, J. (1995). Frontal activation asymmetry and social competence at four years of age: Left frontal hyper and hypo activation as correlates of social behavior in preschool children. *Child Development, 66,* 1770–1784.

France, P. (1997). *Hermits: The insights of solitude.* New York: St. Martin's.

Garcia-Coll, C., Kagan, J., & Reznick, J.S. (1984). Behavioral inhibition in young children. *Child Development, 55,* 1005–1019.

Goncu, A. (1989). Models and features of pretense. *Developmental Review, 9,* 341–344.

Greco, L. A., & Morris, T. L. (2001). Treating childhood shyness and related behavior: Empirically evaluated approaches to promote positive social interactions. *Clinical Child and Family Psychology Review, 4,* 299–318.

Gulranick, M. J., Hammond, M. A., & Connor, R. T. (2003). Subtypes of nonsocial play: comparisons between young children with and without developmental delays. *American Journal on Mental Retardation, 108,* 347–362.

Hammitt, W.E. (1982). Cognitive dimensions of wilderness solitude. *Environment and Behavior*, 14, 478–493.

Harrist, A. W., Zaia, A. F., Bates, J. E., Dodge, K. A., & Pettit, G. S. (1997). Subtypes of social withdrawal in early childhood: Sociometric status and social-cognitive differences across four years. *Child Development*, 68, 278–294.

Hart, C. H. (1993). Children on playgrounds: Research perspectives and applications. SUNY *series, children's play in society*. Albany, NY: State University of New York Press.

Hart, C. H., Yang, C., Nelson, L. J., et al. (2000). Peer acceptance in early childhood and subtypes of socially withdrawn behavior in China, Russia, and the United States. *International Journal of Behavioural Development*, 24, 73–81.

Hastings, P.D., Sullivan, C., McShane, K. E., Coplan, R.J., Utendale, W.T., & Vyncke, J.D. (2008). Parental socialization, vagal regulation and preschoolers' anxious difficulties: Direct mothers and moderated fathers. *Child Development*, 79, 45–64.

Hay, D.F., Caplan, M., & Nash, A. (2006). The beginnings of peer interaction. In K.H. Rubin, W. Bukowski, & B. Laursen (Eds.), *Handbook of peer interactions, relationships, and groups*. New York: Guilford.

Hay, D., & Morisey, A. (1978). Reports of ecstatic, paranormal, or religious experience in Great Britain and the United States – A comparison of trends. *Journal for the Scientific Study of Religion*, 17, 255–268.

Henderson, H., Marshall, P., Fox, N.A., & Rubin, K.H. (2004). Converging psychophysiological and behavioral evidence for subtypes of social withdrawal in preschoolers. *Child Development*, 75, 251–263.

Henninger, M. (1994). Adult perceptions of favorite childhood play experiences. *Early Child Development and Care*, 99, 23–30.

Hirshfeld, D. R., Rosenbaum, J. F., Biederman, J., Bolduc, E. A., Faraone, S. V., Snidman, N., et al. (1992). Stable behavioral inhibition and its association with anxiety disorder. *Journal of the American Academy of Child and Adolescent Psychiatry*, 31, 103–111.

Hogan, L.E. (1898). *A study of a child*. New York: Harper.

Howes, C. (1992). *The collaborative construction of pretend*. New York: State University of New York Press.

Hutt, C. (1970). Specific and diverse exploration. In H. Reese & L. Lipsitt (Eds.), *Advances in Child Development and Behavior* (pp. 119–181). New York: Academic Press.

Johnson, J. (1976). Relations of divergent thinking and intelligence test scores with social and nonsocial make-believe play of preschool children. *Child Development*, 47, 1200–1203.

Kagan, J., Reznick, J.S., Clarke, C., Snidman, N., & Garcia Coll, C. (1984). Behavioral inhibition to the unfamiliar. *Child Development*, 55, 2212–2225.

Kagan, J., Snidman, N., Kahn, V., & Towsley, S. (2007). The preservation of two infant temperaments into adolescence. *Monographs of the Society for Research in Child Development, Serial No. 287*, 72.

Katz, Jill C. & Buchholz, Ester S. (1999). "I did it myself": The necessity of solo play for preschoolers. *Early Child Development and Care*, 155, 39–50.

Kohlberg, L., LaCrosse, J., & Ricks, D. (1972). The predictability of adult mental health from childhood behavior. In B.B. Wolman (Ed.), *Manual of child psychopathology* (pp. 1217–1284). New York: McGraw-Hill.

Ladd, G. W., & Profilet, S. M. (1996). The Child Behavior Scale: A teacher-report measure of young children's aggressive, withdrawn, and prosocial behaviors. *Developmental Psychology*, 32, 1008–1024.

Larson, R.W. (1990). The solitary side of life: An examination of the time people spend alone from childhood to old age. *Developmental Review*, 10, 155–183.

Larson, R. (1997). The emergence of solitude as a constructive domain of experience in early adolescence. *Child Development*, 68, 80–93.

Lehman, H.C. (1926). The play activities of persons of different ages, and growth stages in play behavior. *Pedagogical Seminary*, 33, 250–272.

Lehman, H.C., & Anderson, T.H. (1928). Social participation vs. solitariness in play. *Pedagogical Seminary*, 34, 279–289.

Levy-Shiff, R. & Hoffman, M.A. (1989). Social behavior as a predictor of adjustment among three-year-olds. *Journal of Clinical Child Psychology*, 18, 65–71.

Lloyd, B., & Howe, N. (2003). Solitary play and convergent and divergent thinking skills in preschool children. *Early Childhood Research Quarterly*, 18, 22–41.

Long, C.R., & Averill, J.R. (2003). Solitude: An exploration of benefits of being alone. *Journal for the Theory of Social Behavior*, 33, 21–44.

Martlew, M., Connolly, K. and McLeod, C. (1976). Language use, role and context in a five-year-old. *Journal of Child Language*, 5, 81–99.

Maslow, A.H. (1970). *Motivation and personality* (2nd ed.). New York: Harper & Row.

Marcoen, A., Goossens, L., & Caes, P. (1987). Loneliness in pre- through late adolescence: Exploring the contributions of a multidimentional approach. *Journal of Youth and Adolescence, 16(6)*, 561–577.

Mead, G.H. (1934). *Mind, self, and society*. Chicago: University of Chicago Press.

Moore, N., Evertson, C. and Brophy, J. (1974). Solitary play: Some functional reconsiderations. *Developmental Psychology*, 10, 830–834.

Morris, D.P., Soroker, E., & Buruss, G. (1954). Follow-up studies of shy, withdrawn children – I. Evaluation of later adjustment. *American Journal of Orthopsychiatry*, 24, 743–754.

Nelson, L. J., Hart, C. H., & Evans, C. A. (2008). Solitary-functional play and solitary-pretend play: Another look at the construct of solitary-active behavior using playground observations. *Social Development*, 17, 812–831.

Nelson, L.J., Hart, C.H., Evans, C.A., Coplan, R.J., Olson Roper, S., Robinson, C.C. (2009). Behavioral and relational correlates of low self-perceived competence in young children. *Early Childhood Research Quarterly*, 24, 350–361.

Nelson, L. J., Rubin, K. H., & Fox, N. A. (2005). Social withdrawal, observed peer acceptance, and the development of self-perceptions in children ages 4 to 7 years. *Early Childhood Research Quarterly*, 20, 185–200.

Ness, D. & Farenga, S.J. (2007). Knowledge under construction: The importance of play in developing children's spatial and geometric thinking. Rowman & Littlefield.

Paquette, D., & LaFrenière, P. J. (1994). Are anxious-withdrawn children inhibited in a new social context? *Canadian Journal of Behavioral Science*, 26, 534–550.

Parten, M.B. (1932). Social participation among preschool children. *Journal of Abnormal Psychology*, 27, 243–269.

Pedersen, D.M. (1979). Dimensions of privacy. *Perceptual and Motor Skills*, 48, 1291–1297.

Perez-Edgar, K., Schmidt, L.A., Henderson, H. A., Schulkin, J., & Fox, N.A. (2008). Salivary cortisol levels and infant temperament shape developmental trajectories in boys at risk for behavioral maladjustment. *Psychoneuroendocrinology, 33,* 916–925.

Phillips, R. and Sellitto, V. (1990). Preliminary evidence on emotions expressed by children during solitary play. *Play and Culture,* 3, 79–90.

Piaget, J. (1926). *The language and thought of the child.* London: Routledge & Kegan Paul.

Piaget, J. (1932). *The moral judgment of the child.* Glencoe: Free Press.

Piaget, J. (1962). Play, dreams, and imitation in childhood. New York: Norton.

Purcell, R.Z., & Keller, M.J. (1989). Characteristics of leisure activities which may lead to leisure satisfaction among older adults. *Activities, Adaptation and Aging, 13(4),* 17–29.

Robins, L.N. (1966). *Deviant children grown up.* Baltimore: Williams & Wilkins.

Rosenbaum, J. F., Biederman, J., Gersten, M., Hirshfeld, D. R., Meminger, S. R., Herman, J. B., et al. (1988). Behavioral inhibition in children of parents with panic disorder and agoraphobia. A controlled study. *Archives of General Psychiatry, 45,* 463–470.

Robinson, C. C., Anderson, G. T., Porter, C. L., Hart, C. H. & Wouden-Miller, M. (2003). Sequential transition patterns of preschoolers' social interactions during child-initiated play: Is parallel-aware play a bidirectional bridge to other play states. *Early Childhood Research Quarterly,* 18, 3–21.

Rosenbaum, J. F., Biederman, J., Hirshfeld, D. R., Bolduc, E. A., & Chaloff, J. (1991). Behavioral inhibition in children: A possible precursor to panic disorder or social phobia. *Journal of Clinical Psychiatry, 52,* 5–9.

Rubin, K.H. (1977). The social and cognitive value of preschool toys and activities. *Canadian Journal of Behavioural Sciences, 9,* 382–385.

Rubin, K.H. (1982). Non-social play in preschoolers: Necessary evil? *Child Development, 53,* 651–657.

Rubin, K.H. (1985). Socially withdrawn children: An "at risk" population? In B. Schneider, K.H. Rubin, & J. Ledingham (Eds). *Children's peer relations: Issues in assessment and intervention.* (pp. 125–139), New York: Springer-Verlag.

Rubin, K. H. (2001). *The Play Observation Scale (POS).* University of Waterloo.

Rubin, K. H., & Asendorpf, J. B. (1993). Social withdrawal, inhibition, and shyness in childhood: Conceptual and definitional issues. In J. B. Asendorpf & K. H. Rubin (Eds.), *Social withdrawal, inhibition, and shyness in childhood* (pp. 3–17). Hillsdale, NJ: Lawrence Erlbaum Associates.

Rubin, K.H., & Both, L. (1989). Iris pigmentation and sociability in childhood: A re-examination. *Developmental Psychology, 22,* 717–726.

Rubin, K. H., Bukowski, W. M., & Parker, J. G. (2006). Peer interactions, relationships and groups. In N. Eisenberg (Vol. Ed.), *The handbook of child psychology* (6th ed., pp. 571–645). New York: Wiley.

Rubin, K. H., Burgess, K. B., & Hastings, P. D. (2002). Stability and social-behavioral consequences of toddlers' inhibited temperament and parenting behaviors. *Child Development, 73,* 483–495.

Rubin, K.H., Chen, X., & Hymel, S. (1993). Socioemotional characteristics of withdrawn and aggressive children. *Merrill-Palmer Quarterly, 39,* 518–534.

Rubin, K.H., Coplan, R.J., & Bowker, J. (2009). Social withdrawal in childhood. *Annual Review of Psychology, 60,* 11.1–11.31.

Rubin, K.H., Coplan, R.J., Fox, N.A., & Calkins, S.D. (1995). Emotionality, emotion regulation, and preschoolers' social adaptation. *Development and Psychopathology, 7,* 49–62.

Rubin, K., Fein, G. G., & Vandenberg, B. (1983). Play. In P. Mussen (Series Ed.) & E. M. Hetherington (Vol. Ed.), *Handbook of child psychology* (Vol. 4, 4th ed., pp. 693–774). New York: Wiley.

Rubin, K.H. & Hayvren, M. (1981). The social and cognitive play of children differing with regard to sociometric status. *Journal of Research and Development in Education, 14,* 116–122.

Rubin, K.H., Hymel, S., & Mills, R. S. L. (1989). Sociability and social withdrawal in childhood: Stability and outcomes. *Journal of Personality, 57,* 238–255.

Rubin, K.H. & Krasnor, L.R. (1980). Changes in the play behaviors of preschoolers: A short-term longitudinal investigation. *Canadian Journal of Behavioural Science, 12,* 278–282.

Rubin, K.H., LeMare, L. & Lollis, S. (1990). Social withdrawal in childhood: Developmental pathways to peer rejection. In S. Asher & J. Coie (Eds.), *Peer rejection in childhood.* New York: Cambridge University Press (pp. 217–249).

Rubin, K. H., Maioni, T. L., & Hornung, M. (1976). Free play behaviors in middle- and lower-class preschoolers: Parten and Piaget revisited. *Child Development, 47,* 414–419.

Rubin K.H., & Mills, R.S.L. (1988). The many faces of social isolation in childhood. *Journal of Consulting and Clinical Psychology, 56,* 916–924.

Rubin, K. H., Watson, K., & Jambor, T. (1978). Free play behaviors in preschool and kindergarten children. *Child Development, 49,* 534–536.

Saltz, E., Dixon, D. & Johnson, J. (1977). Training disadvantaged preschoolers on various fantasy activities: Effects on cognitive functioning and impulse control. *Child Development,* 48, 367–380.

Schmidt, L. A., Fox, N. A., Rubin, K. H., & Sternberg, E. M. (1997). Behavioral and neuroendocrine responses in shy children. *Developmental Psychobiology, 30,* 127–140.

Shinn, M.W. (1893). *Note of the development of a child.* University of California studies: Berkeley, California.

Simpson, A. E., & Stevenson-Hinde, J. (1985). Temperamental characteristics of three- to four-year-old boys and girls and child-family interactions. *Journal of Child Psychology and Psychiatry, 26,* 43–53.

Sklare, D. A., Konrad, H. R., Maser, J. D. & Jacob, R. G. (2001). Special issue on the interface of balance disorders and anxiety: An introduction and overview. *Journal of Anxiety Disorders, 15,* 1–7.

Smilansky, S. (1968). The effects of sociodramatic play on disadvantaged preschool children. New York: Wiley.

Smith, P. (1978). A longitudinal study of social participation in preschool children: Solitary and parallel play reexamined. *Developmental Psychology,* 14(5), 517–523.

Spangler, T., & Gazelle, H. (2009). Anxious solitude, unsociability, and peer exclusion in middle childhood: A multitrait-multimethod matrix. *Social Development, 18,* 833–856.

Spenser, H. (1873). Principles of psychology. Vol. 2, 2nd ed. New York: Appleton.

Spinrad, T.L., Eisenberg, N., Harris, E., et al. (2004). The relation of children's everyday nonsocial peer play behavior to their emotionality, regulation, and social functioning. *Developmental Psychology, 40,* 67–80.

Stern, L.W. (1924). *The psychology of early childhood.* New York: Henry Holt.

Storr, A. (1988). *Solitude: A return to the self*. New York: Free Press.

Sullivan, H.S. (1953). *The interpersonal theory of psychiatry*. New York: Norton.

Tracy, F. (1910). *The psychology of childhood*. Boston: D.C. Heath & Co.

Verry, E.E. (1923). A study of mental and social attitudes in the free play of preschool children. Thesis for M.A. degree, State University of Iowa.

Vygotsky, L.S. (1967). Play and its role in the mental development of the child. *Soviet Psychology, 12,* 62–76.

Younger, A.J., & Piccinin, A.M. (1989). Children's recall of aggressive and withdrawn behaviors: Recognition memory and likability judgments. *Child Development, 60,* 580–590.

Internalizing and Externalizing Disorders during Childhood: Implications for Social Play

David Schwartz *and* Daryaneh Badaly

Abstract

This chapter will examine the potential impact of internalizing and externalizing disorders on children's social play. We will contend that the available findings provide preliminary evidence that childhood disorders can have pernicious implications for social play. We will then move on to generate hypotheses regarding the mediating role of disruptions in areas of core competency, including emotion regulation and social cognition. In addition, we will highlight concerns related to the peer relationships that serve as a critical context for social play. Our overall objective will be to identify possible intervening mechanisms as a heuristic for future inquiry.

Keywords: Social play, internalizing disorders, externalizing disorders, emotion regulation, social cognition.

A theme that should be apparent throughout this volume is the centrality of play in children's lives. Play is sometimes viewed as a frivolous diversion by adult caregivers (Sutton-Smith, 1997) but it offers an important context for children to enhance their emerging social skills (Coplan & Arbeau, 2009). Social forms of play, in particular, can serve an organizing function for peer relationships in school peer groups (Howes & Matheson, 1992) and might help foster the development of age-appropriate friendships (Howes, Droege, & Matheson, 1994). These activities can contribute to physical maturation (Pellegrini & Smith, 1998), socialization (Rubin, Fein, & Vandenberg, 1983), and cognitive development (Pellegrini & Bjorklund, 1997).

Theoretical perspectives that emphasize the potential benefits of social play might also suggest a need to carefully examine any factors that interfere with children's involvement in these peer group activities. Insofar as participation in social play is linked to positive developmental outcomes, children who are experiencing disruptions in this aspect of functioning with peers may warrant empirical and clinical attention. We also contend that play is one of the defining behavioral features of childhood so that difficulties in this domain might effectively identify children who are on problematic trajectories. In this chapter, we will be particularly concerned with children who are characterized by internalizing and externalizing disorders. Our objective will be to consider the potential negative implications of these dimensions of psychosocial maladjustment for involvement in social play.

We are highlighting the concept of "social play" given our interest in play activities that involve two or more children. We will only rarely refer to more solitary behaviors and will do so primarily as a contrast. Moreover, our chapter will be oriented specifically toward social play rather than cooperative interactions between peers in general. Arguably, the term "play" has not always been used with precision by past investigators and has sometimes been viewed broadly as a form of prosocial interaction between peers. Our focus will be on the particular behaviors that are the subject of this volume and have been elaborated in past reviews by play researchers (e.g., Pellegrini & Smith, 1998; Rubin et al., 1983)

Goals of this chapter and current state of the literature

Before we proceed with our discussion, we will pause to acknowledge that the relevant empirical literature is currently limited in scope. Research on psychological and behavioral disorders during childhood has sometimes emphasized larger aspects of social maladjustment with peers such as friendlessness (Schwartz, Gorman, Duong, & Nakamoto, 2008), peer rejection (Bierman, 2004), and victimization (Hawker & Boulton, 2000). However, the specific phenomenon of social play has only rarely been addressed in this work. Accordingly, our discussion will necessarily be somewhat speculative.

Given the current state of the literature, we will also not be in a position to focus extensively on subclasses of dysfunction. Instead, we will consider broader dimensions of internalizing and externalizing disorders with preliminary conclusions that summarize across wide literatures. Our conceptualization of "externalizing disorders" will include problems related to undercontrolled, impulsive, or aggressive behavior. Included in this category are conduct disorder, oppositional defiant disorder, and attention deficit hyperactivity disorder (ADHD). Conversely, we use the term "internalizing" to delineate aspects of dysfunction that reflect disorders rooted in distress-related emotions (e.g., depression and anxiety). Although we do not wish to dismiss potentially meaningful differences within these clusters, our goal will be to develop a preliminary theory that is inclusive in nature.

We will begin by examining the small number of relevant studies that have been conducted. As we will discuss, the existing literature is not yet sufficient to support strong conclusions, but some coherent themes have begun to emerge. We will then move on to focus on basic skills and core capacities that may be influenced by childhood disorders. Like other researchers (Smith, 2009), we conceptualize social play as complex behavior that requires competencies in specific areas of functioning. In particular, we will argue that adaptive participation in play requires age-appropriate capacities for emotion regulation and social information-processing. We will also posit that internalizing and externalizing disorders can be associated with significant deficits in these domains and can, accordingly, have a detrimental impact on play behavior. We will then

conclude by examining the idea that childhood disorders result in reduced opportunities for play.

Existing Research

Informed by developmental psychopathology perspectives (e.g., Cicchetti, 2006), a number of investigators have considered the implications of childhood psychopathology and behavioral disorders for social functioning in the peer group. The central assumption underlying much of this research is that normative adjustment with peers is a salient developmental task of childhood so that disruptions in this domain are likely to be indicative of other underlying problems (Deater-Deckard, 2001; Parker & Asher, 1987). Within this larger literature, a relatively small number of researchers have observed children's play behavior. For the most part, play is not the primary focus in these studies but is viewed as a barometer of global adjustment with peers. That is, researchers observe behavior in play interactions as a means of assessing more generalized social adjustment.

Externalizing disorders and social play

In regard to externalizing disorders, the available findings suggest that the play behaviors of children who are characterized by aggression, ADHD, or other disruptive behaviors tend to be somewhat immature in nature and characterized primarily by nonsocial activities. For example, Alessandri (1992) examined the peer relationships of four- to five-year-old children who had ADHD. Compared to their classmates, these children engaged in less constructive and dramatic play. Overall, children with ADHD spent less time involved in social play. Consistent findings were reported by Howes and Matheson (1992; See also Howes, this volume), who investigated friendships and play in preschool peer groups. Howes and Matheson found that aggressive behavior was associated with low rates of complementary and reciprocal play, and high rates of parallel play. Likewise, in a study conducted with elementary school children in German-speaking cantons of Switzerland, Malti (2006) reported that aggression (assessed with a behavior problem checklist) was negatively associated with social competence in cooperative play tasks.

There have also been a number of studies that examine play distribution within dyads that include a child who has an externalizing disorder. These dyads are generally characterized by low rates of cooperative social play. In one relevant investigation, Hubbard and Newcomb (1991) paired unacquainted elementary school boys. For dyads that included a boy with ADHD, the primary play activities were solitary play and solitary behavior. Moreover, when rough-and-tumble bouts did occur, the result was often withdrawal by one of the dyad members. Clark, Cheyne, Cunningham, and Siegal (1988) observed pairs of boys engaging in a cooperative play task. Dyads that included a boy with ADHD engaged in low rates of both joint toy activity and verbal reciprocity.

Interestingly, there is some evidence that particular forms of solitary play are likely to identify youths with externalizing problems. Coplan and colleagues (Coplan, Gavinski-Molina, Lagacé-Séguin, & Wichmann, 2001; Coplan & Rubin, 1998; Coplan, Rubin, Fox, & Calkins, 1994; See also Coplan, this volume) have emphasized links between impulsive dispositions and "solitary-active" play. Solitary-active play features high-energy aimless behavior. A young boy who endlessly roams around a playground banging two toys together instead of engaging in thematic activities might epitomize this type of play. A number of investigators have suggested that solitary-active play is characteristic of children whose disruptive tendencies result in exclusion from social play (Asendorph, 1993; Bowker, Bukowski, & Zargarpour, 1998). The developmental sequence implied by these researchers has impulsive or aggressive behavior leading to rejection by peers and a subsequent emphasis on solitary-active play.

The emerging pattern across these different studies suggests that children with externalizing disorders may have problems with social play primarily as a reflection of their deficits in behavioral and emotional self-regulation. (We will have more to say about this important point in the subsequent sections of this chapter.) Not surprisingly, children with ADHD are more active and inattentive during play than their peers (Campbell, Breaux, Ewing, & Szumowski, 1986). Other researchers have found associations between aggression and poorly organized behavior during play between peers (e.g., Rubin, Coplan, Fox, & Calkins, 1995). Moreover, these findings seem to carry over to play with adult caregivers. Field, Sandberg, Goldstein, and Garcia (1987) observed play interactions between conduct disordered children and their parents. The children were characterized by high rates of unfocused motor activity but tended to avoid engaging in interactive play.

Internalizing disorders and social play

As we shift to the literature on internalizing, the findings that are most apparent relate to avoidance.

Descriptive research on the play interactions of depressed or anxious children indicates that these children tend to orient toward solitary activities including parallel and solitary focused play (Altmann & Gotlib, 1998; Rubin et al., 1995). Adding to the picture is an extensive body of findings linking internalizing disorders to shy or reticent behavior (Coplan et al., 2001; Rubin & Mills, 1988). In fact, investigators have often conceptualized solitary or isolated play as an important indicator of underlying states of depression and anxiety (Cheah, Nelson, & Rubin, 2001; Coplan & Rubin, 1998). To some extent, the timid nature of these children might motivate wariness toward social interactions with peers (Coplan, Rubin, Fox, Calkins, & Stewart, 1994) and subsequent avoidance of social play.

A related issue is that depressed and anxious children can bring a level of negative affectivity to play situations that many peers seem to find aversive (Rudolph, Hamman, & Burger, 1994). These children seem to be unable to inhibit their underlying mood states and, as a result, have difficulties interacting in the context of play (Coplan et al., 2001). For this reason, cooperative play with depressed children may not be very enjoyable for their peers. Consistent with this hypothesis, observational researchers have found that children display relatively high levels of negative emotion and low levels of positive emotion during play with depressed partners (Rockhill, Fan, Katon, McCauley, Crick, & Pleck, 2007).

Internalizing disorders also tend to be associated with play styles that are underdeveloped and characterized by low rates of cognitively sophisticated forms of play. Supporting this conclusion is evidence that depressed children engage in fantasy play (Field et al., 1997) and symbolic play (Lous, de Wit, De Bruyn, & Riksen-Walraven, 2002) less frequently than other children. In addition, high levels of generalized anxiety or separation anxiety can interfere with social play that involves toys and other objects (McIntyre, Lounsbury, Hamilton, & Mantooth, 1980).

Summing up

Taken together, the available studies provide only limited insight into the implications of behavioral and psychological disorders for play but there are some similar results across investigations. More specifically, the available data are indicative of low rates of involvement in social play. Internalizing and externalizing disorders seem to be linked to withdrawal from normative play interaction as well as frequent rebuff by potential play partners (Rubin & Mills, 1988). A second major set of findings relates to affective tone. Displays of dysregulated negative emotional states are a constant background feature for these children. Finally, there is a tendency for children with internalizing and externalizing disorders to eschew complex play behaviors (e.g., fantasy play) and to emphasize less sophisticated forms of play.

Building on these very preliminary findings, our goal in the remainder of this chapter will be to highlight mechanisms that might potentially link internalizing and externalizing to difficulties in the context of play. The limited empirical data that are available suggest that behavioral and psychological disorders have pernicious implications for children's involvement in social play but the underlying processes remain to be identified. We also suggest that a focus on intervening mechanisms could provide a useful heuristic for further investigation.

Hypothesized Underlying Mechanisms
Emotion regulation

As we move toward theoretical models that summarize the potential influence of childhood disorders on social play, we believe that emotion regulation will be an essential domain to consider. The term "emotion regulation" refers to behaviors and psychological attributes that allow children to modulate, and cope with, powerful affective states (Eisenberg & Spinrad, 2004). For example, a child might mitigate the intensity of unpleasant emotional states through soothing self-talk, reframing of upsetting events, attention shifts, or instrumental behavioral strategies (i.e., behaviors that alter emotion-provoking situations). Efficient use of these strategies is necessary for normative social functioning (Schwartz & Proctor, 2000) and is reflected in a child's ability to behave adaptively and strategically during arousing peer group interactions (Shields, Cicchetti, & Ryan, 1994). Research has consistently shown that deficits in emotion regulation are predictive of ostracism, rejection, and other social difficulties with peers (Eisenberg, Fabes, Murphy, Maszk, Smith, & Karbon, 1995; Pope & Bierman, 1999; Shields & Cicchetti, 1998).

Emotion regulation is likely to have critical implications for children's interactions in the context of social play. Negative emotions, such as sadness, anger, and frustration, could exert a disorganizing influence on play (Spinrad et al., 2004) and must be effectively "down regulated" in evocative situations. As an illustration, consider the case of a group of boys who are happily engaging in rough-and-tumble play (Pellegrini, 1987). The boys are excitedly running around in a small area of the school playground taking turns in mock fighting bouts. For this very pleasant activity to continue, each of the boys must modulate their emotional arousal. If the boys become too excited, or fail to inhibit intense negative emotions (e.g., anger or hostility), the prosocial nature of the play interaction will not be maintained.

A child's participation in social play would also benefit from "up regulation" of positive emotional states such as interest/excitement and happiness. Affective states of this nature are likely to have an energizing effect on play. These emotions could also motivate continued engagement in peer interactions and help determine a child's desirability as a potential play partner (Sroufe, Schork, Motti, Lawroski, & LaFreniere, 1988). We suspect that peers will be especially likely to seek out play partners who are fun compatriots because they bring a happy demeanor to social interactions.

For the purposes of this chapter, the hypothesized role of emotion regulation warrants consideration because impairment in these capacities is a central feature of psychological maladjustment during childhood. For example, externalizing disorders have often been viewed as manifestations of problems modulating negative affect. The literature on highly aggressive children, in particular, has emphasized the role of dysregulated anger. Prominent typologies posit the existence of subtypes of aggressive behaviors that are hot-blooded in nature and driven by poorly controlled states of anger and frustration (Card & Little, 2006). Most notably, Dodge and Coie (1987) described distinctions between reactive forms of aggression and more goal-oriented proactive subtypes. Individual differences in reactive aggression can reflect a tendency to respond angrily to benign overtures from peers (Dodge, Lochman, Harnish, Bates, & Pettit, 1997; Hubbard, Dodge, Cillessen, Coie, & Schwartz, 2001; Shields & Cicchetti, 1998). Interestingly, these retaliatory subtypes of aggressive behavior are closely associated with social difficulties in the peer group such as rebuff and mistreatment by peers (Schwartz et al., 1998; Schwartz, 2000).

The wider literature on conduct disorder and oppositional defiant disorder has also incorporated a focus on irritability and hot-tempered anger (Dodge et al., 1997). Emotional reactivity may underlie the defiant or aggressive behavior displayed by these youths (Hubbard et al., 2001). In addition, conduct disorder can be accompanied by other problems with dysregulated negative emotions, including sadness and anxiety. Comorbidity rates for conduct disorder and internalizing disorders are moderately high (e.g., Cole & Carpentieri, 1990; Ingoldsby, Kohl, McMahon, Lengua, & Conduct Problems Prevention Research Group, 2006; Kiesner, 2002).

Similarly, ADHD is an externalizing disorder that is often conceptualized as a fundamental deficit in behavioral and emotional self-regulation (Barkley, 2006). Children with ADHD have difficulty controlling impulses and inhibiting powerful emotional states (Martel, 2009). As a result, these children are easily frustrated and experience irritability, anger, and emotional reactivity (Melnick & Hinshaw, 2000).

With regard to internalizing disorders, investigators have keyed on the notion that distress may occur as a reflection of difficulties coping with sadness and anxiety. In one interesting study, Garber, Braflaadt, and Weiss (1995) investigated the mechanisms that depressed children and adolescents use to modulate negative affective states. Compared to their peers, depressed youths were less likely to utilize efficient tactics, such as distraction and problem-focused coping. Instead, these children and adolescents tended to rely on less competent approaches, including avoidant, passive, and aggressive strategies. Zeman, Shipman, and Suveg (2002) found correlations between children's self-reports of anxiety and depressive symptoms and difficulties controlling anger and sadness. More recently, Feng et al. (2009) conducted a short-term longitudinal study examining regulation of negative emotions as predictors of depressive symptoms for elementary school girls. These researchers found that deficits in the regulation of sadness were predictive of depressive symptoms one year later, although the effects held only for those girls who also reported low parental acceptance.

Internalized distress can also be conceptualized as a manifestation of difficulties with the "up regulation" of more positive emotions. This idea is implicit in existing theoretical models of the processes underlying depressive disorders. Clark and Watson's (1991) influential tripartite model posits that depression is marked by the absence of positive affect. Consistent with such models, a core feature of mood disorders is anhedonia, the inability to experience pleasure or positive affect (Hammen & Rudolph, 1996). From a more empirical perspective, Feng et al. (2009) reported predictive relations between difficulties modulating positive affect and depressive symptoms during middle childhood.

We are essentially hypothesizing a meditational model with childhood disorders predicting difficulties in social play through the mediation of impairments in emotion modulation. To the best of our knowledge, pathways of this nature have not been directly examined in any existing empirical investigations. Nonetheless, the available findings are consistent with the model we are proposing. Earlier, we discussed evidence that the play interactions of children with internalizing and externalizing disorders are likely to be characterized by displays of negative affect and can also be disorganized and immature. It seems reasonable to speculate that these difficulties may reflect poorly modulated states of intense emotions. In any case, we would contend that emotion regulation is a critical domain for future play researchers to consider.

Social cognition

Research on emotional self-regulation during childhood has often been guided by conceptualizations that posit integrated systems of emotion and social cognition (e.g., Lemerise & Arsenio, 2000). The theoretical roots of this work are in social information-processing models (Dodge, 1986; Dodge, Pettit, McClaskey, & Brown, 1986; Crick & Dodge, 1994). These models seek to delineate the cognitive processes underlying social behavior, often with a focus on the mechanisms underlying maladaptive response styles in social situations (Dodge & Schwartz, 1997). Information-processing perspectives have been very influential in research on peer relationships and social development in general. In our view, a social cognitive framework could also have utility in helping investigators to conceptualize play behavior and to explain any potential deficits displayed by children with internalizing or externalizing disorders.

Although it is beyond the scope of this chapter to offer a comprehensive review of the existing literature on social information-processing, several specific areas might merit attention for potential relevance to the phenomenon of social play. We will begin by considering cue encoding and interpretation. Social competence requires children to attend to the peer group context, encode sufficient information (i.e., transform sensory information into internally represented data; Dodge, Murphy, & Buchsbaum, 1984; Spivack & Shure, 1974; See also Lillard, this volume), and then make accurate interpretations of any ambiguous peer behaviors (Dodge & Frame, 1982; Waas, 1988). To demonstrate how these cognitive skills might influence play interactions, return again to our earlier example of boys engaged in mock fighting bouts on a school playground. The behaviors involved in these interactions are topographically similar to aggression and could mistakenly be seen as provocative by some children. For the boys to continue with their prosocial exchanges, they will need to attend to the social cues embedded into the situation, accurately assess the intentions of their peers, and recognize the benign intent of overtures that (on a surface level) might share features with more antisocial behaviors.

Children's capacities to generate, and evaluate, potential responses to peer overtures (Dodge & Price, 1994) will also be central to successful participation in play. To use the metaphor of a computer, in any given social situation, a child must search his or her database for appropriate behavioral strategies and then evaluate the implications of each identified option (Crick & Ladd, 1990; Perry, Perry, & Rasmussen, 1986). Through these information-processing mechanisms, socially competent children are able to generate behaviors that are optimized for specific contexts (Dodge et al., 1986). During play interactions, adaptive outcomes from response search and evaluation will likely be prosocial in nature and will be oriented toward maintaining the enjoyable aspects of the interaction. In contrast, children whose response search processes are biased toward aggression or other inappropriate behaviors will likely have marked difficulty in social play.

These response search processes can be influenced by the goals that guide children's social information-processing and peer group behavior. A number of theorists have described a feedback loop through which children evaluate social situations for consistency with their desired goals (Troop-Gordon & Asher, 2005). Disparities between perceived goals and real-world parameters will result in social cognitive activity designed to alter the situation or reframe the desired objective.

Consider two preschool girls, Hillary and Michelle, who are approaching a sandbox that contains a small number of toys. Hillary has object possession as her primary objective. She wants the toys for herself and is only peripherally concerned with her play partner. In contrast, Michelle is primarily interested in having a fun interaction. Her organizing goals are prosocial and oriented toward engaging a peer in pretend play. How will these different general objectives shape the social cognitive processes through which Hillary and Michelle identify appropriate behavioral strategies for their sandbox interaction? When disagreements occur over the limited resources, which of the two girls will generate solutions that are designed to facilitate social play and maintain the positive tone of the interaction?

This discussion has been brief and limited in scope but the potential importance of effective social information-processing for children's play behavior should be apparent. Thus, it seems worthwhile to consider associations between different dimensions of child maladjustment and social cognitive biases or deficits. The literature on externalizing disorders, in particular, has frequently emphasized the role of social information-processing mechanisms. In fact, there is an extensive body of findings on the social cognitive attributes of highly aggressive children (Dodge & Schwartz, 1997; Huesmann, 1998; Pakaslahti, 2000). With regard to cue encoding and interpretation, aggressive or disruptive children are less likely to internalize relevant information from any social situation (Dodge & Newman, 1981; Dodge et al., 1986). They also to tend to view benign situations as provocative, a propensity that has been labeled "hostile attributional bias" by past researchers (Dodge & Frame, 1982; Waas, 1988). At the stages of response generation and evaluation, these youths generate a high number of aggressive solutions (Asarnow & Callan, 1985). They evaluate the outcomes of aggressive or antisocial behavior positively, believe that such behaviors are efficacious, and are confident in their ability to use aggressive strategies (Crick & Ladd, 1990; Dodge et al., 1986; Perry et al., 1986). Finally, the goals guiding their information-processing and social behavior are generally antisocial in nature (Troop-Gordon & Asher, 2005). Aggressive youths tend to report objectives that are oriented toward dominance or control of others (Lochman, Wayland, & White, 1993), hostility (Slaby & Guerra, 1988), and revenge (Erdley & Asher, 1996).

A smaller number of studies have been conducted to examine social information-processing deficits in children with ADHD. Consistent with the impulsive disposition of these children, they seem to have difficulties with cue encoding and they generate relatively few solutions to problematic social situations (Milich & Dodge, 1984). In addition, there is some evidence that ADHD is linked to response selection biases that tend to favor aggressive strategies (King et al., 2009).

Prominent theoretical perspectives on depression and anxiety have also emphasized the role of maladaptive cognitive schemata or structures (Abramson, Alloy & Metalsky, 1988; Beck, 1963, 1972). Tests of the resulting cognitive models with children have generally been oriented toward more global information-processing deficits rather than the specific cognitive processes that underlie social behavior with peers (Cole & Turner, 1993). Obviously, it is these latter cognitive mechanisms that should be of greatest interest to play researchers. A notable exception is a study conducted by Quiggle, Garber, Panak, and Dodge (1992). These investigators examined the social cognitive tendencies of depressed and aggressive youth. Quiggle et al. found that depressed children are characterized by hostile attributional biases and they generate relatively few assertive solutions to problematic social situations. In a subsequent study, Bell-Dolan (1995) found similar attributional tendencies for children who reported high levels of anxiety. There is also some research that focuses on the social cognitive attributes of reticent or withdrawn children (Wichmann, Coplan, & Daniels, 2004).

Although research on peer relationships (and to a lesser extent psychopathology) during childhood has often highlighted social cognitive mechanisms, a similar emphasis has not always been present in the literature on social play. Nonetheless, current understanding of the factors underlying children's social difficulties with peers has clearly been informed by processing perspectives. We would expect that further investigation conducted from a social cognitive framework could help shed light on the implications of internalizing and externalizing disorders for play.

Social acceptance and friendships as affordances for social play

To this point, we have emphasized the role of core competencies and skills. We have hypothesized that internalizing and externalizing disorders are likely to be associated with significant impairments in emotion regulation and social cognition and that deficits in these domains will interfere with play behavior. These difficulties notwithstanding, a more fundamental issue may be that children who are experiencing psychopathology simply have fewer opportunities for play. As we will argue, internalizing and externalizing problems can lead children to experience social rejection and friendlessness. Social problems of this nature, in turn, will limit options for play.

Our presumption is that positive relationships with peers offer "affordances" for play. In particular, children who have many friends are likely to be sought after as play partners. Early observational studies of friendship support this suggestion, portraying

interactions between friends as a rich context for play (Gottman, 1993). Howes and colleagues (Howes, 1993; Howes et al., 1994; See also Howes, this volume) found that, during preschool, friends tend to play together longer and in more complex ways than do acquaintances. The cooperation and mutuality inherent in friendship might foster the reciprocal exchanges that are fundamental to social play (Hartup, 1996).

It is also important to consider the role of acceptance by the peer group as a whole. Peer relationship researchers have conceptualized friendship as an intimate, dyadic relationship between two peers whereas social acceptance is a construct that reflects liking by the peer group as a whole (Bukowski, Pizzamiglio, Newcomb, & Hoza, 1996). The two aspects of social adjustment are not truly independent because well-accepted youths are likely to be involved in numerous friendships (Gest, Graham-Bermann, & Hartup, 2001; Kupersmidt, DeRosier, & Patterson, 1995). Still, acceptance and friendship may tap different dimensions of social skills (Asher, Parker, & Walker, 1996; Bukowski & Hoza, 1989). We suspect that the dyadic competencies involved in friendships will be particularly relevant for play interactions (Howes et al., 1994). Nevertheless, we would also expect social acceptance to be predictive of opportunities for play.

As an illustration of the hypotheses we are offering, consider the case of two elementary school boys who are happily heading out of the classroom for lunch and recess. The first boy, Bill, has several close friends in the peer group, and is well liked by his classmates. As he walks out onto the playground, Bill's friends are quick to involve him in social play. At recess, and in the hours after school, Bill always has many options for play. The second boy, Al, is not as well accepted by his peers and has relatively few friends at school. He looks forward to his time on the playground but he tends to spend much of that time by himself, building a small fort in the sandbox. When Al does become involved in social play, he is often on the periphery of the interactions.

If we accept the premise that positive relationships with peers provide opportunities for play, the next issue to examine is the impact of externalizing and internalizing disorders on children's peer relationships. Are these dimensions of psychological and behavioral maladjustment associated with friendlessness and/or low acceptance? At least with regard to externalizing disorders, the links with social difficulties in the peer group appear to be quite strong (Coie, Dodge, & Kupersmidt, 1990). In early to middle childhood, aggression and other forms of disruptive behaviors are closely associated with peer rejection (Coie & Kupersmidt, 1983; Dodge, 1983). Children who are impulsive or highly aggressive tend to be disliked by their peers and are often among the most rejected children in the classroom (Bierman, 2004).

Despite their rebuff by the peer group as a whole, children with externalizing disorders are sometimes able to form dyadic affiliations with a small number of friends (Haselager, Hartup, van Lieshout, & Riksen-Walraven, 1998). Typically, these friend-ships involve other children with externalizing tendencies (Dishion & Dodge, 2005). This pattern is notable because friendships between aggressive youths tend to be characterized by low quality features (e.g., suspicion and mistrust; see Dishion, Andrews, & Crosby, 1995; Poulin, Dishion, & Haas, 1999). It is not yet clear how such relationship characteristics influence play behaviors but we would speculate that lower quality friendships are likely to foster less enjoyable play interactions.

The evidence regarding social difficulties associated with internalizing disorders is more equivocal. A number of researchers have reported that depressed youths tend to be disliked by their peers (Cole, 1991; Panak & Garber, 1992) and often have difficulty establishing and maintaining friendships (Rockhill et al., 2007; Schwartz et al., 2008). Nonetheless, in much of this research, depression has been viewed as the outcome rather than the predictor. That is, investigators have hypothesized that the stress associated with social rebuff and friendlessness leads to symptoms of depression. The alternative pathway, with depression predicting later social difficulties, has been less widely supported. In fact, longitudinal research has failed to reveal consistent evidence that depressive symptoms predict social outcomes with peers (Cole, Martin, & Powers, 1997; Nolan, Flynn, & Garber, 2003).

The available findings notwithstanding, interpersonal theories of depression have emphasized the negative implications of depressive symptoms for social relationships (Rudolph, Flynn, & Abaied, 2008). The central assumption is that depression interferes with social behavior and, hence, portends rebuff and avoidance by peers (Rudolph, Hammen, & Burge, 1994). Consistent with these perspectives, there is some evidence that depressed children tend to elicit negative responses from their peers (Connolly, Geller, Marton, & Kutcher, 1992). Of immediate relevance for the current chapter,

Rudolph et al. (1994) found that children tend not to enjoy play interactions with depressed peers.

Children with internalizing disorders may also have difficulties establishing friendships simply because they actively choose to avoid peers. For a subgroup of inhibited children, anxiety and other forms of internalized distress can motivate social withdrawal (Coplan et al., 1994; Harrist, Zaia, Bates, Dodge, & Pettit, 1997). This anxious reticence could have obvious negative implications for social relationships and involvement in play.

To some extent, the ideas that we are proposing here are not new. Research on inhibition and shyness during childhood has often emphasized the need to consider the reasons why different children experience social isolation (Harrist et al., 1997; Rubin & Mills, 1988; See also Coplan, this volume). For some youths, avoidance of social play and other peer group activities may be an active strategy. These children may be characterized by either a lack of interest in cooperative interactions with peers or by anxiety that motivates withdrawal from the peer group. Other children may display a solitary play style primarily because they are unable to find play partners.

Our hypotheses also resonate with themes that are present in the developmental psychopathology literature. Peer relationships researchers have long been concerned that children who experience rebuff and friendlessness may miss critical opportunities for socialization and the development of relationship skills (e.g., Parker & Asher, 1987). We speculate that reduced participation in play may be one aspect of these difficulties. In fact, a number of investigators have found associations between childhood disorders and high rates of solitary play (as discussed earlier in the chapter). Children with internalizing and externalizing disorders will likely spend much of their recreational time in solitary activities because they simply have no other option.

Conclusions and Future Directions

In this chapter, our objective has been to consider the implications of internalizing and externalizing disorders for children's participation in social play. Given the limited availability of relevant empirical findings, our conclusions have been somewhat tentative in nature. Indeed, it seems fair to suggest that a clear picture regarding the impact of internalizing and externalizing on play has yet to emerge. Moreover, investigators have not yet directly considered underlying processes or potential mediator mechanisms.

We advocate for further investigation for a number of different reasons. Earlier in this chapter, we emphasized the potential contributions of play to development. As we discussed, a number of theorists have viewed participation in play as an important component of socialization (Rubin, Watson, & Jambor, 1978). Although a balanced perspective would likely not view play as essential for normative outcomes (e.g., Smith, 2009), we contend that any factors that detract from children's involvement in these activities should merit close attention.

We also suggest that research on play could add to a wider understanding of the meaning of psychosocial maladjustment for children's day-to-day lives. Internalizing and externalizing disorders have powerful implications for children's relationships in the school peer group (Prinstein & Aikins, 2004; Schwartz et al., 2008). Disruptions in social play may be one important indicator of these difficulties. In this case, research on play could help shed light on the true costs of psychological disorder for children's social development. Whether or not researchers view play as an essential component of socialization and development, it does seem clear that play can provide an efficient window into children's relationships with peers. As we gain a better understanding of how disorder affects play, we will gain insight into larger issues related to functioning in the school peer group.

In summary, our goal has been to identify processes through which psychosocial maladjustment could potentially exert a pernicious influence on children's involvement in social play. We have focused particularly on areas of core competency, including emotion regulation and social cognition. We have also raised questions regarding potential disruptions in the peer relationships that serve as a critical context for play. We believe that further research on each of these issues is warranted, and could greatly enhance current perspectives on both social development and childhood psychopathology.

References

Alessandri, S. M. (1992). Attention, play, and social behavior in ADHD preschoolers. *Journal of Abnormal Child Psychology, 20,* 289–302.

Altmann, E. O., & Gotlib, I. H. (1988). The social behavior of depressed children: An observational study. *Journal of Abnormal Child Psychology, 16,* 29–44.

Abramson, L. Y., Alloy, L. B., & Metalsky, G. I. (1988). The cognitive diathesis-stress theories of depression: Toward an adequate evaluation of the theories' validities. In L. B. Alloy (Ed.), *Cognitive processes in depression.* (pp. 3–30). New York: Guilford Press.

Asarnow, J. R., & Callan, J. W. (1985). Boys with peer adjustment problems: Social cognitive processes. *Journal of Consulting and Clinical Psychology, 53,* 80–87.

Asher, S. R., Parker, J. G., & Walker, D. L. (1996). Distinguishing friendship from acceptance: Implications for intervention and assessment. In W. M. Bukowski, A. F. Newcomb, & W. W. Hartup (Eds.), *The company they keep: Friendship in childhood and adolescence.* (pp. 366–405). New York: Cambridge University Press.

Asendorpf, J. B. (1993). Abnormal shyness in children. *Journal of Child Psychology and Psychiatry and Allied Disciplines, 34,* 1069–1081.

Barkley, R. A. (2006). Attention-deficit hyperactivity disorder, 3rd ed.: A handbook for diagnosis and treatment. New York: Guilford Press.

Beck, A. T. (1963). Thinking and depression: Idiosyncratic content and cognitive distortions. *Archives of General Psychiatry, 9,* 324–333.

Beck, A. T. (1972). *Depression: Causes and treatment.* Philadelphia: University of Pennsylvania Press.

Bell-Dolan, D. J. (1995). Social cue interpretation of anxious children. *Journal of Clinical Child Psychology, 24,* 2–10.

Bierman, K. L. (2004). *Peer rejection: Developmental processes and intervention strategies.* New York: Guilford Press.

Bowker, A., Bukowski, W., & Zargarpour, S. (1998). A structural and functional analysis of a two-dimensional model of social isolation. *Merrill-Palmer Quarterly, 44,* 447–463.

Bukowski, W. M., & Hoza, B. (1989). Popularity and friendship: Issues in theory, measurement, and outcome. In T. J. Berndt, & G. W. Ladd (Eds.), *Peer relationships in child development.* (pp. 15–45). Oxford: John Wiley & Sons.

Bukowski, W. M., Pizzamiglio, M. T., Newcomb, A. F., & Hoza, B. (1996). Popularity as an affordance for friendship: The link between group and dyadic experience. *Social Development, 5,* 189–202.

Campbell, S. B., Breaux, A. M., Ewing, L. J., & Szumowski, E. K. (1986). Correlates and predictors of hyperactivity and aggression: A longitudinal study of parent-referred problem preschoolers. *Journal of Abnormal Child Psychology, 14,* 217–234.

Card, N. A., & Little, T. D. (2006). Proactive and reactive aggression in childhood and adolescence: A meta-analysis of differential relations with psychosocial adjustment. *International Journal of Behavioral Development, 30,* 466–480.

Cheah, C. S. L., Nelson, L. J., & Rubin, K. H. (2001). Nonsocial play as a risk factor in social and emotional development. In A. Göncü, & E. L. Klein (Eds.), *Children in play, story, and school.* (pp. 39–71). New York: Guilford Press.

Cicchetti, D. (2006). Development and psychopathology. In D. Cicchetti, & D. J. Cohen (Eds.), *Developmental psychopathology, vol 1: Theory and method (2nd ed.).* (pp. 1–23). Hoboken, NJ: John Wiley & Sons Inc.

Clark, L. A., & Watson, D. (1991). Tripartite model of anxiety and depression: Psychometric evidence and taxonomic implications. *Journal of Abnormal Psychology, 100,* 316–336.

Clark, M. L., Cheyne, J. A., Cunningham, C. E., & Siegel, L. S. (1988). Dyadic peer interaction and task orientation in attention-deficit-disordered children. *Journal of Abnormal Child Psychology, 16,* 1–15.

Coie, J. D., Dodge, K. A., & Kupersmidt, J. B. (1990). Peer group behavior and social status. In S. R. Asher, & J. D. Coie

(Eds.), *Peer rejection in childhood.* (pp. 17–59). New York: Cambridge University Press.

Coie, J. D., & Kupersmidt, J. B. (1983). A behavioral analysis of emerging social status in boys' groups. *Child Development, 54*, 1400–1416.

Cole, D. A. (1991). Preliminary support for a competency-based model of depression in children. *Journal of Abnormal Psychology, 100*, 181–190.

Cole, D. A., & Carpentieri, S. (1990). Social status and the comorbidity of child depression and conduct disorder. *Journal of Consulting and Clinical Psychology, 58*, 748–757.

Cole, D. A., Martin, J. M., & Powers, B. (1997). A competency-based model of child depression: A longitudinal study of peer, parent, teacher, and self-evaluations. *Journal of Child Psychology and Psychiatry, 38*, 505–514.

Cole, D. A., & Turner, J. E. (1993). Models of cognitive mediation and moderation in child depression. *Journal of Abnormal Psychology, 102*, 271–281.

Connolly, J., Geller, S., Marton, P., & Kutcher, S. (1992). Peer responses to social interaction with depressed adolescents. *Journal of Clinical Child Psychology, 21*, 365–370.

Coplan, R. J., & Arbeau, K. A. (2009). Peer interactions and play in early childhood. In K. H. Rubin, W. M. Bukowski, & B. Laursen (Eds.), *Handbook of peer interactions, relationships, and groups.* (pp. 143–161). New York: Guilford Press.

Coplan, R. J., Gavinski-Molina, M. H., Lagacé-Séguin, D. G., & Wichmann, C. (2001). When girls versus boys play alone: Nonsocial play and adjustment in kindergarten. *Developmental Psychology, 37*, 464–474.

Coplan, R. J., & Rubin, K. H. (1998). Exploring and assessing nonsocial play in the preschool: The development and validation of the preschool play behavior scale. *Social Development, 7*, 72–91.

Coplan, R. J., Rubin, K. H., Fox, N. A., & Calkins, S. D. (1994). Being alone, playing alone, and acting alone: Distinguishing among reticence and passive and active solitude in young children. *Child Development, 65*, 129–137.

Crick, N. R., & Dodge, K. A. (1994). A review and reformulation of social information-processing mechanisms in children's social adjustment. *Psychological Bulletin, 115*, 74–101.

Crick, N. R., & Ladd, G. W. (1990). Children's perceptions of the outcomes of social strategies: Do the ends justify being mean? *Developmental Psychology, 26*, 612–620.

Deater-Deckard, K. (2001). Recent research examining the role of peer relationships in the development of psychopathology. *Journal of Child Psychology and Psychiatry, 42*, 565–579.

Dishion, T. J., Andrews, D. W., & Crosby, L. (1995). Antisocial boys and their friends in early adolescence: Relationship characteristics, quality, and interactional processes. *Child Development, 66*, 139–151.

Dishion, T., & Dodge, K. A. (2005). Peer contagion in interventions for children and adolescents: Moving towards an understanding of the ecology and dynamics of change. *Journal of Abnormal Child Psychology, 33*, 395–400.

Dodge, K. A. (1986). A social information processing model of social competence in children. In M. Perlmutter (Ed.), *Minnesota Symposium on Child Psychology* (pp. 77–125). Hillsdale, NJ: Erlbaum.

Dodge, K. A., & Coie, J. D. (1987). Social information-processing factors in reactive and instrumental aggression in children's playgroups. *Journal of Personality and Social Psychology, 53*, 1146–1158.

Dodge, K. A., & Frame, C. L. (1982). Social cognitive biases and deficits in aggressive boys. *Child Development, 53*, 620–635.

Dodge, K. A., Lochman, J. E., Harnish, J. D., Bates, J. E., & Pettit, G. S. (1997). Reactive and proactive aggression in school children and psychiatrically impaired chronically assaultive youth. *Journal of Abnormal Psychology, 106*, 37–51.

Dodge, K. A., Murphy, R. R., & Buchsbaum, K. (1984). The assessment of intention-cue detection skills in children: Implications for developmental psychopathology. *Child Development, 55*, 163–173.

Dodge, K. A., & Newman, J. P. (1981). Biased decision-making processes in aggressive boys. *Journal of Abnormal Psychology, 90*, 375–379.

Dodge, K. A., Pettit, G. S., McClaskey, C. L., & Brown, M. M. (1986). Social competence in children. *Monographs of the Society for Research in Child Development, 51*, 1–85.

Dodge, K. A., & Price, J. M. (1994). On the relation between social information processing and socially competent behavior in early school-aged children. *Child Development, 65*, 1385–1897.

Dodge, K. A., & Schwartz, D. (1997). Social information processing mechanisms in aggressive behavior. In D. M. Stoff, J. Breiling, & J. D. Maser (Eds.), *Handbook of antisocial behavior.* (pp. 171–180). Hoboken, NJ: John Wiley & Sons Inc.

Eisenberg, N., Fabes, R. A., Murphy, B., Maszk, P., Smith, M., & Karbon, M. (1995). The role of emotionality and regulation in children's social functioning: A longitudinal study. *Child Development, 66*, 1360–1384.

Eisenberg, N., & Spinrad, T. L. (2004). Emotion-related regulation: Sharpening the definition. *Child Development, 75*, 334–339.

Erdley, C. A., & Asher, S. R. (1996). Children's social goals and self-efficacy perceptions as influences on their responses to ambiguous provocation. *Child Development, 67*, 1329–1344.

Feng, X., Keenan, K., Hipwell, A. E., et al. (2009). Longitudinal associations between emotion regulation and depression in preadolescent girls: Moderation by the caregiving environment. *Developmental Psychology, 45*, 798–808.

Field, T. M., Sandberg, D., Goldstein, S., & Garcia, R. (1987). Play interactions and interviews of depressed and conduct disorder children and their mothers. *Child Psychiatry & Human Development, 17*, 213–234.

Garber, J., Braafladt, N., & Weiss, B. (1995). Affect regulation in depressed and nondepressed children and young adolescents. *Development and Psychopathology. Special Issue: Emotions in Developmental Psychopathology, 7*, 93–115.

Gest, S. D., Graham-Bermann, S. A., & Hartup, W. W. (2001). Peer experience: Common and unique features of number of friendships, social network centrality, and sociometric status. *Social Development, 10*, 23–40.

Gottman, J. M. (1983). How children become friends. *Monographs of the Society for Research in Child Development, 48*, 86.

Hammen, C., & Rudolph, K. D. (1996). Childhood depression. In E. J. Mash & R. A. Barkley (Eds.), *Child psychopathology* (pp. 153–195). New York: Guilford Press.

Harrist, A. W., Zaia, A. F., Bates, J. E., Dodge, K. A., & Pettit, G. S. (1997). Subtypes of social withdrawal in early childhood: Sociometric status and social cognitive differences across four years. *Child Development, 68*, 278–294.

Hartup, W. W. (1996). The company they keep: Friendships and their developmental significance. *Child Development, 67*, 1–13.

Haselager, G. J. T., Hartup, W. W., van Lieshout, C. F. M., & Riksen-Walraven, J. M. A. (1998). Similarities between friends and nonfriends in middle childhood. *Child Development, 69*, 1198–1208.

Hawker, D. S. J., & Boulton, M. J. (2000). Twenty years' research on peer victimization and psychosocial adjustment: A meta-analytic review of cross-sectional studies. *Journal of Child Psychology and Psychiatry and Allied Disciplines, 41*, 441–455.

Howes, C., Droege, K., & Matheson, C. C. (1994). Play and communicative processes within long- and short-term friendship dyads. *Journal of Social and Personal Relationships. Special Issue: Children's Friendships, 11*, 401–410.

Howes, C., & Matheson, C. C. (1992). Sequences in the development of competent play with peers: Social and social pretend play. *Developmental Psychology, 28*, 961–974.

Hubbard, J. A., Dodge, K. A., Cillessen, A. H. N., Coie, J. D., & Schwartz, D. (2001). The dyadic nature of social information processing in boys' reactive and proactive aggression. *Journal of Personality and Social Psychology, 80*, 268–280.

Hubbard, J. A., & Newcomb, A. F. (1991). Initial dyadic peer interaction of attention deficit-hyperactivity disorder and normal boys. *Journal of Abnormal Child Psychology, 19*, 179–195.

Huesmann, L. R. (1998). The role of social information processing and cognitive schema in the acquisition and maintenance of habitual aggressive behavior. In R. G. Geen & E. Donnerstein (Eds.), *Human aggression: Theories, research, and implications for social policy.* (pp. 73–109). San Diego: Academic Press.

Ingoldsby, E. M., Kohl, G. O., McMahon, R. J., Lengua, L., & Conduct Problems Prevention Research Group. (2006). Conduct problems, depressive symptomatology and their co-occurring presentation in childhood as predictors of adjustment in early adolescence. *Journal of Abnormal Child Psychology, 34*, 603–621.

Kiesner, J. (2002). Depressive symptoms in early adolescence: Their relations with classroom problem behavior and peer status. *Journal of Research on Adolescence, 12*, 463–478.

King, S., Waschbusch, D. A., Pelham, W. E., Jr., Frankland, B. W., Andrade, B. F., Jacques, S., & Corkum, P. V. (2009). Social information processing in elementary-school aged children with ADHD: Medication effects and comparisons with typical children. *Journal of Abnormal Child Psychology, 37*, 579–589.

Kupersmidt, J. B., DeRosier, M. E., & Patterson, C. P. (1995). Similarity as the basis for children's friendships: The roles of sociometric status, aggressive and withdrawn behavior, academic achievement and demographic characteristics. *Journal of Social and Personal Relationships, 12*, 439–452.

Lochman, J. E., Wayland, K. K., & White, K. J. (1993). Social goals: Relationship to adolescent adjustment and to social problem solving. *Journal of Abnormal Child Psychology, 21*, 135–151.

Lous, A. M., de Wit, C. A. M., De Bruyn, E. E. J., & Riksen-Walraven, J. M. (2002). Depression markers in young children's play: A comparison between depressed and nondepressed 3- to 6-year-olds in various play situations. *Journal of Child Psychology and Psychiatry, 43*, 1029–1038.

Malti, T. (2006). Aggression, self-understanding, and social competence in Swiss elementary-school children. *Swiss Journal of Psychology/Schweizerische Zeitschrift Für Psychologie/Revue Suisse De Psychologie, 65*, 81–91.

Martel, M. M. (2009). Research review: A new perspective on attention-deficit hyperactivity disorder: Emotion dysregulation and trait models. *Journal of Child Psychology and Psychiatry, 50*, 1042–1051.

McIntyre, A., Lounsbury, K. R., Hamilton, M. L., & Mantooth, J. M. (1980). Individual differences in preschool object play: The influences of anxiety proneness and peer affiliation. *Journal of Applied Developmental Psychology, 1*, 149–161.

Melnick, S. M., & Hinshaw, S. P. (2000). Emotion regulation and parenting in AD/HD and comparison boys: Linkages with social behaviors and peer preference. *Journal of Abnormal Child Psychology, 28*, 73–86.

Milich, R., & Dodge, K. A. (1984). Social information processing in child psychiatric populations. *Journal of Abnormal Child Psychology, 12*, 471–490.

Nolan, S. A., Flynn, C., & Garber, J. (2003). Prospective relations between rejection and depression in adolescents. *Journal of Personality and Social Psychology, 85*, 745–755.

Pakaslahti, L. (2000). Children's and adolescents' aggressive behavior in context: The development and application of aggressive problem-solving strategies. *Aggression and Violent Behavior, 5*, 467–490.

Panak, W. F., & Garber, J. (1992). Role of aggression, rejection, and attributions in the prediction of depression in children. *Development and Psychopathology, 4*, 145–165.

Parker, J. G., & Asher, S. R. (1987). Peer relations and later personal adjustment: Are low-accepted children at risk? *Psychological Bulletin, 102*, 357–389.

Pellegrini, A. D. (1987). Rough-and-tumble play: Developmental and educational significance. *Educational Psychologist, 22*, 23–43.

Pellegrini, A. D., & Bjorklund, D. F. (1997). The role of recess in children's cognitive performance. *Educational Psychologist, 32*, 35–40.

Pellegrini, A. D., & Smith, P. K. (1998). Physical activity play: The nature and function of a neglected aspect of play. *Child Development, 69*, 577–598.

Perry, D. G., Perry, L. C., & Rasmussen, P. (1986). Cognitive social learning mediators of aggression. *Child Development, 57*, 700–711.

Pope, A. W., & Bierman, K. L. (1999). Predicting adolescent peer problems and antisocial activities: The relative roles of aggression and dysregulation. *Developmental Psychology, 35*, 335–346.

Poulin, F., Dishion, T. J., & Haas, E. (1999). The peer influence paradox: Friendship quality and deviancy training within male adolescent friendships. *Merrill-Palmer Quarterly, 45*, 42–61.

Prinstein, M. J., & Aikins, J. W. (2004). Cognitive moderators of the longitudinal association between peer rejection and adolescent depressive symptoms. *Journal of Abnormal Child Psychology, 32*, 147–158.

Quiggle, N. L., Garber, J., Panak, W. F., & Dodge, K. A. (1992). Social information processing in aggressive and depressed children. *Child Development, 63*, 1305–1320.

Rockhill, C. M., Fan, M., Katon, W. J., McCauley, E., Crick, N. R., & Pleck, J. H. (2007). Friendship interactions in children with and without depressive symptoms: Observation of emotion during game-playing interactions and post-game evaluations. *Journal of Abnormal Child Psychology, 35*, 429–441.

Rubin, K. H., Coplan, R. J., Fox, N. A., & Calkins, S. D. (1995). Emotionality, emotion regulation, and preschoolers' social adaptation. *Development and Psychopathology, 7*, 49–62.

Rubin, K. H., Fein, G., & Vanderberg, B. (1983). Play. In P. Mussen & E. M. Hetherington (Eds.), *Handbook of child psychology: Vol. 4. Socialization, personality, and social development* (pp. 693–774). New York: Wiley.

Rubin, K. H., & Mills, R. S. (1988). The many faces of social isolation in childhood. *Journal of Consulting and Clinical Psychology, 56*, 916–924.

Rubin, K. H., Watson, K. S., & Jambor, T. W. (1978). Free-play behaviors in preschool and kindergarten children. *Child Development, 49*, 534–536.

Rudolph, K. D., Hammen, C., & Burge, D. (1994). Interpersonal functioning and depressive symptoms in childhood: Addressing the issues of specificity and comorbidity. *Journal of Abnormal Child Psychology, 22*, 355–371.

Rudolph, K. D., Flynn, M., & Abaied, J. L. (2008). *A developmental perspective on interpersonal theories of youth depression.* New York: Guilford Press.

Schwartz, D. (2000). Subtypes of victims and aggressors in children's peer groups. *Journal of Abnormal Child Psychology, 28*, 181–192.

Schwartz, D., Dodge, K. A., Coie, J. D., Hubbard, J. A., Cillessen, A. H. N., & Lemerise, E. A. (1998). Social cognitive and behavioral correlates of aggression and victimization in boys' play groups. *Journal of Abnormal Child Psychology, 26*, 431–440.

Schwartz, D., Gorman, A. H., Duong, M. T., & Nakamoto, J. (2008). Peer relationships and academic achievement as interacting predictors of depressive symptoms during middle childhood. *Journal of Abnormal Psychology, 117*, 289–299.

Schwartz, D., & Proctor, L. J. (2000). Community violence exposure and children's social adjustment in the school peer group: The mediating roles of emotion regulation and social cognition. *Journal of Consulting and Clinical Psychology, 68*, 670–683.

Shields, A., & Cicchetti, D. (1998). Reactive aggression among maltreated children: The contributions of attention and emotion dysregulation. *Journal of Clinical Child Psychology, 27*, 381–395.

Shields, A. M., Cicchetti, D., & Ryan, R. M. (1994). The development of emotional and behavioral self-regulation and social competence among maltreated school-age children. *Development & Psychopathology, 6*, 57–75.

Slaby, R. G., & Guerra, N. G. (1988). Cognitive mediators of aggression in adolescent offenders: 1. Assessment. *Developmental Psychology, 24*, 580–588.

Smith, P.K. (2009). *Children's play.* Oxford: Wiley-Blackwell.

Spinrad, T. L., Eisenberg, N., Harris, E., et al. (2004). The relation of children's everyday nonsocial peer play behavior to their emotionality, regulation, and social functioning. *Developmental Psychology, 40*, 67–80.

Spivack, G., & Shure, M. B. (1974). Social adjustment of young children: A cognitive approach to solving real-life problems. Oxford, England: Jossey-Bass.

Sroufe, L. A., Schork, E., Motti, F., Lawroski, N., & LaFreniere, P. (1988). The role of affect in social competence. *Emotions, cognition, and behavior.* (pp. 289–319). New York: Cambridge University Press.

Sutton-Smith, B. (1997). *The ambiguity of play.* Cambridge, MA: Harvard University Press.

Troop-Gordon, W., & Asher, S. R. (2005). Modifications in children's goals when encountering obstacles to conflict resolution. *Child Development, 76*, 568–582.

Waas, G. A. (1988). Social attributional biases of peer-rejected and aggressive children. *Child Development, 59*, 969–975.

Wichmann, C., Coplan, R. J., & Daniels, T. (2004). The social cognitions of socially withdrawn children. *Social Development, 13*, 377–392.

Zeman, J., Shipman, K., & Suveg, C. (2002). Anger and sadness regulation: Predictions to internalizing and externalizing symptoms in children. *Journal of Clinical Child and Adolescent Psychology, 31*, 393–398.

Gender and Temperament in Young Children's Social Interactions

Carol Lynn Martin, Richard A. Fabes, *and* Laura D. Hanish

Abstract

Understanding social interactions occurring in young girls' and boys' lives has long been a topic of interest. During the preschool years, children become increasingly social and spend less time alone. However, young children do not interact with all available peers equally; rather, they narrow their social fields toward a selective set of peers. As such, children interact with some peers frequently, with some peers occasionally, and they rarely or never interact with other peers. In the present chapter, we review the powerful role that gender plays in young children's social interactions and explore the factors that contribute to it, with particular attention paid to temperamental factors that affect the degree to which children engage in gender-segregated interactions. We present some new data highlighting the importance of considering dispositional regulation as a factor that influences the patterns of children's interactions. Directions for future research also are identified.

Keywords: Gender, gender segregation, temperament, social interactions, young children.

Understanding the social interactions that occur in young girls' and boys' lives has long been a topic of interest for developmental scientists (Parten, 1932; Rubin, Watson, & Jambor, 1978). As early as the 1930s, impressive and extensive observational data were collected that addressed questions about who young children interacted with and what they did in those interactions (Challman, 1932; Mallay, 1935). Since that time, researchers have shown that children's social interactions are multi-faceted developmental phenomena.

Developmentally, it is during the preschool years that children become more social—moving from spending time alone to spending time along side others (e.g., parallel play) to being truly interactional and cooperative. In addition, during early childhood, interactions become more sophisticated; involving increasingly complex interactions and activities with peers that are based on elaborate rules and/or role assignments (e.g., complex pretend play) (Howes & Matheson, 1992). Moreover, as children progress through the preschool years, they interact with a larger array of peers and in larger groups (Howes, this volume; Howes & Matheson, 1992; Rubin & Coplan, 1998; Strayer & Santos, 1996). Interacting with peers provides a context for preschoolers' social learning and knowledge exchange that can afford numerous benefits above and beyond the learning opportunities and developmental experiences provided by non-social play or through interactions with adults.

For most young children, it is during play activities that social interactions with peers most often occur. Thus, for young children, initiating and maintaining playful interactions with peers represents important developmental milestones. However, young children do not interact and play with all available peers equally; rather, they narrow their social fields toward a selective set of peers. As such, children interact with some peers frequently, with some peers occasionally, and rarely or never interact with other peers (see Coplan, this volume;

Hanish, Martin, Fabes, & Barceló, 2008; Snyder, Horsch, & Childs, 1997). Children show considerable variability in the selection of partners, types of activities in which they engage, and in the extent of narrowing they show in selecting playmates. This narrowing is not random; instead it is guided by shared interests, preferences, and individual characteristics. From a developmental perspective, this narrowing of partners is important because different types of peers provide different types of interactions and learning opportunities, thereby moving children down different social, emotional, and cognitive developmental pathways.

A major contributor to the narrowing of children's interactional partners is gender—of both the child and her/his peers. Although recognized in early studies, attention did not shift to the importance of gender in children's interactions until the 1980s, when the powerful nature of gender was recognized and its extent widely publicized within the developmental literature (Maccoby, 1988; Maccoby & Jacklin, 1987). Surprisingly, although individual differences have been implicated as factors in gender segregation (Bem, 1996; Fabes, 1994), we still do not have an adequate understanding of the role of individual variability in children's gender-segregated interactions.

The goal of the present chapter is to review the powerful role that gender plays in young children's social interactions and to explore the factors that contribute to it, with particular attention paid to temperamental factors that affect the degree to which children engage in gender-segregated interactions. We begin by introducing the concept of gender segregation and review the developmental patterns of gender segregation over early childhood. We then review the major explanations for gender segregation, and consider how a full understanding requires consideration of how gender segregation begins, how it is maintained, and how it changes over situations and individuals. Next, we discuss an important temperamental factor—regulation—and how variations in regulation relate to children's interactional partner choices. We also present new data highlighting the importance of dispositional regulation in children's gender-segregated interactions. In the final sections, we consider an integrative perspective on gender segregation, the role of temperament, and propose future directions for the study of social interactions in young children. An important caveat: In the literature on gender segregation, little distinction has been made between children's play (e.g., social pretend play, rough and tumble play) and children's social interactions, although play is defined as having different qualities than non-play interactions (Burghardt, 2005; Pellegrini, 2009). For that reason, our review will focus on social interactions of all types. However, it is important to note that most of the literature on young children's gender-segregated interactions has taken place in the context of their play with peers.

Young Children's Preference for Same-Gender Interactional Partners

Perhaps the most fundamental basis upon which children select their peer partners is gender, accounting for 70–80% of the variance in young children's choice of peer partners (Martin & Fabes, 2001). If given a choice of partners, girls tend to interact with girls and boys tend to interact with boys. In fact, it is rare to see children interact solely with peers of the other gender (Fabes, Martin, & Hanish, 2003; Maccoby, 1998; Martin & Fabes, 2001). Similarly, children identify same-gender peers as friends more frequently than other-gender peers (Hayden-Thomson, Rubin, & Hymel, 1987; Kupersmidt, DeRosier, & Patterson, 1995). When encountering unfamiliar peers, children assume that same-gender peers are more similar to themselves and more likable than other-gender peers (Powlishta, 1995). These social preferences are readily observed whenever children are allowed to engage in unstructured activities and have the freedom to select their own partners (i.e., free-play). Moreover, these preferences are resistant to change (Maccoby, 1990; Serbin, Tonick, & Sternglanz, 1977). For instance, in one study, preschool teachers provided reinforcement to children for interacting with other-gender peers. Although the amount of other-gender interactions increased while the contingency was in effect, when the reinforcement was discontinued, the children quickly returned to baseline levels of gender-segregated interactions (Serbin et al., 1977).

This phenomenon of same-gender preference in interactional partners, known as gender segregation, is thought to be one of the strongest, most consistent, and most robust developmental phenomena (Ruble, Martin, & Berenbaum, 2006) and has been observed almost universally across various cultures (Whiting & Edwards, 1973) and across most mammalian species (Ruckstuhl & Neuhaus, 2005). It also has been shown to operate as a driving force in peer selection throughout the lifespan (Mehta & Strough, 2009).

Children's preferences for interacting with same-gender peers begin to emerge between two to three years of age. Girls tend to segregate first and boys follow about six months later. Throughout early childhood, segregation becomes increasingly strong (LaFreniere, Strayer, & Gauthier, 1984; Maccoby & Jacklin, 1987; Serbin, Moller, Gulko, Powlishta, & Colburne, 1994). For example, whereas young pre-schoolers interact with same-gender peers three times as much as they do with other-gender peers, the ratio of time spent increases to 11-to-1 by the time children are in the early elementary years (Maccoby & Jacklin, 1987). Evidence indicates that even though same-gender preferences emerge earlier for girls than for boys, boys show stronger prefer-ences than girls for same-gender interactions by approximately five to six years of age (LaFreniere, Strayer, & Gauthier, 1984).

Gender segregation among preschoolers can be seen in children's responses to play bids from same- and other-gender peers, the amount of time that children spend with same- versus other-gender peers, and in the quality of interactions with same- and other-gender peers. Specifically, as compared to other-gender peers, children respond more favor-ably to same-gender peers' play bids, they engage with same-gender peers more frequently and for longer periods of time, and they provide more posi-tive reinforcement to same-gender peers (Fabes et al., 2003; Howes, 1988; Snyder et al., 1996). Building on the interactional patterns established in early childhood, gender segregation continues to be evident in individuals' choice of social interaction partners across ensuing developmental periods, from middle childhood through late adulthood, although the strength of this varies in adolescence as they show increased interest in other-gender rela-tionships (Maccoby, 1998; Mehta & Strough, 2009).

As noted previously, gender segregation is one of the strongest known social phenomena. Not only is there a preference for children to interact with peers of their own gender, but even interactions with peers of the other gender appear to be dependent on the presence of same-gender peers. In most cases, gender-integrated interactions occurs in the form of groups in which children engage with both male and female peers, such that they have members of the same gender involved in the interactions as well members of the other gender. In comparison, gender-integrated interactions rarely involve a girl interacting solely with one or more boys (or vice versa). Estimates suggest that mixed-gender group interactions occur between one-fourth and one-third of the time in preschools whereas interactions

with only other-gender peers is quite infrequent, accounting for only 10–15% of children's social interactions (Fabes et al., 2003; Martin & Fabes, 2001). Thus, young children's affiliations with oth-er-gender peers primarily occur in the context of same-gender peers. Sroufe and colleagues (Sroufe, Bennett, Englund, & Urban, 1993) demonstrated that, at least for preadolescents, the presence of same-gender peers provides a normative and socially acceptable context in which children may interact with other-gender peers without the stigma that can accompany interactions with other-gender peers and further research is needed to explore whether this is also the case at other ages.

Although gender-segregated interactions are quite ubiquitous, there is variability in young chil-dren's overall level of gender segregation. In addition to the developmental variations in gender-segregated interactions that are typically seen across the pre-school period, the social context and children's indi-vidual characteristics provide an additional basis for variability in gender segregation. Children's tenden-cies to segregate by gender vary across situations. For instance, rates of gender integrated interaction vary according to the nature of the preschool setting (such as number of boys and girls in the classroom; the physical structure of the preschool, presence/absence of adults, etc.) that children experience (Bianchi & Bakeman, 1978). The qualities of the other children in the class also matter: children who are in classrooms with "gender enforcers"—those children who admonish their peers to follow stereo-typic interaction patterns—tend to show stronger segregation than children in classrooms with fewer gender enforcers (McGuire, Martin, Fabes, & Hanish, 2007).

Moreover, even though there is day-to-day vari-ability in gender segregation, some children show stronger tendencies to segregate than others and these patterns are moderately stable over time (Martin & Fabes, 2001; Martin & Ruble, 2010). Thus, relative rates of gender segregation and gender integration may also depend on children's individual characteristics, such as temperament, age, and phys-ical attractiveness (Pellegrini & Long, 2007). Individual variations are not well understood, but the stability of patterns over time suggests that a better understanding of the individual characteristics that contribute to gender segregation is worthy of additional research efforts. Interestingly, recent research suggests that children differ in the types of variations they show in gender-segregated interac-tional partners and in toy play. That is, some children show a flexible pattern that may allow them to adjust to changing contexts with more ease than other children who are more rigidly locked into their partners and toys (DiDonato et al., 2009).

The relative dominance of same-gender interactions is developmentally important because it provides relatively unique social experiences, patterns of interactions, habits, activities, and behaviors for girls and boys. Although boys and girls do share a number of interests and behavioral styles (e.g., Lansford & Parker, 1999), there are also some well-established interactional differences in these that extend along gendered lines. For instance, toys and other play materials may be divided according to gender; feminine toys highlight domestic activities, nurturance, and attractiveness, and girls are more likely than boys to engage in activities such as art, music, dress-up, and dolls (Blakemore & Centers, 2005). Girls' interactions tend to be quiet and sedentary (Maccoby, 1998; Smith & Inder, 1993). They interact close to adults and their interaction styles are responsive to adult-generated structures (Martin & Fabes, 2001; Smith & Inder, 1993). Moreover, girls interact in dyads more frequently than in large groups (Fabes et al., 2003). As such, girls' social interactions are conducive to verbal interactions that are oriented toward the development and maintenance of relationships, and girls manage conflicts by using pacification techniques and compromise (Maccoby & Jacklin, 1987; Rose & Rudolph, 2006).

In contrast, masculine play and toys promote competition, aggressiveness, and construction, and boys are more likely than girls to play with objects such as balls, blocks, cars, and weapons (Blakemore & Centers, 2005). Paralleling these masculine-typed activities, boys' interactions are more physically active, competitive, heavy-handed, and aggressive (Eaton & Yu, 1989; Martin & Fabes, 2001). Boys also gravitate toward larger groups and structure their peer interactions according to peer- rather than adult-generated rules (Carpenter et al., 1986; Fabes et al., 2003). Thus, establishing and maintaining dominance hierarchies are key parts of boys' interactions, and boys manage conflicts using force (Maccoby, 1998). In light of these gender differences in activities and interaction styles, it is not surprising that interactions with same-gender peers provide a social context that supports engagement in gender-typical behaviors and inhibits engagement in gender-atypical behaviors (Goble et al., 2008).

Because gender-segregation is ubiquitous, powerful, and has the potential to shape their skills and interactions patterns into the future (Leaper, 1994; Maccoby, 1998; Martin & Fabes, 2001), it is crucial that we understand this phenomenon. In the following section, we consider the predominant explanations that have been proposed to account for gender segregation.

Explanations for Gender Segregation

Before reviewing theories, we must consider what needs to be explained in gender segregation, and what cautions need to be taken into consideration for any explanation of this phenomenon. At the most basic level, we need to understand why there is an attraction and preference for same-gender peers, and to explore whether there is a corresponding dislike or disinterest in other-sex peers. Furthermore, it is important to explain and understand why these affiliation patterns are so ubiquitous and powerful. Given the strength and ubiquity of gender segregation, it is tempting to hold out for bold explanations that suggest very strong effects. However, caution should be exercised because even small effects can have surprisingly large consequences in group settings (Martin, Fabes, Hanish, & Hollenstein, 2005). For example, studies involving the computerized simulation modeling of segregation (e.g., racial segregation in neighborhoods) have demonstrated that even small preferences for same-race neighbors can, when played out over time and over all members of a neighborhood, appear as very large differences in segregation (e.g., Schelling, 1971). Because of the potential for small effects to be magnified in groups, we should not infer that it is necessary to have extreme levels of liking of same-sex peers and/or high levels of disliking or disinterest in other-sex peers to produce the robust nature of gender segregation seen in young children's freely chosen interactions.

Explanations of gender segregation need to consider more than the positive pulls toward same-gender peers and the negative pushes against other-gender peers; they also need to consider developmental and temporal patterning of these behaviors. Three important questions need addressing. First, what first draws same-gender children together? This is the question of initial attraction. Second, what keeps same-gender children playing together? This question focuses on the factors that maintain same-gender interactions over time (Thorne, 1993). Third, what causes variations in partner choices? This is the question as to how individual and contextual factors influence gender segregation. In the following sections, we review the major explanations that have been given for gender segregation and draw conclusions and inferences about the degree to which each theory provides answers to these important questions.

Evolutionary approaches: Sexual selection

Evolutionary explanations for gender segregation involve considerations of how early behavior may be adaptive for later adult roles. Although several evolutionary hypotheses have been articulated, they converge on the idea that early segregation relates to adult reproductive success and roles. The assumption is that differential male and female roles in reproduction bring about different social behaviors for girls and boys, and these differences contribute to gender-differentiated interaction styles and gender segregation. That is, the underlying cause of segregation is the gender differences in behavior but the reasons for these differences relate to differential male and female roles in reproduction (Geary & Bjorklund, 2000; Pellegrini, 2004). Sexual selection favors males who are larger and stronger because they have to compete for mates; and it favors females who are able to nurture, protect, and provision their offspring. Social behaviors that are congruent with these roles should be selected for in mates, and these behaviors are expected to represent major differences between males and females. In this way, selection increases the likelihood of such characteristics in the population. Furthermore, these differences are thought to lead to segregation of males and females and into groups with peers who have similar skills and interests. Segregation by gender then allows children practice in adult roles and in the skills that will enhance reproductive success later in life.

As expected from evolutionary approaches, girls and boys differ in their social behavior, and one of the most compelling differences between the sexes that may lead to gender segregation involves the vigor of interactions. Although both sexes exhibit active, vigorous, and rough and tumble play, boys tend to engage in this form of interaction considerably more often than girls (Maccoby, 1998; Pellegrini, 2004). Additionally, boys may stand to gain more from active and vigorous play than do girls. Active and energetic play in childhood is hypothesized to maximize behavioral, brain, and muscular systems that are useful for competition with other males, thereby improving sexual success in adult males (Pellegrini, 2004). Thus, boys' competitiveness, striving for dominance and practice of aggression in the form of rough and tumble play may prepare them for their later roles as adult males

in competition with other adult males for access to females (Geary, 1999).

Similarly, girls' strivings for cooperative interactions and social connection are thought to provide practice for later social roles involving kinship networks that join together to provide care for children, as seen in hunter-gatherer societies (Maccoby, 2000). Even girls' expressions of relational aggression (aggression that is intended to disrupt social networks of competitors) may provide practice for later competition for mates and resources (Geary & Bjorklund, 2000).

According to the evolutionary perspective, these early sex differences in behavior draw children together in gender-segregated groups around common goals and behaviors, which then increase children's adaptability by providing them with practice in the behaviors that relate to their upcoming gender-differentiated roles of women and men. Some evidence has been found to support gender differences in these behaviors (Pellegrini, 2004; Ruble et al., 2006), but fewer studies have examined links between these behaviors and levels of gender segregation (e.g., Pellegrini, Long, Roseth, Bohn, & Van Ryzin, 2007).

Interestingly, the evolutionary perspective suggests that gender segregation should be widespread if not universal given the consistency of gender differences in reproductive roles, and this view is supported with evidence reporting that gender segregation is found cross-culturally (Whiting & Edwards, 1973) and even in non-human animals (Conradt, 1998). Also, expressions of gender differences should vary depending on context and culture. For instance, boys' fighting tends to be rougher in societies in which male-on-male aggression is common, and girls are socialized to be less obedient and more achievement oriented in societies where women have more political and economic power (Geary, 1999; Low, 1989).

One major strength of the evolutionary perspective is in addressing the initial attraction aspect of gender segregation—girls and boys segregate because they behave differently and these behavioral differences are in preparation for adult reproductive roles. The theory is less specific about how gender segregated interactions are maintained over time. Gender segregated interactions may be maintained over time because children enjoy the activities of their own gender group, but specific mechanisms involved in the maintenance of same-gender interactions are not clearly addressed in the theory. The theory provides descriptions of how broad societal norms would relate to variability over cultures, but is less explicit about variability over more narrow contexts (e.g., differing classrooms). Although not specifically addressed, implicit in theory is the idea that individual variation may occur: Children with non-typical characteristics relevant to their own gender group should be less likely to be interested in gender-segregated interactions.

Behavioral compatibility explanations

The mechanism that is probably the most commonly employed explanation for gender segregation is behavioral compatibility—referring to the idea that children are drawn to other children who share similar interaction styles and interests (Goodenough, 1934; LaFreniere, Strayer, & Gauthier, 1984; Maccoby, 1988; Maccoby & Jacklin, 1987; Moller & Serbin, 1996; Powlishta, Serbin, & Moller, 1993; Serbin, Moller, Gulko, Powlishta, & Colburne, 1994). Because there are gender differences in children's social behaviors, styles, and interests, children with similar behaviors or interests are likely to be of the same sex, thereby leading to gender segregation (Hoffman & Powlishta, 2001). This explanation can be considered a subset of the sexual selection theory as the behavioral differences that are argued to be essential to promoting segregation may derive from evolutionary pressures.

The range of interaction styles, interests, and behaviors that are presumed to draw boys to boys and girls to girls is vast and includes communication styles, forms of influence, conflict resolution strategies, activity level, play activities, and self regulation. In young children, similarities in toy and activity preferences have been considered to have powerful influences on segregation (LaFreniere et al., 1984). Any or all of these social behaviors can be potential contributors to gender segregation. Boys may be attracted to and to seek out other boys because of shared similarities in interacting around dominance issues, using direct styles of influence and being assertive; resolving conflicts through force or direct requests; playing at high activity levels; enjoying play with cars, trucks, and blocks; and a more rowdy and less controlled style of play. Girls may be attracted to and seek out girls because of similarities in interacting in cooperative ways, using indirect forms of influence, solving conflicts through indirect requests and discussion, playing with lower activity levels and with less vigor, playing house and with dolls, and being well-regulated in their interactions. Gender differences have been identified in these areas that are generally consistent with

expectations of this approach (for reviews see Berenbaum, Martin, Briggs, Fabes, & Hanish, 2009; Mehta & Strough, 2009; Ruble & Martin, 1998; Ruble et al., 2006).

If behavioral compatibility relates to the initial development of gender segregation, it makes sense that these patterns of gender differences would be evident prior to children showing strong segregation. As already noted, gender differences in some social behaviors and in preferences for certain types of toys are evident at an early age, approximately the age at which gender segregation begins (see Maccoby, 1998; Martin, Ruble, & Szkrybalo, 2002; Ruble et al., 2006). However, given that children are socialized in their experiences with peers (Leaper, 1994; Maccoby, 1998; Martin & Fabes, 2001), it is difficult to disentangle who children interact with from what they do and how they act. Furthermore, it is difficult to measure "similarity" in natural settings. Typically, children's behavior is assessed in free-play interactions with others, without having an independent setting for comparing children's behavior away from peers. For these reasons, it is difficult to know whether girls prefer to engage with other girls because they play with dolls or whether girls like to play with dolls and come to prefer interacting with other girls because they are the peers they encounter at the doll area. In both of these cases, the result is segregation by gender.

Despite the challenge of measuring similarity among children, several researchers have found indirect evidence supporting the behavioral compatibility explanation by examining similarity in the social behaviors of children who are friends (Serbin et al., 1994), by comparing similarity in preferred versus non-preferred playmates (Rubin, Lynch, Coplan, Rose-Krasnor, & Booth, 1994), or by comparing similarity in social sensitivity in early versus late segregators (Serbin et al., 1994). But seldom have researchers directly examined the link between similarity and gender segregation. In one such study that involved a sophisticated analytic assessment of effects, levels of gender segregation were not related to a preference for playing with children with similar interaction styles (Hoffman & Powlishta, 2001). Recent evidence using advanced social network analytic techniques that assess changes over time in segregation patterns, however, suggests that sharing similarity in activities relates to increased numbers of ties with same-gender peers over the course of a semester (Martin et al., 2010). Thus, the likelihood of finding supportive evidence may depend on the methods used as well as the type of similarity assessed.

Behavioral compatibility may be a stronger explanation of initial attraction for salient versus less salient features of interactions. For salient features such as activities and toys, it is easy to understand how children are attracted to peers who have similar and compatible interests. As previously noted, a girl who likes dolls may observe another girl playing with dolls (and presume that the girl likes dolls), therefore she becomes interested in interacting with this girl. For less salient features (such as internal qualities) it is more difficult to understand initial attraction based on compatibility, especially for young children. Without having the obvious salient cues about compatibility, how does initial attraction occur? Does it require a longer duration of time from which less salient interactional qualities can be experienced and then acted upon?

Behavioral compatibility also has potential for explaining how children maintain gender segregation. Once children recognize that they share similar interests or behaviors, the theory would predict that children would continue to interact together, with the shared interest or characteristic being the basis of continuing attraction. However, based on the behavior compatibility perspective, children who are atypical in interests or characteristics should be unlikely to be attracted to same-gender peers. Furthermore, this perspective is silent as to why behavior might vary over time, contexts, and situations. Unless children's attributions of compatibility change with situations, there is no clear explanation about why children's preferences for partners would change over differing contexts.

Thus, the behavioral compatibility perspective appears to offer strong explanations for how and why interactions among same-gender children are initiated at least on the basis of salient characteristics, and provides some explanation for why gender segregation might be maintained. The approach is less explicit about why affiliations would change over time but offers some explanations about why individuals might differ from one another. It appears that additional factors must be considered to provide a more robust explanation as to how behavioral compatibility and similarity might contribute to children's gender-segregated interactions.

Gender cognitive explanations

Categorical distinctions drawn about gender may provide strong and salient markers for defining members of one's in-group versus members of the out-group, thereby facilitating initial decisions about playmates. As Maccoby and Jacklin (1987) stated, "the mere fact of knowing that one is a boy or girl might lead a child to prefer other children known to be similar to the self" (p. 252). "I am a girl, and I want to be with other girls" would provide strong motivation for girls to segregate, for instance. Social psychologists label this "similarity-attraction" and posit that gender and other salient visible characteristics (e.g., age, race) contribute to selection processes: Children find peers they perceive as being similar to themselves as attractive and likeable (Epstein, 1989). Moreover, such similarity helps validate children's identities, attitudes, and behaviors, as well as providing a context for sharing mutually enjoyable activities (Aboud & Mendelson, 1996). In a variety of ways, children's recognition of the categories of "male" and "female" facilitates gender development and appears to contribute to gender segregation.

Once children can label themselves and others by gender group, a wide variety of group-related processes are initiated, such as preferences for one's own group over other groups (Maccoby, 1988; Martin & Halverson, 1981). There is evidence in support of this notion: toddlers who are able to label the sexes spend more time with same-sex peers than those who have yet to reach this milestone (Fagot, Leinbach, & Hagan, 1986). By preschool, children draw inferences and show preferences about others based on sex (Berndt, 1986; Martin, 1989; Yee & Brown, 1994).

Simply knowing one's gender group and the gender of others may only represent part of the preference to interact with same-sex others. In addition to coming to recognize gender categories, young children also use gender knowledge to help organize other information and to draw inferences about similarity. For example, children develop gender theories, that is, beliefs about a broadly-shared set of similarities within members of one gender group (Martin, 1994). Evidence for these gender theories about similarity within members of one sex comes from studies of novel toys. When young children are asked to rate their own preferences for novel toys and about how much they expect girls and boys to like the same toys, the expectation is that children would use gender-based reasoning. For instance, a girl might say, "if I like the toy, I expect other girls to like this toy but boys may not". The findings suggest that children make strong positive inferences about shared similarity within their own gender group, but do not make strong negative inferences about the other gender not liking the toys (Martin, Eisenbud, & Rose, 1995).

In a test of whether gender cognitions contribute to gender-segregated interactions, Martin and colleagues (Martin et al., submitted) assessed the degree to which behavioral similarity on rough and tumble play, activity level, and effortful control (regulation) predicted observed interactional patterns, and then tested whether gender cognitions about expected similarity with same-sex peers contributed to these patterns. Rough and tumble play was found to be related to the number of interactions with boys versus girls, and so were their gender cognitions. Children with stronger beliefs about same-sex similarity spent more time with same-sex partners. These findings suggest that both expected and experienced similarity play a role in gender segregation (Barbu, Le-Maner-Idrissi, & Jouanjean, 2000).

Gender cognitive explanations may be strongly implicated in the initial attraction same-gender children show one another; children use gender as a salient marker and then infer that same-gender children will share their interests, and this increases the likelihood of affiliating with same-gender peers. Gender cognitive processes may also relate to the maintenance of gender-segregated interactions to the extent that children continue to hold their gender-typed beliefs about girls and boys. In addition, gender cognitive explanations fill gaps in the literature by providing explanations about why children might show gender segregation even in situations that are not gender-typed (e.g., playing on the swings), and by providing explanations of why children might show gender segregation before they know the behaviors of their peer partners. However, less has been said about how these processes would relate to variability in gender-segregation over situations, or over individuals, but it is consistent with this approach to argue that individuals vary in the degree to which they adhere and accept gender cognitions, and this type of individual variation contributes to variability in tendencies to segregate by gender.

Peer group and institutional influences

Evolutionary, behavioral compatibility, and gender cognitive explanations for gender segregation each tend to focus on factors that direct individual children towards gender-segregated interactions. Although these explanations are the dominant ones found in the literature, it is also important to consider the fact that there are peer and institutional structures that contribute to gender-segregated interactions. We now consider these briefly.

How peers respond to children may also contribute to their tendencies to prefer interacting with same-gender children and certainly contribute to the maintenance of gender-segregated play. Peers typically show negative reactions to crossing of gender boundaries in toy choices and concerning peer playmates (Fagot, 1977, 1984; Lamb, Easterbrooks, & Holden, 1980), and these reactions appear to grow stronger over age, although only a few studies have examined this issue (Carter & McCloskey, 1984). In addition to children reacting negatively to cross-gender interests and to interactions with other-gender peers, they also tease one another about romantic interests when children affiliate with an other-gender playmate, and this has been demonstrated in even young children (Lloyd & Duveen, 1992).

Children appear to adhere to a homo-social norm, and recognize that others will disapprove of violations of the norm to befriend same-sex peers (Mehta & Strough, 2009). Even young children recognize that other people will be more likely to approve of same-gender playmates than other-gender playmates, and the extent to which children hold these beliefs relates to the degree to which they were observed in gender-segregated interactions over the course of several months (Martin, Fabes, Evans, & Wyman, 1999). Teasing about romantic relationships may have immediate effects and may also contribute to moving children's other-gender friendships underground. In preadolescence, children (especially socially competent ones) understand when it is acceptable to move into an other-gender group, such as in structured situations or when with a same-gender friend (Sroufe, Bennett, Englund, Urban, & Shulman, 1993).

Peer responses to children's behavior also have the potential to influence initial attraction. A girl who makes an overture to interact with another girl is less likely to receive negative feedback (either from the girl or other peers) than a girl who makes an overture to interact with a boy. Peers' responses may play a continuing role as children internalize peer expectations and admonitions. Very little attention has been paid to how peer responses might relate to variations in social interactions, but one study suggests that peers show more disapproval in some situations than in others; preadolescents are less likely to show disapproval for crossing gender boundaries when a group engages in this behavior or when it is done in structured settings (Sroufe et al., 1993).

Even less attention has been paid to broader explanations related to institutional practices (see Mehta & Strough, 2009). For instance, some after-school programs segregate children by gender and single-gender classrooms are increasing at rapid rates (Mael, Alonso, Gibson, Rogers, & Smith, 2005). Even in mixed-gender classrooms, teachers often make gender salient by having separate rosters for each gender (Lockheed & Harris, 1984), asking boys and girls to line up by gender, or by addressing them as "boys and girls" (Lloyd & Duveen, 1991). Such practices have been shown to highlight and emphasize the importance of gender and may also influence interactional patterns (Bigler, 1995). Children who spend more time in single-gender classrooms may become more practiced at interacting with same-gender peers, and so may seek out these peers outside of class. Most directly, these practices would influence some of the variations we observe across different contexts and likely serve to maintain gender segregation in some settings. It is less obvious, however, how institutional practices impact initial attraction other than by channeling same-gender children into the same environments, thereby reducing their peer partner choices.

An integration of perspectives

To develop a more comprehensive view of gender-segregated interactions, an integrative approach might be best: that is, one that encompasses evolutionary perspectives focused on adult roles and adaptability, consideration of the many types of behavioral compatibility, recognition that children hold strong gender cognitions about similarity within members of each gender group, and the recognition of the overt and subtle forms of peer and institutional pressures to develop and maintain gender segregated groups. Each of the mechanisms that have been discussed may contribute to young children's gender-segregated interactions and each of these factors also might be a consequence of such interactions. As noted previously, gender-segregated interactions and many of its purported causes likely act in a reciprocal manner, such that, for instance, communication style differences may contribute to initial segregation but also these differences become magnified over time by children learning to communicate with same-sex peers while failing to learn to communicate as well with other-sex peers (Leaper, 1994). Such reciprocity suggests that these are dynamic and on-going processes that occur across multiple timescales including moment-to-moment interactions and longer-term patterns of interaction (Martin & Ruble, 2009).

The extent to which each factor contributes to the process may vary over real and developmental time. Early in development, similarities in specific behaviors (e.g., disruptive behavior and social sensitivity), similarities in interests (e.g., dolls vs. cars), and possibly recognition of one's own gender group, may be important contributors to pulling same-gender children together and to pushing girls and boys apart. As children grow older and have more interactions with each other, children expand the range of experiences they have with same- and other-gender peers, providing more information for making choices about interactional partners. But, to the extent that they have experienced gender-segregated cultures, children may become increasingly comfortable in those worlds, may develop stronger and more gender-stereotyped expectations of both sexes, and these factors may continue to hold gender segregated patterns in place. However, developmental changes in the ability to think about others, increased romantic interests in the other gender, and individual differences in children work to ease gender boundaries as children grow older.

Individual Differences in Gender-Segregated Interactions

Together, the theories of gender segregation provide an adequate explanation of how girls and boys come to choose same-gender partners and why they tend to maintain interactions with same-gender partners over time. However, these theories have less to say about the range of individual variability that is seen in children's tendencies towards gender segregated interactions. At least in part, this may be because individual-level variation in gender segregation has only been recently recognized as a significant phenomenon.

In her initial work, Maccoby (1988; Maccoby & Jacklin, 1987) argued that individual variation in gender-segregated interactions was not an important consideration. She based this conclusion on data that showed that the likelihood of children being observed in gender-segregated interaction was not stable over time. Although the playground was clearly segregated by gender, she argued that there was not significant consistency from day to day in which children engaged in gender-segregated interactions. Boys and girls were observed to be segregated, but she argued that it was not the same boys and girls that segregated from one day to the next. As a result she focused more on group than individual difference processes as factors involved in gender segregation.

Maccoby based her conclusion on data that involved a relatively small number of observations taken at two points in time. When larger amounts of data have been collected over a longer period of time, the results show stronger consistency, suggesting that there is variation day to day but also consistency when longer periods of time are assessed. For instance, Martin and Fabes (2001) collected data over an entire school year and found considerable stability in children's tendencies to be observed in gender-segregated interactions. Moreover, their work (Fabes et al., 2003; Martin & Fabes, 2001) demonstrated important consequences (e.g., interactions became more gender-typed over time) as a result of the amount of segregated interactions children engaged in, and showed that these effects were "dose dependent"—the more children engaged in gender-segregated play, the greater the consequences. Martin and Fabes (2001) argued that individual differences in gender-segregated interactions were important and need to be explored to a greater extent.

Individual differences certainly play a significant role in the behavioral compatibility explanation. However, to date the link between behavioral compatibility and gender-segregated interaction is more theoretical than empirical. Moreover, it is likely that the relation between variation in individual characteristics and gender segregation is more complex than the theory purports and likely depends on the specific nature of the characteristic in question— certain behaviors may be attractive but only up to some point. For example, children who prefer highly active play may be attracted to other children who also prefer and are engaged in highly active play. Because boys typically are more active than girls, this would lead boys to prefer to interact with other boys—creating a context for gender-segregated play. However, even among boys, there is variation in activity level, and interactions can become aversive at very high levels of activity or when a person's activity level is consistently high and inflexible. These scenarios point out the importance of considering exactly how specific behaviors or interactional qualities may lead to gender segregation. To illustrate, we now turn to a discussion of regulation as an important temperamental individual difference factor in gender-segregated interactions (Fabes, 1994; Fabes et al., 1999).

Regulation, gender, and children's interactions

The quantity and quality of children's peer interactions has been theoretically and empirically linked to individual differences in children's ability to regulate their behaviors and emotions (Coplan, Prakash, O'Neil, & Armer, 2004; Fabes, 1994). These regulatory abilities are considered to be part of children's dispositional temperamental qualities and reflect relatively stable and enduring characteristics (Rothbart & Bates, 2006).

Eisenberg and Fabes (1992) proposed that social behaviors, including play-related behaviors, are related to optimal levels of regulation. Optimal regulation is thought to be associated with positive, adaptive behavior, although the strength of this relation is predicted to vary according to the intensity with which emotions, particularly negative emotions, are experienced. To date, several studies provide evidence to support the hypothesized relations between regulation and the qualities of children's interactions with peers (Fabes et al., 1999; Gleason, Gower, Hohmann, & Gleason, 2005; Rothbart, Ahadi, & Hershey, 1994). For example, Eisenberg et al. (1993) found that the combination of high emotional intensity and low attentional regulation was associated with low social skills and poor social status among peers and these relations held in a follow-up conducted two years later (Eisenberg et al., 1997).

What has not typically been considered in these data is the role that children's gender may play in the relations of regulation to interaction-related behaviors and outcomes. This is true despite the fact that there have been relatively consistent differences found in boys' and girls' abilities to regulate their behaviors and emotions—with girls typically perceived to be more competent at regulating their behaviors and emotions. Moreover, these gender differences in regulatory abilities have been found to appear early (Weinberg, Tronick, Cohn, & Olson, 1999) and to be relatively robust and stable (Else-Quest, Hyde, Goldsmith, & Van Hulle, 2006).

Such gender differences in regulation are likely to contribute to gender-segregation. For example, boys' more forceful, heavy-handed and active interactional qualities are relatively unappealing to girls. In contrast, the more regulated, controlled, and low-key interactional styles of girls are relatively unappealing to and ineffective with boys. In an effort to find complementary interactional styles, dispositional regulatory differences between boys and girls may lead them to interact more often with same- versus other-gender peers. Some evidence for this exists— when a broad construct of arousability was assessed (i.e., activity level, vigorousness, and impulsivity), more arousable boys showed more same-gender interactions (Fabes, 1994). However, as noted above, even among boys, dysregulated play styles are likely to be accepted only up to a point and then children may be at risk for peer rejection (in other words, fewer interactions with same-gender peers) as the intensity and frequency of dysregulated play leads to aversive levels of negative emotionality within the context of peer interactions.

Efforts to examine the relations between regulation and qualities of boys' and girls' peer interactions have been hampered because of measurement issues. For example, self-reports of regulation are susceptible to issues of comprehension and production for younger children, and self-presentational and demand characteristics for older children. Teacher and parent reports of children's regulation are likely to be significantly influenced by the overlap between regulation and quality of peer interactions—teachers and parents often use qualities of peer interactions to make judgments about children's dispositional characteristics. For example, children who frequently are alone are likely to be judged to be shy and inhibited. Or, children who have problems maintaining peer interactions are likely to be judged to have difficult temperaments. Moreover, parents' and teachers' judgments about children's behaviors and qualities are likely influenced by gender stereotypes with the same behavior leading to different judgments for boys than for girls (see Ruble et al., 2006). Given these issues, for much of the extant research it is difficult to disentangle regulatory and peer qualities.

Heart rate variability: An internal marker of regulation

Physiological assessments of regulation can be used to overcome some of these issues in measurement. Several researchers have suggested that heart rate variability (HRV) may be a useful internal marker of an individual's ability to regulate affective states and to emit age and socially appropriate responses (Fox, 1989; Izard, Porges, Simons, Haynes, et al., 1991). HRV involves the timing between heartbeats and is thought to reflect vagal control of the autonomic nervous system. High HRV reflects greater regulation, whereas low HRV reflects relatively weak regulation. HRV appears to provide an internal marker of individual differences in physiological responsiveness and adaptation to one's environments and does not depend on child or adult reports and issues associated with these. As such, HRV is considered to be a useful marker of individual differences in one's capability to physiologically react and self-regulate (see Porges, 1991).

Support for the usefulness of HRV in relation to children's socio-emotional behavior has been found. For example, Fabes and colleagues (1993) found that HRV was positively related to children's expressions of sympathy and inversely related to distress responses when exposed to someone in need of help. In addition, children with high HRV appear to be sociable, expressive, and uninhibited, whereas children with low HRV tend to be shy, fearful, and inhibited (Kagan, Reznick, & Gibbons, 1989). These findings suggest that individual differences in HRV might be useful markers of variations in how young children adapt to social interaction situations and to the quality of their interactions with peers. However, to date no one has directly examined these hypotheses, and HRV has not been examined in relation to gendered interactional patterns.

We explored the relation of HRV to children's interaction-related behaviors in an sample of 33 preschoolers (17 boys and 16 girls, mean age = 50 months). Three minutes of children's resting heart rate was acquired using a Nasiff CardioCard PC ECG System and AcqKnowledge software. Children were asked to lie down and be still while the heart rate data were collected (note: Children were previously introduced to the equipment and electrodes to reduce reactivity). After the child was calm (about a minute), three minutes of continuous HR data were collected. HRV was computed as the variance of the beat-to-beat heart rates. In addition, we collected children's nominations of peers they like to interact with, as well as brief observations of children's interactional partners over eight weeks of the fall semester (see Martin & Fabes, 2001 for a description of the observational procedures).

Because girls are less likely to tolerate dysregulated behaviors in the context of their social interactions, HRV might relate more to interacting with girls than to interacting with boys. Some evidence of this was provided in the correlation between HRV and children's nominations of preferred play partners. HRV was related to being nominated as preferred partners by girls but not by boys (for girls: rs = .51 for boy nominations and .60 for girl nominations). Thus, children with high HRV (who are relatively higher in self-regulation) were likely to be socially accepted as girls' (but not boys') partners than were those low in HRV. As such, girls show a preference for partners who are relatively high in regulation. Given the previously described gender differences in regulation, such preferences may contribute to gender-segregated interactional patterns.

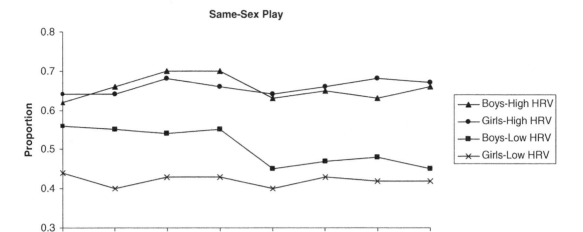

Fig. 17.1 Mean proportion of same-sex peer interactions over time: By level of heart rate variance and sex. (Note: HRV = heart rate variance).

Further evidence of the role of individual differences in regulation in children's interactional patterns was found in observations of peer partners. To explore this, we calculated the weekly proportion of same-gender interactions (out of the total number of social interactions/child) and plotted this over the eight weeks of the fall semester. We did this for high versus low HRV boys and girls (based on median split). As indicated in Figure 17-1, boys and girls who were high in HRV had relatively high and consistent proportions of same-gender interaction across the eight-week period. In contrast, girls who were low in HRV had consistent but relatively low proportions of same-sex interaction across the eight weeks. For boys low in HRV, they started out relatively high in interacting with other boys but dropped off about mid-way through the semester to levels comparable to girls low in HRV. Thus, girls who were low in HRV were relatively unaccepted by their female peers. Boys who were low in HRV were initially accepted but after a few weeks these boys also came to be accepted less by their male peers.

Next, based on the Eisenberg and Fabes (1992) model, we explored the possible role that negative emotionality may play in these findings. We did this by examining the degree to which children's interactions with peers involved the expression of negative affect. For each observed social interaction, observers used a four-point scale (1 = no expression to 4 = highly intense expression) to rate the level of negative affect that occurred during the interaction. We again plotted this over the course of each of the eight weeks of observations. As indicated in

Figure 17-2, boys and girls who were high in HRV were relatively low in the degree of negative affect within their social interactions, and negative affect was low and stable over the eight weeks.

In contrast, boys and girls who were low in HRV were observed to have had higher mean levels of negative affect during their social interactions. For low HRV girls, this level was consistent and stable over time. However, low HRV boys started at about the same level of negative affect as low HRV girls, but increased linearly across the eight week period.

These descriptive findings suggest that boys may not initially react negatively to dysregulated interactional styles and emotions (and may initially find such interactions attractive). Over time, however, they appear to find these interactional partners difficult and aversive and are less willing to include them in their social interactions due possibly to the escalating rates of negative affect. Thus, this is likely a reciprocally dynamic process in which low regulatory abilities contribute to dysregulated and negatively charged peer interactions. In turn, these strained peer interactions create a context that makes it more difficult for these children to interact effectively, contributing to even greater dysregulated interactions and enhanced chances of being excluded and mistreated by peers.

With our small sample size, caution is warranted in generalizing these findings. However, the findings are compelling and are consistent with the Eisenberg and Fabes (1992) model. As such, it appears that the combination of dysregulated tendencies and heightened negative emotion affect the quality and quantity of young children's peer

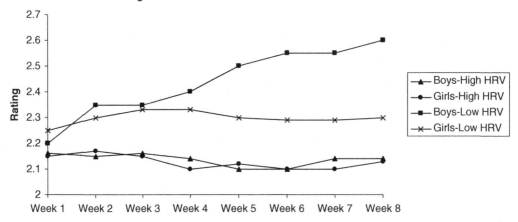

Fig. 17.2 Mean negative affect in peer interactions over time: By level of heart rate variance and sex. (Note: HRV = heart rate variance.)

interactions with same-gender peers. Moreover, although there is some similarity for boys and girls, the patterns suggest that the combination is more detrimental to boys over time.

Note, however, that even for those children who are relatively dysregulated and have relatively high levels of negative affect, the mean level of same-gender interaction is just below 50% of their social interactions. Thus, even for these children, they spend a considerable amount of time with same-gender peers and their patterns of gender-segregated interaction are not dramatically altered. What may occur is that these children tend to find same-gender peers who are like themselves as fewer same-gender peers will play with them. Thus, for these children, the breadth of their same-gender peer networks may be more restricted than is the case for children who are high in HRV. Overall, HRV as an indicator of regulation, activity level, impulsivity, and other dimensions of temperament may contribute to segregation and to the breadth of children's networks, and additional attention given to these topics is warranted.

Conclusions and Future Directions

The material reviewed and presented in this chapter highlights the important role that young children's gender plays in influencing social interaction patterns. Gender segregation is a powerful phenomenon that appears early in development and that is easily and readily recognized. Despite this, it is not well understood. The theories that have been put forward to explain it focus mainly on its initiation and less so on the factors and processes that maintain it. More attention to these processes is needed

if we are to fully understand gender segregation and its effects. Furthermore, more attention needs to be paid to the extent to which segregation varies over differing situations and in different forms of interaction (e.g., play vs non-play interactions).

The theoretical and empirical evidence reviewed in this chapter suggest that gender-segregation is both a group-level and an individual-level phenomenon. At the group level, gender segregation is known to be widespread and robust, emerging during early childhood and is evident across species, cultures, contexts, and developmental levels. Despite the ubiquity of gender segregation, variations occur across cultures, settings, time, and individuals, and exploring the factors associated with variations in this type of social interaction is interesting and important. Yet, relatively little is known about how and why variation occurs and what the meaning of such variation is— whether across individuals or across time and contexts. Thus, we suggest that one of the next frontiers in research on children's social play should be to address variability in children's interactions with same-gender peers and the consequences and outcomes associated with this variability.

Most explanations of gender segregation focus on the broad patterns of social interaction and are less concerned about individual differences in gender-segregated interactions. More attention needs to be paid to individual variability because evidence has accumulated suggesting that the consequences of gender-segregated interactions depend on the amount of time boys and girls spend playing with same-sex peers (Martin & Fabes, 2001). Thus, we need a better understanding of the factors that relate to the amount of time spent in gender-segregated interactions if we are going to understand its effects. One important individual difference is that of temperament, with data suggesting that self-regulation in particular warrants continued consideration. For example, Fabes et al. (1997) found that the consequences of interactions with same-gender peers were moderated by temperamental self-regulation and that the pattern of findings differed for boys and girls. For dysregulated boys, interactions with same-gender peers increased problem behaviors a semester later. In contrast, dysregulated girls who interacted with other girls were relatively unlikely to show problem behaviors. Thus, temperamental and contextual factors, in the forms of temperamental arousability and the tendency to interact with same-gender peers, differentially influenced preschool boys' and girls' social adaptation and adjustment. Moreover, the new data presented in this chapter also suggest an important interaction of temperamental regulation (HRV) and gender-based interactional patterns.

Such data support some intriguing considerations for future research and its application. First, the pattern of findings for girls suggests that highly arousable girls who interact more often with same-gender peers show relatively low levels of problem behaviors, implying that interacting with other girls can inhibit the likelihood (or expression) of problem behaviors. Thus, one avenue for helping girls improve their social adjustment is to encourage and facilitate their interactions with same-gender peers. For boys, it may be necessary to examine the characteristics of the same-gender peers they interact with and be more proactive in structuring the composition of these groups.

Findings such as these suggest that we need to better understand mixed-gender (interacting with both a boy and girl) and other-gender (interacting with only an other-gender peer or peers) interactions. Furthermore, more attention must be paid to the balance of the different types of interactions. Is a balance of same- and other/mixed-gender interactions beneficial because it promotes the learning of a wide range of interaction styles and behaviors? Knowing the consequences of each type of interaction and the importance of the balance of each type of social interaction would help in the development of peer-based interventions for young children, such as how to 'buddy' up children with peers in ways that could have positive effects on children's adjustment and well-being. We also need to better understand the consequences (both within and across gender groups) of children associating with peers

with specific qualities. For example, Fabes et al. (2010) found that high levels of interaction with prosocial peers subsequently led to enhanced positive and decreased negative emotions expressed within their peer interactions. Furthermore, additional research and theorizing is needed to discover in what ways and how peers influence one another. Although we are gaining a considerable understanding of how peers come to exert influence on one another from research conducted with older children and adolescents, the findings from recent research suggest that young children also influenced by peers. Because young children's peer interactions revolve primarily around play, the context of play is important to our overall understanding of gendered peer influences. Thus, we call for more attention to be paid to the consequences social play in early child development and suggest that researchers should not ignore the important effects of gender and individual differences in peer influence processes and effects.

Author's note

Support for the authors was provided in part by grants from the National Institute of Child Health and Human Development (1 R01 HD45816-01A1), the National Science Foundation (0338864), and the T. Denny Sanford Foundation.

References

Aboud, F. E. & Mendelson, M. J. (1996). Determinants of friendship selection and quality: Developmental perspectives. In W. M. Bukowski, A. F. Newcomb, & W. W. Hartup (Eds.), *The company they keep: Friendship in childhood and adolescence.* (pp. 87–114). New York: Cambridge.

Barbu, S., Le-Maner-Idrissi, G., & Jouanjean, A. (2000). The emergence of gender segregation: Towards an integrative perspective. *Current Psychology Letters: Behavior, Brain, and Cognition, 3*, 7–18.

Bem, D. J. (1996). Exotic becomes erotic: A developmental theory of sexual orientation. *Psychological Review, 103*, 320–335.

Berenbaum, S. A., Martin, C. L., Briggs, P., Fabes, R. A., & Hanish, L. D. (2008). Sex differences in children's play. In J. Becker, K. Berkley, N. Geary, E. Hampson, J. Herman, & E. Young (Eds.), *Sex on the brain: From genes to behavior.* (pp. 275–290). New York: Oxford University Press.

Berndt, T. & Heller, K. A. (1986). Gender stereotypes and social inferences: A developmental study. *Journal of Personality and Social Psychology, 50*, 889–898.

Bianchi, B. D. & Bakeman, R. (1978). Sex-typed affiliation preferences observed in preschoolers: Traditional and open school differences. *Child Development, 49*, 910–912.

Bigler, R. S. (1995). The role of classification skill in moderating environmental effects on children's gender stereotyping: A study of the functional use of gender in the classroom. *Child Development, 66*, 1072–1087.

Blakemore, J. E. O. & Centers, R. E. (2005). Characteristics of boys' and girls' toys. *Sex Roles, 53*, 619–633.

Burghardt, C. M. (2005). *The genesis of animal play: Testing the limits.* Cambridge, MA: MIT Press.

Carpenter, C. J., Huston, A. C., & Holt, W. (1986). Modification of preschool gender-typed behaviors by participation in adult-structured activities. *Sex Roles, 14,* 603–615.

Carter, D. B. & McCloskey, L. A. (1984). Peers and the maintenance of sex-typed behavior: The development of children's conceptions of cross-gender behavior in their peers. *Social Cognition, 2,* 294–314.

Challman, R. C. (1932). Factors influencing friendships among preschool children. *Child Development, 3,* 146–158.

Conradt, L. (1998). Measuring the degree of sexual segregation in group-living animals. *Journal of Animal Ecology, 67,* 217–226.

Coplan, R. J., Prakash, K., O'Neil, K., & Armer, M. (2004). Do you "want" to play? Distinguishing between conflicted shyness and social disinterest in early childhood. *Developmental Psychology, 40,* 244–258.

DiDonato, M., Martin, C. L., Hessler, E., Amazeen, N., Hanish, L. D., & Fabes, R. A (2009). Children's gendered behavior: Longitudinal and dynamic relations. Paper in preparation.

Eaton, W. O. & Yu, A. P. (1989). Are sex differences in child motor activity level a function of sex differences in maturational status? *Child Development, 60,* 1005–1011.

Eisenberg, N., & Fabes, R. A. (1992). Emotion, regulation, and the development of social competence. In M. S. Clark (Ed.), *Emotion and social behavior* (Vol. 14, pp. 119–150). Newbury Park, CA: Sage.

Eisenberg, N., Fabes, R. A., Bernzweig, J., Karbon, M., Poulin, R., & Hanish, L. (1993). The relations of emotionality and regulation to preschoolers' social skills and sociometric status. *Child Development, 64,* 1418–1438.

Eisenberg, N., Fabes, R. A., Shepard, S. A., Murphy, B. C., Guthrie, I. K., Jones, S., et al. (1997). Contemporaneous and longitudinal prediction of children's social functioning from regulation and emotionality. *Child Development, 68,* 642–664.

Else-Quest, N. M., Hyde, J. S., Goldsmith, H. H., & Van Hulle, C. A. (2006). Gender differences in temperament: A meta-analysis. *Psychological Bulletin, 132,* 33–72.

Epstein, J. L. (1989). The selection of friends: Changes across the grades and in different school environments. In T. J. Berndt & G. W. Ladd (Eds.), *Peer relationships in child development.* (pp. 138–187). New York: Wiley.

Fabes, R. A. (1994). Physiological, emotional, and behavioral correlates of gender segregation. In C. Leaper (Ed.), *Childhood gender segregation: Causes and consequences. New directions for child development* (Vol. 65, pp. 19–34). San Francisco: Jossey-Bass.

Fabes, R. A., Eisenberg, N., & Eisenbud, L. (1993). Behavioral and physiological correlates of children's reactions to others in distress. *Developmental Psychology, 29,* 655–663.

Fabes, R. A., Eisenberg, N., Jones, S., Smith, M., Guthrie, I. K., Poulin, R., et al. (1999). Regulation, emotionality, and preschoolers' socially competent peer interactions. *Child Development, 70,* 432–442.

Fabes, R. A., Hanish, L. D., Martin, C. L., Moss, A., & Reesing, A. (2010). *The effects of young children's affiliations with prosocial peers on subsequent emotionality in social interactions.* Manuscript submitted for publication.

Fabes, R. A., Martin, C. L., & Hanish, L. D. (2003). Young children's play qualities in same-, other-, and mixed-sex peer groups. *Child Development, 74,* 921–932.

Fagot, B. I. (1977). Consequences of moderate cross-gender behavior in preschool children. *Child Development, 48,* 902–907.

Fagot, B. I. (1984). Teacher and peer reactions to boys' and girls' play styles. *Sex Roles, 11,* 691–702.

Fagot, B. I., Leinbach, M. D., & Hagan, R. (1986). Gender labeling and the adoption of sex-typed behaviors. *Developmental Psychology, 22,* 440–443.

Fox, N. A. (1989). Heart-rate variability and behavioral reactivity: Individual differences in autonomic patterning and their relation to infant and child temperament. In J. S. Reznick (Ed.), *Perspectives on behavioral inhibition* (pp. 177–195). Chicago, IL: University of Chicago Press.

Geary, D. C. (1999). Evolution and developmental sex differences. *Current Directions in Psychological Science, 8,* 115–120.

Geary, D. C., & Bjorklund, D. F. (2000). Evolutionary developmental psychology. *Child Development, 71,* 57–65.

Gleason, T. R., Gower, A. L., Hohmann, L. M., & Gleason, T. C. (2005). Temperament and friendship in preschool-aged children. *International Journal of Behavior Development, 29,* 336–344.

Goble, P. M., Hanish, L. D., Fabes, R. A., Martin, C. L., Clary, L. K., & Palermo, F. (2008, April). *Exploring the influence of social context on young children's gender-typed activity choices.* Poster presented at the Third Gender Development Research Conference, San Francisco, CA.

Goodenough, F. (1934). Developmental psychology: An introduction to the study of human behavior. New York: Appleton-Century.

Hanish, L. D., Martin, C. L., Fabes, R. A., & Barcelo, H. (2008). The breadth of peer relationships among preschoolers: An application of the Q-connectivity method to externalizing behavior. *Child Development, 79,* 1119–1136.

Hayden-Thomson, L., Rubin, K. H., & Hymel, S. (1987). Sex preferences in sociometric choices. *Developmental Psychology, 23,* 558–562.

Hoffman, M. L. & Powlishta, K. K. (2001). Gender segregation in childhood: A test of the interaction style theory. *Journal of Genetic Psychology, 162,* 298–313.

Howes, C. (1988). Same- and cross-sex friends: Implications for interaction and social skills. *Early Childhood Research Quarterly, 3,* 21–37.

Howes, C. & Matheson, C. C. (1992). Sequences in the development of competent play with peers: Social and social pretend play. *Developmental Psychology, 28,* 961–974.

Izard, C. E., Porges, S. W., Simons, R. F., Haynes, O. M. et al. (1991). Infant cardiac activity: Developmental changes and relations with attachment. *Developmental Psychology, 27,* 432–439.

Kagan, J., Reznick, J. S., & Gibbons, J. (1989). Inhibited and uninhibited types of children. *Child Development, 60,* 838–845.

Kupersmidt, J. B., DeRosier, M. E., & Patterson, C. P. (1995). Similarity as the basis for children's friendships: The roles of sociometric status, aggressive and withdrawn behavior, academic achievement, and demographic characteristics. *Journal of Social and Personal Relationships, 12,* 439–452.

LaFreniere, P., Strayer, F. F., & Gauthier, R. (1984). The emergence of same-sex affiliative preferences among preschool peers: A developmental/ethological perspective. *Child Development, 55,* 1958–1965.

Lamb, M. E., Easterbrooks, M. A., & Holden, G. W. (1980). Reinforcement and punishment among preschoolers: Characteristics, effects, and correlates. *Child Development, 51,* 1230–1236.

Lansford, J. E., & Parker, J. G. (1999). Children's interactions in triads: Behavioral profiles and effects of gender and patterns of friendships among members. *Developmental Psychology, 35,* 80–93.

Leaper, C. (1994). Exploring the consequences of gender segregation on social relationships. In C. Leaper (Ed.), *Childhood gender segregation: Causes and consequences* (pp. 67–86). San Francisco: Jossey-Bass.

Lloyd, B. & Duveen, G. (1991). Expressing social gender identities in the first year of school. *European Journal of Psychology of Education, 6,* 437–447.

Lloyd, B. & Duveen, G. (1992). Gender identities and education: The impact of starting school. New York: St. Martin's Press.

Lockheed, M. E. & Harris, A. M. (1984). Cross-sex collaborative learning in elementary classrooms. *American Educational Research Journal, 21,* 275–294.

Low, B. S. (1989). Cross-cultural patterns in the training of children: An evolutionary perspective. *Journal of Comparative Psychology, 103,* 311–319.

Maccoby, E. E. (1988). Gender as a social category. *Developmental Psychology, 24,* 755–765.

Maccoby, E. E. (1990). Gender and relationships: A developmental account. *American Psychologist, 45,* 513–520.

Maccoby, E. E. (1998). *The two sexes: Growing up apart, coming together.* Cambridge, MA: Belknap Press.

Maccoby, E. E. (2000). Perspectives on gender development. *International Journal of Behavioral Development, 24.*

Maccoby, E. E., & Jacklin, C. N. (1987). Gender segregation in childhood. In W. R. Hayne (Ed.), *Advances in child development and behavior, Vol. 20.* (pp. 239–287). Orlando, FL: Academic Press.

Mael, F., Alonso, A., Gibson, D. Rogers, K., & Smith, M. (2005). *Single-sex versus coeducational schooling: A systematic review.* Washington, DC: US Department of Education.

Mallay, H. (1935). A study of some of the techniques underlying the establishment of successful social contacts at the preschool level. *Pedagogical Seminary and Journal of Genetic Psychology, 47,* 431–457.

Martin, C. L. (1989). Children's use of gender-related information in making social judgments. *Developmental Psychology, 25,* 80–88.

Martin, C. L. (1994). Cognitive influences on the development and maintenance of gender segregation. In L. Campbell (Ed.), *Childhood gender segregation: Causes and consequences. New directions for child development, No. 65.* (pp. 35–51). San Fransisco, CA: Jossey-Bass Inc, Publishers.

Martin, C. L., Eisenbud, L., & Rose, H. (1995). Children's gender-based reasoning about toys. *Child Development, 66,* 1453–1471.

Martin, C. L. & Fabes, R. A. (2001). The stability and consequences of young children's same-sex peer interactions. *Developmental Psychology, 37,* 431–446.

Martin, C. L., Fabes, R. A., Evans, S. M., & Wyman, H. (1999). Social cognition on the playground: Children's beliefs about playing with girls versus boys and their relations to sex segregated play. *Journal of Social and Personal Relationships, 16,* 751–771.

Martin, C. L., Fabes, R. A., Hanish, L. D., & Hollenstein, T. (2005). Social dynamics in the preschool. *Developmental Review, 25,* 299–327.

Martin, C. L., Fabes, R. A., Hanish, L. D., Leonard, S., & Dinella, L. (submitted). The roles of behavioral qualities and gender cognitions about perceived similarity to young children's same- and other-sex peer play.

Martin, C. L., & Halverson, C. (1981). A schematic processing model of sex typing and stereotyping in children. *Child Development, 52,* 1119–1134.

Martin, C. L., Kornienko, O., Schaefer, D., Hanish, L. D., Fabes, R. A., & Goble, P. (2010). The role of sex of peers and gender-typed activities in young children's peer affiliative networks: A longitudinal analysis of selection and influence. Paper in preparation.

Martin, C. L. & Ruble, D. N. (2009). Patterns of gender development. *Annual Review of Psychology, 61,* 353–381.

Martin, C. L., Ruble, D. N., & Szkrybalo, J. (2002). Cognitive theories of early gender development. *Psychological Bulletin, 128,* 903–933.

McGuire, J., Martin, C. L., Fabes, R. A., & Hanish, L. D. (March, 2007). The role of "gender enforcers" in young children's peer interactions. Poster presented at the Biennial Meeting of the Society for Research in Child Development, Boston, MA.

Mehta, C. M. & Strough, J. (2009). Sex segregation in friendships and normative contexts across the life span. *Developmental Review, 29,* 201–220.

Moller, L. C. & Serbin, L. A. (1996). Antecedents of toddler gender segregation: Cognitive consonance, gender-typed toy preferences and behavioral compatibility. *Sex Roles, 35,* 445–460.

Parten, M. B. (1932). Social participation among preschool children. *Journal of Abnormal and Social Psychology, 27,* 243–269.

Pellegrini, A. D. (2004). Sexual segregation in childhood: Review of evidence for two hypotheses. *Animal Behavior, 68,* 435–443.

Pellegrini, A. D. (2009). Research and policy on children's play. *Child Development Perspectives, 3,* 131–136.

Pellegrini, A. D. & Long, J. D. (2007). An observational study of early heterosexual interaction at middle school dances. *Journal of Research on Adolescence, 17,* 613–638.

Pellegrini, A. D., Long, J. D., Roseth, C. J., Bohn, C. M., & Van Ryzin, M. (2007). A short-term longitudinal study of preschoolers' (*Homo sapiens*) sex segregation: The role of physical activity, sex, and time. *Journal of Comparative Psychology, 121,* 282–289.

Porges, S. W. (1991). Vagal tone: An autonomic mediator of affect. In J. Garber & K. A. Dodge (Eds.), *The development of emotion regulation and dysregulation* (pp. 111–128). New York: Cambridge University Press.

Powlishta, K. K. (1995). Intergroup process in childhood: Social categorization and sex role development. *Developmental Psychology, 31,* 781–788.

Powlishta, K. K., Serbin, L. A., & Moller, L. C. (1993). The stability of individual differences in gender typing: Implications for understanding gender segregation. *Sex Roles, 29,* 723–737.

Rose, A. J. & Rudolph, K. D. (2006). A review of sex differences in peer relationship processes: Potential trade-offs for the emotional and behavioral development of girls and boys. *Psychological Bulletin, 132,* 98–131.

Rothbart, M. K. & Bates, J. E. (2006). Temperament. In N. Eisenberg, W. Damon, & R. Lerner (Eds.), *Handbook of Child Psychology* (6 ed., pp. 99–166). New York: Wiley.

Rothbart, M. K., Ahadi, S. A., & Hershey, K. L. (1994). Temperament and social behavior in childhood. *Merrill-Palmer Quarterly, 40,* 21–39.

Rubin, K. H. & Coplan, R. J. (1998). Social and nonsocial play in childhood: An individual differences perspective. In O. N. Saracho & B. Spodek (Eds.), *Multiple perspectives on play in early childhood education* (pp. 144–170). Albany, NY: State University of New York Press.

Rubin, K. H., Lynch, D., Coplan, R., Rose-Krasnor, L., & Booth, C. L. (1994). "Birds of a feather…": Behavioral concordances and preferential personal attraction in children. *Child Development, 65,* 1778–1785.

Rubin, K. H., Watson, K. S., & Jambor, T. W. (1978). Free-play behaviors in preschool and kindergarten. *Child Development, 49,* 534–536.

Ruble, D. N. & Martin, C. L. (1998). Gender development. In D. W. (Ed.), *Handbook of child psychology* (Fifth ed., Vol. 3). New York: J. Wiley.

Ruble, D. N., Martin, C. L., & Berenbaum, S. (2006). Gender development. In W. Damon (Ed.), *Handbook of child psychology* (Vol. 3, pp. 858–932). New York: Wiley.

Ruckstuhl, K. E. & Neuhaus, P. (2005). *Sex segregation in vertebrates: Ecology of the two sexes.* New York: Cambridge University Press.

Schelling, T. C. (1971). Dynamic models of segregation. *Journal of Mathematical Sociology, 1,* 143–186.

Serbin, L. A., Moller, L. C., Gulko, J., Powlishta, K. K., & Colburne, K. A. (1994). The emergence of gender segregation in toddler playgroups. In C. Leaper (Ed.), *Childhood gender segregation: Causes and consequences. New directions for child development, No. 65.* (pp. 7–17). San Fransisco, CA: Jossey-Bass Inc, Publishers.

Serbin, L., Tonick, I. J., & Sternglanz, S. H. (1977). Shaping cooperative cross-sex play. *Child Development, 48,* 924–929.

Smith, A. B. & Inder, P. M. (1993). Social interaction in same- and cross-gender preschool peer groups: A participant observation study. *Educational Psychology, 13,* 29–42.

Snyder, J., Horsch, E., & Childs, J. (1997). Peer relationships of young children: Affiliative choices and the shaping of aggressive behavior. *Journal of Clinical Child Psychology, 26,* 145–156.

Snyder, J., West, L., Stockemer, V., & Gibbons, S. (1996). A social learning model of peer choice in the natural environment. *Journal of Applied Developmental Psychology, 17,* 215–237.

Sroufe, L. A., Bennett, C., Englund, M., Urban, J., & Shulman, S. (1993). The significance of gender boundaries in preadolescence: Contemporary correlates and antecedents of boundary violation and maintenance. *Child Development, 64,* 455–466.

Strayer, F. F. & Santos, A. J. (1996). Affiliative structures in preschool peer groups. *Social Development, 5,* 117–130.

Thorne, B. (1993). *Gender play: Girls and boys in school.* New Brunswick, NJ: Rutgers University Press.

Weinberg, M. K., Tronick, E. Z., Cohn, J. F., & Olson, K. L. (1999). Gender differences in emotional expressivity and self-regulation during early infancy. *Developmental Psychology, 35,* 175–188.

Whiting, B. & Edwards, C. (1973). A cross-cultural analysis of sex-differences in the behavior of children age three through 11. *Journal of Social Psychology, 91,* 171–188.

Yee, M. & Brown, R. (1994). The development of gender differentiation in young children. *British Journal of Social Psychology, 33,* 183–196.

Social Play of Children with Adults and Peers

Carollee Howes

Abstract

The development of social play in children in the toddler and preschool periods of development is placed within a theoretical framework that integrates theories of development with theories of development within context, as well as with theories of cultural community. The practices and activities of a cultural community are the socio-cultural context for adult socialization of children's forms and styles of social play. Social play is a behavioral manifestation of social competence. Antecedents of social play development include the child capacities, relationships with adult caregivers, and the social and emotional climate of the social setting of play. Future research on social play needs to examine and understand the development of children's play when the play partner, adult or peer, comes from a different home cultural community than the child. Future social policy-directed research needs to examine trends in opportunities to play within programs for young children.

Keywords: cultural community; social competence; social play; attachment relationships; social climate; emotion regulation; communicative competence

Introduction: Theory of Social Play Development within Cultural Community

A theoretical formulation to explain and understand children's development of social play must be sufficiently complex to account for influences of individual children's development as well as for dyadic and group processes, and must include dimensions of the social context. In my work, I find that the theoretical framework that best meets these constraints integrates theories of development with theories of development within context, as well as with theories of cultural community (Howes, 2008, 2009).

Cultural community

A cultural community is defined as a grouping of people who share goals, beliefs, and everyday practices, and often a racial or ethnic identity (Rogoff, 2003). An assumption of Rogoff's theory of human development within cultural communities is that by participation in a cultural community children

develop similar social interaction forms and styles through joint participation with adults, siblings, and peers in common activities. These activities—for example, washing dishes, hearing stories, playing outside—are guided by adult practices also common to the cultural community (Howes, 2009; Rogoff, 2003).

SOCIALIZATION OF SOCIAL PLAY WITHIN CULTURAL COMMUNITIES

The practices and activities of a cultural community are the socio-cultural context for adult socialization of children's forms and styles of social play. By the kinds of activities, for example, going to the park or helping fix dinner; practices, for example, sitting on the floor and having a "tea party" or having a school age-sibling responsible for a toddler; and their interactions with the children, the adults communicate their beliefs about and goals for their children's development of social play. There is often general agreement within the adult members of a cultural community on the value of children's social play and the relative roles and importance of adult-child social play and of sibling and age-mate social play. For example, mothers in rural Mexico and many Mexican-heritage mothers in the United States believe that social play activities are best when composed of siblings and age-mates, and that while mothers may encourage their children to play versions of household work alongside them as they complete domestic tasks, mother–child play is not valued or in the repertoire of maternal practices (Farver & Howes, 1993; Howes, Guerra Wishard, & Zucker, 2008). Thus, one important aspect of the cultural community construct for understanding the development of social play with adults and children is that it assists in explaining the well-established differences in the importance adults of different cultural communities place on children's social play (Haight, Wang, Fung, Williams, & Mintz, 1999; Keller et al., 2004; Lancy, 2007). Participating with other community members in activities and practices of social play with adults, with age-mates, and/or with older children provides children within the cultural community opportunities for developing forms and styles of playing as well as their own beliefs about play. Differences in children's play forms and styles from different cultural communities reflect these differences in children's experiences of participation (Haight, 1999; Lancy, 2007).

DEVELOPMENT ROOTED WITHIN CULTURAL COMMUNITY IS NOT CROSS-CULTURAL RESEARCH

Cross-cultural research on social play (see chapters by Bock and Tudge et al., this volume) is designed to elaborate observed differences in social play between children and adults belonging to different cultural communities. While beliefs, activities, and practices are often common to a cultural community, they are also contested within cultural communities (Rogoff, 2003). In other words, there are individual differences within a cultural community in adult beliefs, activities, and practices. Some of these differences are dispositional; not all mothers enjoy the same mother–child activities. Other differences are based in differences in generation or experiences of cultural community members. For example, differences in immigrant Mexican mothers' ongoing social connections to their family of origin, and the physical location of this family, are associated with differences in maternal interaction with their children and their provision of activities

related to social play (Howes, Wishard Guerra, & Zucker, 2008; Howes, Wishard Guerra, & Zucker, 2007).

Furthermore, few adults belong to only one cultural community; in our sample of Mexican-heritage mothers, one group of mothers actively participated in a local all-Latino evangelical church group while others worked almost full-time as housekeepers and nannies for well-educated European-American families who promulgated a child-initiated style of interaction with children. These two groups of mothers were exposed to and expressed very different ideas about practices and activities around how to engage in social play with children. Mothers whose cultural community was primarily composed of Latinas were less likely to engage their children in play while the mothers who worked as housekeepers tended to believe that their children would do better in school if they played with them.

Most toddler and preschool children in the United States experience caregiving from adults who belong to different cultural communities. For example, in my Los Angeles neighborhood, many European-American infants and toddlers spend their weekdays with Latina nannies and weekends with their parents. Informal observations suggest that for these children, play activities and interactions with an adult who is their nanny is different in form and style than play with a parent. Furthermore, individual differences in play within both the nanny and parent groups are striking. In another Los Angeles neighborhood, African American caregivers increasingly care for Latino/a children and are challenged by differences in adult expectations for social interaction (Sanders, Deihl, & Kyler, 2007).

When children experience regular caregiving outside of their home in formal early childhood or informal childcare arrangements, cross-cultural community engagement between adults and children and between peers is common. Adults who work in early childhood programs often come from different cultural communities as children, experience learning activities and practices around play in their education and/or training to become teachers, and then must negotiate with other teachers the form and style of play activities and practices with children. Therefore, while understanding the development of social play by placing it within a cultural community construct is useful, it is not sufficiently comprehensive to explain children's development.

As a developmental psychologist researcher of play I believe that to fully explain children's development of social play, theories of development must be nested within theories of cultural community. Attachment theory provides an explanation of how children develop relationships and patterns of social interaction with adults and peers. (Thompson & Raikes, 2003). Theories of development in context assume that describing dimensions of the social context, family, and classroom environments will help explain differences in children's social play. In particular, a person-environment theoretical perspective suggests that social interaction with others can be understood by examining interactions between child characteristics and the environment in which social interaction is developed (Lochman, 2004).

Social Play as a component of social competence as defined by developmental psychology

There is a rich literature in developmental psychology that defines and examines children's social competence as a developmental construct (Vaughn et al., 2009; Waters & Sroufe, 1983). In this research tradition the specific behaviors included in social competence change with developmental period, but social competence remains a central developmental goal during each period. Children who are socially competent at any developmental period are able to engage with others in an affectively and cognitively flexible way to cooperatively and collaboratively achieve social goals of both partners (Bost, Vaughn, Washington, Cielinski, & Bradband, 1998; Howes, 1988; Rose-Krasnor, 1997; Vaughn et al., 2009).

Within this developmental psychology research tradition, social play with adults and children during the toddler and preschool developmental periods is seen as a behavioral manifestation of social competence. Within social play, participants share meaning; an intrinsic part of social play is to communicate to the partner the symbolic meanings embedded in the play. It requires cognitive and communicative skills for both the partners to understand and expand on meanings within the play, for example to communicate and understand that the green block stands for the tea cup and the blue block for the tea pot. Social play also requires children to regulate their emotions, for example to take turns "pouring the tea" and to express emotion, for example to express and communicate shared pleasure in the play. Social play also requires that children and their partners exercise reciprocity. Both partners need to want to play together for the play to be satisfying for both partners.

Control over the course of play is optimally balanced between partners in social play. Reciprocity and mutual pleasure in playing rather than frustration is more difficult to achieve when one partner is dominant. Often when adult or child partner would rather not be playing or when one partner is bossy, play ends (Howes, Unger, & Matheson, 1992). However, in some instances social play continues with one partner dominating. In peer social play, the joint negotiation of the play may be as important as the play itself (Doyle & Connolly, 1989). In adult-child social play, control may be unbalanced because the adult is teaching shared meaning by scaffolding the child's symbolic meaning, that is, "let's use the block as a tea cup" (Haight & Miller, 1992; Haight, Masiello, Dickson, Huckely, & Black, 1994; Lillard, this volume).

A final component of studying social play within a developmental psychology research tradition is that it is firmly rooted in observational methodology. Valid and reliable independent behavioral observations of children' social interaction during social play rather than teacher or parent reports of social play are the best predictors of concurrent and future social competence (Vaughn et al., 2009). Within developmental psychology, distinctions are made between core or universal developmental constructs and goals, activities, and practices that are particular to a cultural community (Howes & Wishard Guerra, 2009; Rogoff, 2003). Following this distinction, researchers assume that parents and teachers view social play through the lens of their cultural community while independent observations are assumed to capture core or universal constructs.

Social play components: Structure, affective content, and interactive content

STRUCTURE OF SOCIAL PLAY

The structural component of social play assumes that with development and experiences with play, the social play of children becomes progressively complex. The Peer Play Scale (Howes, 1980, 1988; Howes & Matheson, 1992), developed for peer partners but applicable to the structure of adult-child social play, is one system for describing social play structure. There are several assumptions underlying examining the structure of social play. One assumption is that a necessary condition for children to be considered engaged in social play is that adult observers can infer from their behavior that each child understands the other to be a social actor and that social actions between partners can be coordinated and communicated (Howes, 1983, 1996). Therefore, as a starting place, research had to establish that children behaved as if they had these understandings. A second assumption is that later development in social play could occur only as the child increasingly understood the role of the other, incorporated symbolic play, and communicated shared meaning (Howes et al., 1992). These assumptions are the bases for the behaviors that are captured in the Peer Play Scale. Initially, children are expected to show signs of each of these three components, but eventually they are expected to use them fluidly and communicate negotiations with each other about their play.

There are two key aspects of early social play that presuppose such social understanding: mutual social awareness and coordination of action. Together, these two markers represent the necessary components for what the Peer Play Scale called complementary and reciprocal play (Howes, 1980). Specifically, each play partner's actions reverse the actions of the other. A child chases his or her partner, then is chased. One child peeks at his or her partner, the partner says boo, and then peeks back. Research in cognitive and communicative development (Howes, 1988) suggests that the representational underpinnings of these understandings are present in children as young as the toddler developmental period. The next developmental step of social play structure is to incorporate symbols into shared play. Children in peer group settings first begin to use symbols or to play pretend alone or with a competent adult player (Brody & Stoneman, 1981; Howes, 1985; Howes & Matheson, 1992), but symbolic play soon enters the realm of peer play. Pretend play with a partner requires both that the child manipulate symbolic transformations and communicate the resulting symbolic meaning to a partner. The simplest form of social pretend play, called *cooperative social pretend play*, requires that children enact nonliteral role exchanges (Howes, 1985; Howes, Unger, & Seidner, 1989; Kavanaugh, this volume). Play partners integrate their pretend actions by using a familiar pretend theme or script such as a tea party. Similarly to complementary and reciprocal play, *cooperative social pretend play* requires that children reverse the actions of the other, but in this form of play, the actions are nonliteral or symbolic. The actions of the children presuppose that each partner understands that each player may engage in the symbolic behaviors. The children are able to share understanding about the symbolic meaning of their play, but this is communicated through the implicit script of the play rather than explicit talk about the play. For example, when a toddler offers a cup to a partner who is holding a pitcher, the child is engaged in a very simple form of social pretend play compared to the preschool-age child who discusses the play script, sets the table, brings festively dressed toy bears to the table, and gives the bears a tea party. Nonetheless, toddler-age children are beginning to understand the role of the partner in constructing social sequences.

Despite the new skills incorporated into cooperative social pretend play, it is only a rudimentary version of the well-developed fantasy play of older children that we label *complex social pretend play*. Toddlers have only just begun to transform symbols, so their transformations are not fluid and may be only partially developed. By preschool age, children's symbolic, linguistic, and communicative development permits meta-communication about social pretend play. Children can plan and negotiate the sequences of symbolic actions with fluidity, modify the script as it progresses, and step out of the pretend frame to correct the actions or script. These behaviors, such as those seen in a tea party for the toy bears, indicate the most structurally complex play captured in the Peer Play Scale.

Perhaps because it captures structural complexity rather than the content of peer play, the Peer Play Scale has been successfully used in cultures other than the United States. Farver has used the Peer Play Scale to describe and examine peer interaction in such diverse cultures and ethnic groups as Mexican children (Farver, 1992), Latino and African American Head Start children in Los Angeles (Farver & Frosch, 1996; Farver, 1996), Indonesian children (Farver & Howes, 1988; Farver & Wimbarti, 1995), and Korean American children (Farver & Shin, 1997; Farver, Kim, & Lee, 1995; Farver, 2000). Across studies, children's play was represented at each structural play level, and play forms emerged at similar ages.

AFFECTIVE CONTENT OF SOCIAL PLAY

When researchers use only the structural components to describe social play, aggressive acts are coded according to their complexity and the aggressive content is lost. Thus, an episode of social play that includes a reciprocal and complementary fight between partners receives the same structural complexity code as a run-chase game filled with laughter. Affective content is an important component of social play in the toddler and preschool periods. Shared positive affect is often a component of play between adults and children and within peer play. Furthermore, children as young as toddler age engage in social aggressive acts, including bullying and social withdrawal from adult and peer partners (Rubin, Burgess, & Hastings, 2002).

The affective content of social play can be captured using many different rating schemes. In my own work I use one devised by Ladd and colleagues because it captures a range of agonistic and aggressive behaviors (Ladd, Birch, & Buhs, 1999). In this rating scheme, behaviors including aggression toward the partner, exclusion from social activity, withdrawal from social activity, anxious/fearful behavior towards social partners, being a victim of aggression, prosocial behaviors towards partners, sociability with peers, dominating peers, and being distracted from social play can be coded and used to describe social play.

Including affective content as a component when describing social play is necessary for describing children as socially competent. Socially competent children do not aggress against or bully peers, nor do they anxiously withdraw from the give and take of peer games. Instead, socially competent children act as leaders in generating games, share toys, and generally engage in a prosocial manner. Using a definition of social competence that includes affective content, children who are socially competent with peers as toddlers and preschoolers tend to be socially competent as older children (Howes, Hamilton, & Phillipsen, 1998; Rubin, Burgess, Dwyer, & Hastings, 2003; Rubin et al., 2002).

INTERACTIVE CONTENT OF SOCIAL PLAY

Most recent research on social play among peers has focused on describing structural complexity and affective content. In contrast, research on social play between adults and children and between older and younger siblings has focused on actions of the partner that expand or inhibit play. Much of the literature on the development of social play in the United States suggests that children need interested and responsive adults in order to become proficient in complex social interaction, including playing pretend with peers (Haight & Miller, 1992; Thompson & Raikes, 2003). When mothers are directly involved in play interaction (i.e., becoming a play partner and scaffolding children's attempts to share symbols) rather than directing children's play actions, children are later rated as more socially competent (Farver & Howes, 1993; Goncu, Mistry, & Mosier, 2000; Haight et al., 1994; Haight et al., 1999; Howes, with Unger, & Matheson, 1992).

Haight and colleagues (Haight et al., 1999) argue that there are universal as well as cultural community-specific aspects to adult-child social play. For example, in most cultural communities mothers and children include objects in their play, perhaps to facilitate toddler-age children's transition from literal to symbolic play. The didactic (or not) content communicated by the adult partner in adult-child play appears to vary according to the adult's goal or intention in play. For example, Chinese mothers use adult-child social play to instruct children in manners while dominant-culture mothers in the United States use adult-child social play as a school readiness activity.

Siblings as well as parents and teachers engage in social play with younger children. Research on older siblings' play with younger siblings is a rich source of description of interactions that shape the play behaviors of the younger child (Dunn & Dale, 1984; Youngblade & Dunn, 1995). Sibling dyads can become very skillful at scaffolding one another's ideas; over time the story lines of sibling social play become more and more rich and sophisticated (Howe, Petrakas, & Rinaldi, 1998; Howe, Rinaldi, Jennings, & Petrakos, 2002; Howe, Rinaldi, & LeFebvre, 2005). These descriptions suggest that both siblings benefit from social play as they learn together how to create complex play sequences when one child is less skillful than the other.

SOCIAL PLAY AND GROUP FORMATION

The study of social development involves the study of individual children, of dyads, and of social groups. Social play between age-mates monitored by adult caregivers leads to the development of early friendships (Howes, 1983). Within groups of children, some dyads catch on to mutual games quickly and repetitively. With repeated experiences in mutual social play and if the play includes shared positive affect, friendship relationships develop. Likewise, some children are more sought after as play partners, and some children are avoided as play partners (Vaughn & Waters, 1981). With repetition of these patterns, children cluster into groups that are more and less popular with others, and a social status structure emerges. Furthermore, when children are playing, adults in formal children's groups tend to monitor but not facilitate positive interaction with peers (Howes & Galluzzo, 1994). In these ways children can be said to co-construct their peer group.

However, it is rare that all the children in the peer group are the same, or even similar, in home cultural communities, and therefore the peer group cultural community is important to consider when understanding the development of social play within children's peer groups. Children in the same classroom may not all speak the same home language and may come from homes with different ideas and expectations about how to engage with others, for example, to share materials or not to share. Construction of interactions and relationships among children from different home cultural communities may require different skills or different adult support than when all children are similar (Howes & Lee, 2007).

SOCIAL PLAY CHANGES FROM TODDLER-AGE TO PRESCHOOL PERIODS OF DEVELOPMENT

Simply from everyday observations in parks, neighborhoods, and children's programs, there is little doubt that toddler-age children's social play with peers is less sophisticated than preschool-age children's peer play and that younger children require and receive more scaffolding and direction within social play from adults or older playmates than older children. What is surprising is the lack of research, particularly recent research, on developmental changes in play across this period. Developmental trends reported in the older literature on social play include increases in symbolic or pretend play, greater emphasis on negotiating the roles within play, and decreases in objects within play (Doyle & Connolly, 1989; Haight et al., 1999; Howes & Matheson, 1992).

ARE SOCIAL PLAY WITH ADULTS AND SOCIAL PLAY WITH PEERS IN THE SAME DOMAIN OF DEVELOPMENT?

The development of children's early social play behaviors may be semi-independent of their relationships with adults (Hay, 1985). This argument is based in part on the premise that the construction of social interaction with a peer is different than with an adult. Peers, unlike adults, are not particularly more knowledgeable or skillful in social interaction than the infant or toddler. But, to their advantage, peers share interests in activities that adults generally do not. Most adults quickly tire of games like run-chase or jumping off a step.

As discussed earlier, adults from different cultural communities place more or less importance on adult-child social play. In some cultural communities, social play belongs to the world of children. Older siblings and neighborhood children are responsible for taking care of and playing with children (Goncu & Gaskins, this volume; Mosier & Rogoff, 2003; Rogoff, Mistry, Goncu, & Mosier, 1993; Tudge et al., this volume). In other cultural communities, social play between mothers and children is seen as extremely important (Haight et al., 1994).

The perspective that peer relations are primarily constructed within peer groups is not necessarily at odds with an attachment theory perspective. It is possible that early adult-child attachment relationships serve to orient children towards or away from the peer group. Children with secure adult-child attachment relationships may perceive peers as potentially fun and interesting social partners, enter into peer play, and, with experience, become socially skilled. Children with insecure adult-child attachments may perceive peers as hostile or threatening and withdraw from or aggress towards peers. Once a child has withdrawn from peers or has constructed antagonistic patterns of interaction and relationships, it may be especially difficult to develop alternative behaviors with peers (Howes & Phillipsen, 1998). Unlike some sensitive adults who can understand that what appear to be maladaptive behaviors are instead based on mistrust, peers may perceive the potential peer partner as unpleasant and to be avoided. A skillful adult can work to disconfirm a child's hostile or withdrawing behavior. A peer is more likely to react in ways that maintain the maladaptive sequences.

Antecedents of Social Play Development
The development of social play from an attachment theory perspective

Attachment theory informs the framework of this chapter primarily through the assumption that the affective nature of children's relationships with adults, both parents and teachers, influences their development of social competence, including social play (Howes & Spieker, 2008; Thompson & Raikes, 2003). A central assumption of attachment theory is that representations of relationship—internal working models of relationships—are formed through iterative interactions between social partners. Thus the affective nature of social play episodes between children and their caregivers are part of the interactive materials that a children draws upon in forming a representation of the other. Children who have secure representations of the interactive other are more likely to approach potential partners with the expectation of positive social interaction. These expectations, in turn, lead to more positive social play sequences. Moreover, children who have developed more secure relationships with their caregivers are more fun to play with, increasing the experiences a child has in social play. Positive experiences with social play lead in turn to increasing sophistication in the structure of play (Slade, 1987).

While having a secure adult-child relationship is not independent of engaging in positive adult-child play, the playmate function of adult-child relationships is independent of the caregiving function of adult-child relationships (Cassidy, 1999). Children can and do have secure mother–child attachments in families where mother–child social play is infrequent (Howes et al., 2008). Secure adult-child attachment relationships in these instances may serve primarily as a secure base from which the child feels comfortable exploring social play with others (Howes & Spieker, 2008). This may be particularly true for children whose mother–child attachment was constructed within a cultural community where adult-child social play is not a parental goal. Children who have secure mother–child attachments may readily engage in social play with others upon entering an early childhood education social group where the children and adults do engage in adult-child play (Howes et al., 2008).

Many if not most children in contemporary United States families engage in social play with adults and peers who are not family members. Children are taken care of by nannies, by family childcare providers, or by teachers in center-based early childhood programs. In these instances the children's peer group consists of the other children at the playground where the nannies hang out or the other children in the childcare setting.

When the practices of the adults in charge of children are very different from practices at home, and particularly if the differences are confounded by discrimination, children fare in better social situations if there are bridges between home and the setting of play (Baker, 1999; Johnson et al., 2003). For example, young children who are still learning how to play with peers may find forming play sequences and relationships across language groups and interaction styles challenging. A trusted adult, perhaps one similar in ethnic and/or language background, may serve as a bridge because the children can use an adult with familiar interaction styles as a base for social play.

There is some evidence that having a childcare teacher who is an ethnic match is particularly important for children who are less able to modulate their negative emotions. For example, African American and Latino children who were observed to have difficult interactions with adults and peers within a few weeks of entering new childcare classrooms were observed to have less positive teacher-child

relationships six months later only when their teacher was different in ethnic background (Howes & Shivers, 2006). Within this same sample, African American children were observed as less aggressive when their peers were also African American rather than of another ethnic background (Howes, Sanders, & Lee, 2008). African American teachers may be particularly significant for African American children because of a common belief that teachers are responsible for mothering all of the children of the wider community (Sanders et al., 2007). Likewise, beliefs in the differential roles of teacher and mothers and of play within Latino communities may lead to Latina teachers being relatively less willing to take on a mothering role rather than that of a respected authority (Arcia & Johnson, 1998; Halgunseth, Ispa, & Rudy, 2006).

Social play in formal children's groups: The role of particular experiences

With notable exceptions (Farver & Howes, 1993; Haight, 1999; Howes, Wishard Guerra et al., 2008), most research on social play with adults and peers in the United States is based on children's interactions in early childhood education or childcare settings. Children in these settings tend to be in relatively small, single-age groups. Children tend to remain with these potential playmates for a school year, although many children remain in the same early childhood setting for two or three years. In this case, children who remain tend to be in the same peer group across time with some additions and losses, and usually with a different teacher. In these situations children construct patterns of play over time that are particular to the peer group (Howes & Ritchie, 2002). Children who remain longer in these peer groups tend to be rated as more socially competent than children who join the peer group after it is well established (Howes, 1988).

The social climate of social play

Children's play with others is not only nested within a cultural community, it is in the most proximal sense embedded within a social climate, of a family or in the case of formal children's groups, a classroom. Family climates are characterized by social interactions that range from calm and harmonious to hostile and belittling and from vivacious to withdrawing. Warm and harmonious parenting interactions contribute to children's competent play interactions (Ross & Howe, 2008). Parents also can facilitate opportunities for children to develop and maintain positive social play with others through their social planning and supervision of children's activities. Some parents plan supervised play activities while others leave children's opportunities for social play with others up to chance. Some families have rich and complex social networks that include other children and adults while other families are socially isolated. Some parental discipline practices indirectly foster harmonious social play by modeling social skills and conflict resolution while others do not.

Consistent with a cultural communities perspective, there are of course ethnic and language differences in home environments. However, relations between positive home climates within cultural communities and children's development of social competence tend to be similar across ethnic and language groups (Bradley, Corwyn, Burchinal, McAdoo, & Coll, 2001; Bradley, Corwyn, McAdoo, & Coll, 2001; Duncan et al., 2007).

Individual children's social play within classrooms is embedded within the social climate of the classroom. Interactions between children and teachers and the affective tone the teacher sets for the entire group contribute to the social and emotional climate of the classroom. Thus social play within classrooms that are generally negative and conflictual tends to be negative in affective content (Fabes, Hanish, & Martin, 2003). Within classrooms characterized by harmonious child-teacher interactions and where the teacher effectively manages the classroom so that children feel included and safe, children tend to engage in social play with positive affective content (Howes & Ritchie, 2002). Social pretend play themes in these peer groups may be scary or wild, but the interactions among children in the play are harmonious.

Interactions between children and teacher and among peers, as well as the tone the caregivers set for the entire group, all contribute to the social and emotional climate of the classroom. Imagine a classroom in which most of the interactions are harmonious and respectful, in which children and adults work together on projects, in which a child who is distressed or frustrated is comforted and helped, and in which laughter and other expressions of positive affect predominate. Contrast this with a classroom in which children are ridiculed for being different; talked to and touched in a harsh, rejecting manner; compete with each other rather than help each other; and where the general tone includes mistrust and anger. We can imagine that the social play of children would take different paths in these two extremes. Because for the child the classroom is

ultimately an experience of "living" within a group; it is impossible to understand the social play development of a child as isolated from the group.

The social-emotional climate of the classroom can enhance or impede the social development of children. Although there is an extensive literature describing the interactions of teachers and children and classroom management strategies (see Pianta, Hamre, & Stuhlman, 2002 for a review of this literature), only recently has attention turned to the general climate that is created within the classroom from the interactions of participants. Several recent large-scale observational studies of classrooms for young children identified two dimensions of classroom climate: instructional support and social-emotional support (Hamre & Pianta, 2005; La Paro, Pianta, Hamre, & Stuhlman, 2002; NICHD ECCRN, 2002; Pianta et al., 2005). Classrooms that score high on the measure of social-emotional support are pleasant places where there are conversations, spontaneous laughter, and enjoyment expressed as children and teachers engage in various activities and interactions. Teachers are warm and sensitive to all of the children; they are emotionally and physically involved with the children's activities and they rarely are intrusive, angry, or annoyed. In these classrooms there are clear but flexible rules and expectations for classroom routines. Children tend to follow these rules so that teachers rarely have to employ control techniques. In contrast, classrooms with negative climates are characteristically filled with relational as well as physical aggression among children and hostile conflictual interactions between children and teachers. Children in these classrooms have few options for activities. Interactions and activities are adult-driven and most often based on behavioral management of out-of-control children.

Classrooms with positive emotional climates are associated with positive teacher-child relationships (Howes, 2000); children in classrooms with high scores for positive emotional climate are likely to construct positive relationships with teachers. But beyond the secure base that positive teacher-child relationships provide, a positive emotional climate appears to facilitate social play development by providing rules for engagement that promote prosocial rather than hostile peer social play. If it is difficult for young children to construct play sequences when they are just developing the capacity to do so, it is even more difficult to do so when they are interrupted by conflict occurring around them. In one longitudinal study, children who experienced positive emotional climates as three-year-olds were also likely to have positive peer relationships as second graders (Howes, 2000).

Positive social-emotional climates also can facilitate positive peer social play in newly formed peer groups. In most large-scale studies of preschool classrooms, climate scores are on the average fairly positive, above the median of the scale (see for example Pianta et al., 2005). However, in our recent study of children entering preschool, the average social-emotional climate scores were near the negative end of the scale (Howes & Shivers, 2006). As such, it was a challenge for children in these classrooms to create relationships and complex play within these newly formed peer groups (Howes, Sanders et al., 2008).

Individual children's development

Children have individual differences in dispositions and skills, in sociability and wariness, in emotional regulation, and in communicative skills, all of which influence their social play with adults and peers.

DISPOSITIONS AND SOCIABILITY

Some children approach social play with others with enthusiasm. They run, wiggle, and shout their way into children's formal groups. They can't wait to climb, run, and explore the block corner. Others are slow to find their place, sad to leave the side of the parent, and slow to find playmates and activities pleasurable. Children who are able to strike a balance between their own desires and interests and those of the other children and caregivers are those who are able to regulate and control their emotions and impulses (Eisenberg, Fabes, & Losoya, 1997; Fabes et al., 1999; Rothbart, Ahadi, & Hershey 1994). If children have these more sociable dispositions or are helped to develop them, they are more likely to engage in harmonious social play interactions. Children who are shy or slow to warm may fare better when parents or teachers provide support for their social play interactions with others (Coplan, this volume; Coplan & Prakash, 2003).

EMOTIONAL REGULATION

Children's emotional regulation development also contributes to positive social play with peers once the child has entered the play group (Eisenberg, Vaughan, & Hofer, 2008). Children who have difficulty modulating their negative emotions are more likely to engage in aggressive social interactions with peers, while children who have more emotional regulation skills are more likely to engage in interactive

social play and sociable behavior (Dunn, 2004; Spinrad et al., 2004). Children's ability to regulate their emotions and engage with their peers may be particularly important when adults in classrooms are less likely to monitor and facilitate children's encounters (Deynoot-Schaub & Riksen-Walraven, 2006).

LANGUAGE AND COGNITIVE DEVELOPMENT

In addition to dispositions and regulation, children more skillful in verbal, nonverbal, and emotional decoding are more able to communicate with peers and teachers or caregivers (Dunn, 2004; Spinrad et al., 2004). Sharing meanings and engaging in verbal exchanges are important aspects of young children's play sequences (Brenner & Mueller, 1982; Howes, Sanders et al., 2008; Mueller, Bleir, & Krakow, 1977). Furthermore, children who are more language and communication proficient are more able to engage in prosocial social play with peers (Ensor & Hughes, 2005). Not understanding what peers are saying can inhibit children's ability to engage in mutual social play because they do not understand how to play or they miss verbal cues for playing. Children who cannot communicate with their peers may engage in conflict with or withdrawal from peers. Communicative skills may interact with dispositions; for example, in one study shy preschool-age children who had larger expressive vocabularies seemed to have more confidence in their interactions with peers than shy children with smaller expressive vocabularies (Coplan & Armer, 2005).

Developmental Consequences of Social Play Development
Continuity in social competence

Assuming that social competence is a developmental construct and that social play is a marker of social competence in the toddler and preschool periods leads to the expectation that children who engage in relatively high frequencies of social play with positive affective tones as younger children will be rated as more socially competent as older children. These assumptions are supported in a number of longitudinal studies from the toddler to the school-age periods of development (Howes & Phillipsen, 1998, Early Child Care Research Network, 2008). Although, to my knowledge, there are not research studies that support this, it also seems reasonable that children who early on master the social interactive skills found in early social play will be able to engage in social conversations, games, and eventually adult collegial interactions with others.

Consequences across developmental domains

The consequences of children's engaging in early social play across developmental domains are not as straightforward. There is some evidence to support associations between opportunities to engage in social play and children's later school readiness, especially in the areas of narrative and reading development, persuasive talk and argument, and emotion regulation. Social play is linked to narrative development and hence to success in literacy and reading through proto-narratives. These are collaborative undertakings co-constructed by two or more participants in an effort to interpret and anticipate experiences together (Gleason & Melzi, 1997; Lucariello & Nelson, 1987; McCabe, 1997; Ochs, 2001). Similarly to social pretend play, proto-narratives are easier for very young children to produce when their partner is more knowledgeable about narratives. When the toddler is engaged with an adult or older child, they can rely on extensive scaffolding and prompts of their more advanced conversational partners, both in terms of the technical structure of their narratives and in terms of content orientation (Gleason & Melzi, 1997; Imbens-Bailey, 1997; Ochs, 2001; Snow & Imbens-Bailey, 1997). For these reasons, research on proto-narratives is almost exclusively placed within the context of adult-child talk. However, in the preschool context when literacy props are placed within creative play activity centers (such as dress-up or coloring table), oral narratives, with the assistance of the teacher, begin to transform into more formal written narratives. Social play development is linked to proto-narrative development because complex social pretend play requires the verbal negotiation of a script and differentiated roles. These scripts provide opportunities for children to jointly construct narratives (Howes & Wishard-Guerra, 2004).

Experiences in social pretend play also may be implicated in another school readiness skill—talk that is shaped to assist in the comprehension of the listener as well as persuading the partner to take on the other's point of view (Connolly & Doyle, 1984; de Lorimier, Doyle, & Tessier, 1995; Doyle & Connolly, 1989; Doyle, Doehring, Tessier, deLorimier, & Shapiro, 1992; Dunn & Dale, 1984; Farver, 1992b; Howe et al., 2002). In particular, Doyle's studies of the complex and lengthy negotiations that precede and interrupt social pretend play suggest that within complex social pretend play, children learn to persuade and resolve such discrepancies (de Lorimier et al., 1995; Doyle & Connolly, 1989; Doyle et al., 1992).

When children experience resolving difference in imagined and communicated meaning of the play, they also have the satisfaction of play continuing. When these differences are not resolved, children have less experience in emotion regulation. As we have discussed, children who are better able to regulate their own emotions or who have monitoring adults who can help them regulate negative emotions are better able to engage in the initiating, cooperating, and negotiating involved in more complex forms of social play. Because play will end if children "fall apart" in tantrums or retreat in sulks, for some children social play becomes a powerful incentive for emotion regulation. If children are willing to adapt their behavior in order to keep on playing, they can experiment with strategies that are more or less successful in continuing the play. These opportunities for learning can help children develop emotion regulation, another component of school readiness.

Conclusion and Commentary on State of Theory and Research in Social Play

The study of play, in general, draws from many theoretical traditions. In this chapter I have introduced a relatively new framework for examining the development of social play in young children. This framework integrates a relatively old theoretical and empirical research tradition—the development of social competence within developmental psychology—with a relatively new one: human development within cultural communities. The older research tradition of social competence drew primarily on studies of children within the dominant culture of the United States, and tended to assume that all children, regardless of cultural community, developed play in similar universal ways. A review of this literature suggests that there is some truth to that assumption in terms of some universal developmental features of social play. However, nesting the development of social play within a cultural community perspective provides a theoretical perspective for examining cultural community specificity in children's social play. I hope that future research will continue this analysis.

In terms of future directions for research on children's development of social play, I perceive two pressing and difficult problems to address. The first issue is to further examine and understand the development of children's play when the play partner, adult or peer, comes from a different home cultural community than the child. Social policy advocates tend to argue that for very young children, particularly minority children or poor children, optimal development may occur when the child remains within their home cultural community (Johnson et al., 2003). The case of children's development of social pretend play may provide a counter-argument. In one of our studies, Mexican-heritage children who did not engage in social pretend play at home or in informal childcare settings with Mexican-heritage caregivers did begin to play social pretend with peers when enrolled in center-based childcare programs with European-American teachers trained in traditional child development ideas of learning through play (Howes, Wishard Guerra & Zucker, 2008).

The second pressing problem involves the larger social context of where children play. For many years researchers have assumed that children's groups in childcare, early education, and preschool would be where children played with peers. In this chapter we have reviewed numerous studies that suggest social play within these settings is enhanced with positive social and emotional climates. But what if there is no time to play within these programs, as anecdotal reports suggest that programs are providing relatively little unstructured time for children to play? In 2004 we compared children's time in social pretend play across 20 years of data collection using three comparable studies with data collected at ten-year intervals (Howes, Wishard, & Guerra, 2004). The children who participated in these studies, consistent with the child population of Los Angeles, were predominantly Latino (45% to 60%) and African American (20% to 25%), with a small percent Asian American and the remainder white (Howes, 1988; Howes & Matheson, 1992; Howes & Shivers, 2006). The children in these studies were all enrolled full-time in center-based childcare programs, including a substantial number of programs sampled at all three time points. Complementary and reciprocal play and cooperative social pretend and complex social pretend play were defined using the same coding scheme across studies. This analysis found that the proportion of time spent in social play and social pretend play decreased from almost half of the observation time to less than 10% of the observation time over this 20-year period.

In conclusion, as researchers we know a great deal about the development of social play in young children and about the antecedents of such play. In a world that appears to be giving children less time to play, it is noteworthy to have this Handbook. It is my hope that it will lead to a rich and current body of contemporary research on children's play.

References

Arcia, E., & Johnson, A. (1998). When respect means to obey: Immigrant Mexican mothers' values for their children. *Journal of Child and Family Studies, 7*, 79–95.

Baker, J. A. (1999). Teacher-student interaction in urban at-risk classrooms: Differential behavior, relationship quality, and student satisfaction with school. *Elementary School Journal, 100*, 57–70.

Bost, K. K., Vaughn, B. E., Washington, W. N., Cielinski, K. L., & Bradband, M. R. (1998). Social competence, social support, and attachment: Demarcation of construct domains, measurement, and paths of influence for preschool children attending Head Start. *Child Development, 68*, 192–218.

Bradley, R. H., Corwyn, R. F., Burchinal, M., McAdoo, H. P., & Coll, C. G. (2001). The home environments of children in the United States Part II: Relations with behavioral development through age thirteen. *Child Development, 72*, 1868–1886.

Bradley, R. H., Corwyn, R. F., McAdoo, H. P., & Coll, C. G. (2001). The home environments of children in the United States Part I: Variations by age, ethnicity, and poverty status. *Child Development, 72*, 1844–1867.

Brenner, J., & Mueller, E. (1982). Shared meaning in boy toddler peer relations. *Child Development, 53*, 380–391.

Brody, G., & Stoneman, Z. (1981). Selective imitation of same age older and younger peer models. *Child Development, 52*, 717–720.

Cassidy, J. (1999). The nature of the child's ties. In J. Cassidy & P. Shaver (Eds.), *Handbook of attachment* (pp. 3–20). New York: Guilford.

Connolly, J. & Doyle, A. (1984). Relation of social fantasy play to social competence in preschoolers. *Developmental Psychology, 20*, 797–806.

Coplan, R. J. & Armer, M. (2005). Talking yourself out of being shy: Shyness, expressive vocabulary, and socioemotional adjustment in preschool. *Merrill Palmer Quarterly, 52*, 20–41.

Coplan, R. J. & Prakash, K. (2003). Spending time with teacher: Characteristics of preschoolers who frequently elicit versus initiate interactions with teachers. *Early Childhood Research Quarterly, 19*, 1–16.

de Lorimier, S., Doyle, A.-B., & Tessier, O. (1995). Social coordination during pretend play: Comparison of nonpretend play and effects on expressive content. *Merrill Palmer Quarterly, 41*, 497–516.

Deynoot-Schaub, M. J., & Riksen-Walraven, J. M. (2006). Peer contacts of 15-month-olds in child care: Links with child temperament, parent–child interaction and quality of child care. *Social Development, 15*, 709–729.

Doyle, A.-B. & Connolly, J. (1989). Negotiation and enactment in social pretend play Relations to social acceptance and social cognition. *Early Childhood Research Quarterly, 4*, 289–302.

Doyle, A. B., Doehring, P.,Tessier,S., deLorimier, D., & Shapiro, S. (1992). Transitions in children's play: A sequential analysis of states preceding and following social pretense. *Developmental Psychology, 28*, 137–144.

Duncan, G. J., Dowsett, C. J., Classens, A., Magnuson, K., Huston, A., Klebanov, P., et al. (2007). School readiness and academic achievement. *Developmental Psychology, 43*, 1428–1446.

Dunn, J. (2004). *Children's friendships.* Malden, MA: Blackwell.

Dunn, J. & Dale, N. (1984). I a Daddy: 2-year-olds' collaboration in joint pretend with a sibling and with a mother.

In I. Bretherton (Ed.), *Symbolic play* (pp. 131–158). New York: Academic.

ECCRN, N. (2008). Social competence with peers in third grade: Associations with earlier peer experiences in child care. *Social Development, 17,* 419–454.

Eisenberg, N., Fabes, R. A., & Losoya, S. (1997). Emotional responding: Regulation, social correlates, and socialization. In P. Salovey & D. J. Sluyter (Eds.), *Emotional development and emotional intelligence: Educational implications* (pp. 129–163). New York: Basic Books.

Eisenberg, N., Vaughan, J., & Hofer, C. (2008). Temperament, self regulation and peer social competence. In K. H. Rubin, W. M. Bukowski, & B. Laursen (Eds.), *Handbook of peer interactions, relationships, and groups* (pp. 473–489). New York: Guilford.

Ensor, R. & Hughes, C. (2005). More than talk: Relations between emotional understanding and positive behavior in toddlers. *British Journal of Developmental Psychology, 23,* 343–363.

Fabes, R. A., Eisenberg, N., Jones, S., Smith, M., Guthrie, I., Poulin, R., et al. (1999). Regulation emotionality and preschoolers' socially competent peer interactions. *Child Development, 70,* 432–442.

Fabes, R. A., Hanish, L. D., & Martin, C. L. (2003). Children at play: The role of peers in understanding the effects of child care. *Child Development, 74,* 1039–1043.

Farver, J. (1992). Communicating shared meaning in social pretend play. *Early Childhood Research Quarterly, 7,* 501–516.

Farver, J., & Howes, C. (1988). Cross-cultural differences in peer interaction: A comparison of American and Indonesian Children. *Journal of Cross-Cultural Psychology, 19,* 203–215.

Farver, J. M., & Howes, C. (1993). Cultural differences in American and Mexican mother–child pretend play. *Merrill Palmer Quarterly, 39,* 344–358.

Farver, J. A., & Shin, Y. L. (1997). Social pretend play in Korean- and Anglo-American preschoolers. *Child Development, 68,* 544–556.

Farver, J. A. M. (1992). An analysis of young American and Mexican children's play dialogues. In C. Howes (Ed.), *The collaborative construction of pretend* (pp. 55–66). Albany. NY: SUNY Press.

Farver, J. A. M., & Frosch, D. (1996). L. A. Stories: Aggression in preschoolers' spontaneous narratives after the riots of 1992. *Child Development, 67,* 19–32.

Farver, J. A. M., Kim, Y. K., & Lee, Y. (1995). Cultural differences in Korean- and Anglo-American social interaction and play behaviors. *Child Development, 66,* 1088–1099.

Farver, J. A. M. & Lee-Shin, Y. (2000). Acculturation and Korean American children's social and play behavior. *Social Development, 9,* 316–336.

Farver, J. A. M. & Wimbarti, S. (1995). Indonesian children's play with their mothers and older siblings. *Child Development, 66,* 1493–1503.

Farver, J. M. (1996). Aggressive behavior in preschoolers' social networks: Do birds of a feather flock together? *Early Childhood Research Quarterly, 11,* 333–350.

Farver, J. M. & Howes, C. (1993). Cultural differences in American and Mexican mother–child pretend play. *Merrill Palmer Quarterly, 30,* 344–358.

Gleason, J. B. & Melzi, G. (1997). The mutual construction of narratives by mothers and children: Cross-cultural observations. *Journal of Narrative and Life History, 7,* 217–222.

Goncu, A., Mistry, J., & Mosier, C. (2000). Cultural variations in the play of toddlers. *International Journal of Behavior Development, 24,* 321–329.

Haight, W. L. (1999). The pragmatics of caregiver-child pretending at home: Understanding culturally specific socialization practices. In A. Goncu (Ed.), *Children's engagement in the world* (pp. 128–147). New York: Cambridge University Press.

Haight, W. L., Masiello, T., Dickson, L., Huckely, E., & Black, J. E. (1994). The everyday contexts and social functions of mother–child pretend play in the home. *Merrill Palmer Quarterly, 40,* 509–522.

Haight, W. L. & Miller, P. (1992). The development of everyday pretend play: A longitudinal study of mothers' participation. *Merrill Palmer Quarterly, 38,* 331–349.

Haight, W. L., Wang, X.-L., Fung, H. H., Williams, K., & Mintz, J. (1999). Universal, developmental, and variable aspects of young children's play: A cross-cultural comparison of pretending at home. *Child Development, 70,* 1477–1488.

Halgunseth, L. C., Ispa, J., & Rudy, D. D. (2006). Parental control in Latino families: An integrative review. *Child Development, 77,* 1282–1297.

Hamre, B. & Pianta, R. C. (2005). Can instructional and emotional support in the first grade classroom make a difference for children at risk for school failure? *Child Development, 76,* 949–967.

Hay, D. (1985). Learning to form relationships in infancy: Parallel attainments with parents and peers. *Developmental Review, 5,* 122–161.

Howe, N., Petrakas, H., & Rinaldi, C. M. (1998). "All the sheeps are dead. He murdered them." Sibling pretense, negotiation, internal state language, and relationship quality. *Child Development, 69,* 1820–1912.

Howe, N., Rinaldi, C. M., Jennings, M., & Petrakos, H. (2002). "No! The lambs can stay out because they got cozies": Constructive and destructive sibling conflict, pretend play, and social understanding. *Child Development, 73,* 1460–1473.

Howe, N., Rinaldi, C. M., & LeFebvre, R. (2005). "This is a bad dog, you know…": Constructiong shared meanings during sibling pretend play. *Child Development, 76,* 783–794.

Howes, C. (1980). Peer play scale as an index of complexity of peer interaction. *Developmental Psychology, 16,* 371–372.

Howes, C. (1983). Patterns of friendship. *Child Development, 54,* 1041–1053.

Howes, C. (1985). Sharing fantasy: Social pretend play in toddlers. *Child Development, 56,* 1253–1258.

Howes, C. (1988). Peer interaction in young children. *Monograph of the Society for Research in Child Development, #217 Vol. 53 No. 1.*

Howes, C. (1996). The earliest friendships. In W. M. Bukowski, A. F. Newcomb, & W. W. Hartup (Eds.), *The company they keep: Friendships in childhood and adolescence.* (pp. 66–86). New York: Cambridge.

Howes, C. (2000). Social-emotional classroom climate in child-care, child-teacher relationships, and children's second grade peer relations. *Social Development, 9,* 191–204.

Howes, C. (2008). Peer relationships in early childhood: Friendship. In K. Rubin, W. Bukowski, & B. Laursen (Eds.), *Handbook of peer interactions, relationships, and groups* (pp. 180–194). New York: Guilford.

Howes, C. (2009). *Culture and child development in early childhood education: Practices for quality education and care.* New York: Teacher's College Press.

Howes, C., & Galluzzo, D. C. (1994). Adult socialization of children's play in child care. In H. Goelman (Ed.), *Play and child care* (pp. 20–36). Albany. NY: SUNY Press.

Howes, C., Guerra Wishard, A., & Zucker, E. (2008). Migrating from Mexico and sharing pretend with peers in the United States. *Merrill Palmer Quarterly, 54*, 256–288.

Howes, C., Hamilton, C. E., & Phillipsen, L. (1998). Stability and continuity of child-caregiver and child-peer relationships. *Child Development, 69*, 418–426.

Howes, C., & Lee, L. (2007). If you are not like me, can we play? Peer groups in preschool. In B. Spodek & O. Saracho (Eds.), *Contemporary perspectives on research in social learning in early childhood education*. Durham, NC: Information Age Publishing.

Howes, C., & Matheson, C. C. (1992). Sequences in the development of competent play with peers: Social and social pretend play. *Developmental Psychology, 28*, 961–974.

Howes, C. & Phillipsen, L. C. (1998). Continuity in children's relations with peers. *Social Development, 7*, 340–349.

Howes, C., & Ritchie, S. (2002). *A matter of trust: Connecting teachers and learners in the early childhood classroom.* New York: Teachers College Press.

Howes, C., Sanders, K., & Lee, L. (2008). Entering a new peer group in ethnically and linguistically diverse childcare classrooms. *Social Development, 17*(4), 922–940.

Howes, C., & Shivers, E. M. (2006). New child-caregiver attachment relationships: Entering child care when the caregiver is and is not an ethnic match. *Social Development, 15*, 343–360.

Howes, C., & Spieker, S. (2008). Attachment relationships in the context of multiple caregivers. In J. Cassidy & P. R. Shaver (Eds.), *Handbook of attachment theory and research: Second edition*. New York: Guilford Publications.

Howes, C., Unger, O., & Seidner, L. (1989). Social pretend play in toddlers: Social pretend play forms and parallels with solitary pretense. *Child Development, 60*, 132.

Howes, C., Unger, O., & Matheson, C. C. (1992). *The collaborative construction of pretend: Social pretend play functions.* Albany, NY: SUNY Press.

Howes, C. & Wishard, A. (2004). Revisiting shared meaning: Looking through the lens of culture and linking pretend play through proto-narrative development to emergent literacy. In E. Zigler, D.G. Singer, & S.J. Bishop-Josef (Eds.) *Children's play: the roots of literacy*. Pp. 173–185, Washington: DC: Zero to Three.

Howes, C. & Wishard Guerra, A. (2009). Networks of attachment relationships in low-income children of Mexican heritage: Infancy through preschool. *Social Development, 18*(4), 896–915.

Howes, C., Wishard Guerra, A., & Zucker, E. (2008). Migrating from Mexico and sharing pretend with peers in the United States. *Merrill Palmer Quarterly, 54*, 256–288.

Howes, C., Wishard Guerra, A., & Zucker, E. (2007). Cultural communities and parenting in Mexican-heritage families. *Parenting: Science and Practice, 7*, 1–36.

Howes, C., with Unger, O. A., & Matheson, C. C. (1992). *The collaborative construction of pretend: Social pretend play functions*. New York: SUNY Press.

Imbens-Bailey, A. & Snow, C. (1997). Making meaning in parent–child interaction: A pragmatic approach. In C. M. A. McCabe (Ed.), *The problem of meaning: Behavioral and cognitive perspectives*. New York: Elsevier Science.

Johnson, D. J., Jaeger, E., Randolph, S. M., Cauce, A. M., Ward, J., & NICHD ECCRN (2003). Studying the effects of early child care experiences on the development of children of color in the United States: Towards a more inclusive research agenda. *Child Development, 74*, 1227–1244.

Keller, H., Lohaus, A., Kuensmueller, P., Abels, M., Yovsi, R., Voelker, S., et al. (2004). The bio-culture of parenting: Evidence from five cultural communities. *Parenting: Science and Practice, 2*(1), 25–50.

La Paro, K. M., Pianta, R. C., Hamre, B., & Stuhlman, M. (2002). *Classroom Assessment Scoring System (CLASS) Pre-K version*. Charlottesville: University of Virginia.

Ladd, G. W., Birch, S., & Buhs, E. S. (1999). Children's social and scholastic lives in kindergarten: Related spheres of influence. *Child Development, 70*, 1373–1400.

Lancy, D. (2007). Accounting for variability in mother–child play. *American Anthropologist, 109*(2), 273–284.

Lochman, J. E. (2004). Contextual factors in risk and prevention research. *Merrill Palmer Quarterly, 50*, 311–325.

Lucariello, J., & Nelson, K. (1987). Remembering and planning talk between mothers and children. *Discourse Processes, 10*, 219–235.

McCabe, A. (1997). Developmental and cross-cultural aspects of children's narration. In M. Bamberg (Ed.), *Narrative development: Six approaches*. Mahwah, NJ: Lawrence Erlbaum Associates.

Mosier, C. E. & Rogoff, B. (2003). Privileged treatment of toddlers: Cultural aspects of individual choice and responsibility. *Developmental Psychology, 39*, 1047–1060.

Mueller, E., Bleir, M., & Krakow, J. (1977). The development of peer verbal interaction among two-year-old boys. *Child Development, 48*, 284–297.

NICHD ECCRN (2002). The relation of global first grade environment to strucutual classroom features, teacher, and student behaviors. *Early Elementary School Journal, 102*, 367–387.

Ochs, E. C., L. (2001). *Living narrative: Creating lives in everyday storytelling*. Cambridge, MA: Harvard University Press.

Pianta, R. C., Hamre, B., & Stuhlman, M. (Eds.). (2002). *Relationships between teachers and children* (Vol. 7). New York: Wiley.

Pianta, R. C., Howes, C., Burchinal, M., Bryant, D., Clifford, R., Early, D., et al. (2005). Features of pre-kindergarten programs, classrooms, and teachers: Do they predict observed classroom quality and child-teacher interactions? *Applied Developmental Science, 9*, 144–159.

Rogoff, B. (2003). *The cultural nature of human development*. New York: Oxford University Press.

Rogoff, B., Mistry, J., Goncu, A., & Mosier, C. (1993). Guided participation in cultural activity by toddlers and caregivers. *Monograph of the Society for Research in Child Development, 58*, pp. 7, serial No. 236.

Rose-Krasnor, L. (1997). The nature of social competence A theoretical review. *Social Development, 111*–135.

Ross, H. & Howe, N. (2008). Family influences on children's peer relations. In K. H. Rubin, W. M. Bukowski, & B. Laursen (Eds.), *Handbook of peer relationships, relationships, and groups* (pp. 508–531). New York: Gilford.

Rothbart, M. K., Ahadi, S. A., & Hershey, K. L. (1994). Temperament and social behavior in childhood. *Merrill Palmer Quarterly, 40*, 21–39.

Rubin, K. H., Burgess, K. B., Dwyer, K. M., & Hastings, P. P. (2003). Predicting preschoolers' externalizing behaviors from toddler temperament, conflict, and maternal negativity. *Developmental Psychology, 39*, 164–176.

Rubin, K. H., Burgess, K. B., & Hastings, P. D. (2002). Stability and social-behavioral consequences of toddlers' inhibited temperament and parenting behaviors. *Child Development, 73*, 483–495.

Sanders, K. E., Deihl, A., & Kyler, A. (2007). DAP in the 'hood: Perceptions of child care practices by African American child care directors caring for children of color. *Early Childhood Research Quarterly, 22*, 394–406.

Slade, A. (1987). Quality of attachment and early symbolic play. *Developmental Psychology, 23*, 78–85.

Snow, C. & Imbens- Bailey, A. (1997). Beyond Labov and Waletzy: The antecedents of narrative discourse. *Journal of Narrative and Life History, 7*, 197–207.

Spinrad, T. L., Eisenberg, N., Harris, E., Hanish, L., Fabes, R. A., Kupanoff, K., et al. (2004). The relation of children's everyday nonsocial peer play behavior to their emotionality, regulation and social functioning. *Developmental Psychology, 40*, 67–80.

Thompson, R. A. & Raikes, H. A. (2003). Towards the next quarter-century: Conceptual and methodological challenges for attachment theory. *Develpment and Psychopathology, 15*, 691–718.

Vaughn, B. E., Shin, N., Kim, M., Coppola, G., Krzysik, L., Santos, A., et al. (2009). Hierarchical models of social competence in preschool children: A multisite, multinational study. *Child Development, 80*(6), 1775–1796.

Vaughn, B. E. & Waters, E. (1981). Attention structure sociometric status and dominance: Interrelations, behavioral correlates, and relationships to social competence. *Developmental Psychology, 17*, 275–288.

Waters, E. & Sroufe, L. A. (1983). Social competence as a developmental construct. *Developmental Review, 3*, 79–97.

Youngblade, L. M. & Dunn, J. (1995). Individual differences in young children's pretend play with mother and siblings: Links to relationships and understanding of other people's feelings and beliefs. *Child Development, 66*, 1472–1492.

Rough-and-Tumble Play: Training and Using the Social Brain

Sergio M. Pellis *and* Vivien C. Pellis

Abstract

A central feature of rough-and-tumble play is reciprocity, requiring that the competition to win be attenuated by the need to maintain cooperation. This feature of rough-and-tumble play appears to be put to good use during childhood for the development of nuanced social skills, and can be used to good effect, throughout the life cycle, to deal with ambiguous social situations. The experimental and comparative literature on non-human animals provide a guide both for characterizing the brain mechanisms involved and for identifying the behavioral rules by which such play can be effectively deployed.

Keywords: play, rough-and-tumble, fighting, development, social factors, behavior

Introduction

Play fighting, or rough-and-tumble play, is one of the most commonly reported forms of play in non-human animals (Aldis, 1975; Burghardt, 2005; Fagen, 1981) and is certainly the most studied (Pellis & Pellis, 1998a). In the literature on human play, play fighting has received some attention (see Fry, 2005 for a review), but more often than not it is raised in the context of whether it is truly play (Hughes, 1999), or is simply ignored as a subject of study (Clements & Fiorentino, 2004). While studies of spontaneously occurring play in places such as school playgrounds do indeed show that such play constitutes no more than 10% of all play (Smith, 1997), for several reasons, the relative neglect of this form of play is unfortunate. First, play is still a poorly understood phenomenon especially with regard to what benefits it may accrue for the performer (Power, 2000). Second, as critical experiments are either impractical or unethical in their application to human children, most studies are forced to involve correlations (Pellegrini, 1995). Third, many forms of play in children, such as

sociodramatic play, have no counterparts in other species (Burghardt, 1998). Focusing on a form of play that is widespread among a variety of species, including humans, can be advantageous in these regards: By using appropriately chosen species, critical experiments can be performed to characterize at least some of the key features that constitute play and so provide insight into new questions that can then be investigated in humans (Pellis & Pellis, 2007).

Play Fighting: Fairness and Ambiguity

Despite cultural differences in the imaginary themes within which play fighting is couched, there is a consistent human-typical behavioral pattern present in play fighting across all children (Fry, 2005; Smith, 1997), as well as an underlying similarity in the play fighting of humans when compared to that of other species (Aldis, 1975; Power, 2000). The core similarity in play fighting across all species is that it is a blend of competition and cooperation. It is competitive because the participants attempt to gain some advantage over one another, such as throwing and pinning the partner to the ground in humans or successfully delivering a bite, albeit gentle, to a species-typical bodily target in many species of mammals (Aldis, 1975; Pellis, 1988). It is cooperative because the participants seem to refrain from taking advantage of their success in a way that does not occur during serious fighting (Pellis & Pellis, 1998b). During serious fighting, the participants will take advantage of an opening in their opponent's defensive posturing to deliver a bite or blow (Blanchard, Blanchard, Takahashi & Kelley, 1977; Geist, 1978; Pellis, 1997). In contrast, game theory models have shown that as the win-loss ratio deviates further from 50:50, it is less likely that play fighting will be sustained (Dugatkin & Bekoff, 2003); this conforms to the general observation of play in animals, that winning needs to be reciprocal (Altmann, 1962; Fagen, 1981). Of course, how reciprocity is achieved during play fighting need not be the same in all species.

The basis of fairness in play

During serious fighting, animals will integrate some defensive action when launching an attack (Geist, 1978). For example, consider using your left hand to block an opponent's right arm when you throw a punch at an opponent's jaw. In these actions, attack and defense are simultaneously engaged, reducing the likelihood of a successful counterattack. Similarly, an attack should be met as swiftly as possible with a defensive reaction. Studies of serious fighting and play fighting in many different species of rodents have shown that, unlike the case in serious fighting, during play fighting, animals do not simultaneously defend themselves when attacking and their response speed in engaging a defensive reaction is relatively slower (Pellis & Pellis, 1998b). That is, during play fighting, animals will engage in behavior that facilitates their partner's chances of gaining or regaining the advantage. As in rodents, many species of primates also behave in a manner that increases their partner's chances of successfully retaliating (Biben, 1998; Pellis & Pellis, 1997; Reinhart et. al, 2010), and thus are not appearing to play to win! There are, however, studies with rodents, primates, dogs, and ungulates that do suggest that when play fighting, animals do not show such restraint, and hence do play to win (Bauer & Smuts, 2007; Thompson, 1998; Symons, 1978).

The resolution for these apparently contradictory findings arises from different species adopting different strategies to ensure reciprocity during play fighting. For example, rats, grasshopper mice, and

ground squirrels do not simultaneously incorporate defense during play fighting as they do during serious fighting and so their play fighting facilitates successful retaliatory contact by the partners at any point during the encounter (Pasztor, Smith, MacDonald, Michener & Pellis, 2001; Pellis & Pellis, 1987; Pellis, MacDonald & Michener, 1996; Pellis, Pasztor, Pellis & Dewsbury, 2000). However, the South American rodent, the degu, a relative of the better-known chinchilla, does not hold back in this manner. During both serious and playful fighting, these animals will attempt to deliver bites to their opponents' upper, mid-back. To block access to this target, opponents will face one another and rear up on their hind legs and grab, push, and hit with their forepaws. Once in this boxing position, the animal will maneuver in such a manner as to balance against its opponent with its forepaws and push upwards as it leaps up and around, kicking the opponent in the ventrum with both of its hind feet as it does so. If the kick is successfully delivered, the opponent is knocked backwards onto the ground. To this point in the sequence, playful and serious encounters in degus look identical—that is, in play fighting, the attacker uses a combination of offensive and defensive maneuvering to gain the advantage, just as that which occurs in serious fighting. The difference between serious and playful fighting can be seen once the opponent is successfully knocked over.

During serious fights, if the degu delivering the kick manages to regain its footing before its opponent does, it will rush over to it and attempt to deliver a bite. In contrast, during play fights, the animal delivering the successful kick does not take advantage of its partner's loss of balance. Rather, after a successful hind leg kick, it does not follow-up the attack; instead, the animals may move apart, re-engage in play, or the animal delivering the successful kick may even remain passive when its partner comes over to it and nuzzles its shoulders and neck (Pellis, Pellis & Reinhart, 2010). That is, during play fighting, when maneuvering to deliver the hind leg kick, opponents do not show restraint in their actions, but unlike the case in serious fighting, they do show restraint after the kick is successfully delivered. Thus, while the play fighting of both rats and degus involves restraint, the restraint occurs at different points in the interaction. Our ongoing studies on several species of pigs suggest a third avenue for restraint. Pigs, like degus, when play fighting, do not show restraint during the execution of tactics of attack and defense (Estes, 1993;

Rushen & Pajor, 1987). Unlike degus, however, once a pig gains the advantage, it does not withhold from further attack. To block further attack, the pig that has been unbalanced has to signal submission by either lying prostrate or fleeing (Pellis & Pellis, work in progress). In pigs, then, it seems up to the loser to ensure reciprocity. No doubt, as more species are studied, other ways by which reciprocity is sustained during play fighting will be identified.

There appear, then, to be multiple ways in which different species fulfill the reciprocity rule, or, to phrase it another way, fairness during play fighting can be achieved in various ways. Understanding how different species maintain fairness during play fighting is critical for making cross-species comparisons, but what does seem to be true across all species that engage in play fighting is that some mechanism exists to ensure that the behavior has an element of reciprocity. Because of the inherent involvement of such fairness (Bekoff, 2001), a second element intrudes into play fighting—ambiguity.

How to deal with ambiguity

When engaged in play fighting, animals have continually to assess the actions of their partners to determine whether actions that overstep the species-specific rules for fairness are the result of one partner taking unfair advantage or are accidental. Only about 1% of play fights among rats escalate to serious fighting and when they do, they do so when one partner retaliates against the other's transgression of the typical reciprocal exchange (Pellis & Pellis, 1998b). For many of us, schoolyard experiences provide a confirmation of this dilemma. As a child, when playing, you may remember having been thrown on the ground by another a little too hard or prevented by them from getting to your feet just that little too long: Was this due to your partner's playful exuberance or was it a deliberate attempt on their part to put you in your place? Ambiguity thus goes hand in hand with fairness, the hallmark of play fighting.

For many species, ambiguity during play fighting can be attenuated by the use of play signals that inform one's partner that a momentary transgression was unintended (Aldis, 1975). Not surprisingly, play signals are frequently delivered prior to making contact (Bekoff, 1995), especially when the play is between animals of disparate size or age (Palagi, 2008; Pellis & Pellis, 1997). However, many species do not have obvious play signals (e.g., rats) and even when present, there is no guarantee that they represent the performer's actions honestly

(Pellis & Pellis, 1996, 2009). The problem still remains, how are transgressions to the rules of play fighting to be assessed and acted upon? In our view, it is this combination of reciprocal fairness with the attendant problem of ambiguity that makes play fighting during the juvenile period a valuable tool for the training of social skills and for increasing the subtlety of social interactions that enable more sophisticated social networks to be developed in adulthood. Work on rats and other species provide compelling evidence for these two roles of play fighting.

Play Fighting as a Tool for Training the Social Brain

Studies of children indicate that those who engage in more social play at one age are more skilled at solving social problems at another age (Pellegrini, 1995). Of course, depending on what is being measured, studies have yielded differing results (Power, 2000). Indeed, even if there is a correlation between the two, the result may not be saying anything about play, it could simply be that socially competent children are also more playful, rather than play having a causal influence on the development of social skills. However, non-human animals provide the means by which to test, experimentally, whether there is a causal relationship between the experience of play and the development of social skills. In particular, decades of research from many different laboratories on the play of rats provide some of the best evidence that play fighting aids the development of social skills.

The consequences of play deprivation

In rats, play involves locomotor play, social play and, to a lesser extent, object play (Hole & Einon, 1984). These begin to appear in the week preceding weaning, which occurs around 21–23 days after birth, and peaks in the middle of the juvenile period, around 30–40 days, steadily declining with the approach of puberty, around 60 days (Bolles & Woods, 1964; Meaney & Stewart, 1981; Panksepp, 1981; Thor & Holloway, 1984). Although solitary locomotor play does occur in rats, especially at the younger ages, most locomotor play, by the juvenile period, occurs in the context of social play (Pellis & Pellis, 1983) and most social play involves play fighting (Pellis & Pellis, 1990, 1997b). Therefore, if rats are isolated during the juvenile period, they are largely prevented from the opportunity to engage in play fighting, and the consequences of this absence of social partners results in adults that are deficient in sexual, social, and cognitive skills (C. Moore, 1985; Hole & Einon, 1984). But it may not be the absence of play fighting that is critical; after all, being separated from social partners over the juvenile period involves the absence of all kinds of social experiences (Bekoff, 1976; Burghardt, 1973). Several lines of evidence, however, implicate play as being an element critical for the development of these skills (Pellis & Pellis, 2006).

Naturalistic studies of litters of rats in laboratory conditions have shown that over the course of 24 hours, juveniles engage in play (mostly play fighting) for about an hour. Rats that are reared over the juvenile period in social isolation, but are housed with a peer for one hour per day, grow into adults that are without the deficits present in rats that have been reared in complete social isolation. However, if juveniles that have been isolated socially are given one hour of daily exposure to an adult female rat, they will still grow into adults with deficits that are typical of rats that have been reared in complete social isolation. The difference between daily exposure to a peer or to an adult female is that, while in both cases the rats experience a range of social stimuli, odors, grooming, huddling, and so forth, it is only with peers that juvenile rats will experience play fighting, since adult females rarely engage juveniles in play (Einon & Morgan, 1977; Einon, Morgan & Kibbler, 1978; Einon, Humphreys, Chivers, Field & Naylor, 1981). Similarly, a rat that is reared with a peer that is not playful will have abnormal patterns of brain development as would happen if it were reared in complete social isolation (Hall, 1998). These and other findings (see Pellis & Pellis, 2006, for a more detailed review) strongly implicate play fighting as being essential to the development of important social, emotional, and cognitive skills. These conclusions do not mean that non-play social experiences are not important—indeed, we will provide below some evidence for one role for such experiences.

The evidence that play is important for the development of two types of skills is particularly strong. First, experiences that are derived from play fighting appear critical for the development of skills that are related to coordinating one's movements with those of one's social partner in both sexual (C. Moore, 1985) and non-sexual (Pellis, Field & Whishaw, 1999) contexts. Second, experiences derived from play fighting appear critical for the development of skills that are related to solving social problems. This latter deficiency is well illustrated when adult male rats are placed in a new colony.

If adult male rats are placed in a colony of unfamiliar rats, they will attract the attention of, and be attacked by, the resident dominant male. After several attacks by the dominant male occur, intruding males will adopt submissive postures and curtail their movements in the colony, so as to escape his notice (Blanchard & Blanchard, 1990). However, male rats that have been reared in social isolation fail to display appropriately submissive behavior and they do not curtail their movements in the colony, and so continue to provoke attacks (e.g., Byrd & Briner, 1999; Einon & Potegal, 1991; van den Berg, Hol, van Ree, Spruijt, Everts & Koolhaas, 1999). Furthermore, when rats that have been reared socially are given the opportunity to escape the notice of a colony's dominant male by moving onto and remaining on a raised platform, they do so. In contrast, rats that have been reared in social isolation, fail to do so (von Frijtag, Schot, van den Bos & Spruijt, 2002). Thus, rats reared in isolation have difficulty solving social problems.

That the lack of play fighting is particularly damaging to the development of social skills is further indicated by the finding that whereas it only takes a week or so of isolation during the juvenile period to affect later social behavior, it takes longer periods of isolation—the entire prepubescent period (25–60 days)—to erode the development of non-social cognitive skills (Arakawa, 2003, 2007). The evidence is thus strong that rats reared in social isolation grow into adults that are socially deficient.

Peering into the social brain......

Adult rats that have been reared socially, but have been given brain damage to the whole cortex, have deficits in social behavior comparable to intact rats that have been reared in social isolation (Pellis, Pellis & Whishaw, 1992). Indeed, damage restricted to the prefrontal cortex (PFC) seems sufficient to produce the social deficits otherwise seen in rats reared in isolation (Bell, McCaffrey, Forgie, Kolb & Pellis, 2009; Pellis, Hastings, Shimizu, Kamitakahara, Komorowska, Forgie & Kolb, 2006). These data suggest that the experiences derived from play fighting during the juvenile period influence the development of the PFC—the part of the cortex shown to be critical for making decisions, the 'executive brain' (Goldberg, 2001). Recent work supports this conclusion. Juvenile rats were reared with either an adult female or with another peer from 25–60 days after birth. The animals were then sacrificed and their brains removed. Of particular interest was whether the neurons of the PFC were altered by these different rearing experiences (Bell, Pellis & Kolb, 2010).

Neurons are composed of a cell body, an axon, which is a long projection that connects to distant cells, and a number of dendrites, which are shorter projections that connect to neighboring cells. The interconnections among dendrites of neighboring cells provide a network of cells that operate as neural circuits. Experiences during development can either increase or prune the number of branches of dendrites depending on whether mature neural circuits function more optimally with more or less connections (Kolb, Gorny, Soderpalm & Robinson, 2003). The core finding of the experiment was that the experience of play fighting in the juvenile period altered the pattern of dendritic branching (Bell et al., 2010). This completes the causal circle: Deprivation of play fighting experience in the juvenile period leads to impoverished social skills as adults; normally reared rats given brain damage to the PFC have social deficits similar to those of play deprived rats; and the experience of play in the juvenile period affects the development of the neurons of the PFC. The details of these findings provide an interesting and nuanced dimension to the role of play in shaping the social brain.

.... and its development

Brain damage to different areas of the PFC appears to influence different social skills. Damage to the orbital frontal cortex (OFC) leads to animals that can behave normally, but fail to modify their behavior in response to the identity and status of the social partner (Pellis et al., 2006). Damage to the medial prefrontal cortex (mPFC) leads to animals that appear to have difficulty in coordinating their movements, particularly complex motor actions, to those of their social partner (Bell et al., 2010). Intriguingly, in the experiment to evaluate the effects of rearing conditions on the development of the neurons of the PFC, it was found that different types of social experience occurring during the period of juvenile differentially influenced the development of the OFC and the mPFC (Bell et al., 2010).

In this experiment, as well as rearing a single juvenile with either a single peer or a single adult female to contrast the effects of play on the cells of the PFC, another experimental condition was used—juveniles were reared with three other juveniles. The rationale for this third condition arose from the finding that play is contagious, in that less playful rats can be stimulated to play more when in the presence of more playful partners (Pellis & McKenna, 1992;

Reinhart, Metz, McIntyre & Pellis, 2006). Juveniles reared with the adult female would gain social experiences arising from social grooming, huddling, and other bodily contact, but not play (see above). In contrast, juveniles reared with another juvenile would gain all social experiences, including play fighting, and juveniles reared with three other juveniles would not only gain a complete complement of social experiences, but would also experience greater amounts of play. It was expected that the juveniles experiencing the hyper-play rearing condition would have exaggerated changes to those neurons sensitive to the experience of play (Bell, 2008). It was found that, while the branches of the dendrites of the OFC were increased with the appropriate experience, the branches of the mPFC were reduced by the appropriate experience. The relevant experiences that produced these changes in the neurons of the OFC and the mPFC, however, differed. For the mPFC, it was the experience of play that mattered: as it did not matter whether the juvenile had one peer or three peers with whom to play, what must be critical is for the rat to experience some minimal, threshold level of play. However, for the OFC, it was the number of partners that mattered to the rat, but not whether they played or not, as follow-up experiments show that being housed with three adults is just as effective as being reared with three peers (Bell et al., 2010). To reiterate, while the crucial experience for the mPFC is in the play, for the OFC it is in the number of social partners.

Even though the experiences crucial for the development of the OFC do not directly involve play, the OFC may be indirectly influenced by play. Rats, during the juvenile period, are particularly motivated to make social contact through play (Varlinskaya, Spear & Spear, 1999). Furthermore, in natural colonies, it is likely that there exist many juveniles from litters from many different females from which to choose to play. This strong motivation to engage in play fighting may indirectly ensure that young rats have social interactions with a wide range of animals and so experience the diversity of partners so critical to the development of the OFC (Pellis & Pellis, 2009). Therefore, both directly and indirectly, play in the juvenile period of rats provides a vehicle by which the development of the social brain is facilitated, which then leads to adults with more nuanced social skills. But when it comes to the direct effects of play on development, what are the relevant experiences and what exactly are they influencing?

The unique experiences that play provides

Play fighting interactions, which are fast-paced, may provide young animals with many opportunities to experience the problem of calibrating their movements with those of partners. The impoverished ability in adults that have not engaged in playful fighting as juveniles to coordinate movements with those of a partner (C. Moore, 1985; Pellis et al., 1999) supports this possibility. Another possibility may be that play fighting provides young animals with the experience of uncertainty, and so, influences their ability to deal with the vicissitudes of life (Spinka, Newberry & Bekoff, 2001). Pain inducing and stressful stimuli abound in life, generally, and in social life, in particular, and living socially is rare among mammals. Increased sociality that involves the formation of permanent or semi-permanent groups most often occurs in cases where the advantages that are gained from such a grouping afford an advantage, such as defense against predators, and outweigh the costs of social living, such as an increased risk of disease, an increased competition for food, mates, and shelter and an increased inter-animal conflict (Eisenberg, 1981). To gain the advantages of social living an individual must accept some level of physical and psychological discomfort.

Animals that have been reared in social isolation show either hyposensitivity (Fox, 1967) or hypersensitivity (Einon & Potegal, 1991) to pain. This suggests that one of the ways in which social experiences during early development influence social competency may be in that they afford the individual animal the opportunity to calibrate pain thresholds in a variety of contexts. Being pushed, bitten, kicked or thrown to the floor during play fighting is not without its discomfort, yet, as already discussed above, if these painful stimuli occur in a context in which animals are seemingly following the appropriate, species-typical rules for play, they are accepted and do not disrupt the play mood. Play fighting, then, is ideally suited for animals to learn to discriminate between acceptable and unacceptable levels of pain in a context of social actions that are performed by particular individuals. Indeed, studies on humans have shown that experimental subjects will treat the same absolute pain stimulus as more painful when the supposed perpetrator 'intended' to induce pain compared to one in which the pain was delivered 'accidently' (Gray & Wegner, 2008). That is, the same stimulus can be perceived as more or less painful depending on the social context!

Young animals have been shown to be highly plastic in the development of their defensive responses, in that learning to match threat with context can modify their responses. Maturation and modulation of the neural circuits that regulate fear appear to be critical in enabling animals to become more sophisticated in matching an appropriate defensive reaction to an environmental context (Weidenmayer, 2009). In the subcortical neural circuitry that mediates fear is the amygdala. In turn, the amygdala has reciprocal connections to the PFC (Damasio, 1996). One means by which play experiences can influence the development of appropriately scaled fear responses, is to strengthen the regulation of the amygdala by the PFC (e.g. Rempel-Clower, 2007). We have already shown above how experiences derived from play fighting can modify the neurons of the PFC.

Pain and fear-inducing stimuli activate an animal's stress response system and stressed animals are less able to execute movements or engage their cognitive skills to solve problems as effectively as unstressed animals (McEwen & Sapolsky, 1995; Metz, Jadavji & Smith, 2005). Adult rats that have been reared in social isolation during the juvenile period overreact to benign social contact (Einon & Potegal, 1991) and have an over responsive stress-response system, with stress hormones maintaining heightened levels for longer (von Frijtag et al. 2002). These animals also become excessively fearful in non-social situations, such as when exploring a maze, and their performance can be made normal by pretreatment with an anxiolytic, such as diazepam (da Silva, Ferreria, de Padua Gorabrez, & Morato, 1996). However, rats that have had play fighting experience as juveniles appear better able to restrain their reaction to potentially unpleasant situations, so utilizing, more effectively, their motor, social and cognitive skills.

Indeed, at the peak of juvenile period when play is at its most frequent, rats reorganize their play fighting in a way that increases the unpredictability of events and do so by behaving in ways that reduce the control they have over their own movements and those of their partners (Pellis, Pellis & Foroud, 2005). Furthermore, this reorganization depends on a specific neural mechanism (Kamitakahara, Monfils, Forgie, Kolb & Pellis, 2007); this suggests that the juvenile-typical pattern of play is an adaptation designed to provide the rat with the experiences needed to refine the development of their social brain. Therefore, play in the juvenile period appears to be organized to train animals for the unexpected (Spinka et al., 2001) and may do so by attenuating their fear responses to unpredictable events so that they are more likely to react to situations in an appropriate manner (Pellis & Pellis, 2009).

Play is not just for rats

These avenues by which rats, when play fighting, can modify their performance suggest that individuals with experience of play are better able to make more nuanced judgments about social actions and to engage emotions that promote social contact. Some evidence from the human literature supports these predictions. In one set of experiments, videotaped sequences of young boys were obtained that showed them engaged in either play fighting or serious fighting. Only those sequences that were unambiguously playful or serious were selected. Sequences were then randomly spliced together and shown to subjects whose task it was to label each sequence as playful or serious. All subjects claimed to use a variety of bodily, facial, and movement cues to make their decisions, with subjects from several countries found to have a similar level of performance (Costabile, Smith, Matheson, Aston, Hunter, & Boulton, 1991; Smith, Hunter, Carvalho & Costabile, 1992). Boys who were twelve years old or younger were correct most of the time. Adult men were correct about 70% of the time and adult women performed at around chance (Pellegrini, 2003; Smith & Boulton, 1990). A closer inspection of the women's performance was quite revealing. When the responses by the women were separated into two categories, those who had been reared with brothers and those who had not, and were then compared, it was found that the women who had brothers, and hence, those who were also more likely to have had personal experience with play fighting, performed about as well as the adult men. In contrast, those women who had not had personal experience with play fighting tended to see all the sequences as serious (Conner, 1989). Clearly, experience with play fighting in childhood can influence one's ability to make subtle distinctions about social behavior that superficially looks similar.

Unlike social play in rats that occurs between peers with the onset of the juvenile period, social play in humans, and many other primates, first begins with the mother (Biben & Suomi, 1993). Mothers use play to engage their infants in interactions that induce a positively affective state. Children who, as infants, have experienced such positive affect are better able to engage in interactions with peers and do so in positively affective states (Denham, Mitchell-Copeland, Strandberg, Auerbach, & Blair, 1997; Parke, Cassidy, Burks, Carson & Boyum, 1992). In late infancy, fathers often engage their children in play also, and this frequently takes the rougher form of play fighting. Again, infants, especially boys, who have experienced such play with their fathers are better able to develop peer friendships and engage in play fighting with their peers (Paquette, 2004; Paquette, Carbonneau, Dubeau, Bigras & Tremblay, 2003). However, for play with one's father to have a positive effect on subsequent peer play, it seems that the father must exert dominance in these contests (Flanders, Leo, Paquette, Pihl & Séguin, 2009). Clearly, the relationships between parent and child are important in influencing how play experience exerts its effect on subsequent behavior, although the exact mechanisms involved remain to be determined.

In situations where these positively affective experiences are compromised, such as when there is marital discord, there is a negative impact on the child's ability to interact in a positive manner with their peers. Yet, for parents able to sustain positively affective interactions with their infants in these situations, the beneficial effects of such interactions can persist into later life (Lindsey, Caldera & Tankersley, 2009). Even though the PFC is not fully developed until one is in their early twenties, there is growing evidence that engaging in routines that require the use of PFC-involving skills can facilitate the development of these skills in young children. Indeed, many of the routines used in such training involve contexts of social play, requiring skills such as turn taking or reciprocity, an essential ingredient of play fighting (Diamond, Barnett, Thomas & Munro, 2007). Training of social skills is even possible to some degree in children with autism spectrum disorder (White, Koenig & Scahill, 2007), a condition known for its deficits in reciprocity and social play (Jordan, 2003).

Classic studies, done by Harlow and others, have shown that, for young monkeys, the quality of the early maternal experiences can greatly influence the development of social competence (Blum, 2002). Inanimate surrogate mothers simply do not provide the relevant stimuli to train such skills. Some of these studies point to the important role of play-like experiences in the development of these skills. For example, infant monkeys were either 'reared' by a standard surrogate terry toweling cloth mother or by such a mother that was hooked to springs that made it mobile. This mobile mother moved around the enclosure in a random pattern, either towards the infant or away from it, bumping it here and moving it there. The infants with the mobile surrogate mothers initiated more play fights with their mothers and experienced the unpredictable behavior of the mother and hence, the ambiguity of play. As juveniles, these monkeys were better able to develop normal play relations with peers, and, as adults, were better able to engage in sex and integrate into troops (Anderson, Kenney & Mason, 1977; Eastman, & Mason, 1975; Mason & Berkson, 1975). Moreover, those monkeys reared with standard mother surrogates who exhibited pathological behavior as juveniles could be coaxed into more normal social behavior by 'therapist' juveniles, monkeys reared by real mothers who had had the opportunity to integrate into normal peer relationships (Harlow & Suomi, 1971; Suomi, Harlow & McKinney, 1972).

The data on monkeys and children are consistent with the findings from the experiments with rats—play interactions with parents and peers help to calibrate one's ability to maintain a positive affective state in situations of uncertainty and refine one's ability to read subtle social cues. Either directly or indirectly, the experiences derived from play fighting appear critical for sharpening the skills of the social brain.

On Using Play for Social Advantage

So far, we have examined how play fighting, with its properties of fairness and ambiguity, provides a fertile training ground for the social brain and its skills. In many species, including rats and humans, play can continue well into adulthood (Pellis, 2002a; Pellis & Iwaniuk, 1999, 2000). However, at this age, it is unlikely to function as training for some future benefit. Rather, play fighting, with its properties of fairness and ambiguity, has more immediate payback in adulthood: it is used as a means for assessing and manipulating social partners (Brueggeman, 1978).

The view from the rat colony

In rats, play fighting not only continues into adulthood, but also appears to be used by male rats to negotiate dominance relationships (Pellis, 2002a). The subtle ways in which different defensive tactics are used reveal how play fighting is involved. During play fighting, rats compete for access to the nape of the neck (Pellis & Pellis, 1987; Siviy & Panksepp, 1987), which, if contacted, is gently nuzzled with the snout (Pellis, 1988). There are many different tactics available for avoiding, or extricating from, nape contact (Pellis & Pellis, 1987; Pellis et al., 1992). One class of tactics involves evasion, where

the defender runs, leaps or swerves away from the attacker, and, in doing so, removes its nape from the vicinity of its partner's snout. Evasive tactics account for about 20–30% of defense at all ages and for both sexes (Pellis & Pellis, 1990, 1997b). The other class of tactics is more common and involves turning to face the attacker, and this can occur in one of two ways—the defender can either roll over to supine or remain standing (Pellis & Pellis, 1987). While from both these positions the defender moves its nape away and can use its forepaws to block further attack, the standing position affords more options for suppressing further attack as well as for launching counterattacks (Pellis & Pellis, 1998b). It is facing defense that varies most with age, between the sexes and in dominance-influenced interactions.

For both sexes, when play fighting first emerges, the more common defensive tactic used is to face the attacker while remaining standing. Following weaning, facing the attacker by turning supine becomes the more common tactic. With the onset of puberty, another switch occurs in the use of defensive tactics, but this time, the sexes differ in their choices. Whereas post-pubescent females continue to use the juvenile-typical pattern of rolling over to supine as the primary tactic of defending against nape contact, males revert to mainly using the standing tactic (Pellis, 2002b). However, for males, this switch is context-dependent. With the onset of puberty, groups of cohabiting males begin to form dominance relationships, in which one male typically becomes dominant over the other males in the colony (Barnett, 1975; Lore & Flannelly, 1977). Subordinate males playing with other subordinate males or with females will use the adult male typical pattern of primarily using the standing tactic when attacked, as will a dominant male. However, when a subordinate male plays with a dominant male, it will revert to the juvenile-typical pattern of primarily using supine defense (Pellis & Pellis, 1991, 1992).

One way to view the subordinate males' switching from adult-typical to juvenile-typical defense is that by behaving in a more juvenile manner, the subordinate is demonstrating its subordinate status (Pellis & Pellis, 1991). There is evidence that using infantile or juvenile behavior patterns can reduce the aggressiveness of the social partner (e.g., Fox, 1971; Glocker, Langleben, Rupare, Loughead, Gur, & Sachser, 2009; Mischkulnig, 1989). In the case for rats, the juvenile-typical play by the subordinate male rats may be a form of obsequiousness—by remaining on friendly terms with the dominant male in the colony, the subordinate may be more readily tolerated and less likely to be attacked and pummeled by the dominant animal. Indeed, in large colonies, the subordinate males that are the less frequently encountered are the ones more likely to be attacked aggressively (Blanchard, Flannelly & Blanchard, 1988). Consistent with this interpretation is that both subordinate males and females are more likely to initiate amicable contact—including play, grooming and huddling—with the colony's dominant male than they are with one another (Adams & Boice, 1983, 1989; Pellis & Pellis, 1991).

That this partner-related modulation of play fighting is indeed a property of dominance is illustrated by the following experiment. Colonies, each consisting of three, young, adult male rats were formed. After a couple of weeks of cohabitation, the play of all combinations of dyads in each colony was compared. Subordinate rats were more likely to use the standing tactic in defense against each other's playful attacks, but both these animals mainly used the supine tactic when they defended themselves against the dominant. Once the dominant was identified, he was permanently removed from the colony, and the two subordinates were left to re-establish their relationships. When retested two weeks later, one of the animals behaved like a subordinate—using the supine tactic—and the other switched to the dominant role and continued to use mainly standing defense (Pellis, Pellis & McKenna, 1993). That is, the same individual switched from using the adult-typical pattern of defense to the juvenile-typical when interacting with the same partner! These dominance-related changes in play have been verified with regard to the animals' status, by using independent (i.e., non-play) measures for identifying dominants and subordinates (Pellis et al., 1993; Smith, Fantella & Pellis, 1999).

So, by using play in a partner-modulated manner, subordinate males can maintain a friendly relationship with a dominant male. But it can be subtler than this. Some subordinates in a natural colony seem to accept the role, but others do not. Those that do not will seek to leave their current colony and usurp a colony that is controlled by another dominant or to establish their own colony (Calhoun, 1962). When constrained to remain in the current colony, these reluctant subordinates are the ones that keep to the periphery and away from the dominant (Blanchard et al., 1988). Also, when they play with the dominant, their relative balance of standing versus supine defense is much smaller than that of other subordinates. Indeed, in the three-male

experiment we significantly predicted which would become the dominant pair mate once the dominant was removed based on the relative reluctance of the other to adopt the supine defense (Pellis et al., 1993). Again, fairness and ambiguity are at work here.

The reluctant subordinate can bias its play to its own advantage by increasing its use of standing defense, thus increasing its chance of gaining the advantage over its partner. If the partner accepts this level of 'rough' play, the subordinate can make it even rougher, and so on, until the dominant retaliates with very rough play or an outright aggressive attack—by biting the subordinate's lower back or flanks (Blanchard et al., 1977; Pellis & Pellis, 1987), or by acquiescing to the rough play and so acknowledging that the dominance relationship has been reversed. While play is inherently fair, transgressions to that fairness create ambiguity for the partner who has to decide whether it was a transgression, how serious it was, and whether to do something about it. These situations of dominance contests can make use of the properties of play fighting to negotiate possible changes in relationships. This usage is well illustrated when unfamiliar males meet.

When an unfamiliar adult male rat is placed into the territory of an existing colony, the dominant male of the colony will aggressively attack the intruder (Blanchard & Blanchard, 1990). In contrast, when unfamiliar males are placed together in a neutral arena, dominance relationships will eventually be formed, but only occasionally does this involve aggressive fighting. Rather, the animals will engage in play fighting, but of the roughest version of the adult male-typical form. Again, over time, the animals will increase the roughness of their play until one animal concedes and starts playing in a more subordinate-typical manner or until they engage in a serious fight, which then leads to the establishment of the dominance relationship (Smith et al., 1999). The beauty of play fighting is that because of the ambiguity involved, the animal pushing the envelope can, when faced with a severe response, back down. After all, it was only 'play.'

Beyond the social world of rats
Adult rats can use playful modes of interaction during courtship and during dominance-related interactions among males (Pellis, 2002a; Pellis & Iwaniuk, 2004). Furthermore, in dominance-related interactions, play can be used to reinforce submission, to overturn existing dominance relationships, or establish new ones. For many species that retain

play fighting in adulthood, play can be used in all or some of these ways. For some, play fighting can be incorporated into courtship, but not dominance contests, and for others, play can be used for challenging existing dominance relationships but not to establish new ones (Pellis, 2002a; Pellis & Iwaniuk, 1999, 2000). But rats do not exhaust all the options. In a series of studies on bonobos and chimpanzees, Palagi and her colleagues have shown that these species can use play fighting prior to feeding time as a means of establishing ties within the group that will permit the animals to tolerate each other's presence during feeding. That is, those that play together, stay together (Palagi, 2006). However, there are subtle differences between these species. In chimpanzees, adults seek out, and play with, the young of adult females with whom they wish to remain near. Although adult bonobos will, like chimpanzees, seek to play with the appropriate juveniles in these situations, they will also, unlike chimpanzees, seek out, and play with, the adults directly (Palagi, Cordoni & Borgognini Tarli, 2004; Palagi, Paoli & Borgognini Tarli, 2006). Clearly, we are only in the early stages of documenting and characterizing the play of adult animals, and play in adulthood has been greatly neglected (Cohen, 2006), but the insight by Brueggeman (1978), that adults use play fighting for assessment and manipulation of social relationships, seems to be the direction most worthy of further investigation.

Two predictions arise from Brueggeman's hypothesis: First, adult-adult play should be more common in species facing greater ambiguity in their social relationships; second, species that have retained play fighting into adulthood should have more complex and subtle ways to deal with social situations. Some of the accumulated data on primates and rodents support these two predictions. Although the presence of play, especially social play in adults, is not infrequent, it is understudied relative to the focus on the play of younger animals. Where it is studied, it is often in the context of adults playing with younger animals, yet, it is estimated that in primates, about 50% of species engage in adult-adult play (Pellis & Iwaniuk, 1999, 2000). If such play is part of the animals' tool kit for assessment and manipulation of social relationships, then it is expected that variation in social organization should significantly predict for which primates play as adults.

Play and social complexity

Primates are highly social mammals, but the pattern of aggregation can vary greatly across the order

(Fuentes, 2007). For some lineages, such as many species of Old World Monkeys, social life involves tight knit groups of female kin, in which females spend their entire lives. Males typically leave by adulthood to attach themselves to other troops, and their tenure with a troop may be limited to only a portion of their adult lives. Macaques and baboons nicely illustrate this pattern. But even in this lineage there is significant deviation from this pattern. Hamadryas baboons, for example, form small harems, whereby an adult male accumulates a number of females, which need not be related to one another, and actively maintain their proximity to him. These single male harems coalesce into large troops containing multiple harems. In other lineages, males and females form monogamous pairs (e.g., gibbons), and, in some, a female may actually have cohabiting multiple males who share the burden of rearing offspring (e.g., callitrichids, a family of New World Monkeys). In others, the males form lasting bonds and it is the females that move to a new troop when sexually mature (e.g., chimpanzees), or both sexes move to new troops when reaching sexual maturity (e.g., spider monkeys).

At the other extreme, some primates spend a lot of time alone and only congregate periodically with other members of their species, either only during mating (e.g., aye-aye, a nocturnal lemurid) or sporadically throughout the year (e.g., orangutans, a Great Ape; loris, a nocturnal prosimian). Even though the troops of some species, such as chimpanzees and spider monkeys, may contain the same individuals for years on end, large troops can fragment, with the fragments remaining out of contact for days or weeks, and then recombine. Such fission-fusion style of social arrangement creates many opportunities for uncertainties in social relationships. Therefore, primate social life may involve daily, constant contact with the same social partners, sporadic encounters with known individuals or encounters with strangers—both sexual and nonsexual social behavior then, can involve interactions with partners differing degrees of familiarity.

As predicted, species with lower familiarity are the ones significantly more likely to use play fighting in their sexual (Pellis & Iwaniuk, 1999) and non-sexual (Pellis & Iwaniuk, 2000) social interactions. That is, species that have more fluid and uncertain relationships are the ones most likely to use play fighting, as has become dramatically apparent by detailed studies of chimpanzees and bonobos (Palagi, 2006). The fairness and inherent ambiguity of play seems to provide an excellent milieu for helping deal with ambiguous social relationships.

Those species with play in their tool kit appear better able to deal with nuanced gradations in their social interactions. For example, as noted above, when unfamiliar adult male rats meet in a neutral arena, they are most likely to engage in a rough form of play to establish their relative status. In contrast, other territorial rodents, such as house mice and Syrian golden hamsters, species that do not have such play as adults, have but two choices—fight or flee (Pellis, 2002a; Pellis & Iwaniuk, 2004). That is, rats have a richer set of options for negotiating their relationships, with play offering a middle ground. Not surprisingly perhaps, species that retain play in adulthood also tend to be more flexible and nuanced in several domains of their behavior, social and non-social. For example, rats outperform mice in virtually all domains that have been examined (Whishaw, Metz, Kolb & Pellis, 2001). Several species have been shown to have such play-based capacity for negotiating social relationships (see Pellis, 2002a, for a review of some of this literature). For example, in striped hyenas, following puberty, individuals preferentially seek out and engage older members of the group in play fighting, in an apparent bid to identify their potential slot in the dominance hierarchy (Mills, 1990). In howler monkeys, dominant troop members use a rough version of play fighting as a means by which to 'punish' lower ranking members, thus reinforcing their status without risking retaliation from the subordinates (Jones, 1983). Again, the fairness and ambiguity of play can be very useful in developing more subtle social relationships and testing them.

What about humans?

Although others are better placed to review the situation in humans, it is worth pointing out that play fighting is used in adolescent boys as a means by which to test social relationships and either reinforce or challenge one's position in the status hierarchy (Fry, 2005). Similarly, playful interactions form part of the courtship process, as documented in both adolescents and young adults (Ballard, Green & Granger, 2003; M. Moore, 1985, 1995; Ryan & Mohr, 2005). Playful teasing can test the qualities of the participants—for example, by assessing how sensitive the other person is to one's feelings. It can allow the partners to assess each other's interest in pursuing the courtship further—for example, by assessing how much and how rough the contact that is tolerated. It may also provide clues as to the potential partners' compatibility—for example, by assessing the degree of compatibility of the participants through how quickly they reach a consensus on the degree of roughness acceptable to both. Humor and joking is widespread in the school, workplace and, indeed, any social gathering, and it too, in many ways, may be thought of an extension of play fighting. Through jokes, subordinates can be put in their place or dominants tested for their ability to sustain their status. Both play fighting and non-touch-based joking have the same basic properties of fairness and ambiguity, and both can be used to test the relationship and one is able to back down with "I was only playing/joking" in case of a brusque response from the recipient (for a review see Pellis & Pellis, 2009). Taken together, then, play and play-like patterns of interactions provide a means of expanding the range of subtlety in social relationships and interactions.

Conclusion

Using play in childhood to increase social competency or in adulthood to increase complexity in social relationships, may, at some level, be connected. Relative to other rodents studied, rats have the most complex pattern of play fighting, with juvenile-typical patterns of play that appear designed to facilitate the development of the social brain. Also, relative to other rodents, rats retain play fighting into adulthood for use in non-sexual social relationships. It may be the case, then, that species that retain play in adulthood as a social tool are more likely to have modified the role of play in childhood to maximize the development of their social capabilities. Certainly, among primates, it does appear that those species with the most versatile and spectacular patterns of play as juveniles are also the ones that have the most complex and nuanced social behavior as adults, which includes liberal uses of play. The four most extraordinary examples are spider monkeys, chimpanzees, bonobos and, of course, humans. Whether this relationship between childhood and adult play is real, remains to be tested empirically, but the evidence to date suggests that this may be a valuable direction for future studies of play. Indeed, it is one way to bring together otherwise disparate research on play at these different stages of life.

References

Adams, N. & Boice, R. (1983). A longitudinal study of dominance in an outdoor colony of domestic rats. *Journal of Comparative Psychology, 97*, 24–33.

Adams, N., & Boice, R. (1989). Development of dominance in rats in laboratory and seminatural environments. *Behavioral Processes, 19*, 127–142.

Aldis, O. (1975). *Play fighting*. New York, NY: Academic Press.

Altmann, S. A. (1962). Social behavior of anthropoid primates: Analysis of recent concepts. In E. L. Bliss (Ed.), *Roots of behavior* (pp. 277–285). New York, NY: Harper.

Anderson, C. O., Kenney, A. M., & Mason, W. A. (1977). Effects of maternal mobility, partner, and endocrine state on social responsiveness of adolescent rhesus monkeys. *Developmental Psychobiology, 10*, 421–434.

Arakawa, H. (2003). The effects of isolation rearing on open-field in male rats depends on developmental stages. *Developmental Psychobiology, 43*, 11–19.

Arakawa, H. (2007). Ontogeny of sex differences in defensive burying behavior in rats: Effect of social isolation. *Aggressive Behavior, 33*, 38–47.

Ballard, M. E., Green, S., & Granger, C. (2003). Affiliation, flirting, and fun: Mock aggressive behavior in college students. *The Psychological Record, 53*, 33–49.

Barnett, S. A. (1975). *The rat: A study in behavior*. The University of Chicago Press: Chicago, IL.

Bauer, E. B. & Smuts, B. B. (2007). Cooperation and competition during dyadic play in domestic dogs, *Canis familiaris*. *Animal Behaviour, 73*, 489–499.

Bekoff, M. (1976). The social deprivation paradigm: Who's being deprived of what? *Developmental Psychobiology, 9*, 499–500.

Bekoff, M. (1995). Play signals as punctuation: The structure of social play in canids. *Behaviour, 132*, 419–429.

Bekoff, M. (2001). Social play behavior: Cooperation, fairness, trust and the evolution of morality. *Journal of Consciousness Studies, 8*, 81–90.

Bell, H. C. (2008). *Playful feedback and the developing brain*. Unpublished M.Sc. Thesis. University of Lethbridge: Lethbridge, Alberta, Canada.

Bell, H. C., Pellis, S. M., & Kolb, B. (2010). Juvenile peer play experience and the development of the orbitofrontal and medial prefrontal cortex. *Behavioural Brain Research, 207*, 7–13.

Bell, H. C., McCaffrey, D., Forgie, M. L., Kolb, B., & Pellis, S. M. (2009). The role of the medial prefrontal cortex in the play fighting of rats. *Behavioral Neuroscience, 123*, 1158–1168.

Biben, M. (1998). Squirrel monkey play fighting: Making the case for a cognitive training function for play. In M. Bekoff & J. A. Byers (Eds.), *Animal play: Evolutionary, comparative, and ecological perspectives* (pp. 161–2). Cambridge, UK: Cambridge University Press.

Biben, M. & Suomi, S. J. (1993). Lessons from primate play. In K. MacDonald (Ed.), *Parent–child play. Descriptions and implications* (pp. 185–196). Albany, NY: State University of New York Press.

Blanchard, D. C. & Blanchard, R. J. (1990b). The colony model of aggression and defense. In D. A. Dewsbury (Ed.), *Contemporary issues in comparative psychology* (pp. 410–430). Sunderland, MA: Sinauer Associates.

Blanchard, R. J., Flannelly, K. J., & Blanchard, D. C. (1988). Life-span studies of dominance and aggression in established colonies of laboratory rats. *Physiology & Behavior, 43*, 1–7.

Blanchard, R. J., Blanchard, D. C., Takahashi, T., & Kelley, M. J. (1977). Attack and defensive behaviour in the albino rat. *Animal Behaviour, 25*, 622–634.

Blum, D. (2002). *Love at Goon Park: Harry Harlow and the science of affection*. Cambridge, MA: Perseus.

Bolles, R. C. & Woods, P. J. (1964). The ontogeny of behavior in the albino rat. *Animal Behaviour, 12*, 427–441.

Brueggeman, J. A. (1978). The function of adult play in free-ranging *Macaca mulatta*. In E. O. Smith (Ed.), *Social play in primates* (pp. 169–192). Routledge: London, UK.

Burghardt, G. M. (1973). Instinct and innate behavior: Toward an ethological psychology. In J. A. Nevin & G. S. Reynolds (Eds.), *The study of behavior: Learning, motivation, emotion and instinct* (pp. 322–400). Glenview, IL: Scott Foresman.

Burghardt, G. M. (1998). Play. In G. Greenberg & M. Haraway (Eds.), *Comparative psychology: A handbook* (pp. 757–767). New York, NY: Garland.

Burghardt, G. M. (2005). *The genesis of play. Testing the limits*. Cambridge, MA: MIT Press.

Byrd, K. R. & Briner, W. E. (1999). Fighting, nonagonistic social behavior, and exploration in isolation-reared rats. *Aggressive Behavior, 25*, 211–223.

Calhoun, J. B. (1962). *The ecology and sociology of the Norway rat*. US Public Health Service Publication, 1008. Washington, D.C.: US Government Printing Office.

Clements, R. L., & Fiorentino, L., (2004). *The child's right to play. A Global Approach*. Westport, CN: Praeger.

Cohen, D. (2006). *The development of play*. London, UK: Routledge.

Conner, K. (1989). Aggression: Is in the eye of the beholder? *Play & Culture, 2*, 213–217.

Costabile, A., Smith, P. K., Matheson, L., Aston, J., Hunter, T., & Boulton, M. J. (1991). A cross-national comparison of how children distinguish serious and playful fighting. *Developmental Psychology, 27*, 881–887.

Damasio, A. R. (1994). *Descartes' error*. New York, NY: Avon.

da Silva, N. L., Ferreria, V. N. M., de Padua Gorabrez, A., & Morato, G. S. (1996). Individual housing from weaning modifies the performance of young rats on elevated plus-maze apparatus. *Physiology & Behavior, 60*, 1391–1396.

Denham, S. A., Mitchell-Copeland, J., Strandberg, K., Auerbach, S., & Blair, K. (1997). Parental contributions to preschoolers' emotional competence: Direct and indirect effects. *Motivation & Emotion, 21*, 65–86.

Diamond, A., Barnett, W. S., Thomas, J., & Munro, S. (2007). Preschool program improves cognitive control. *Science, 318*, 1387–1388.

Dugatkin, L. A. & Bekoff, M. (2003). Play and the evolution of fairness: A game theory model. *Behavioural Processes, 60*, 209–214.

Eastman, R. F. & Mason, W. A. (1975). Looking behavior in monkeys raised with mobile and stationary artificial mothers. *Developmental Psychobiology, 8*, 213–222.

Einon, D. F. & Morgan, M. J. (1977). A critical period for social isolation in the rat. *Developmental Psychobiology, 10*, 123–132.

Einon, D. & Potegal, M. (1991). Enhanced defense in adult rats deprived of playfighting experience in juveniles. *Aggressive Behavior, 17*, 27–40.

Einon, D. F., Morgan, M. J., & Kibbler, C. C. (1978). Brief periods of socialization and later behavior in the rat. *Developmental Psychobiology, 11*, 213–225.

Einon, D. F., Humphreys, A. P., Chivers, S. M., Field, S., & Naylor, V. (1981). Isolation has permanent effects upon the behavior of the rat, but not the mouse, gerbil, or guinea pig. *Developmental Psychobiology, 14*, 343–355.

Eisenberg, J. F. (1981). *The mammalian radiations*. The University of Chicago Press: Chicago, IL.

Estes, R. D. (1993). *The safari companion. A guide for watching African mammals.* Post Mills, VT: Chelsea Green Publishing Company.

Fagen, R. A. (1981). *Animal play behavior.* New York, NY: Oxford University Press.

Flanders, J. L., Leo, V., Paquette, D., Pihl, R. O., & Séguin, J. R. (2009). Rough-and-tumble play and the regulation of aggression: An observational study of father-child play dyads. *Aggressive Behavior, 35,* 285–295.

Fox, M. W. (1967). The effects of short-term social and sensory isolation upon behavior, EEG and averaged evoked potentials in puppies. *Physiology & Behavior, 2,* 145–146.

Fox, M. W. (1971). Socio-infantile and socio-sexual signals in canids: A comparative and ontogenetic study. *Zeitschrift für Tierpsychologie, 28,* 185–210.

Fry, D. P. (2005). Rough and tumble social play in humans. In A. D. Pellegrini & P. K. Smith (Eds.), *The nature of play* (pp. 54–85). New York, NY: Guilford Press.

Fuentes, A. (2007). Social organization. Social systems and the complexities in understanding the evolution of primate behavior. In C. J. Campbell, A. Fuentes, K. C. MacKinnon, M. Panger, & S. K. Bearder (Eds.), *Primates in perspective* (pp. 609–621). Oxford University Press: Oxford, UK.

Geist, V. (1978). On weapons, combat and ecology. In L. Krames, P. Pliner, & T. Alloway (Eds.), *Advances in the study of communication and affect,* Vol. 4, *Aggression, dominance and individual spacing* (pp. 1–30). Plenum Press: New York, NY.

Glocker, M. L., Langleben, D. D., Rupare, K., Loughead, J. W., Gur, R. C., & Sachser, N. (2009). Baby schema in infant faces induces cuteness perception and motivation for caretaking in adults. *Ethology, 115,* 257–263.

Goldberg, E. (2001). *The executive brain. Frontal lobes and the civilized mind.* New York, NY: Oxford University Press.

Gray, K. & Wegner, D. (2008). The sting of intentional pain. *Psychological Science, 19,* 1260–1262.

Hall, F. S. (1998). Social deprivation of neonatal, adolescent, and adult rats has distinct neurochemical and behavioral consequences. *Critical Reviews in Neurobiology, 12,* 129–162.

Harlow, H. F. & Suomi, S. J. (1971). Social recovery by isolation-reared monkeys. *Proceedings of the National Academy of Sciences, USA, 68,* 1534–1538.

Hole, G. J. & Einon, D. F. (1984). Play in rodents. In P. K. Smith (Ed.), *Play in Animals and Children* (pp. 95–117). Basil Blackwell: Oxford, UK.

Hughes, F. P. (1999). *Children, play and development.* 3rd Ed. Allyn & Bacon: Needham Heights, MA.

Jones, C. B. (1983). Social organization of captive black howler monkeys (*Aloutta caraya*): Social competition and the use of non-damaging behavior. *Primates, 24,* 25–39.

Jordan, R. (2003). Social play and autistic spectrum disorders. *Autism, 7,* 347–360.

Kamitakahara, H., Monfils, M.-H., Forgie, M. L., Kolb, B., & Pellis, S. M. (2007). The modulation of play fighting in rats: Role of the motor cortex. *Behavioral Neuroscience, 121,* 72–84.

Kolb, B., Gorny, G., Soderpalm, A. V. H., & Robinson, T. E. (2003). Environmental complexity has different effects on the structure of neurons of the prefrontal cortex versus the parietal cortex or nucleus accumbens. *Synapse, 48,* 149–153.

Lindsey, E. W., Caldera, Y. M., & Tankersley, L. (2009). Marital conflict and the quality of young children's peer play behavior: The mediating and moderating role of parent–child emotional reciprocity and attachment security. *Journal of Family Psychology, 23,* 130–145.

Lore, R. K. & Flannelly, K. (1977). Rat societies. *Scientific American, 236,* 106–118.

McEwen, B. S., & Sapolsky, R. M. (1995). Stress and cognitive function. *Current Opinions in Neurobiology, 5,* 205–216.

Mason, W. A. & Berkson, G. (1975). Effects of maternal mobility on the development of rocking and other behaviors in rhesus monkeys: A study with artificial mothers. *Developmental Psychobiology, 8,* 197–211.

Meaney, M. J. & Stewart, J. (1981). A descriptive study of social development in the rat (*Rattus norvegicus*). *Animal Behaviour, 29,* 34–45.

Metz, G. A., Jadavji, N. M., & Smith, L. K. (2005). Modulation of motor function by stress: A novel concept of the effects of stress and corticosterone on behavior. *European Journal of Neuroscience, 22,* 1190–1120.

Mills, M. G. L. (1990). *Kalahari hyaena. Comparative behavioural biology of two species.* Unwin Hyman: London.

Mischkulnig, M. (1989). Babyishness and anger reduction. *Zeitschrift für Experimentelle und Angewante Psychologie, 36,* 567–578.

Moore, C. L. (1985). Development of mammalian sexual behavior. In E. S. Gollin (Ed.), *The comparative development of adaptive skills* (pp. 19–56). Lawrence Erlbaum: Hillsdale, NJ.

Moore, M. M. (1985). Non-verbal courtship patterns in women: Contact and consequences. *Ethology & Sociobiology, 6,* 237–247.

Moore, M. M. (1995). Courtship signaling and adolescents: "Girls just want to have fun"? *Journal of Sex Research, 32,* 319–328.

Palagi, E. (2006). Social play in bonobos (*Pan paniscus*) and chimpanzees (*Pan troglodytes*): Implications for natural social systems and interindividual relationships. *American Journal of Physical Anthropology, 129,* 418–426.

Palagi, E. (2008). Sharing the motivation to play: The use of signals in adult bonobos. *Animal Behaviour, 75,* 887–896.

Palagi, E., Cordoni, G., & Borgognini Tarli, S. M. (2004). Immediate and delayed benefits of play behavior: New evidence from chimpanzees (*Pan troglodytes*). *Ethology, 110,* 949–962.

Palagi, E., Paoli, T. & Borgognini Tarli, S. (2006). Short-term benefits of play behavior and conflict prevention in *Pan paniscus*. *International Journal of Primatology, 27,* 1257–1270.

Panksepp, J. (1981). The ontogeny of play in rats. *Developmental Psychobiology, 14,* 327–332.

Paquette, D. (2004). Theorizing the father-child relationship: Mechanisms and developmental outcomes. *Human Development, 47,* 193–219.

Paquette, D., Carbonneau, R., Dubeau, D., Bigras M., & Tremblay, R. (2003). Prevalence of father-child rough-and-tumble play and physical aggression in preschool children. *European Journal of Psychology & Education, 18,* 171–189.

Parke, R. D., Cassidy, J., Burks, V. S., Carson, J., & Boyum, L. (1992). Familial contributions to peer competence among children: The role of interactive and affective processes. In R. D. Parke & C. Ladd (Eds.), *Family-peer relationships* (pp. 107–134). Erlbaum: Hillsdale, NJ.

Pasztor, T. J., Smith, L. K., MacDonald, N. L., Michener, G. R., & Pellis, S. M. (2001). Sexual and aggressive play fighting of sibling Richardson's ground squirrels. *Aggressive Behavior, 27,* 323–337.

Pellegrini, A. D. (1995). Boys' rough-and-tumble play and social competence: Contemporaneous and longitudinal relations.

In A. D. Pellegrini (Ed.), *The future of play theory: A multidisciplinary inquiry into the contribution of Brian Sutton-Smith* (pp. 107–126). State University of New York Press: Albany, NY.

Pellegrini, A. D. (2003). Perceptions and possible functions of play and real fighting in early adolescence. *Child Development, 74*, 1552–1533.

Pellis, S. M. (1988). Agonistic versus amicable targets of attack and defense: Consequences for the origin, function and descriptive classification of play-fighting. *Aggressive Behavior, 14*, 85–104.

Pellis, S. M. (1997). Targets and tactics: The analysis of moment-to-moment decision making in animal combat. *Aggressive Behavior, 23*, 107–129.

Pellis, S. M. (2002a). Keeping in touch: Play fighting and social knowledge. In M. Bekoff, C. Allen, & G. M. Burghardt (Eds.), *The cognitive animal: Empirical and theoretical perspectives on animal cognition* (pp. 421–427). MIT Press: Cambridge, MA.

Pellis, S. M. (2002b). Sex-differences in play fighting revisited: Traditional and non-traditional mechanisms for sexual differentiation in rats. *Archives of Sexual Behavior, 31*, 11–20.

Pellis, S. M. & Iwaniuk, A. N. (1999). The problem of adult play: A comparative analysis of play and courtship in primates. *Ethology, 105*, 783–806.

Pellis, S. M. & Iwaniuk, A. N. (2000). Adult-adult play in primates: Comparative analyses of its origin, distribution and evolution. *Ethology, 106*, 1083–1104.

Pellis, S. M. & Iwaniuk, A. N. (2004). Evolving a playful brain: A levels of control approach. *International Journal of Comparative Psychology, 17*, 90–116.

Pellis, S. M. & McKenna, M. M. (1992). Intrinsic and extrinsic influences on play fighting in rats: Effects of dominance, partner's playfulness, temperament and neonatal exposure to testosterone propionate. *Behavioural Brain Research, 50*, 135–145.

Pellis, S. M. & Pellis, V. C. (1983). Locomotor-rotational movements in the ontogeny and play of the laboratory rat *Rattus norvegicus*. *Developmental Psychobiology, 16*, 269–286.

Pellis, S. M. & Pellis, V. C. (1987). Play-fighting differs from serious fighting in both target of attack and tactics of fighting in the laboratory rat *Rattus norvegicus*. *Aggressive Behavior, 13*, 227–242.

Pellis, S. M. & Pellis, V. C. (1990). Differential rates of attack, defense and counterattack during the developmental decrease in play fighting by male and female rats. *Developmental Psychobiology, 23*, 215–231.

Pellis, S. M. & Pellis, V. C. (1991). Role reversal changes during the ontogeny of play fighting in male rats: Attack versus defense. *Aggressive Behavior, 17*, 179–189.

Pellis, S. M. & Pellis, V. C. (1992). Juvenilized play fighting in subordinate male rats. *Aggressive Behavior, 18*, 449–457.

Pellis, S. M. & Pellis, V. C. (1996). On knowing it's only play: The role of play signals in play fighting. *Aggression & Violent Behavior, 1*, 249–268.

Pellis, S. M. & Pellis, V. C. (1997a). Targets, tactics and the open mouth face during play fighting in three species of primates. *Aggressive Behavior, 23*, 41–57.

Pellis, S. M. & Pellis, V. C. (1997b). The pre-juvenile onset of play fighting in rats (*Rattus norvegicus*). *Developmental Psychobiology, 31*, 193–205.

Pellis, S. M. & Pellis, V. C. (1998a). The play fighting of rats in comparative perspective: A schema for neurobehavioral analyses. *Neuroscience & Biobehavioral Reviews, 23*, 87–101.

Pellis, S. M. & Pellis, V. C. (1998b). Structure-function interface in the analysis of play. In M. Bekoff & J. A. Byers (Eds.), *Animal play: Evolutionary, comparative, and ecological perspectives* (pp. 115–140). Cambridge, UK: Cambridge University Press.

Pellis, S. M. & Pellis, V. C. (2006). Play and the development of social engagement: A comparative perspective. In P. J. Marshall & N. A. Fox (Eds.), *The development of social engagement: Neurobiological perspectives* (pp. 247–274). Oxford, UK: Oxford University Press.

Pellis, S. M. & Pellis, V. C. (2007). Rough-and-tumble play and the development of the social brain. *Current Directions in Psychological Science, 16*, 95–98.

Pellis, S. M. & Pellis, V. C. (2009). *The playful brain. Venturing to the limits of neuroscience.* Oxford, UK: Oneworld Press.

Pellis, S. M., Field, E. F., & Whishaw, I. Q. (1999). The development of a sex-differentiated defensive motor-pattern in rats: A possible role for juvenile experience. *Developmental Psychobiology, 35*, 156–164.

Pellis, S. M., MacDonald, N., & Michener, G. R. (1996). The lateral display as a combat tactic in Richardson's ground squirrel *Spermophilus richardsonii*. *Aggressive Behavior, 22*, 119–134.

Pellis, S. M., Pellis, V. C., & McKenna, M. M. (1993). Some subordinates are more equal than others: Play fighting amongst adult subordinate male rats. *Aggressive Behavior, 19*, 385–393.

Pellis, S. M., Pellis, V. C., & Foroud, A. (2005). Play fighting: Aggression, affiliation and the development of nuanced social skills. In R. Tremblay, W. W. Hartup, & J. Archer (Eds.), *Developmental origins of aggression* (pp. 47–62). New York, NY: Guilford Press.

Pellis, S. M., Pellis, V. C., & Reinhart, C. J. (2010). The evolution of social play. In C. Worthman, P. Plotsky, & D. Schechter (Eds.), *Formative experiences: The interaction of caregiving, culture, and developmental psychobiology* (pp. 406–433). Cambridge, UK: Cambridge University Press.

Pellis, S. M., Pellis, V. C., & Whishaw, I. Q. (1992). The role of the cortex in play fighting by rats: Developmental and evolutionary implications. *Brain, Behavior & Evolution, 39*, 270–284.

Pellis, S. M., Pasztor, T. J., Pellis, V. C., & Dewsbury, D. A. (2000). The organization of play fighting in the grasshopper mouse (*Onychomys leucogaster*): Mixing predatory and sociosexual targets and tactics. *Aggressive Behavior, 26*, 319–334.

Pellis, S. M., Hastings, E., Shimizu, T., Kamitakahara, H., Komorowska, J., Forgie M. L., & Kolb, B. (2006). The effects of orbital frontal cortex damage on the modulation of defensive responses by rats in playful and non-playful social contexts. *Behavioral Neuroscience, 120*, 72–84.

Power, T. G. (2000). *Play and exploration in animals and children.* Mahwah, NJ: Lawrence Erlbaum Associates.

Reinhart, C. J., Metz, G., Pellis, S. M., & McIntyre, D. C. (2006). Play fighting between kindling-prone (FAST) and kindling-resistant (SLOW) rats. *Journal of Comparative Psychology, 120*, 19–30.

Reinhart, C. J., Pellis, V. C., Thierry, B., Gauthier, C.-A., VanderLaan, D. P., Vasey, P. L., & Pellis, S. M. (2010). Targets and tactics of play fighting: Competitive *versus* cooperative styles of play in Japanese and Tonkean macaques. *International Journal of Comparative Psychology, 23*, 166–200.

Rempel-Clower, N. L. (2007). Role of orbitofrontal cortex connections in emotion. *Annals of the New York Academy of Sciences, 1121,* 72–86.

Ryan, K. M. & Mohr, S. (2005). Gender differences in playful aggression during courtship in college students. *Sex Roles, 53,* 591–601.

Rushen, J., & Pajor, E. (1987). Offence and defense in fights between young pigs (*Sus scrofa*). *Aggressive Behavior, 13,* 329–346.

Siviy, S. M. & Panksepp, J. (1987). Sensory modulation of juvenile play in rats. *Developmental Psychobiology, 20,* 39–55.

Smith, L. K., Fantella, S.-L., & Pellis, S. M. (1999). Playful defensive responses in adult male rats depend upon the status of the unfamiliar opponent. *Aggressive Behavior, 25,* 141–152.

Smith, P. K. (1997). Play fighting and real fighting. Perspectives on their relationship. In Schmitt, A., Atzwanger, K., Grammar, K., & Schäfer, K. (Eds.), *New aspects of human ethology* (pp. 47–64). New York, NY: Plenum Press.

Smith, P. K. & Boulton, M. (1990). Rough and tumble play, aggression and dominance: Perception and behavior in children's encounters. *Human Development, 33,* 271–282.

Smith, P. K., Hunter, T., Carvalho, A. M. A., & Costabile, A. (1992). Children's perceptions of playfighting, playchasing and real fighting: A cross-national interview study. *Social Development, 1,* 211–229.

Spinka, M., Newberry, R. C., & Bekoff, M. (2001). Mammalian play: Can training for the unexpected be fun? *Quarterly Review of Biology, 76,* 141–176.

Suomi, S. J., Harlow, H. F., & McKinney, W. T. (1972). Monkey psychiatrists. *American Journal of Psychiatry, 128,* 927–932.

Symons, D. (1978). *Play and aggression. A study of rhesus monkeys.* New York, NY: Columbia University Press.

Thompson, K. V. (1998). Self assessment in juvenile play. In M. Bekoff & J. A. Byers (Eds.), *Animal play: Evolutionary, comparative, and ecological perspectives* (pp. 183–204). Cambridge, UK: Cambridge University Press.

Thor, D. H., & Holloway, W. R., Jr. (1984). Developmental analysis of social play behavior in juvenile rats. *Bulletin of the Psychonomic Society, 22,* 587–590.

van den Berg, C. L., Hol, T., van Ree, J. M., Spruijt, B. M., Everts, H., & Koolhaas, J. M. (1999). Play is indispensable for an adequate development of coping with social challenges in the rat. *Developmental Psychobiology, 34,* 129–138.

Varlinskaya, E. I., Spear, L. P., & Spear, N. E. (1999). Social behavior and social motivation in adolescent rats: Role of housing conditions and partner's activity. *Physiology & Behavior, 67,* 475–482.

von Frijtag, J. C., Schot, M., van den Bos, R., & Spruijt, B. M. (2002). Individual housing during the play period results in changed responses to and consequences of a psychosocial stress situation in rats. *Developmental Psychobiology, 41,* 58–69.

Weidenmayer, C. P. (2009). Plasticity of defensive behavior and fear in early development. *Neuroscience & Biobehavioral Reviews, 33,* 432–441.

White, S. W., Koenig, K., & Scahill, L. (2007). Social skills development in children with autism spectrum disorders: A review of the intervention research. *Journal of Autism & Developmental Disorders, 37,* 1858–1868.

Whishaw, I. Q., Metz, G., Kolb, B., & Pellis, S. M. (2001). Accelerated nervous system development contributes to behavioral efficiency in the laboratory mouse: A behavioral review and theoretical proposal. *Developmental Psychobiology, 39,* 151–170.

Children's Games and Playground Activities in School and Their Role in Development

Ed Baines *and* Peter Blatchford

Abstract

This chapter examines the role of school playground games in children's development. Games and play take place in a range of settings, both in and outside of the home, in gardens, parks, on the streets, designated playgrounds, or other locations. They also take place and are often studied on the school playground and this will be the main context in which the role of games and other playground activities will be discussed here. The school playground is a useful research site because it is one of the few locations where children interact in a relatively safe environment, free of adult control, and when their play, games, and social relations are more their own. There is an appreciation by many researchers that much can be learned about children from studying their behavior and experiences whilst engaged in play and games (see Blatchford & Sharp, 1994; Pellegrini, 2005; Pellegrini & Blatchford, 2000; Smith, 1994; Sutton-Smith, 1982). Although playground activities express something about the individual child, individuals on the playground are situated and live their lives in complex social structures. Social structures involve and are expressed through, for example, play, games, even hanging around, and the study of playground activity can help with the understanding of peer relations in terms of friendship, peer groups, and social status. A key message in this chapter therefore is that if we want to find out about children's social and psychological development, including their relationships with peers and the acquisition of social and cognitive skills, then we need to study how these arise out of the everyday reality of children's playful activities and interactions with others in everyday contexts.

The chapter draws mainly on psychological research on games and social activities that children participate in during middle childhood and to some extent adolescence. There are five main sections which cover the following issues.

- The current status and context of play outside and inside school.
- Definitions of games and perspectives on their role in development.
- How games and social activities change with development during and beyond middle childhood, how this varies by sex, and how games are learned from other children.
- The role playground games have in supporting peer relationships and the development of social-cognitive skills.
- The role of games in relation to learning and engagement in the classroom, school belonging, and adjustment.

For illustration, we draw on several of our own research projects, in particular the Nuffield Foundation-funded national surveys of recess (or breaktime as it is called in the UK) in schools (conducted in 1995 and 2006) and pupil views on recess and social life outside of school (Blatchford & Baines, 2006; Blatchford & Sumpner, 1996), and a Spencer Foundation-funded project on playground activities and peer relations in UK and US schools (Baines & Blatchford, 2009; Blatchford, Baines & Pellegrini, 2003; Pellegrini, Kato, Blatchford & Baines, 2002; Pellegrini, Blatchford, Kato & Baines, 2004). Reported data will come in the main from the UK part of this project, including unreported data from a three-year follow up, unless otherwise stated. We will refer to these as the 'Nuffield' and 'Spencer' projects, respectively.

Keywords: Games; games-with-rules; recess; breaktime; peer relations; friendships; peer groups; sex differences; school adjustment

Introduction

In the US and UK, play and games and the contexts within which they occur are different to those 20 or even 10 years ago. These changes provide insights into the way games and play more generally are viewed and valued within our societies and school systems. The complex social, economic, and cultural changes over this period have inevitably affected opportunities for children and young people to engage in games and other social activities outside of school and the home (Elkind, 2007; Furedi, 2002; Gill, 2007; Nichols & Good, 2004). While advanced communication technologies have led to increased social connection at one level, people are leading increasingly separate lives with fewer opportunities for face-to-face interactions with peers and friends (see Goldstein, this volume). The rise in home entertainment, modern constraints such as increased traffic, pressure on space in cities, and policies and behaviors prompted by concerns about risk taking, bullying, and strangers are functioning to keep children inside the home. Parents are discouraged from allowing their children unsupervised movement out of the home so that they become unable to benefit from free play and opportunities to learn through experience, appropriate risk, and even mistakes. For example, surveys since the early 1990s show that students in the UK, at least, are less likely to walk to school, that large proportions of 8–10 year olds had never been to a park, shops, or played out with their friends unsupervised, and that nearly a third of 8–15 year olds rarely meet friends outside of school (Blatchford & Baines, 2006; Hillman, 1993; Home Office & DCSF, 2005). An unlikely source of reduction in free play opportunities comes from the increase in adult-led after-school provision designed to provide care and/or additional learning opportunities while busy parents work.

There are suggestions that these constraints are affecting the well-being of our children as illustrated by public debate and concerns about bullying, anti-social behavior, and youth violence (Margo & Dixon, 2006; Nichols & Good, 2004) as well as concerns about physical and mental health (Layard & Dunn, 2009; Nichols & Good, 2004) and declining moral values (Public Agenda, 1999, cited in Nichols & Good, 2004). A recent report from UNICEF (2007) indicated that on several indices US and UK children were less happy and had more difficulties with peers than those in other OECD countries. The Children's Society national enquiry in the UK indicated that the number of teenagers with no best friends had increased over the past 16 years, while those who reported being assaulted or threatened by a peer had also increased (Layard & Dunn, 2009).

Within schools there are also limited opportunities for play and social interaction with peers. Studies of classroom practice highlight that at primary and to some extent secondary levels, classroom life is dominated by whole class teaching and independent seatwork (Baines, Blatchford & Kutnick, 2003; Galton, Hargreaves, Comber, Wall & Pell, 1999; Weinstein, 1991). Within school classrooms students are given few opportunities to work and interact with peers and friends (Epstein, 1989). Children that are friends are often separated for fear of increased off-task activity or disruption (Zajac & Hartup, 1997).

Such reduced opportunities for play and peer interactions emphasize the importance of those few remaining times, such as at recess in school, which provide opportunities for children to play and interact with peers and develop friendships. But here, too, there are indications of progressive reductions in time available for recess in the US, UK, and Australia (Evans, 1990; Patte, 2006; Pellegrini, 2005). In the US, many states do not require a statutory recess break and many school systems have abolished recess (Jarrett & Maxwell, 2000; Simon & Childers, 2006) sometimes in favor of additional physical education (Pellegrini, 2005). In the UK, the current situation is slightly better with most students experiencing a short morning break of approximately 15 minutes as well as a lunch time of up to one hour. The Nuffield research, which consisted of two recent national surveys of approximately 6–7% of all primary and secondary schools in the UK, found a growing trend over the past 15–20 years for a reduction in the length, or even virtual elimination, of recess from the school day (Blatchford & Baines, 2006; Blatchford & Sumpner, 1998). Previously, longer lunch times and an afternoon recess were common. Reasons presented for reductions in recess were to increase curriculum time and as a response to worsening behavior of students. Ongoing concerns about anti-social behavior in school have led to calls for the reduction and elimination of recess (Galton & MacBeath, 2004) and the construction of new schools without space or opportunities for unstructured play activity (The Observer, 2007). The Nuffield survey indicated that school staff views on the value of recess varied, with the majority highlighting it as an opportunity to let off steam, get physical exercise, and for the development of social skills, though secondary schools valued it in more functional terms (e.g., as a time to eat). In contrast to concerns about bullying and disruptive behavior, we found that the large majority of children enjoy recess and valued it in terms of the opportunities it provided for meeting with friends and other peers. The Nuffield research, which also involved a survey of over 1300 children and adolescents, suggests that only 4–6% of pupils are negative about recess. There is no evidence at all that pupils feel recess should be further eroded, in fact many expressed the view, and increasingly with age, that it should be extended or remain the same length.

The current lack of opportunities outside of school for young people to engage in playful recreation highlights the importance of a prescribed school recess for all children. A positive view of recess highlights the inherent value and positive benefits it may have on a number of fronts. During middle childhood, recess (where it exists) is often a time for vigorous physical activity, and has an obvious function in relation to worries about sedentary life styles and childhood obesity (Stratton & Mullan, 2005). Indeed, a recent review suggests that recess in primary school can contribute up to 40% of boys' and 30% of girls' recommended amount of daily physical activity (Ridgers, Stratton, & Fairclough, 2006). As highlighted by folklorists, recess is a main context for cultural transmission through participation in a wide array of play, games, rituals, and social activities that are instigated and controlled by children and where adult involvement undermines the spontaneity, creativity, and delight of the game (Bishop & Curtis, 2001; Opie & Opie, 1969; Opie, 1993). Recess, like play, has an intrinsic value in allowing children to have fun, to engage in social interaction with peers where friendships and peer groups (we use the term 'peer groups' to refer to 'cliques,' 'social networks,' and 'peer networks') are formed and maintained, and where important social-cognitive skills are developed and social lessons learned (Sluckin, 1981). Recess also has important implications for school learning, engagement, and overall adjustment (Blatchford & Baines, 2010).

The Nature of Games and Perspectives on Their Role in Development

In this section we examine the notion of games in relation to views of play and outline main perspectives on games relative to human development.

What are games and how are they different from play?

To date, psychological research on children's games is relatively limited. This is particularly the case over the last 25 years or so. As noted by Pellegrini (2005), the most recent editions of the *Handbook of Child Psychology* (published in 1998, but also the more recent edition published in 2006) on social and personality development make little reference to games-with-rules. A main reason is the absence of a chapter on play. Pellegrini suggests this is due to the difficulties associated with undertaking research on children's play and games in school settings, but it may also reflect an ambivalent view of the role of games in social and cognitive development. While games have been located in relation to play in traditional theoretical works in this area (Garvey, 1990; Piaget, 1962), more recent writings about play have aimed to disassociate games from play (Pellegrini, 2005; Rubin, Fein & Vandenberg, 1983; Smith, 2010). Much of this stems from efforts to clearly define play and this is seen most notably in the work of Rubin et al. (1983) in their review of play in the 4th edition of the *Handbook of Child Psychology*, which specifically excludes games on definitional grounds as well as a practical need to focus the review. But as we shall see in this section, although games have distinctive features that suggest that they may be different from play, a clear boundary is not easily drawn between them.

A main characteristic particular to games is that they involve rules and roles that have previously been established by others, are probably codified in some way, and thus can be explicitly communicated. The existence of rules and roles places constraints on children's behavior within the game. These rules are much less flexible than the implicit rules and roles evident in peek-a-boo, rough-and-tumble (R&T) play, and those negotiated during fantasy play (Smith, 2010; Vygotsky, 1978). As Garvey (1990) suggests, the existence of codified rules renders games as "*social objects*" which can be "*recalled, talked about, evaluated, or planned in advance*" (p. 104). Rules associated with a game are set in advance and players must subordinate their desires and behavior to them (Pellegrini, 2005).

But in reality, games are more flexible than this. For example, the simple game of 'it' involves a chaser and chased but there are plenty of additional features that can be introduced to make the game more complex. Similarly, there are multiple ways of playing a version of soccer where some rules are adapted or not applied (Opie & Opie, 1969). The rules used can involve extended negotiations between players, sometimes taking longer to decide than the playing of the game (Garvey, 1990). Similarly, in practice the rules and roles in many types of 'games' are locally negotiated and adapted to the local context (e.g. numbers of players). Children may play some of the roles or rules involved in one game and apply them to another or adapt the rules or structure to match the numbers of players, space, and props available.

Determining whether children are playing a 'game' or engaged in play can be quite difficult for an observer and children may not make a clear distinction either. In the Spencer project, the traditional game of 'cops and robbers,' which involves both specific rules relative to chaser and chased but also a fantasy theme, was played in one school both as purely a chasing game with little reference to the theme but also by another group of children as a primarily fantasy play activity with some chasing. Other groups of children highlighted both components to provide a real mix of the fantasy and chasing elements. In practice, sustaining a clear distinction between play and games is not straightforward. There is also nothing precluding the possibility of a game being played with a slightly different emphasis each time.

Another feature of games, highlighted by Rubin et al. (1983) and Piaget (1962), is that games require at least two people to engage in competitive activity. This is a main reason given for not including games in a definition of play since they involve an ulterior motive or goal, that is, for a person or team 'to win,' and are thus not engaged in for their own sake. This characterization of games draws on Piaget's investigation and definition of games. Piaget's work was limited to two types of games in particular—that of marbles and a relatively simple game played mainly by girls (the equivalent of which might be '40:40' or 'hide and seek'). Despite this limited investigation of games, Piaget indicated that children were less concerned about the competitive component of games.

> "As a matter of fact, no child even from among the older ones, ever attributes very great importance to the fact of knocking out a few more marbles than his opponents. Mere competition is therefore not what constitutes the affective motive power of the game" (p.33, *Piaget*, 1932).

Piaget was keen to emphasize that children value games because they enjoy getting to know the rules of the game but more importantly the opportunity they provide to participate socially with others in joint activity. This emphasis is much more on the 'means' rather than the outcome of the activity.

There is no denying that some games do involve competition between persons. Racing games often pit individuals against each other and it may be that ranking in the social network hierarchy is based on how a child fares, over time, relative to peers. Equally, there are many types of games which involve relatively minimal amounts of competition (e.g., chasing games). In some cases a better term might be a 'challenge'—for example, in various types of jump-rope (or skipping as it is called in the UK) games it is the challenge of how long a child can jump for, rather than competition with other participants. Peers may be quick to point out where players have gone wrong but there is little emphasis on winners and losers. If the game were just about the winning, then many children might not participate in these activities. Those children not skilled at these games are often still keen to participate. Participation in games is an opportunity to hone and publicly demonstrate individual skills. Demonstrations of 'facility' in the activity may lead to enhanced social status and thus may represent competition within the peer group. But this is not the full story since other types of games also involve a social coordinative or collaborative element (particularly some girls' games but also team games). Success in these collaborative elements may also be necessary for social success. Bruner (1972) refers to anthropological research by Burridge in New Guinea where games have less of a competitive component and the aim of the game is for players to tie and receive equal shares. This type of game exists in a culture where equal sharing is highly valued.

For Rubin et al. (1983), both the presence of codified rules and competition are in direct conflict with at least two main components of play—its flexibility and engagement in the activity for its own sake. The overriding question is whether this formalization, due to rules, and varying emphasis on competition or social challenge, is enough to separate games from play. The play criteria suggested by Krasnor and Pepler (1980) emphasizes that play can involve flexibility in content and form, non-literality of the meaning of behavior and situation, intrinsic motivation or engagement in the activity for its own sake, and involves enjoyment or positive affect (Krasnor and Pepler indicate that the more criteria that are present the more likely something can be considered to be play than not play). Games certainly involve positive affect, engagement in the activity for its own sake as well as to compete with others or demonstrate skill and social coordination. Many games also have varying levels of non-literality as can be illustrated by 'cops and robbers,' 'duck, duck, goose,' and 'what's the time Mr. Wolf?' While admittedly there is a tendency for the rules of games to be established by tradition and to be set prior to children embarking on the game, children are often innovative in their adjustment of games to suit the local constraints and conditions. In short, there is little to suggest that games cannot be considered a form of play. In fact we might want to argue (consistent with the views of Piaget, 1932; Sutton-Smith, 1976; and Vygotsky, 1978) that the nature of play develops within the child alongside cognitive and social development and that game play is part of this process.

An important feature of games is that they are invariably social activities conducted in small, large, or very large groups of people (though some games can be solitary, e.g., patience and console activities). By contrast, much play activity can be either solitary or social. Games can be less focused than play; the activity of a game may stretch all across the playground and/or involve multiple sites of action and multiple clusters of children interacting. There are also differences in the nature of the social interaction involved in play and games. Within social fantasy play there is an expectation of a certain amount of coordination between those involved, but it is also acceptable for players to decide where their particular role or individual activity might go next. Children do cooperate and collaborate in fantasy play but there is less necessity for this to take place in order for the activity to exist. Participation in games is more about cooperating or collaborating in an activity where players assume or expect other players to abide by the rules and within the boundaries of fair play. In games such as 'hide and seek' a player would be perfectly within their right to assume that the hider had not 'hot-footed' it off home or somewhere completely out of the current context. Similarly, some players within a game of soccer or 'British Bulldogs' would be expected to collaborate together in their endeavor to catch others.

Theoretical perspectives on games and development

There are a number of theories that relate to the development of play and games. Many of these will not be covered here since their primary focus is on play rather than games and readers are referred elsewhere (Goncu & Gaskins, this volume; Rubin et al.,

1983; Ortega, 2003; and chapters in Pellegrini & Smith, 2005). Of the 20th century theorists, Piaget's work holds the most relevance to a discussion of games and social activities on the school playground. For Piaget, play and games were not of intrinsic interest but reflected social-cognitive development of the child and thus he did not discuss them in detail (Piaget, 1926, 1932, 1962).

Piaget (1962) suggested that game play emerged during the early years in school and was associated with the beginnings of operational thought where children begin to take account of alternate perspectives, control their own views and desires, and to adapt their behavior to comply with the abstract publicly accepted rules of the game. In contrast to earlier forms of play, games-with-rules represent an interest in the social regulation of activity by way of adherence to codified rules. Children begin to coordinate their behavior and action with others (via rules), to cooperate, and ultimately to collaborate in playful activity. Piaget suggested that early game play involved imitation of the play of older children to feel part of a larger and older social group rather than a real desire to engage or cooperate with playmates. During this period the child may adhere to the rules or make them up as he/she sees fit. Development in game play involves increasing personal knowledge of game rules to an appreciation that rules are collectively agreed but modifiable according to the needs of the group.

Such development is supported by an increasing ability to engage in coherent and complex dialogues, disputes, and negotiations involving increasingly abstract content (Piaget, 1926) initially with another peer and later in larger groups (Baines & Howe, in press; Goncu, 1993). This final stage is often described as peers collaborating in abstract thought (e.g. discussions about game rules). Others have argued that experiences during games and play may be wrapped up in provoking developmental change (Garvey, 1990); when peers challenge each other on their understanding (e.g. of roles, rules, stereotypes, cheating and other aspects of the world around them) this may lead to socio-cognitive conflict and the development of new understandings.

AN ECOLOGICAL PERSPECTIVE

Drawing on the work of Bronfenbrenner, we can apply an ecological approach to understanding the role of games and play in development. In his highly influential ecological systems model, Bronfenbrenner (1979) conceptualized the individual at the center of a range of ecologically meaningful nested contexts from the 'microsystem,' which relates to the school or family context, to more distant contexts such as the neighborhood and the political system. More recent authors have highlighted the presence of other smaller, more locally defined, contexts that exist within Bronfenbrenner's notion of the 'microsystem' of a school, such as the classroom and the playground and even within these contexts we can distinguish further nested contexts of formally or informally organized groups or groupings that the individual is involved in (Pellegrini & Blatchford, 2000; Baines et al., 2003; Kindermann & Valsiner, 1995). These contexts involve qualitatively distinct sets of relationships, rules, and dynamics that promote certain types of behavior and activity while hindering others. This connects very closely with work by ecological psychologists who highlighted the important role of the immediate environment as a factor in explaining everyday behavior (Barker & Wright, 1951), and the important notion of proximal, as opposed to distal, processes that arise in everyday interactions with others and are likely to have a profound effect on individual development (Bronfenbrenner & Ceci, 1994). Related to an ecological perspective is the following point from Sutton-Smith (1982) who argues that

> "the most important thing to know about peer culture is what is going on there. That is, that we might learn more of the structure and more of the function if we first studied what the action is (that is) the performances that are central to children…"
> (p. 68).

The centrality of everyday activities and interactions (with peers, adults etc.) is paramount since this is the location where the proximal processes and the more distal features of culture, school policies, classroom ethos, peer group attitudes, and so on interconnect. Though we might view contexts as nested circles (Bronfenbrenner, 1979), or as a rope of twisted threads (Cole, 1996), the place where the proximal and distal features of social and cultural life converge on the individual child is through that child's direct actions and interactions with others in the ongoing context. It is during these interactions with others that proximal and distal processes are conveyed, imposed, negotiated, and constructed.

How Games Change with Development

The nature of play changes markedly with development, from simple forms of object play in the early years, increasing amounts of fantasy play and vigorous and sedentary object play, to activities often described as games-with-rules in middle childhood (Pellegrini, 2005; Smith, 2010). Such development is associated more broadly with changes in social and cognitive development. However, there is little understanding of how play and games change during middle childhood, once children begin to engage in games-with-rules.

Taking account of Piaget's developmental model, we might expect games that involve rules to increasingly predominate activity at recess during middle childhood, at the expense of other forms of play, as they require experience and maturation for children to learn the rules. Furthermore, there might be changes in the complexity of games played. In learning the rules, children will need to use them when engaged in the game and to subordinate (or not) their perspectives to those of their peers and other players. Pellegrini et al. (2004) suggest that children move from simple chase activities to games such as soccer, American football, basketball, etc. Similarly, Blatchford (1998) reported that 'traditional' chasing, catching and seeking games, such as 'What's the time Mr. Wolf' and 'hide 'n seek' declined over the year (8–9 years), perhaps as a result of inherent limitations in the games. However, some chasing games (e.g. 'British bulldogs,' 'cops and robbers,' and so on) can involve rather more complex rules, roles, and characteristics than more simplistic chase activities. Therefore, an increase in game play and game complexity might be expected with development.

A further aspect of game play that may change over middle childhood is the tendency for games to become increasingly a forum for social activity with increasing numbers of playmates and interaction partners. Middle childhood is about the time that the dominance of play in early childhood is joined by the emergence of friendships and social conversation (Hartup, 1996).

Descriptions of the types of play and games engaged in during middle childhood identify the vivacity and social complexity shown in the play of primary school children (Bishop & Curtis, 2001; Opie & Opie, 1969). However, in contrast with other aspects of children's play, there is little descriptive data on the frequency with which different types of games are played, (e.g., Holland, 2003; Pellegrini & Smith, 1998; Rubin et al., 1983). Boulton (1992; 2005) found that sociable contact between children, and rule games such as football, rounders, and tag, as well as R&T play, were common activities. Similarly, drawing on self-report data, Blatchford (1998) found that at 11 years, playground activities were dominated by active games, in particular ball games and chasing games but also straightforward social activity such as talking to friends, hanging around, and sitting down. While this study provides insights into the range and popularity of particular activities it does not tell us actual levels of engagement in these activities. In the Spencer project, which involved repeated systematic scan sampling observations of seven- to eight-year-old children over a period of two weeks at the start (September) and the end of a year (June) in four schools in London, children spent recess primarily engaged in social activity (solitary activity was observed only 10% of the time) (Blatchford et al., 2003). There were three main types of activity, all of which usually involved peer interaction: first, conversation; second, play (vigorous, sedentary, and fantasy play); and third, game playing (chasing, catching and seeking games, racing games, ball games, jump skipping, games with materials, verbal games). Play and games each accounted for about a third of activities observed and conversation a fifth of activities. The remaining 11% represented no activity (i.e., when they were solitary or parallel onlooking/ unoccupied etc). A longitudinal follow up three years later (June), when the children were ten to eleven years old, found a reduction in play activities to 14% of observations and an increase in conversational activities to 39% of observations. Levels of game play increased slightly to 37% and 'no activity' remained constant at 10%.

Of the types of games played over the three time points, there was an increase in ball games (8% to 15% to 25% across the three time points) and a decrease in racing and jump rope but chasing, catching, and seeking games, and verbal-hand clapping games remained constant at 7% and 2% respectively. These findings are broadly consistent with the theory that children play increasingly complex rule-bound games (Pellegrini et al., 2004). Chasing, catching, and seeking games did not decrease in incidence possibly because children engaged in more advanced forms. Such games may reduce substantially once children transfer to secondary school. As well as the influence on games of materials and spaces provided by schools, and the fact that secondary school playgrounds tend to be barren landscapes, there are also social processes that might discourage game play. Older children may influence the games that are played by determining what is and is not considered 'appropriate' (Blatchford, 1998). Views on the intrinsic value of certain types of games might change over time with some being considered dull or childish. More careful exploration of the nature and balance of social and non social factors affecting changes in games over time is still needed.

In the Spencer study, levels of R&T behavior were surprisingly low, accounting for about 5% of observations at each time point. These estimates are low in comparison to other studies (e.g. Jarrett & Duckett-Hedgebeth, 2005), though the difference may be explained by the different sampling methods used (instantaneous as used in the Spencer study versus one-zero sampling over two minutes) and the age ranges studied (5th–9th graders). The most clearly anti-social behaviors in the Spencer study, such as aggression, teasing/taunting, disputing, were all infrequent at all three time points (with each accounting for 1-2% of observations), as were incidents when children were disciplined by an adult. Aggression, though rare, was most common during vigorous play and conversation, but not ball games (Blatchford et al., 2003; Pellegrini, et al., 2002). This is surprising given that ball games involve higher competitive spirits, physicality and a higher likelihood of accidental harm, than other activities but the presence of game rules may function to provide order and reduce flashpoints. In general, findings suggest that social activities and games are common on the playground and that negative experiences are relatively rare (Jarett & Duckett-Hedgebeth, 2005; Pellegrini et al., 2002; 2004).

Another aspect of games that appears to change over the course of middle childhood is the size of the social grouping engaged in the activity. Few studies provide full details of numbers of children involved in playground groups but Ladd, Price and Hart (1988) in a study of preschoolers between the ages of 3;6 and 4;6 report that average game-group sizes were around 1.48–1.62. These are rather smaller than the groups observed in the Spencer study where game networks ranged from 3.5 at the start of the year (7–8 year olds) to 3.9 at the end of the year and showed a further increase to 4.5 three years later (10–11 years old). Similar group sizes are reported by Boulton and Smith (1993) for 8–9 year olds. This suggests, as indicated earlier, that children socialize in increasingly larger groups with development. Such a pattern may reflect increasing social and communicative competence since the communication skills required to coordinate dialogue, sustain a joint topic of conversation and/or joint activity in larger groupings may be beyond many young children (Baines & Howe, in press). Alternatively, this may be a result of increased participation in team games that require greater numbers of players.

There have been few observational studies of games and activities during recess in secondary school. However, in a self-report study of young people followed up at 16 years, after being originally questioned at 11 years (Blatchford, 1998), the main change was that games other than soccer had all but disappeared. By 16 years the most popular activity was conversing with friends, hanging around, and socializing (72%). The physically active nature of recess in primary school therefore contrasts with the more covert, sedentary, and sometimes apparently unfocused activities of the last years at school. We should, however, be cautious about concluding that secondary recess activities are of less social importance. As they move through secondary school, pupils' social lives become important in new and deeper ways and are vital in their developing sense of who they are (Brown, 1990; Furman, 1989). The Nuffield pupil survey indicated that older children, more so than younger children, wanted longer recess periods (Blatchford & Baines, 2006).

Though secondary school playgrounds are not sites for play and games, the social groups that exist may be centered on a common activity or joint interest (Brown, 1990). Similarly, such 'socializing' (particularly in mixed sex groups) can involve simple and complex forms of social play such as 'poke-and-push' and R&T activity, teasing, practical joking, chasing and catching, daring, and other individual-group affiliating activities. Differences in recess activities between primary and secondary sectors no doubt owe a lot to developmental factors but may also be connected to different policy and practice in the two sectors. This was suggested in the Nuffield study where it was found that recess in secondary schools was perceived by staff as more problematic but also received less attention and planning, less staff support and training, and fewer facilities (Blatchford & Baines, 2006). Staff also viewed recess in functional terms as time for a break and something to eat and drink rather than to socialize and play; it is little wonder that secondary schools are reducing opportunities for unstructured social time.

Although development moves from simple forms of play to games to socializing behaviors and activity, it should not be assumed that play and games die out during adolescence. On the contrary, the substantial computer/console gaming leisure industry is a testament to the longevity of game play outside childhood. Furthermore, throughout childhood and adolescence, children become involved in formalized groups outside school that provide opportunities to engage in sports, cultural, fantasy, and adventure (e.g. scouts) activities; may include training; and are more serious than their equivalents on the playground. Successful transition into university life for young adults may be facilitated by the existence of organized interest-based clubs and groups. Such activities and leisure pursuits clearly indicate that play, broadly conceived, continues long into adulthood and in many instances provides the glue that sustains and enhances friendship and family relationships (Argyle, 1992).

Sex differences in games and play activities

We have seen how games and other recess activities vary with age; however, they also vary by sex. There is a substantial literature focused on the play and other activities of boys and girls highlighting that differences in early play styles and behavior may have a central role in explaining sex differences observed at later points in development (Maccoby, 1998; Serbin, Moller, Gulko, Powlishta & Colbourne, 1994). In this section we will examine sex differences in games and play activities during middle childhood. Reasons for these differences and the formation of single sex groups will be discussed later in this chapter.

Studies of sex differences in play and games have tended to highlight boys' greater engagement in physically vigorous activity (Maccoby, 1998; Pellegrini, 2005; Pellegrini et al., 2002; Rubin et al., 1983) and girls' preference for games requiring verbal facility (Maccoby, 1998). Findings from the Spencer study are consistent, with boys (at 7–8 and 10–11 years) being more likely to engage in physically vigorous fantasy play, ball games, R&T play, aggression, and to be disciplined by adults. In contrast, girls were more likely to engage in conversation and verbal games and to show more positive affection. At 7–8 years, girls engaged in more sedentary play than boys and at 10–11 years higher levels of disputing were recorded. There were few changes in differences over time except, interestingly, girls doubled the amount of participation in ball games from 6% to 12% of observations, a finding consistent with Piaget's view that rule games will become increasing popular among girls and boys.

Studies of sex differences in the levels of fantasy play appear to be relatively equivocal about whether boys or girls engage in more fantasy play (Rubin et al., 1983; Smith, 2010). Pellegrini (2005) suggests that girls engage more frequently in fantasy play during preschool. In contrast, the Spencer study found that boys engaged in fantasy play more frequently than girls, at all three time points, and even at 10 to 11 years, the levels of boys' fantasy play (7%) were still slightly higher than they were for girls at any of the time points (2–6%). For boys, fantasy play is a context for R&T and physical activity, while for girls fantasy play tends to be more sedentary (Fein, 1981). Boys' fantasy play is often based on action heroes in media (computer games, films, TV cartoons), while girls' fantasy play combines media characters with domestic and caring themes (Holland, 2003). The differences between studies in the levels of fantasy play for boys and girls might be explained by different definitions or differences between schools in the availability of play materials. Developmental changes are also a reasonable explanation with girls initially engaging in more fantasy play but then moving on to other activities once they reach school. One possible reason for the sex difference in levels of fantasy play reported in the Spencer study is that it offered those boys that do not engage in athletic/sporting games an outlet for physical activity.

Overall patterns of recess activity from the Spencer study indicate that boys spend more time engaged in games than girls, and their involvement in games and conversation increases over middle childhood (36% to 50% and 15% to 25% respectively). At the same time, involvement in play declines (40% to 19%). Girls' interest in social conversation increases (from 26% to 52%) over middle childhood, while their interest in play and to some extent games, already less than boys', declines (32% to 11% and 30% to 26% respectively). Such findings are not dissimilar to those reported by Boulton and Smith (1993) who observed 8–9 year olds and Crombie and Desjardins (1993) (cited in Maccoby, 1998) who observed the free play of 9–10 and 11–12 year olds. Predictions that participation in games would increase over time at the expense of play therefore apply to boys but less so for girls. It is difficult to say that girls' involvement in games reduces between 8 and 11 years because we do not have data for the three years in between. However, findings do attest to the increasing dominance for girls of conversation over play and possibly also games.

These findings introduce difficulties for Piagetian ideas about the development of games being driven by the cognitive complexity of rules but are consistent with ideas about play reflecting increased social coordination, interaction, and intimacy, issues that girls appear to be more interested in. In comparing boys and girls, Piaget (1932) suggested that girls were less interested in a detailed understanding of game rules. However, some of the game-like (since the rules are not really codified) dancing routines that girls participate in on playgrounds can involve high levels of individual and social coordination and collaboration. These activities may be of equal complexity to many traditional rule games and are similar to jump-rope performances. Some groups of girls spend hours discussing, arranging, and perfecting routines. Similarly, as suggested by Goodwin (2006), girls are often equally concerned with issues of rules, rights, and social justice within games and peer relationships. What we are suggesting here is that the increased interest during middle childhood, in socially coordinated and regulated activity, can express itself in different ways and different activities.

How games are passed on

Games and play activities at recess can have a life of their own and some games are sustained in a school for generations while others are dropped, maybe to resurface a few years later, possibly under a different name (Blatchford, 1998). The cutting back or even abolition of recess as evidenced in parts of the US and UK may threaten the existence and transfer of playground culture across generations of children (Jarrett & Duckett-Hedgebeth, 2005).

Piaget (1932) and Opie and Opie (1969) suggest that games and their rules are passed down by older children. The processes involved in transmission are complex and may be via peers, older siblings, or even the supervising adults that exist on the playground. The most likely process is through observation of older children playing such games or actual participation in these games. Field notes from the Spencer study illustrate how a young group of boys (7–8 year olds) played a chasing and catching game of 'British Bulldogs' in parallel and overlap with a group of older boys (10–11 year olds) playing the same game. Only the more popular boys from the younger group participated in both games; interacting and talking with the older boys, helping them chase others, running in parallel with them as they were being chased or by actually chasing them. Younger boys were not chased by older boys. The remainder of the group played the game in parallel with the older group. Similar forms of transmission were observed within girls' games. Transmission may be related to social status and function to reinforce social hierarchy such that game rules may be passed down by older children to the popular children in the peer group. In turn, these rules may be conveyed to same-age peers through information exchange or rebuke when a rule is broken.

The Role of Games and Playground Activities in Peer Relations and the Development of Social-Cognitive Skills

Games and playground activities in school are also of interest because of their role in the social organization and status of children relative to peers (Boulton, 1992, 2005; Sutton-Smith, 1982) and in the development of friendships and social-cognitive skills (Sluckin, 1981). These aspects are, of course, intimately connected in that social-cognitive skills, and the ability to adapt them, have implications for sociometric status and the nature of relationships with peers in school. In turn, the nature and quality of one's peer relations can have implications for the development of particular social and cognitive skills. Games and playground activities can also have a negative side. Social relations can be fractious, and the misery caused by bullying and harassment has to be recognized and dealt with. But it is a salutary finding that students say that the best thing about school is the chance to meet their friends (Layard & Dunn, 2009), and games and play at recess provide the main forum for their social life in school (Blatchford, 1998; Blatchford & Baines, 2006). The negative side of peer experiences during recess such as bullying, deviant peer relations, and aggression are relatively rare and will not be covered here (see the following for further coverage: Garandeau & Cillessen, 2006; Hartup, 1996; Nishina, 2004; Smith & Sharp, 1994). In this section we examine the role of games and play activities in developing and supporting peer relationships and providing opportunities for the development of social-cognitive skills.

Playground activities, peer networks, and friendship

There is a large literature on the development of children's friendships and peer groups. This research is too numerous to be covered here (see reviews in Cairns, Xie, & Leung, 1998; Dunn, 2004; Gest, Graham-Bermann, & Hartup, 2001; Hartup, 1992; Rubin, Bukowski, & Parker, 2006; Schneider, 2000). Here we concentrate on friendship relations and peer groups in the context of games and informal contacts between pupils in school.

Playground games and other social activities have a main role to play in friendship relations and the formation of peer groups because it is at recess that peers, perhaps not in the same class at school, have a chance to meet; a time when important social skills can be learned; a time when they can fall out, but can also develop strategies for avoiding conflict. Given the difficulties children may face in meeting out of school (Blatchford & Baines, 2006), recess may be the main setting within which friendships are formed and develop. Similarly, games and other social activities are of particular interest to those studying peer networks. Whilst many studies utilize questionnaires to identify the existence of children's groups (Cairns et al., 1998), there are few that explore how they operate in practice (Adler & Adler, 1998; Baines & Blatchford, 2009). It is very easy to assume that peer groups have an everyday reality, and that there is a clear boundary between membership and non-membership. Inevitably this is harder to pin down. Peer group membership is reflected by repeated and sustained social interactions during joint activity or 'hanging' around together as well as a psychological sense of identity or belonging. Research on games and playground activities can examine the nature and development of these groups by observing those children that regularly play and socialize together, the relations within these groups, and the activities that bind them together.

There are several ways in which activities at recess and in particular games may have a social role in peer relations during the primary school years. Drawing on Blatchford (1998), Hartup (1992), and Pellegrini and Blatchford (2000), we identify a number of roles for playground activities in social relations. A first main role is that play and games can function as a social scaffold which supports social interactions between children when they are relatively new to each other (e.g. after transition to a new school). While the possibility of all children in a class being completely new to each other is rare, there may be a large number that are not familiar with others. The game can support and give a reason for talking to and getting to know peers. Davies (1982) notes how the inherently motivating nature of a game can draw children in, thus assisting with friendship formation and enabling access to a shared peer culture. In their year-long observational study of young children interacting on the playground, Ladd et al., (1988) found that the range of children played with at the start of the year was highest and that this decreased over the year, suggesting that children try to maximize potential relationships with others and then allow particular relationships to take priority while others fade. The notion of ready-made games as social scaffolds removes the cognitive challenge of setting up and negotiating the rules and procedures of a new activity, allowing players to focus on socialization, learning rules, and developing relationships.

A related function of games and other play activities is as a consolidator of peer networks and friendships. We know that children with similar interests and characteristics are likely to form groups and become friends (Cairns et al., 1998; Epstein, 1989; Schmuck & Schmuck, 2001) and the style of game is one main reflection of this, with some social groups selecting activities that may involve either vigorous, competitive, sedentary, fantasy, intellectual activity, or others. The games children play can contribute to their identity as a group and also represent the means through which social understanding between peers develops. As social groups stabilize so there is a marked reduction in the range of games played (Pellegrini et al., 2004), though there may be an increase in the versions of types of games played (Blatchford, 1998). Games may function to consolidate peer groups first, with friendships within the group developing later. If this is the case, friendship formation may have less to do with the types of games and activities played as other more personal and social factors. On the other hand, friendships and groups may be established in a more bottom up fashion with friendship relations being established first on the basis of a common interest in an activity and then dyads of children with similar activity interests coming together to form groups. Such a model would be consistent with the changes in game group size with age observed earlier (Blatchford et al., 2003; Ladd et al., 1988; Lewis & Phillipsen, 1998), but research is needed to examine this in more detail. Games and other play activities are crucial in supporting these processes and little work has examined friendship and group formation patterns in this context. During adolescence, when students are more concerned with establishing their own identity, common interest in activity continues to have a key role in bringing individuals together. There may be groups with particular interests and identities, for example, skateboarders, console gamers, sporty groups, and groups with an interest in fashion and/or music (Brown, 1990).

Though playground activities can reinforce group differences, they can also help bridge differences, for example, between different ethnic groups. Social psychologists have long been aware that some form of 'super-ordinate goal' is needed over and above contact and proximity to bring about integration and cooperation (Sabini, 1992). Games and play activities may be more successful at achieving 'real' and lasting integration than artificial and adult-imposed classroom interventions designed to bring ethnic groups together.

Games and play activities can also provide opportunities for social exploration and may lead to the development of new social relationships. This may take place when new games arrive on the playground, when there is a new 'craze' for a toy, activity, or media (e.g., cartoons), or when children's interests change. During the Spencer study, many of the friendship groups were temporarily disrupted halfway through the year by the arrival of the 'Pokémon' card game and TV cartoon. Children that rarely interacted were observed trading in cards, playing the game, or engaging in fantasy play based on this theme. Similarly, an interest in exploring new social relations with members of the opposite sex often referred to as 'border work,' can result in new provocative games like 'kiss chase' (Thorne, 1993). Such cross-sex encounters act to reaffirm single-sex groups but also represent covert interest in and learning about the opposite sex. We know relatively little about these encounters, the persons involved, and the implications of participating in them.

SEX DIFFERENCES IN FRIENDSHIPS AND PEER GROUPS

Sex cleavage in peer groups and differences in their size may be explained by diverse play and social interaction styles. In turn, these dissimilar group contexts may have implications for other sex differences (Maccoby, 1998) and may act as principle socialization contexts for future social, gender, and peer-related behavior (Harris, 1995; Kindermann & Valsiner, 1995). The existence of single sex peer groups is so robust that even efforts on the part of teachers to increase sex mixing are short lived when reinforcement is reduced (Serbin, Tonick, & Sternglanz, 1977). The formation of single sex play partnerships begins around the fourth year and continues throughout childhood (Maccoby, 1998). The Spencer research covering middle childhood also found sex cleavage in playground groups with approximately 87% of observations being of same sex groups at 7–8 years and only a slight reduction by 10–11 years (approx 83%). There are suggestions that the existence of sex cleavage in social groups continues into early adolescence and arguably beyond (Maccoby, 1998). Certainly in adulthood divisions between the sexes are sustained in UK and US cultures (at least) in the form of separate socializing practices and work practices (Gosso, 2010).

Theories explaining the formation of single sex groups have focused on a range of social, cultural, and biological/evolutionary factors. While many potential explanations are possible, the view that a complex combination of biological adaptation and social-cultural factors play a role is most likely (Benenson, Apostoleris, & Parnass, 1998; Maccoby, 1998; Pellegrini & Smith, 1998; Zarbatany, McDougall, & Hymel, 2000). Pellegrini (2005) suggests that the formation of homogeneous social groups is an example of children finding physically compatible play partners. Such differences may be the result of prenatal hormones as well as males' tendency to be physically larger, which in turn requires more physical exercise than smaller bodies (Pellegrini & Smith, 1998). These factors, subsequently, lead to greater levels of vigorous and R&T play, competitiveness, and aggression (Pellegrini, 2005). Research findings are consistent with this model in that during the period when sex cleavage in play groups increases, boys' play together tends to be more active than that of girls (Pellegrini, Huberty, & Jones, 1995; Ridgers et al., 2006). On the other hand, girls form homogenous groups to engage in more co-operative and sedentary play with shared outcomes and interactions involving greater intimacy and exclusivity (Eder & Hallinan, 1978; Maccoby, 1990). A play preference based explanation also accounts for cross sex game involvement, for example, Alexander & Hines (1994) found that when pushed to choose members of the opposite sex as a playmate, choices were based on similar play interests and play styles. A compatible explanation for sex segregation might arise from a need to develop skills associated with different sex roles. These might be facilitated by parents and other adults (Carson, Burks & Parke, 1993) encouraging particular styles of playful interaction which are then transmitted into the playgroup (Maccoby, 1998). Single sex groups may provide opportunities for practicing and applying the skills and roles that children observe and identify in adult life. Another possible explanation focuses on the motivation for coming together. Girls may be primarily motivated to form groups to establish and enjoy social relationships with friends and participate in games in this context, boys on the other hand, come together to engage in joint games and play and develop relationships with other boys in this context. That is, for boys the game is the motivation for coming together, for girls it is the social relationship (Eder & Hallinan, 1978; Maccoby, 1990).

Such explanations not only need to explain sex cleavage, but also the existence of multiple play groups within each sex. Might these multiple groups be related to differing levels of physical activity or need for intimacy? More research attention needs to focus on these within-sex sub-groups to see whether explanations also account for these segregations. In the Spencer project groups of males (and to a less extent females) tended to be separated on the basis of the activity with some male groups being associated with team games while others were associated with fantasy play or disruptive activity. Such distinctions might reflect parental interests and socialization. Maccoby (1998) suggests, however, that the influence of parents is more modest and highlights the important role that other aspects of society and culture might play in the formation of single sex peer groups. It may be the case that general preferences for vigorous activity or social intimacy account for sex division and specific play interests account for sub-group formation.

Similarly, Goodwin (2006) has questioned the generality of the view that girls' cliques are based on a need to engage in intimacy-enhancing activities and positive relationships. Through an examination of girls' talk within peer groups, her work provides valuable insights into the coalition forming, exclusion creating, and relational aggression practices that girls participate in and direct at members of other groups as well as their own groups. The shortcoming in this research is that these analyses are based on observations of a few select groups but it is clear that current understanding is limited in terms of the reasons for segregation and the nature of the social activity that takes place within girls' and boys' groups.

Another trend inconsistent with explanations for single-sex group formation is that outside of school, children in the US and UK are reportedly more likely to play in mixed sex groupings (Pellegrini, 2005; Thorne, 1993). Evidence exploring this trend is sparse, and it might be explained by a limited availability of same sex and age playmates in the home setting (Edwards, 1992). Nevertheless, the boundaries between boys' and girls' groups seem much stronger inside school, during middle childhood at least, and this may be related to the presence of many same age and older children along with an overriding peer and school culture. The presence of other peers that can comment on and influence one's social status and relationships with others, either positively or negatively, might function to discourage close associations with the opposite sex and encourage conformity to the expectations of peers and older schoolmates.

Peer group size
Related to the existence of sex-segregated groups is the observation that boys play in larger groups than girls and that girls tend to exist in dyads or small groups (Belle, 1989; Benenson et al., 1998; Feiring & Lewis, 1989; Ladd et al., 1988). A difference in play styles or play interests is reportedly responsible with girls' underlying preference for intimacy-enhancing activities causing them to form small groups (Belle, 1989; Zarbatany et al., 2000) and boys' interest in playing competitive team games requiring larger groups (Hartup, 1992). An alternative explanation offered by Belle (1989) and later discussed by Benenson et al. (1998) suggests that boys have an inherent preference for forming larger groups and that boys play team games because of this. While neither Belle nor Benenson offer further explication of the nature of this force, participation in and an opportunity to be promoted up through a competitive social hierarchy might require a need for larger social groups where boys can demonstrate their prowess or become associated with those considered popular.

Findings from the Spencer project indicated sex differences in the size of playground game networks and enduring peer groups (based on the aggregation of the playground game networks over two weeks of observations). When instances of team game activities were removed from the data set and the game networks re-calculated, boys' and girls' game networks became similar in size. This suggests that play preference determines the larger networks reported for boys. However, when the enduring peer groups are re-examined, surprisingly, boys were still found to sustain larger peer groups than implied by the smaller game networks (Baines & Blatchford, 2009). The implication is that while girls consistently socialize in their peer groups, some boys interact and play games with different portions of their peer group at different times, thus sustaining an overall group which occasionally comes together as a whole during team games. This suggests that both the centripetal force and 'games determine group size' interpretations may apply—the former being associated with enduring peer groups and the latter game networks. The existence of a second male peer group in every class studied, smaller than the large male group yet comparable in size to those of girls,

suggests that the 'centripetal force' model does not relate to all boys. Finally, the simple observation that social networks vary in size in an inverted 'U' fashion between childhood and late adolescence (see Cairns et al., 1998), when social activities change from the playing of games to socializing and hanging around (Blatchford, 1998), provides further support for the 'team games' explanation.

The size, structure, and stability of peer groups are likely to have implications for the nature of interactions within them and individual children's self perceptions and social development. For instance, group size positively predicts changes in self perceptions of self worth and peer acceptance (Boulton, 2005). Spencer study findings suggested that girls' groups consisted mainly of friends and those of boys were composed of both friends and non-friends. Girls were more likely than boys to have friends outside of the group, thus enabling them to draw on these friends if their own group separates. Peer group stability was found to be lower for girls than boys, indicating that girls were far more likely to be in a position of having to draw on relationships outside of their group and to forge new relationships (Baines & Blatchford, 2009).

Peer groups as socializing contexts
Segregated male and female play groups may act as socializing contexts such that activities and experiences within these peer groups may lead to the development of different behavioral norms and interaction styles (Maccoby, 1998; Fabes, Martin & Hanish, 2004). In a longitudinal study of preschoolers, Martin and Fabes (2001) found that those boys that played most frequently with other boys at the start of the year engaged in increased gendered activity later in the year. This suggests that the level of same sex involvement is related to level of adoption of stereotyped behaviors at a later point.

Gendered behaviors are also most evident during same sex play interactions with peers rather than when playing alone, indicating that gendered behavior is an important group level phenomenon (Fabes et al., 2004). These experiences with same sex peers may have a self-perpetuating effect on learning about and abiding by gender norms. This raises questions about the nature and location of the socializing processes. A number of possibilities are suggested in the literature on peer influence (Brown, Bakken, Ameringer & Mahon, 2008) including direct efforts of coercion by peers (e.g., group leaders or supporters), indirect efforts through the use of antagonistic (e.g., teasing) or rewarding behaviors (e.g., deviancy training—see Dishion, Spracklen, Andrews & Patterson, 1996) and via indirect internal pressures (e.g., to become more accepted by peers, children may be motivated to conform with gender stereotypes). According to Maccoby (1998), boys are quick to establish a stable hierarchy while girls' hierarchies are more fluid and less stable. Given earlier points about the number and size of groups in a class and the overlap between friendships and group membership, this may suggest that boys, who have more to lose if ostracized, might be more likely to be influenced by peers (Baines & Blatchford, 2009).

The existence of a range of male and female peer groups based around common interest in different games and social activity may involve quite different peer influence processes and lead to a wide range of different values, outcomes, gendered stereotypes, and behaviors. Further research in this area could examine interaction and activity in relation to the development and expression of norms, values, and socializing influences within peer groups.

Social Status, Leadership and Other Roles

Involvement in games and other activities during recess can provide substantial social knowledge about the nature and behavior of peers. This can be gained through direct interaction, observation of others, or more indirectly through the sharing of peer experiences and views. Those children who are unnecessarily aggressive, hotheaded, engage in inappropriate behavior, cheat at games, and so forth, are likely to be avoided or mistrusted, while those who are dominant, prosocial, good at playing, leading, and organizing games are likely to be preferred.

Research on sociometric status and dominance in the peer group is substantial and readers are referred to other sources for more comprehensive reviews (Gifford-Smith & Brownell, 2003; Ladd, 2005). Such measures of status, usually derived through peer ratings or nominations of liking, assume that children's preferences are based on their experiences with others. Little recent work has examined the behavioral expression of social status in playground settings. Games and other playground activities are main contexts where social status may be determined and some studies have examined the behavioral correlates of social status. Research by Ladd et al. (1988) examined the play styles of peer accepted and rejected 3½–4½ year olds and found that higher levels of cooperative play and interaction with many different peers at the start of the year predicted gains in social preference

at the end of the year. High conflict at the beginning of the year was related to lower social preference, and unoccupied behavior was predictive of social neglect later in the year. Importantly, peer status at the start of the year did not explain behavioral change over the year, though children with low peer acceptance at the start of the year interacted with a wide range of peers at later points in the year. While popular and average peers are quick to find play partners, rejected children wander from group to group, often have difficulties being accepted into play activities and frequently end up playing with younger peers. Marginalized children may eventually come together to form homogeneous groups of aggressive youth which may lead to problems later (Cairns et al., 1998).

A range of other associations between playground activity, behavior, and social status have been found. Research by Pellegrini (1988) demonstrates that among boys higher levels of vigorous activity and R&T play were positively related to peer acceptance and social problem solving a year later, while aggression was negatively related to acceptance. Pellegrini (2005) suggests that one of the purposes of R&T play is to establish dominance status in boy's peer groups, though given that it tends to take place within the group suggests that it could have an affiliative function as well. Maccoby (1998) suggests that leadership in boys' play groups is connected to toughness, and physical and athletic prowess to assert dominance, while in girls' groups leadership may be affected by different qualities such as peer acceptance. Peer acceptance seems to be associated with positive social interaction with peers (Dodge, Coie, Pettit & Price, 1990; Ladd et al., 1988). But data from Boulton (2005) highlights an important link between playground activity and self perceptions of social status. Boulton found a positive relation between the frequency of game play and self perceptions of social acceptance among boys (of 8–9 years) but this was negative for girls. Conversely, a positive relation was found between conversation and status perceptions for girls but this relation was negative for boys.

One limitation of research on peer relations and interaction is that invariably children are observed in an already functioning peer system and therefore research is unable to examine how particular relationships and statuses form or to posit a causal relationship between behavior and social status. In a pioneering study, Dodge (1983) determined that particular behavior patterns were predictive of peer status. In his study, Dodge examined 7–8 year olds who did not know each other at the start of the study, playing in simulated play groups of eight members for eight one-hour sessions over two weeks. At the end of the fortnight, pupils completed sociometric nomination questionnaires. Popular boys had tended to be more cooperative during their play, were the most sought after by peers, and sustained interactions for the longest. Rejected boys often displayed hostile, excluding, and aggressive behavior. Neglected children also demonstrated inappropriate behavior, though this was less aggressive than for rejected children, and were often observed to engage in solitary play and lower levels of social conversation than other children.

Although some studies have examined the behavioral correlates of acceptance and rejection, much research has tended to focus on the difficult or troubled child. This can be seen in the many studies of the aggressive, rejected, bullied, victimized, or withdrawn children (see Ladd, 2005). But the majority of children on the playground do not fall into these categories and there is a more positive side to individual differences in peer relations during games and activities on the playground. Other researchers have aimed to go beyond abstract conceptions of social status based on acceptance and rejection to identify alternative ways of examining and representing status in every day settings. Such studies aim to identify different types of persons on the playground relative to leadership and social involvement in playground activities. Iona Opie (1993) refers to the 'kingpins of the playground' who through their ability to tell stories and jokes enjoy great popularity among peers. Haslett and Bowen (1989, reviewed in Erwin, 1993) classified differences in the social skills of five-year olds in terms of three types: 'agenda setters,' who tended to initiate and dominate play and to be active physically and verbally; 'responders' who reacted appropriately to play bids and maintained interaction without establishing the play agenda or initiating change; and 'isolates' who responded inappropriately and were insufficiently persistent and often overlooked.

Adler and Adler (1998) in an ethnographic longitudinal study also refer to different positions in a status hierarchy within the whole peer network (e.g., a class) and within peer groups. Within peer groups, Adler and Adler differentiate between leaders, second tier members, followers, wannabes, and others that are not part of the clique, either because they have been ejected or because they were never involved with the clique. Children in more dominant and senior positions utilize a range of inclusion and exclusion strategies to sustain their dominance and position. However, the various intra- and inter-group strategies outlined present a negative picture of peers engaging in highly competitive and cut-throat strategies to sustain their power and dominance. Little mention is made of positive attributes such as cooperation, prosociability, joking, storytelling, and so forth that have often been associated with more conventional characterizations of popularity and dominance. The extent to which the patterns outlined by Adler and Adler are representative of peer relations processes more generally needs further investigation.

The Spencer project examined the degree to which children were actively involved in instigating and engaging in games and other activities and proposed the notion of 'game involvement' which involved five types of player. These were: Key, Central, Team, Hoverer, and Solitary (Blatchford, Baines & Pellegrini, 2001). 'Key players,' as Blatchford (1998) referred to them, appeared to have a central role in the organization and development of playground activities and peer groups and friendships. Playground observations and interviews with children identified other children who were also heavily involved in playground activities but who tended to follow the key players. These were central and team players with the former being far more vocally and actively involved in the organization of the activity than the latter who tended to listen and follow the game. There were also others who were less involved, and more on the edge of activities, sometimes hovering from game to game and group to group, and there were some who were disconnected from any peer groups or playground activities (Blatchford et al., 2001). Research by Goodwin (2006) provides insights into the social activity and conversations of girls that might be described as key and central players and how these girls can act to intimidate and exclude a 'hoverer,' or 'tag along,' as Goodwin refers to them.

Medium strength correlations (r=0.6) were found between the game involvement measure and nomination measures of leadership and suggesting games to play, observed frequency of social involvement on the playground (r=0.5), active network size (r=0.5), and nominations of peer acceptance, friendship, and athleticism (all above r≥0.3). However, game involvement was not related to measures of observed, peer-nominated, and teacher-rated aggression, nor was it related to a measure of teacher-rated prosociability (Blatchford et al., 2001). This finding is consistent with measures that acknowledge a role of dominance, aggression, and cooperation in leadership and popularity (Adler & Adler, 1998; Parkhurst & Hopmeyer, 1998). Sex differences in the predictors of game involvement were found which indicated that for males becoming more involved in playground games was more connected to suggesting games, while for females game involvement is more connected to social relations with peers. Highlighting a similar construct, Pellegrini et al. (2004) found that game facility (the aggregate of nominations of athletic, teacher ratings of good at games and sport, observed frequency engaged in games, and the number of peers in their immediate game group) among first graders was related to social competence and school adjustment later in the year in US children but not those from the UK.

Notions of agenda setters or key players are connected more closely to peer groups than the whole peer network (e.g., class) and strong overlaps may be expected with constructs such as leadership and network centrality, dimensions that are, according to Gest et al. (2001), themselves correlated (r=0.39). This implies that the key player might be the day-to-day behavioral expression of a person with high network centrality, at least with regard to children's peer groups. Key players may be the most influential in relation to their own peer group and the playground activities that they are engaged in but, given the varying overall status of different groups, may hold varying levels of influence outside of the group.

Changes in individual status may take place when there is a dramatic shift in social context. Sluckin (1981) describes a boy who on transition between schools lost status from what looked like being a key player to someone rather excluded and on the edge of peer friendship groups. This reflected sadly on his drop in social standing, which had previously depended on an aggressive style not now taken seriously by others. It may be that particular values and forms of behavior linked with popularity in one context may or may not be associated with acceptance in another. Peer groups in different schools can have different sets of values and a child's sociometric status may be determined partly by these values (see Blatchford & Baines, 2010). Alternatively, transitions may accelerate changes that might have happened anyway with development—that is, a child's declining popularity might decline more rapidly between schools. At transitions, peer relations and status have to be renegotiated and successful adjustment depends on how many supportive and/or friendly peers there are from one's previous school (Berndt & Keefe, 1995).

Games as a context for the acquisition of social-cognitive skills

At an individual level, participation in activities during recess involves children drawing on and potentially developing various social, cognitive, and linguistic skills (Sluckin, 1981). Observations of the behavior and language that takes place in these settings can inform us about children's cognitive and social development. The cognitive, social, and organizational skills involved in initiating, developing, and playing games with a number of peers may be relatively unique to this context and will contribute to their development (Waters & Sroufe, 1983). Bruner (1972) emphasized that games and play allow opportunities for the playful practice of important behaviors that can be combined into more useful problem-solving strategies and skilled activities. Different aspects and types of games and activities might contribute to social and cognitive skills in different ways. Some straightforward games (such as chase and be chased) may require few cognitive skills (Pellegrini, 2005), while others that involve hiding, seeking, rescuing, physical and social coordination, and so forth, may help the child develop more sophisticated cognitive, social, and motor skills. Children go to great lengths to decide the game they will play, the roles that players will adopt, and to negotiate the rules that will be in place. Such occasions often lead to arguments and heated discussions and may therefore exercise children in their decision making, problem solving, conflict resolution, and reasoning skills, which can lead to improved social understanding and perspective taking. A one-year longitudinal study of second and fifth graders by Borman and Kurdek (1987) found that observed game complexity was positively related to interpersonal understanding for girls but negatively related for boys. However, the Spencer study found that in the US but not the UK, game facility was related to social competence (Pellegrini et al., 2004). Other studies have suggested that reduced opportunities for, and experiences of, play with peers may result in lower levels of perspective taking (Hollos, 1975; Le Mare & Rubin, 1987).

Bruner (1972) also suggested that play may contribute to first language development in the early years and later, the development of essential skills for engaging in conversations and negotiations with peers. In playground contexts children must use language to negotiate access to games (Putallatz &

Gottman, 1981). Games provide rare opportunities for children to engage in and sustain group talk, effective conflict management, and to use many other forms of advanced communication skills that children and young people often have difficulties with (Baines & Howe, in press; Baines, Rubie-Davies & Blatchford, 2009). While many of these skills are not particular to games, there is a sense in which these peer contexts are particularly powerful given the highly motivating nature and absence of adult involvement. However, games and play contexts are relatively unique in the opportunities they provide for children to collaborate with peers and thus may be one of the main settings in which collaborative skills are developed. This highlights the importance of such opportunities given the absence of opportunities for collaborative learning and collaborative skills training in classrooms (Baines et al., 2003; Galton et al., 1999).

Sluckin (1981) argued that recess offers children opportunities for peer interaction in the context of which many lessons relevant to adult life are learned. He draws out rules that are implicit in the ways children play and deal with each other on the playground. These rules, originally negotiated in the playground, form the bases for broader peer interaction patterns in school. As more recent commentators have highlighted, these skills are also important for social success during childhood (Pellegrini, 2005; Smith 2010).

Games, Learning and School Adjustment

Games and social activities may have important implications for learning and adjustment to school. We have just discussed how games in themselves and as a context for peer interaction may contribute to the development of social-cognitive skills and a number of theorists have discussed the connections between play, games, and learning or cognitive development (Bruner, 1972; Piaget, 1962; Vygotsky, 1978). Games and playground activities in school may contribute to learning and engagement in class, both directly in terms of the development or consolidation of academic skills, but also more indirectly through the development of positive peer relationships and by providing enjoyable experiences in school. In this section we consider firstly how games and playground activities might relate to learning and engagement in class and then in relation to school belonging and adjustment.

Learning and engagement in the classroom

Play can be conceived as a natural inclination of an organism to learn, adapt, and develop the skills required for immediate and eventual later use. That is, play assists with the development and informal education of the child to adapt to their environment and learn the skills that will enable them to survive and succeed. This view is consistent with that conveyed by Pellegrini, Dupius, and Smith (2007), who emphasize that formal schooling is a relatively recent phenomenon and that play, along with exploration, may previously have been the main way that children acquire the skills and innovative abilities associated with everyday life. Gosso et al. (2005) go so far as to question whether formal education replaces the types of learning benefits resulting from participation in games and other play activities. Indeed, the skills learned within the context of games and activities (especially in terms of social development and collaboration) may not be supported by formal learning opportunities within classrooms.

But are play and games related to engagement and learning in the classroom? Though rare, some research has examined the effects of games and playground activity on children's learning and engagement in school during middle childhood. Borman and Kurdek (1987) failed to find any connection between the complexity of the game engaged in and non-verbal logical reasoning. But both UK and US components of the Spencer research found game involvement or facility with games to be associated with school adjustment and achievement but also were related uniquely to progress over time (Pellegrini et al., 2002; Blatchford et al., 2001). This suggests that those most involved in games and the most facile in game activity are likely to adapt better to school. However, given the correlational nature of the data, other interpretations cannot be ruled out.

Play can be highly repetitive in character and thus useful for children to consolidate their understanding and learning (Gosso et al., 2005; Rubin et al., 1983). There are also resemblances between games and classroom learning activities (e.g., counting rhymes and numbers, creativity in fantasy play and creative writing skills). But these commonalities are limited and the extent to which skills transfer across contexts is also questionable. Games and other social activities may have more of an impact on social understanding, perspective taking, an ability to sustain attention and activity, to regulate one's own behavior as well as that of peers, to engage in team work and communication skills, and other 'life' or 'soft' skills. Though often considered secondary to main areas of learning, such life skills are the ones reportedly missing from the curriculum and that are highly valued in the workplace (Cowie & Ruddock, 1988).

There have been a range of studies undertaken that examine the effects of games and play, broadly defined, on children's attention in the classroom. These studies have primarily involved manipulating the length of a lesson leading up to a recess period and/or students' ability to engage in physical activity. These studies have suggested that the longer children are expected to focus their attention on a task the less likely they are to be attentive (Stevenson & Lee, 1990; Pellegrini et al., 1995), and that task attention is greater after a period of recess than towards the end of the lesson immediately prior to recess (Pellegrini et al., 1995). Another study found that children aged 9–10 years were more engaged and less restless in the classroom on days when they had had recess period (Jarrett et al., 1998). These studies are somewhat limited, not least because it is impossible to determine whether the effects are due to having a break, or opportunities for play, physical activity, or for socializing with peers. Where games might more clearly support learning and engagement in the classroom is indirectly through the general positive effects they have on helping children to foster social interactive, cognitive, and problem-solving skills and most importantly in their support and development of children's relationships and friendships. Games and friendships offer opportunities for cooperation, reciprocity, effective conflict management, intimacy, commitment, and self disclosure (Hartup, 1992). All of these skills are important for learning interactions within the classroom (Zajac & Hartup, 1997). There is evidence that when working together, friends perform better than non-friends, especially on complex tasks. This is because they know each other better and thus their collaboration is more effective with more evidence of cooperation and productive conflict supported by reasoning (Zajac & Hartup, 1997). It may be the case that a history of interactions with friends during games and play activities at recess provides friends with the skills required to be successful at complex interactive tasks in classroom settings. The possible connections between game play, peer relations, and learning within the classroom deserve more attention from researchers.

School belonging and adjustment

Games and play activities may not, on first look, be considered to have an immediate relevance to adjustment to school. Yet the fact that recess can take up a sizable portion of the school day in many communities, that it is almost unanimously cited by children as a main reason for coming to school, one of main things enjoyed at school, and that it forms some of the most memorable experiences of children's school lives is a testament to its importance in school life. The inherently motivating nature of participation with friends in games and activities during recess may significantly affect feelings of school belonging. Integration into playground groups and positive social relationships with peers may play a key role in children positively adjusting to school. Recent motivational theories have emphasized the importance of belonging or relatedness for adjustment to school (Connell & Wellborn, 1991; Osterman, 2000). The extent to which this need is fulfilled predicts engagement and performance within the school context, and contributes to the adoption of goals defined by the institution and the social groups within it (Connell & Wellborn, 1991). But it might not always be the case that games and other social activities are positively related to school adjustment and belonging. Sociological research suggests that schools can have a cohesive peer culture that is anti-school and anti-learning; it is quite possible for students to feel a sense of involvement and belonging to the peer group but not feel any connection with the ethos or values of the school and academic life (Schmuck & Schmuck, 2001). There is a clear need for further research to begin examining the important role that games and activities during recess may play in adjusting to school.

Conclusions and Future Directions

There is a wide range of literature related to a discussion of children's games and activities on the playground which is testament to the relevance and importance of games for the child's approach to and location in society and their social and cognitive development. This chapter provides just a snapshot of this work and we hope we have done it some justice. We have discussed how games, on the one hand, are quite different from some other forms of play, whilst also trying to present games as a continuation of the development of play in children. Both Sutton-Smith (1976) and Vygotsky (1978) highlight the changing nature of the motivations for engaging in play such that the emphasis and nature of play changes with development. Games and play activities in school both reflect cognitive and social development but also appear to provide a main opportunity for experiences to influence development, for skills and knowledge to be tested, and social issues examined in more detail. We have tried to highlight the important role that games have in peer relationships both in terms of the functioning of peer groups and friendships but also as occasions where they can find out about peers and themselves. Games and social activities seem to have a particular role in supporting the formation and sustaining of peer groups and friendships during middle childhood and adolescence. It is within and between these groups that powerful socialization effects have been proposed by the likes of Harris (1995) and Fabes et al. (2004) and there is a need for a fuller understanding of the processes that are associated with peer influence. A main way that this can be achieved is by undertaking research that examines interactions during play and games at recess. Similarly, given the different structure and size of these peer groups there are constraining effects that might have implications for the types of experiences that children will have and in turn these will influence the types of social-cognitive skills developed.

Games and playground activities are particularly important for the development of a wide range of skills associated with interactions with people of similar status, including social-cognitive skills as well as others not discussed here (e.g., emotional skills and moral understanding). This is simply because there appear to be few opportunities for these skills and relationships to be developed elsewhere inside or outside of school without the presence of a potentially over-dominating adult. We have also suggested that games are important for learning and engagement in class as well as school adjustment. This principally seems to be an indirect relationship through peer relations and the development of other social-cognitive skills but also emphasizes that pupils' significant enjoyment of recess may contribute to feelings of school belonging which may also enhance school adjustment.

One question that might be raised given the broad importance suggested here of games for children's peer relations and their development of social-cognitive skills, is whether games are necessary for children's development. There are at least two ways in which we might see play and games as enhancing development. The first is in terms of it offering up special experiences and opportunities for the development of particular skills that other everyday non-play activities do not provide and which are necessary for development. The second way of viewing the value of play is as an extension of everyday experiences where play provides a further context for the development of particular skills and involvement in processes. Smith (2010), on reviewing the

evidence, suggests that currently it does not support the view that play is a developmental necessity. Most studies in this area involve correlational designs and thus our ability to infer causality is extremely limited. Determining whether play or games are a necessity requires a clear conceptualization of what play is and is not; unfortunately, this is not by any means clear and play involves a multiplicity of social, cognitive, and emotional 'activity' and experiences. Furthermore, it might not be play that is important but rather the opportunity that play provides for peer interaction and the learning of associated skills. While many children will have multiple opportunities to socialize with peers, there are also a number that have few opportunities for engaging in social interaction and play with a range of peers outside of school. It is these children that may be at a disadvantage when it comes to socializing with peers and the development of particular social and cognitive skills. While these skills will not be an absolute necessity to their development, they may be at a distinct disadvantage without them.

There is a need for further detailed work in this area that can examine children's day-to-day experiences during games, play, and other social activities. In order to capture important detail in terms of interactions as well as how they relate to broader social structures like peer groups and sociometric status, research will need to involve complex multimethod and even mixed method designs that can focus on the specifics of rich and meaningful interactions as well as provide insights into general patterns across pupils and playgrounds. The work of ethnographers and others in this tradition is extremely valuable, particularly in providing new insights, but needs to be combined with other approaches to provide insights into how widespread and exclusive such findings are.

We have noted the importance of taking account of the school and playground context and materials available to children which may influence the types of play and games in which children participate. In the Spencer project we identified a number of ways in which pupils' experience of recess and peer relations varied across schools (Blatchford et al., 2001). The nature of the school grounds as well as the policies and ethos of the school can affect games and the relationships between peers in distinctive ways (Titman, 1994). There is evidence in the literature that classroom organization (e.g., in terms of seating, teaching approach, and tracking) may influence the relationships between peers (Schmuck & Schmuck, 2001). Playground culture and peer relations in schools are therefore likely to be best conceived as something emerging in context and affected by the school culture and environment. Epstein (1989) has said:

> "It is no longer feasible to study or explain the selection of friends with attention only to psychological constructs and child development terms. It is also necessary to give attention to the designs of the school, classroom, family, and other environments in which peer relations and the selection and influence of friends take place" (p.183).

But we know very little about how schools affect children's games, peer relations and their experiences of recess. This is clearly an area requiring future study.

We have considered how games and playground activities and peer relations may be associated with learning, engagement, and school adjustment, but there is a tendency for teachers and schools to view playground activities and peer relations as separate to what goes on inside school. In other work we have suggested that teaching and learning practices in classrooms, particularly during group work, can beneficially utilize the positive ethos and relationships that are constructed on the playground (Blatchford & Baines, 2010). We have suggested the value in a 'relational approach' to classroom teaching and learning which aims to develop, extend, and make use of the processes developed in friendship relations to support the development of further communication, group planning, and advanced group working skills for implementing group interactions in the classroom (Baines, Blatchford, Kutnick et al., 2008). The processes involved in group learning and in informal interactions between friends may involve similar skills and qualities (e.g. perspective taking, mutuality, conflict resolution, problem solving, and trust). Informal relationships between peers can allow feelings of 'psychological safety' (Van den Bossche, Gijselaers, Segers, & Kirschner, 2006), where children feel comfortable expressing their views and opinions publicly because they know that these will be listened to, valued, and respected.

Experiences of games and behaviors during recess can also be utilized in classroom learning in another way too. There are a rich set of social and moral dilemmas and experiences that take place on the playground. The difficulties that teachers know arise at recess can be viewed as positive opportunities to engage in discussions with pupils about social and

moral dilemmas and provide greater involvement of pupils in school decisions and management (Blatchford, 1998) within a social and moral framework provided by the school.

We end this chapter by returning to the discussion of the importance of recess in schools. As we have suggested, opportunities for play, games, and social activities outside of school appear to be declining and there is a trend toward restrictions on pupils' unsupervised activities with friends. Greater control of children's freedom and independence risks losing the positive benefits of play, games, and peer relations for social-cognitive and moral development and wellbeing more generally. There are, however, moves in this direction (Margo & Dixon, 2006) with schools reducing or abolishing recess or flooding it with adult-led activities. However, in cases where there is bullying, aggression, and anti-school feelings among peers, the danger of not acting could lead to the same conclusions and destructive effects on social well-being and learning. An important issue for schools is to get the balance right and Blatchford (1998) discusses ways to achieve this.

Recess can also be seen as part of a solution to many modern social and moral problems. Whilst schools and teachers can be effective in teaching children about social and moral understanding, children also learn from their own experiences, mistakes, and reflections. Similarly, recess offers the main opportunity outside of physical education to get exercise that contributes toward a child's daily requirement and thus may help resolve problems with sedentary behavior. It is clearly difficult to get the balance right, but a coherent approach to the provision, timing, and management of recess and peer relations in schools could do much to improve children's experiences of learning and school.

References

Adler, P.A. & Adler, P. (1998). *Peer power: Preadolescent culture and identity*. New Brunswick, NJ: Rutgers University Press.

Alexander, G.M. & Hines, M. (1994). Gender labels and play styles: Their relative contributions to children's selection of playmates. *Child Development, 65*, 869–879.

Argyle, M. (1992). *The social psychology of everyday life*. London: Routledge.

Baines, E., & Blatchford, P. (2009). Sex differences in the structure and stability of children's playground social networks and their overlap with friendship relations. *British Journal of Developmental Psychology, 27*, 743–760.

Baines, E., Blatchford, P., & Kutnick, P. (2003). Changes in grouping practice over primary and secondary school, *International Journal of Educational Research, 39*, 9–34.

Baines, E., Blatchford, P., Kutnick, P., with Chowne, A., Ota, C., & Berdondini, L. (2008). *Promoting effective group work in the primary classroom: A handbook for teachers and practitioners.* London: Routledge.

Baines, E. & Howe, C.J. (in press). Discourse topic management skills in 4-, 6- and 9-year-old peer interactions: Developments with age and the effects of task context. *First Language.*

Baines, E., Rubie-Davies, C., & Blatchford, P. (2009). Improving pupil group work interaction and dialogue in primary classrooms: Results from a year-long intervention study. *Cambridge Journal of Education, 39,* 95–117.

Barker, R.G. & Wright, H.F. (1951). *One boy's day.* New York: Harper and Brothers.

Belle, D. (1989). Gender differences in children's social networks and supports. In D. Belle (Ed.). *Children's social networks and social supports* (pp. 173–188). New York: Wiley.

Benenson, J.F., Apostoleris, N.H., & Parnass, J. (1998). The organization of children's same sex peer relationships. In W. Bukowski & A. Cillessen (Eds.). *Sociometry then and now. New directions for child development no. 80* (pp. 5–23). San Francisco: Jossey-Bass Publishers.

Berndt, T. & Keefe, K. (1995). Friends' influence on adolescents' adjustment to school. *Child Development, 66,* 1312–1329.

Bishop, J. C. & Curtis, M. (Eds.). (2001). *Play today in the primary school playground.* Philadelphia: Open University Press.

Blatchford, P. (1998). *Social life in schools: pupils' experiences of breaktime and recess from 7 to 16 years.* London: Falmer Press.

Blatchford, P. & Baines, E. (2006). *A follow up national survey of breaktimes in primary and secondary schools* (Report to Nuffield Foundation Ref: EDV/00399/G). Retrieved September 10, 2009, from http://www.breaktime.org.uk/NuffieldBreakTimeReport-WEBVersion.pdf.

Blatchford, P. & Baines, E. (2010). Peer relations in school. In K. Littleton, C. Wood, & K. Staarman (Eds.). *Elsevier handbook of educational psychology: New perspectives on learning and teaching.* New York: Elsevier.

Blatchford, P., Baines, E., & Pellegrini, A. (2001). *A typology of playground game involvement: individual differences and their correlates.* Paper presented at Society of Research in Child Development, Minneapolis USA, April 2001.

Blatchford, P., Baines, E., & Pellegrini, A. (2003). The social context of school playground games: Sex and ethnic differences, and changes over time after entry to junior school. *British Journal of Developmental Psychology, 21,* 481–505.

Blatchford, P. & Sharp, S. (1994). *Breaktime and the school: Understanding and changing playground behavior.* London: Routledge.

Blatchford, P. & Sumpner, C. (1996). Changes to breaktime in primary and secondary schools. Final Report to Nuffield Foundation.

Blatchford, P. & Sumpner, C. (1998). What do we know about breaktime?: Results from a national survey of breaktime and lunchtime in primary and secondary schools. *British Journal of Educational Research, 24,* 79–94.

Borman, K. & Kurdek, L. (1987). Grade and gender differences in the stability and correlates of the structural complexity of children's playground games. *International Journal of Behavioral Development, 10,* 241–251.

Boulton, M. (1992). Participation in playground activities at middle school. *Educational Research, 34,* 167–182.

Boulton, M. (2005). Predicting changes in children's self-perceptions from playground social activities and interactions. *British Journal of Developmental Psychology, 23,* 1–19.

Boulton, M. & Smith, P. (1993). Ethnic, gender partner, and activity preferences in mixed race schools in the UK: Playground observations. In C. Hart (Ed.). *Children on playgrounds* (pp. 210–238). Albany: SUNY Press.

Bronfenbrenner, U. (1979). *The ecology of human development.* Cambridge, MA: Harvard University Press.

Bronfenbrenner, U. & Ceci, S.J. (1994). Nature-nurture reconceptualized in developmental perspective: A bioecological model, *Psychological Review, 101,* 568–86.

Brown, B.B. (1990). Peer groups and cultures. In S.S. Feldman & G.R. Elliott (Eds.). *At the threshold: The developing adolescent.* Cambridge, MA: Harvard University Press.

Brown, B., Bakken, J., Ameringer, S., & Mahon, S. (2008). A comprehensive conceptualization of the peer influence process in adolescence. In M. Prinstein & K. Dodge (Eds.). *Understanding peer influence in children and adolescents* (pp. 17–44). London: Guildford Press.

Bruner, J. (1972). Child's play. *New Scientist, 62,* 694, London: IPC Magazines Ltd.

Cairns, R.B., Xie, H., & Leung, M-C. (1998). The popularity of friendship and the neglect of social networks: Toward a new balance. In W. Bukowski & A. Cillessen (Eds.). *Sociometry then and now. New directions for child development, no.80* (pp. 25–53). Jossey-Bass Publishers: San Francisco.

Carson, J., Burks, V., & Parke, R. (1993). Parent–child physical play: Determination and consequences. In K. MacDonald (Ed.). *Parent–child play* (pp. 197–220). Albany: State University of New York Press.

Cole, M. (1996). *Cultural psychology: A once and future discipline.* Cambridge, MA: Harvard University Press.

Connell, J., & Wellborn, J. (1991). Competence, autonomy and relatedness: A motivational analysis of self-system processes. In Gunnar M. R., & Sroufe L. A. (Eds.). *Self-processes and development.* Hillsdale, NJ: Erlbaum.

Cowie, H. & Ruddock, J. (1990). *Cooperative learning: Traditions and transitions.* London: BP Educational Service.

Davies, B. (1982). *Life in the classroom and the playground: The accounts of primary school children.* London: Routledge and Kegan Paul.

Dishion, T., Spracklen, K., Andrews, D., & Patterson, G. (1996). Deviancy training in male adolescent friendships. *Behavior Therapy, 27,* 373–390.

Dodge, K. (1983). Behavioral antecedents of peer social status. *Child Development, 54,* 1386–1399.

Dodge, K., Coie, J., Pettit, G., & Price, J. (1990). Peer status and aggression in boys' groups: Developmental and contextual analyses. *Child Development, 61,* 1289–1309.

Dunn, J. (2004). *Children's friendships: The beginnings of intimacy.* Malden, MA: Blackwell.

Eder, D. & Hallinan, M. (1978). Sex differences in children's friendships. *American Sociological Review, 43,* 237–250.

Edwards, C. (1992). Cross cultural perspectives on family-peer relations. In R. Parke & G. Ladd (Eds.). *Family-peer relationships: Modes of linkage.* Hillsdale, NJ: Erlbaum.

Elkind, D. (2007). *The power of play: How spontaneous imaginative activities lead to happier, healthier children.* New York: Cambridge University Press.

Epstein, J. (1989). The selection of friends: changes across the grades and the different school environments. In T. Berndt & G. Ladd (Eds.). *Peer relationships in child development.* New York: Wiley.

Erwin, P. (1993). *Friendship and peer relations in children.* Chichester: Wiley.

Evans, J. (1990). The teacher role in playground supervision. *Play and Culture, 33,* 219–234.

Fabes, R. A., Martin, C. L., & Hanish, L. D. (2004). The next 50 years: Considering gender as a context for understanding young children's peer relationships. *Merrill-Palmer Quarterly, 50,* 260–273.

Feiring C. & Lewis, M. (1989). The social networks of girls and boys from early through middle childhood. In D. Belle (Ed.). *Children's social networks and social supports* (pp. 173–188). New York: Wiley.

Furedi, F. (2002). *Paranoid parenting: Why ignoring the experts may be best for your child.* Chicago: Chicago Review Press.

Furman, W. (1989). The development of children's networks. In D. Belle. (Ed.). *Children's social networks and social supports* (pp. 151–172). New York: Wiley.

Galton, M.J., Hargreaves, L., Comber, C., Wall, D., & Pell, A. (1999). *Inside the primary classroom: 20 years on.* London: Routledge.

Galton, M., MacBeath, J., with Steward, S., Page, C., & Edwards, J. (2004). *A life in secondary teaching: Finding time for learning,* (Report for NUT). Cambridge: Cambridge Printing.

Garandeau, C. F., & Cillessen, A. H. N. (2006). From indirect aggression to invisible aggression: A conceptual view on bullying and peer group manipulation. *Aggression and Violent Behavior, 11,* 612–625.

Garvey, C. (1990). *Play* (2nd Ed.). Cambridge, MA: Harvard University Press.

Gest, S.D., Sandra A. Graham-Bermann, S.A., & Hartup, W.W. (2001). Peer experience: Common and unique features of number of friendships, social network centrality, and sociometric status. *Social Development, 10,* 23–40.

Gifford-Smith, M. & Brownell, C. (2003). Childhood peer relationships: Social acceptance, friendships, and peer networks. *Journal of School Psychology, 41,* 235–284.

Gill, T. (2007). *No fear: Growing up in a risk averse society.* Calouste Gulbenkian Foundation.

Goncu, A. (1993). Development of intersubjectivity in the dyadic play of preschoolers. *Early Childhood Research Quarterly, 8,* 99–116.

Goodwin, M.H. (2006). *The hidden life of girls: Games of stance, status, and exclusion.* Oxford, UK: Blackwell.

Gosso, Y. (2010). Play in different cultures. In P. Smith (Ed.). *Children and play.* Oxford: Wiley-Blackwell.

Gosso, Y., Otta, E., Morais, M., Ribeiro, F. & Bussab, V. (2005). Play in hunter-gatherer society. In A. Pellegrini & P. Smith (Eds.). *The nature of play: Great apes and humans* (pp. 213–253). New York: Guilford Press.

Harris, J.R. (1995). Where is the child's environment? A group socialization theory of development. *Psychological Review, 102,* 458–489.

Hartup, W.W. (1992). Friendships and their developmental significance. In H. McGurk (Ed.). *Childhood social development: Contemporary perspectives.* Hove: LEA.

Hartup, W.W. (1996). The company they keep: Friendships and their developmental significance. *Child Development, 67,* 1–13.

Hillman, M. (1993). One false move… In M. Hillman (Ed.). *Children, transport and the quality of life.* London: Policy Studies Institute.

Holland, P. (2003). *We don't play with guns here.* Philadelphia: Open University Press.

Hollos, M. (1975). Logical operations and role taking abilities in two cultures: Norway and Hungary. *Child Development, 46,* 638–649.

Home Office & Department of Children Schools and Families (UK), (2005). *2003 Home Office Citizenship Survey: Top-level findings from the Children's and Young People's Survey.* Retrieved 10th October 2007: http://www.dcsf.gov.uk/research/data/uploadfiles/RW29.pdf

Jarrett, O. S. & Dickett-Hedgebeth, M. (2003). Recess in a middle school: What do the students do? In D. Lytle (Ed.). *Play and educational theory and practice* (pp. 227–241). Westport, CT: Ablex Publishing.

Jarrett, O. S. & Maxwell, D. M. (2000). What research says about the need for recess. In R. Clements (Ed.). *Elementary school recess: Selected readings, games, and activities for teachers and parents.* Lake Charles, LA: American Press.

Jarrett, O. S., Maxwell, D. M., Dickerson, C., Hoge, P., Davies, G., & Yetley, A. (1998). The impact of recess on classroom behavior: Group effects and individual differences. *Journal of Educational Research, 92,* 121–126.

Kindermann, T., & Valsiner, J. (1995). *Development of person-context relations.* Hillsdale, NJ: Erlbaum.

Krasnor, L., & Pepler, D. (1980). The study of children's play: Some suggested future directions. In K. Rubin (Ed.). *Children's play* (pp. 85–95). San Francisco: Jossey-Bass.

Ladd, G. W. (2005). *Children's peer relations and social competence: A century of progress.* New Haven, CT: Yale University Press.

Ladd, G.W., Price, J.M., & Hart, C.H. (1988). Predicting preschoolers' peer status from their playground behaviors. *Child Development, 59,* 986–992.

Layard, R. & Dunn, J. (2009). *A good childhood: Searching for values in a competitive age.* London: Penguin.

LeMare, L.J. & Rubin, K.H. (1987). Perspective taking and peer interaction: structural and developmental analyses. *Child Development, 58,* 306–315.

Lewis, T. & Phillipsen, L. (1998). Interactions on an elementary school playground: Variation by age, gender, race, group size and playground area. *Child Study Journal, 28,* 309–320.

Maccoby, E.E. (1990). Gender and relationships: A developmental account. *American Psychologist, 45,* 513–520.

Maccoby, E. E. (1998). *The two sexes: growing up apart, coming together.* London: Harvard University Press.

Margo, J. & Dixon, M. with Pearce, N. & Reed, H. (2006). *Freedom's orphans: Raising youth in a changing world.* London: Institute for Public Policy Research.

Martin, C.L. & Fabes, R.A. (2001). The stability and consequences of young children's same sex peer interactions. *Developmental Psychology, 37,* 431–446.

Nichols, S.L. & Good, T.L. (2004). *America's teenagers – myths and realities: Media images, schooling, and the social costs of careless indifference.* Mahwah: LEA.

Nishina, A. (2004). A theoretical review of bullying: Can it be eliminated? In C. Sanders, & G. Phye (Eds.). *Bullying: Implications for the classroom* (pp. 36–62). London: Elsevier.

The Observer (2007). 'No break, no bells in school of the future' Sunday 26 August 2007 written by Anushka Asthana. Retrieved on 5th October 2009 from: http://www.guardian.co.uk/uk/2007/aug/26/newschools.schools.

Opie, I. (1993). *The people in the playground.* Oxford: Oxford University Press.

Opie, I. & Opie, P. (1969). *Children's games in street and playground.* Oxford: Oxford University Press.

Ortega, R. (2003). Play, activity and thought: Reflections on Piaget's and Vygotsky's theories. In D. Lytle (Ed.). *Play and educational theory and practice* (pp. 99–116). Westport, CT: Praeger.

Osterman, K. (2000). Students' need for belonging in the school community. *Review of Educational Research, 70*, 323–367.

Parker, J.G., & Gottman, J.M. (1989). Social and emotional development in a relational context: Friendship interaction from early childhood to adolescence. In T.J. Berndt & G.W. Ladd (Eds.). *Peer relationships in child development*. New York: Wiley.

Parkhurst, J. T., & Hopmeyer, A. (1998). Sociometric popularity and peer-perceived popularity: two distinct dimensions of peer status. *The Journal of Early Adolescence, 18*, 125–144.

Parten, M. (1932). Social participation among preschool children. *Journal of Abnormal and Social Psychology, 27*, 243–269.

Patte, M. (2006). What happened to recess: Examining time devoted to recess in Pennsylvania's elementary schools. *Play and Folklore, 48*, 5–16.

Pellegrini, A. (1988). Elementary school children's rough-and-tumble play and social competence. *Developmental Psychology, 24*, 802–806.

Pellegrini, A. (2005). *Recess: Its role in education and development*. Mahwah, NJ: LEA.

Pellegrini, A. & Blatchford, P. (2000). *The child at school: Interactions with peers and teachers*. London: Arnold.

Pellegrini, A., Kato, K., Blatchford, P., & Baines, E. (2002). A short-term longitudinal study of children's playground games across the first year of school: Implications for social competence and adjustment to school. *American Educational Research Journal, 39*, 991–1016.

Pellegrini, A., Blatchford, P., Kato, K., & Baines, E. (2004). A short term longitudinal study of children's playground games in Primary school: Implications for adjustment to school and social adjustment in the USA and UK. *Social Development, 13*, 105–123.

Pellegrini, A., Dupuis, D., & Smith, P. (2007). Play in evolution and development. *Developmental Review, 27*, 261–276.

Pellegrini, A., Huberty, P., & Jones, I. (1995). The effects of recess timing on children's playground and classroom behaviors. *American Educational Research Journal, 32*, 845–864.

Pellegrini, A. & Smith, P. (1993). School recess: implications for education and development. *Review of Educational Research, 63*, 51–67.

Pellegrini, A. & Smith. P. (1998). Physical activity play: The nature and function of a neglected aspect of play. *Child Development, 68*, 577–598.

Pellegrini, A. & Smith. P. (2005). *The nature of play*. New York: Guilford Press.

Piaget, J. (1926). *The language and thought of the child*. London: Kegan Paul & Co.

Piaget, J. (1932). *The moral judgment of the child*. London: Kegan Paul and Co.

Piaget, J. (1962). *Play, dreams and imitation in childhood*. New York: Norton.

Putallatz, M. & Gottman. J. (1981). An interactional model of children's entry into peer groups. *Child Development, 52*, 986–994.

Ridgers, N., Stratton, G., & Fairclough, S. (2006). Physical activity levels of children during school playtime. *Sports Medicine, 36*, 359–371.

Rubin, K., Bukowski, W., & Parker, J. (2006). Peer interactions, relationships, and groups. In W. Damon, R. M. Lerner, & N. Eisenberg (Vol. Eds.), *Handbook of child psychology: Vol. 3, Social, emotional, and personality development* (6th ed., pp. 571–645). New York: Wiley.

Rubin, K., Fein, G., & Vandenberg, B. (1983). Play. In E.M. Hetherington (Vol. Ed.) & P.H. Mussen (Series Ed.). *Handbook of child psychology, Vol. IV: Socialization, personality and social development* (pp. 103–196), New York: Wiley.

Sabini, J. (1992). *Social psychology*. Norton: New York.

Schmuck R. & Schmuck, P. (2001). *Group processes in the classroom*. Boston: McGraw-Hill.

Schneider, B.H. (2000). *Friends and enemies: Peer relations in childhood*. London: Arnold.

Serbin, L., Moller, L., Gulko, J., Powlishta, K. & Colbourne, K. (1994). The emergence of gender segregation in toddler play groups. In C. Leaper (Ed.). *New Directions for Child Development no 65. Childhood gender segregation* (pp. 7–17). San Francisco: Jossey-Bass.

Serbin, L., Tonick, I., & Sternglanz, S. (1977). Shaping cooperative cross-sex play. *Child Development, 48*, 924–929.

Simon, J., & Childers, H. (2006). Principals' perceptions of school recess: Sources of information, benefits, and drawbacks. *Research in the Schools, 13*, 37–46.

Sluckin, A. (1981). *Growing up in the playground: The social development of children*. London: Routledge & Kegan Paul.

Smith, P. (1994). What children learn from playtime, and what adults can learn from it. In P. Blatchford & S. Sharp (Eds.). *Breaktime and the school*. London: Routledge.

Smith, P.K. (2010). *Children and play*. Oxford: Wiley-Blackwell.

Smith, P.K. & Sharp, S. (Eds.) (1994). *School bullying: Insights and perspectives*. London: Routledge.

Stevenson, H., & Lee, S. (1990). Contexts of achievement: A study of American, Chinese, and Japanese children. *Monographs of the Society for Research in Child Development, 55* (n221).

Stratton, G. & Mullan, E. (2005). The effect of multicolor playground markings on children's physical activity level during recess. *Preventive Medicine, 41*, 828–833.

Sutton-Smith, B. (1976). Current research and theory on play, games and sports. In T. Craig (Ed.). *The humanistic and mental health aspects of sports, exercise and recreation*. Chicago: American Medical Association.

Sutton-Smith, B. (1982). A performance theory of peer relations. In K.M. Borman (Ed.). *The social life of children in a changing society*. Hillsdale, New Jersey: LEA.

Thorne, B. (1993). *Gender play: girls and boys in school*. Buckingham: Open University Press.

Titman, W. (1994). *Special places: special people: the hidden curriculum of the school grounds*. Godalming, Surrey, World Wildlife Fund for Nature/Learning Through Landscapes.

UNICEF (2007). Child poverty in perspective: An overview of child well-being in rich countries: A comprehensive assessment of the lives and well-being of children and adolescents in the economically advanced nations UNICEF Innocenti Research Centre Report Card 7. Retrieved December 16, 2008 from: www.unicefirc.org/presscentre/presskit/reportcard7/rc7_eng.pdf.

Van den Bossche, P., Gijselaers, W.H., Segers, M., & Kirschner, P.A. (2006). Social and cognitive factors driving teamwork in collaborative learning environments: Team learning beliefs and behaviors. *Small Group Research, 37*, 490–521.

Vygotsky, L. (1978). *Mind in society: Development of higher psychological processes.* Cambridge, MA: Harvard University Press.

Waters, E., & Sroufe, L. (1983). Social competence as developmental construct. *Developmental Review, 3,* 79–97.

Weinstein, C.D. (1991). The classroom as a social context for learning. *Annual Review of Psychology, 42,* 459–491.

Zajac, R. & Hartup, W. (1997). Friends as coworkers: Research review and classroom implications. *The Elementary School Journal, 98,* 3–13.

Zarbatany, L., McDougall, P., & Hymel, S. (2000). Gender-differentiated experiences in the peer culture: Links to intimacy in preadolescence. *Social Development, 9,* 62–79.

Mother–Child Fantasy Play

Angeline S. Lillard

Abstract

Although historically theorists ignored the role of parents in children's pretending, recent research has shown that American mothers model pretense behaviors for infants and coach young children's early pretense attempts. In this chapter I first highlight four features that distinguish mothers' pretending from children's pretending with peers or solo. Next I discuss how mothers might help avert confusion in their early presentations of pretense, namely by changing their canonical behaviors in ways that might signal pretense (or "don't' take this seriously") to their children.

Keywords: Pretend play, mother–child interaction

Introduction

Jean Piaget discussed pretending as an autistic behavior, emerging solely within the child as the result of a maturing semiotic function. In more recent analyses, particularly for American children, pretending is believed to emerge socially, with mothers often providing early tutelage. In this chapter I define pretend play and discuss how mothers behave when pretending with children. The initial discussion of maternal pretend behavior focuses on macro-level issues, like the objects employed and roles taken. The chapter ends with micro-level analyses of how mothers' behaviors change when pretending, and how these changes might signal to very young infants not to mistake pretense events as real.

Defining Pretend Play

Whereas "play" is difficult to define (Burghardt, this volume), the subtype of "pretend play" is much less obtuse (Pellegrini, 2009). Pretend play occurs when an alternative reality is superimposed on the present one, so one is living in as "as-if" world. Objects in the real world "stand in for" or symbolize what is

imagined. In earlier discussions I spelled out a more specific set of criteria (Lillard, 1993, 2002):

1. There is a sentient being (a person or perhaps an animal) carrying out the pretense.
2. There is some reality (omnipresent, of course, but worth noting)
3. There is an alternative reality that is mentally represented by the pretender. Even if this alternative is similar to what is real, it always is different in the sense that it is pretend and therefore more free to vary.
4. This alternative reality is projected—at least mentally and possibly via action as well (see below)—onto the real.
5. The pretender is aware that he or she is engaged in this projection, and that what is being projected is not real. They might not know that the projection is mental, but they are aware that they are superimposing a different reality
6. The pretender is projecting the imagined reality intentionally; such a projection performed unintentionally would be a mistake rather than a pretense.

All of these criteria must be present for us to claim pretense is occurring. A seventh feature often accompanies pretend: action. Thus, in addition to the mental projection (#4), pretenders often carry out what they are imagining. If I am pretending that a bowl contains soup, I might well pretend to drink the soup, carrying out to some degree the actions I would carry out were the soup real. As Bateson (1972) aptly pointed out, the actions might be truncated in some way, for example, I might not actually put the spoon all the way in my mouth and close my lips around it were I merely pretending to drink soup. They also might be exaggerated, for example, I might slurp very loudly when pretending to drink soup. But the actions are not essential to pretense; the other six criteria set out above are.

Why is Pretend Play so Interesting?

The mind has evolved to help us operate in the world. Thus it is very good at setting up representations of space (Newcombe & Huttenlocher, 2003; Wang & Spelke, 2000) and it even represents space according to how our body would need to move in it (Proffit, 2006) in a "Gibsonian affordance" sense. Even monkeys mentally represent social relations, keeping track of hierarchies and dominance/subordinance relationships (Seyfarth & Cheney, 2000). We also mentally track time (Large & Jones, 1999). All this is done in a personal-veridical fashion that corresponds to what we need to know to operate in the environment. Even forward-looking hypothetical thinking focuses on what really might be the case. Our minds are quite sensibly geared to represent the world such that we can interact with the veridical environment.

Pretend play presents a mystery because it subverts the veridicality which is so important to human cognition: Pretense is a case when the mind willingly misrepresents reality, and acts on that misrepresentation as if it were true. The fact that a child's mind can do this at a very young age, when the child still lacks an enormous amount of common knowledge about reality, is mysterious. And children are not even very good at hypothetical thinking (Kuczaj, 1981; Sodian, Zaitchik, & Carey, 1991), which pretending seems to rest on. At age four, their abilities improve *if* a verbal hypothetical is couched in pretense (Dias & Harris, 1988; Dias & Harris, 1990). However, at younger ages, around two years of age, they can even respond to action-based hypotheticals—namely hypotheticals couched in present objects and pretend scripts (Harris & Kavanaugh, 1993; Kavanaugh, this volume). How and why

young children can do this is a mystery. And yet they can do it, and from a very young age.

Development of Pretend Play

Although pretend play is not difficult to define, and one knows oneself when one is pretending (the "awareness" criteria), one cannot always tell when a child is pretending. Piaget (1962) used his children's smiles and laughter to indicate the production of *play* acts, a broader category than pretense. For example, "At 0;3 T. played with his voice, not only through interest in the sound, but for 'functional pleasure,' laughing at his own power" (p. 91). There is no hint here of some alternative reality being pulled over the actual one, for example representing one's own voice as the voice of a teacher or fairy. It is play, but not pretend play. At nine months, J. was observed, while engaged in physical play with her pillow, suddenly sucking its fringe, and then re-enacting "going to sleep" behaviors which she typically did with the pillow (p. 93). According to Piaget, this "ritualization"

"is a preparation for symbolic games. All that is needed for the "ludic" ritual to become a symbol is that the child, instead of merely following the cycle of his habitual movements, should be aware of the make-believe, *i.e.*, that he should "pretend" to sleep" (pp 92–3).

Six months later Piaget claimed that J. finally appeared aware that she was engaged in pretense or make-believe, when she grabbed some fringes that

"vaguely recalled those of her pillow; she seized it, held a fold of it in her right hand, sucked the thumb of the same hand, and lay down on her side, laughing hard. She kept her eyes open, but blinked from time to time, as if she were alluding to closed eyes. Finally, laughing more and more, she cried, Néné (Nono)" (p. 96).

This laughter indicated awareness for Piaget, and therefore marked the beginning of pretense. In Piaget's scheme pretending appeared with the sixth substage of the sensory motor period, along with language and deferred imitation, the other two hallmarks of the semiotic function.

In Piaget's writing, adults appear to have had nothing to do with pretending's arrival; pretending arose strictly out of the child's own developing cognitive capacities. Circular reactions were performed in play, ritualized, and then performed in altered versions as symbols for the real thing. Some classic reviews on pretend play have maintained this view that pretending is initially a solitary activity, and even have claimed that mothers would be unlikely to engage in and model pretense for young children (Fein, 1981).

In contrast to this solitary view of the onset of pretense, and more in keeping with a Vygotskian approach (Goncu, this volume), more recent theorists have situated the development of pretense in a social context (Garvey, 1990; Lillard & Witherington, 2004; Smolucha & Smolucha, 1998; Tomasello & Rakoczy, 2003). Over 25 years ago, several chapters in Bretherton's (1984b) edited volume, *Symbolic Play: The Development of Social Understanding*, examined the play of two- and three-year-olds in the company of their mothers, peers, and siblings. More recently, an observational study of eight middle-class American children ranging from 12 to 48 months of age showed that almost all of the children's pretending at 12 months was done with the mother, and even at 48 months, half of it was with the mother (Haight & Miller, 1993). At 12 months, four children and all eight of the mothers produced a pretend act. Pretending in these middle-class American homes apparently began with the mother, and transferred to the child. In a study including American children in lower-class homes, Dunn and Wooding (1977) found that 40% of the symbolic play bouts of 18- to 24-month-olds were mother-initiated. In some cultures mothers are much less apt to pretend with young children (Farver & Wimbarti, 1995; Gaskins, 1999; Goncu, Mistry, & Mosier, 2000; Tudge et al., this volume); the development of pretending in cultures where parents do not play with their young children would be a worthy topic of inquiry. Discussion here is limited to the cultures where most of pretense research has occurred, particularly North America (but see Tamis-LeMonda, Bornstein, Cyphers, Toda, & et al., 1992).

Four features characterize American mother's pretending with young children: It is more advanced than solo play; mothers tend to be spectators and directors more than actors; mothers use more replica objects than do peers; and mothers' pretending tends to re-enact real events, whereas with peers children make up things that never happened, create more imaginary objects, and so on. These are discussed in turn.

Pretending with mother is initially more advanced

Several studies have noted that when young children pretend with their mothers, their pretending is more advanced than it is when they pretend alone or with peers (e.g., Bornstein, Haynes, Legler, O'Reilly, & Painter, 1997; DeLoache & Plaetzer, 1985; Fiese, 1990). For example, at 18–24 months of age, children were much less likely to pretend at all when their mothers were doing housework than when their mothers were actively engaged with them (Dunn & Wooding, 1977). When pretending with their mothers, 2.5-year-olds can take on reciprocal mother-baby roles; with peers this type of play emerged at three years of age (Miller & Garvey, 1984). Two-year-olds' play with mothers is also more diverse in its themes than is their play alone (O'Connell & Betherton, 1984).

The reason for this increase in the amount, level, and diversity of pretending appears to be that mothers scaffold pretend behaviors, actively demonstrating and suggesting behaviors the child might engage in to fulfill the role (Dunn & Wooding, 1977). In this latter study, conversations with mothers revealed that most of the child-initiated play had been previously demonstrated by adults. Likewise, Haight and Miller (1993) found that 75% of 12-month-olds' utterances when pretending repeated the mother's prior utterance; at 24-months, this figure dropped to 30%, and thereafter it was near 0. Early on, young children often do not even continue the mother's pretend initiatives, thus failing to continue the pretense. Mothers of eight 12- to 15-month-olds produced 75 pretend utterances in a 40-minute observation (typically attributions about feelings and functions of animate and inanimate objects), but the children rarely responded in a way that allowed the pretense theme to continue (Kavanaugh, Whittington, & Cerbone, 1983). This changed dramatically by 18 months, when children "were virtually certain to find some way to continue their mothers' fantasy initiatives" (p. 52).

Mothers initially on appear to provide the ideas for what to do, in some cases being more directive (Miller & Garvey, 1984) and in others more suggestive (DeLoache & Plaetzer, 1985; Haight & Miller, 1993). Probably because of this input, young children's pretend play sessions with mothers are more sustained (Dunn & Wooding, 1977) and complex (Fiese, 1990; Slade, 1987) than is their pretend play alone or with peers. By age four, Haight and Miller (1993) observed a complete reversal, such that pretend play bouts with peers were twice as long as pretend play bouts with mothers.

Mothers also provide ideas about how to pretend. For example, by convention people tend to use a differently-pitched voice when speaking for others in pretense, such as a higher pitch for a baby or a mouse, and a lower pitch for a man or a bear. Haight and Miller (1993) described how a mother modeled this behavior when playing with her son, and how initially he overextended the convention and spoke in a higher pitch during all of his pretense; by age three he only used a higher pitch when speaking for the mouse, used a lower pitch when speaking as a man, and used his normal voice when speaking out of frame (pp. 61–2). The child was apparently taught this convention by maternal modeling.

There are varying findings regarding whether mothers modify their behaviors during pretense to fit the child's level. O'Connell and Bretherton (1984) found no differences in maternal structuring of pretense at 20 and 28 months of age, but others have found that mothers of children whose pretending was more advanced (Damast, Tamis-LeMonda, & Bornstein, 1996) or who were gifted (Morrissey & Brown, 2009) gave more advanced directives, scaffolding children in their individual zones of proximal development (see also Kavanaugh, et al., 1983; Miller & Garvey, 1984; Sachs, 1980). Related to this is the degree to which mothers are spectators or actors in their children's pretense.

Mothers are more spectators than actors

When children pretend with siblings and peers, both parties are engaged in the action. The older partner tends to take on a more directive role (Dunn & Dale, 1984) but both parties have "within frame" parts in the play. Mothers, in contrast, initiate pretending from a within-frame position around one year, but by age two are frequently taking an off-stage role (Haight & Miller, 1993), commenting on the child's pretend action and making suggestions, but not actively participating themselves. They set up and encourage pretending by providing props, like dolls and dollhouse furniture, miniature cars, trains, and train tracks (Miller & Garvey, 1984), but they hang back from within-frame participation. In Dunn and Dale's (1984) study of two-year-olds' play with mother and older sibling, mothers were spectators in 85% of play bouts and were actively involved in 15%; the levels for the four- to five-year-old *siblings* were 40% and 60%, respectively. The levels in Haight and Miller's (1993) observations were even more discrepant: At 48 months, children pretended (thus were in frame) about six times more than their mothers.

Mothers focus on replica objects

Whereas pretend play with siblings and peers often involves pulling themes seemingly out of thin air,

adopting roles and inventing internal states, mothers tend to focus on replicas in their play with toddlers. In one study, 97% of mothers' play bouts involved replica objects, in contrast to 27% of siblings' (Dunn & Dale, 1984). Across the board children's play frequently involves replicas (Haight & Miller, 1993) and at least among low income children provision of replicas increases some forms of pretend play (McLoyd, 1983). Particularly with girls, the replicas mothers tend to bring into play are dolls, and the behaviors mothers enact or encourage in their daughters are nurturing (Dunn & Dale, 1984). Siblings, in contrast, are likely to enact household routines, or everyday scripts like school and birthday party. No props are needed to get this sibling play off the ground.

Mothers re-enact; peers and sibs enact

Consistent with their reliance on replicas, mothers' play seems to be more often following a cultural script; peers and siblings are more apt to deviate from such scripts. Bretherton (1984a) distinguished as-if from what-if behavior. In the former, she wrote, one simulates everyday behaviors: pretending to eat, to drink, and to sleep. In what-if behavior, reality is transformed, so one object can become another, people can take on different roles, and the impossible can occur. Dunn and Dale (1984) noted that whereas maternal behavior tends to be of the as-if variety, play with siblings is more often of the what-if type.

Given mothers' reliance on the here-and-now—the replicas, the enactments of everyday behavior, the movement away from really joining in the pretense to instead hanging on the outskirts and directing it—the primary finding that pretense with the mother is more advanced is puzzling. This apparent contradiction can be explained developmentally. People have tended to study children's play with mothers when children are very young, and pretending is just emerging. Early pretending is characterized by the mini-moves into the fantastic realm that mothers are willing to make, and thus their scaffolding of those moves does advance the play of young children. As children get older, these moves would no longer be an advance, but the mother–child play is less frequent. Perhaps in keeping with this, Tamis-LeMonda and Bornstein (1994) found specific relations between symbolic play at 13 and 20 months, with children's levels of play correlating with mothers' levels at, but not across, each age. Thus mother's behaviors drove 13-month-olds' behaviors, but did not predict their behavior seven months later. By 24 or 28 months, one might expect no concurrent relationship between mother and child level of play.

Given that adults pretend with very young children, who are not yet pretending themselves, a question arises as to how children know how to interpret pretense acts? How do they know not to take them literally?

Sachs (1980) provided an example of the puzzle:

> A two-year-old and her father were talking together when the child put some blocks on top of her doll in her doll's bed. Her father said, "Don't put the blocks on her. That isn't comfortable." A few minutes later, they left the doll lying in a heap in the toy box while they went to lunch, and it appeared that neither worried about whether the doll was comfortable.
> (pp. 46–7)

Sachs goes on to comment that there was no "overt signal" in the father's initial utterance indicating that it referred to a pretend world in which the doll had real feelings of comfort. Why did it not confuse the child? How did she know to put a pretend frame around the first event and step out of it to go get lunch?

In a series of studies, we have examined how mothers might signal to very young children that they are pretending, and (later) which of those signals young children appear to be able to use when.

What do Mothers do Differently When They Pretend?

To study how mothers' behavior in pretend situations differs from what they do in real situations, we (Lillard & Witherington, 2004) devised two laboratory situations that were virtually the same in all ways but three: 1) the mother was asked to pretend in one situation and not the other, 2) when pretending, some real objects were absent that would normally be present in a real situation and 3) the color of the objects was red in one condition and blue in the other (varied across mothers). Specifically, we asked mothers to have a real snack and a pretend snack with their child "just like you would at home."

The setting was a table, about three feet square in size, with the baby in a clip-on high chair and the mother across the table in a desk chair on wheels. On the table in both conditions were a small metal pitcher, a metal serving bowl, a paper napkin, two plastic bowls for eating from, and two plastic cups for drinking from. In the real condition only, the pitcher contained apple juice and the serving bowl

contained Cheerios cereal. Cameras were positioned behind the mother to capture the baby, and behind a one-way glass to capture the mother. A fly-swatter microphone was positioned on the wall. In addition, some of the mothers' hands were monitored by a Flock of Birds motion detector which delivered x,y,z coordinates of their place in space each millisecond.

Across two experiments, 55 18-month-olds came to the laboratory with their mothers, and half of the mothers were first asked to pretend to have a snack of Cheerios and juice, and the other half were first asked to have a snack for real. They were left alone in the room to do this for two minutes, after which the experimenter came back, changed out the snacking materials, and told them about the second condition. Afterwards, mothers were asked to rate their comfort level in the experiment (to indicate if they felt they behaved artificially), what they thought the purpose of the experiment was (we had told them it was to study parent–child interaction, but wanted to be sure they hadn't figured out that we were interested specifically in pretense), and how much experience their child had pretending. Sessions were then coded for a variety of features that we expected might differ across pretend and real situations, based on the existing literature with animals and humans. These are discussed in turn.

Smiles

From the chimpanzee "play face" (Eibl-Eibesfeldt, 1989; Palagi, this volume; van Hooff, 1972) to Piaget's (1962) claims of his children's tell-tale smiles, there is suspicion that we communicate pretense via smiling (Boulton, 1993). In our experiment, mothers did smile more when pretending to have a snack than when really snacking; they also engaged in more "long smiles," ones over four s in length, making for more smiling overall when pretending. Long facial expressions are more often "fake" ones (Frank, Ekman, & Friesen, 1993), and young children are sensitive to the timing of events (see below) so this could conceivably be a signal. However, whereas on average 3.3 smiles in the pretend condition were long ones, 1.75 long smiles occurred (on average) in the real condition, so if children relied on this as a cue, they might mistake some pretend events for real. Of course, it is possible that when really having a snack, something happened that was "faked," so looking at referents of smiles also seemed important.

One cannot know for sure what mothers' smiles referred to, but coders' reasonable guesses about what they referred prove to be reliable (kappa = .81). Based on preliminary data, coders categorized smile referents into five types: mother action, child action, child's confusion, greeting smiles, or ambiguous. Results showed that in the pretend condition, as compared to the real one, twice as many maternal smiles appeared to be about mother action; in contrast, in the real condition, mothers smiled more about (apparently) the child's actions. One might speculate that in the real condition mothers were smiling to encourage their children's behaviors, whereas in the pretend one they were smiling to let the child know not to take their actions seriously. As will be discussed later in this chapter, we have discussed this behavior as a type of social referencing that might serve to signal pretend play (Lillard, 2007; Nishida & Lillard, 2007).

Looks

Looking at people often serves a communicative function (Fehr & Exline, 1987), and after viewing actions that were ambiguous with respect to goal, infants look immediately to the actor's eyes (Phillips, Baron-Cohen, & Rutter, 1992). Infants are also sensitive to adult gaze, and smile more during eye contact (Hains & Muir, 1996). When pretend snacking, mothers looked at their children much more than they looked at the task implements (like the bowl and pitcher); in real snacking, they looked only slightly more at the child. Looked at another way, they looked at the task implements more in real snacks than in pretend ones, and they looked at the child more in pretend snacks than real snacks. Thus, looking behavior supports pretending involving communication from mother to child, whereas really snacking requires more looking at the task. The increased looking to task in pretense makes sense: If you do not look when pouring, for example, you are more likely to spill. The increased looking in pretense supports the idea that mothers are engaging in a communicative act.

Words

The words mothers used also differed by condition. First, note that most mothers did not simply outright tell children, "I'm pretending." On average, the explicit labeling of the event type was used once in every pretend session, but many mothers did not use the word at all. Second, one might expect that mothers would frequently talk about Cheerios and juice in the pretend session, since the only way to instantiate these specific absent objects is to name them. One can mime eating to evoke generic food, but to evoke Cheerios specifically requires labeling. On the other hand, 18-month-olds are just learning language, and labeling invisible objects constitutes "representational abuse" (Leslie, 1987). In fact, although mothers talked overall more in the pretend condition, mothers were equally likely in pretend as in real snacks to refer to the absent objects. They did not go overboard with referential abuse by referring even more to these objects. Instead, they referred proportionally twice as often to their actions (eating, pouring, and drinking) in the pretend condition, and somewhat more often to the concrete objects (the cup and plate). The increased talk while pretending was thus more about things that were or at least were closer to the real.

One might wonder if mothers talked more while pretending because they could: they were not really eating. In fact, in the real condition, mothers often talked just after popping a Cheerio into their mouths; these snacks did not appear to inhibit their talking. Instead, it seems they were talking more while pretending in order to communicate about what they were doing.

Sound effects

One might expect sound effects to be a standard way to get pretense across: pouring noises, "glug-glugs" for drinking, and so on. This was a stark difference across conditions: while pretending, mothers averaged 11 sound effects in one experiment and 6 in the other, and while really eating, there were virtually none. On the other hand, the amount of maternal laughter was less likely to differ across conditions.

Movements

Overall, mothers moved faster when pretending than when really eating. This is consistent with research on the pace of pantomime (Weiss, Jeannerod, Paulignan, & Freund, 2000): people pantomime faster than they engage in those same actions for real. Mothers moved their hand to their mouth faster, and away faster, they lifted the cup to their mouths faster, they rotated the pitcher faster, and so on. The exception to this was pretend eating: while pretending to eat, mothers held their hands at their mouths longer than they did when really eating. This is probably a conventionalized pretense behavior. In real eating, we tend to drop the food off in our mouths and move our hands away quickly. In pretend eating, though, we often leave the hand there while we tap our lips together and make a smacking noise with the tongue. (It would be interesting to know if this is universal or culturally-specific way to mime eating.) Babies might be able to recognize this special pretense behavior as pretense at an early age. Later research, however, suggests that children fail to understand that these conventionalized behavior, at least when enacted by strangers, are more likely than are real behaviors to involve pretend or imaginary content (Ma & Lillard, 2006; Ma & Lillard, in preparation).

Mothers also engaged in more snack-related acts overall in the pretend condition: they sipped from their cups more, brought Cheerios to their mouths more, and so on. Thus they provide an abundance of evidence suggesting that they are snacking, and that these different component acts constitute snacking. Tomasello (1999) discussed pretending as an opportunity to learn culture, and this extensive provision of the components of a cultural act (eating involves a different set of components in different cultures) supports the view that pretending with more knowledgeable others is a setting for the transmission of culture.

People often suggest that pretend actions are exaggerated. We noted exaggeration in just one way in this study: mothers raised the pitcher higher when pretend pouring than when really pouring. In a later study, described next, we also found they exaggerated the pouring angle of the pitcher. One might think of the long hold at the mouth in pretend eating to be a form of exaggeration, but it does not seem to be in that the hand, in real eating, the hand only goes to the mouth briefly to deposit the food. The hand at the mouth in pretend eating is not a drawn-out deposit; rather it seems to mark the location of interest while the pretender "eats."

An additional experiment (Lillard, et al., 2007, Exp. 1) involving snacking tested developmental change: whether mothers change their behaviors in pretense in ways that are consistent across ages of children, from 15 months, when children are still on the verge of entering this realm, to 24 months, when most children have become established pretenders, often initiating pretense episodes themselves (Haight & Miller, 1993). Overall, results were consistent with the first study and there were no differences across this nine-month age range. A few exceptions were found.

First, although with the older two ages groups mothers again placed smiles after their own actions more in the pretend condition, they did not do so with 15-month-olds. This is surprising, in that children at this age clearly share affect and even use adult affect as a cue to how to respond to ambiguous situations (Walden & Ogan, 1988), although more so in response to vocal than facial expressions (Mumme, Fernald, & Herrera, 1996). Fifteen-month-olds would seem to need *more* signals about pretense than older children need, and yet mothers were less apt to provide of one seemingly obvious cue—smiles—in this situation. Mothers do tend to provide signals (facial and vocal) to infants around this age for social referencing in real contexts, signaling whether something ambiguous is dangerous or safe, for example. And it is not simply that mothers smiled so much with younger babies that they maxed out the possibility for smiles in both conditions: Mothers were overall more smiley when pretending with 24-month-olds than with younger children. Why mothers give the signals to older children but not 15-month-olds in a pretense context is unclear.

One potential cue that was provided *more* for younger children was holding the hand at the mouth while eating. Mothers did not produce this conventionalized cue for 24-month-olds, but did for both of the younger groups. Another possible motor cue that was provided more for younger children was the angle to which the pitcher was rotated for pouring (something not measured in the first study). Mothers exaggerated this angle for all children, but the exaggeration was particularly marked for younger groups. We know that children are sensitive to how long events should take from at least five months of age (Dannemiller & Freedland, 1991); the path of motion difference in pretend pouring is probably also noticeable to them since in other domains they show sensitivity to different paths of motion (Rochat, Morgan, & Carpenter, 1997). Very young infants likely can use these kinds of variations in hand movements to assist their comprehension (Zukow-Goldring, 1996), and either the long hold or the exaggerated pouring angle could conceivably be a cue to pretense for 15-month-olds.

Two additions to the data set in this second study were the pitch and amplitude of mothers' voices, as measured with the Computer Speech Lab (CSL); another was data on word use provided by the Linguistic Word Count (LIWC) program (Pennebaker, Francis, & Booth, 2001). The CSL analysis detected a difference in behavior dependent on the age of the infant: although mothers used more variable pitch and talked more loudly when pretending for the sample overall, pitch variation was not used for 18-month-olds. We do not know why mothers used more "sing-songy" voices at the two outside ages and not the middle one. Increased pitch variation in pretense is consistent with research by Reissland and Snow (1996): they found more pitch variation in pretend at 11–12 months, and hypothesized that its role was to signal pretending.

The LIWC analysis revealed that overall, mothers repeated the same words more in pretense (e.g., used fewer unique words even though they talked more) and used more "we" talk when pretending. More "we" talk fits with pretending being a communicative act involving joint attention. The mother sees herself and the child as being in the pretend world together, even more so than they are when having a snack together for real. In joint pretense, shared meaning is crucial but not for granted. It must be created via communication and action, whereas in the real snack situation it is part of the cultural knowledge the child by this age already possesses. Repeating the same words more in pretense can also be explained by a heightened need for clear communication.

Finally, for one experiment (Lillard, et al., 2007, Exp. 2) we changed the pretense scenario, to allow us to determine whether the behavioral changes we observed were unique to snacks, a behavior which roughly half of mothers said they had pretended with their children before (more at older ages). The new scenario was one of personal grooming. Although many mothers said they had done this before, we suspect it is less frequent that pretend eating, given that most people self groom just once in the morning, but eat several times a day. Pretend eating-related toys (kitchen sets, wooden fruit to cut, tea party sets) also seem to be much more common than pretend grooming toys, and mothers are inclined towards using replicas in their play. Yet despite its probably being done less than eating, grooming is something that many mothers do pretend with their children; it may well even be the second-most common pretense after eating, thus it was the choice for this experiment.

In each condition mothers were provided with a brush (the bristles were removed for pretend), a small lotion bottle (no lotion in pretend), a small sponge (wetted in real), and a face towel. Of 37 mother–child pairs, 25 were run with the CSL and 12 with the motion monitor (the two technologies were incompatible). We found some differences in mothers' behaviors across pretend and real grooming scenarios. First, they were less smiley at baseline than they had been when snacking, and they did not increase smiling when pretending to groom. However, mothers were again more apt to place smiles after actions in the pretend condition, consistent with the first studies. This consistency with the three prior studies using a snack scenario suggests smile placement might be a particularly important cue to pretense. As in the prior studies, mothers also looked more at their children when pretending than when doing things for real, highlighting the possible import of this cue. Differences for movements were less strong, but there was a trend towards more activity in the pretense scenario, thus giving more instances of the behavior to interpret in the pretense mode. Only one of the motions we analyzed was faster in pretend: mothers rubbed "lotion" into their faces more quickly when pretending. Consistent with findings for 18-month-olds in the prior experiment, the CSL detected no differences in maternal speech with these 18-month-olds.

In sum, in a new, less-frequently pretended activity, personal grooming, mothers continued to look more at their 18-month-olds and to engage in more "social referencing smiles," and to provide (somewhat) more instances of behaviors, one of which they did faster. The use of these potential cues across scenarios suggests that they might be especially important generic means to communicate pretense.

We summarized across our research concerning signs of pretense as follows:

> In four experiments thus far, either significantly or as a trend, mothers have used more words in pretense (two experiments), they have referred more to pretense behaviors (three experiments) and objects (two experiments), and they have used more sound effects (three experiments); they have smiled more at baseline (three experiments) and have smiled more often (three experiments) and used longer smiles (three experiments), and more of those smiles appear to be in reference to the mothers' own behaviors (four experiments); they have looked more frequently at the child (three experiments) and have been more often judged to be looking predominantly at the child (four experiments); they have engaged in more scenario-related behaviors (four experiments) and have done at least some of those behaviors faster (four experiments) with the exception of a conventionalized behavior, holding the hand at the mouth longer while pretend eating (seen in all three snack experiments). In addition, of the three experiments examining links to engagement, at least a trend toward a relation has been seen for the number of words mothers spoke (two experiments), the proportion of references to scenario-related behaviors (two experiments), the frequency and duration of smiles and the tendency for smiles to be

about the mothers' behaviors (all three experiments, and especially for experienced pretenders), duration and frequency of looking at the child (two experiments), and shorter durations of some movements (which may help more experienced pretenders, and interfere with less experienced ones).

(*Lillard* et al 2007, p. 27)

Given that mothers are providing these cues, how is the use of each cue related to children's understanding that their mothers were pretending?

Two lines of research in our laboratory have examined when and how children might know that others are pretending. One approach, enacted largely by Lili Ma, was to show young children actors pretending to eat with the "signs" mothers (generically) used, side by side with another actor who was really eating, and see whether they detected the meaning of the pretend variations (Ma & Lillard, 2006; Ma & Lillard, in preparation). The test of whether they got pretense in this case was to see if children realized that only the pretender lacked real food in their bowl ("Where is the real cheese?"). Surprisingly, children did not show a really solid understanding until 2.5 years of age (although 2-year-olds showed implicit signs of understanding earlier, for example smacking their lips more during real eating). Further studies have also looked at how other adults and four-year-olds interpret "thin slices" (Ambady, Bernieri, & Richeson, 2000) of pretend and real behaviors based on the signs, and in this case were simply asked outright if people were pretending or not (Ma & Lillard, under review; Richert & Lillard, 2004); however, because these two lines do not involve children's interpretations of their mothers' behaviors, they are not discussed further here.

The other approach is less definitive, but involved children and their mothers' pretending: We looked at the children's behaviors in the experiments above in terms of when the children *seemed* to understand pretense, and what maternal behaviors accompanied their apparent understanding. This culminated in a sequential analysis (Nishida & Lillard, 2007) also described below.

Children's smiles and pretense behaviors in the experiments just described were taken to be indicators that children in some sense understood the pretense snack scenario, and were summed for an "understanding" score. This is of course not a rock-solid indicator of understanding; for this reason in the Lillard et al. (2007) study we even downgraded the term from "understanding" to "engagement." Our research since has further supported our initial

hunch that smiles and pretense behaviors while their mothers pretend indicates understanding, and it is the term used here.

Supporting this supposition, babies' smiles and snack-related behaviors in the pretend session increased with age (Lillard et al, 2007). In addition, even just among 18-month-olds, those whose mothers reported that they had more experience pretending engaged in more pretense behaviors during the pretense sessions; smiling was equivalent with an average of two baby smiles per session. Lillard et al (2007) wrote, "This might suggest that young children's snack-related actions are a better indicator of understanding than are their smiles, but viewing of the tapes suggested that both are important" (p. 106): Some children never engaged in snacking behaviors themselves but smiled and giggled at their mothers throughout the pretend session, very much appearing to understand she was pretending but not themselves partaking. The increase with age and experience in smiling and pretend snacking behaviors suggests that combined they are an indicator of understanding.

The levels of baby understanding and the different maternal behaviors were initially subjected to correlational analyses to see whether particular mother behaviors were associated with apparent understanding. Across the four experiments just reviewed, one consistent relationship was between baby understanding and mother smiling, particularly the placement of her smiles just after, and thus apparently in reference to, the pretend behavior. This was especially the case for children who had more experience pretending, as reported by their mothers. Mothers looking at their children while pretending also was associated with higher understanding scores; again, in some studies this relationship was significant only for more experienced pretenders.

These experience-driven findings are interesting. It is possible that mothers reserve these signs until children in other ways show they "get it." This would fit with their using these kinds of signs less with 15-month-olds. Alternatively, it could be that children of mothers who use these signs get pretending earlier, and thus came into the experiment with more understanding. Further research could tease apart these possibilities.

There were also some indications that when mothers talked a lot, and specifically when they talked about their behaviors (used snack- or grooming-related verbs), children had higher understanding scores. Thus, maternal language is probably one avenue into understanding for children, as mothers repeatedly emphasize "I'm pouring" and "We're eating a good snack now!" offering an interpretation of acts that could be ambiguous given the lack of real content. Young children are sensitive to goals from an early age (Gergely, Nadasdy, Csibra, & Biro, 1995; Woodward, 2008), and the goal of pouring is to move liquid!

Recall that mothers used more motor cues for younger babies, exaggerating the angle of the pour and the timing of hold the hand at the mouth while pretend eating. These are both cases of slowing the action down. An interesting pattern of relationships was found for baby understanding and maternal movement in pretense. It appeared that the *less* experience children had pretending, the more mothers' canonically short, fast movements in pretense confused them, resulting in significantly lower understanding scores. As children grew older or had more pretense experience, these canonical pretense movements were associated with *more* understanding. Slowing the pace of motor actions apparently helps get the point across to younger babies, and as they come to get pretense (perhaps learning to rely on other cues like the placement of smile), then faster movements cue pretense. Pretending generally involves "speeded-up" time, like other forms of fiction. The assistance provided by slower motion is implied by research on "motionese" (Brand, Baldwin, & Ashburn, 2002) as well.

Correlation, of course, could work either way: mothers' behaviors might have been in response to children's. To address this and get a better sense of whether mother's behaviors might be cueing children, we subjected the data by time stamp to sequential analyses.

Specifically, mothers' actions, looks to the child, and smiles—in that order—were looked at in terms of how frequently they immediately preceded child understanding behaviors (smiles and snack-related movements). The frequency of these sequences of mother–child behaviors was compared with the frequency of two alternative sequences: generalized imitation (mother snack-related behavior followed by child snack-related behavior) and affective mirroring (mother smiles-child smiles). All three sequences were examined in both pretend and real scenarios for 32 mother–child pairs from Lillard and Witherington (2004, Exp. 1). Each behavior had to occur within a second after its prior behavior in a sequence to be considered part of a sequence. These analyses revealed that the first sequence occurred significantly more often in the pretend condition than the real one, and significantly more often than the imitation and affective mirroring sequences in the pretend condition.

From this and the prior studies, we concluded that mothers and children use something like social referencing in their pretend interpretations. In the ambiguous situation that mother's pretense behavior presents, mothers look to their child to establish joint attention, act, then signal to their child by smiling not to take that action seriously. Young children read the situation correctly, responding in kind.

How does pretending with the mother begin to generalize to pretending with peers and strange adults? Paul Harris and Robert Kavanaugh (1993) have provided crucial information relevant to this extension. They found that around 2.5 years of age, children seem to understand when pretense is occurring (corroborated by the Ma and Lillard study just described). In their studies, an experimenter engaged in pretense acts and children were asked to continue those acts, or repeat them on other entities. For example, the experimenter pretended to pour water on one of two bears, and asked children to dry the Teddy who was wet. Two-year-olds were at chance but by 2.5 the one who had been "poured" on was selected significantly more often. What is especially interesting here is that in these studies the experimenters did not give signs they were pretending— they did not smile, vary their pitch, say the word "pretend," and so on. Thus, by 2.5 in a tightly controlled situation with a strange experimenter, children are far enough along with pretense understanding that they can be cued simply by the unreal situation; interpersonal cues are not necessary. On the other hand, what children were able to do in these studies was continue the sequence of pretend actions; in Ma and Lillard (2006) they could not infer that pretending implies lack of real content until around three. The pretending that begins with the mother in the first year, and is elaborated on by and with the mother in the second, is operative in the world of strange adults midway through the third.

Summary

Piaget and other earlier Western theorists discussed pretending as emerging in the child alone; in contrast, Vygotsky and more recent theorists have discussed pretending emerging in the context of parent–child play, at least in cultures where parents engage in such play. Mothers' play with very young children is different than such young children's play alone or with peers: it occurs at a higher level and is more sustained and includes more diverse themes. In addition, mothers more often involve replica objects rather than imaginary or substitute ones; they more often re-enact scripts from everyday life, whereas more "wild" things happen in play with peers; and mothers move quickly from initially being actors into director or spectator roles in pretend play with very young children.

The issue of how mothers initially bring children into pretense is an important one, given that the cognitive system would logically be set up to apprehend reality. Mothers behave differently when they pretend than when they do those same things for real, and some of those changes in behavior might signal to young children that they are pretending. Specifically, mothers engage in behavior sequences when pretending that are akin to what occurs in social referencing. Mothers appear to establish joint attention with the child by looking at them, then engage in a pretend act, then smile, as if to comment on the act just performed. When mothers present such sequences more often to 18-month-olds, children appear to "get" pretend more often, in that they more smile back and perform additional pretend acts themselves.

References

Ambady, N., Bernieri, F. J., & Richeson, J. A. (2000). Toward a histology of social behavior: Judgmental accuracy from thin slices of the behavioral stream. In M. P. Zanna (Ed.), *Advances in experimental social psychology, Vol. 32* (pp. 201–271). San Diego, CA: Academic Press.

Bateson, G. A. (1972). A theory of play and fantasy. In G. A. Bateson (Ed.), *Steps to an ecology of mind* (pp. 177–193). New York: Chandler.

Bornstein, M. H., Haynes, O. M., Legler, J. M., O'Reilly, A. W., & Painter, K. M. (1997). Symbolic play in childhood: Interpersonal and environmental context and stability. *Infant Behavior & Development, 20*, 197–207.

Boulton, M. J. (1993). A comparison of adults' and children's abilities to distinguish between aggressive and playful fighting in middle school pupils: Implications for playground supervision and behaviour management. *Educational Studies, 19*, 193–203.

Brand, R. J., Baldwin, D. A., & Ashburn, L. A. (2002). Evidence for 'motionese': Modifications in mothers' infant-directed action. *Developmental Science, 5*(1), 72–83.

Bretherton, I. (1984a). Representing the social world in symbolic play: Reality and fantasy. In I. Bretherton (Ed.), *Symbolic Play* (pp. 3–41). New York: Academic Press.

Bretherton, I. (Ed.). (1984b). *Symbolic play: The development of social understanding.* Orlando: Academic Press.

Damast, A., Tamis-LeMonda, C., & Bornstein, M. (1996). Mother–child play: Sequential interactions and the relation between maternal beliefs and behaviors. *Child Development, 67*(4), 1752–1766.

Dannemiller, J. L., & Freedland, R. (1991). Speed discrimination in 20-week-old infants. *Infant Behavior & Development, 14*(2), 163–173.

DeLoache, J. S., & Plaetzer, B. (1985). *Tea for two: Joint mother–child symbolic play.* Paper presented at the Bienniel meeting for the Society for Research in Child Development, Toronto.

Dias, M. G. & Harris, P. L. (1988). The effect of make-believe play on deductive reasoning. *British Journal of Developmental Psychology, 6*, 207–221.

Dias, M. G. & Harris, P. L. (1990). The influence of the imagination on reasoning by young children. *British Journal of Developmental Psychology, 8*, 305–318.

Dunn, J. & Dale, N. (1984). I a daddy: 2-year-olds collaboration in joint pretend play with sibling and with mother. In I. Bretherton (Ed.), *Symbolic play* (pp. 131–158). London: Academic Press.

Dunn, J. & Wooding, C. (1977). Play in the home and its implications for learning. In B. Tizard & D. Harvey (Eds.), *Biology of play* (pp. 45–58). London: Spastics International.

Eibl-Eibesfeldt, I. (1989). *Human ethology.* New York: Aldine de Gruyter.

Farver, J. A. & Wimbarti, S. (1995). Indonesian children's play with their mothers and older siblings. *Child Development, 66*, 1493–1503.

Fehr, B. J. & Exline, R. V. (1987). Social visual interaction: A conceptual and literature review. In A. W. Siegman & S. Feldstein (Eds.), *Nonverbal behavior and communication* (2nd ed., pp. 225–326). Hillsdale, NJ: Lawrence Erlbaum Associates.

Fein, G. G. (1981). Pretend play in childhood: An integrative review. *Child Development, 52*, 1095–1118.

Fiese, B. H. (1990). Playful relationships: A contextual analysis of mother-toddler interaction and symbolic play. *Child Development, 61*, 1648–1656.

Frank, M. G., Ekman, P., & Friesen, W. V. (1993). Behavioral markers and recognizability of the smile of enjoyment. *Journal of Personality & Social Psychology, 64*, 83–93.

Garvey, C. (1990). *Play* (2 ed.). Cambridge, MA: Harvard University Press.

Gaskins, S. (1999). Children's daily lives in a Mayan village: A case study of culturally constructed roles and activities. In A. Goncue (Ed.), *Children's engagement in the world: Sociocultural perspectives* (pp. 25–60). New York, NY, USA: Cambridge University Press.

Gergely, G., Nadasdy, Z., Csibra, G., & Biro, S. (1995). Taking the intentional stance at 12 months of age. *Cognition, 56*, 165–193.

Goncu, A., Mistry, J., & Mosier, C. (2000). Cultural variations in the play of toddlers. *International Journal of Behavioral Development, 24*(3), 321–329.

Haight, W. L., & Miller, P. J. (1993). *Pretending at home.* Albany: SUNY Press.

Hains, S. M. J. & Muir, D. W. (1996). Infant sensitivity to adult eye direction. *Child Development, 67*(5), 1940–1951.

Harris, P. L. & Kavanaugh, R. D. (1993). Young children's understanding of pretense. *Monographs of the Society for Research in Child Development, 58*, (1, Serial No. 231).

Kavanaugh, R. D., Whittington, S., & Cerbone, M. J. (1983). Mothers' use of fantasy speech to young children. *Journal of Child Language, 10*, 45–55.

Kuczaj, S. A. (1981). Factors influencing children's hypothetical reference. *Journal of Child Language, 8*, 131–137.

Large, E., & Jones, M. (1999). The dynamics of attending: How people track time-varying events. *Psychological Review-New York, 106,* 119–159.

Leslie, A. M. (1987). Pretense and representation: The origins of "theory of mind". *Psychological Review, 94,* 412–426.

Lillard, A. S. (1993). Pretend play skills and the child's theory of mind. *Child Development, 64,* 348–371.

Lillard, A. S. (2002). Just through the looking glass: Children's understanding of pretense. In R. Mitchell (Ed.), *Pretending in animals and children* (pp. 102–114). Cambridge, England: Cambridge University Press.

Lillard, A. S. (2007). Guideded participation: How mothers structure and children's understanding of pretend play. In A. Goncu & S. Gaskins (Eds.), *Play and development: Evolutionary, sociocultural, and functional perspectives.* Mahwah, NJ: Erlbaum.

Lillard, A. S., Nishida, T., Massaro, D., Vaish, A., Ma, L., & McRoberts, G. (2007). Signs of pretense across age and scenario. *Infancy, 11*(1), 1–30.

Lillard, A. S. & Witherington, D. (2004). Mothers' behavior modifications during pretense snacks and their possible signal value for toddlers. *Developmental Psychology, 40*(1), 95–113.

Ma, L., & Lillard, A. S. (2006). Where is the real cheese? Young children's ability to discriminate between real and pretend acts. *Child Development, 77*(6), 1762–1777.

Ma, L., & Lillard, A. S. (in preparation). Two-year-olds' understanding of real-pretend contrasts: The case of real versus substitute or imaginary content.

Ma, L., & Lillard, A. S. (under review). What makes an act a pretense one? Young children's pretend-real judgments and explanations.

McLoyd, V. (1983). The effects of the structure of play objects on the pretend play of low-income preschool children. *Child Development,* 626–635.

Miller, P., & Garvey, C. (1984). Mother-baby role play: Its origins in social support. In I. Bretherton (Ed.), *Symbolic play* (pp. 101–158). London: Academic Press.

Morrissey, A. & Brown, P. (2009). Mother and toddler activity in the zone of proximal development for pretend play as a predictor of higher child IQ. *Gifted Child Quarterly, 53*(2), 106–120.

Mumme, D. L., Fernald, A., & Herrera, C. (1996). Infants' responses to facial and vocal emotional signals in a social referencing paradigm. *Child Development, 67,* 3219–3237.

Newcombe, N. & Huttenlocher, J. (2003). *Making space: The development of spatial representation and reasoning.* Boston: The MIT Press.

Nishida, T. & Lillard, A. S. (2007). The informative value of emotional expressions: Social referencing in mother-infant pretense. *Developmental Science, 10*(2), 205–212.

O'Connell, B. & Betherton, I. (1984). Toddler's play, alone and with mother: The role of maternal guidance. In I. Bretherton (Ed.), *Symbolic play* (pp. 337–368). London: Academic Press.

Pellegrini, A. (2009). *The role of play in human development.* New York: Oxford University Press.

Pennebaker, J. W., Francis, M. E., & Booth, R. J. (2001). *Linguistic Inquiry and Word Count (LICW): A computerized text analysis program.* Mahwah NJ: Erlbaum.

Phillips, W., Baron-Cohen, S., & Rutter, M. (1992). The role of eye contact in goal detection: Evidence from normal infants and children with autism or mental handicap. *Development & Psychopathology, 4,* 375–383.

Piaget, J. (1962). *Play, dreams, and imitation in childhood* (G. Gattegno & F. M. Hodgson, Trans.). New York: Norton.

Proffit, D. R. (2006). Embodied perception and the economy of action. *Perspectives in Psychological Science, 1*(2), 110–122.

Reissland, N. & Snow, D. (1996). Maternal pitch height in ordinary and play situations. *Journal of Child Language, 23*(2), 269–278.

Richert, R. & Lillard, A. S. (2004). Observers' proficiency at identifying pretense acts based on behavioral cues. *Cognitive Development, 19,* 223–240.

Rochat, P., Morgan, R., & Carpenter, M. (1997). Young infants' sensitivity to movement information specifying social causality. *Cognitive Development, 12,* 441–465.

Sachs, J. (1980). The role of adult-child play in language development. In K. H. Rubin (Ed.), *Children's play* (Vol. 9, pp. 33–48). San Francisco: Jossey-Bass.

Seyfarth, R. & Cheney, D. (2000). Social awareness in monkeys. *Integrative and Comparative Biology, 40*(6), 902.

Slade, A. (1987). Quality of attachment and early symbolic play. *Developmental Psychology, 23*(1), 78–85.

Smolucha, L. & Smolucha, F. (1998). The social origins of mind: Post-Piagetian perspectives on pretend play. In O. N. Saracho & S. Bernard (Eds.), *Multiple perspectives on play in early childhood education. SUNY series, early childhood education: Inquiries and insights* (pp. 34–58). Albany, NY: State University of New York Press.

Sodian, B., Zaitchik, D., & Carey, S. (1991). Young children's differentiation of hypothetical beliefs from evidence. *Child Development, 62*(4), 753–766.

Tamis-LeMonda, C. & Bornstein, M. (1994). Specificity in mother-toddler language-play relations across the second year. *Developmental Psychology, 30,* 283–292.

Tamis-LeMonda, C. S., Bornstein, M. H., Cyphers, L., Toda, S., & et al. (1992). Language and play at one year: A comparison of toddlers and mothers in the United States and Japan. *International Journal of Behavioral Development, 15,* 19–42.

Tomasello, M. (1999). *The cultural origins of human cognition.* Cambridge, MA: Harvard.

Tomasello, M. & Rakoczy, H. (2003). What makes human cognition unique? From individual to shared to collective intentionality. *Mind & Language, 18*(2), 121–147.

van Hooff, J. A. R. A. M. (1972). A comparative approach to the phylogeny of laughter and smiling. In R. A. Hinde (Ed.), *Non-verbal communication* (pp. 209–237). Cambridge, England: Cambridge U.

Walden, T. A. & Ogan, T. A. (1988). The development of social referencing. *59,* 1230–1240.

Wang, R. & Spelke, E. (2000). Updating egocentric representations in human navigation. *Cognition, 77*(3), 215–250.

Weiss, P. H., Jeannerod, M., Paulignan, Y., & Freund, H. J. (2000). Is the organisation of goal-directed action modality specific? A common temporal structure. *Neuropsychologia, 38*(8), 1136–1147.

Woodward, A. (2008). Infants learning about intentional action. In A. Woodward & A. Needham (Eds.), *Learning and the infant mind* (pp. 227–249). New York: Oxford.

Zukow-Golding, P. (1996). Sensitive caregiving fosters the comprehension of speech: When gestures speak louder than words. *Early Development and Parenting, 5,* 195–211.

Origins and Consequences of Social Pretend Play

Robert D. Kavanaugh

Abstract

During early childhood, play with peers becomes an important form of social interaction for many children. Among the various ways that children play together, pretend play, often in the form of sociodramatic or role play, has received considerable attention due to its potential influence on children's understanding of the beliefs and emotions of others. This chapter places social pretend play in two broad contexts. One is the similarities and differences between animal and human pretense. The other is the influence of culture, including family and community values and activities, on the frequency and type of make-believe play with others. Potential consequences of role play are evaluated through a discussion of empirical work on a number of possible contributors to the development of belief-emotion understanding, including family interactions and language abilities. Possible models are discussed for evaluating the influence of role play, language, and family relationships on children's understanding of other minds.

Keywords: imagination, role play, theory of mind, simulation, language

Although play has been notoriously difficult to define, the playful actions of primates are usually fairly easy to recognize. One reason is that playful actions do not have an immediate purpose or goal (Bateson, 2005; Burghardt, this volume). Yet despite this characteristic, play has long been recognized as an important aspect of primate development due, at least in part, to its apprenticeship quality (Fagen, this volume). In broad perspective, play offers primates an extended period of freedom and exploration that provides "a low cost way to develop alternate responses to new and challenging environments" (Pellegrini, Dupuis, & Smith, 2007. p. 272).

Among humans, play takes many different forms some of which overlap. Object play, characterized by sensorimotor exploration, is typical of infants and toddlers (see Bjorklund and Gardiner, this volume). In its earliest manifestations, pretend play incorporates objects but adds a critical 'as if' element, for example, sipping 'tea' from an empty cup (see Lillard, this volume). Playful physical activities, often called rough and tumble (see Pellegrini, this volume), are also part of the human play landscape as are electronic or computer-based games now popular in the middle childhood years and beyond (see Goldstein, this volume).

My focus is on pretend play and, particularly, pretending that involves one or more play partners, typically referred to as social pretend play. At the outset, it is worth noting that there are at least two important problems to confront in determining what constitutes pretense. One is the issue of closely related terms, such as make-believe or fantasy. Although it is certainly possible to make distinctions, the terms pretend, make-believe, and fantasy are often used interchangeably as attributes of human or animal play. A second and thornier problem is how pretense relates to imagination. Imagination is a more difficult term to circumscribe (Mitchell, 2006), its breadth perhaps best captured in Walton's (1990) critical analysis of the representational arts. Imagination is broader in scope than pretense, involving, for example, what if counterfactual scenarios, but it is also central to the concept of pretense. As Mitchell (2006, p. 53) noted, "the goal of pretense (behaviors) is to enact imagination."

Although there is no general agreement on a concise definition, there are at least three identifiable features of pretense that allow us to consider how it is manifested in both humans and animals. One is that pretense involves an animate being "acting as if" (Fein, 1981; Leslie, 1987). This simple but descriptive statement captures the notion of non-literal, simulated activity that it is at the core of pretense. A second feature is that pretend actions incorporate both actual and non-actual properties of objects involving what McCune-Nicolich (1981) referred to as "double knowledge." A third important feature is that pretense is a mental activity—an idea—that is intentionally projected on to something, for example, a box that the pretender transforms into a boat (Lillard, 2001).

There are a number of different and competing theoretical explanations of pretense. In an early influential paper, Leslie (1987) linked pretense to metarepresentational thought. He posited the early development of 'primary representations' that allow us to perceive the world "in an accurate, faithful, and literal way" but that are ill-suited to cope with non-literal situations. Leslie argued that a theory of pretense had to account for the fact that by the second year a child can use primary representations to categorize objects (e.g., a banana is a yellow concave object) but can also pretend that an object is something that it is not (e.g., banana is a telephone). To overcome the problem that the child's real and pretend worlds could become hopelessly intertwined and subject to "representational abuse," Leslie posited that during pretend play children create a "decoupled" copy of the primary representation (e.g., 'this banana is a telephone'). Because the decoupled copy is "quarantined" from the primary representation, children can distinguish between actual and pretend scenarios.

A number of authors have either challenged or modified the claim that pretend play requires metarepresentation. Some of the opposition is empirical involving research which shows that children do not infer the mental states involved in pretense until age three or four years at the earliest (Hickling, Wellman, & Gottfried, 1997; Lillard, 1993; Rosen, Schwebel, & Singer, 1997). In addition, there are alternative theoretical explanations that have emphasized that pretense is possible without metarepresentation. One competing theory

involves the notion of simulation, which posits that young children use their own mental abilities to imagine what the world is like from a perspective different from their own (Harris, 2000). Social pretend play and, in particular, socio-dramatic or role play illustrates how children use simulation. For example, in adopting complementary roles, such as doctor and patient, children create elaborate dialogues that involve contingent exchanges consistent with the actions of their pretend characters. Through role play, children have the opportunity "to imagine the world from the point of view of another person" (Harris, 2000, p. 48).

Lillard's (2001) social-cognitive analysis of pretend play offers a somewhat different challenge to metarepresentation. Lillard argued that early social experiences, such as play with parents, combine with emerging cognitive skills, such as intention reading and symbolic competence, to foster an understanding of pretense in young children. These combined skills allow children to make sense of the otherwise puzzling non-literal actions of others, such as someone who appears to 'sip' tea from an empty cup (Harris & Kavanaugh, 1993). Similar to Harris (2000), Lillard viewed children's later engagement in sociodramatic as a vehicle by which they may come to appreciate the imagined thoughts and feelings of others.

Pretense among Animals

The question of whether the capacity for pretense is exclusively human has generated a fairly passionate debate (see Mitchell, 2002a). On the one hand, there are well-documented examples of mammals, primarily great apes raised in captivity, who appear to engage in make-believe actions, such as sipping loudly from a toy tea cup or offering food to a toy animal (Matevia, Patterson, & Hillix, 2002). On the other hand, there is a mix of caution in interpreting acts of pretense in animals (Mitchell, 2002b), skepticism that animal pretense exists, with the possible exception of the great apes (Smith, 2006), and judgments that true expressions of pretend play are limited to humans (Tomasello & Call, 1997).

The debate about animal pretense appears to center around several questions. One is whether definitions of pretense include "unnecessary and inappropriate criteria" that weigh against observing animal pretense (Mitchell, 2006). If so, then the doubt about pretense in other species is primarily a reluctance to acknowledge what would be "obvious examples of pretense" were the same behaviors observed in human infants (Matevia et al, 2002). At the same time, there are questions about one of the defining features of pretense, performing intentional "as if" acts, as opposed to the use of one object "instead of" another (Gómez & Martín-Andrade, 2002). These questions align with assertions that pretend acts in animals are present but limited in scope, that is, pretense does not progress in animals in the same fashion that it does in humans from simple iconic or "feature dependent" actions, such as 'sipping' from an empty cup, to less iconic and more social actions, such as imaginary companion (role) play (Bering, 2001).

There is a large body of research on pretense and fantasy in animals by which to evaluate these questions. While there is some suggestion of pretending among wild (non-captive) primates (Gómez & Martín-Andrade, 2005) and among dolphins (Mitchell, 2006), the clearest and most numerous examples come from captive primates. A number of authors have provided detailed accounts of simple pretend acts in captive primates, such as feeding, bathing, and cooking, particularly among those who have some language or symbol training (Gómez & Martín-Andrade, 2005: Matevia et al, 2002; Mitchell, 2002b, 2006; Zeller, 2002). These include the behavior of well-known human-reared (enculturated) primates studied over many years: Washoe (chimpanzee) (Gardner & Gardner, 1969); Kanzi (bonobo) (Savage-Rumbaugh, Shanker, & Taylor, 1998); Koko (gorilla) (Patterson & Linden, 1981); and Chantek (orangutan) (Miles, Mitchell, & Harper, 1996). There are also well-substantiated examples of human-reared primates using inanimate objects (toy animals) to simulate biting and feeding (Mitchell, 2006). Koko, for example, animated her dolls quite frequently in this manner and also showed evidence of object substitution, for example, placing a bottle on her head and signing 'hat' (Matevia et al, 2002). There is even some evidence of play with imagined objects. Chantek is reported to have engaged in this type of play by using his fingers and mouth to simulate blowing up a non-existent balloon (Mitchell, 2006).

In overview, the literature on enculturated great apes shows ample evidence of simple pretend acts similar to those that a young child might carry out. Furthermore, some of these acts are clearly social in that they involve interactions with a human trainer. However, they differ noticeably from the simulated acts of great apes observed *in situ*. One example from ethological research that is particularly relevant to the goals of this chapter is social play fighting, which is characterized by rough and tumble movement, chasing, and mock biting (Lewis, 2005). Animals show their interest in this type of play with particular bodily, facial, and vocal expressions typically executed as they run after each other.

It is possible to consider social pretend fighting as a form of metacommunication that involves signals between conspecifics that the fighting is playful rather than serious (Bekoff, 1998; Pellegrini, this volume; Smith, this volume). Such an interpretation could mean that social pretend fighting has a non-literal quality that makes it quite similar to, if not a form of, pretend play. However, as Gómez and Martín-Andrade (2005) note, the arguments against this interpretation are formidable. First, social play fighting appears in young juveniles reared in captivity. Among these animals, it cannot be thought as a reciprocal game modeled on observed adult behavior (though see Pellis this volume). Second, and related to the first point, the running and chasing of social play fighting appear to be intrinsic, and phylogenetically older, elements of the behavioral repertoire of primates (Gómez & Martín-Andrade, 2005).

It seems unlikely that social play fighting evolved to support intentional simulated acts among primates. In a broader sense, however, it may contribute to reading and interpreting play signals which, in turn, assists in the management of social interactions among conspecifics (Pellegrini & Bjorklund, 2004). Interpreting play signals is, of course, an important part of human social interactions as well. However, the type of social play that has evolved in human has a more elaborate pretense component. In childhood, it allows the shared creation of make-believe roles, often modeled on adult activity, and maintained by a cognitive system that permits flexible exchanges of information mediated by language. In adulthood, this same system may serve the appreciation of the performing arts (Walton, 1990). As Pellegrini and Bjorklund (2004) point out, while there is "phenotypic" similarity between the social interactions of humans and other primates, they represent "phylogenetically independent solutions" to social group pressure.

Cultural Influences on Pretend Play

Cultural influences on pretending are but one part of the broader question of how cultures differ in attitudes towards children's play (see also chapters by Göncü and Gaskins and Tudge et al.). There a number of reasons for cultural differences including the economic structure of a community, community beliefs about the value of play, and how beliefs about play are conveyed to children (Göncü, Tuermer, Jain, & Johnson, 1999; see also Bock, this volume). Of these reasons, one that is often overlooked is the impact of economic circumstances on the time and resources available for play. For example, Göncü and colleagues have shown that workload prevents non-Western parents from participating in children's play. Furthermore, in rural communities the work required of children may result in less time for play than is typically found among Western children (Göncü, Jain, & Tuermer, 2006). These findings support the argument that theories about the development of play too often over represent the experiences of European-American children (Gaskins, Haight, & Lancy, 2006).

Anthropological studies have revealed that pretend play, including role play, is found in all cultures (Bornstein, 2006; Schwartzman, 1976). This includes the play of children in contemporary foraging groups. Blurton Jones (1993), for example, reported on the play of children in two such groups, the !Kung and Hazda, and found imaginative play among children in both groups, including role play as predators and foreigners. What appears to differ notably by culture is not the presence of pretend play but the frequency with which children engage in pretense, the make-believe themes that children enact, and how involved parents are in children's pretending (Bornstein, Haynes, Liliana, Painter, & Galperín, 1999; Haight, Wang, Fung, Williams, & Mintz, 1999).

Parental and community values are an important source of differences in how frequently children engage in pretend play as well as the make-believe themes they enact. Parents may encourage particular themes or, alternatively, discourage pretending altogether (Bornstein et al, 1999; Gaskins et al, 2006; Göncü et al, 1999; Haight et al, 1999; Farver & Shin, 1997). Several authors have made direct comparisons of parental involvement in pretend play in different cultural communities. Bornstein and colleagues examined the play of Argentine and European American mothers with their toddlers (age 20 months). They found higher rates of symbolic play among Argentine mothers, particularly other-directed pretense play, for example, putting a doll to sleep (Bornstein et al, 1999). Haight and colleagues compared pretend play among European American and Chinese (Taiwanese) parents and their young children. They observed that American parents often selected and endorsed fantasy themes whereas Chinese parents were more likely to use pretend play to instruct children about proper conduct (Haight et al, 1999). In an extensive study of play among toddlers in four different cultural communities, American, Turkish, Indian and Guatemalan toddlers, Göncü and colleagues found more pretend and language play among the American and Turkish toddlers than among the Indian and Guatemalan toddlers, along with different levels of parental involvement. The American and Turkish parents, for example, entered in to role play games with their children. At the same time, the authors observed play themes in the two non-Western communities (Turkey and India) that differed from those typically found in pretend play research on Western children (Göncü et al, 1999).

Parents' beliefs about and involvement with children's play vary widely across cultures (Bornstein, 2006; Gaskins et al, 2006). As noted, research has shown that parents in Argentinean, European American, Chinese (Taiwan), and Turkish communities support and participate in children's pretend play. While parents in these communities are similar in that they encourage pretend play, the differences in how they accomplish this are quite notable. One proposed reason for these differences is the degree to which Western cultures emphasize individuality, autonomy, and self expression versus an emphasis on collectivism and social relatedness in non-Western communities (Kitayama & Uchida, 2005). This broad conceptualization of cultural influences holds that parents will differ in their socialization goals which in turn will reflect on how they play with their children. In the realm of pretend play, parents from middle-class European American families often subscribe to the notion that fantasy exploration is important for intellectual and social development (Haight et al, 1999). Parents in these communities, typically mothers, serve as pretend play partners for the children, provide children with toys that elicit pretend actions, and encourage make-believe themes and fantasy exploration during pretend play (Haight & Miller, 1993; Haight et al, 1999). This type of play contrasts with what might be called 'instructional pretense,' in which the goal is to use pretending as a vehicle to teach children to respect and adhere to community values. For example, parent-child play in Taiwanese families emphasizes harmonious social interactions and respect for elders, with Taiwanese parents often taking the lead in using pretense as a way to instill proper conduct in young children (Gaskins et al, 2006). Similarly, Bornstein (2006) noted that in contrast to American mothers, Japanese mothers encouraged other-directed pretend play that was consistent with the collectivist orientation of Japanese society. These parental differences likely shape the form of social pretend play among children as they reach the preschool years (age two and beyond). When Farver and Shin (1997) contrasted the social pretend play of European American and Korean American preschool children, they found that both play themes and styles of interaction differed notably. Among European-American children, fantasy and danger themes predominated and the children frequently engaged in dialogues that corrected or rejected the partner's suggestion. Among Korean-American preschoolers, whose parents were all raised in Korea, the pretend themes involved daily activities and family roles and the play interactions among the children were typically non-assertive.

There are some cultural communities in which parents limit or curtail children's play. These include peasant communities where the physical surroundings combined with children's required daily chores limit the opportunities for play (Gaskin et al, 2006). In her intensive study of one such community, the Mayan Indians of Yucatan, Mexico, Gaskins (1996, 1999) noted that parents generally discourage play, particularly if it conflicts with the work required of children to assist the family. Not surprisingly, parents in this community viewed adult participation in children's pretend play as neither appropriate nor central to children's development. Farver and Howes (1993) found similar beliefs about pretend play among traditional Spanish-speaking Mestizos' mothers living in a small working class town in southern Mexico. Unlike American mothers who often initiate pretend play with young children, the Mestizos mothers made play with children part of a shared work routine (see also Howes this volume). Among the children in this community, pretend play occurred more regularly with older siblings and in mixed-age peer groups (Farver, 1993).

Within the United States, there are a variety of parental attitudes towards pretense, ranging from very favorable to concerns about a possible negative impact on children's development. One parental concern is that full-fledged involvement in fantasy play, such as having an imaginary companion, may bring about confusion between fantasy and reality. This is likely to be a particular concern of working class families (Taylor, 1999). In Newson and Newson's sample of British working class families, as reported by Taylor, parents expressed concerns that children's involvement in fantasy might lead them to lose touch with reality. Some parents in fundamentalist

Christian communities have expressed a different concern about pretense and fantasy. They worry that fantasy will lead children into lying and deceitful practices, and these parents may admonish children about telling stories that do not describe real events (Taylor & Carlson, 2000). Among some fundamentalist parents, there is a particular concern about the consequences of Christian myths, such as gifts brought by Santa Claus, because of the possibility that children's belief in the reality of a fantasy figure will ultimately undermine parental credibility about the existence of God (Clark, 1995). Furthermore, in some communities there is a concern that involvement in fantasy is unproductive. Taylor and Carlson (2000), for example, found that the adults in a Mennonite community viewed pretend as wasteful, a form of "idleness" that undermined children's development. Not surprisingly, teachers in this community typically did not have positive views about the value of pretend play. Interestingly, however, when comparing the play at recess of Mennonite children with children attending a non-Mennonite school in the same region, there were no meaningful differences in the proportion of time devoted to pretend play (Carlson, Taylor, & Levin, 1998).

In sum, pretend play emerges amidst a complex intersection of community values and parental beliefs about play, the time and opportunity for children to play with others, the age and ability of children's play partners, and the props and objects available for pretending. Variability of this sort argues against a common developmental sequence of pretend play yet, notably, there is persuasive evidence that pretend play with others occurs in all cultures (Bornstein, 2006; Schwartzman, 1976).

Development of Pretend Play

The ecology of pretend play highlights variation. Children can pretend with objects found in their everyday environment or with miniature toys that adults provide for them. Pretend play with others may involve either same age peers or, alternatively, older peers or adults who scaffold the young child's entry into pretense. As the cultural studies reveal, the possibilities for pretend scenarios are many and varied. Pretenders can change a wooden block into a bar of soap, teach a lesson about proper conduct, or make a friend in to a marauding pirate. In constructing make-believe scenarios, pretenders can recruit objects to help transform the scene they envision or conjure up a make-believe object, situation, or companion. Amidst the variation, one important feature remains constant, the mind of the pretender deliberately transforming the actual— "the here and now, the you and me, the this or that…"—into the imagined (Garvey, 1977, p.82).

Two traditions define much of the research on pretend play in children. One is the cognitive-developmental framework inspired by the observations and theoretical force of Piaget's (1962) classic work, *Play, Dreams, and Imitation*. In Piaget's view, pretense began with self-referenced actions, often while playing alone, that involved behaviors enacted outside of their usual context, e.g., Piaget's 15-month old daughter using a frayed cloth to knowingly simulate being asleep. These actions gradually came to involve others, such as at 19 months when Piaget's daughter pretended to drink from a box and then held the empty box up to the mouths of people nearby. Paradoxically, despite Piaget's strong influence on research that examined young children's ability to generate pretend actions, he did not believe that pretending was critical to the development of the logical thought processes that he sought to describe (Bretherton, 1984; Harris, 2000). Rather, Piaget (1962) saw pretense (symbolic games) as a form of assimilation that interfered with accommodation to the world and, as such, was ultimately a maladaptive process that children outgrew over time (Harris, 2000). Nevertheless, Piaget inspired a large number of studies of pretend play that investigated the relationship between varying levels of pretense and representational abilities as well as parallels between pretend actions and the development of language (Fein, 1981; McCune, 1993; McCune, 1995).

A different tradition, with conceptual roots that trace to Vygotsky's (1978) work on higher mental processes, emphasized the importance of the social context of pretend play. The theoretical and empirical work emerging from this tradition underscore the positive impact of collaborative play (Rogoff, 1990) as well as the various ways in which particular play partners—parents, siblings, and peers—influence children's make-believe play (Youngblade & Dunn, 1995). A large body of research points to the impact of mothers on young children's social pretend play skills. A review of the initial wave of these studies showed that maternal involvement typically increased the duration and diversity of children's pretend play (Kavanaugh, 2002). Furthermore, this literature makes clear that mothers engage in a number of different behaviors, such as prompts, explicit directions, and self demonstrations, that support more complex levels of pretense in children. More recently, Lillard and colleagues'

micro analysis of mother–child social interactions (see this volume) has identified the particular signs and signals that mothers use to convey to children that they are engaged in play with pretend objects (Lillard & Whitherington, 2004; Lillard, Nishida, Massaro, Vaish, Ma, & McRoberts, 2007).

The majority of the research on maternal involvement in pretend play has focused on young children, often under the age of two years. Between the ages of two and six years, peer relationships become increasingly important in children's play (Howes, 2009). Of the various ways for children in this age range to play together, role play has been a central concern in cognitive developmental research. Quite often children enact make-believe roles taken from the work of adult members of their community. As noted earlier, the anthropological record makes clear that role play occurs in many different cultural communities although the amount of time that children spend in role play varies considerably due, in part, to parental resources and encouragement (Smith, 2005).

Role play and understanding others

One reason to pay particular attention to role play is because of its potential to assist children in understanding the mental states of others (Harris, 2000). The potential exists because in full-throated form role play involves pretend identities that are negotiated and assigned to each player, dialogue between players that is rich and contingent, and the construction of make-believe scenarios that may help children to extrapolate how others think and feel (de Lorimier, Doyle, & Tessier, 1995; Kavanaugh & Engel, 1998).

One source of evidence for a relationship between role play and mental state understanding comes from Dunn and colleagues' extensive program of research on the antecedents and sequelae of belief-emotion understanding in young children (Dunn, 1991; Dunn, 1995; Dunn, 2000), including work on role play and theory of mind (Dunn & Cutting 1999; Hughes & Dunn, 1997; Youngblade & Dunn, 1995). In one study (Hughes & Dunn, 1997), pairs of four-year-olds were videotaped in an area of their school that was provisioned with props that encouraged pretend play. The analysis of the children's play focused strongly on role enactment as well as the statements children made about their roles. When the children were assessed one week later on false belief and deception tasks, Hughes and Dunn (1997) found that role play showed a positive relationship to performance on the theory of mind tasks. In a similar study, Dunn and Cutting (1999) examined the social pretend play of pairs of friends and found that various elements of role play, such as discussing a joint pretend episode, assuming a pretend role, or following the pretend suggestion of a play partner, showed a positive relationship with both theory of mind and emotion understanding tasks. A longitudinal study (Youngblade & Dunn, 1995) in which children were observed interacting at home with their mothers and siblings at 33 months and then again at 40 months confirmed a role play-theory of mind relationship. Several play measures were taken at 33 months but when the children were seen again at 40 months only role enactment showed a significant relationship with false belief understanding.

The specificity of a relationship between role play and theory of mind is important because theoretical claims, such as those found in simulation theory, rest on the assumption that it is role play, and not pretend play or play more generally, that fosters an understanding of the mental states of others. Two studies have investigated specific elements of the role play-theory of mind relationship while controlling for both age and verbal abilities (Astington & Jenkins, 1995; Schwebel, Rosen, & Singer (1999). Astington and Jenkins (1995) found that among three- to five-year-old children observed playing together in small groups, involvement in role play through joint proposals and assignment of roles, but not total amount of play, showed a positive relationship with performance on false belief tasks. Schwebel et al. (1999) carried out two experiments with three- to five-year-olds that investigated the relationship between pretending during free play activities and two theory of mind measures, appearance-reality and false-belief understanding. In both experiments, they found that role play, versus solitary pretend play, showed a significant positive relationship with children's performance on an appearance reality measure but not on a false belief task.

It is possible to argue that children who have an imaginary companion are also engaged in role play (Harris, 2000). Effectively, the child who creates a make-believe companion is deeply absorbed in a form of role play in which the child is the sole creator of the imagined scenarios. If this argument holds, then there should be a relationship between developing an imaginary companion and performance on theory-of-mind tasks. Two studies suggest that such a relationship exists. One is Taylor and Carlson's (1997) investigation of imaginary companions in three- and four-year-old children.

With verbal ability controlled, Taylor and Carlson found that four year olds who either had an imaginary companion or were classified as impersonators—children who spent considerable time pretending to be a particular animal or character—had reliably higher theory-of-mind scores than those who had neither an imaginary companion nor were thought to be impersonators. LaLonde and Chandler (1995) used teachers' ratings of three-year-old children on several dimensions of social interaction and play and compared them to the children's performance on false-belief tasks. The analyses revealed that most of the teacher-rated characteristics, such as showing good social skills, showed no significant correlation with false-belief performance. However, there was a reliable positive relationship between having an imaginary companion, as well as other forms of make-believe play, and false-belief understanding.

Models of understanding others

There is little doubt of a positive relationship between role play and theory of mind but there are questions about the nature of the relationship and its place in the larger context of the development of social cognition. One concern is that most of the supporting data are correlational and therefore offer no clear indication of directionality. Furthermore, as Smith (2005) noted, many of the role play-theory of mind correlations are modest. There are several ways to address these problems; though to date there have been relatively few attempts to do so. One is to use a training study to determine if improved role-play skills lead to advances in theory of mind. The best example of this type of study is Dockett's (1998) research with four-year olds who were taken to a local pizza shop to observe how pizza is made. The children were then trained in role-play activities that involved making and serving pizza for approximately three weeks during the course of a ten-week preschool session. Compared to controls who experienced only the regular curriculum, the role-play trained children showed significant improvement on both immediate and delayed theory-of-mind posttests. Using a different approach, Jenkins & Astington (2000) assessed three- and four-year olds on both role play and theory of mind on three different occasions. Independent of verbal ability, children's understanding of theory of mind at an earlier time point predicted key elements of their subsequent role play while the converse relationship, role play predicting later theory-of-mind performance, was not significant.

Jenkins and Astington's (2000) study underscores the point that other developing abilities, particularly language, may play a critical role in children's understanding of the beliefs and emotions of others. In fact, both Dunn and Astington and their colleagues, who have found positive and specific relationships between role play and theory of mind, have also uncovered important relationships between language and theory of mind. Cutting and Dunn (1999), for example, noted that among four-year olds receptive and expressive language ability correlated significantly with both false belief and emotion understanding while Hughes and Dunn (1997) found that when preschoolers played together, genuine mental state talk, such as references to the play partner's thoughts, was related significantly to false belief understanding. Similarly, Jenkins and Astington (1996) found a significant correlation among three- to five-year olds' scores on false-belief tasks and their scores on the Test of Early Language Development (TELD), a basic measure of syntactic and semantic ability. Astington and Jenkins (1999) later demonstrated the importance of language ability by testing three-year olds on both the TELD and a theory of mind measure on three occasions over a seven month period. The results showed that TELD scores predicted subsequent theory of mind performance while the reverse relationship was not significant. A recent meta-analysis of over 100 studies further strengthened this argument by showing a substantial effect size of general language ability (e.g., TELD) on false belief understanding with age controlled (Milligan, Astington, & Dack, 2007).

As is the case for role play, however, mastery of the basic elements of language is but one alternative explanation for children's progress in the development of the understanding of other minds. Other promising avenues include research on attachment and mental state talk, broadly conceived. Attachment security at 12 months, for example, has been shown to predict comprehension of complex emotions at age six (Steele, Steele, Croft, & Fonagy, 1999). Related research on this topic suggests that the attachment-emotion understanding relationship may be mediated in turn by the larger construct of maternal sensitivity and attunement to the child's emotional needs (Meins, 1998). Equally promising is research on mental state talk, essentially discourse about thoughts and feelings, and its relationship to belief-emotion understanding. As noted, role play among peers invites mental state talk (Hughes and Dunn, 1997) but so too do a number of different interactions between parents and children, including everyday conversations and book reading. Studies on both of these topics have shown a positive relationship between parental discourse about mental states and belief-emotion understanding in children (Ruffman, Slade, & Crowe, 2002; Adrian, Clemente, & Villanueva, 2005; Slaughter, Peterson, & Mackintosh, 2007).

One bottom line conclusion from this large body of research is that the development of belief-emotion understanding unfolds in the crucible of community values and family interactions, a position that Dunn (1991; 2008) and Nelson (2005, 2007) have advanced convincingly. Nelson (2005) argues that as children reach age 3 and beyond they become participants in "mind exchanges" determined by the activities of their particular community and mediated by developing language abilities. Beginning in infancy, children enter a "community of minds" where over time they learn to "represent mental states and actions… that take their meaning from agreement within the community" (Nelson, 2005, p. 35). Dunn's work points to the complementary position that children learn from and about other minds though intense "social exchanges" that involve humor, arguments, threats to self, and discussions of causality (Dunn, 1991). Families are a prime source for these various social interactions and children who participate in them generally perform well on tests of belief and emotion understanding (Youngblade & Dunn, 1995). Still, it is possible to argue that neither Nelson's nor Dunn's position diminishes the role of shared imaginative play in children's understanding of mental states. Rather, the argument they make locates any potential benefits of involvement in social pretending within the larger context of community and family relationships.

Pretend Play After Early Childhood

The intense interest in social pretend play fades noticeably after the early childhood years. One reason may be the connection between pretend play with others and theory of mind, a relationship that is thought to develop primarily during early childhood. Another is that opportunities for role play, at least in small groups, may decline as children's schooling becomes more formal and classrooms become less likely to provide particular areas that foster make-believe play. Furthermore, there is some evidence that children become more self conscious, and parents less supportive, of overt manifestations of make-believe play, such as open involvement with imaginary companions (Taylor, 1999).

However, there is no reason to assume that children's interest and involvement in social pretend play ends at early childhood. It seems more likely that interest in shared imaginative play shifts to participation in structured games and activities. *Dungeons and Dragons,* a fantasy role playing game in which each player assumes the role of a particular character, is one example of social pretend play that has attracted a wide following during the middle childhood years (see Goldstein, this volume). Perhaps due in part to the success of games like *Dungeons and Dragons,* role playing games (RPGs) are now widely available electronically. Despite the interest in RPGs and electronic gaming more generally, there has been relatively little research on the potential benefits and hazards of this type of play. Dorothy and Jerome Singer have brought together much of what is known on this topic in their seminal work on imagination in the electronic age (Singer & Singer, 2005). As the Singers note, there are established risks to electronic games, particularly in the violent themes of video games, but there is also evidence that computer-based games allow participants to construct fantasy figures and scenarios that have the potential to contribute positively to the development of imaginative abilities in middle childhood.

If interest in pretend play in middle childhood has been modest, there has been even less focus on the question of what happens to pretend play beyond the childhood years. One possible reason is the far reaching influence of Piaget and Vygotsky, whose differences on play are well known, but who converged on the idea of play as primarily a childhood activity. As a result, researchers rarely study play from a life-span perspective (Göncü & Perone, 2005). According to Göncü and Perone (2005), one unfortunate consequence of an exclusive child focus on play is that we have missed both the parallels and continuities between social pretend play in children and adults. In particular, they cite the inventiveness and negotiation among players and audiences that characterize improvisational theater, suggesting that it is effectively a form of adult role play. In his philosophical analysis of make-believe, Walton (1990) put forth a related argument about the continuity between engagement in the pretend activities of childhood and adult interest in fiction and the representational arts (see also Fagen, this volume). At present, however, there appears to be very limited interest in pursuing questions about adult involvement in play and activities related to pretense.

Conclusion

There is evidence that animals, particularly those raised in captivity, have the ability to produce simple pretend acts, but social pretend play, at least in its most advanced form, appears to be unique to humans. In Western cultures, children's first pretend play partners are often parents, and there is an extensive literature showing how mothers in particular model and elicit pretend play in interactions with very young children. Children also engage with peers in spontaneous episodes of social pretend play at an early age. We know from the anthropological record that one particular type of play, sociodramatic or role play, has widespread appeal among young children.

Beyond its appeal to children, role play has attracted considerable interest because of its potential link to belief-emotion understanding. Simulation theory, as articulated through a proposal offered by Harris (2000), posits that role play may well be a significant source of individual differences in theory of mind understanding. This proposal gathers support from a number of studies of role play and theory of mind, both when role play is assessed in dyadic or small group play, and when children are involved in what might be thought of as solitary role play with an imaginary companion. Still, the evidence supporting a role play-theory of mind relationship is far from conclusive. For the most part, support comes from correlational studies; and, while the correlations are positive, most fall in the low to moderate range (see Smith, 2005). One relevant training study (Dockett, 1998) did find support for an effect of role play on theory of mind but the sample size was relatively small and no alternative model was tested, for example, training children on theory of mind to determine if role play skills improved.

On the whole, the evidence suggests that role play is but one of several possible antecedents of the development of mental state understanding. In terms of a single variable, language ability, measured by basic syntactic and semantic skills, has more direct empirical support as a predictor of theory of mind. With age controlled, Astington and colleagues demonstrated that language ability predicted theory of mind while the converse relationship did not hold (Astington & Jenkins, 1999) and that basic language ability, again with age controlled, had a substantial effect on false belief understanding (Milligan et al, 2007). Similarly, Dunn and colleagues (Dunn & Cutting, 1999; Hughes & Dunn, 1997; Youngblade & Dunn, 1995) found support for a relationship between role play and theory of mind but, in broad perspective, Dunn's work (1991, 1995, 2000) points to multiple effects of parental, sibling, and friends on belief-emotion understanding (Dunn, 2008).

One approach to the issue of multiple effects is to control for or partial out different variables. There is certainly merit to this approach and longitudinal studies, using multiple regression or modeling techniques, may help to identify some variables as particularly important, and others as less important, to children's understanding of other minds. However, there is also a risk that this approach may discount the intersection of key elements of children's social-cognitive development. As Astington (2003) noted, the most telling story of the relationships between language, theory of mind, and social behaviors may unfold in the overlap of those three variables. In his analysis of parent–child conversations, Harris (2000) makes a related point. In the course of parent–child conversations, parents may ask children to consider how others feel. In doing so, parents may mirror a process that unfolds during role play when children try to imagine how their play partner thinks or feels. The intersection of these two types of interaction is what Harris (2000) referred to as a virtuous circle. Social pretend play is a good candidate to be part of a comprehensive analysis of the development of belief-emotion understanding in children. The challenge is to determine its relationship to other fundamental contributors.

Future Directions

1. How to develop measures of thoughts and beliefs of others that go beyond standard assessment of theory of mind.

2. How to develop models of social cognition that recognize the importance of the intersection of family interactions, peer relationships, and language ability

3. Research on what happens to social pretend play, including the form that it takes and its potential consequences, beyond the early childhood years.

References

Adrian, J. E., Clemente, R. A., & Villanueva, L. (2005). Parent-child picture-book reading, mothers' mental state language, and children's theory of mind. *Journal of Child language, 32,* 673–686.

Astington, J. W. (2003). Sometimes necessary never sufficient: False belief understanding and social competence. In B. Repacholi and V. Slaughter (Eds.), *Individual differences in theory of mind: Implications for typical and atypical development* (pp. 13–38). New York: Psychology Press.

Astington, J. W. & Jenkins, J. J. (1995). Theory of mind development and social understanding. *Cognition and Emotion, 9,* 151–165.

Astington, J. W. & Jenkins, J. J. (1999). A longitudinal study of the relation between language and theory-of-mind development. *Developmental Psychology, 35,* 1311–1320.

Bateson, P. (2005). The role of play in the evolution of great apes and humans. In Pellegrini, A. D. & Smith, P. K. (Eds.), *The nature of play: Great apes and humans* (pp. 13–24). New York: Guilford Press.

Bekoff, M. (1998). Playing with play: What can we learn about cognition, negotiation, and evolution? In D. D. Cummins & C. Adams (Eds.), *The evolution of mind* (pp. 162–182). New York: Oxford University Press.

Bering, J. (2001). Theistic percepts in other species: Can chimpanzees represent the minds of non-natural agents. *Journal of Cognition and Culture, 1,* 107–137.

Blurton Jones, N. (1993). The lives of hunter-gatherer children: Effects of parental behavior and parental reproductive strategy. In M. E. Pereira & L. A. Fairbanks (Eds.), *Juvenile primates: Life history, development, and behavior* (pp. 309–326). New York: Oxford University Press.

Bornstein, M. H. (2006). On the significance of social relationships in the development of children's earliest symbolic play: An ecological perspective. In A. Göncü & S. Gaskins (Eds.), *Play and development: Evolutionary, sociocultural, and functional perspectives* (pp. 101–129). Mahway: N.J.: Erlbaum.

Bornstein, M. H., Haynes, O. M., Liliana, P., Painter, K. M., & Galperín, C. (1999). Play in two societies: Pervasiveness of process, specificity of structure. *Child Development, 70,* 317–331.

Bretherton, I. (1984). Representing the social world in symbolic play: Reality and fantasy. In I. Bretherton (Ed.), *Symbolic play: The development of social understanding* (pp. 3–41). New York: Academic Press.

Carlson, S. M., Taylor, M., & Levin, G. R. (1998). The influence of culture on pretend play: The case of Mennonite children. *Merrill-Palmer Quarterly, 44,* 538–565.

Clark, C. D. (1995). *Flights of fancy, leaps of faith: Children's myths in contemporary America.* Chicago: University of Chicago Press.

Cutting, A. L., & Dunn, J. (1999). Theory of mind, emotion understanding, language, and family background: Individual differences and interrelations. *Child Development, 70,* 853–865.

de Lorimier, S., Doyle, A-B, & Tessier, O. (1995). Social coordination during pretend play: Comparisons with nonpretend play and effects on expressive content. *Merrill-Palmer Quarterly, 41,* 497–516.

Dockett, S. (1998). Constructing understandings through play in the early years. *International Journal of Early Years Education, 6,* 105–116.

Dunn, J. (1991). Understanding others: Evidence from naturalistic studies of children. In A. Whiten (Ed.), *Natural theories of mind: Evolution, development, and simulation in everyday mindreading* (pp. 51–61). Oxford: Blackwell.

Dunn, J. (1995). Children as psychologists: The later correlates of individual differences in understanding of emotions and other minds. *Cognition and Emotion, 9,* 187–201.

Dunn, J. (2000). Mind-reading, emotion understanding, and relationships. *International Journal of Behavioral Development, 24,* 142–144.

Dunn, J. (2008). Relationships and children's discovery of the mind. In U. Müller, Carpendale, J. I. M., Budwig, N., & Sokol, B. W. (Eds), *Social life and social knowledge: Toward a process account of development* (pp. 171–182). New York: Erlbaum/Taylor & Francis Group.

Dunn, J., & Cutting, A. L. (1999). Understanding others, and individual differences in friendship interactions in young children. *Social Development, 8,* 201–219.

Farver, J. M. (1993). Cultural differences in scaffolding pretend play: A comparison of American and Mexican-American mother–child and sibling-child dyads. In K. MacDonald (Ed.), *Parent–child play: Descriptions and implications* (pp. 349–366). Albany, NY: SUNY Press.

Farver, J. M. & Howes, C. (1993). Cultural differences in American and Mexican mother–child pretend play. *Merrill-Palmer Quarterly, 39,* 344–358.

Farver, J. M. & Shin, Y. L. (1997). Social pretend play in Korean- and Anglo-American preschoolers. *Child Development, 68,* 544–556.

Fein, G. (1981). Pretend play in childhood: An integrative review. *Child Development, 52,* 1095–1118.

Gardner, R. A. & Gardner, B. T., (1969). Teaching sign language to a chimpanzee. *Science, 165,* 664–672.

Garvey, C. (1977). *Play.* Cambridge, MA: Harvard University Press.

Gaskins, S. (1996). How Mayan parental theories come into play. In S. Harkness & C. Super (Eds.), *Parents' cultural belief systems* (pp. 345–363). New York: Guilford.

Gaskins, S. (1999). Children's daily lives in a Mayan village: A case study of culturally constructed roles and activities. In A. Göncü (Ed.), *Children's engagement in the world: A sociocultural perspective* (pp. 25–61). Cambridge, UK: Cambridge University Press.

Gaskins, S., Haight, W., & Lancy, D. F. (2006). The cultural construction of play. In S. Gaskins & A. Göncü (Eds.), *Play and development: Evolutionary, sociocultural, and functional perspectives* (pp. 179–202). Mahway: N.J.: Erlbaum.

Gómez, J. C. & Martín-Andrade, B. (2002). Possible precursors of pretend play in nonpretend actions of captive gorillas (Gorilla gorilla). In R. W. Mitchell, *Pretending and imagination in animals and children* (pp. 255–268). Cambridge, U.K.: Cambridge University Press.

Gómez, J. C. & Martín-Andrade, B. (2005). Fantasy play in apes. In A. D. Pellegrini & P. K. Smith (Eds.), *The nature of play: Great apes and humans* (pp. 139–172). New York: Guilford Press.

Göncü, A. & Perone, A. (2005). Pretend play as a life-span activity. *Topoi, 24,* 137–147.

Göncü, A., Tuermer, U., Jain, J. (2006). Children's play as cultural interpretation. In A. Göncü & S. Gaskins (Eds.), *Play and development: Evolutionary, sociocultural, and functional perspectives* (pp. 155–178). Mahway: N.J.: Erlbaum

Göncü, A., Tuermer, U., Jain, J., & Johnson, D. (1999). Children's play as cultural activity. In A. Göncü (Ed.), *Children's engagement in the world: A sociocultural perspective* (pp. 148–170). Cambridge, U.K.: Cambridge University Press.

Haight, W. L. & Miller, P. J. (1993*). Pretending at home: Early development in a sociocultural context.* Albany, NY: SUNY Press.

Haight, W. L., Wang, X.-l, Fung H., Williams, K., & Mintz, J. (1999). Universal, developmental, and variable aspects of young children's play: A cross-cultural comparison of pretending at home. *Child Development, 70,* 1477–1488.

Harris, P. L. (2000). *The work of the imagination.* Oxford: Blackwell.

Harris, P. L. & Kavanaugh, R. D. (1993). Young children's understanding of pretense. *Monographs of the Society for Research in Child Development, 58,* (1, Serial No. 231).

Hickling, A. K., Wellman, H. M., & Gottfried, G. M. (1997). Preschoolers' understanding of others' mental attitudes toward pretending. *British Journal of Developmental Psychology, 15,* 339–354.

Howes, C. (2009). Friendship in early childhood. In K. Rubin, W. M. Bukowski, & Laursen, B., *Handbook of peer interactions, relationships, and groups* (pp. 180–194). New York: Guilford Press. SUNY Press.

Hughes, C. & Dunn, J. (1997). "Pretend you didn't know": Young children's talk about mental states in pretend play. *Cognitive Development, 12,* 477–499.

Jenkins, J. M. & Astington, J. W. (1996). Cognitive factors and family structure associated with theory of mind development in young children. *Developmental Psychology, 32,* 70–78.

Jenkins, J. M. & Astington, J. W. (2000). Theory of mind and social behavior: Causal models tested in a longitudinal study. *Merrill-Palmer Quarterly, 46,* 203–220.

Kavanaugh, R. D. (2002). Pretend play and theory of mind. In L. Balter & C.S. Tamis-LeMonda (Eds.), *Child psychology: A handbook of contemporary issues. Vol. 2* (pp. 153–166). Philadelphia: Psychology Press.

Kavanaugh, R. D. & Engel, S. (1998). The development of pretense and narrative in early childhood. In O. N. Saracho and B. Spodek (Eds.), *Multiple perspectives on play in early childhood education* (pp. 80–99). Albany, N.Y.: SUNY Press.

Kitayama, S. & Uchida. Y. (2005). Interdependent agency: An alternative system for action. In R. Sorrentino, D. Cohen, J. M. Olson, & M. Zanna (Eds.), *Culture and social behavior: The Ontario Symposium, Vol. 10* (pp. 137–164). Mahway, NJ: Erlbaum.

Lalonde, C. E. & Chandler, M. J. (1995). False belief understanding goes to school: On the social-emotional consequences of coming early or late to a first theory of mind. *Cognition and Emotion, 9,* 167–185.

Leslie, A. M. (1987). Pretense and representation: The origins of "theory of mind." *Psychological Review, 94,* 412–426.

Lewis, K. P. (2005). Social play in the great apes. In A. D. Pellegrini & P. K. Smith (Eds.), *The nature of play: Great apes and humans* (27–53). New York: Guilford Press.

Lillard, A. S. (1993). Young children's conceptualization of pretense: Action or metarepresentational state? *Child Development, 64,* 372–386.

Lillard, A. S. (2001). Pretend play as twin earth: A social-cognitive analysis. *Developmental Review, 21,* 495–531.

Lillard, A. S., Nishida, T., Massaro, D., Vaish, A., Ma, L., & McRoberts, G. (2007). Signs of pretense across age and scenario. *Infancy, 11,* 1–30.

Lillard, A. S. & Whitherington, D. (2004). Mothers' behavior modifications during pretense snacks and possible signal value for toddlers. *Developmental psychology, 40,* 95–113.

Matevia, M. L., Patterson, G. P., & Hillix, W. A. (2002). Pretend play in a signing gorilla. In R. W. Mitchell (Ed.), *Pretending and imagination in animals and children* (pp. 285–304). Cambridge, UK: Cambridge University Press.

McCune, L. (1993). The development of play as the development of consciousness. In M. Bornstein & A. W. O'Reilly (Eds.), *The role of play in the development of thought* (pp. 67–79). San Francisco: Jossey-Bass.

McCune, L. (1995). A normative study of representational play at the transition to language. *Developmental Psychology, 31*, 198–206.

McCune-Nicolich, L. (1981). Toward symbolic functioning: Structure of early use of early pretend games and potential parallels with language. *Child Development, 52*, 785–797.

Meins, E. (1998). The effects of security of attachment and maternal attribution of meaning on children's linguistic acquisitional style. *Infant Behavior and Development, 21*, 237–252.

Miles, H. L., Mitchell, R. W., & Harper, S. E. (1996). Simon says: The development of imitation in an enculturated orangutan. In A. E. Russon, K. A. Bard, & S. T. Parker (Eds.), *Reaching in to thought: The minds of great apes* (pp. 278–299). New York: Cambridge University Press.

Milligan, K., Astington, J. W., & Dack, L. A. (2007). Language and theory of mind: Meta-analysis of the relation between language ability and false-belief understanding. *Child Development, 78*, 622–646.

Mitchell, R. W. (Ed.) (2002a). *Pretending and imagination in animals and children*. Cambridge, U.K.: Cambridge University Press.

Mitchell, R. W. (2002b). A history of pretense in animals and children. In R. W. Mitchell (Ed.), *Pretending and imagination in animals and children* (pp. 3–22). Cambridge, U.K.: Cambridge University Press.

Mitchell, R. W. (2006). Pretense in animals: The continuing relevance of children's pretense. In S. Gaskins & A. Göncü (Eds.), *Play and development: Evolutionary, sociocultural, and functional perspectives* (pp. 51–75). Mahway: N.J.: Erlbaum

Nelson, K. (2005). Language pathways into the community of minds. In J. W. Astington & J. A. Baird (Eds.), *Why language matters for theory of mind* (pp. 26–49). New York: Oxford University Press.

Nelson, K. (2007). *Young minds in social worlds: Experience, meaning, and memory*. Cambridge, MA: Harvard University Press.

Patterson, F. & Linden, E. (1981). *The education of Koko*. New York: Holt, Rinehart, & Winston.

Pellegrini, A. D. & Bjorklund, D. E. (2004). The ontogeny and phylogeny of children's object and fantasy play. *Human Nature, 15*, 23–43.

Pellegrini, A. D., Dupuis, D., & Smith, P. K. (2007). Play in evolution and development. *Developmental Review, 27*, 261–276.

Piaget, J. (1962). *Play, dreams and imitation in childhood*. New York: Norton.

Rogoff, B. (1990). *Apprenticeship in thinking: Cognitive development in social context*. New York: Oxford University Press.

Rosen, C. S., Schwebel, D. C., & Singer, J. (1997). Preschoolers' attributions of mental states in pretense. *Child Development, 68*, 1133–1142.

Ruffman, T., Slade, L., & Crowe, E. (2002). The relation between children's and mothers' mental state language and theory of mind understanding. *Child Development, 73*, 734–751.

Savage-Rumbaugh, W., Shanker, S. G., & Taylor, T. T. (1998). *Apes, language, and the human mind*. New York: Oxford University Press.

Schwebel, D. C., Rosen, C. S., & Singer, J. L. (1999). Preschooler's pretend play and theory of mind: The role of jointly constructed pretense. *British Journal of Developmental Psychology, 17*, 333–348.

Schwartzman, H. B. (1976). The anthropological study of children's play. *American Review of Anthropology, 5*, 290–328.

Singer, D.G. & Singer, J. L. (2005). *Imagination and play in the electronic age*. Cambridge, MA: Harvard University Press.

Slaughter, V., Peterson, C. C., & Mackintosh, E. (2007). Mind what mother says: Narrative input and theory of mind in typical children and those on the autism spectrum. *Child Development, 78*, 839–858.

Smith, P. K. (2005). Social and pretend play in children. In Pellegrini, A. D. & Smith, P. K. (Eds.), *The nature of play: Great apes and humans* (pp. 173–209). New York: Guilford Press.

Smith, P. K. (2006). Evolutionary functions and foundations of play. In S. Gaskins & A. Göncü (Eds.), *Play and development: Evolutionary, sociocultural, and functional perspectives* (pp. 21–49). Mahway: NJ: Erlbaum.

Steele, H., Steele, M., Croft, C., & Fonagy, P. (1999). Infant-mother attachment at one year predicts children's understanding of mixed emotions at six years. *Social Development, 8*, 161–178.

Tomasello, M. & Call, J. (1997). *Primate cognition*. New York: Oxford University Press.

Taylor, M. (1999). *Imaginary companions and the children who create them*. New York: Oxford University Press.

Taylor, M., & Carlson, S. M. (2000). The influence of religious beliefs on parental attitudes about children's fantasy behavior. In K. Rosengren, C. Johnson, & P. Harris (Eds.), *Imagining the impossible: The development of magical, scientific, and religious thinking in contemporary society* (pp. 247–268). Cambridge, UK: Cambridge University Press.

Youngblade, L. M. & Dunn, J. (1995). Individual differences in young children's pretend play with mother and sibling: Links to relationships and understanding of other people's feelings and beliefs. *Child Development, 66*, 1472–1492.

Vygotsky, L. S. (1978). *Mind in society: The development of higher mental processes*. Cambridge, MA: Harvard University Press.

Walton, K. L. (1990). *Mimesis as make-believe: On the foundations of the representational arts*. Cambridge, MA: Harvard University Press.

Zeller, A. (2002). Pretending in monkeys. In R. W. Mitchell (Ed.), *Pretending and imagination in animals and children* (pp. 183–195). Cambridge, UK: Cambridge University Press.

The Development of Pretend Play in Autism

Christopher Jarrold *and* Carmel Conn

Abstract

Individuals with autism tend to produce much less pretense in free play contexts than one would expect, and understanding the reason for this deficit has implications for theories of pretend play in general. A particularly influential account (Leslie, 1987) suggests that problems in pretense in autism result from deficits in theory of mind that are known to be associated with the condition, thereby drawing a link between the representational processes involved in pretend play and theory of mind. Here we review evidence that suggests that the deficits in pretend play seen in autism are not as marked as this account would predict. Instead, problems in producing creative pretend play might result from executive difficulties in the control of behavior or might reflect the fact that play behavior in autism develops in an atypical sociocultural context. These suggestions are more consistent with theoretical accounts that emphasize the gradual development of pretend play skills in childhood. However, a remaining question is whether the pretend play that one observes on occasions among individuals with autism is associated with the same motivation, playfulness, and symbolism as is pretend play in typically developing children.

Keywords: Autism, pretend play, metarepresentation, theory of mind, executive dysfunction, sociocultural context

Introduction

Autism is a condition that is clearly caused by genetic factors (see Bailey, Phillips, & Rutter, 1996), although the nature of this genetic etiology is far from being fully specified (see Rutter, 2005; Ronald, Happé, & Plomin, 2005). Consequently, the condition is diagnosed on the basis of its characteristic behavioral features. All diagnostic schemes currently require individuals to show evidence of atypicalities in a 'triad' of domains, namely socialization, communication, and imagination (cf. Wing & Gould, 1979), which relate closely to the behaviors identified by individuals who first recognized the syndrome (Asperger, 1944; Kanner, 1943). It should be noted that autism is often, though not necessarily, associated with some degree of intellectual retardation over and beyond these characteristic features,

and as a result the manifestation of the condition differs considerably between individuals. Given this range of behaviors, and the very fact that diagnosis rests on the inexact science of judging behavioral features, there is a degree of debate about the boundaries of autism, and its incidence. Most would argue that autism is best viewed as a spectrum condition, with the degree of severity ranging across individuals along this spectrum. Depending on where one draws the cut-off for an autism spectrum disorder, current estimates of incidence range from 1 per 1000 to 1.6 per 1000 (Fombonne, 2005).

Spontaneous Pretend Play in Autism

The fact that problems of imagination form a core part of current diagnostic schemes for autism clearly suggests that the condition is associated with difficulties in play, and in pretend play in particular. In fact, while a lack of pretend play is specifically mentioned as a characteristic of autism in DSM-IV (American Psychiatric Association, 1994) and ICD-10 (World Health Organization, 1992) diagnostic schemes, this appears under the list of communication difficulties associated with the condition. Nevertheless, there is evidence that individuals with autism differ markedly from typically developing individuals in the amount of pretend play they spontaneously engage in (see Jarrold, Boucher, & Smith, 1993; Jarrold, 2003 for previous reviews). Indeed, in their pioneering study of the constellation of behavioral features seen in children with impaired 'social interaction,' Wing and Gould (1979) noted that 55% showed no "symbolic, imaginative activities, including pretend play" (p. 16). Furthermore, an absence of pretend play at 18 months of age has been shown to be a predictive indicator of a future diagnosis of autism (Baron-Cohen, Allen, & Gillberg, 1982).

Of course, one might well expect individuals with autism to show low levels of pretend play given that intellectual difficulties are often associated with the condition. Among typically developing individuals language skills in particular are clear correlates of level of pretend play (e.g., Fein, 1981; see also Kavanaugh & Lillard this volume), and the same appears to be true in autism (Riguet, Taylor, Benaroya, & Klein, 1981; Sigman & Ungerer, 1984; Stanley & Konstantareas, 2007). Consequently, the key question is whether individuals with autism show less pretend play than one would expect given their developmental level, and, in particular, their level of language skill (Jarrold et al., 1993). A number of studies have compared the extent of pretend play shown by individuals in free play situations with, often younger, typically developing children of a comparable verbal mental age. These have tended to show clear impairments in the degree of pretend play shown by individuals with autism (Baron-Cohen, 1987; Blanc, Adrien, Roux, & Barthélémy, 2005; Jarrold, Boucher, & Smith, 1996; Libby, Powell, Messer, & Jordan, 1998; though see also Hobson, Lee, & Hobson, 2009; Morgan, Maybery, & Durkin, 2003). For example, Blanc et al. (2005) compared the play behaviors shown by children with autism, children with general development delay, and typically developing children, during a ten-minute free play session in which a variety of toys were available. Play was coded as 'symbolic' (pretend) when the child used an object in a non-literal way; 'functional' when a toy was used appropriately such as when a spoon was used to feed a doll (cf. Huttenlocher & Higgins, 1978); and 'sensorimotor.' A larger proportion of the play activities produced by the children with autism involved sensorimotor play than in either of the other two groups. Correspondingly, the children with autism produced proportionally less functional play than the typically developing group (but not the individuals with developmental delay), and proportionally less symbolic play than either of the other groups (cf. Jarrold et al., 1996).

The Relevance for Theories of Pretense

The finding of impoverished spontaneous pretend play in autism is clearly relevant to our understanding of the condition, but arguably its most important implication is for theories of pretense in general. Baron-Cohen (1987) argued that a specific deficit in pretend play reflected an impaired ability to symbolize in autism. Pretend play is often termed symbolic play, following Piaget's (1962) assertion that in pretense an object (the 'signifier') comes to represent another (the 'signified'); the classic example cited in the literature is a child pretending that a banana is a telephone. Others have since extended the definition of pretense to encompass three characteristic behaviors: object substitution (as just described), the attribution of absent properties (e.g., a toy teapot is hot), and imaging absent objects or entities (e.g., the toy toothbrush has imaginary toothpaste on it) (e.g., Leslie, 1987). In Baron-Cohen's (1987) terminology a child engaged in these forms of pretense is using a prop to 'symbolize' another, non-present, imaginary target or a modified version of the prop itself. However, this terminology is potentially open to confusion, as many would argue that language is a symbolic system and individuals with autism can show impaired pretend play in the presence of intact vocabulary.

Leslie (1987) extended Baron-Cohen's analysis and argued that, in pretense, a child does not simply use one object to stand for (or represent) another. Leslie argued that this would cause potentially disastrous consequences for the child's understanding of the world as it risks confusing and blurring the child's representations of objects' meaning and function. He therefore claimed that when pretending, the child has to acknowledge, or represent, its own or another's pretend 'attitude' to the imaginary state of affairs that pertains in that situation. More specifically, Leslie's argument is that when a child makes sense of what mother is doing when pretending, for example when she holds a banana to her ear and starts talking into it, they have to represent how the mother herself represents the banana being used 'as if it were a telephone.' In Leslie's terminology this is a particular form of secondary representation, as the child is taking a representational perspective on another representational relation. Indeed, as a direct result of this analysis Leslie (1987) claimed that pretend play is 'metarepresentational' in nature.

The importance of this seminal work follows from the fact that Leslie drew a direct link between the metarepresentational nature of pretense and the development of theory of mind in children. Theory of mind is the ability to attribute propositional attitudes (e.g., beliefs) to another person (Wimmer & Perner, 1983), and is classically tested using variants of false belief tasks (Dennett, 1978) in which the participant has to appreciate that a protagonist holds a (false) belief that differs from their own. This requires the participant to represent how another misrepresents the world, and is therefore assumed to involve metarepresentation (Perner, 1991). Leslie's (1987) argument was that there is a "deep isomorphism" between theory of mind and pretend play, precisely because both require metarepresentational abilities. Potentially crucial support for this claim comes from the clear evidence that individuals with autism have severe difficulties in understanding theory of mind tasks (Baron-Cohen, Leslie, & Frith, 1985; see Yirmiya, Erel, Shaked, & Solomnica-Levi, 1998).

Two Problems with the Metarepresentational Account

Despite the intuitive appeal of this account, the first author has argued on a number of occasions that a detailed analysis of pretend play in autism poses problems for Leslie's account (Jarrold, 2003; Jarrold et al., 1993; Jarrold, Carruthers, Smith, & Boucher, 1994). There seems little doubt that individuals with autism do suffer from theory of mind difficulties, although there is considerable debate as to what causes this problem (Baron-Cohen, 2002; Hobson, 1990; Russell, 1996). Consequently, one would expect individuals with autism to have problems in other situations that require metarepresentational understanding. Clearly, the above review shows that children with autism do tend to produce very little pretend play in free play situations. However, there is evidence to suggest that, first, these difficulties may extend into other areas of play, and, second, that these problems might be much less marked in other contexts. Both of these suggestions are problematic for Leslie's (1987) account (Jarrold et al., 1994; Williams, Reddy, & Costall, 2001).

Do impairments extend beyond pretend play in autism?

In his analysis of pretend play in autism, Baron-Cohen (1987) drew a clear distinction between symbolic (or pretend) play and functional play. As noted, above, the latter involves appropriate use of miniature props, such as brushing a doll's teeth with a miniature toothbrush; in other words, using toy objects as their play function suggests. While one might argue that this looks very much like pretend play activity, Huttenlocher and Higgins (1978) argued strongly that children might carry out such play without any attempt to mentally represent the play object as signifying (or symbolizing) a non-present object. Rather, they suggested, children might simply be using these objects in line with their observed conventional usage. For that reason, authors have tended to restrict the attribution of pretending to situations where it is clear that the child is using a play prop in a method which clearly differs from its suggested function, or where it is apparent that absent properties or objects are being imagined. In line with this, Baron-Cohen (1987) argued that functional play did not require the kind of symbolic representation needed for pretend play. Similarly, Leslie (1987) claimed that functional play does not require metarepresentation.

Given this, individuals with autism should have no difficulties in engaging in functional play if their problems in pretense stem solely from a fundamental difficulty in metarepresentational thought. Indeed, this is what Baron-Cohen found, as comparable numbers of individuals with and without autism produced some evidence of functional play in his study. A number of other studies have similarly shown that children with autism produce as many functional play acts as controls (Charman & Baron-Cohen, 1997; Lewis & Boucher, 1988; Libby et al., 1998). However, other work has suggested that children with autism might spend less time engaged in functional play in free play settings than one would expect (Blanc et al., 2005; Lewis & Boucher, 1988; Jarrold et al., 1996; Sigman & Ungerer, 198; Trillingsgaard, Ulsted Sørensen, Nêmec, & Jørgensen, 2005). A possible reconciliation of these apparently contradictory findings comes from a study by Williams, Reddy, and Costall (2001). These authors looked in detail at the different types of functional play shown by very young children and controls who had a developmental level of between one and two years. Overall, the children with autism did not produce significantly less functional play than controls, but the functional play they did show was less sophisticated and elaborated. They produced fewer new acts, and instead repeated functional acts with the available props, and they combined toys and play acts (e.g., stirring a spoon in a cup) significantly less often than controls. As a result of these data Williams et al. (2001) argued that the functional play shown by individuals with autism is impaired. Other studies that have suggested that functional play is intact in autism may have done so solely by virtue of coding the number of functional play episodes without examining the duration or quality of that play.

It is unclear too whether other types of play are unaffected in children with autism. Not only do children with autism show a preference for sensorimotor play compared to typical and developmentally delayed children matched for language and comprehension (Boucher, 1999; Blanc et al., 2005; Jarrold et al., 1996; Libby et al., 1998), they also display preferences for specific ways of playing. Physical, non-verbal play seems to hold an appeal, with evidence of a preference for rough and tumble play (Boucher, 1999; El-Ghoroury & Romanczyk, 1999), as does social play provided that it has well-defined interactive turns and a clear purpose (El-Ghoroury & Romanczyk, 1999).

Are deficits in pretend play less marked in other contexts?

It is worth noting that even those studies that provide clear evidence of impaired spontaneous pretense in autism indicate that at least some of the individuals in these samples do show some pretend play on occasion. Baron-Cohen (1987) found that 20% of his sample showed 'unambiguous pretend play,' and similarly Libby et al. (1998) note that five of their nine individuals with autism showed some evidence of pretending at some stage of their study. Blanc et al.'s (2005) data suggest that very small but measureable levels of pretense were seen in their sample of children with autism, and Jarrold et al. (1996) found that individuals with autism spent, on average, about 7% of their free play time in pretend play.

In addition, studies that have provided a more structured environment than a free play setting have observed what appear to be higher levels of pretense among individuals with autism. When pretend play is 'encouraged,' 'elicited,' or 'prompted,' individuals with autism benefit from these manipulations. Typically, the degree of improvement in amount of pretend play produced under structured relative to free play conditions is comparable in groups of individuals with autism and controls (Blanc et al., 2005; Lewis & Boucher, 1998; Jarrold et al., 1996), meaning that individuals with autism still tend to show impaired levels of pretend play (Blanc et al., 2005; Jarrold et al., 1996).

However, a slightly different result emerged from a particularly careful examination of this issue carried out by Rutherford et al. (2007). These authors built on a previous study which they had conducted (Rutherford & Rogers, 2003), that had shown evidence of impaired spontaneous pretend play in a sample of children with autism relative to non-verbal mental age-matched groups of children with developmental delay and typically developing individuals. In their follow-up study Rutherford et al. (2007) returned to these samples to repeat their measures at a second time point. On both occasions participants were given the Fewell Play Scale (Fewell & Rich, 1987), which allows individuals to engage with toy props spontaneously, but then moves through a series of increasingly 'scaffolded' elicitation and prompting phases. At time 2, the individuals with autism were impaired, relative to controls, on both spontaneous and scaffolded pretend play scores. However, an analysis of the relative levels of performance shown by each group across spontaneous and scaffolded conditions revealed that children with autism showed significantly better scaffolded than spontaneous performance; in contrast, the two control groups performed comparably across conditions. In other words, although individuals with autism still showed impaired pretend play under scaffolded conditions, the degree of this impairment was significantly less than that observed in free play (see also Hobson et al., 2009).

Arguably the most extreme forms of experimenter-determined scaffolding one can employ in a play study are to either instruct the participant to carry out a particular act, or to carry that act out oneself and test the participant's comprehension of the outcome. Both approaches have been adopted in studies of pretend play in autism. When children with autism are instructed to carry out pretend acts with particular props they appear to perform as well as do controls (Charman & Baron-Cohen, 1997; Jarrold et al., 1996; Lewis & Boucher, 1988, 1995). The first studies to test individuals' comprehension of pretend play acts also found unimpaired performance among individuals with autism (Jarrold, Smith, Boucher, & Harris, 1994; Kavanaugh & Harris, 1994). These findings have recently been qualified in a study from the first author's research group (Jarrold, Mansergh, & Whiting, 2010) that examined children with autism's ability to understand multiple pretend transformations (cf. Harris & Kavanaugh, 1993). Specifically, we wanted to test Leslie's (1987) assertion that in order to make sense of pretense one needs to represent how the 'other' represents the pretend relation between signifier and signified. A number of theorists (e.g., Harris, 1991, 1994; Nichols & Stich, 2000; Perner, 1991) have argued that this invokes an unnecessary level of complexity, and instead that individuals can make sense of pretense by simply making their own pretend reading of the current state of affairs. In other words, rather than 'going inside the other's head' to attribute to them a pretend representation (metarepresentation), children might instead simply apply a non-literal representation of what they themselves observe (the banana is being used 'as-if' it were a telephone) (Lillard, 1993; this volume). Certainly, the initial evidence of unimpaired comprehension of pretense in autism appeared consistent with this view, but we wanted to test the limits of this account by creating a situation in which the participant was forced to attribute a pretend representation to a protagonist.

This was done by borrowing a 'false pretense' paradigm from Hickling, Wellman, and Gottfried (1997). Participants were shown a pretense version of a false belief task in which two protagonists sequentially acted out different pretend acts on the same object. For example, Protagonist A might pretend than an empty paint pot contained green paint, but when they left the room Protagonist B would change the situation by pretending to empty the paint pot and to fill it with red paint. On Protagonist A's return the child was asked what Protagonist A was pretending when they acted on the target object (what color was A pretending to paint when they dipped their brush into the pot and started 'painting'). Crucially, this condition was contrasted with an extremely similar condition in which Protagonist A remained present when B switched the pretend stipulation (what we termed a true pretense trial). We reasoned that in true pretense trials the child could keep track of the pretend situation by simply updating their own pretend representation of the state of affairs. In contrast, in false pretense trials they would need to correctly represent the pretend representation of Protagonist A, because this differed from the current state of affairs.

These predictions were borne out. Individuals with autism and typically developing comparison children were divided into subgroups on the basis of

their performance on a separate false belief task, in order to determine whether they had developed the ability to engage in metarepresentational reasoning or not. In both individuals with and without autism performance on this theory of mind task was unrelated to performance on the true pretense trials, but had a large impact on performance on false pretense trials. In the latter case, individuals who failed the theory of mind task struggled much more on the false pretense trials than did those individuals who passed the theory of mind task. As a result, we argued that false pretense trials involved metarepresentational competence, but that this was not the case for true pretense trials. While the first aspect of this claim might be rather unsurprising, given the clear structural similarities between our false pretense and false belief tasks, it nevertheless shows that one can generate tests of comprehension of pretend play that do require metarepresentation. More importantly, the findings from true pretense trials add further support to the view that one can very often make sense of observed pretend play acts without having to use metarepresentational skills to attribute a pretend representation to another.

In the studies of comprehension of pretense in autism just reviewed, participants were tested on their understanding of the outcome of a pretend transformation. Bigham (2008) extended this work by examining children with autism's ability to understand object substitutions carried out by the experimenter. In addition, Bigham varied the extent to which the different props (the signifiers) used in different conditions of her study matched the imagined target objects (the signifieds) in terms of both form and function. The typically developing literature has shown that, as children age, they become increasingly willing to use props that differ considerably in form and function to the imagined target—a trend termed 'decontextualization' (Bigham & Bourchier-Sutton, 2007; Corrigan, 1987; Fein, 1981; Jackowitz & Watson, 1980; Lyytinen, 1990). Bigham (2008) replicated these decontextualization effects in children with autism and in verbal mental age-matched controls with and without developmental delay, but children with autism were significantly less able than controls to identify the imagined object that was the subject of the experimenter's pretend action. This group difference was observed on all conditions, apart from a 'similar form and function' condition in which the prop was very closely matched to the target. However, ceiling effects on this similar form and function condition may well have obscured a general deficit among individuals with autism. Certainly, Bigham's (2008) data suggest that individuals with autism struggle to understand modeled object substitutions, in contrast to their apparent strengths in comprehending pretend actions involving the attribution of absent properties.

The question of whether individuals with autism have a fundamental deficit in making sense of pretense, as Leslie (1987) suggested, or instead have difficulty in producing pretend play in some situations, is a classic 'competence versus performance' issue (Jarrold et al., 1993; Rutherford et al., 2007). An obvious way of testing whether individuals with autism can overcome an apparent problem in pretense (a performance account) is by looking at the results of intervention studies that have attempted to train pretend play. Luckett, Bundy, and Roberts (2007) have recently provided a detailed review of 'behavioral' play interventions in autism, including those that have sought to improve pretend play by selectively reinforcing appropriate behaviors. Luckett et al. highlight four previous studies that have made claims for the effectiveness of this form of behavioral pretend play training (Lifter, Sulzer-Azaroff, Anderson, & Cowdery, 1993; Newman, Reinecke, & Meinberg, 2000; Stahmer, 1995; Thorp, Stahmer, & Schreibman, 1995). Luckett et al. note that in each case there is evidence that the training led to generalized pretend play behaviors using props not employed in the intervention, but no strong evidence that problems in pretend play in autism are 'removed' by these interventions.

Similar findings emerged from a further study carried out by Kasari, Freeman, and Paparella (2006) that again applied behavioral play training to individuals with autism. This study had the advantage that individuals with autism were randomly assigned to one of two treatment groups—one training joint attention, the other symbolic play—or a control group. Kasariet et al. found that play training led to a greater increase in the 'highest level' of play behavior in the play intervention group than in controls. They also claimed that "children in the play intervention showed more novel types of symbolic play" (p. 616). However, a comparison of free play sessions before and after the interventions provided no evidence that children in either intervention group increased their amount of symbolic play more than controls. Taken together, the results of these studies suggest that while such interventions do appear to lead to some degree of generalization and greater creativity in pretend play in children who receive training, there is no clear evidence as yet that such

children end up playing (or in this case pretending) in the same way and with the same internal motivation as would a typically developing child (Luckett et al., 2007).

In summary, there is certainly evidence to suggest that individuals with autism can produce, and make sense of, pretend play in some circumstances. At the same time, this evidence is not completely conclusive, and there remain questions as to the nature of the type of pretend play that appears to be occurring in these studies. We return to these questions in the final section of the chapter, but before doing so we turn instead to alternative, non-metarepresentational explanations for the pattern of deficits seen in the pretend play of individuals with autism.

Executive Dysfunction as an Explanation of Impaired Pretend Play in Autism

The notion of executive control refers to high-level planning and control functions typically associated with the human prefrontal cortex (Barkely, 1997; Passingham, 2003; Shallice, 1998). Typically, definitions of the 'executive functions' that go together to allow for the deliberate control of human action take the form of a list of candidate processes such as 'inhibition, set-shifting, monitoring, planning, and working memory' (e.g., Hill, 2004) and there is evidence that many, though perhaps not all, of these functions are impaired in autism (Hill, 2004; Kenworthy, Yerys, Anthony, & Wallace, 2008; Pennington & Ozonoff, 1996). This is relevant because alternative accounts of the typical development of pretend play to Leslie's place considerable emphasis on the child's need to distance themselves from the real nature of objects in order to engage in pretense. This idea is central to Vygotsky's analysis of pretense (e.g., Vygotsky, 1966; See Goncu & Gaskins, this volume), which argues that the development of the ability to pretend reflects the child's increasing ability to move from a position in which meaning is dictated by external factors (in this case the object) to one where meaning is dictated by internal factors (the child's own intentions). In this sense the child becomes 'emancipated' from the real world form and functions of the objects that they use in play and becomes able to use these objects flexibly, creatively, and non-literally in pretense. Support for this more gradual development of pretend play skills comes from the observed developmental trend of decontextualization referred to above. This is entirely consistent with the idea that true pretend competence emerges gradually as the child learns to distance themselves from objects' functions.

Authors have therefore argued that a failure to inhibit objects' forms and functions, which follows directly from general executive dysfunction, may make pretend play particularly difficult for individuals with autism. Jarrold, Boucher, and Smith (1994) therefore examined this suggestion directly by looking for any particular reluctance among children with autism to select unsuitable props for a prompted object substitution task. In this experiment participants were shown a functional play act that was modeled to them (e.g., brushing a doll's teeth) and were then given a set of props from which they could select one to carry out a pretend re-enactment of that action. The prop set contained objects with no obvious function that varied in their similarity to the target object (in this case, a miniature toothbrush) in size and shape (i.e., dissimilarity of form). In addition, each prop set contained one item that matched the target for size and shape but had a clearly defined function of its own (e.g., a pencil, dissimilarity of function). Comparison individuals showed the expected decontextualization effects, preferring to initially select props that were similar in form to the target, and showing some reluctance to select the prop with its own defined function. However, these effects were no more marked among individuals with autism, contrary to what would be predicted if a problem in inhibition underpinned problems of pretend play in autism.

Depending on how one reads the data, Bigham's (2008) study arguably produced somewhat similar findings. As noted above, in this experiment Bigham looked at individuals' ability to understand object substitutions that were demonstrated to them, and employed props that differed in both form and function from the intended target. Although Bigham did report an interaction in her data, such that individuals with autism were unimpaired only when making sense of object substitutions using props with a similar form and function to the target, ceiling effects appeared to be operating in this condition. In all other conditions individuals with autism showed the same decontextualization effects as did controls. This again suggests that individuals with autism do not have *particular* difficulties in over-riding the apparent form and function of objects being used in pretense.

Having said this, Bigham's study did show impaired comprehension of object substitutions in autism, which contrasts with findings of unimpaired performance on tests of the comprehension of the pretend attribution of absent properties (see above). One possible explanation for this contrast is that object substitution is particularly difficult for individuals with autism because it involves the inhibition of objects' functions in a way that other forms of pretend play do not. Some preliminary support for this suggestion comes from a recent study from the first author's group (Jarrold & Goyder, 2010). In this work children with and without autism were shown a series of pretend scenarios that were carried out by protagonists; each scenario involved the protagonist acting on three similar props. In trials in one condition the protagonist pretended that one prop acquired an absent property (e.g., they pretended to pour tea into the yellow cup, while washing up and putting away the blue and red cup respectively). In trials in the other condition each prop was the subject of a different object substitution (e.g., the protagonist pretended that the yellow cup was a drum, the blue cup a hat, and the red cup a vase). At the end of the trial a second protagonist was introduced and the child was told that this character needed one of the props to fulfil a certain task (e.g., have a drink, make some music). The child therefore had to keep track of either the attribution of absent properties or object substitution in order to select the correct prop. The results showed that type of task interacted with group, such that individuals with autism actually did better than controls on the attribution of absent properties trials but less well on the object substitution trials. This is therefore consistent with the notion that difficulties in over-riding object functions is particularly problematic for individuals with autism, perhaps as a result of inhibitory problems associated with executive dysfunction.

A slightly different 'executive' account was advanced by Lewis and Boucher (1995). They reanalyzed data from their earlier 1988 study to examine the extent to which pretend play acts produced by individuals with and without autism in response to elicited and instructed prompts were novel or not. This showed some evidence that individuals with autism produced fewer novel acts than controls. Indeed, the above review of both symbolic and functional play in autism provides further suggestions that individuals with autism produce as many play acts as controls, but that more of these acts are repetitive and fewer novel (e.g., Williams et al., 2001). Jarrold et al. (1996) extended this line of argument and examined the rate of generation of pretend play acts shown by children with autism and controls across a six-minute elicited play session. They found that while individuals with autism did engage in some pretend play (in line with the findings reviewed above) they produced novel pretend acts at a significantly slower rate than controls.

It has therefore been suggested that problems of set-shifting and flexibility in autism, which might well arise from general executive dysfunction, hamper pretend play by impairing individuals' ability to generate the ideas for flexible creative pretend play (Honey, Leekam, Turner, & McConachie, 2007; Jarrold et al., 1996; Jarrold, 1997; Rutherford et al., 2007). This form of deficit would clearly explain why individuals struggle most to engage in pretend play in free play situations, and why the deficit is reduced when the 'ideas' for pretense are provided by the experimenter. Similarly, such an account would sit well with the suggestion that problems in play are not restricted to pretend play in autism, but rather might extend to functional play. Indeed, Rutherford and Rogers (2003) provided evidence that supported this account when they observed that scores on a test of generativity, in which individuals were asked to generate as many uses of a set of toys as they could, were correlated with levels of spontaneous pretend play among individuals with and without autism. It should, however, be noted, that their individuals with autism did not produce significantly fewer play ideas on the generativity task than did controls, which is not what one would expect given a generativity account. Indeed, other studies that have looked at the generation of ideas, or category examples, in autism have provided mixed evidence for the kinds of problems in generativity that this account would predict (see Dichter, Lam, Turner-Brown, Holtzclaw, & Bodfish, 2009; Robinson, Goddard, Dritschel, Wisley, & Howlin, 2009; Scott & Baron-Cohen, 1996; Spek, Schatorjé, Scholte, & van Berckelaer-Onnes, 2009; Turner, 1999).

Atypical Sociocultural Learning as an Explanation of Impaired Pretend Play in Autism

The notion that deficits in pretend play in autism might follow from executive dysfunction draws directly on Vygotsky's analysis of the development of pretense. However, central to Vygotsky's theorizing on the development of the capacity for symbolic thought is the claim that this depends on the actual social relations between people, with all 'higher mental functions' being socially formed and culturally transmitted through language. Importantly, his theory of human development consists of two parts, social conditions and biological behavior, where one is in constant interaction with the other so that "an experimenter must study both components and the laws which govern their *interlacement* at each stage of a child's development" (John-Steiner, & Souberman, 1978, p 123).

However, until recently researchers and theorists have tended to focus on the internalization of learning, thereby reducing Vygotsky's analysis of culture to simply a trigger for development. Such a reading served to reinforce the idea of development as an essentially individual enterprise, where individuals exist as entities that are separate from cultural processes and where culture itself exists apart from the actions of its individual members. Recent developments in theory have, however, questioned this assumption and reemphasized the sociocultural basis of development (Rogoff, 2003). From birth, children have continuous experiences of social routines and engage in activities on the environment in close cooperation with others. Using his extensive research with preschool children, the sociologist Bill Corsaro notes how profoundly social children are and describes their persistent attempts to understand and gain a footing in social activity (Corsaro, 1988, 1992). Children do not always have social knowledge, but try to make sense of what is going on around them and interact anyway. Corsaro argues that children do not simply learn about culture, but produce it themselves in creative ways. They do not carry round culture in their heads, but reproduce it continuously in shared, public, performative social acts with each other, in their play and with the adults with whom they come into contact.

Such an interpretation of children's actions does not distinguish between different types of social activity. Social play, pretend play, social interaction, and friendship can all be described as 'temporal sites of cultural reproduction,' where children learn about culture and reproduce it (James, Jenks, & Prout, 1998). Indeed, in contrast to Leslie's (1987) analysis, which draws a qualitative distinction between 'pretense' and 'non-pretense,' a sociocultural perspective highlights the social in pretend play and simply positions it as an extension of the other activities children do with each other and with objects (Rakoczy, Tomasello, & Striano, 2005; Striano, Tomasello, & Rochat, 2001). Thus, imaginative pretense, even in solitary play, closely follows real life rules and social narratives, however creatively reproduced. Pretend play, like social play, is about coordinated interaction and shared ideas, albeit at a more complex level (Howes, Unger, & Seidner, 1989;

Howes, this volume; Rakoczy, 2008a; Rakoczy et al., 2005). Shared pretend play involves the recognition of other children's aims and negotiation of individual play interests (Rakoczy, 2008b; Wyman, Rakoczy, & Tomasello, 2009) all of which is made possible by spending time together and enjoying each other's company (Dunn, 2005). Pretend play is more common in siblings who are fond of each other (Dunn, 1991) and is an important indication of friendship in peers (Corsaro, 2003). It is about connectedness of communication and is characterized by its compelling emotional quality, the excitement of the engagement in pretense and the pleasure to be had from that (Hobson et al., 2009).

This form of analysis suggests two related explanations of impaired spontaneous pretend play in autism. First, the social difficulties that are clearly associated with the condition will inevitably mean that children with autism do not participate in cultural routines in the same way as typically developing children and do not therefore have the same amounts of social knowledge. It could be said, indeed, that the effect of autism on the way individuals perceive, understand, and act upon the world contributes to a form of development that is qualitatively different to the typical case. Whilst recognizing that it is a development disorder, some accounts of autism argue that the sociocultural impact of the condition in effect leads to a kind of cultural diversity in people with autism (Mesibov & Shea, 1998). It is possible that children with autism have different ways of playing that are less social and more sensory-based (Libby et al., 1998) and a different way of being friends, too, that is more about actual physical presence and less a mental form of companionship (Chamberlain, Kasari, & Rotherham-Fuller, 2007).

Second, individuals with autism may lack the motivation or drive to carry out pretend play. Almost by definition pretending has a particularly playful quality—there is no obvious functional benefit to play, and Piaget (1962) suggested that individuals engage in pretense partly because of the playful desire to manifest their own mastery over these symbolic routines. Hobson et al. (2009) examined this issue by comparing the pretend play shown by individuals with autism and language-matched controls with learning difficulties in both free play and 'modeled' play sessions. They rated pretend play behaviors in terms of two factors related to the 'mechanics' of pretense ('attribution of symbolic meaning' and 'flexible prop use') and four related to the 'playful' nature of pretense ('self-awareness,'

'degree of investment,' 'creativity,' and 'fun'). They found that individuals with autism showed a comparable ability to controls to engage in the mechanics of pretending, but lower playfulness scores. In terms of Hobson and colleagues' general account (Hobson, 1990; 1993; Hobson et al., 2009) this absence of playfulness in autism follows from a biological predisposition that adversely affects individuals with autism's intersubjective engagement with others. However, despite the biological underpinnings of this account, it clearly places an emphasis on the need to understand the individual with autism's "social-emotional" (Hobson et al., 2009) state.

It is worth noting that, in line with Hobson et al.'s recent work, there is increasing recognition of the need for a deeper sociocultural perspective to the study of pretend play in autism, particularly the need to carry out naturalistic research into the actual play behaviors of children who know each other (Boucher & Wolfberg, 2003). For example, a number of play interventions have taken seriously the need to consider the 'cultural context' of children with autism's play, with apparent success. Wolfberg has developed integrated play groups (IPGs) that bring together 'expert' players without autism, with 'novice' players with autism (cf. Herman, Paukner, & Suomi, this volume). The focus of these groups is on play skills as well as the quality of the play, with social guidance techniques used to support both expert and novice players in sibling or peer groups, in classroom and home settings (Wolfberg 1999). Careful consideration is given to the preferred forms of play of the children involved in the groups, to the play materials used, and to the organization of the play space. Adult guidance involves developing what children are presently doing together by suggesting new events, actions, or things to say.

A range of quantitative and qualitative methods have been used to gauge the effectiveness of IPGs and gains in the amount of children's play engagement, sophistication of play skill, and level of language use are reported across a number of studies (Wolfberg & Schuler, 1999; Yang, Wolfberg, Wu, & Hwu, 2003). However, what is less clear is which aspects of this rich and complex model underpin this success. In an interesting use of the IPG model by Zercher, Hunt, Schuler, & Webster (2001), the difficulty of measurement in a social developmental approach is highlighted. In this study, a small group of peers—three sisters—were trained to be more effective in their play with two boys with autism without ongoing adult guidance. The sisters were trained to use discrete prompting behaviors with the boys to gain their attention, offer play ideas, and repair social breakdown, including specific nonverbal behaviors (e.g., touching arm to get attention) and verbal scripts (e.g., asking 'What are you doing?'). The authors report that though the girls were highly motivated and followed instructions generally with great fidelity, they did not use discrete prompt procedures as instructed. Instead, their input was highly complex, embedded within the context of the pretend play itself. They gained attention by performing pretend actions, prompted responses by offering pretend choices, and repaired breakdown in the play by being more persistent in their pretending. The results of this study serve to remind us that culture and thought are mutually constituting processes, not easily picked apart as sets of independent variables. As Hobson et al. (2009) point out, it is probable that the process of pretense in play rests on a collection of cognitive, generative, motivational, social, and cultural components, the interaction of which is not necessarily quantifiable.

Conclusion

The first question facing the researcher who wishes to synthesize the findings regarding pretend play in autism is whether the deficits which are clearly observed in spontaneous play settings reflect a competence or performance deficit. Under a competence deficit account difficulties in spontaneous pretend play reflect the fact that individuals with autism have a fundamental deficit in the ability to produce pretense in any situation. Under a performance deficit account problems in spontaneous pretense are less marked in other situations because individuals with autism have the capability to pretend, but struggle to show this in free play situations for whatever reason. This distinction is both relevant and important because it maps onto a distinction between the major theoretical accounts of the development of pretend play in general. On the one hand, Leslie (1987) argues that pretend play is qualitatively different from other types of play behavior, an analysis that sits happily with the suggestion of a competence deficit in autism. On the other, more traditional accounts such as those of Piaget (e.g., Piaget, 1962) and Vygotsky (e.g., Vygotsky, 1966) emphasize the gradual development of pretend play and so draw a more quantitative distinction between, for example, symbolic and functional play. This view is more in line with the performance deficit notion that individuals with autism have difficulties

in producing pretend play, but difficulties that can be overcome in certain circumstances with the right support.

The above review suggests that there is considerable evidence that appears to support the performance deficit account of pretend play deficits in autism. Individuals with autism do produce some pretend play even in free play situations; they appear to produce more when encouraged to do so, and in many instances they are as able as controls to carry out instructed pretend acts or to make sense of pretend scenarios that they witness. In addition, when one observes pretend play deficits in autism these most often reflect problems in producing as many pretend acts, or as rich and creative pretense, as seen in controls. Similar findings appear when one focuses on functional play, and together these data certainly suggest that problems in play reflect *difficulties* in production rather than a general *inability* to engage in pretense. In turn, this would suggest that Piaget and Vygotsky were right not to draw too firm a distinction between pretend play on the one hand and other types of play on the other.

Having said this, a key issue that one must also address is whether the type of play that one observes in individuals with autism in these more structured situations really merits the label of symbolic pretend play. Baron-Cohen (1990) was the first, at least in the context of autism research, to question what one can infer from the case where a child responds appropriately to an instruction to pretend (see also Charman & Baron-Cohen, 1997). His argument was that the child might simply select the prop that most closely resembles the target pretend object and use that appropriately, without making any attempt to mentally represent the symbolic relationship between prop and target. Similarly, when a child makes sense of a pretend act that has been demonstrated to them, might they simply be drawing probabilistic inferences about what normally happens when, for example, one empties a teapot, rather than actually representing the absent objects or properties (in this case, the hot tea now on the table)?

Of course, many would argue that the comprehension of pretense in fact does involve little more than a plausible reading of the observed situation (Harris, 1991, 1994; Perner, 1991), albeit with the proviso that the child is aware at some level at least that this behavior is non-literal. However, Leslie would argue that a strong case could be made that such a process should not be termed 'pretend proper' (e.g., Friedman & Leslie, 2007). Our data (Jarrold et al., 2010), and our analysis of others' findings, suggest to us that individuals can make sense of many pretend play acts without recourse to metarepresentational abilities, but might Leslie be right to suggest that proper pretend play requires an 'awareness' of the intentional act of pretending (see also Lillard, 2001; Rakoczy, Tomasello, & Striano, 2004)?

Certainly we agree with Hobson and colleagues that a distinction can be drawn between the 'mechanics' of pretense and the playful 'attitude' associated with it. The above review is consistent with Hobson et al.'s (2009) analysis that individuals with autism can engage in what looks like the mechanics of pretense, but do so without the playful attitude that attends pretend play in typical development. In addition, a common assumption underlying much of the cognitive research into play in autism is that its development, if and when it occurs, follows the typical case, moving from sensorimotor to functional and symbolic play. However, there is no evidence that the play experience of a child with autism is 'typical' at any of these stages. It is possible that the sensory aspects of every level of play are more emotionally compelling for a child with autism and that 'cultural reproduction' is a much less important factor. When we see pretense in the actions of a child with autism, for example when a child pretends to drive a car across the floor, we cannot assume it is pretense as we understand it. It is perhaps the case that, rather than an engagement in the familiar social routine of going from A to B or an identification with the mastery of being a driver, the child's experience of playing with a car is the much more sensory one of being the car itself, of wheels going round, the white markings of the road passing underneath and the lines of fencing moving in the peripheral vision.

Hobson et al. (2009, p. 19) summarized this issue when they wrote:

> "whatever means children with autism do make one thing stand for another and/or invent imaginary objects and/or attribute pretend properties and/or show flexibility in using the objects of play, in important respects … these means do *not* correspond with those of children without autism. This is betrayed by the fact that only among the latter are the qualities of self-awareness in creating new meanings, investment in symbolic meanings, creativity/generativity and fun *also* part and parcel of the playful symbolizing activity."

The point we make here, in line with Hobson and colleagues, and perhaps also Leslie, is that one is then forced to ask the question of whether 'just going through the motions' of pretending (Jarrold, 2003) should really be classed as pretend play proper.

This question is unlikely to be resolved without further theoretical developments in the general pretend play literature. However, the contribution of autism research to this issue might well be to highlight this potential distinction between the mechanics of carrying out or understanding pretense and the attitude associated with these behaviors. The current review suggests that individuals with autism can engage in what one might term the mechanics of pretense in some contexts, although we suggest that their executive problems in overriding the known function of pretend objects might make this particularly difficult in free-play situations. However, we have also highlighted the problems that individuals with autism have in playing flexibly and creatively, and with the engagement and affect that would be expected to accompany pretense. Whether this problem results directly from a metarepresentational deficit linked to theory of mind problems associated with the condition, or as a secondary consequence of the atypical sociocultural environment experienced by individuals with autism, remains to be resolved.

Future Directions

1. How and when do the problems that individuals with autism have in mental metarepresentation impact on their pretend play?

2. Are apparently executive problems in producing pretense in autism due to a failure to inhibit objects' functions, or in generating the ideas for pretense? Are the two in some way related?

3. Do individuals with autism struggle to produce typical patterns of pretend play because they develop in an atypical sociocultural context, and is the playful nature of pretend play lacking for them for this (or some other) reason?

4. Would we want to call the type of pretending that we see in autism 'pretend play proper'? Is it atypical, or is it rather the individual just pretending in a way that is most appropriate for them?

5. Should theories of pretend play development in general distinguish between the mechanics and motivational aspects of pretense? Does this distinction relate to a distinction between the cognitive and social aspects of pretense, or is that an oversimplification?

References

American Psychiatric Association (1994). *Diagnostic and statistical manual of mental disorder* (4th ed.) Washington DC: American Psychiatric Publishing, Inc.

Asperger, H. (1944). Die "autistischen psychopathen" im kindesalter. *Archiv für Psyciatrie und Nervenkrankheiten, 117*, 76–113.

Bailey, A., Phillips, W., & Rutter, M. (1996). Autism: Towards an integration of clinical, genetic, neuropsychological, and neurobiological perspectives. *Journal of Child Psychology and Psychiatry, 37*, 89–126.

Barkley, R. A. (1997). Behavioral inhibition, sustained attention, and executive functions: Constructing a unifying theory of ADHD. *Psychological Bulletin, 121*, 65–94.

Baron-Cohen, S. (1987). Autism and symbolic play. *British Journal of Developmental Psychology, 5*, 139–148.

Baron-Cohen, S. (1990). Instructed and elicited play in autism: A reply to Lewis and Boucher. *British Journal of Developmental Psychology, 8*, 207.

Baron-Cohen, S. (2002). The extreme male brain theory of autism. *Trends in Cognitive Sciences, 6*, 248–254.

Baron-Cohen, S., Allen, J., & Gillberg, C. (1992). Can autism be detected at 18 months? The needle, the haystack, and the CHAT. *British Journal of Psychiatry, 161*, 839–843.

Baron-Cohen, S., Leslie, A. M., & Frith, U. (1985). Does the autistic child have a 'theory of mind'? *Cognition, 21*, 37–46.

Bigham, S. (2008). Comprehension of pretence in children with autism. *British Journal of Developmental Psychology, 26*, 265–280.

Bigham, S., & Bourchier-Sutton, A. (2007). The decontextualization of form and function in the development of pretence. *British Journal of Developmental Psychology, 25*, 335–351.

Blanc, R., Adrien, J. L., Roux, S., & Barthélémy, C. (2005). Dysregulation of pretend play and communication development in children with autism. *Autism, 9*, 229–245.

Boucher, J. (1999). Interventions with children with autism: Methods based on play. *Child Language Teaching and Therapy, 15*, 1–5.

Boucher, J. & Wolfberg, P. (2003). Editorial. *Autism, 7*, 339–346.

Chamberlain, B., Kasari, C., & Rotherham-Fuller, E. (2007). Involvement or isolation? The social networks of children with autism in regular classrooms. *Journal of Autism and Developmental Disorders, 37*, 230–242.

Charman, T. & Baron-Cohen, S. (1997). Brief report: Prompted pretend play in autism. *Journal of Autism and Developmental Disorders, 27*, 325–332.

Corrigan, R. (1987). A developmental sequence of actor-object pretend play in young children. *Merrill-Palmer Quarterly, 33*, 87–106.

Corsaro, W. A. (1988). Routines in the peer culture of American and Italian nursery school children. *Sociology of Education, 61*, 1–14.

Corsaro, W. A. (1992). Interpretive reproduction in children's peer cultures. *Social Psychology Quarterly, 55*, 160–177.

Corsaro, W. A. (2003). *We're friends right? Inside kid's culture.* Washington D. C.: Joseph Henry Press.

Dennett, D. C. (1978). Beliefs about beliefs. *Behavioral and Brain Sciences, 4*, 568–570.

Dichter, G., Lam, K., Turner-Brown, L., Holtzclaw, T., & Bodfish, J. (2009). Generativity abilities predict communication deficits but not repetitive behaviors in autism spectrum disorders. *Journal of Autism and Developmental Disorders, 39*, 1298–1304.

Dunn, J. (1991). Understanding others: Evidence from naturalistic studies of children. In A Whiten (Ed.), *Natural theories of mind* (pp. 51–61). Oxford: Blackwell.

Dunn, J. (2005). Naturalistic observations of children and their families. In S. Greene & D. Hogan (Eds.), *Researching children's experience: Methods and approaches* (pp. 87–101). London: Sage Publications.

El-Ghoroury, N. H., & Romanczyk, R. G. (1999). Play interactions of family members towards children with autism. *Journal of Autism and Developmental Disorders, 29*, 249–258.

Fein, G. G. (1981). Pretend play in childhood: An integrative review. *Child Development, 52*, 1095–1118.

Fewell, R. R., & Rich, J. S. (1987). Play assessment as a procedure for examining cognitive, communication, and social skills in multi-handicapped children. *Journal of Psychoeducational Assessment, 5*, 107–118.

Fombonne, E. (2005). Epidemiological studies of pervasive developmental disorders. In F. R. Volkmar, R. Paul, A. Klin, & D. Cohen (Eds.) *Handbook of autism and pervasive developmental disorders* (pp. 42–69). Hoboken, New Jersey: John Wiley & Sons.

Friedman, O. & Leslie, A. M. (2007). The conceptual underpinnings of pretense: Pretending is not 'behaving-as-if.' *Cognition, 105*, 103–124.

Harris, P. L. (1991). The work of the imagination. In A. Whiten (Ed.), *Natural theories of mind* (pp. 283–304). Oxford: Blackwell.

Harris, P. L. (1994). Understanding pretence. In C. Lewis & P. Mitchell (Eds.), *Children's early understanding of mind* (pp. 235–259). Hove: Lawrence Erlbaum Associates.

Harris, P. L. & Kavanaugh, R. D. (1993). Young children's understanding of pretense. *Monographs for the Society of Research in Child Development, 58*.

Hickling, A. K., Wellman, H. M., & Gottfried, G. M. (1997). Preschooler's understanding of others' mental attitudes towards pretend happenings. *British Journal of Developmental Psychology, 15*, 339–359.

Hill, E. L. (2004). Executive dysfunction in autism. *Trends in Cognitive Sciences, 8*, 26–32.

Hobson, R. P. (1990). On acquiring knowledge about people and the capacity to pretend: Response to Leslie (1987). *Psychological Review, 97*, 114–121.

Hobson, R. P. (1993). Autism and the development of mind. Hove, Sussex: Erlbaum.

Hobson, R. P., Lee, A., & Hobson, J. A. (2009). Qualities of symbolic play among children with autism: A social-developmental perspective. *Journal of Autism and Developmental Disorders, 39*, 12–22.

Honey, E., Leekam, S., Turner, M., & McConachie, H. (2007). Repetitive behavior and play in typically developing children and children with autism spectrum disorders. *Journal of Autism and Developmental Disorders, 37*, 1107–1115.

Howes, C., Unger, O., & Seidner, L. B. (1989). Social pretend play in toddlers: Parallels with social play and solitary pretend. *Child Development, 60*, 77–84.

Huttenlocher, J., & Higgins, E. T. (1978). Issues in the study of symbolic development. In W. A. Collins (Ed.), *Minnesota symposia on child psychology, vol. 11.* Hillsdale, NJ: Erlbaum.

Jackowitz, E. R., & Watson, M. W. (1980). Development of object transformations in early pretend play. *Developmental Psychology, 16*, 543–549.

Jarrold, C. (2003). A review of research into pretend play in autism. *Autism, 7*, 379–390.

Jarrold, C. (1997). Pretend play in autism: Executive explanations. In J. Russell (Ed.), *Autism as an executive disorder* (pp. 101–140). Oxford: Oxford University Press.

Jarrold, C., Boucher, J., & Smith, P. K. (1993). Symbolic play in autism: A review. *Journal of Autism and Developmental Disorders, 23*, 281–307.

Jarrold, C., Boucher, J., & Smith, P. K. (1994). Executive function deficits and the pretend play of children with autism: A research note. *Journal of Child Psychology and Psychiatry, 35*, 1473–1482.

Jarrold, C., Boucher, J., & Smith, P. K. (1996). Generativity deficits in pretend play in autism. *British Journal of Developmental Psychology, 14*, 275–300.

Jarrold, C., Carruthers, P., Smith, P. K., & Boucher, J. (1994). Pretend play: Is it metarepresentational? *Mind and Language, 9*, 445–468.

Jarrold C. & Goyder, J. (2010). Problems in understanding object substitution suggest that executive dysfunction may limit pretend play in autism. *Manuscript in preparation*.

Jarrold, C., Mansergh, R., & Whiting, C. (2010). The representational status of pretence: Evidence from typical development and autism. *British Journal of Developmental Psychology, 28*, 239–254.

Jarrold, C., Smith, P., Boucher, J., & Harris, P. (1994). Comprehension of pretense in children with autism. *Journal of Autism and Developmental Disorders, 24*, 433–455.

James, A., Jenks, C., & Prout, A. (1998). *Theorizing childhood.* Cambridge: Polity Press.

John-Steiner, V. & Souberman, E. (1978). Afterword. In M. Cole, V. John-Steiner, S. Scribner, & E. Souberman (Eds.) *Mind in Society* (pp. 121–133). Cambridge, MA, Harvard University Press.

Kanner, L. (1943). Autistic disturbances of affective contact. *Nervous Child, 2*, 217–250.

Kasari, C., Freeman, S., & Paparella, T. (2006). Joint attention and symbolic play in young children with autism: A randomized controlled intervention study. *Journal of Child Psychology and Psychiatry, 47*, 611–620.

Kavanaugh, R. D. & Harris, P. L. (1994). Imagining the outcome of pretend transformations: Assessing the competence of normal children and children with autism. *Developmental Psychology, 30*, 847–854.

Kenworthy, L., Yerys, B., Anthony, L., & Wallace, G. (2008). Understanding executive control in autism spectrum disorders in the lab and in the real world. *Neuropsychology Review, 18*, 320–338.

Leslie, A. M. (1987). Pretence and representation: The origins of 'theory of mind'. *Psychological Review, 94*, 412–426.

Lewis, V. & Boucher, J. (1988). Spontaneous, instructed and elicited play in relatively able autistic children. *British Journal of Developmental Psychology, 6*, 325–339.

Lewis, V. & Boucher, J. (1995). Generativity in the play of young people with autism. *Journal of Autism and Developmental Disorders, 25*, 105–121.

Libby, S., Powell, S., Messer, D., & Jordan, R. (1998). Spontaneous play in children with autism: A reappraisal. *Journal of Autism and Developmental Disorders, 28*, 487–497.

Lifter, K., Sulzer-Azaroff, B., Anderson, S. R., & Cowdery, G. E. (1993). Teaching play activities to preschool children with disabilities. The importance of developmental considerations. *Journal of Early Intervention, 17*, 139–159.

Lillard, A. S. (1993). Pretend play skills and the child's theory of mind. *Child Development, 64*, 348–371.

Lillard, A. (2001). Pretend play as twin earth: A social-cognitive analysis. *Developmental Review, 21*, 495–531.

Luckett, T., Bundy, A., & Roberts, J. (2007). Do behavioral approaches teach children with autism to play or are they pretending? *Autism, 11*, 365–388.

Lyytinen, P. (1990). Developmental trends in children's pretend play. *Child: Care, Health and Development, 17*, 9–25.

Mesibov, G. & Shea, V. (1998). *The culture of autism: From theoretical understanding to educational practice.* New York: Plenum Publishing Corporation.

Morgan, B., Maybery, M., & Durkin, K. (2003). Weak central coherence, poor joint attention, and low verbal ability: Independent deficits in early autism. *Developmental Psychology, 39*, 646–656.

Newman, B., Reinecke, D. R., & Meinberg, D. L. (2000). Self-management of varied responding in three students with autism. *Behavioral Interventions, 15*, 145–151.

Nichols, S. & Stich, S. (2000). A cognitive theory of pretense. *Cognition, 74*, 115–147.

Passingham, R. E. (1993). *The frontal lobes and voluntary action.* Oxford: Oxford University Press.

Pennington, B. F. & Ozonoff, S. (1996). Executive functions and developmental psychopathology. *Journal of Child Psychology and Psychiatry, 37*, 51–87.

Perner, J. (1991). *Understanding the representational mind.* Cambridge, MA: MIT press/Bradford Books.

Piaget, J. (1962). *Play, dreams and imitation in childhood.* London: Routledge & Kegan Paul.

Rakoczy, H. (2008a). Pretence as individual and collective intentionality. *Mind & Language, 23*, 499–517.

Rakoczy, H. (2008b). Taking fiction seriously: Young children understand the normative structure of joint pretence games. *Developmental Psychology, 44*, 1195–1201.

Rakoczy, H., Tomasello, M., & Striano, T. (2004). Young children know that trying is not pretending: A test of the "behaving-as-if" construal of children's early concept of pretense. *Developmental Psychology, 40*, 388–399.

Rakoczy, H., Tomasello, M., & Striano, T. (2005). On tools and toys: How children learn to act on and pretend with 'virgin objects'. *Developmental Science, 8*, 57–73.

Riguet, C. B., Taylor, N. D., Benaroya, S., & Klein, L. S. (1981). Symbolic play in autistic, down's and normal children of equivalent mental age. *Journal of Autism and Developmental Disorders, 11*, 439–448.

Robinson, S., Goddard, L., Dritschel, B., Wisley, M., & Howlin, P. (2009). Executive functions in children with autism spectrum disorders. *Brain and Cognition, 71*, 362–368.

Rogoff, B. (2003). *The cultural nature of human development.* Oxford and New York: Oxford University Press.

Ronald, A., Happé, F., & Plomin, R. (2005). The genetic relationship between individual differences in social and nonsocial behaviors characteristic of autism. *Developmental Science, 8*, 444–458.

Russell, J. (1996). *Agency: Its role in mental development.* Hove: Erlbaum (UK) Taylor & Francis.

Rutherford, M. D. & Rogers, S. J. (2003). Cognitive underpinnings of pretend play in autism. *Journal of Autism and Developmental Disorders, 33*, 289–302.

Rutherford, M., Young, G., Hepburn, S., & Rogers, S. (2007). A longitudinal study of pretend play in autism. *Journal of Autism and Developmental Disorders, 37*, 1024–1039.

Rutter, M. (2005). Aetiology of autism: Findings and questions. *Journal of Intellectual Disability Research, 49*, 231–238.

Scott, F. J., & Baron-Cohen, S. (1996). Imagining real and unreal things: Evidence of a dissociation in autism. *Journal of Cognitive Neuroscience, 8*, 371–382.

Shallice, T. (1988). *From neuropsychology to mental structure.* Cambridge: C.U.P.

Sigman, M., & Ungerer, J. A. (1984). Cognitive and language skills in autistic, mentally retarded, and normal children. *Developmental Psychology, 20*, 293–302.

Spek, A., Schatorjé, T., Scholte, E., & van Berckelaer-Onnes, I. (2009). Verbal fluency in adults with high functioning autism or Asperger syndrome. *Neuropsychologia, 47*, 652–656.

Stahmer, A. C. (1995). Teaching symbolic play skills to children with autism using pivotal response training. *Journal of Autism and Developmental Disorders, 25*, 123–141.

Stanley, G. & Konstantareas, M. (2007). Symbolic play in children with autism spectrum disorder. *Journal of Autism and Developmental Disorders, 37*, 1215–1223.

Striano, T., Tomasello, M., & Rochat, P. (2001). Social and object support for early symbolic play. *Developmental Science, 4*, 442–455.

Thorp, D. M., Stahmer, A. C., & Schreibman, L. (1995). Effects of sociodramatic play training on children with autism. *Journal of Autism and Developmental Disorders, 25*, 265–282.

Trillingsgaard, A., Ulsted Sørensen, E., Nêmec, G., & Jørgensen, M. (2005). What distinguishes autism spectrum disorders from other developmental disorders before the age of four years? *European Child & Adolescent Psychiatry, 14*, 65–72.

Turner, M. A. (1999). Generating novel ideas: Fluency performance in high-functioning and learning disabled individuals with autism. *Journal of Child Psychology and Psychiatry, 40*, 189–201.

Vygotsky, L. S. (1966). Play and its role in the mental development of the child. *Soviet Psychology, 12*, 62–76.

Williams, E., Reddy, V., & Costall, A. (2001). Taking a closer look at functional play in children with autism. *Journal of Autism and Developmental Disorders, 31*, 67–77.

Wimmer, H., & Perner, J. (1983). Beliefs about beliefs: Representation and constraining function of wrong beliefs in young children's understanding of deception. *Cognition, 13*, 103–128.

Wing, L., & Gould, J. (1979). Severe impairments of social interaction and associated abnormalities in children: Epidemiology and classification. *Journal of Autism and Developmental Disorders, 9*, 11–29.

World Health Organization (1992). *International classification of diseases: diagnostic criteria for research* (10th ed.). Geneva: Author.

Wolfberg, P. J. (1999). *Play and imagination in children with autism.* New York and London: Teachers College Press.

Wolfberg, P. J., & Schuler, A. L. (1999). Fostering peer interaction, imaginative play and spontaneous language in children with autism. *Child Language Teaching and Therapy, 15*, 41–52.

Wyman, E., Rakoczy, H., & Tomasello, M. (2009). Normativity and context in young children's pretend play. *Cognitive Development, 24*, 146–155.

Yang, T.-R., Wolfberg, P. J., Wu, S. –C., & Hwu, P.-Y. (2003). Supporting children on the autism spectrum in peer play at home and school: Piloting the integrated play groups in Taiwan. *Autism, 7*, 437–453.

Yirmiya, N., Erel, O., Shaked, M., & Solomonica-Levi, D. (1998). Meta-analyses comparing theory of mind abilities of individuals with autism, individuals with mental retardation, and normally developing individuals. *Psychological Bulletin, 124*, 283–307.

Zercher, C., Hunt, P., Schuler, A. & Webster, J. (2001). Increasing joint attention, play and language through peer supported play. *Autism, 5*, 374–398.

Technology and Play

Jeffrey Goldstein

Abstract

Toys have always reflected the latest developments in science and technology, from music boxes to electric trains to computer games and robots. This chapter considers how children learn to play with modern technology, and what they learn through that play. Playful learning, or guided learning (see Fisher, et al., this volume), is illustrated through selected studies conducted in schools, homes, hospitals, and play settings.

Children often use smart toys in traditional ways, bypassing the technology. There is little research on whether smart toys increase children's cognitive or social skills, although some toys are designed with these goals in mind. Electronic toys and digital games keep children on task for a longer period of time. New media do not necessarily displace older media so much as add to the range of play options available.

Children learn to use new technologies largely through trial and error—through exploration, experimentation, and play—and in collaboration with others, both face to face and online. A computer game is learned by playing it. The typical computer game involves a range of cognitive activities: remembering, hypothesis testing, and strategic planning. Games involve written text, visual environments, and speech. Examples are given of videogames in health, education, medicine, and science.

Modern technologies are also used to study play, with data collected via the Internet, with mobile phones and video cameras. Global positioning systems allow researchers to study play in vivo, tracing children's outdoor movement over time. New forms of play objects and interactivity bring with them questions about our relationship with nature and with one another.

Keywords: smart toys, interactive toys, videogames, science and modern technology, Internet, learning, education, health, research methods.

Every month two hundred million people play games through their Microsoft computer operating systems, or on one of more than 150 million Sony PlayStation consoles, Nintendo Wii's, or Microsoft Xbox-es, or are downloading one of the more than 16,000 casual game apps for an iPhone (http://www.casualconnect.org/newscontent/112007/CasualGamesMarketReport2007_Summary.pdf). New technologies, those that include electronic and digital components, give rise to new forms of play, like *FarmVille*, a virtual farm that requires timely planting, harvesting, milking of cows, and fertilizing of fields. More than 66 million people play *FarmVille*, while there are only about 2 million actual farms in America. Smart phones with global positioning systems and accelerometers enable new forms of play, such as virtual golf in real settings. Digital and electronic forms of play snare a growing part of our leisure time. We live in a world of iPods, mobile telephones, portable wireless computers, and devices of every description, including toys that contain computer chips, memory, voice recognition, and interactive connectivity. User-generated content allows players not only to play, but to shape the games they play, and by so doing shape the effects that play has on them. In this chapter I define play, following Huizinga (1950), as a voluntary activity standing outside 'ordinary' life, being 'not serious' but at the same time absorbing the player intensely (see also Burghardt, this volume).

With this alteration of the division of leisure come changes in the way traditional play consequences come about. In this chapter I review selected studies of how technology has broadened the range of play possibilities and created new paths for the satisfaction of personal and social goals.

Learning to Play with Technology

Toys, games, and electronic media are merging into a seamless blend of entertainment, information, education, and play. Technological developments in the past 25 years have led to a radical shift in which familiarity with electronic and digital equipment is essential for success in both leisure and work (Marsh, 2002). In their everyday lives, children come across barcode scanners in supermarkets, mobile telephones, portable computers, cash dispensers, and parking lot ticket machines, all of which confront them with modern technology (electronic and digital objects). Electronic toys and digital games are the child's first hands-on introduction to this world, giving children an opportunity to learn about technology as well as with technology.

Chips with that? technology-enhanced toys

From music boxes, crying dolls, kaleidoscopes, and stereoscopes to electric trains, remote controlled vehicles, and robots, toys have always reflected the latest developments in science and technology. The idea of mixing play, technology, and learning is hardly new. In establishing the first kindergarten in 1837, Froebel used the technology of his time to develop a set of toys to help young children learn important concepts such as number, size, shape, and color (Resnick, 2006). According to Marsh (2002), toys have always inducted children into the practices and values of their society. It is not surprising that toy shops and catalogues are filled with plastic representations of the technological objects that clutter adult lives—laptops, mobile phones, and DVDs.

'Smart toys' contain embedded electronics that appear to have the capacity to adapt to the abilities or actions of the player. *Tamagotchi* (BanDai) was the first smart toy, appearing in 1996. The *Tamagotchi* was programmed to be nurtured by a child. The more it was fed and cared for, the stronger it became, and if neglected it eventually died. In 1997, *Furby* (Tiger Electronics) appeared, followed by other interactive toys including *Poo-Chi*, *Interactive Barney*, and *Me Barbie*. Today's smart toys may include speech recognition software, touch or motion sensors, and the ability to be networked together with other smart toys or a PC. Many traditional toys are found in multiple media and embodiments. Action Man, Batman, and Thomas the Train exist as toys, as interactive computer games, in illustrated books, and in animated videos.

Who plays and why?

Surveys and in-home studies of children's use of technology and play activities sketch a picture of moderate involvement with technology on a daily basis. A survey in Ireland described patterns of technology usage in children's play (Downey, Hayes & O'Neill, 2007). Children, aged 4 to 12, from ten primary schools throughout the country participated in the study. Data were also gathered from parents and teachers. Most of the children have a high degree of access to technology. Children preferred to play outdoors, but when the weather discouraged this, they played console or computer games, mostly against another person. Mobile phones are increasingly desirable as a child gets older. Most children said that their main use was to text friends or to play games. Console gaming increases with age. Games based on racing and sports were the most popular. Most children had seen or played *Grand Theft Auto San Andreas* (rated 18+). Some children also talked about their role in the household as someone who understands technology—teaching parents or carers on how to use a mobile phone or control a game console.

In contrast to play, *games* typically follow a priori rules and guide interactions with both peers and technology (see also Baines & Blatchford, this volume). The stereotype of the typical gamer as an inactive, overweight, socially isolated adolescent is false on all counts. Nearly every study finds that videogamers play in moderation, and typically engage in sports and other social activities, besides. Surveys report that adolescents spend from 3–4 hrs/day watching TV, and from 1–2 hrs/day playing videogames. The average age of videogamers is steadily rising and now approaches 30 years of age (http://www.theesa.com/facts/index.asp). In one nationwide American survey, boys age 8 to 18 played videogames an average of 16.4 hrs/week while girls played 9.2 hrs (Gentile, 2009). In another survey with children age 9 to 23, boys played videogames an average of 16.9 hours/wk, while females played an average of 6.3 hrs/wk (Sherry, et al., 2006). A survey of online gamers found that they play massively multiplayer online role-playing games (23%), first-person shooters (23%), strategy games (17%), and action-adventure games (15%) (Przybylski, et al., 2009).

Williams, Yee, and Caplan (2008) surveyed 7,000 players of *EverQuest 2*, a massively multiplayer online game (MMO), and collected in-game data on their behaviors. The researchers compared gamers to the general population in terms of physical and mental health. Among all players, the mean hours played per week was 26. Gamers were primarily adult (31.2 years old on average), male (80%), white, and middle class. EQ2 players are healthier than the general population. EQ2 players have an average BMI (body mass index) of 25, making them slightly overweight, but less so than the average American adult, who has a BMI of 28. Twenty-two percent of EQ2 players are technically obese, compared to 31% of American adults. On average, EQ2 players describe their health as slightly better than "good" and report engaging in vigorous exercise between one and two times a week. EQ2 players have a higher rate of physical impairments than the general population, 9.5% vs. 7.3%. EQ2 players have lower levels of mental health on two of three indicators. Twenty-three percent of EQ2 players reported having been diagnosed with depression. EQ2 players reported slightly lower levels of anxiety than the general population. It is possible that game play created these outcomes, but it is equally possible that people who are depressed are more likely to seek out MMOs. *EverQuest 2* players' media use data were compared with national data to explore what activities were displaced by game play. The most apparent difference lies in the number of hours spent watching television vs. playing online. EQ2 players spent 22 hours per week watching television, compared to 32 per week for the general population. It seems that game play takes time away predominantly from television viewing.

In general, videogames are used by children to make and maintain friends, to experience competition and competence, and to regulate emotional and physical states, something games share with all leisure activities (Wack & Tantleff-Dunn, 2009). Motivations for playing videogames vary with age and developmental stage. Younger players, age 9 to about 13, are motivated primarily by challenge, while older players find competition the most attractive reason to play (Sherry, Greenberg, Lucas & Lachlan, 2006; Williams, et al., 2008).

GENDER DIFFERENCES

An overview of research published in the last 20 years concluded that females are at a disadvantage relative to males when learning about computers or learning with the aid of computer-assisted software (Cooper, 2006). Cooper suggests that the digital divide is fundamentally a problem of computer anxiety whose roots lie deep in socialization patterns of boys and girls, combined with the stereotype that computers are for boys (Kelan, 2007).

Children as young as age eight months already display marked preferences for sex-typed toys. By 36 months, pronounced sex differences in toy preferences and play styles are reliably established. Sex differences in toy preferences have been observed in two nonhuman primate species, which is compelling evidence that sex differences in toy preferences can exist without the social pressures to engage in gender-typical behavior (Alexander & Hines, 2002). Alexander, Wilcox, and Woods (2009) examined interest in a doll and a toy truck in 30 infants ranging in age from three to eight months using eye-tracking technology that provides indicators of visual attention. Sex differences in visual interest in sex-linked toys were found, with girls showing a visual preference for the doll over the toy truck, while boys showed a greater number of visual fixations on the truck. The findings suggest that the conceptual categories of "masculine" and "feminine" toys are preceded by sex differences in the preferences for perceptual features (movement, color, shape) associated with such objects.

How do children use technology-enhanced toys?

Whether we are talking about traditional toys or hi-tech toys, children do not always play with toys in predictable ways. Although toys may come with programmed responses, we cannot assume that they will be used only in pre-scripted ways (Bergen, 2004; Kline, 2004; Stephen, McPake, Plowman, & Berch-Heyman, 2008; Marsh, 2002). When playing with smart toys, children do not discover their full functionality. They behave much like adults, who know how to use their computer to accomplish the tasks that they want, but who never discover its full capabilities.

Plowman and Luckin (2004) investigated children's use of smart toys. Two toy aardvark characters from stories and cartoon series familiar to most of the children were used in the study. The toys are 60 cm tall, have a vocabulary of about 4,000 words, motors to provide movement, and an electronic chip to recognize inputs. If a child squeezes a toy's hand or wristwatch, the toy will ask questions. If a child squeezes the toy's toe, it will suggest a game. Activities include estimating a time—5, 10, 15, or 20 seconds—by squeezing the toy's hand when the time is up and saying the alphabet backwards. (However, these latter convergent activities are more didactic than playful.) Children also can use the toys in conjunction with CD-ROMs that feature language and number games. Thirty-four children aged five to six participated in the home or in after-school clubs. There was considerable diversity in the extent to which children attributed human characteristics to the toys. Some knew batteries powered the toy, but younger children tended to think the toy had feelings and could think and talk by itself (see Turkle, 2005; Francis & Mishra, 2009.) Most children eventually switched off the toy's talking mode. Plowman and Luckin found no evidence that these toys have either a beneficial or detrimental influence on the children's ability to engage in child-led imaginative play.

Bergen (2004) observed boys and girls ages 3½ to 5 years while playing with 'talking' (computer-chip enhanced) and 'non-talking' *Rescue Heroes* figures (firemen, police officers). After an initial exploratory period, most of the children used the toys in generally similar ways. The children with technology-enhanced toys repeated some phrases and sounds that the toy made and initially activated the sound/talk mechanisms, but in their free play most of them used actions and language narratives similar to those of the children with the non-talking toys.

LEARNING TO PLAY VIDEOGAMES

Until around age two years, flat monitors do not hold much interest to a child, and the child's limited fine motor control make using computers and electronic play and game devices difficult. Preschoolers, age three to five, increasingly realize their ability to influence events on a flat screen, and use and pretend using cell phones and computers (Lauricella, Barr & Calvert, 2009). TV plug-in toys and videogame consoles, as well as portable game systems, are increasingly appealing to this age group. From ages 6 to 12 the full plethora of contemporary media becomes available. The child's ability to reason logically makes strategy games appealing at this age, and with growing communication and social skills comes heightened interest in multi-player games, cell phones, and social networking.

How does a child learn to play a videogame? Boys and girls who play videogames most often teach themselves to learn game strategies, while those who play less often tend to ask others for assistance (Blumberg & Sokol, 2004).

In an effort to study how intrinsically motivated tasks like playing videogames might relate to attention and performance, Blumberg (1998) investigated age differences in children's performance on a popular videogame (Sega's *Sonic the Hedgehog 2*). Forty-three girls and 61 boys aged 7–12 years played the videogame for 10 mins and then were questioned about the game features that they paid attention to, and about specific game strategies that they would recommend to a novice player. Younger children focused more on evaluative assessments, emphasizing whether they liked the game or not. Older children focused more on specific goals for the game, explaining what one must do to attain a high score; such a focus was correlated with better performance on the game.

Digital games seem to have the same basic functions as other media in serving adolescents' mood management, stimulation seeking, sociality, and self-presentation. The challenge and mastery that accompany play and games, involvement, and opportunities for social contact, both during and after play online and on the playground, are all powerful attractors (Colwell, 2007; Yee, 2006). The reasons play is initiated affect the outcomes of that play (Przybylski, et al. 2009; Wallenius, et al. 2009).

Learning Through Play with Technology

Playing with electronic toys and digital games complement but do not replace the valuable activities and materials of early childhood, such as sand, blocks, books and storytelling, art and crafts, board games, movement and dance, and dramatic play. Technology broadens the range of play possibilities but does not replace any. There are many technology-based products for young children, including toys, software, hand-held computers, dance mats, Websites, Wii's, smart phones, an assortment of playforms and platforms. Technology-assisted learning no longer means being stuck behind a computer.

Games do not have to be designed specifically for an educational purpose in order for learning to occur (Gee, 2003; Prensky, 2005; Shaffer, 2008). All videogames may promote learning, but not always the content-based learning supported in school systems (Martin & Murray, 2006).

Recently there has been a surge of computer-based products that claim to integrate play and learning, under the banner of 'edutainment.' But these edutainment products often miss the spirit of play. Often, education is seen as a bitter medicine that needs the sugar coating of entertainment to become palatable. "They provide entertainment as a reward if you are willing to suffer through a little education," writes Resnick (2006, p. 195). Much edutainment, indeed much formal education, sees the learner as passive. But the best way to learn is through active engagement with an activity.

Games and technology in the classroom

Computer games are engaging, deploying rich visual and spatial aesthetics that draw players into fantasy worlds that seem very real. Games are fast and responsive, and can be played against real people anywhere in the world, or against a computer. They handle huge amounts of content and can be instantly updated and customized by individual players. Computer games incorporate many learning principles by putting learners in the role of decision-maker, confronting them through ever harder challenges, and engaging the player in experimenting with different ways of learning and thinking. Well-produced simulation games encourage visualization, experimentation, and creativity in finding new ways to tackle the game. The combinations of video, audio, and text are useful in accommodating different learning styles, thereby promoting multi-modal literacy. Games enable engagement in activities otherwise too costly or too dangerous, difficult, or impractical to implement in the classroom. Simulation games can prepare learners for engagement with the outer world. This is active learning, as players experience the subject domain or situation in new ways, and prepare for future learning and problem solving in the domain or transfer learning to related domains. Gaming expertise is linked to executive functioning, self-monitoring, pattern recognition, problem solving, decision-making, qualitative thinking, and superior short-term and long-term memory. By looking at what and how children learn from their out-of-school activities with devices such as smart toys, computers, videogames, and mobile telephones, we may find ways to improve formal education (Gee, 2003; Hsi, 2007; Prensky, 2001, 2010; Shaffer, 2008). As all toys do, electronic toys and digital games keep children on task for a longer period of time, giving whatever benefits they may offer a greater probability of materializing (Owston, et al. 2009).

RESISTANCE TO GAMES IN SCHOOL

Schools have been slow to adopt computers and related technologies, often overlooking the educational potential of children's knowledge of popular culture and enthusiasm for games (see Baines & Blatchford, this volume). Objections to using electronic games and smart toys in the classroom are that they limit the child's imagination, and may lead to addiction, social isolation, and aggressive behavior. The evidence to support these positions is equivocal. Indeed, as documented in the chapter by Baines and Blatchford (this volume), children's games with their peers during the school recess period predict a number of positive social and academic outcomes.

Specific to technology, in a study in Irish primary schools, Downey, et al. (2007) found that both teachers and parents believed that technology was central to children's lives, though one teacher described it as 'a mixed blessing.' One concern was about children becoming lazy, mentally as well as physically. Teachers were especially aware of the issues surrounding the appropriateness of content that children consume or are exposed to. Teachers appeared to be more concerned than parents about the level of mobile phone ownership among the children at school. Like teachers (Tondeur, et al., 2008), students are not entirely enthusiastic about the use of games as educational tools in the classroom (Sheehy & Bucknall, 2008). They see technology as something that could make the learning process more efficient, but not transformative. Technology can enhance traditional educational media, for example, a broadcast educational television program must be viewed when transmitted and offers little or no opportunities for learners to control or interact with the linear structure. The same program on DVD or the Internet allows learners to exercise control over when and how the contents are viewed, stopping, replaying, or skipping sections as they choose. In this respect, using new media more closely resembles the act of reading a newspaper than of watching television or a film in the theater.

Selected studies of games and learning

Young people's everyday uses of computer games and the Internet involve a range of informal learning processes (see also Fisher, Hirsh-Pasek, Golinkoff, Singer, & Berk, this volume). Children learn to use these media largely through trial and error—through exploration, experimentation, and play; and collaboration with others, both in face-to-face and virtual forms. Electronic game playing is a 'multi-literate' activity: it often involves interpreting complex three-dimensional visual environments, reading both on-screen and off-screen texts (such as games magazines and websites) and processing auditory information. In computer games, success derives from the acquisition of skills and knowledge. Online chat and instant messaging require specific skills in language and interpersonal communication. Young people have to learn to 'read' subtle nuances, often on the basis of minimal cues. They have to learn the rules and etiquette of online communication, and to shift quickly between genres or language registers. Provided they are sensible about divulging personal information, chat rooms and social netowrking sites provide young people with a safe arena for rehearsing and exploring aspects of identity and personal relationships that may not be available elsewhere. Again, much of this learning is carried out without explicit teaching: it involves active exploration, 'learning by doing,' apprenticeship rather than direct instruction. Above all, it is profoundly social (Buckingham, 2008). From these premises, interaction with technology probably relates positively to learning and cognition.

Following are selected studies of toys, games, and learning.

COGNITION AND LANGUAGE

Parents and teachers believe that educational media are important to children's intellectual development (Rideout et al., 2003). According to research by the Consumer Electronics Association and the Toy Industry Association, three-quarters of consumers who purchase an electronic toy for an infant or child up to 15 years old do so for its educational value. There is little research on whether 'smart' toys and digital games increase children's cognitive or social skills, although some toys and games are designed with these goals in mind. Research has begun to ask how new play and games technologies might be used to support learning.

The cognitive processes involved in play are similar to those involved in all learning: motivation, meaning, repetition, self-regulation, and higher-order information processing. Young pre-readers or early readers, ages three to five, may benefit from electronic toys that provide spoken instructions and reading help. Book readers allow the child to touch a page or a word to hear letters, words, or entire stories read aloud. Computers, smart toys, and other new media have the potential to facilitate language development if parents mediate the experience, for example labeling objects, asking questions,

repeating dialogue, and describing the content (Weber, 2006; Lemish & Rice, 1985).

Play with traditional building blocks promotes language, cognitive schema, and impulse control (Christakis, Zimmerman, & Garrison, 2007). Does manipulating blocks on a computer screen, as in *Tetris*, promote the same abilities? Computerized blocks were devised by Itoh, Yamaguchi, Kitamura, & Kishino (2005), using a simple interface that requires no computer expertise. The shapes in the physical environment are matched by their representation in cyberspace, enabling users to interact with cyberspace via these physical objects. First, using a set of computerized blocks, children construct a shape with which they want to play in cyberspace. The computer automatically recognizes the constructed structure in real time, and then retrieves 3D virtual models closely matching the constructed structure (see Figure 24-1). Children then play the virtual model's multimedia contents. Children can play in cyberspace while manipulating the constructed object in their hands.

Educational theorists argue that gaming embodies a new kind of literacy, one that combines significant elements of traditional reading and writing with new literacies that pertain to accessing and evaluating information, constructing complex narratives, decision-making, and navigating rich multimedia environments (Gee, 2003; Owston, et al., 2009; Shaffer, 2008; Prensky, 2010). While some of these activities are more didactic than playful, as it is defined in the developmental literature, they do relate to positive school-related outcomes.

HI-TECH TOYS AND THE CHILD'S IMAGINATION

Many critics contend that children are no longer able to engage in authentic, spontaneous play, that the narratives, symbols, and scenarios of their pretend play have been taken over by the media, depriving children of the opportunity to develop their imagination and autonomy (e.g., Cordes and Miller, 2000; Levin and Rosenquest, 2001; Palmer, 2006). There is concern that technology will displace more desirable activities, like outdoor play, reading, or socializing with friends, and there is some support for this view (Kline, 2004; Valkenburg, 2001). Yet much research suggests that children are far from being passive recipients of media. In their play and games, children actively appropriate cultural commodities, making their own discriminations and judgments, while combining and reworking them in myriad ways. Contemporary children's culture depends not

Fig. 24.1 Computerized blocks. Reprinted with kind permission of Yuichi Itoh and Springer Science + Business Media.

on passive consumption, but on the energetic activity of the child (Goldstein, Buckingham and Brougére, 2004; Götz, et al., 2005).

Do children who play with electronic toys play less creatively or imaginatively than children who play with more traditional toys—blocks and dolls, paper and crayons—that do not involve electronics? Although there is insufficient research to provide a clear answer, the concerns do not seem to be justified (Bergen, 2004; Plowman & Lucvkin, 2004). In one experiment, 6–8 year-old children displayed the same reasoning skills and performed similarly (required the same number of moves for the solution) whether a task was in the form of a board game or a computer game (Ko, 2002), though level of imagination and creativity were not assessed directly.

Research on television and children's imaginative play finds that the content, but not the quantity, of fantasy is affected by program content (Valkenburg & van der Voort, 1995). Some technologies, rather than stunting imaginative thinking, could actually foster and support the development of creative thinking and creative expression. Contemporary play objects, by virtue of their electronic functions and affordances, invite exploration and discovery, learning activities *par excellence*. Children discover an object and its uses, learn the means by which to communicate this to others, share in and eventually create new meanings around the object (Goldstein,

Buckingham and Brougére, 2004; Grugeon, 2004). According to Resnick (2006, p. 192), "today's technology can open new opportunities for children to playfully explore, experiment, design, and invent."

Götz, Lemish, Aidman, and Moon (2005) conducted a multi-national study of the fantasy worlds of eight- to ten-year-old children in Germany, Israel, South Korea, and the U.S. Children built upon a wealth of information gathered from a wide range of sources, including their own personal experience and mediated sources, and freely interweave them to create rich fantasy backdrops for play. Some children stayed fairly close to the original media script in their fantasy play. Götz et al. write,

"This raises the question of whether such media texts inhibit children's imagination, so that there is less originality and more imitation in the fantasy. According to our study, this is the exception rather than the rule... Contrary to popular belief, children make sophisticated use of these mediated worlds. They mix and match settings and specific objects within them in ways that facilitate their own fantasy worlds and allow them to best experience their wishes in these worlds. They highlight and expand on those aspects of the original media worlds that are particularly attractive to them and adapt or erase those that hinder or are not relevant to the wished for experience. One might say they play the role of editor..."
(*Götz*, et al., 2005, pp. 197-199).

The findings suggest that the media are simply another resource that children use to create worlds of fantasy.

VIDEOGAMES AND LEARNING

This chapter does not review the controversies surrounding violent media content or addiction to videogames. For conflicting positions on the violent content issue see Anderson, Gentile, and Buckley (2007), Goldstein (2005), Grimes, Anderson, and Bergen (2008), and Kutner and Olson (2008). Differing positions on addiction to videogames and the Internet can be found in Gentile (2009) and Wood (2008).

Games create opportunities for situated learning by providing immersive and motivating contexts for players to engage in a wide variety of activities and to develop and practice the skills necessary to be successful in those activities (Gee, 2003). A number of attributes common to computer games are critical in fostering active engagement, motivation, and high levels of persistence in game play. Games have been used both to promote and to study learning (Blumberg & Sokol, 2004), memory (Shewokis, 1997), attention (Garris, et al. 2002), self-esteem (Lou, et al., 2001), motivation (Wong, 1996), cognitive processes (Kappas & Pecchinenda, 1999) and spatial abilities (Greene & Bavelier, 2006, 2007). Games have taught reading, vocabulary, and math to elementary school pupils (Rosas et al., 2003), and health care and safe sexual practices to adolescents (Lieberman, 2001). Multiplayer online games are valuable means to promote collaborative learning (Williamson & Facer, 2004). Designing games is also regarded as a form of digital literacy entailing new approaches to deal with information and representation.

The studies reviewed here, with both commercially available computer games and purpose-made 'serious games,' illustrate how games can teach academic skills to children and adults. The important questions are whether what is learned is transferred to non-play situations, and whether game-mediated learning is superior to other forms of learning (Okita, 2004). When games have a specific educational goal, we can speak of playful learning, a combination of free play and guided play (Fisher, Hirsh-Pasek, Golinkoff, Singer & Berk, this volume). The capacity model developed by Fisch (2000) to account for transfer of learning from television is applicable to other media, including videogames. Transfer is most likely when four conditions are met: The child must understand the content, must create an abstract mental representation of that content, must remember the content and see its relation to the new problem or setting, and must apply the remembered content to the new problem.

Results of game-based learning are not always consistent. In one study, kindergarten children performed better on language tests, but not on math (Din & Calao, 2001), while in another study with first and second grade pupils, significant results were obtained for math, but not for language (Rosas, et al., 2003).

Rosas, Nussbaum, Cumsille, Marianov, Correa, Flores, et al. (2003) developed computer games in which the incidental learning that occurred while playing the games matched the school curriculum in reading and math skills for first and second grade. Five computer games were written for a GameBoy-like device, each with educational components. For example, in one game, Hermes is the messenger of the Gods who must save his friends imprisoned inside the temples of the city. In each of the temples, an instruction is presented with two possible answers. If the player chooses the correct answer, a prisoner is released and, after completing all the exercises of a scene, the player may enter the next city. The game requires identification of initial phonemes and syllabic analysis of words. It requires addition and subtraction and identification of symbols $<$, $+$, $-$, and $>$. Pupils played for 30 hours over a period of three months. The results show significant differences in Math, but not in Reading Comprehension or Spelling. Teacher reports and classroom observations confirm an improvement in motivation to learn and a positive effect on 'classroom dynamics.'

Between 2000 and 2005 approximately 450,000 students graduated annually in the United States with an undergraduate degree in science, technology, engineering, or mathematics (Mayo, 2009). These numbers pale in comparison to the reach of a single computer videogame, such as *World of Warcraft*, a fantasy game with over 12 million subscribers. According to Mayo, videogames can yield a 7% to 40% positive learning increase over a lecture. Videogames allow the player control over navigation, which enhances learning. Game-based learning often requires the formation of hypotheses, experimentation, and discovery, the very bases of science. Furthermore, games invite more time spent on the (learning) task. Assessment of game-based learning allows one to track sequences of actions and communications and relate these to more complex skills and abilities. Game-based learning has the potential to deliver science and math education to millions of users simultaneously. Unlike other mass-media experiments in education (e.g., TV, Webinars), games are a highly interactive medium with many key attributes shared with sophisticated pedagogical approaches. Some games have been developed with the goal of teaching science, for example, *Food Force*, a game produced for the United Nations on the mechanics of food aid distribution, which had 4 million players in its first year [http://www.food-force.com]. Designed for ages 8 to 13, *Food Force* is designed to teach history, geography, social studies, and mathematics. Likewise, Dormann and Biddle (2006) created a role playing game based on *Neverwinter Nights*, to teach about climate change.

VIDEOGAMES AND PERCEPTION
Playing videogames promotes a variety of visual skills and abstract thinking (DeLisi & Wolford, 2002; Subrahmanyan & Greenfield, 1994). Research by Green and Bavelier can serve as a model of how laboratory research on videogames might be conducted. After observing consistent differences in visual attention skills between players of first person shooter games and nonplayers, Green and Bavelier (2003, 2006, 2007) then trained nonplayers to become proficient in the videogame before measuring their perceptual and cognitive competences. In one study (Green and Bavelier, 2003), 16 university students who had little or no experience in the previous six months with videogames trained either on the action videogame *Medal of Honor – Allied Assault*, or on *Tetris*, in which only one task is attended to at a time. Three visual tasks were measured (attention, spatial distribution, and temporal resolution) before and after the ten-day training period. Those who played the action videogame showed significant improvement on all three visual skills. The control group trained with *Tetris* showed no such improvement, thereby establishing the causal role between complex games and improved visual abilities.

Electronic games have been among the most successful means for reducing the typically reported sex differences in spatial abilities. Subrahmanyam and Greenfield (1994) found that practice with a video game improved the spatial scores of both fifth grade (10–12 yrs. old) boys and girls. Furthermore, the improvements transferred from video games to other spatial activities. Videogame practice was most effective for children who started out with relatively poor spatial skills.

Design for learning
While there is increasing research on the potential of gaming for learning, the benefits of game-making activities have only recently been examined. According to Kafai and Ching (1996) there is a need for educational researchers to find connections between formal education and the many other activities and contexts which inhabit the "real world" of children. Ten and 11-year-old children who are proficient videogamers were found to display high levels of competence when explaining games to others, displaying pattern recognition, decision making, qualitative thinking, and superior memory (Vandeventer & White, 2002). Kafai (2006) says that traditional thinking is in terms of designing instructional educational games. Far fewer people have sought to turn the tables by making games for learning instead of playing games for learning. Rather than embedding lessons directly in games, the focus is on providing students with opportunities to construct their own games.

Owston, Wideman, Ronda, and Brown (2009) examined computer game development as a pedagogical activity to motivate and engage elementary school students in curriculum-related literacy activities. Fourth grade students were assigned to either an experimental or control group. Both groups studied the same curriculum over a ten-week period, but the experimental group also developed computer games related to the unit using a game development shell (Education Games Central. http://egc.savie.ca/), which simplifies the construction of electronic versions of popular board games. To create a game, students must develop a set of questions and answers and enter them into online forms. Game developers have the option of specifying the feedback a player receives when a question is correctly or incorrectly answered. A step-by-step guide on the game creation page verifies whether all questions are entered correctly and if the game is ready to play. Two standardized literacy test batteries were administered prior to and following the ten-week period. A total of 285 games were developed during the study, containing more than 7,000 questions written by the students. On literacy tests, the experimental students performed significantly better on a measure of logical sentence construction. Qualitative data in the form of field notes and teacher interviews indicated that game development helped improve student content retention, ability to compare and contrast information presented, utilize more and different kinds of research materials including digital resources, editing skills, and develop an insight into questioning skills.

To conclude this section, I have illustrated how interacting with and making videogames can facilitate a variety of cognitive processes. It is important to recognize, however, that these technologies guide individuals in rather convergent ways to solve a variety of problems. Again, these processes are not "play" as typically defined, but more akin to "guided play" as defined by Fisher, Hirsh-Pasek, Golinkoff, Singer, and Berk (this volume).

Further Applications and Future Directions

As early as 1991, Kinder could write that video games

"have considerable educational and therapeutic value for a diverse range of groups—including adolescents, athletes, would be pilots, the elderly in old age homes, cancer patients undergoing chemotherapy, stroke victims, quadriplegics, and young children suffering from palsy, brain damage, and Down's syndrome" (p. 112).

Health

Play has long been used in child clinical psychology and pediatrics as a diagnostic tool and therapeutic treatment for physical and emotional trauma (Singer, 2004). Hi-tech forms of play and videogames are increasingly used with both children and adults in a growing variety of health care settings to impart information, promote adherence to exercise and medical regimens, and even for training physicians (Jannink, et al., 2008; Petersson & Brooks, 2006; Rosser, et al., 2007).

In randomized clinical trials, children and adolescents improved their self care and significantly reduced their use of emergency clinical services after playing health education and disease management videogames (Lieberman, 2001). In games for asthma self-management, diabetes self-management, and smoking prevention, players assume the role of a character who also has their chronic condition or is battling the effects of smoking and nicotine addiction. For example, the videogame *Rex Ronan* graphically portrays the physiological effects of smoking. Children who took these games home and used them for one week (smoking prevention) to six months (diabetes self care) increased their resolve not to smoke, markedly improved their ability to manage their asthma or diabetes, and significantly reduced their emergency care visits related to their illness.

Videogames and/or interactive multimedia tools can help to improve health-related behaviors in pediatric populations. In the first large-scale, randomized, intervention trial conducted with a population composed of adolescent and young adults with cancer, the intervention focused on treatment adherence, a pervasive problem in this age group (Kato, et al. 2008). The purpose of the study was to determine the effectiveness of a videogame intervention for improving adherence and other behavioral outcomes for adolescents and young adults with malignancies including acute leukemia, lymphoma, and soft-tissue sarcoma. The videogame *Re-Mission* was developed in consultation with patients and medical staff (http://www.re-mission.net/site/game/). See Figure 24-2. The game is described as

"An epic battle deep in the realms of the human body. Colonies of microscopic cancer cells replicate, attack, and damage healthy organs. Enter Roxxi, your gutsy and fully armed nanobot, and medicine's mightiest warrior. Lead her through challenging missions and her rapid-fire assaults on malignant cells, wherever they hide. It's the world's smallest battlefield, yet the stakes have never been higher."

A randomized trial with baseline and one- and three-month follow-up assessments was conducted at 34 medical centers in the United States, Canada, and Australia. A total of 375 male and female patients age 13–29 years old and currently undergoing treatment were randomly assigned to the intervention or control group. Outcome measures included adherence, self-efficacy, knowledge, control, stress, and quality of life. For 200 patients who were prescribed prophylactic antibiotics, adherence was tracked by electronic pill-monitoring devices. Adherence to 6-mercaptopurine was assessed through serum metabolite assays. Results show that adherence to medications was greater in the intervention group. Self-efficacy and knowledge also increased in the intervention group compared with the control group. The intervention did not affect self-report measures of stress, control, or quality of life. Kato, et al. concluded that the videogame intervention significantly improved treatment adherence and indicators of cancer-related self-efficacy and knowledge in adolescents and young adults. The findings support current efforts to develop effective videogame interventions for education and training in health care.

SPECIAL NEEDS POPULATIONS

Because games and programmable toys can be adapted easily to the user's specifications, videogames

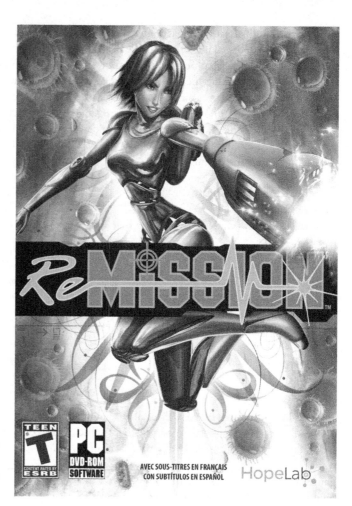

Fig. 24.2 *Re-Mission*, a game for young cancer patients.

Reprinted with kind permission of Pamela Kato and HopeLab.

and smart toys have been altered for a variety of populations with particular requirements or limitations. In one case, ride-on vehicles were outfitted with a global positioning system (GPS) to prevent collisions for children one to seven years old who are blind or partially sighted (Fabregat, Costa, & Romero, 2004). Robots have been developed that enable children with severe limitations to manipulate toys (Kronreif, et al., 2007). (See Figure 24-3).

Developed by NASA, video games can use biofeedback to train pilots to stay alert during long flights and calm during emergencies (Pope and Bogart 1996; Mason et al. 2004). Signals from sensors attached to the player's head and body are fed through a signal-processing unit to a videogame joystick. As the player's brainwaves come closer to an optimal, stress-free pattern, the joystick becomes easier to control. The technology is now commercially available for Sony PlayStation and Microsoft X-box to target symptoms arising from brain injuries, attention deficit hyperactivity disorder, and

learning disabilities. The system allows off-the-shelf video games (racing games are best) to be controlled through brain wave activity. The more focused and faster the brain is working, the faster the car accelerates, and the easier it is to play the game. Children with ADHD have been found to increase attention span through this device (Pope and Bogart, 1996). Video games can be controlled using many forms of biofeedback, including galvanic skin response (GSR), heart rate, and temperature (Parente & Parente, 2006).

VIDEOGAMES AND THE ELDERLY

For the elderly, the main cognitive abilities that change over time are perception, attention, memory, and executive functioning (Gamberini, et al., 2006). As with designing games for children, the cognitive and perceptual capabilities of users must be considered. Studies of the non-institutionalized elderly suggest that electronic games can speed reaction time, and may have cognitive, social, and emotional

Fig. 24.3 PlayBOT robot system to facilitate manipulation of toys.

Adapted from Kronreif et al. (2007). Reprinted with permssion of Gernot Kronreif.

benefits (Dustman, et al., 1992; Goldstein, Cajko, Oosterbroek, Michielsen, van Houten, & Salverda, 1997; Quandt, et al., 2009). Cognitive effects of video games have not been consistently obtained in studies of the elderly, although improved knowledge acquisition and retention among videogame-playing adults was reported by Ricci, Salas and Cannon-Bowers (1996).

COMPUTER GAMES IN THE WORKPLACE

Many companies prohibit their employees from playing computer games during working hours, based on the assumption that all work and no play is the most efficient use of company time. However, there is little research on how playing computer games might affect employee productivity, job satisfaction, or absenteeism. A variety of factors associated with play and games, including perceived control, reduced stress, and incubation, could result in more positive attitudes toward the workplace, increased job satisfaction, and heightened productivity (Beck & Wade, 2004). Bogers, Sijbrandij, Wiegers, and Goldstein (2003) conducted an experiment at a health insurance company in the Netherlands, in which some employees were permitted to play computer games during the workday. Employees were randomly assigned to an experimental condition in which computer games were permitted for up to one hour per day, for a period of

four weeks, or to a non-playing control group, in which no change in company policy against computer games was made. Before and after the gaming period began, employees took the Job-related Affective Well-being Scale and a 20-item scale of job involvement and productivity. Follow-up interviews were done with a sample of those in the experimental group to gain insight into their use of play during the course of the workday. Games led to a small but significant increase in positive attitudes toward work. There was no change in the control group. Games were seen by employees as a way to relax at one's desk, a way of alternating tasks, and as a reward for a successfully completed task. These effects are not unlike those observed for the effects of recess on children's attention to class work, which were explained in terms of distributed vs. massed practice (see Baines & Blatchford, this volume).

VIDEOGAMES IN SPACE

During ultra long space missions (e.g., to Mars), the isolated environment affects a number of physiological, psychological, and mental processes critical to human performance. Past experiences in space have shown that the mental health of a crew can have a great effect on the success or failure of a mission. Stress, interpersonal problems, and lack of capability to rescue crew members, isolation, monotony, and tedium of life aboard an autonomous shuttle develop slowly over time and are difficult to detect and remedy by observers on the ground. Computer games can be used to both assess and train astronauts in perceptual, cognitive, and social communication areas necessary for the smooth functioning of a multi-year space mission. Furthermore, the games are enjoyable in themselves and contribute to emotion regulation (Rauterberg, et al., 2008).

Using technology to study play and games

New technologies are quickly adopted as research tools in the study of play. We have already referred to the use of videogames and smart toys to study and develop perception, cognition, and motivation. Cell phones and inexpensive digital cameras, global positioning systems, robotics, and eye tracking technology have all been used to study children's play and toy preferences (Alexander, Wilcox & Woods, 2009; Mikkelsen and Christensen, 2009; Plowman, Stephen, & McPake, 2009; Kronreif, et al., 2007).

Handheld portable game devices have much to recommend them as psychological tests. The equipment is robust, inexpensive, small, light, and portable. Jones (1984) describes an American mountaineering expedition to the 7,700 meter high Tirich Mir, the highest peak in the Hindu Kush range. Two games were used to measure performance, *Simon Says* to measure short-term memory, and *Split Second* to measure pattern recognition and reaction time. The expedition placed four men on the summit of Tirich Mir. The games operated normally even at 7,000 meters under the extreme conditions of the climb (but the batteries had to be warmed by the climbers). Performance on the games did not degrade until a very high altitude. When it did deteriorate, it did so mainly on *Simon Says*. It took the climbers considerable effort to play this game on the mountain. The problem seems to have been more a matter of maintaining attention than of impaired short-term memory. This study demonstrates the possibility of testing performance under extreme conditions by means of electronic games.

Much research requires children to play on demand, thus violating the voluntary nature of play, rendering it something else. In laboratory experiments of videogames, for example, participants are required to play a game not of their choosing, at a fixed time and location, alone, and for a limited period of time, usually 10 to 20 minutes. The outcome of such experiments has little to do with play (Goldstein, 2005). Research by Allen (2004) and Bekker, Sturm & Barakova (in press) induce children to play by placing attractive and unfamiliar potential play objects in their environments and allowing the children to discover, explore, and play with them as they choose.

Future directions

Our improved understanding of human cognitive and physiological processes enhances possibilities for novel human/machine interfaces. Eye-movements, brain activity, and speech are far more natural ways to interact with a machine, as we would with another human. When this technology will be incorporated into toys and games is dependent on the development of reliable systems and sustainable costs. Similarly, as hardware improves, this permits developments in software, for example 3-D movies and virtual sports, like Nintendo's Wii. According to Allen (2004) perhaps the greatest impediment to the further growth of smart toys is the lack of development of artificial intelligence and speech recognition. Present artificial intelligence capabilities are too expensive to implement in a toy, but this will change as computational power and speed come down in price. Eventually this will result in cheaper

technology, enhanced functionality, and a richer play experience.

Future discoveries and new hybrids will add to the possibilities for play, games, and recreation. Traditional forms of play and toys are not likely to disappear, but they are being squeezed from all sides. Where people play and with whom is increasingly virtual and remote, and this trend is likely to continue. At the same time, new technologies free us from chairs and computer screens to allow mobile and active play, virtual and otherwise.

The first generation of digital natives, children who grew up with electronic toys and games, see computers as rational machines and people as emotional beings, a formulation destined to be challenged (Kahn, et al., 2009; Martin & Murray, 2006; Turkle, 2007). By the mid-1990s, computational creatures, such as robots and Tamagochi, were presented as 'relational artifacts'—beings with feelings and needs. One consequence of this development is a sense of uncertainty about what is authentic and what is alive (Turkle, 2007). Robotic animals were used by Francis and Mishra (2009) to study children's beliefs about what is real. Twenty-five children from three to eight years old played with three different toys with different levels of interactivity. They were then interviewed about what makes something real. Even though children said the toys were not real, they treated the more interactive toys as if the toys had real and intentional qualities. Developments in technology not only impact on the possibilities for play, health, and well-being, but confront children and adults with deeply profound philosophical questions about what it means to be alive.

Author's note

I am grateful to Lydia Plowman for comments on a previous version of this chapter.

References

Alexander, G. M. (2003). An evolutionary perspective of sex-typed toy preferences: Pink, blue, and the brain. *Archives of Sexual Behavior, 32*, 7–14.

Alexander, G. M. & Hines, M. (2002). Sex differences in response to children's toys in nonhuman primates. *Evolution & Human Behavior, 23*, 467–479.

Alexander, G. M., Wilcox, T., & Woods, R. (2009). Sex differences in infants' visual interest in toys. *Archives of Sexual Behavior, 38*(3), 427–433.

Allen, M. (2004). Tangible interfaces in smart toys. In J. Goldstein, D. Buckingham, & G. Brougére (Eds.). *Toys, games, and media*. (pp. 179–194). Mahwah, NJ: Lawrence Erlbaum Associates.

Beck, J. C. & Wade, M. (2004). *Got game: How the gamer generation is reshaping business forever.* Cambridge MA: Harvard Business School Press.

Bekker, T., Sturm, J., & Baralova, E. I. (2010). Design for social interaction through physical play in diverse contexts of use. *Personal & Ubiquitous Computing, 14,* 285–296.

Bergen, D. (2004). Preschool children's play with "talking" and "nontalking" Rescue Heroes: Effects of technology-enhanced figures on the types and themes of play. In J. Goldstein, D. Buckingham, & G. Brougére (Eds.), *Toys, games, and media.* (pp. 295–206). Mahwah, NJ: Lawrence Erlbaum Associates.

Blumberg, F. C. (1998). Developmental differences at play: Children's selective attention and performance in videogames. *Journal of Applied Developmental Psychology, 19*(4), 615–624.

Bogers, S., Sijbrandij, K., Wiegers, M., & Goldstein, J. (2003). *Computer games in the workplace.* Paper presented at Digital Games Research Association meeting. Utrecht, The Netherlands. http://www.gamesconference.org/2003/index.php?Abstracts/Bogers%2C+et+al.

Buckingham, D. (2008). *Beyond technology: Children's learning in the age of digital culture.* Cambridge: Polity.

Christakis, D. A., Zimmerman, F. J., & Garrison, M. (2007). Effect of block play on language acquisition and attention in toddlers a pilot randomized controlled trial. *Archives of Pediatric and Adolescent Medicine, 161*(10), 967–971.

Colwell, J. (2007). Needs met through computer game play among adolescents. *Personality and Individual Differences, 43,* 2072–2082.

Cooper, J. (2006). The digital divide: The special case of gender. *Journal of Computer Assisted Learning, 22,* 320–334.

Cordes, C. & Miller, E. (2000). *Fool's gold: A critical look at computers in childhood.* www.allianceforchildhood.net.

De Kort, Y. A. W., & Ijsselsteijn, W. A. (2006). Reality check: The role of realism in stress reduction using media technology. *CyberPsychology and Behavior, 9*(2), 230–233.

DeLisi, R. & Wolford, J. L. (2002). Improving children's mental rotation accuracy with computer game playing. *Journal of Genetic Psychology, 163,* 272–282.

Din, F. S. & Calao, J. (2001). The effects of playing educational videogames on kindergarten achievement. *Child Study Journal, 31,* 95–102.

Dormann, C. & Biddle, R. (2006). Humor in game-based learning. *Learning, Media and Technology, 31,* 411–424.

Downey, S., Hayes, N., & O'Neill, B. (2007). *Play and technology for children aged 4-12.* Centre for Social and Educational Research. Dublin Institute of Technology. Office of the Minister for Children.

Dustman, R. E., Emerson, R. Y., Steinhaus, L. A., Shearer, D. E., & Dustman, T. J. (1992). The effects of videogame playing on neuropsychological performance of elderly individuals. *Journal of Gerontology, 47,* 168–171.

Fabregat, M., Costa, M., & Romero, M. (2004). Adaptation of traditional toys and games to new technologies: New products generation. In J. Goldstein, D. Buckingham, & G. Brougére (Eds.). *Toys, games, and media.* (pp. 225–240). Mahwah, NJ: Lawrence Erlbaum Associates.

Fisch, S. (2000). A capacity model of children's comprehension of educational content on television. *Media Psychology, 2,* 63–92.

Francis, A. & Mishra, P. (2009). Is AIBO real? Understanding children's beliefs about and behavioral interactions with anthropomorphic toys. *Journal of Interactive Learning Research, 20*(4), 405–422.

Gamberini, L., et al. (2006). Cognition, technology and games for the elderly: An introduction to ELDERGAMES Project. *PsychNology Journal, 4*(3), 285–308.

Gee, J. P. (2003). *What video games have to teach us about learning and literacy.* New York: Palgrave Macmillan.

Gentile, D. A. (2009). Pathological video-game use among youth ages 8 to 18: A national study. *Psychological Science, 20,* 594–602.

Goldstein, J. (2005). Violent video games. In J. Raessens & J. Goldstein (Eds.), *Handbook of computer game studies.* (pp. 341–358) Cambridge, MA: MIT Press.

Goldstein, J., Buckingham, D., & Brougère, G. (2004). Introduction: Toys, games, and media. In J. Goldstein, D. Buckingham, & G. Brougére (Eds.). *Toys, games, and media.* (pp. 1–8). Mahwah, NJ: Lawrence Erlbaum Associates.

Goldstein, J., Cajko, L., Oosterbroek, M., Michielsen, M., van Houten, O., & Salverda, F. (1997). Videogames and the elderly. *Social Behavior and Personality, 25,* 345–352.

Götz, M., Lemish, D., Aidman, A., & Moon, H. (2005). *Media and the make-believe worlds of children. When Harry Potter meets Pokémon in Disneyland.* London: Lawrence Erlbaum Associates.

Green, C. S. & Bavelier, D. (2003). Action videogame modifies visual selective attention. *Nature, 423*(6939), 534–537.

Green, C.S. & Bavelier, D. (2006). Enumeration versus multiple object tracking: The case of action videogame players. *Cognition, 101*(1), 217–245.

Green, C.S. & Bavelier, D. (2007). Action-video-game experience alters the spatial resolution of vision. *Psychological Science, 18*(1), 88–94.

Grimes, T., Anderson, J. A., & Bergen, L. (2008). *Media violence and aggression: Science and ideology.* Los Angeles: Sage.

Hsi, S. (2007). Conceptualizing learning from the everyday activities of digital kids. *International Journal of Science Education, 29,* 1509–1529.

Huizinga, J. (1950). *Homo ludens.* Boston: Beacon Press.

Itoh, Y., Yamaguchi, T., Kitamura, Y., & Kishino, F. (2005). A computerized interactive toy: TSU.MI.KI. *Entertainment Computing, ICEC 2005,* pp. 507–510.

Jannink, M. J.A., van der Wilden, G. J., Navis, D.W., Visser, G., Gussinklo, J., & Ijzerman, M. (2008). A low-cost videogame applied for training of upper extremity function in children with cerebral palsy: A pilot study. *CyberPsychology and Behavior, 11,* 27–32.

Jones, M. B. (1984). Video games as psychological tests. *Simulation and Gaming, 15,* 131–157.

Kafai, Y. B. (2006). Playing and making games for learning: Instructionist and constructionist perspectives for game studies. *Games and Culture, 1,* 36–40.

Kafai, Y. B., & Ching, C. C. (1996). *Meaningful contexts for mathematical learning: the potential of game making activities.* Proceedings of the 1996 international conference on learning sciences. Evanston, Illinois. Pages: 164–171.

Kahn, P. H., Jr., Severson, R. L., &. Ruckert, J. H. (2009). The human relation with nature and technological nature. *Current Directions in Psychological Science, 18,* 37–42.

Kato, P. M., Cole, S. W., Bradlyn, A. S., & Pollock, B. H. (2008). A videogame improves behavioral outcomes in adolescents and young adults with cancer: A randomized trial. *Pediatrics, 122,* e305–e317.

Kelan, E. K. (2007). Tools and toys: Communicating gendered positions towards technology. *Information, Communication and Society, 10*(3), 358–383.

Kinder, M. (1991). *Playing with power.* Berkeley: University of California Press.

Kline, S. (2004). Learners, spectators, or gamers? An investigation of the impact of digital media in the media-saturated household. In J. Goldstein, et al., *Toys, games and media.* (pp. 131–156).

Ko, S. (2002). An empirical analysis of children's thinking and learning in a computer game context. *Educational Psychology, 22,* 219–233.

Kronreif, G., Kornfeld, M., Prazak, B., Mina, S., & Furst, M. (2007). Robot assistance in playful environment – User trials and results. Proceedings IEEE – International Conference on Robotics and Animation. article 4209529, pp. 2898–2903.

Lauricella, A. R., Barr, R. F., & Calvert, S. L. (2009). Emerging computer skills: Influences of young children's executive functioning abilities and parental scaffolding techniques in the U.S. *Journal of Children and Media, 3*(3), 217–233.

Levin, D. E. & Rosenquest, B. (2001). The increased role of electronic toys in the lives of infants and toddlers: Should we be concerned? *Contemporary Issues in Early Childhood, 2,* 242–247.

Lieberman, D.A. (2001). Management of chronic pediatric diseases with interactive health games: Theory and research findings. *Journal of Ambulatory Care Management, 24* (1), 26–38.

Marsh, J. (2002). Electronic toys: Why should we be concerned? A response to Levin and Rosenquest (2001). *Contemporary Issues in Early Childhood, 3* (1), 132–138.

Martin, C. & Murray, L. (2006). Digital games in the 21st Century. *Learning, Media and Technology, 31,* 323–327.

Mason, S. G., Bohringer, R., et al. (2004). Real-time control of a video game with a direct brain-computer interface. *Journal of Clinical Neurophysiology, 21,* 404–408.

Mayo, M. J. (2009). Videogames: A route to large-scale STEM education? *Science, 323,* 2 January, 79–82.

Mikkelsen, M. R. & Christensen, P. (2009). Is children's independent mobility really independent? A study of children's mobility combining ethnography and GPS/mobile phone technologies. *Mobilities, 4*(1), 37–58.

Myers, D. G. (2009). Using new interactive media to enhance the teaching of psychology (and other disciplines) in developing countries. *Perspectives on Psychological Science, 4*(1), 99–100.

Nardo, R. (2008). Music technology in the preschool? Absolutely! *General Music Today, 22,* 38–39.

Okita, S. (2004). Effects of age on associating virtual and embodied toys. *Cyberpsychology and Behavior, 7,* 464–471. http://www.liebertonline.com/doi/abs/10.1089/cpb.2004.7.464.

Owston, R., Wideman, H., Sinitskaya Ronda, N., & Brown, C. (2009). Computer game development as a literacy activity. *Computers and Education, 53,* 977–989.

Parente, A. & Parente, R. (2006). Mind-operated devices: Mental control of a computer using biofeedback. *CyberPsychology and Behavior, 9*(1), 1–4. http://www.liebertonline.com/doi/abs/10.1089/cpb.2006.9.1.

Petersson, E. & Brooks, A. (2006). Virtual and physical toys: Open-ended features for non-formal learning. *Cyberpsychology and Behavior, 9,* 196–199.

Pivic, M. & Pivic, P. (2008). *Games in schools.* http://games.eun.org.

Plowman, L. (2004). "Hey, hey, hey! It's time to play": Children's interactions with smart toys. In J. Goldstein, D. Buckingham, & G. Brougére (Eds.). *Toys, games, and media.* (pp. 207–223). Mahwah, NJ: Lawrence Erlbaum Associates.

Plowman, L. & Luckin, R. (2004). Interactivity, interface, and smart toys. *Computer. (IEEE).* February. pp. 98–100.

Plowman, L., Stephen, C., & McPake, J. (2010). *Growing up with technology: Young children learning in a digital world.* London: Routledge.

Pope, A.T., & Bogart, E.H. (1996). Extended attention span training system: Video game neurotherapy for attention deficit disorder. *Child Study Journal, 26* (1), 39–50.

Prensky, M. (2001). *Digital game-based learning.* New York: McGraw-Hill.

Prensky, M. (2010). *Teaching digital natives.* Corwin Press.

Przybylski, A. K., Weinstein, N., Ryan, R. M., & Rigby, C. S. (2009). Having to versus wanting to play: Background and consequences of harmonious versus obsessive engagement in video games. *Cyberpsychology and Behavior, 12,* 485–492.

Quandt, T., Grueninger, H., & Wimmer, J. (2009). The gray haired gaming generation: Findings from an explorative interview study on older computer gamers. *Games and Culture, 4*(1), 27–46.

Rauterberg, M., Neerincx, M., Tuyls, K., & van Loon, J. (2008). Entertainment computing in the orbit. In P. Ciancarini, et al. (Eds.), *International Federation for Information Processing, 279. New Frontiers for Entertainment Computing.* (pp. 59–70). Boston: Springer.

Resnick, M. (2006). Computer as paintbrush: Technology, play, and the creative society. In D.G. Singer, R. M. Golinkoff, & K. Hirsh-Pasek (Eds.). *Play = learning: How play motivates and enhances children's cognitive and social-emotional growth.* Oxford University Press.

Rideout V.J., Vandewater E.A., & Wartella E.A. (2003). *Zero to six: Electronic media in the lives of infants, toddlers, and preschoolers.* Menlo Park, CA: Kaiser Family Foundation.

Rosas, R., Nussbaum, M., Cumsille, P., et al. (2003). Beyond Nintendo: Design and assessment of educational videogames for first and second grade students. *Computers and Education, 40,* 71–94.

Rosser, J. C., et al. (2007). Impact of videogames on training surgeons in the 21st Century. *Archives of Surgery, 142,* 181–187.

Shaffer, D. W. (2008). *How computer games help children learn.* Palgrave Macmillan.

Sheehy, K. & Bucknall, S. (2008). How is technology seen in young people's visions of future educational systems? *Learning, Media and Technology, 33,* 101–114.

Sherry, J. L., Greenberg, B. S., Lucas, K., & Lachlan, K. (2006). Video game uses and gratifications as predictors of use and game preference. In P. Vorderer & J. Bryant (Eds.), *Playing video games: Motives, responses and consequences.* (pages 248–262). Lawrence Erlbaum Associates.

Singer, D. (2004). Play as healing. In J. Goldstein (Ed.), *Toys, play, and child development.* (pages 147–165). New York: Cambridge University Press.

Stephen, C., McPake, J., Plowman, L., & Berch-Heyman, S. (2008). Learning from the children: Exploring preschool children's encounters with ICT at home. *Journal of Early Childhood Research, 6,* 99–117.

Subrahmanyam, K. & Greenfield, P. M. (1994). Effect of video game practice on spatial skills in girls and boys. *Journal of Applied Developmental Psychology, 15,* 13–32.

Tondeur, J., Hermans, R., van Braak, J., & Valcke, M. (2008). Exploring the link between teachers' educational belief profiles and different types of computer use in the classroom. *Computers in Human Behavior, 24,* 2541–2553.

Turkle, S. (2007). Authenticity in the age of digital companions. *Interaction Studies: Social Behavior and Communication in Biological and Artificial Systems, 8,* 501–517.

Turkle, S. (2005). Computer games as evocative objects. In J. Raessens & J. Goldstein (Eds.), *Handbook of computer game studies.* Cambridge, MA: MIT Press. (pp. 267–282).

Valkenburg, P. M. & Peter, J. (2009). Social consequences of the internet for adolescents. *Current Directions in Psychological Science, 18,* 1–5.

Vandeventer, S. S. & White, J. A. (2002). Expert behavior in children's video game play. *Simulation & Gaming, 33,* 28–48.

Wack, E. & Tantleff-Dunn, S. (2009). Relationships between electronic game play, obesity, and psychosocial functioning in young men. *CyberPsychology and Behavior, 12,* 241–244.

Wallenius, M., Rimpelä, A., Punamäki, R-L., & Lintonen, T. (2009). Digital game playing motives among adolescents: Relations to parent–child communication, school performance, sleeping habits, and perceived health. *Journal of Applied Developmental Psychology, 30,* 463–474.

Weber, D. S. (2006). Media use by infants and toddlers: A potential for play. In D.G. Singer, R. M. Golinkoff, & K. Hirsh-Pasek (Eds.). *Play = learning: How play motivates and enhances children's cognitive and social-emotional growth.* Oxford University Press.

Williams, D., Yee, N., & Caplan, S. E. (2008). Who plays, how much, and why? Debunking the stereotypical gamer profile. *Journal of Computer-Mediated Communication, 13,* 993–1018.

Wood, Richard T. A. (2008). Problems with the concept of videogame "addiction": Some case study examples. *International Journal of Mental Health and Addiction, 6,* 169–178.

Yee, N. (2006). Motivations for play in online games. *CyberPsychology and Behavior, 9,* 772–775.

PART 6

Education

Playing Around in School: Implications for Learning and Educational Policy

Kelly Fisher, Kathy Hirsh-Pasek, Roberta M. Golinkoff,
Dorothy G. Singer, *and* Laura Berk

Abstract

A fundamental question has spawned fervent debates in classrooms and on Capitol Hill: *How* do we best educate children to be successful in a global, ever-changing world? Here we present the evidence that playful learning pedagogies not only promote important academic learning but also build the skills required for success in the 21st century. A brief review of current educational trends and their underlying philosophies is followed by the introduction to of the concept of "playful learning," a teaching approach that uses free-play and guided-play activities to promote academic, socio-emotional, and cognitive development. The chapter then reviews correlational, observational, and experimental literature on playing around in school and offers suggestions and future directions for research in the emerging playful learning domain.

Keywords: Play, playful learning, guided play, early childhood education, elementary, learning, informal learning, academic readiness, academic achievement

"If education is always to be conceived along the same antiquated lines of a mere transmission of knowledge, there is little to be hoped from it in the bettering of man's future."
—*Maria Montessori, The Absorbent Mind,* 1995 (p. 04)

In an era marked by globalization and advancing technology, 21st century children must do more than just learn facts. They must engage in the world around them, actively seeking new knowledge and solving problems. They must persevere in the face of complex challenges and must generate solutions by synthesizing, transforming, and applying information in novel ways. They must be able to communicate, collaborate, and lead effectively. In short, 21st century children must be creative, flexible thinkers and lifelong learners who can achieve significant change in the world (Bell-Rose & Desai,

2005; Fromberg, 2002; Hirsh-Pasek, Golinkoff, Berk, & Singer, 2009; Resnick, 2007). In this review we present the evidence that playful learning pedagogies promote key cognitive and social skills while continuing to build the academic content knowledge required for success in what has been deemed the "knowledge age" (Edersheim, 2007; Gardner, 1999).

The great divide: Academics versus play
A fundamental question has spawned fervent debates in classrooms and on Capitol Hill: *How* do

we best educate children to meet these goals (Brown, 2009; Jones, 2008; Pellegrini, 2009; Rothstein, 2008)? In the wake of recent education reform (NCLB, 2001), reports show that many prekindergarten and early elementary classrooms have replaced playful experiences with scripted curricula that directly link to state education standards and assessments (e.g., Miller & Almon, 2009; Pellegrini, 2005; Sunderman et al., 2004). Children in full-day kindergartens in Los Angeles and New York, for example, commonly spend three to four hours per day in literacy and math instruction and test preparation compared to 30 minutes or less in free play (Miller & Almon, 2009). This trend extends into elementary school, where instruction and test preparation have replaced art, music, physical education, and recess (Abril & Gault, 2006; Graber, Locke, Lambdin, & Solmon, 2008; Spohn, 2008; Resnick, 2003; Wright, 2002). Many have come to believe that play and academics are polar extremes that are fundamentally incompatible: educators feel that they must choose to teach or let children play (Kochuk & Ratnaya, 2007; Viadero, 2007).

Historical reviews reveal that this represents a much deeper ideological debate about *how* children learn (Glickman, 1984; Zigler, Singer & Bishop-Josef, 2004). Arising from the essentialist and behaviorist philosophies, some believe that there is a core set of basic skills that children must learn and a carefully planned, scripted pedagogy is the ideal teaching practice. In this 'direct instruction' perspective, teachers become agents of transmission, identifying and communicating need-to-know facts that define academic success. Learning is compartmentalized into domain-specific lessons (mathematics, reading, language) to ensure the appropriate knowledge is being conveyed. Worksheets, memorization, and assessments often characterize this approach—with little academic value associated with play, even in preschool. As a result, this approach commonly emphasizes short-term cognitive gains (Kagan & Lowenstein, 2004; Stetcher, 2002). Some have referred to this as the "empty vessel" approach where children, void of information, are to be filled with facts by supportive teachers.

Conversely, the whole-child perspective assumes children play an active role in the learning process. Arising from experimentalism and constructivist philosophies (See Goncu & Gakins, this volume), children's needs, interests, and immediate experiences define what is *meaningful* and *useful* to learn. For example, a child who plays with another peer's shape sorter will learn about shapes and the social

skills required for sharing. In this view, learning is not compartmentalized into separate domains; rather, cognitive, social, and motor learning are inextricably intertwined (Copple, Sigel, & Saunders, 1989; Froebel, 1897; Piaget, 1970). Furthermore, the learner is seen as an active explorer who—through interactions in the world—constructs knowledge, which continually evolves and adapts with new experiences (Bransford, Brown, & Cooking, 2000; Glickman, 1984; Hirsh-Pasek et al., 2009). Play, in particular, represents a predominant method for children to acquire information, practice skills, and engage in activities that expand their repertoire (Elkind, 2007). Here, the child defines learning processes and outcomes while teachers are seen as collaborative partners that enrich and support the learning process (Vygotsky, 1978).

Dispelling the debate: Academic learning through play

A wealth of research demonstrates that play and academic learning *are not* incompatible. From dress-up to board games, from stacking blocks to art activities, research suggests that children's free-play fosters mathematics, language, early literacy, and socioemotional skills for children from both low- and higher income environments (Campbell, Pungello, Miller-Johnson, Burchinal, & Ramey, 2001; Campbell & Ramey, 1995; Campbell, Ramey, Pungello, Sparling, & Miller-Johnson, 2002; Duncan et al., 2007; Gardner, 1995; Reynolds, Ou, & Topitzes, 2004; Schweinhart, 2004; Weikart, 1998; Zigler & Bishop-Josef, 2006). The literature on guided play is also compelling. An emerging area, the findings show that play can be gently scaffolded by a teacher/adult to promote curricular goals while still maintaining critical aspects of play (Berk, 2001; Berger, 2008; Hirsh-Pasek et al., 2009; Marcon, 2002; Schweinhart, 2004).

In this paper, we argue that playful learning offers a middle ground between the warring factions in early education (pre-K–3rd grade; Bodrova, 2008; Bogard & Takanishi, 2005). Using the best available data as our foundation, we show that children who are exposed to rich academic content through free and guided play acquire a cadre of cognitive and social skills beyond those taught via traditional, direct instruction practices (Hirsh-Pasek & Golinkoff, 2003; Ladd, Herald, & Kochel, 2006). Moreover, when we view play as a *learning process,* we gain a broader perspective on the key skill sets that young children must develop to be successful in school and in the 21st century (e.g., Bell-Rose

& Desai, 2006; Hirsh-Pasek, Golinkoff, Berk, & Singer, 2009).

Expounding on Playful Learning

Playful learning defined as both free play and guided play—is a whole-child educational approach that promotes academic, socio-emotional, and cognitive development (Hirsh-Pasek et al, 2009; Resnick, 2003; Singer, Hirsh-Pasek, & Golinkoff, 2006). Representing a broad array of activities, including object play, pretend and sociodramatic play, and rough-and-tumble play, free play has been notoriously difficult to define (see Burghardt, this volume for a review). Contemporary play researchers generally agree that play activities are fun, voluntary, flexible, involve active engagement, have no extrinsic goals, involve active engagement of the child, and often contain an element of make-believe (Johnson, Christie, & Yawkey, 1999; Pellegrini, 2009; Sutton-Smith, 2001).

Guided play, on the other hand, fosters academic knowledge through play activities. Guided play itself falls on a continuum. The extent to which the adult sets up the environment and participates in the play varies according to the adults' curricular goals and the child's developmental level and needs. The dimension along which guided play varies is degree of adult guidance. For example, consider research conducted by Neuman and Roskos (1992), who provisioned a preschool classroom with literacy-related materials but did not direct children in their use. Findings indicate that children's literacy play increases dramatically. In such guided play contexts, adults provide materials but children discover their affordances on their own. Eventually children will want to know how to read words and write letters to accomplish their play goals (such as making a sign for the cost of bananas during grocery store dramatic play). Teacher guidance will be essential for this purpose. Thus, the guided play involved in teaching these concepts and skills must naturally involve more input from the teacher. It occurs in playful contexts where children are actively engaged and involved in their literacy play while the adult is responsive to children's literacy queries and capitalizes on them to enrich children's knowledge. In Bellin and Singer's (2006) Magic Story Car work, adults lead children in playful activities to promote emergent literacy skills, such as phonological awareness, alphabet letters, print knowledge, and vocabulary. While the adult leads the activity, it is playful and engaging and offers many opportunities for child input. Children begin to play Magic Story Car

without adult guidance as they continue with the curriculum.

Thus, guided play has two aspects (Ashiabi, 2007; Blanc, Adrien, Roux, & Barthélémy, 2005; Christie, 2001; Fisher, 2009; Hirsh-Pasek et al., 2009; Moyles, 2001; Plowman & Stephen, 2005; Singer, Singer, Plaskon, & Schweder, 2003). First, adults enrich the environment with objects/toys that provide experiential learning opportunities infused with curricular content (Berger, 2008). In a Montessori classroom, for example, the well chosen play materials enable children to discover and practice basic principles of math and reading. Another example is the Neuman and Roskos literacy materials study described above. Second, in guided play teachers enhance children's exploration and learning by commenting on children's discoveries; by co-playing along with the children; through asking open-ended questions about what children are finding; or exploring the materials in ways that children might not have thought to do (Ash & Wells, 2007; Berk & Winsler, 1995; Callanan & Braswell, 2006; Callanan & Oakes, 1992; Copple, Sigel, & Saunders, 1979; Rogoff, 2003). For example, although the child initiates the action on a particular toy (e.g., a farm animal), the teacher may model ways to expand the child's repertoire (e.g., make sounds, talk to other animals, use it to 'pull' a wagon). The new dimensions might then be incorporated into the child's spontaneous play activities. Importantly, Nicolopoulou (2006) argues,

> "although this is a structured and teacher-facilitated activity, it is simultaneously child-centered...the child is able to participate according to his or her own individual interests, pace, inclination and developmental rhythms" (p. 129).

Teachers play a unique role in guided play experiences. They can sensitively guide learning, creating flexible, interest-driven experiences that encourage children's autonomy/control over the process. Teachers subtly intervene as play partners or curious onlookers asking questions/making suggestions to help children when they have difficulty. As a result, play *and* guided play may foster intrinsic motivation and learning in similar ways (e.g., Deci, 1992; Harter, 1992; Parker-Rees, 1997; Reiber, 1996; Renninger, 1990; Schiefele, 1991). However, guided play may transform into adult-directed experiences when teachers/parents intervene too much. Shmukler (1981) found that when adults make suggestions and then let free-play continue, children engaged in the most creative play; however, when adults become too imposing, children stopped play- ing altogether (see also Pellis & Pellis's work with animals, this volume; Bonawitz, Shafto, Gweon, Chang, Katz, & Schulz, 2009; Dodd, Rogers, & Wilson, 2001). This suggests that many factors will impinge on the definition of guided play. These include, among others, teachers' sensitivity to the line between child-centered learning activities and direct instruction. Teachers must continually evalu- ate and adapt their behaviors to foster learning yet not become overly intrusive (e.g., 'hovering' over children's play activities, interjecting too much). It also includes teacher's acceptance of variability in children's answers (rather than demanding one cor- rect response). Finally, there are individual differ- ences and possibly socioeconomic class differences in the nature of and opportunities of free play and guided play that can weigh on when adult presence is more or less obtrusive (e.g., Dansky, 1980 Feitelson & Ross, 1973; Rosen, 1974; Rubin, Maioni, & Horung, 1976).

How might playful learning work in the context of a classroom? A teacher may introduce a variety of shapes to promote the exploration and learning of shapes in preschool. After initial free play activities, the teacher might also encourage children to play "Dora the Explorer" and find shapes. Conceptual understanding is promoted when the teacher asks children to compare shapes in a 'show and tell' activity. Guided play is a synergistic learning process, in which learning continually oscillates between planned, teacher-enriched contexts and self-directed, emergent learning contexts over time (Fisher, 2009). Guided play is a concept that deserves serious consideration by educators.

Playful Learning: Presenting the Evidence
According to NAEYC (2006),

> "…play provides a context for children to practice newly acquired skills and also to function at the edge of their developing capacities, to take on new social roles, attempt novel or challenging tasks, and solve complex problems that they would not (or could not) otherwise do" (p.1).

With a focus on children in pre-k to third grade, in the following sections we explore how different play- ful experiences promote a cadre of knowledge and skills in math/science, literacy, social understanding, and self-regulation (Copple & Bredekamp, 2009). For the purpose of this review, we adopt the broad- est sense of guided play activities, including teacher- and computer-facilitated activities that maintain play-like qualities and child-directed characteristics as described in the previous section (Plowman & Stephen, 2005; Singer & Singer, 2005).

The Role of Play in Mathematics and Science

> Through the various stages of development, children at play begin to learn essential math skills such as counting, equality, addition and subtraction, estimation, planning, patterns, classification, volume and area, and measurement. Children's informal understanding provides a foundation on which formal mathematics can be built.
> *Shaklee et al., 2008 (p. 3).*

A plethora of research demonstrates that early math- ematical thinking undergoes substantial develop- ment during the preschool and primary years (see Clements & Sarama, 2007). Theorists suggest that the building blocks of mathematic knowledge arise from a variety of self-directed, exploratory play activities and become further developed through playful learning (Ginsburg, 2006). In particular, observational research shows that children spend substantial amounts of self-directed, free play expe- rience in exploring and practicing math concepts.

Free play: Math and science
A landmark experiment conducted by Ginsburg, Pappas, and Seo (2001) examined the frequency of mathematic-related activities in four- and five-year- old children's free play period in daycare. During this time, children engaged in a variety of activities, including symbolic and object play. Regardless of gender and ethnicity, over half of children's playtime was spent in some form of mathematic or science- related activity: 25% was spent examining patterns and shapes, 13% on magnitude comparisons, 12% on enumeration, 6% on dynamic change, 5% on spatial relations (e.g., height, width, location), and 2% on classifying objects. Sarama and Clements (2009) replicated these findings, concluding that free play is a rich experience for children to practice and expand their foundational math and spatial knowledge. In the scientific reasoning domain, a series of studies have shown that children use play to disentangle ambiguities they find in the world and to test their incipient hypotheses about how things work (see Bonawitz, Chang, Clark, & Lombrozo, 2008; Bonawitz, Fischer, & Schulz, 2008; Schulz & Bonawitz, 2007) When toddlers were given toys with ambiguous causal mechanisms, they immedi- ately engaged in exploratory play to determine how

the toys worked (e.g., touching, moving levers on the object).[1]

The frequency of math-related play has been linked to increases in mathematical knowledge and achievement (e.g. Ginsburg, Lee, & Boyd, 2008). Preschool children who participate in manipulative activities (e.g., block play, model building, carpentry) or play with art materials do better in spatial visualization, visual-motor coordination, and creative use of visual materials (e.g., Caldera, McDonald, Culp, Truglio, Alvarez, & Huston, 1999; Hirsch, 1996). A longitudinal study by Wolfgang, Stannard and Jones (2001) indicated that complexity of block play in preschool was significantly related to number of math courses taken, number of honors courses, mathematics grades achieved, and weighted mathematics points' scores in junior and senior high schools. Even when controlling for IQ and gender, the authors found that block play still accounted for significant portions of variability in math performance, suggesting that complex block play may be one mode in which children practice rudimentary math knowledge.

Guided play: Math and science

Research also shows that the integration of math-related materials into children's early free play environments promote math-relevant behaviors (e.g., Arnold, Fisher, Doctoroff, & Dobbs, 2002; Griffin & Case, 1996; Griffin, Whyte & Bull, 2008). For example, Cook (2000) found that when preschoolers' pretend play environments were enriched with artifacts emphasizing number symbols, children engaged in more talk and activity related to mathematical concepts. Such evidence suggests environmental enrichment with curricular content facilitates learning in a developmentally meaningful way.

Similarly, Ness and Farenga (2007) found that children use spatial and geometric thinking during spontaneous play activities. They explore shapes through drawing, manipulation of blocks, and even through language and explanation of their constructions. The authors suggest that math teachers use a guided play approach to introduce spatial and geometric problems into children's natural free play activities. Ness and Farenga outline thirteen space-geometry- architecture codes (e.g., such as symmetry, shapes, patterns, enumeration, etc.) to help teachers determine what types of problems children can perform during the given play activity. The teacher uses questions "…to determine what the child actually knows and where the child needs guidance" (p. 218).

Few have examined how teacher commentary on children's play directly influences *developing* math knowledge (Clements & Sarama, 2007; Fisher, 2009). Fisher and colleagues explored the impact of guided play and direct instruction on preschoolers' developing shape concepts (Fisher et al., 2009; Fisher et al., 2010). Children were randomly assigned to a guided play, direct instruction, or control condition. In the guided play condition, they were encouraged to discover the 'secret of the shapes.' Experimenters facilitated children's discovery of shape properties by prompting exploration of the shapes and asking leading questions (e.g., "How many sides are there?"). They were then asked to draw newly learned shapes. In the direct instruction condition, the experimenter verbally described the secret shape properties, pointed out the properties on the shapes, and practiced drawing the shapes while children watched. In the control condition, a story was read in place of the learning activity.

Results from a shape-sorting task revealed that guided play and direct instruction appear equal in learning outcomes for simple, familiar shapes (e.g., circles). However, children in the guided play condition showed significantly superior geometric knowledge for the novel, highly complex shape (pentagon) than the other conditions. For the complex shapes, the direct instruction and control conditions performed similarly. The findings suggest discovery through engagement and teacher commentary (dialogic inquiry) are key elements that foster shape learning in guided play. These two potential mechanisms may also help children hone in on the particular key learning elements of complex concepts beyond those of direct instruction. More research is needed to isolate these mechanisms and assess the generalization of these findings to other domains.

Technology is proliferating at an unprecedented rate and this too simulates the kind of guided play found in the Fisher et al. study. Although many of the claims that educational videos and games promote learning are largely unfounded (Kaiser Family Foundation, 2005) and considered inappropriate for children under the age of three (Roseberry et al., 2009), research has shown specific electronic manipulative activities may augment learning for older children. For example, Papert (1980) described a LOGO software program that allows users to type in commands on a computer keyboard that moved a robotic turtle in real life. The turtle has wheels, a dome shape, and a pen that can draw shapes when it moves. On the computer screen a child sees a "light turtle" and must think about how she wants the turtle to move. The child must then translate this to "turtle talk" and then type in the appropriate commands. Papert suggests such programs help children transfer knowledge from their own play experiences (i.e., body movement) to new contexts and situations while simultaneously learning geometric and spatial concepts.

Using the LOGO software, Clements and Sarama (1997) also show that children learn best when they direct action in both a physical and a virtual world. Activities in which children first move their bodies (for instance, walking around a shape on the floor) and then use commands to direct an onscreen turtle to make the same motions, improve mathematical understanding and problem-solving skills. This may be due to the fact that children have additional practice with the concepts (e.g., moving bodies, walking around, and then translating it to turtle commands). Others have shown mixed results in achievement of kindergarten and elementary students using physical manipulatives, virtual manipulatives, or a combination of the two (Reimer & Moyer, 2005; Sarama & Clements, 2009). Thus, the role of guided play in multiple domains is an area that demands further research.

Researchers are also examining the use of mathematics computers games in the classroom (Sarama & Clements, 2009). According to Bitter and Hatfield (1998), use of technology for mathematics enhances "mathematical thinking, student and teacher discourse, and higher-order thinking by providing the tools for exploration and discovery" (p. 39). In one such study, the inclusion of a software program called Skills Arena in a second grade classroom showed that children enjoyed playing the game and completed three times more math problems in a 19-day period compared to what they would have using traditional worksheets (Lee, Luchini, Michael, Norris, & Soloway, 2004). Electronic games harness some of the guided play elements, such as "built-in scaffolding" as students are presented with harder material as the games progress; however, little research has explored how these influence interest in the subject and how math knowledge fostered in games transfers to other math-related experiences (Rieber, 1996; Squire, 2006).

Today, a variety of U.S. and European educators are implementing math-related playful learning practices in classroom settings (Casey, 2008; Kamii & Kato, 2006; Kindergarten heute, 2003; Friedrich, 2003). Sarama and Clements (2009), for example, designed Building Blocks, an early childhood math

curriculum, that helped young children meet the new pre-K to grade 2 standards by weaving three types of math media—print, manipulatives, and computer programs—into many preschool daily activities, from building blocks to art and stories. Compared with age-mates randomly assigned to other preschool programs, low-income preschoolers experiencing Building Blocks showed substantially greater year-end gains in math concepts and skills, including counting, sequencing, arithmetic computation, and geometry (including shapes, spatial sense, measurement, and patterning) (Sarama & Clements, 2002).

Taken together, research suggests that when children engage in free play and guided play activities, they learn about core properties, spatial relations, and causal processes, priming early mathematical and scientific concepts (see Baroody, Lai, & Mix; 2006; Ginsburg, Cannon, Eisenband, & Pappas, 2005; Seo & Ginsburg, 2004). Parents, teachers, and older peers may scaffold learning in a variety of ways, including populating children's environments with math-related games and toys, labeling new concepts (e.g., shapes, counting), modeling novel ways of interacting with objects (e.g., different ways to play with a ball), fostering conceptual knowledge through exploratory talk (e.g., what makes this a triangle?), or through co-play. These newly learned skills might later be practiced and expanded while children play on their own or with peers. Such knowledge becomes the foundation on which more formal, higher-order knowledge is built (e.g., a rudimentary concept of weight facilitates learning weight systems). Additional experimental research with traditional checks for experimenter bias is necessary to provide direct links between specific elements of free and guided play activities and academic outcomes.

The Role of Play in Language and Literacy

Children naturally incorporate language into their play activities. In the toddler years, children explore and practice the fundamental components of their language system through private speech, word games, and complex language use during social play (e.g., Garvey, 1977; Hirsh-Pasek & Golinkoff, 1996; Hirsh-Pasek & Golinkoff, 2006; Roskos & Christie, 2000, 2001; Rowe, 1998; Zigler, Singer, & Bishop-Josef, 2004). During the elementary years, children engage in different forms of play compared to toddlers. Symbolic play becomes integrated into games with rules, such as competitive board games. Play also becomes more abstract, with an increasing focus on mental and language play. Eight to twelve-year-olds like to invent "riddles, puns, tongue twisters, insults, chants, rhymes, and secret codes that may involve playing with syntax and semantics of language" (Manning, 2006, p.23). Imaginative play, on the other hand, tends to become more private as children write poetry or short stories or engage in dramatic activities. A substantial body of research shows that play activities serve as contexts in which language and literacy skills advance to new heights.

Free play: Language and literacy

The evidence suggests that free play activities relate to the development of language and literacy. Dramatic play, in particular, consists mostly of enacted narratives that naturally require instructional discourse between play partners (Nicolopoulou et al., 2006; Pellegrini & Galda, 1990). Specifically, children must convey their thoughts to their play partners, synthesize their individual thoughts into a shared play context, and integrate these components into a coherent story (e.g., Cloran, 2005). To accomplish this task, play partners often describe *how* to act out a story through instructive dialog or 'metacommunications' (Fein, 1975). For example, a four-year-old who wants to play 'fairy princess' must communicate this idea to her partner, negotiate roles, and describe how props may be used for the setting (e.g., the cardboard box will be the castle, the stuffed teddy bear will be the prince). The children must then synthesize their ideas into a logical storyline that can then be acted out.

Several observational studies focused on the roots of instructional discourse in symbolic play (Cloran, 2005; Lloyd & Goodwin, 1993; Tykkyläinen & Laakso, 2009). Sachs (1987) examined speech during a pretend play session among 46 same-sex dyads, ranging from 21–61 months of age, in a room containing doctor theme toys as well as nondescript toys (e.g., fabric, hats, Styrofoam, and dolls). Children engaged in a variety of communicative styles with one another, including directive statements (e.g., "Use this for a sling"), information requests (e.g., "Are you using that toy? Are you sick?"), and attentional requests (e.g., "Lookit.").

Theorists suggest that this form of dialogue plays a key role in developing language and literacy skills (e.g., Bruner, 1983; Dickinson, Cote, & Smith, 1993; Pellegrini & Galda, 1990). Children may be better prepared to recognize vital aspects that underlie narratives when they have engaged in activities that parallel these components, such as the identification

and implementation of roles, communication styles to enhance roles, and the use of props and contextual descriptions to foster a story-related reality; however, very little research has explored the relationship between components of make-believe play and later reading and communicative activities.

Correlational research typically examines the relationship between the frequency of specific forms of literacy-related play activities and school readiness. (Roskos & Christie, 2001; Pellegrini et al., 1991; Pellegrini & Galda, 1993). Bergen and Mauer (2000), for example, found a higher rate of literacy-related play at age four (e.g., rhyming games and pretend reading to stuffed animals) predicted language and reading readiness in kindergarten. Kindergartners with increased rhyming and phonological awareness relative to their peers also had more diverse vocabularies, used more complex sentences, and showed the extent of their competencies most often in playful environments. Additionally, Dickinson and Moreton (1991) noted that the amount of time three-year-olds spent talking with peers while pretending was positively associated with the size of their vocabularies two years later after they had begun kindergarten.

Guided play: Literacy development

Intervention studies have examined how embedding literacy materials within play settings enhances children's engagement in literacy activities during free play (Christie & Enz, 1992; Christi & Roskos, 2006; Einarsdottir, 2000; Roskos & Christie, 2004; Saracho & Spodek, 2006). Neuman and Roskos (1992) for example, explored how the incorporation of literacy props in three- to five-year-old children's free play environments increased literacy-related activities compared to a control group. At the intervention site, three theme-based play areas (e.g., housekeeping, reading, and manipulatives) were enriched with literacy objects. Children in the intervention group showed significantly higher rates of handling and reading of literacy materials as well as writing compared to their baseline (e.g., touching materials, using materials during play activities, pretend writing). Further, they engaged in longer and more complex literacy-related activities than those in the control group.

Others have focused on how a variety of play activities influence emergent literacy skills, including story-telling, story-acting, and journal writing (Nicolopoulou, 2005). In one such study, Nicolopoulou et al. (2006) reported that Head Start preschool children who engaged in story-telling and dramatization of their stories created longer, more complex storylines and more often used the third person in their narratives over time. Children were also encouraged to "write" stories in journals so they could experience the process of converting those stories to written form. Since children have not mastered writing at this age, stories were depicted in drawings. Over the course of the intervention, children's stories became more complex. The authors also noted that interest and enthusiasm grew over time. Thus, playful learning activities build emergent literacy competencies over time.

Pellegrini and Galda (1982) examined whether different types of play enhance story comprehension and recall in K–2nd grade children. Children were read the same book and placed in one of three experimental conditions: (1) thematic-fantasy play, in which they acted out the story they had just heard; (2) discussion, in which they talked about the story; and (3) drawing, in which they drew pictures of the story. The three groups were then compared on their performance on both a story comprehension and a story recall task. Results indicated that children in the thematic-fantasy condition fared better on both tasks than children in the discussion and drawing conditions. In the thematic-fantasy condition, children who played roles calling for more active participation in the story re-enactment scored better on recall than children with less active roles, indicating that the more verbal exertion the child must put into a dramatic fantasy, the better he or she is able to retell the story. Others experimental studies found thematic-fantasy play, compared to other less active play activities (e.g., puppet thematic play, coloring), promote more complex narratives (Ilgaz & Aksu-Koç, 2005) and increased language recall (Marbach & Yawkey, 1980).

These findings lend credence to the belief that play and literacy development are inextricably intertwined. First, children's surrounding environment provides a wealth of props/materials that are naturally guide imaginative activities toward specific themes and learning outcomes (Christi & Roskos, 2006). Second, symbolic play and literacy appear to share similar mental processes (Nicolopoulou et al., 2006; Neuman & Roskos, 1992). Symbolic play, defined as make-believe play and storytelling, draw upon children's representational skills, in which "play... [is] story in action, just as storytelling is play put into narrative form" (Paley, 1990, p. 4).

A key question that arises from the literature is how parent and teacher training in guided play may influence academic outcomes. Singer and colleagues conducted a series of studies on the effectiveness of

Learning through Play, an intervention program designed to teach parents and educators how to engage in learning-oriented, imaginative play games with children (Singer, Plaskon, & Schweder, 2003). In the initial evaluation of the program, kindergarten children of low-SES parents who participated in the intervention showed significant gains on an academic readiness assessment than those whose parents did not participate. Modest improvements were found in subcomponents of the test, including vocabulary, knowledge about nature, general information knowledge, and knowledge about manners. Subsequent studies examined the impact of training educators, parents, and children in guided, imaginary play and found significant gains in academic measures, spontaneous imaginativeness, pro-social skills, task persistence, and positive emotions (Bellin & Singer, 2006).

Another area of research asked how adult interaction and instruction influences literacy-related free play in preschool and early elementary school (Baumer, Ferholt, & Lecusay, 2005; Christie & Enz, 1992; Christie, Enz, & Vukelich, 1997; Farran, Aydogan, Kang, & Lipsey, 2006; Kontos, 1999; Saracho, 2004). How do guiding or co-playing teaching approaches positively influence the quality and longevity of dramatic play activities compared to more uninvolved or overly controlling teaching styles (Enz & Christie, 1997; Neuman & Roskos, 1992)? Some query how teachers' modeling behaviors and intermittent guidance influence literacy-related play. For example, Morrow and Rand (1991) randomly assigned children to one of four conditions: adult-guided free play with paper, pencils, and books, adult-guided free play with thematic materials (e.g., veterinarian's office with pet-related books, signs, etc), free play with thematic materials without adult guidance, and traditional curriculum play centers. In the guided play activities, adults made suggestions on how the materials may be used during play. Results revealed children in the guided play conditions showed stronger gains in the use of literacy-related materials during play (e.g., using literacy materials as play props, engaging in 'pretend reading and writing') than those without guidance. Importantly, the physical materials in the environments influenced what types of literacy-related behaviors the children engaged in. Those given access to papers and pencils were more likely to simulate writing while those in the thematic conditions engaged in more pretend reading activities. Thus, adults who create optimal playful learning opportunities (free-enriched play & adult guidance) may foster specific literacy skills associated with curricular goals.

These studies provide an initial glimpse into how playful learning pedagogies can be integrated to support literacy, yet there is additional work to be done. Research must isolate the causal mechanisms underlying the impact of each of these practices on reading development. Teachers in these studies used *a combination* of pedagogical techniques, materials, and motivational approaches to foster learning. What are the optimal combinations for literacy development (e.g., number of literacy learning activities, length of time per activity, time devoted to free vs. guided play)?

Free play: Social and self-regulatory skills

Social competence and self-regulatory skills are also critical for optimal functioning in learning environments and are predictive of later school success. Through play, children recreate roles and situations that reflect their sociocultural world, where they learn how to subordinate desires to social rules, cooperate with others willingly, and engage in socially appropriate behavior (Berk, Mann, & Ogan, 2006; Hirsh-Pasek et al., 2009; Krafft & Berk, 1998; Saltz, Dixon, & Johnson, 1977; Udwin, 1983; Vygotsky, 1978). Over time, these competencies are transferred to children's everyday behaviors, which foster a positive social environment that is conducive to learning and lifelong success (Brown, Donelan-McCall, & Dunn, 1996; Hirsh-Pasek et al., 2009; Vygotsky, 1986).

Theorists suggest that social play is a key factor in developing a sense of self-awareness and theory-of-mind (Ashiabi, 2007; Flavell, 1999; Lillard, 1993). Through play activities (sociodramatic play, rule-based games, imaginative play), children become aware that they have desires and intentions that may not match those of others. For example, a boy who wants to play with blocks tries to take them from a girl who reacts by crying, yelling, and pushing the boy away. Startled, the boy forms a rudimentary notion that children have different goals and desires.

Pretend play is a conduit for theory-of-mind development in several distinct ways. First, discussing feelings and emotions during play activities with peers may prime children's perspective-taking ability, which, in turn, may promote positive-peer relations (Brown, Donelan-McCall, & Dunn, 1996; Hughes & Dunn, 1998). Fabes, Eisenberg, Hanish, and Spinrad (2001), for example, found that the more preschoolers refer to feelings when interacting with playmates, the better liked they are by their peers. Second, talking about mental-states (e.g., beliefs, desires, etc) during pretend play may also advance children's theory-of-mind understanding (Rosnay & Hughes, 2006). Thus, pretend play encourages these skills as well as may indirectly promote theory-of-mind development, as it fosters both language and self-regulation, which in turn, is important in understanding another's perspective while suppressing their own (Sabbagh, Xu, Carlson, Moses, & Lee, 2006; Milligan, Astington, & Dack, 2007; Whitebread, Coltman, Jameson, & Lander, 2009). Examining children's behavior in groups, a study by Schwebel, Rosen and Singer (1999) found evidence that children's understanding of reality and fantasy and theory of mind were related to how much they engaged in spontaneous imaginative play.

Additional findings are consistent with the notion that make-believe play enhances effective management of emotion. For example, high levels of sociodramatic play and conflict resolution themes in play narratives in preschool are positively related to children's effective emotional self-regulation (Fantuzzo, Sekino, & Cohen, 2004; Lemche, Lennertz, Orthmann, Ari, Grote, Hafker, et al., 2003). During sociodramatic play, preschoolers engage in rich emotion talk with age-mates. Through these experiences, make-believe contributes to emotional understanding, which assists children greatly with positive peer relations. (Smith, 2002). As early as three to five years, knowledge about emotions is related to friendly, considerate behavior, willingness to make amends after harming another, and constructive responses to disputes with age-mates (Brown, & Dunn, 1996; Dunn, Brown, & Macquire, 1995; Garner & Estep, 2001).

Siblings appear to play a crucial role in the relationship between pretend play and perspective-taking (Volling, Youngblade, & Belsky, 1997; Youngblade & Dunn, 1995). Volling, Youngblade and Dunn (1995), for example, compared children's pretend play with peers to parents. They found that children's play at 33 months was significantly related to their developing understanding of false-beliefs seven months later. Thus, play with siblings has a more powerful impact on understanding of others' emotions and beliefs.

As children develop social relationships, they encounter conflicting desires and must discover strategies that solve those conflicts in an effort to sustain playful relationships. A variety of social skills develop from these interactions, including perspective taking to predict potential problems, turn-taking, self-restraint, negotiation, cooperation, problem-solving, and even respecting others desires/roles (Smith, 2003; Thompson, Easterbrooks, & Padilla-Walker, 2003; VanderVen, 2008). Children who fail to develop these skills are more likely to exhibit behavioral misconduct in school. Indeed, several studies have demonstrated that toddlers and pre-schoolers who had prosocial attitudes and behaviors during play activities were more likely to make new friends, be accepted by their peers, and form secure relationships with their teachers, which was predictive of later achievement (Birch & Ladd, 1997; Ladd, Birch, & Buhs, 1999; Ladd, Kochenderfer, & Coleman, 1997).

An emerging literature also indicates that play contributes vitally to children's self-regulation—advancing mastery over their own thinking, emotions, and behavior (see Berk, Mann, & Ogan, 2006, for a recent review). Vygotsky's (1978) view of make-believe play as a paramount early childhood context for development of self-regulation has served as the springboard for this line of research. The creation of imaginary situations in play, Vygotsky explained, helps young children use symbols—most importantly, language, but also gestures and other symbols—to overcome impulse and manage their own behavior. In addition, drawing on experiences in their families and communities, children continuously devise and follow social rules in pretense, striving to bring their behavior in line with social expectations and to act in socially desirable ways.

Free-play observations in classrooms support the contribution of make-believe to self-regulating language and to social skills. In one study of three- to five-year-olds in two preschools, among children's free-play pursuits, fantasy play emerged as the strongest correlate of children's use of private speech, including self-directed verbalizations aimed at both working out pretend characters' actions and guiding behavior during non-pretend tasks, such as solving puzzles (Krafft & Berk, 1998). Furthermore, these two types of private speech were positively correlated, suggesting that self-regulating language, richly stimulated by make-believe, might facilitate children's use of self-guiding speech when faced with real-world challenges.

Complex sociodramatic play in the block and housekeeping areas positively predicted school-year gains in three- and four-year-olds' self-regulation during classroom clean-up periods (the extent to which they independently picked up materials)—a commonly used measure of socially responsible

behavior (Elias & Berk, 2002). The self-regulatory benefits of sociodramatic play were greatest for least well-regulated preschoolers—those rated high in impulsivity on a parent report measure of temperament. Measured as early as three to five years of age, other research shows cognitive control predicts reading and math achievement from kindergarten through high school (Blair & Razza, 2007; Duncan, Dowsett, Claessens, Magnuson, Huston, Klebanov, et al., 2007; Gathercole, Tiffany, Briscoe, & Thorn, 2005). Thus, the self-regulatory gains that accrue from make-believe likely contribute to its academic benefits.

Guided play: Social and self-regulatory skills

What role do adults take in playful social learning? Ashiabi (2007) examined the role of teacher interaction in sociodramatic play and developing social skills. Findings suggest successful preschool practices for promoting social learning through play embrace a combination of free- and guided-play. Sociodramatic play in the classroom requires a range of teacher observation of play, encouragement/support of appropriate social skills, and mediation of conflicts to guide these developing skills. Others have found a higher frequency of adult-initiated play activities with preschool children was associated with higher levels of prosocial behavior, lower levels of nonsocial behavior, and, among boys, greater peer acceptance in preschool (Ladd & Hart, 1992).

A recent intervention study examined the effect of socio-emotional skills training on social and academic outcomes. The Emotional Literacy in the Classroom (ELC) program (Brackett, Rivers & Salovey, in press) teaches children (grades 5th – 6th) to recognize, understand, label, and regulate emotions and to express their emotions using diverse playful self-directed *and* guided learning activities (e.g., self-reflection, critical analysis of academic material and current events, interactions with family members, divergent thinking tasks, and creative writing). Children were randomly assigned to the ELC program or a control group. During the program, children engage in directed role-play that involves a particular emotion.

Results showed that students in classrooms in which ELC was implemented for a period of seven months had higher end-of-year grades and higher ratings in some areas of social and emotional competence compared to the control group.

Specifically, their grades in writing, reading, social studies, listening, and work habits/social development were significantly higher than were the control group. The ELC group also had fewer school problems, such as those related to learning and paying attention, and had more adaptability, including showing more skills related to social relationships, leadership, and studying.

Harris (2000) demonstrated how six-year-old children can regulate their emotions after hearing a story under varied instructions. He divided the children into three groups. One group was given instructions likely to increase emotional absorption: They were asked to become involved with the story, and to feel sad along with the main character. Another group was given instructions likely to diminish absorption: They were asked to remain detached, to listen to the story in such a way "that you won't become sad yourself." Finally, a third, control group, was given no instructions, except "to listen carefully" to the story. Results indicated that the children were differentially influenced by these instructions. Those asked to involve themselves more reported a sadder mood afterwards. They also emphasized more sadness details in their subsequent report of the story and did not do as well as the other groups on a standard memory test. In effect, the children in the absorption group imagined the situation as actually happening to themselves while those with detachment instructions were capable of inhibiting emotional identification. Children's ability to control their emotional state is impressive.

Importantly, it is difficult to ascertain whether the observed outcomes in play training studies are due to adult tuition or to increased frequencies of play activities (e.g., Christie & Johnsen, 1983). Some evidence suggests play and adult tutoring result in similar cognitive gains (e.g., Pellegrini, 1984) while others have found adult tuition is more beneficial for young children (Dansky, 1980) and those from disadvantaged backgrounds (e.g., Saltz, Dixon, & Johnson, 1977). Additional research is necessary to tease apart the differential impact of these two constructs.

To learn in a formal school environment, children must be able to regulate their behaviors and emotions and communicate and engage with others in socially appropriate ways (e.g., Blair & Razza, 2007; Duncan et al., 2007; Gathercole et al., 2005). The current research clearly highlights a relationship between playful learning experiences, social and self-regulatory skills, and academic achievement.

Future experimental research is necessary to explore the *mechanisms* that underlie these relations.

The Big Picture: Research Comparing Pedagogies

Real measures of learning come not only from immediate mastery of information but also from long term retention and transfer. Specifically, comparative education program research shows that playful learning programs promote academic knowledge and cognitive and socio-emotional competencies beyond those attained in traditional, academically focused programs. The majority of the research reviewed in this section uses random assignment designs and compares child-centered, playful learning preschool and kindergarten models to traditional, academically regimented programs.

Montessori schools are characteristically known for creating classrooms in which children choose from a number of playful, hands-on activities that have been prearranged by adults. Importantly, there may be substantial variations in how instructors interpret and implement the philosophical tenets of the program; some are more play-oriented while others are less so (e.g., inclusion of free-play, fantasy-play, or lessons during the day; Daoust, 2004). In the optimal Montessori approach, teachers use a variety of free play and guided play techniques to promote holistic development. In particular, teaching materials are specially designed to promote exploration and discovery, long time periods are given for individual and small-group learning in child-chosen activities, and educators place equal emphasis on academic and social development. Importantly, the children might not even know that there was a learning goal in mind.

Lillard and Else-Quest (2006) examined the differential impact of a Montessori and state-funded education programs on children's social development and academic achievement. Montessori kindergarten children were significantly more likely (43% versus 18% of responses) to use a higher level of reasoning by referring to justice or fairness to convince another child to relinquish an object. Playground observations indicated that Montessori children were significantly more likely to be involved in positive shared peer play and significantly less likely to be involved in rough play that was ambiguous in intent, such as wrestling where there was no evidence of positive emotion. By the end of kindergarten, the Montessori children performed better on standardized tests of reading and math, engaged in more positive interaction on the playground, and showed more advanced social cognition and executive control.

Similarly, Marcon (1993; 1999; 2002) demonstrated that children who were exposed to playful, child-centered preschool environments at age four showed enhanced academic performance in mathematics, reading, language, spelling, handwriting, and science compared to children who experienced more direct instruction. Other researchers documented similar gains in academic knowledge *and* social skills in play-based learners over traditional instruction learners (Burts et al., 1990; Burts et al., 1992; Hirsh-Pasek et al., 1991). A key question that remains is whether certain components of the education experience (e.g., the materials, or the opportunities for collaborative work) are associated with particular outcomes. Montessori and other guided play education systems have a fundamentally different structure from traditional education. Experimental research is necessary to identify what mechanisms in these approaches facilitate the robust learning observed in these studies (i.e., long-term retention, transfer of knowledge, etc.).

Support for playful learning also comes from a rigorously conducted field experiment evaluating Tools of the Mind, an innovative preschool to second grade program inspired by Vygotsky (Barnett et al., 2008; Bodrova & Leong, 1996; Bodrova & Leong, 2007; Bodrova & Leong, 2001; Diamond et al., 2007). A central feature of the Tools curriculum is teacher encouragement of complex socio-dramatic play and games. Scaffolding of cognitive control is woven into virtually all classroom activities. For example, teachers encourage complex make-believe play, guiding children in jointly planning of play scenarios before enacting them. Teachers also lead rule-switching games in which regular movement patterns shift often, requiring flexibility of attention. In addition, Tools teachers model and encourage use of private speech as a means of regulating behavior.

Diamond et al. (2007) randomly assigned 150 preschoolers from low-income families to either Tools classrooms or comparison classrooms with similar content and activities, but without addressing cognitive control. Children from the Tools classrooms differed in end-of-year performance on a battery of laboratory tasks designed to measure cognitive control, a construct that subsumes three core self-regulatory abilities: inhibiting irrelevant thought and action, effortfully holding and operating on information in working memory, and flexibly adjusting attention to changes in task requirements. Tools children were especially advantaged on the more demanding tasks—ones taxing all three aspects of cognitive control—which also correlated significantly with their scores on standardized academic measures. The authors concluded, "Although play is often thought frivolous, it may be essential... yet preschools are under pressure to limit play" (p. 1388). For a more thorough review of the Tools of the Mind research, see Chapter 23.

Comparative research also shows not only the benefits of guided play, but possible dampening effects for children in direct instruction programs. Hart, Yang, Charlesworth, and Burts (2003) confirmed these findings in a longitudinal study that compared children who received direct instruction with those who received developmentally appropriate pedagogical practices—which included playful experiences. Results indicated that those children who received direct instruction experienced more stress than children who received developmentally appropriate curricula. Stress seemed to play a causal role in Hart et al.'s model as it predicted the appearance of hyperactive and distractible behaviors as well as greater hostility and aggression. These findings emerged regardless of gender, race, and socioeconomic status. Boys who were in a direct instruction classroom had lower achievement, mediated by the stress of being in such a classroom. These children grew more slowly in reading (vocabulary and comprehension) and language expression than did their peers in more developmentally appropriate classrooms. Thus, instructional practices consistent with the "empty vessel" view may have aversive socio-emotional effects that, in turn, undermine learning, motivation, and achievement (Hart et al., 1998; Ruckman, Burts, & Pierce, 1999; Burts et al., 1992; Rescorla, Hyson, & Hirsh-Pasek, 1991).

Lastly, a landmark longitudinal study presents a telling account of early education program's impact on socio-emotional factors. In the 1960s, a large-scale study compared a direct instruction program (Direct Instruction System for Teaching Arithmetic and Reading, DISTAR) to two playful learning programs (High/Scope and another child-centered nursery school). High-risk children were randomly assigned to one of the three preschool models and followed until they were 23 (Schweinhart, Weikart, & Larner, 1986; Schweinhart, 2004). During the primary years, no significant differences were found between groups in intellectual and academic performance; however, the direct instruction group reported increasing numbers of misconduct, delinquent behavior, and emotional disturbances from ages 15 to 23. Specifically, the direct instruction group had three times as many felony arrests per person, and 47% of the group was treated for emotional impairment or disturbance during their schooling. The findings suggest that the emphasis on planning, reasoning, and social competencies in the play-based programs may be key factors contributing to positive social outcomes (Bodrova & Leong, 2001; Mills, Cole, Jenkin, & Dale, 2002).

Concluding Thoughts

"The power of play as the engine of learning in early childhood and as a vital force for young children's physical, social, and emotional development is beyond question. Children in play-based kindergartens have a double advantage over those who are denied play: they end up equally good or better at reading and other intellectual skills, and they are more likely to become well-adjusted healthy people"
(*Miller & Almon*, 2009, p. 8).

Playful learning, defined as a combination of free play and guided play, offers a very promising pedagogy for learning academic and social outcomes (Broadhead, & van der Aalsvoort, 2009; Copple, Sigel, & Saunders, 1979; Korat, 2002; Seo & Ginsburg, 2004; Singer & Singer, 2004). The value of playful pedagogy emerges in observational and correlational studies and in studies that use the gold standard of random assignment. The value of this pedagogical approach emerges in preschool settings and in elementary school settings.[2] Play supports both short term and long-term mastery. While there is an accumulating body of research, this area is ripe for future research.

In the so-called "knowledge age," a variety of skills are necessary for success (Cavanagh, Klein, Kay, & Meisinger, 2006). Children must learn content in math, literacy and science (Duncan et al, 2007). They must also learn to synthesize information and to use it creatively, persevere in the face of challenge, and work in a culturally diverse world (Bell-Rose & Desai, 2005; Hirsh-Pasek et al., 2009). The question before us is how to best instill these competencies in our educational settings. The data strongly suggest that playful learning offers one way to achieve these ends. Play and learning are not incompatible. It is not play *versus* learning, but rather play *via* learning for which we must strive.

Future Directions

There are further areas of play research that need to be addressed:

1. What are the defining features of guided play? More specifically, what elements differentiate guided play, directed play, and direct instruction and do such distinctions influence learning outcomes?

2. What mechanisms drive the association between play and learning?

3. How do playful learning experiences change over time? In other words, as children get older how does the nature of their playful learning change?

4. How do playful learning experiences foster lifelong learning approaches?

5. How might different experimental approaches, such as microgenetic analysis of learning (Van der Aalsvoort, van Geert, & Steenbeek, 2009), shed light on playful learning processes?

Notes

1 There is a substantial literature debating whether exploratory behavior is "play" (e.g., Hutt, Tyler, Hutt, & Christopherson, 1989; Keller & Boigs, 1991; Weisler & McCall, 1976). While exploration and play share some common attributes (e.g., intrinsic motivation, interest; Weisler & McCall, 1976), some scholars argue there are significant differences between the two. Hutt (1970) suggests exploration is concerned with understanding the object's featural properties and characteristics (i.e., "What is this object?") whereas play focuses on how the object can be used (i.e., "What can I do with the object?"). Thus, children's exploration and play behaviors may be driven by fundamentally different goals (discovery-oriented versus interest-oriented) and likely operate through different learning processes (e.g., explicit learning versus implicit, unconscious learning or incidental learning). This may be a key element in differentiating forms of play, including guided play, and requires additional exploration.

2 We must be careful not to adopt the "play ethos," in which all play is deemed positive (Smith, 1995). Play can have a dark side, including bullying and compulsory "play" (i.e., forced participation in a game/activity), which may negate the potential benefits reviewed here.

References

Abril, C. R. & Gault, B. M. (2006). The state of music in the elementary school: The principal's perspective. *Journal of Research in Music Education*, 54, 6–20.

Arnold, D., Fisher, P., Doctoroff, G., & Dobbs, J. (2002). Accelerating math development in Head Start classrooms. *Journal of Educational Psychology*, 94, 762–770.

Ash, D. & Wells, G. (2006). Dialogic inquiry in classroom and museum: Action, tools, and talk. In Z. Bekerman, N. Burbules, & D. Silberman-Keller (Eds.), *Learning in places: The informal education reader* (pp. 35–54). New York, NY: Peter Lang Publishing, Inc.

Ashiabi, G. S. (2007). Play in the preschool classroom: Its socioemotional significance and the teacher's role in play. *Early Childhood Education Journal, 35,* 199–207.

Baroody, A.J., Lai, M.L., & Mix, K.S. (2006). The development of young children's number and operation sense and its implications for early childhood education. In O. Saracho & B. Spodek (Eds.), *Handbook of research on the education of young children* (pp. 187–221). Mahwah, NJ: Lawrence Erlbaum Associates.

Baumer, S., Ferholt, B., & Lecusay, R. (2005). Promoting narrative competence through adult–child joint pretense: Lessons from the Scandinavian educational practice of playworld. *Cognitive Development, 20,* 576–590.

Bell-Rose, S. & Desai, V. (2006). *Educating leaders for a global society.* New York, NY: Asia Society.

Bellin, H.F. & Singer, D.G. (2006). My magic story car: Video–based intervention to strengthen emergent literacy of at-risk preschoolers. In D.G. Singer, R.M. Golinkoff, & K. Hirsh-Pasek, (Eds), *Play=Learning: How play motivates and enhances children's cognitive and social-emotional growth* (pp. 101–123). New York, NY: Oxford University Press.

Belsky, J. & Most, R. K. (1981). From exploration to play: A cross-sectional study of infant free play behavior. *Developmental Psychology, 17,* 630–639.

Bergen, D. (1988). Using a schema for play and learning. In D. Bergen (Ed.), *Play as a medium for learning and development* (pp. 169–179). Portsmouth, NH: Heinemann Educational Books.

Bergen, D. & Mauer, D. (2000). Symbolic play, phonological awareness, and literacy skills at three age levels. In Kathleen A. Roskos & James F. Christie (Eds.), *Play and literacy in early childhood: Research from multiple perspectives* (pp. 45–62). New York: Erlbaum.

Berger, K. (2008). *The developing person through childhood and adolescence* (8th ed.). New York, NY: Worth Publishers.

Berk, L. E. (2001). *Awakening children's minds: How parents and teachers can make a difference.* New York, NY: Oxford University Press.

Berk, L. E., Mann, T.D., & Ogan, A.T. (2006). Make-believe play: Wellspring for development of self-regulation. In D. Singer, R.M. Golinkoff, & Hirsh-Pasek (Eds.), *Play =Learning: How play motivates and enhances children's cognitive and social-emotional growth.* New York, NY: Oxford University Press.

Berk, L. E., & Winsler, A. (1995). *Scaffolding children's learning: Vygotsky and early childhood education.* Washington, DC: NAEYC.

Birch, S. H., & Ladd, G. W. (1997). The teacher–child relationship and children's early school adjustment. *Journal of School Psychology, 35,* 61–79.

Bitter, G. & Hatfield, M. (1998). The role of technology in the middle grades. In L. Leutzinger (Ed.), *Mathematics in the Middle* (pp. 36–41). Reston, VA: National Council of Teachers of Mathematics.

Blair, C. & Razza, R. P. (2007). Relating effortful control, executive function, and false belief understanding to emerging math and literacy ability in kindergarten. *Child Development, 78,* 647–663.

Blanc, R., Adrien, J. L., Roux, S., & Barthélémy, C. (2005). Dysregulation of pretend play and communication development in children with autism. *Autism, 9,* 229–245.

Bodrova, E. (2008). Make-Believe play versus academic skills: A Vygotskian approach to today's dilemma of early childhood education. *European Early Childhood Education Research Journal, 16,* 357–369.

Bodrova, E. & Leong, D. J. (1996). *Tools of the mind: The Vygotskian approach to early childhood education.* Englewood Cliffs, NJ: Prentice Hall.

Bodrova, E. & Leong, D.J. (2001). Tools of the mind: *A case study of implementing the Vygotskian approach in American early childhood and primary classrooms.* Switzerland: The International Bureau of Education.

Bogard, K. & Takanishi, R. (2005). PK-3: An aligned and coordinated approach to education for children 3 to 8 years old. *SRCD Social Policy Report, 19,* 415–429.

Bonawitz, E. B., Shafto, P., Gween, H., Chang, I., Katz, S., & Schulz, L. (2009). The double-edged sword of pedagogy: Modeling the effect of pedagogical contexts on preschoolers' exploratory play. *Proceedings of the Thirty-first Cognitive Science Society.*

Bonawitz, E.B., Chang, I., Clark, C., & Lombrozo, T. (2008). Ockham's razor as inductive bias in preschoolers causal explanations. *Proceedings of the 7th International Conference of Development and Learning.* Monterey, CA.

Bonawitz, E.B., Fischer, A., Schulz, L.E. (2008). Training a Bayesian: Three-and-a-half-year-olds' reasoning about Ambiguous Evidence. *Proceedings of the Thirtieth Annual Conference of the Cognitive Science Society.* Washington, DC.

Bowman, B., Donovan, S., & Burns, M. S. (2001). *Eager to learn.* Washington, DC: National Academy Press.

Brackett, M. A., Rivers, S. E., & Salovey, P. (in press). Enhancing academic performance and social and emotional competence with emotional literacy training.

Bransford, J., Brown, A., & Cooking, R. (Eds.). (2000). How children learn. In *How people learn: Brain, mind, experience, and school* (pp. 79–113). Washington, DC: National Academy of Sciences.

Broadhead, P. & van der Aalsvoort (2009). Play and learning in educational settings. *Educational & Child Psychology, 26,* 5–8.

Brown, E. (2009, Nov. 21). *The playtime's the thing.* Washington Post.

Brown, J. R., Donelan-McCall, N., & Dunn, J. (1996). Why talk about mental states? The significance of children's conversations with friends, siblings, and mothers. *Child Development, 67,* 836–849.

Brown, J. R. & Dunn, J. (1996). Continuities in emotion understanding from 3 to 6 years. *Child Development, 67,* 789–802.

Bruner, J. (1983). *Child's talk: Learning to use language.* New York, NY: Norton Publishers.

Burts, D. C., Hart, C. H., Charlesworth, R., & Kirk, L. (1990). A comparison of frequencies of stress behaviors observed in kindergarten in classrooms with developmentally appropriate versus inappropriate instructional practices. *Early Childhood Research Quarterly, 5,* 407–423.

Burts, D. C., Hart, C. H., Charlesworth, R., Fleege, P., Mosley, J., & Thomasson, R. H. (1992). Observed activities and stress behaviors of children in developmentally appropriate and inappropriate kindergarten classrooms. *Early Childhood Research Quarterly, 7,* 297–318.

Caldera, Y. M., Culp, A. M. D., O'Brien, M., Truglio, R. T., Alvarez, M., & Huston, A. C. (1999). Children's play preferences, construction play with blocks, and visual-spatial skills: Are they related? *International Journal of Behavioral Development, 23*, 855–872.

Callanan, M.A. & Braswell, G. (2006). Parent–child conversations about science and literacy: Links between formal and informal learning. In Z. Bekerman, N. Burbules, & D. Silberman-Keller (Eds.), *Learning in places: The informal education reader.* New York, NY: Peter Lang Publishing, Inc.

Callanan, M. & Oakes, L. (1992). Preschoolers' questions and parents' explanations: Causal thinking in everyday activity. *Cognitive Development, 7*, 213–233.

Campbell, F. A., Pungello, E. P., Miller-Johnson, S., Burchinal, M., & Ramey, C. T. (2001). The development of cognitive and academic abilities: Growth curves from an early childhood education experiment. *Developmental Psychology, 37*, 231–242.

Campbell, F. A. & Ramey, C. T. (1995). Cognitive and school outcomes for high-risk African-American students at middle adolescence: Positive effects of early intervention. *American Educational Research Journal, 32*, 743–772.

Campbell, F. A., Ramey, C. T., Pungello, E. P., Sparling, J., & Miller-Johnson, S. (2002). Early childhood education: Young adult outcomes from the Abecedarian Project. *Applied Developmental Science, 6*, 42–57.

Casey, J. (2008, Dec, 28). Lebanon schools turn algebra into child's play. *The Oregonian.* Retrieved from http://oregonlive.com/news/index.ssf/2008/12/math_education.

Cavanagh, R., Klein, D., Kay, K., & Meisinger, S.R. (2006). Ready to work: Employers perspectives on the basic knowledge and applied skills of new entrants to the 21st century U.S. workforce. New York: The Conference Board, Corporate Voices, Partnership for 21st Century Skills, Society for Human Resource Management.

Christie, J. F. (2001). Play as a learning medium-revisited. In S. Reifel (Ed.), *Theory in context and out* (Vol. 3, pp. 358–365). Westport, CT: Ablex Publishing.

Christie, J. F. & Enz, B. (1992). The effects of literacy play interventions on preschoolers' play patterns and literacy development. *Early Education and Development, 3*, 205–220.

Christie, J. F. & Johnsen, E. P. (1983). The role of play in social-intellectual development. *Review of Educational Research, 53*, 93–115.

Christie, J. F. & Roskos, K. (2006). Standards, science, and the role of play in early literacy education. In D. Singer, R. M. Golinkoff, & K. Hirsh-Pasek (Eds.), *Play = learning: How play motivates and enhances children's cognitive and social-emotional growth* (pp. 57–73). New York, NY: Oxford University Press.

Christie, J., Enz, B., & Vukelich, C. (1997). *Teaching language and literacy: Preschool through the elementary grades.* Reading, MA: Addison-Wesley-Longman, Inc.

Clements, D. H. & Sarama, J. (1997). Research on Logo: A decade of progress. *Computers in the Schools, 14*, 9–46.

Clements, D.H., & Sarama, J. (2007) Early childhood mathematics learning. In F.K. Lester (Eds.) *Second handbook of research on mathematics teaching and learning* (pp. 661–555). New York: Information Age Publishing.

Clements, D.H. & Sarama. J. (2009). Learning and teaching early math: The learning trajectories approach. New York, NY: Routledge.

Cloran, C. (2005). Contexts for learning. In F. Christie (Ed.), *Pedagogy and the shaping of consciousness: Linguistic and social processes* (pp. 31–65). London: Continuum.

Cook, D. (2000). Voice practice: social and mathematical talk in imaginative play. *Early Child Development and Care, 162*, 51–63.

Copple, C. & Bredekamp, S. (2009). *Developmentally appropriate practice in early childhood programs serving children from birth through Age 8* (3rd ed.). Washington, D.C.: National Association for the Education of Young Children.

Copple, C., Sigel, I. E., & Saunders, R. (1979). *Educating the young thinker: Classroom strategies for cognitive growth.* New York, NY: D. Van Nostrand Co.

Dansky, J. L. (1980). Cognitive consequences of sociodramatic play and exploration training for economically disadvantaged preschoolers. *Journal of Child Psychology and Psychiatry, 20*, 47–58.

Daoust, C. J. (2004). An examination of implementation practices in Montessori early childhood education. Doctoral dissertation, University of California, Berkeley.

de Rosnay, M. & Hughes, C. (2006). Conversation and theory of mind: Do children talk their way to socio-cognitive understanding? *British Journal of Developmental Psychology, 24*, 7–37.

Deci, E. L. (1992). The relation of interest to the motivation of behavior: A self-determination theory perspective. The role of interest in learning and development. In A. Renninger, S. Hidi, & A Krapp (Eds.), *Interest in learning and development* (pp. 43–70). Hillsdale, NY: Erlbaum.

Diamond, A., Barnett, W. S., Thomas, J., & Munro, S. (2007). Preschool program improves cognitive control. *Science, 318*, 1387–1388.

Dickinson, D.K., Cote, L.R., & Smith, M.W. (1993). Learning vocabulary in preschool: Social and discourse contexts affecting vocabulary growth. In W. Damon (Series Ed.) & C. Daiute (Vol. Ed.), *New directions in child development: The development of literacy through social interaction* (vol. 61, pp. 67–78). San Francisco, CA: Jossey-Bass.

Dickinson, D. & Moreton, J. (1991, April). *Predicting specific kindergarten literacy skills from 3-year-olds' preschool experiences.* Paper presented at the biennial meeting of the Society for Research in Child Development, Seattle, WA.

Dodd, A. T., Rogers, C.S., & Wilson, J. T. (2001). The effects of situational context on playful behaviors of young preschool children. In S. Reifel (Ed.), *Theory in context and out* (Vol. 3, pp. 367–390). Westport, CT: Ablex Publishing.

Duncan, G., Claessens, A., Huston, A., Pagani, L., Engel, M., Sexton, H., et al. (2007). School readiness and later achievement. *Developmental Psychology, 43*, 1428–1446.

Duncan, G. J., Dowsett, C. J., Claessens, A., Magnuson, K., Huston, A. C., Klebanov, P., et al. (2007). School readiness and later achievement. *Dev Psychology, 43*, 1428–1446.

Dunn, J., Brown, J. R., & Maguire, M. (1995). The development of children's moral sensibility: Individual differences and emotion understanding. *Dev Psychology, 31*, 649–659.

Edersheim, E. H. (2007). *The definitive drucker.* New York: McGraw-Hill.

Einarsdottir, J. (2000). Incorporating literacy resources into the play curriculum of two Icelandic preschools. *Play and literacy in early childhood: Research from multiple perspectives* (pp. 77–90). New York: Erlbaum.

Elias, C. L. & Berk, L. E. (2002). Self-regulation in young children: Is there a role for sociodramatic play? *Early Childhood Research Quarterly, 17*, 216–238.

Elkind, D. (2007). *The power of play.* Cambridge, MA: Da Capo Press.

Enz, B. & Christie, J. (1997). Teacher play interaction styles: Effects on play behavior and relationships with teacher training and experience. *International Journal of Early Childhood Education, 2*, 55–69.

Fabes, R. A., Eisenberg, N., Hanish Fabes, R. A., Eisenberg, N., Hanish, L. D., & Spinrad, T. L. (2001). Preschoolers' spontaneous emotion vocabulary: *Relations to likability. Early Education and Development, 12*, 11–27.

Fantuzzo, J., Sekino, Y., & Cohen, H. L. (2004). An examination of the contributions of interactive peer play to salient classroom competencies for urban head start children. *Psychology in the Schools, 41*, 323–336.

Farran, D. C., Aydogan, C., Kang, S. J., & Lipsey, M. W. (2006). Preschool classroom environments and the quantity and quality of children's literacy and language behaviors. In D. K. Dickenson & S. B. Neuman (Eds.), *Handbook of early literacy research.* (pp. 257–68). New York, NY: The Guilford Press.

Fein, G. (1981). Pretend play in childhood: An integrative review. *Child Development, 52*, 1095–1018.

Feitelson, D. & Ross, G. S. (1973). The neglected factor-play. *Human Development, 16*, 202–223.

Feldman, C. F. (2005). Mimesis: Where play and narrative meet. *Cognitive Development, 20*, 503–513.

Fisher, K., Ferrara, K., Hirsh-Pasek, K., Newcombe, N., & Golinkoff, R. (2009, October). *Transforming preschoolers' geometric shape knowledge: Exploring verbalizations and behaviors during a categorization task.* Paper presented at the biennial Cognitive Development Society conference, San Antonio, TX.

Fisher, K., Ferrara, K., Hirsh-Pasek, K., Newcombe, N. & Golinkoff, R. (2010, March). *Exploring the role of dialogic inquiry and exploration in guided play: An experimental study.* Paper presented at the biennial International Conference on Infant Studies, Baltimore, MD.

Flavell, J. H. (1999). Cognitive development: Children's knowledge about the mind. *Annual Review of Psychology, 50*, 21–45.

Friedrich, G. (2003). friedrich-lahr@t-online.dk Kindergarten heute, 1/2003.

Froebel, F. (1897). *Pedagogics of the kindergarten.* (J. Jarvis, Trans.). London: Appleton.

Fromberg, D.P. (2002). *Play and meaning in early childhood education.* Boston, MA: Allyn & Bacon.

Gardner, H. (1995). The unschooled mind: How children think and how schools should teach. New York, NY: Basic Books.

Gardner, H. (1999). Intelligence reframed: Multiple intelligences for the 21st century. LOC: Basic Books.

Garner, P. W. & Estep, K. M. (2001). Emotional competence, emotion socialization, and young children's peer-related social competence. *Early Educ and Development, 12*, 29–48.

Gathercole, S., Tiffany, C., Briscoe, J., & Thorn, A. (2005). ALSPAC team: Developmental consequences of phonological loop deficits during early childhood: A longitudinal study. *Journal of Child Psychology and Psychiatry, 46*, 598–611.

Garvey, C. (1977). *Play.* Cambridge, MA: Harvard University Press.

Ginsburg, H. P. (2006). Mathematical play and playful mathematics: A guide for early education. In D. Singer, R. M. Golinkoff, & K. Hirsh-Pasek (Eds.), *Play = learning: How play motivates and enhances children's cognitive and social-emotional growth* (pp. 145–68). New York, NY: Oxford University Press, USA.

Ginsburg, H. P., Cannon, J., Eisenband, J. G., & Pappas, S. (2005). Mathematical thinking and learning. In K. McCartney & D. Phillips (Eds.), *Handbook of early child development.* Oxford, England: Blackwell.

Ginsburg, H.P., Lee, J.S., Boyd, J. S. (2008). Mathematics education for young children: What it is and how to promote it. *SRCD Social Policy Report*, XXII.

Ginsburg, H. P., Pappas, S., & Seo, K. H. (2001). Everyday mathematical knowledge: Asking young children what is developmentally appropriate. *Psychological perspectives on early childhood education: Reframing dilemmas in research and practice* (pp. 181–219). Mahwah, NY: Lawrence Erlbaum Associates.

Glickman, C. D. (1984). Play in public school settings: A philosophical question. In T. D. Yawkey & A. D. Pellegrini (Eds.), *Child's play: Developmental and applied* (pp. 255–271). Hillsdale, NJ: Lawrence Erlbaum Associates.

Graber, K. C., Locke, L. F., Lambdin, D., & Solmon, M. A. (2008). The landscape of elementary school physical education. *The Elementary School Journal, 108*, 151–159.

Griffin, S.A. & Case, R. (1996). Evaluating the breadth and depth of training effects, when central conceptual structures are taught. In R. Case & Y. Okamoto (Eds.), *The role of central conceptual structures in the development of children's thought. Monographs of the Society for Research in Child Development, 61*, 83–102.

Harris, P. (2000). *The work of the imagination.* Oxford, UK: Blackwell Publishers.

Hart, C., Yang, C., Charlesworth, R., & Burts, D. (2003). *Kindergarten teaching practices: Associations with later child academic and social/emotional adjustment to school.* Symposium paper presented at Society for Research in Child Development conference, Tampa, FL.

Hart, C. H., Burts, D. C., Durland, M. A., Charlesworth, R., DeWolf, M., & Fleege, P. O. (1998). Stress behaviors and activity type participation of preschoolers in more and less developmentally appropriate classrooms: SES and sex differences. *Journal of Research in Childhood Education, 12*, 176–196.

Harter, S. (1992). The relationship between perceived competence, affect, and motivational orientation within the classroom: Processes and patterns of change. In A.K. Boggiano & T.S. Pittman (Eds.), *Achievement and motivation: A social developmental perspective* (pp. 77–114). Cambridge, MA: Cambridge University Press.

Hirsch, E.S. (1996). *The block book* (3rd ed.). Washington, DC: National Association for the Education of Young Children.

Hirsh-Pasek, K. (1991). Pressure or challenge in preschool? How academic environments affect children. In L. Rescorla, M. C. Hyson, & K. Hirsh-Pasek (Eds.), *New directions in child development. Academic instruction in early childhood: Challenge or pressure?* (No. 53, pp. 39–46). San Francisco, CA: Jossey-Bass.

Hirsh-Pasek, K. & Golinkoff, R. M. (1999). The origins of grammar: Evidence from early language comprehension. The MIT Press.

Hirsh-Pasek, K. & Golinkoff, R.M. (2003). *Einstein never used flash cards: How our children really learn and why they need to play more and memorize less.* Emmaus, PA: Rosedale.

Hirsh-Pasek, K. & Golinkoff, R. M. (2006). *Action meets word: How children learn verbs.* New York, NY: Oxford University Press.

Hirsh-Pasek, K., Golinkoff, R. M., Berk, L.E., & Singer. D.G. (2009). *A mandate for playful learning in school: Presenting the evidence.* New York, NY: Oxford University Press.

Hughes, C. & Dunn, J. (1998). Understanding mind and emotion: Longitudinal associations with mental-state talk between young friends. *Developmental Psychology, 34*, 1026–1037.

Hutt, S., Tyler, S., Hutt, C., & Cristopherson, H. (1989). *Play, exploration, and learning: A natural history of the preschool.* London: Routledge.

Ilgaz, H. & Aksu-Koc, A. (2005). Episodic development in pre-school children's play-prompted and direct-elicited narratives. *Cognitive Development, 20,* 526–544.

Johnson, J. E., Christie, J. F., & Yawkey, T. D. (1999). *Play and early childhood development.* New York, NY: Addison Wesley Longman.

Jones, M. (2008, April). Children have to grow up too fast. *Edutopia: The George Lucas Educational Foundation.* Retrieved December 15, 2009, from http://www.edutopia.org/childhoods-end-accountability-forces-children-grow-up-too-fast.

Kagan, S. L. & Lowenstein, A. E. (2004). School readiness and children's play: Contemporary oxymoron or compatible option? In E. F. Zigler, D. G., Singer, & S. J. Bishop-Josef (Eds.), *Children's play: The roots of reading* (pp. 59–76). Washington, DC: Zero to Three Press.

Kaiser Foundation Report (December, 2005). *A teacher in the living room: Educational media for babies, toddlers and pre-schoolers.* Washington. D.C.: Kaiser Foundation.

Kamii. C. & Kato, Y, (2006). Play and mathematics at ages one to ten. In D. P. Fromberg & D. Bergen (Eds.), *Play from birth to twelve: Contexts, perspectives, and meanings* (pp. 187–198). New York, NY: Routledge.

Kavanaugh, R. D. & Engel, S. (1998). The development of pretense and narrative in early childhood. In O. N. Saracho & B. Spodek (Eds.), *Multiple perspectives on play in early childhood education* (pp. 80–99). Albany: State University of New York Press.

Keller, H. & Boigs, R. (1991). The development of exploratory behavior. In M. E. Lamb & H. Keller (Eds.), *Infant development: Perspectives from German-speaking countries* (pp. 275–298). Hillsdale, NJ: Lawrence Erlbaum Associates, Inc.

Klahr, D. (2005). Addressing fundamental issues. *Psychological Science, 16,* 871–872.

Klahr, D. & Li, J. (2005). Cognitive research and elementary science instruction: From the laboratory, to the classroom, and back. *Journal of Science Education and Technology, 14,* 217–238.

Klahr, D., Triona, L. M., & Williams, C. (2007). Hands on what? The relative effectiveness of physical versus virtual materials in an engineering design project by middle school children. *Journal of Research in Science Teaching, 44,* 183–203.

Kochuk, N. & Ratnayaka, M. (2007). *NCLB/ESEA: It's time for a change! Voices from America's classrooms.* National Education Association.

Kontos, S. (1999). Preschool teachers' talk, roles, and activity settings during free play. *Early Childhood Research Quarterly, 14,* 363–382.

Korat, O., Bahar, E., & Snapir, M. (2002). Sociodramatic play as opportunity for literacy development: The teacher's role: In this study in Israel, one teacher supported literacy through play in her kindergarten class with promising results. *The Reading Teacher, 56,* 386–394.

Krafft, K. C. & Berk, L. E. (1998). Private speech in two pre-schools: Significance of open-ended activities and make-believe play for verbal self-regulation. *Early Childhood Research Quarterly, 13,* 637–658.

Ladd, G. W., Birch, S. H., & Buhs, E. S. (1999). Children's social and scholastic lives in kindergarten: Related spheres of influence? *Child Development, 70,* 1373–1400.

Ladd, G.W. & Hart, C. H. (1992). Creating informal play opportunities: Are parents' and preschoolers' initiations related to children's competence with peers? *Developmental Psychology, 28,* 1179–1187.

Ladd, G. W., Kochenderfer, B. J., & Coleman, C. C. (1997). Classroom peer acceptance, friendship, and victimization: Distinct relational systems that contribute uniquely to children's school adjustment. *Child Development, 68,* 1181–1197.

Ladd, G.W., Herald, and Kochel K.P. (2006). School readiness: Are there social prerequisites? *Early Education and Development, 17,* 115–150.

Lee, J., Luchini, K., Michael, B., Norris, C., & Soloway, E. (2004). More than just fun and games: Assessing the value of educational video games in the classroom. In *CHI '04: CHI '04 extended abstracts on human factors in computing systems.* ACM.

Lemche, E., Lennertz, I., Orthmann, C., Ari, A., Grote, K., Häfker, J., et al. (2003). Emotion regulatory processes in evoked play narratives. *Prax Kinderpsychol Kinderpsychiatr, 52,* 156.

Lillard, A. S. (1993). Pretend play skills and the child's theory of mind. *Child Dev, 64,* 348–371.

Lillard, A. & Else-Quest, N. (2006). The early years: Evaluating Montessori education. *Science, 311,* 1893–1894.

Lloyd, B. & Goodwin, R. (1993). Girls' and boys' use of directives in pretend play. *Social Development, 2,* 122–130.

Manning, M.L. (2006). Play development from ages eight to twelve: Contexts, perspectives, and meanings. In D. P. Fromberg & D. Bergen (Eds.), *Play from birth to twelve* (2nd ed.) (pp. 21–29). New York, NY: Routledge.

Marbach, E. S. & Yawkey, T. D. (1980). The effect of imaginative play actions on language development in five-year-old children. *Psychology in the Schools, 17,* 257–263.

Marcon, R. (1993). Socioemotional versus academic emphasis: Impact on kindergartners' development and achievement. *Early Child Development and Care, 96,* 81–91.

Marcon, R. (1999). Differential impact of preschool models on development and early learning of inner-city children: A three cohort study. *Developmental Psychology, 35,* 358–375.

Marcon, R. (2002). Moving up the grades: Relationships between preschool model and later school success. *Early Childhood Research and Practice, 4,* 517–530.

Miller, E. & Almon, J. (2009). *Crisis in the kindergarten: Why children need to play in school.* College Park, MD: Alliance for Childhood.

Milligan, K., Astington, J. W., & Dack, L.A. (2007). Language and theory of mind: Meta-analysis of the relation between language ability and false-belief understanding. *Child Development, 78,* 622–646.

Mills, P., Cole, K., Jenkins, J., & Dale, P. (2002). Early exposure to direct instruction and subsequent juvenile delinquency: A prospective examination. *Exceptional Children, 69,* 85–96.

Morrow, L. M. & Rand, M. K. (1991). Promoting literacy during play by designing early childhood classroom environments. *Reading Teacher, 44,* 396–402.

Moyles, J. (2001). Just for fun? The child as active learner and meaning maker. In N. Kitson & R. Merry (Eds.), *Teaching in the primary school: A learning relationship* (pp. 9–26). London: Routledge.

Ness, D. & Farenga, S.J. (2007). *Knowledge under construction: The importance of play in developing children's spatial and geometric thinking.* Lanham, MD: Rowman & Littlefield Publishers, Inc.

Neuman, S., & Roskos, K. (1992). Literacy objects as cultural tools: Effects on children's literacy behaviors during play. *Reading Research Quarterly, 27,* 203–223.

Nicolopoulou, A. (2005). Play and narrative in the process of development: Commonalities, differences, and interrelations. *Cognitive Development, 20,* 495–502.

Nicolopoulou, A., McDowell, J., & Brockmeyer, C. (2006). Narrative play and emergent literacy: Storytelling and story-acting meet journal writing. In D. Singer, R. Golinkoff, & K. Hirsh-Pasek (Eds.), *Play = learning: How play motivates and enhances children's cognitive and social-emotional growth* (pp. 124–44). Oxford University Press, USA.

No Child Left Behind Act. (NCLB, 2001). *Public Law 107–110,* USA.

Paley, V. G. (1990). *The boy who would be a helicopter: The uses of storytelling in the classroom.* Cambridge, MA: Harvard University Press.

Papert, S. (1980). *Mindstorms: Children, computers, and powerful ideas.* New York: Basic Books.

Parker-Rees, R. (1997). Learning from play: design, technology, imagination, and playful thinking, *Proceedings of the International Conference on Design and Technology Education Research.* Retrieved December 1, 2009 from http://hdl.handle.net/2134/1458.

Pellegrini, A. D. (1984). Identifying causal elements in the thematic-fantasy play paradigm. *American Educational Research Journal, 21,* 691–701.

Pellegrini, A. D. (2009). Research and policy on children's play. *Child Development Perspectives, 3,* 131–136.

Pellegrini, A. D. & Galda, L. (1982). The effects of thematic-fantasy play training on the development of children's story comprehension. *American Educational Research Journal, 19,* 443–452.

Pellegrini, A. D., & Galda, L. (1990). Children's play, language, and early literacy. *Topics in Language Disorders, 10,* 76–88.

Pellegrini, A. D., & Galda, L. (1993). Ten years after: A reexamination of symbolic play and literacy research. *Reading Research Quarterly, 28,* 163–175.

Pellegrini, A. D., Galda, L., Dresden, J., & Cox, S. (1991). A longitudinal study of the predictive relations among symbolic play, linguistic verbs, and early literacy. *Research in the Teaching of English, 25,* 219–235.

Plowman, L., & Stephen, C. (2007). Guided interaction in pre-school settings. *Journal of Computer Assisted Learning, 23,* 14–21.

Piaget, J. (1970). *Science of education and the psychology of the child.* New York: Orion Press.

Reimer, K., & Moyer, P. S. (2005). Third-graders learn about fractions using virtual manipulatives: A classroom study. *Journal of Computers in Mathematics and Science Teaching, 24,* 5–25.

Renninger, K. A. (1990). Children's play interests, representation, and activity. In R. Fivush & J. Hudson (Eds.), *Knowing and remembering in young children* (pp. 127–65). New York, NY: Cambridge University Press.

Rescorla, L., Hyson, M., & Hirsh-Pasek, K. (Eds.). (1991). Academic instruction in early childhood: Challenge or pressure? In W. Damon (Ed.), *New directions in developmental psychology, 53,* New York, NY: Jossey-Bass.

Resnick, M. (2003). Playful learning and creative societies. *Education Update.*

Resnick, M. (2007). *All I really need to know (about creative thinking) I learned (by studying how children learn) in kindergarten.* Paper presented at the ACM Creativity & Cognition conference, Washington DC.

Reynolds, A., Ou, S., & Topitzes, J.W. (2004). Paths of effects if early childhood intervention on educational attainment and delinquency: A confirmatory analysis of the Chicago Child-Parent Centers. *Child Development, 75,* 1299–1328.

Rieber, L. P. (1996). Seriously considering play: Designing interactive learning environments based on the blending of microworlds, simulations, and games. *Educational Technology Research and Development, 44,* 43–58.

Rogoff, B. (2003). *The cultural nature of human development.* New York, NY: Oxford University Press.

Roseberry, S., Hirsh-Pasek, K., Parish-Morris, J., & Golinkoff, R. M. (2009). Live action: Can young children learn verbs from video? *Child Development, 80,* 1360–1375.

Rosen, C. E. (1974). The effects of sociodramatic play on problem-solving behavior among culturally disadvantaged preschool children. *Child Development, 45,* 920–927.

Roskos, K. & Christie, J. (2001). Examining the play-literacy interface: A critical review and future directions. *Journal of Early Childhood Literacy, 1,* 59–89.

Roskos, K. A. & Christie, J. F. (Eds.). (2000). *Play and literacy in early childhood: Research from multiple perspectives* (2nd ed). Mahwah, NJ: Erlbaum.

Roskos, K, & Christie, J. (2004). Examining the play-literacy interface: A critical review and future directions. In E. F. Zigler. D.G. Singer, & S.J. Bishop-Josef (Eds.), *Children's play: Roots of reading* (pp. 95–123). Washington D.C: Zero to Three Press.

Rowe, D. W. (1998). The literate potentials of book-related dramatic play. *Reading Research Quarterly, 33,* 10–35.

Rubin, K., Maioni, T., & Horung, M. (1976). Free play behaviors in middle- and lower-class preschoolers: Parten and Piaget revisited. *Child Development, 47,* 414–419.

Ruckman, A. Y., Burts, D. C., & Pierce, S. H. (1999). Observed stress behaviors of 1st-grade children participating in more and less developmentally appropriate activities in a computer-based literacy laboratory. *Journal of Research in Childhood Educ, 14,* 36–47.

Sabbagh, M. A., Xu, F., Carlson, S. M., Moses, L. J., & Lee, K. (2006). The development of executive functioning and theory of mind: A comparison of Chinese and U.S. preschoolers. *Psychological Science, 17,* 74–81.

Sachs, J. (1987). Preschool boys' and girls' language use in pretend play. In S.U. Philips, S. Steele, & C. Tanz (Eds.), *Language, gender, and sex in comparative perspective.* Cambridge, NY: Cambridge University Press.

Saltz, E., Dixon, D., & Johnson, J. (1977). Training disadvantaged preschoolers on various fantasy activities: Effects on cognitive functioning and impulse control. *Child Development, 48,* 367–380.

Saracho, O. N. (2004). Supporting literacy-related play: Roles for teachers of young children. *Early Childhood Education Journal, 31,* 201–206.

Saracho, O. N. & Spodek, B. (2006). Young children's literacy-related play. *Early Child Development and Care, 176,* 707–721.

Sarama, J., & Clements, D. H. (2002). Building blocks for young children's mathematical development. *Journal of Educational Computing Research, 27,* 93–110.

Sarama, J. & Clements, D.H. (2009). Building blocks and cognitive building blocks: Playing to know the world mathematically. *American Journal of Play, 1,* 313–337.

Sarama, J. & Clements, D. H. (2009). "Concrete" computer manipulatives in mathematics education. *Child Development, 3,* 145–150.

Schiefele, U. (1991). Interest, learning, and motivation. *Educational Psychologist, 26,* 299–323.

Schultz, L. & Bonawitz, E.B. (2007). Serious fun: Preschoolers engage in more exploratory play when evidence in confounded. *Developmental Psychology, 43*, 1045–1050.

Schwebel, D., Rosen, C., & Singer, J. L. (1999). Preschoolers' pretend play and theory of mind: The role of jointly conducted pretense. *British Journal of Developmental Psychology, 17*, 333–348.

Schweinhart, L. (2004). *The High/Scope Perry preschool study through age 40.* Ypsilanti, MI: High/Scope Educational Research Foundation.

Schweinhart, L. J., Weikart, D. Larner, M.B. (1986). Consequences of three preschool curriculum models through age 15. *Early Childhood Research Quarterly, 1*, 15–45.

Senechal, M. & LeFevre, J.A. (2002). Parental involvement in the development of children's reading skill: A five-year longitudinal study. *Child Development, 73*, 445–461.

Seo, K. H. & Ginsburg, H. P. (2004). What is developmentally appropriate in early childhood mathematics education? Lessons from new research. In D. H. Clements, J. Sarama, & A. M. DiBiase (Eds.), *Engaging young children in mathematics: Standards for early childhood mathematics education* (pp. 91–104). Hillsdale, NJ: Erlbaum.

Shaklee, H., O'Hara, P., & Demarest, D. (2008, March) *Early math skills: Building blocks for the future.* Research Brief, University of Idaho Extension.

Shmukler, D. (1981). Mother–child interaction and its relationship to the predisposition of imaginative play. *Genetic Psychology Monographs, 104*, 215–235.

Singer, D. G. & Singer, J. L. (2004). Encouraging school readiness through guided pretend games. In E. F. Zigler, D. G. Singer, & S. J. Bishop-Josef (Eds.), *Children's play: The roots of reading* (pp. 175–187). Washington, D.C.: Zero to Three Press.

Singer, D. G., Golinkoff, R. M., & Hirsh-Pasek, K. (2006). *Play=Learning: How play motivates and enhances children's cognitive and social-emotional growth.* New York, NY: Oxford University Press.

Singer, D.G. & Singer, J.L (2005). *Imagination and play in the electronic age.* Cambridge, MA: Harvard University Press.

Singer, D. G., Singer, J. L., Plaskon, S. L., & Schweder, A. E. (2003). The role of play in the preschool curriculum. In S. Olfman (Ed.), *All work and no play: How educational reforms are harming our preschoolers.* (pp. 43–70). Westport, CT: Praeger Publishers.

Smith, P. K. (1995). Play, ethology, and education: A personal account. In A. D. Pellegrini (Ed.), *The future of play theory: A multidisciplinary inquiry into the contributions of Brian Sutton-Smith,* (pp. 3–21). Albany, NY: State University of New York Press.

Smith, P. K. (2002). Pretend play, metarepresentation and theory of mind. In R. W. Mitchell (Ed.), *Pretending and imagination in animals and children* (pp. 129–141). Cambridge, MA: Cambridge University Press.

Smith, P. K. (2003). Play and peer relations. In A. Slater & G. Bremner (Eds.), *An introduction to developmental psychology* (pp. 311–333). Malden, MA: Blackwell.

Snow, C. E., Tabors, P. O., & Dickinson, D. K. (2001). Language development in the preschool years. In D. K. Dickinson & P. O. Tabors (Eds.), *Beginning literacy with language: Young children learning at home and school* (pp. 1–30). Baltimore, MD: Paul H. Brooks.

Spohn, C. (2008). Teacher perspectives on No Child Left Behind and arts education: A case study. *Arts Education Policy Review, 109*, 3–12.

Squire, K. (2006). From content to context: Videogames as designed experience. *Educational Researcher, 35*, 19–29.

Stecher, B. M. (2002). Consequences of large-scale, high-stakes testing on school and classroom practice. In L. S. Hamilton, S. P. Klein, & B. M. Stecher Rand (Eds.), *Making sense of test-based accountability in education* (pp. 79–100). Santa Monica, CA: Rand Corporation.

Stipek, D. J., Feiler, R., Daniels, D., & Milburn, S. (1995). Effects of different instructional approaches on young children's achievement and motivation. *Child Development, 66*, 209–223.

Sunderman, G. L., Tracey, C. A., Kim, J., & Orfield, G. (2004). Listening to teachers: Classroom realities and No Child Left Behind. *Childhood Education, 82*, 19–23.

Sutton-Smith, B. (2001). *The ambiguity of play.* Cambridge, MA: Harvard University Press.

Takanishi, R. & Bogard, K. L. (2007). Effective educational programs for young children: What we need to know. *Child Development Perspectives, 1,* 40–45.

Thomas, L., Howard, J., & Miles, G. (2006). The effectiveness of playful practice for learning in the early years. *Psychology of education review, 30,* 52–58.

Thompson, R., Easterbrooks, M.A., & Padilla-Walker, L. (2003). Social and emotional development in infancy. In I.B. Weiner (Ed.), *Handbook of psychology: developmental psychology* (pp. 91–112). New York, NY: Wiley.

Tykkyläinen, T., & Laakso, M. (2009). Five-year-old girls negotiating pretend play: Proposals with the Finnish particle jooko. *Journal of Pragmatics, 42,* 242–256.

Udwin, O. (1983). Imaginative play training as an intervention method with institutionalized preschool children. *British Journal of Educational Psychology, 53,* 32–39.

Van der Aalsvoort, G., van Geert, P., & Steenbeek, H.W. (2009). Microgenetic methodology: Possibilities with regard to research on learning and instruction. In K. Kumpulainen, C.E. Hmelo-Silver, & M. Cesar (Eds.), *Investigating classroom interaction: Methodologies in action* (pp. 203–299). Rotterdam: Sense.

Van der Ven, K. (2008). *Promoting positive development in early childhood. Building blocks for a successful start.* Verlag: Springer.

Viadero, D. (2007, June 20). Teachers say NCLB has changed classroom practice. *Education Week, 26,* 6–22.

Volling, B. L., Youngblade, L. M., & Belsky, J. (1997). Young children's social relationships with siblings and friends. *American Journal of Orthopsychiatry, 67,* 102–111.

Vygotsky, L. S. (1978). *Mind in society: The development of higher mental processes* (M. Cole, V. John-Steiner, S. Scribner, & E. Souberman, Eds. and Trans.). Cambridge, MA: Harvard University Press. (Original work published 1930–1935)

Vygotsky, L. (1986). *Thought and language.* (A. Kozulin, Trans.). Cambridge, MA: MIT Press. (Original work published 1930, 1933, and 1935).

Weikart, D. P. (1998). Changing early childhood development through educational intervention. *Preventive Medicine, 27,* 233–237.

Weisler, A. & McCall, R. B. (1976). Exploration and play: Resume and redirection. *American Psychologist, 31,* 492–508.

Whitebread, D., Coltman, P., Jameson, H., & Lander, R. (2009). Play, cognition and self-regulation: What exactly are children learning when they learn through play? *Educational & Child Psychology, 26,* 40–52.

Whyte, J.C. & Bull, R. (2008). Number games, magnitude representation, and basic number skills in preschoolers. *Developmental Psychology, 44,* 588–96.

Wolfgang, C.H., Stannard, L. L., & Jones, I. (2001). Block play performance among preschoolers as a predictor of later school achievement in mathematics. *Journal of Research in Childhood Education, 15*, 173–180.

Wright, W. E. (2002). The effects of high stakes testing in an inner-city elementary school: The curriculum, the teachers, and the English language learners. *Current Issues in Education, 5*, 1–6.

Youngblade, L. M. & Dunn, J. (1995). Individual differences in young children's pretend play with mother and sibling: Links to relationships and understanding of other people's feelings and beliefs. *Child Development, 66*, 1472–1492.

Zigler, E. & Bishop-Josef, S. (2006). The cognitive child vs. The whole child: Lessons from 40 years of head start. In D. Singer, D. M. Golinkoff, & K. Hirsh-Pasek (Eds.), *Play = learning: How play motivates and enhances children's cognitive and social-emotional growth.* New York, NY: Oxford University Press.

Zigler, E., Singer, D. G., & Bishop-Josef, S. J. (2004). *Children's play: The roots of reading.* Zero to Three.

PART 7

Conclusion

Conclusion

Anthony D. Pellegrini

Abstract

The contributors to this *Handbook* have shown that play is an important aspect of human and nonhuman development such that it not only enables individuals to adapt to their immediate ecology but it also may enable individuals to adjust the course of their evolution. With this sort of claim, it is not hard to understand why scholars from a variety of disciplines have suggested that play is indispensible to the healthy development of children; thus play has assumed an important place in public policy relevant to children.

Keywords: play, immediate and deferred benefits, development, educational policy

As the varied contributions to this volume have illustrated, the study of play has been an integral part of the study of human and nonhuman animals well over a century (e.g., Bateson, 1981; 2005; Groos, 1898; 1901; Pellegrini & Smith, 2005). For example, Groos' two volumes on the play of nonhuman (Groos, 1898) and human animals (Groos, 1901) suggested that play during animals' juvenile period, or period of immaturity, was "critical" in shaping later development. This notion of the deferred importance of juvenile play for subsequent development was later incorporated into Piaget's (1962) and Vygotsky's (1967) theories of play in human development, as argued by Goncu and Gaskins in this volume. Robert Fagen (1981), like Groos, concluded that the importance of play, as a quintessential juvenile behavior, stems, in part, from the notion that an organism's early experiences are critical to subsequent development and functioning.

More recently, Burghardt (2005; this volume) examined the place of animal play in the phylogenetic order in light of his Surplus Resource Theory. For Burghardt, the extended juvenile period is crucial to the role of play in developing the complex set of skills necessary for survival and reproduction especially true for animals whose ecology is varied or unstable. From this position, individuals' behaviors are not triggered by an anticipated set of contingencies. Instead, juveniles use the resources afforded them (safety and provisioning by a parent) during this period to explore their environment and experiment with a variety of strategies that may be effective in that niche. These environmental and behavioral factors, in turn, should indirectly affect subsequent gene expression, frequency, and evolution.

In Burghardt's chapter, play behavior of nonhuman animals was of central concern, though he did speculate about the role of play in the human condition. Arguably, the study of play in humans from a broad phylogenetic and ontogenetic perspective has been less systematic. Rubin, Fein, and Vandenberg (1983) provided a thorough psychological overview in their chapter in volume four of the *Manual of Child Psychology*, and Smith's 1982 article and 1984 book compared nonhuman animal and human play. With the exception of this *Handbook*, this has not been taken up to any great extent in the subsequent 20 years, though recent work by Power (2000),

Pellegrini and Smith (1998; 2005), Pellegrini (2009) and Sutton-Smith (1997) have included discussions of both human and nonhuman play. This is a puzzling state of affairs because, from our view, play represents a paradigm example of the place of a behavior in both ontogenetic and phylogenetic development.

During ontogeny, play is observed primarily during the juvenile period in forms that are qualitatively different from seemingly similar adult behaviors. For example, children often playfully enact adult roles and behaviors they have observed. These play behaviors, relative to more serious and functional adult variants, are typically exaggerated (Pellegrini, this volume) and have hypothesized importance for subsequent development (Fagen, this volume; Smith, 1982).

The more complex and flexible the organism, the longer the period of immaturity (Bjorklund, 2006; Bjorklund & Rosenberg, 2005). Humans have an extended period of immaturity, relative to other mammals including primates (Bjorklund & Pellegrini, 2002; Herman et al., this volume; Kaplan, Lancaster, Hill & Hurtado, 2000; Paligio, this volume) and rodents (Pellis & Pellis, this volume). Lancaster and Lancaster (1987) have argued that the long period of immaturity in humans (until sexual maturity) was adaptive for an environment in which extensive parental investment could pay off in terms of skill acquisition by offspring, in a situation in which immediate productive activity by children might be difficult due to hazards (e.g., hunting) or difficulty of extracting resources (e.g., foraging). Although in contemporary environments children learn mostly through formal teaching, in traditional human environments this was not the case (Roopnarine, this volume; Tudge et al, this volume). Learning mostly occurs through observation, exploration and play (Lancy, 1996).

In modern society, formal schooling was created to educate children as an extension of the rationalizing associated with industrialization (e.g., social engineering, specialization, and efficiency) (Chadacoff, this volume; Glickman, 1981; Golinkoff et al., this volume). In pre-industrial times (Thomas, 1964), and currently in pastoral and foraging societies, learning is more integrated into the fabric of a child's daily life—not set off into a separate institution (Bock, 2005; Rogoff, 1995; Tudge et al., this volume). For example, contemporary Botswana girls learn to process grain through a seamless process whereby they first play at pounding grain, where pounding with sticks and reeds is typically embedded in a fantasy theme. As girls become proficient in this activity in play, they move into "work"-related grain pounding with mortar and pestles (Bock, 2005). From this position, one of the primary purposes of the extended period of immaturity is for organisms to sample their environment so as to development behaviors and strategies that are adaptive.

Play is a central component of the immature child. Indeed, an extended period of immaturity is typical when play is observed in most species. This correspondence between play and an extended period of immaturity is not trivial. Following Bateson (2005, this volume), it may be that play during the extended period of immaturity is an important strategy used to develop behaviors that are adaptive to the niches that young children and adults inhabit. Children may sample their environment and through play learn and practice behaviors adaptive to that environment. Bateson (2005, this volume) speculates that play behaviors in ontogeny may be in the forefront of ways in which phenotypes affect subsequent evolutionary processes. This position turns Hall's characterization that ontogeny recapitulates phylogeny on its head by suggesting that ontogeny affects phylogeny.

In short, this volume has shown that play is an important aspect of human development such that it not only enables individuals to adapt to their immediate ecology but it also may enable individuals to adjust the course of their phylogenetic development.

Play and Education Policy
So what are the educational policy implications of the contributions to this volume? First, and perhaps most importantly, educators should label as play only behavior that fits explicated definitions of the construct—this is the only way that we can carry out construct—and content-valid assessments of the educational benefits of play-oriented curricula. From the definitions of play proffered here (Bateson, this volume; Burghardt, this volume), not everything that children do is play and play is multidimensional—not a unitary construct (Bateson, this volume), even though educators may label it as such. For example, it is not play when teachers or researchers tell children to "play" a phonemic awareness game or require them to sing a scripted letter-sound correspondence song. Correspondingly, different forms of play in school can be maximized by giving children opportunities for interaction with familiar peers, with minimal adult intervention.

The notion of "guided play," in Fisher and colleagues' chapter, is an important step in the sort of careful word usage necessary if both science and policy are to advance.

During preschool "free play periods," for example, children expend moderate levels of resources in object play (Bjorklund & Gardiner, this volume; Pellegrini & Gustafson, 2005), pretend play (Kavanaugh, this volume; Lillard, this volume; Rubin et al., 1983), social play (Howes, this volume; Pellegrini & Smith, 1998), and locomotor play (Pellegrini, this volume; Pellegrini et al., 1998), and there have been correlated benefits associated with each form of play. Research on play after the preschool period is very limited (Fagen, this volume; Harris, 2007; Sutton-Smith, this volume), but extant data do suggest that play decreases with age, and so too should benefits. For example, the pretend dimension of social pretend play becomes less important than other forms of peer interaction in facilitating literacy as children move across the primary school grades (Kavanaugh, this volume; Pellegrini & Galda, 1993).

Benefits associated with locomotor play, on the other hand, may be immediate and observed across the lifespan (Bateson, this volume; Pellegrini, this volume). They are also relatively easily to facilitate in schools. For example, increased opportunity, in the form of recess (see Baines & Blatchford, this volume), for outdoor, large motor exercise play and games is related to children's and early adolescents' modest caloric expenditure (Pellegrini et al., 1998), and this exercise may have immediate benefits for cardiovascular functioning and motor skills (Pellegrini & Smith, 1998; Stamps, 1995). Experimental evidence also demonstrates that recess breaks during the school day both maximize students' attention to subsequent class work and facilitate children's peer relationships as they make the transition into primary school (Pellegrini, 2005). However, we do not know the optimal form or duration that these breaks should take in various ecologies. Research in the tradition of massed versus distributed practice suggests that frequent, short breaks would be more effective than fewer and longer breaks in maximizing cognitive performance (e.g., Ebinghaus, 1885/1964). The cognitive immaturity hypothesis (Bjorklund & Green, 1992), on the other hand, suggests that breaks for preschool children should be more "play oriented" and those for older youngsters might involve just taking a break from traditional preschool work, such as listening to music.

In the final analysis, theory and data should guide policy governing the place of play in schools.

Resources are too limited to do otherwise. Although there is a real danger that opportunities for children's play will be minimized, there is also a corresponding danger that advocates of play for children are overzealous in attributing benefits of play. This is understandable in the current educational environment, but such a position also jeopardizes the possibility of future inclusion of play in educational programs because policymakers and parents will equate play with overblown claims.

References

Bateson, P.P.G. (1981). Discontinuities in development and changes in the organization of play in cats. In K. Immelmann, G. Barlow, L. Petrinovich & M. Main (Eds.), *Behavioral development* (pp. 281–295). New York: Cambridge University Press.

Bateson, P. P. G. (2005). Play and its role in the development of great apes and humans. In A. D. Pellegrini & P. K. Smith (Eds.), *The nature of play: Great apes and humans* (pp. 13–26). New York: Guilford.

Bjorklund, D. F. (2006). Mother knows best: Epigenetic inheritance. Maternal effects and the evolution of human intelligence. *Developmental Review, 26,* 213–242.

Bjorklund, D. F. & Green, B. L. (1992). The adaptive nature of cognitive immaturity. *American Psychologist, 47,* 46–54.

Bjorklund, D. F. & Pellegrini, A. D. (2002). *Evolutionary developmental psychology.* Washington, DC: American Psychological Association.

Bjorklund, D. F. & Rosenberg, J. S. (2005). The role of developmental plasticity in the evolution of human cognition: Evidence from enculturated, juvenile, great apes. In B. J. Ellis and D. F. Bjorklund (Eds.) *Origins of the social mind* (pp. 76–107). New York: Guilford.

Bock, J. (2005). Farming, foraging, and children's play in the Okavango Delta, Botswana. In A. D. Pellegrini and P. K. Smith (Eds.), *The nature of play: Great apes and humans* (pp. 254–284). New York: Guilford.

Burghardt, G. M. (2005). *The genesis of animal play: Testing the limits.* Cambridge, MA: MIT Press.

Ebinghaus, H. (1885/1964). *Memory.* New York: Teachers College Press.

Fagen, R. (1981). *Animal play behavior.* New York: Oxford University Press.

Glickman, C. D. (1981). Play and the school curriculum: The historical context. *Journal of Research and Development in Education, 14,* 1–10.

Groos, K. (1898). *The play of animals.* New York: Appleton.

Groos, K. (1901). *The play of man.* London: Heinemann.

Harris, P.L. (2006). Hard work for the imagination. In A. Göncü and S. Haskins (Eds.). *Play and development: Evolutionary, sociocultural and functional perspectives* (pp. 205–226). Mahwah, N.J.: Lawrence Erlbaum Associates.

Kaplan, H. S., Lancaster, J. B., Hill, K., & Hurtado, A. M. (2000). A theory of human life history evolution: Diet, intelligence, and longevity. *Evolutionary Anthropology, 9,* 156–183.

Lancaster, J. B. & Lancaster, C. S. (1987). The watershed: Change in parental-investment and family-formation strategies in the course of human evolution. In J. B. Lancaster,

J. Altmann. A. S. Rossi, & L. R. Sherrod (Eds.), *Parenting across the life span: Biosocial dimensions* (pp. 187–205). New York: Aldine de Gruyter.

Lancy, D. F. (1996). *Playing on the mother-ground.* New York: Guilford.

Pellegrini, A. D. (2005). *Recess: Its role in education and development.* Mahwah, NJ: Erlbaum.

Pellegrini, A. D. (2009). *The role of play in human development.* New York: Oxford Unviersity Press.

Pellegrini, A. & Galda, L. (1993). Ten years after: A reexamination of symbolic play and literacy research. *Reading Research Quarterly, 28,* 163–175.

Pellegrini, A. D. & Gustafson, K. (2005). Boys' and girls' uses of objects for exploration, play, and tools in early childhood. In A. D. Pellegrini and P. K. Smith (Eds.), *The nature of play: Great apes and humans* (pp. 113–138). New York: Guilford.

Pellegrini, A. D. & Smith, P. K. (1998). Physical activity play: The nature and function of a neglected aspect of play. *Child Development, 69,* 577–598.

Piaget, J. (1962). *Play, dreams, and imitation in childhood.* (Trans. C. Gattengno & F.M. Hodgson) New York: Norton. (Original work published 1951).

Rogoff, B. (1994). Developing understanding of the idea of a community of learners. *Mind, Culture, and Activity, 1,* 209–229.

Rubin, K. H., Fein, G., & Vandenberg, B. (1983). Play. In E.M. Hetherington (Ed.), *Handbook of child psychology: Vol. IV. Socialization, personality and social development,* (pp. 693–774). New York: Wiley.

Smith, P.K. (1982). Does play matter? Functional and evolutionary aspects of animal and human play. *The Behavioral and Brain Sciences, 5,* 139–184.

Stamps. J. (1995). Motor learning and the value of familiar space. *American Naturalist, 146,* 41–58.

Sutton-Smith, B. (1997). *The ambiguity of play.* Cambridge, MA: Harvard University Press.

Thomas, K. (1964). Work and leisure in pre-industrial society. *Past & Present, 29,* 50–66.

Vygotsky, L. (1967). Play and its role in the mental development of the child. *SovietPsychology, 12,* 62–76.

INDEX

A

act of representation, 49–51
Ada (Nabokov), 95
ADHD. *See* attention deficit hyperactivity disorder
adolescent period
  play fighting during, 255
  popular activities during, 267
  solitude during, 188
  video games during, mood management from, 325
adult-constructed play, 102
  with children, 236
adulthood, play during, 90–91
  scaffolding in, 91
adults
  children's play with, 231–41
  children v., in social play, 236
  guided play by, 343–44
  imitation of, in child's play, 15
  play fighting for, juvenile v., 252
  supervision by, for children's play, 238
  symbolic play and, in educational settings, 55
The Adventures of Tom Sawyer (Twain), 102
affective content, 233–34
  of social play, 234–35
affordances, 159–60
  through exploration, 159–60
  friendships and, 208–9
  hidden, 160
  pretend play as, 285
  social acceptance as, 208–9
  in tool use and play, 159–60
African Americans
  children's play, observations of, 129–33, 130*t*
  parent–child play for, 22–23
afterschool programs, 222
agenda setters, 274–75
aggression
  density effects on, 142
  observational methods for, in play study, 141–42
  play fighting as regulation for, 79
  social cognition and, 207
  toys and, 217
Albee, John, 105
alloparenting, 23
The Ambiguity of Play (Sutton-Smith), 111

American Journal of Play, 11
Among School Children (Yeats), 94
animal models, play in. *See also* nonhuman primates, social play among; Rhesus macaques, social play among
  fairness in play fighting among, 246–47
  in Gene X Environment, 60, 65
  locomotor play in, 247
  object play in, 247
  play fighting, 247–55
  social play in, 247
  social pretend play, 297–98
animals, play among, 10–11
  object, 10
  rotational, 10
  social, 10–11
  solitary locomotor, 10
antipathy, of play, 110–14
  emotional role, 112–14
antisocial behavior, 261. *See also* social withdrawal; solitary-active play; solitary-passive play
  in Spencer study, 266
apes, social play among, 76–79
  for bonobos, 78–79
  for courtship, 76
  as nonsexual, 76–77
  social structures as influence on, 77
approach-avoidance conflict
  solitary-active play and, 190
  solitary-passive play and, 193
arousability
  emotion regulation and, assessment of, 223–24
  temperament and, 227
arts, play with, 10
attachment theory, 236–37
  mother–child attachments in, 237
  teachers in, 237
attention deficit hyperactivity disorder (ADHD), 11
  emotion regulation and, 206
  information-processing with, 207
  social play and, 203–4
  solitary play and, 204
  technology and play applications, 332
Auguries of Innocence (Blake), 91
autism, pretend play in, 308–18
  atypical sociocultural learning and, 315–17

  decontextualization for, 312, 314
  deficits in, 311–13, 317
  executive control dysfunction and, 313–15
  false pretense paradigms, 312
  Fewell Play Scale for, 311
  functional v. pretend play and, 310–11
  future directions for, 318
  genetic factors for, 308
  motivation as factor in, 316
  object function inhibition, 314
  physical play and, 311
  rough-and-tumble play and, 311
  scaffolding and, 311
  sensorimotor play and, 311
  social interaction impairment and, 309
  social play and, 311
  spontaneous, 308–9, 316
An Autobiography (Frame), 90

B

Badaly, Daryaneh, 5
Baines, Ed, 5
"Baldwin effect," 45
Barnard, John, 103
Barnett, Lisa, 12
Bateson, Gregory, 92
Bateson, Mary Catherine, 90
Bateson, Patrick, 4, 53, 92–93
Bayley Scales of Infant Development, 177
behavioral biology, theories of play and, 42–43
behavioral patterns, of play, 15, 17, 70–71
behavior drift, 147
belief systems, play and, 21–24
  variations within, 21
Berner, Loretta, 105
bias, in play fighting, 253
Bjorklund, Dave, 4
Blake, William, 91
Blatchford, Peter, 5
Bohm, David, 95
bonobo apes, social play among, 78–79, 79*f*
  as contact play, 78
  gender and, 78
boys, play for
  emotion regulation and, 223
  fantasy play, 267–68
  games in, 267–68

boys, play for (*cont.*)
  HRV and, emotion regulation
      from, 224–25
  in peer groups, hierarchical
      organization among, 273
  play fighting as, 255
  with tool use, 164*t*
  with toys, 217
  in US, 106
Brazil, play in
  cultural ecology of, 120, 124–30
  observations of children's
      play, 129–33, 131*t*
Bretherton, Inge, 286
bubblegum years, play during, 90
building blocks, 327, 328*f*
bullying
  playground games and, 261–62
  play v., 9
Burarrwanga, George, 94
Burghardt, Gordon, 4, 42, 45, 111

C

Canby, Henry Seidel, 105
capital theory, 32
capuchin monkeys, tool use by, 162
caregiving, play and
  within cultural community, 232
  cultural development and, 22
  among Rhesus macaques, 62, 65
Chase, Martha Jenks, 105
Chatwin, Bruce, 93
childcare programs, 241
children's play, as social play, 30–34,
      231–41. *See also* human develop-
      ment, play and; social interactions,
      among children
  with adults, 231–41
  adult supervision of, 238
  adults v. children and, 236
  affective content in, 233–34
  in agricultural societies, 33–34
  attachment theory for, 236–37
  in Brazil, 129–33, 131*t*
  in classrooms, 238
  cognitive development and, 239
  as complementary, 234
  components of, 233–34
  within cultural community, 231–36
  developmental stages of, 236
  in different settings, 30–34
  dispositions as influence on, 239
  in dyads, 235
  emotion regulation and, 233, 239
  in formal groups, 237
  individual developments for, 239
  interactive content in, 233–34
  in Kenya, 129–33, 131*t*
  language development and, 239
  during latency period, 4, 102
  object play and, 157, 163–64
  in peer groups, 231–41
  Peer Play Scale for, 233–34

physical settings for, 32–33
potential benefits, 33–34
pretend play, 234
  as reciprocal, 234
  reciprocity in, 233
  as reflection of adult activities, 30–31
  scaffolding in, 235
  with siblings, 235
  sociability as influence on, 239
  social climate of, 237–39
  social competence and, 233
  structure of, 233–34
  symbols in, 234
  tool use in, 163–64, 164*t*
  in US, 129–33, 130*t*
  work/play combinations, 31–32
chimpanzees, social play among, 75
  tool use and, 162
Chudacoff, Howard, 4
'chumships,' 186
classrooms
  children's play in, 238
  gender segregation in, 222
  negative climates in, 238
  play technology applications in, 326
  positive climates in, 238–39
The Cobblers (Sutton-Smith), 90
cognitive development
  children's play and, 239
  from games, 275–76
  games and, 265, 269–73
  playground games and, 269–73
  from social play, 202
  technology and play for, 327
cognitive immaturity hypothesis, 365
Coming, Peter, 114
commitment, from games, 277
communication
  in social bridge hypothesis, 75
  social play as, among nonhuman
      primates, 72
communicative musicality, 85
complementary play, 234
  social play development theory
      and, 241
complex social pretend play, 234
  social play development theory
      and, 241
computer games, 267–68
Computer Speech Lab (CSL), 290–91
conduct disorder, 205–6
conflict resolution
  from games, 277
  from social play, 59
constructive play, 10, 14, 189
  object play and, 154
contextualist theories, of play, 125–29
cooperation, from games, 277
cooperative social pretend play, 234
  social play development theory
      and, 241
Coplan, Rob, 5
'cops and robbers,' 263–64

Corsaro, Bill, 315
co-sleeping, 23
courtship
  among apes, social play as, 76
  play fighting within, 253–55
  play v., 9
Craske, Margaret, 94
Crosby, Mary, 104
cross-sex games, 270–71
Crosswell, T.R., 105
CSL. *See* Computer Speech Lab
Culin, Stewart, 105
cultural community, 231–36
  adult involvement in, 232
  caregiving within, 232
  children's play in, 231–36
  cross-cultural research on, 232–33
  definition of, 231–33
  socialization of social play
      within, 231–32
  theory of human development
      and, 231–33
cultural-ecological theory, for
      play, 125–29
  activities of interest in, 127
  context in, 128
  instantiation of culture in, 128
  methods in, 127–29
cultural ecology of play, 119–34
  anthropological approaches to, 122–23
  in Brazil, 120, 124–33, 131*t*
  contextualist methods for, 121–22
  contextualist theories in, 125–29
  cultural-ecological theory for, 125–29
  ethnographic approaches
      to, 119–20, 122
  ethologists and, 119–20
  in Kenya, 120, 124–25, 129–33, 131*t*
  mother–child play, 122
  neo-positivist methods for, 121
  non-positivist methods for, 121
  paradigms for, 121–23
  PPCT model for, 125
  in Senegal, 124
  in Six Cultures Study, 120
  study methods for, 121–23
  in US, 120, 123–24, 129–33, 130*t*
  Western theories for, 123
Cultural Ecology of Young Children
      project, 127
culture, play and, 19–34. *See also*
      parent–child play
  acculturation status, 21
  agricultural development and, 22–24
  assimilation and, 30
  belief systems about, 21–24
  caregiving and, 22
  causal models for, 21
  among children, 30–34
  conceptual issues with, 20–21
  concerted cultivation and, 21
  definitions within, 21
  differential opportunities in, 31–32

in different settings, 30–34
employment factors, 32
enculturation function, 31
in hunting-gathering
communities, 23–24
infant social contingency play
and, 87–88
maternal beliefs, 24
neighborhood characteristics for, 22
parent–child play, 19–30
physical play, 25–27
in playground games, 278–79
as reflection of adult activities, 30–31
in Six Culture study, 31–32
social pretend play and, influences
on, 298–300
symbolic, differences among, 53–55
theoretical frameworks for, 21
working models for, 22
work/play combinations in, 31–32

D

Damasio, Antonio, 112
primary/secondary emotions, 113*t*
Dancing in the Streets (Ehrenreich), 111
Darwin, Charles, 89–90, 112–13
Darwinism, human development and, 85
deferred adaptations, 155
defiant disorder, 205–6
depression, social play and, 204, 210
development. *See* human development,
play and
developmental scaffolding, 46
developmental theories, play in, 10
Dickinson, Emily, 86
direct instruction programs, 352–53
direct observational methods, in play
study, 140–41
*Direct Observation and Measurement of
Behavior* (Hutt/Hutt), 139
dispositions, children's play and, 239
distress, 206
double-knowledge, 297
Dream Days (Grahame), 90
Dungeons and Dragons, 304
dyads. *See also* peer groups
in children's play, 235
externalizing disorders within, 203–4
girls in, 217

E

ecology theory. *See also* cultural ecology
of play
for social play, among nonhuman
primates, 71
educational applications, technology
and play, 325–31
capacity models in, 329
children's imagination influenced
by, 327–29
in classrooms, 326
for cognition, 327
design for, 330–31

functional benefits of, 326
incidental learning in, 329
for language skills, 327
program content as factor, 328
resistance to, 326
selected studies for, 326–27
with video games, 329–30
educational policy, play in schools
and, 341–53, 364–65
cognitive immaturity hypothesis
and, 365
debates over, 341–42
with direct instruction
programs, 352–53
free play, 344–45, 347, 349–50
free play periods, 365
guided play and, 342–44, 347–51
historical development of, 341–42
"knowledge age," 341, 353
for language skills, 346–49
for literacy skills, 346–49
LOGO software programs, 345–46
for mathematics and science, 344–46
in Montessori schools, 351–52
pedagogical research for, 351–53
playful learning and, 343–44
state standards for, 342
with Tools of the Mind program, 352
educational theories, play in, 10
Ehrenreich, Barbara, 111
Eisen, George, 91
ELC program. *See* Emotion Literacy in
the Classroom program
elderly, technology and play for, 332–33
Eliot, T.S., 94–95
Elkind, David, 11
Emotion Literacy in the Classroom (ELC)
program, 350–51
emotion regulation, from social play, 59,
205–6
ADHD and, 206
arousability assessment and, 223–24
among boys, 223
among children, 233, 239
conduct disorder from, 205–6
defiant disorder from, 205–6
deficits in, 205
distress and, 206
gender segregation and, 221, 223–26
among girls, 223
HRV and, 224–27
hypothesized role of, 205
negative, 205–6
ostracism from, 205
social interactions and, 223–26
social rejection from, 205
emotions, play and, 112–14
antipathetical role of, 112–14
primary, 112
secondary, 112
strategy games and, 113
empathy, from social play, 59
emulation, 165

enculturation function, 31
Erikson, Erik, 91
European Americans, parent–child
play for, 23
evolution, of play, 44–46
adaptability drivers in, 45
"Baldwin effect," 45
as form of plasticity, 45–46
organic selection in, 45
evolutionary developmental psychology,
object play and, 154–55
deferred adaptations in, 155
ontogenetic adaptations in, 155
skeletal competencies in, 155
social signaling in, 155
executive control dysfunction, 313–15
exercise play, locomotor play and, 174–75
benefits of, 182
ethological studies of, 174
by gender, 175
MVPA, 175
during preschool period, 174
during primary school period, 174–75
exploratory behavior, as play, 353n1
The Expression of the Emotions in Man
(Darwin), 112–13
externalizing disorders, social play
and, 202–10
within dyads, 203–4
literature for, 207
peer relationships and, 203
solitary-active play and, 204
solitary play and, 204

F

facial expressions
for nonhuman primates, in social
play, 79
play and, 17
Fagen, Robert, 4
fairness, in play fighting, 245–47
among animals, 246–47
fantasy play
by gender, 267–68
mother–child, 284–94
within parent–child play, 24
fathers, parent–child play for, 25–26
with infants, 251
fear responses, play fighting and, 250
Fewell Play Scale, 311
fighting
as play, 15
play v., 9
Flannagan, William, 104
Four Quartets (Eliot), 94–95
Frame, Janet, 90
free play, 11
for language skills, 347
for literacy skills, 347
for mathematics and science, 344–45
organized v., 11
self-regulatory skills from, 349–50
for social skills, 349–50

friendship
  as affordances, 208–9
  biological adaptation of, 271
  playground games and, 269–70
  sex differences in, 270–73
  sociocultural factors for, 271
functional play, 189
  in autism, pretend play v., 310–11

G

games, 262–70. *See also* playground
    games, in schools
  appropriateness of, as
      peer-influenced, 266
  basic requirements of, for
      participants, 263
  among boys, 267–68
  cognitive development and, 265,
      269–73
  commitment from, development
      of, 277
  complexity of, increase in, 266
  computer, 267–68
  conflict resolution from, 277
  cooperation from, 277
  'cops and robbers,' 263–64
  cross-sex, 270–71
  by developmental stage, 265–69
  development of, 262–65
  ecological perspectives of, 264–65
  by gender, 265–68
  through generations, 268–69
  among girls, 267–68
  group identity from, 270
  'hide and seek,' 264
  intimacy as result of, 277
  language skills development from,
      275–76
  learning development from, 276–77
  in literature, 267
  marbles, 263
  during middle childhood, 265–66
  peer groups and, 269–73
  Piaget on, 264–65, 268
  play v., 262–64
  racing, 263
  reciprocity from, 277
  rules in, 262–63, 266
  school adjustment from, 276–77
  school belonging from, 277
  self-disclosure from, 277
  social-cognitive skills from, 275–76,
      278
  social groupings and, changing
      size of, 266
  as social objects, 262
  as social scaffold, 269–70
  in Spencer study, 266
  theoretical perspectives on, 264–65
  video games, 325
The Games of New Zealand Children
    (Pellegrini), 112
game theory models, 246

Gardiner, Amy, 4
gelada baboons, social play among, 75–76
  adult distribution within, 76
  OMUs and, 75–76
  play fighting as, 76f
gender
  arousability assessment by, 223–24
  cross-sex games, 270–71
  exercise play by, 175
  fantasy play by, 267–68
  friendship by, 270–73
  games by, 265–68
  HRV by, emotion regulation
      from, 225f
  locomotor play by, 173, 175–76
  nonsocial play by, 195–96
  object play by, 156–57, 163–64
  peer groups by, 270–73
  social interactions among children and,
      215–27
  technology play by, 324
  tool use by, 161–64, 164t
gender, social play by
  among bonobo apes, 78
  among children, 215–27
  among gorillas, 73
  object play and, 163–64
  role reinforcement through, 119
  tool use and, 164t
"gender enforcers," 216
gender segregation, 215–26
  activity levels and, 219
  in afterschool programs, 222
  from behavioral compatibility, 219–20
  in classrooms, 222
  cognitive explanations for, 220–21
  communication styles with, 219
  conflict resolution strategies and, 219
  development of, 215–17
  emotion regulation and, 221, 223–26
  evolutionary approaches to, 218–19
  explanations for, 217–22
  forms of influence with, 219
  future research for, 226–27
  "gender enforcers" for, 216
  by girls, 217
  homo-social norms and, 221
  individual differences in, 222–26
  institutional influences on, 221–22
  integrative approach to, 222
  level variability of, 216
  partner choice variations with, 217–18
  peer groups and, 221–22
  during preschool period, 216
  research data on, 222–23
  as resistant to change, 215
  rough-and-tumble play and, 221
  self-regulation and, 219
  "similarity-attraction" with, 221
  social network analytic techniques
      for, 219–20
  toy play and, 216–17
The Genesis of Animal Play (Burghardt), 111

genetics
  Gene X Environment, 59–60
  polymorphisms and, 63, 65
  for Rhesus macaques, social play
      influenced by, 62–63
  social play and, factors for, 59–65
Gene X Environment, 59–60
  in animal models, 60, 65
  in Rhesus macaques, 63–64
gestures, play and, 17
  among nonhuman primates, 79
Gilder, Jeannette Leonard, 104
girls, play for
  compromise among, 217
  in dyads, 217
  emotion regulation and, 223
  fantasy play, 267–68
  games in, 267–68
  gender segregation and, 217
  HRV and, emotion regulation
      from, 224–25
  pacification techniques with, 217
  in peer groups, hierarchical
      organization among, 273
  social conversation as, 268
  with tool use, 164t
  with toys, 217
  in US, 106
The Golden Age (Grahame), 90
Goldstein, Jeff, 6
Goodall, Jane, 84
Goodrich, Samuel, 103
gorillas, social play among, 72–75, 73f
  gender as influence on, 73–74
  play frequency for, 73
  size matching in, 74
  social contexts for, 73
Gould, Stephen Jay, 85, 94
Grahame, Kenneth, 90
grooming, among nonhuman primates, 75
group identity, from games, 270
guided play, 342–44
  adult guidance in, 343–44
  definition of, 344
  ELC program, 350–51
  for literacy skills, 347–49
  for mathematics and science, 345–46
  self-regulatory skills and, 350–51

H

Hagan, Theresa, 177
Handbook of Child Psychology, 3, 172, 262
Harris, Paul, 293
Havens, Catherine Elizabeth, 101–2
'Hawthorne effect,' 147
heart rate variability (HRV), emotion
    regulation from, 224–27
  among boys, 224–25
  distress and, 224
  by gender, 225f
  among girls, 224–25
  negative emotions and, 225, 226f
  software technology for, 224

Henricks, Thomas, 11
hide and seek, 264. *See also* peek-a-boo
The High Jump (Knox), 90
hostile attribution bias, 207–8
Howells, William Dean, 108
Howes, Carollee, 5
HRV. *See* heart rate variability, emotion regulation from
Huizinga, Johan, 13, 101–2
human development, play and, 83–98. *See also* infant social contingency play; musicality
   adaptability hypothesis for, 92
   during adulthood, 90–91
   behavioral-flexibility and, 83
   during bubblegum years, 90
   communicative musicality in, 85
   corollaries for, 96–97
   criteria for, 85
   Darwinism as influence on, 85
   ecology theories in, 93
   embodiment and, 93–96
   flexibility hypothesis for, 92
   future directions of, 97–98
   geographies as influence on, 85
   historical account of, 87
   hypotheses for, 91–96
   Implicit Function Theorem for, 94
   infant-mother contingency play, 96
   infant social contingency play, 87–88
   intersubjectivity in, 84, 93, 95–96
   kinetic melodies and, 93–96
   metaphors about, 85–86
   during middle infancy, 89–90
   milk availability and, 87
   moments of awareness in, 93–96
   musicality hypothesis for, 92–95
   nature-nurture dualism for, 84
   null hypothesis, 91–92
   play ethos and, 83
   rates of, 86–89
   rhythm in, 94–97
   scaffolding in, 86, 97–98
   science media reform for, 97–98
   scope of, 86
hunting, play v., 9
Hutt, Corinne, 139
Hutt, S.J., 139

I

imaginary companions, 302
imagination
   in social pretend play, 296–97
   technology and play as influence on, 327–29
Implicit Function Theorem, 94
infancy, play fighting during, with fathers, 251
"infant handling," among nonhuman primates, 75
infant-mother contingency play, 96
infant social contingency play, 87–88
   cross-cultural information on, 87–88

hypotheses of, 88
integrated play groups (IPGs), 316
interactive content, 233–34
   of social play, 235
internalizing disorders, social play and, 202–10
   depression and, 204, 209
   distress, 206
   parallel play and, 204
   solitary focused play and, 204
intersubjectivity, 52–53
   about metacommunication, 53
   construction of, 52
   in human development, for play, 84, 93, 95–96
   interpretive role of play, 54
   peer groups and, 52–53
   in scripts, 53
intimacy, from games, 277
IPGs. *See* integrated play groups

J

Job-related Affective Well-being Scale, 333
joking, as play fighting, 255
Jones, Blurton, 139, 142, 299
Jordan, Barbara, 106

K

Kavanaugh, Robert, 5, 293
Kenya, play in
   cultural ecology of, 120, 124–25
   observations of children's play, 129–33, 131*t*
key players, 274–75. *See also* agenda setters
'kingpins of the playground,' 274
"knowledge age," 341, 353
Knox, Elizabeth, 90
Kraus-Bolte, Maria, 101–2

L

language play, 10
language skills
   children's play and, 239
   educational policy for, with play, 346–49
   free play for, 347
   games and, as factor in development of, 275–76
   parent–child play and, 24
   for Piaget, 51
   role playing and, 303
   technology and play for, 327
   TELD measurements for, 303
large-motor play, 10
latency period, play during, 4, 102
leadership, playground games and, 273–76
learning development, from games, 276–77
lemurs, social play among, 77
   play fighting as, 77, 79

Levenson, Sam, 106
Lillard, Angeline, 5
Linguistic Word Count (LIWC), 290–91
literacy skills
   educational policy for, with play, 346–49
   free play for, 347
   guided play for, 347–49
litotes, 70
LIWC. *See* Linguistic Word Count
locomotor play, 172–83
   age trends in, 173, 175, 182
   animal models for, 247
   benefits of, 365
   cognitive effects of, 179–81
   definition of, 172–73
   deprivation studies for, 176–77
   dimensions of, 176
   endurance training for, 178–79
   ethological studies for, 178
   exercise play and, 174–75
   functional attributes of, 173
   functions of, 176–77
   by gender, 173, 175–76
   methodological approaches to, 181–82
   physical components of, 173
   physical training for, 177–79
   physiological development from, 177–78
   research on, 180, 182–83
   rhythmic stereotypies in, 174, 176–77, 182
   rough-and-tumble play and, 173
   scaffolding in, 176
   sex segregation and, 181–82
   social effects of, 181–82
   socialization pressures with, 181
   as social play, 173
   Surplus Energy Theory for, 179
LOGO software programs, 345–46
looks, in mother–child pretend play, 289
Lore and Language of School Children (Opie/Opie), 112

M

make-believe play, 10
Manual of Child Psychology, 363
marbles, 263
massive multiplayer online (MMO) game, 324
mastery play, 10
medical prefrontal cortex (mPFC), 249
mental play, 17
metacommunication, 53
metarepresentational thought, 297
   functional v. pretend play, 310–11
   in pretend play, 310–13
   in theory of mind, 310–13
Mickey Mouse Club, 107
middle childhood, games during, 265–66
middle infancy, play during, 89–90

MMO game. *See* massive multiplayer online game
moderate to vigorous physical activity (MVPA), 175
Montessori schools, educational policy in, 351–52
Morgan, Lloyd, 45
Morris, Desmond, 45
mother–child play, 284–94
  cultural ecology of, 122
  fantasy play, 284–94
mother–child pretend play, 29, 286–93. *See also* movement, in mother–child pretend play
  infant comprehension in, 292
  language in, 292–93
  looks in, 289
  mothers as spectators in, 287
  mothers' behaviors in, 288–93
  motor cues in, 293
  movements in, 289–93
  peers in, 287–88
  reenactments in, 287–88
  replica objects in, 287
  research on, 291–92
  scaffolding in, 286–87
  siblings and, 287–88
  smiles in, 288–89
  social referencing in, 291, 293
  solitary play v., 286–87
  sound effects in, 289
  voice pitch in, 286–87, 290–91
  Vygotsky on, 293–94
  word use in, 289
  Zone of Proximal Development and, 287
motivation, in theories of play, 42–43
movement, in mother–child pretend play, 289–93
  exaggeration in, 290
  pantomime, 289
  snack-related behaviors, 290, 292
mPFC. *See* medical prefrontal cortex
Muir, John, 104
musicality, 92–95. *See also* communicative musicality
  communicative, 85
  in human development, play and, 92–95
  rhythm and, 94–95
MVPA. *See* moderate to vigorous physical activity

N

Nabokov, Vladimir, 95, 97
negative emotions, 205–6
  HRV and, 225, 226*f*
Newcomb, Harvey, 104
"No Child Left Behind," 23
nonhuman primates, social play among, 70–80. *See also* apes, social play among; bonobo apes, social play among; gelada baboons, social play among; gorillas, social play among; social bridge hypothesis
  for apes, 76–79
  behavioral plasticity for, 71
  for bonobo apes, 78–79, 78*f*
  for chimpanzees, 75
  ecology theory for, 71
  facial displays in, 79
  for gelada baboons, 75–76
  gender as influence on, 73–74
  gestures in, 79
  for gorillas, 72–75, 73*f*
  grooming and, 75
  "infant handling" and, 75
  for lemurs, 77
  object play, 157–58
  playfighting as, 254–55
  during puberty, 71–75
  for Rhesus macaques, 60–64
  size-matching for, 74–75
  social bridge hypothesis, 75–79
  as social communication, 72
  social competence from, 71–72
  social signaling and, 72
  among spider monkeys, 72*f*
  for spider monkeys, 72*f*
  surplus resource theory for, 71
  tool use and, 162–63
non-literality, play and, 13
non-participant observational methods, in play study, 139–40
nonsexual play, among apes, 76–77
nonsocial play, 185–97. *See also* reticent behavior; solitary-active play; solitary-passive play
  'chumships' and, 186
  contextual differences for, 196–97
  definition of, 186
  developmental differences for, 195
  development of, 185–86
  disadvantages of, 187
  empirical studies of, 186
  by gender, 195–96
  historical perspectives for, 186
  methodological issues with, 194–95
  onlooking with, 188
  for peer groups, 186–87
  real world implications of, 197
  reticent behavior as, 189–91
  sampling techniques for, 194
  scale assessment of, 194
  shyness and, 196
  social context for, 186, 188
  social participation and, 188–89
  social withdrawal and, 187
  socio-emotional outcomes, 195
  solitary play v., 188
  solitude and, 187–88
  subtypes of, 186, 189–94
  theoretical perspectives for, 186
  unoccupied behaviors and, 188
null hypothesis, for human development and play, 91–92

O

object-oriented play. *See* object play
object play, 10, 153–58. *See also* evolutionary developmental psychology, object play and
  among animals, 247
  among children, 157, 163–64
  children's folk psychology and, 167
  constructive play and, 154
  definition of, 153–54
  evolutionary developmental psychology and, 154–55
  experiential learning for, 165–66
  exploration v., 154
  by gender, 156–57, 163–64
  in nonhuman primates, 157–58
  observational learning for, 165–66
  perception v. action with, 166–67
  social learning and, 165
  social pretend play and, 296
  tool use and, 163–64
observational methods, in play study, 138–48
  for aggression, 141–42
  behavior analysis, 146
  behavior drift in, 147
  categorization of, 138, 143–44
  constraint setting in, 140–41
  developmental differences in, 156–57
  direct, 140–41
  ethological methodology for, 138–39
  familiarization of, 142–43
  gender differences in, 156–57
  'Hawthorne effect' in, 147
  history of, 139–40
  measures of behavior in, 144–45
  in natural environments, 140–41
  with non-participants, 139–40
  observer effects in, 147
  parallel play, 144
  with participants, 139–40
  pilot work in, 142–43
  POS in, 143
  recording techniques, 144
  reliability of, 146–47
  sampling in, 145–46
  sequence analysis in, 148
  theoretical suppositions in, 142–43
  with tool use, 165–66
  validity of, 146–47
observer effects, 147
OFC. *See* orbital frontal cortex
one-male units (OMUs), 75–76
ontogenetic adaptations, 155
Opie, Iona, 112, 274
Opie, Peter, 112
orbital frontal cortex (OFC), 249
organized play, free v., 11
Osborne, Nigel, 97
ostracism, 205
Our Street (Sutton-Smith), 90

P

parallel play, 144
  internalizing disorders and, 204
parent–child physical play, 25–27
  child form attachments, 27
  purpose of, 26–27
parent–child play, 19–30. *See also* fathers,
    parent–child play for; mother–child
    play; mother–child pretend play;
    parent–child physical play;
    parent–child pretend play
  for African Americans, 22–23
  alloparenting and, 23
  among Asians, 23
  co-sleeping and, 23
  as culture-specific, 20
  ethno-theories about, 21
  among European Americans, 23
  fantasy play within, 24
  for fathers, 25–26
  language skills and, 24
  maternal cognitions in, 22–23
  modernization and, 19
  modes of, 24–30
  with non-parental figures, 25
  as object-mediated, 25
  peek-a-boo in, 28
  physical, 25–27
  pretend, 28–30
  for Puerto Ricans, 22–23
  in socialization models, 20
  stimulation activities for, 27–28
  universal claims of, 20
parent–child pretend play, 28–30
  adult initiation of, 28
  child initiation of, 28
  for mothers, 29
  peer group influence on, 28
  siblings and, 29
  socialization and, 29
participant observational methods, in play
    study, 139–40
"pay-for-play" sites, 107–8
peek-a-boo, 28
peer groups
  biological adaptation of, 271
  for boys, hierarchical organization
    among, 273
  children's play among, 231–41
  in different schools, 275
  externalizing disorders and, 203
  formation of, 235–36
  games among, changing size of, 266
  by gender, 270–73
  gender segregation and, 221–22
  for girls, hierarchical organization
    among, 273
  intersubjectivity and, 52–53
  membership in, 269
  mother–child pretend play and,
    287–88
  nonsocial play for, 186–87
  playground games and, 267, 269–73

psychological safety within, 279
  among Rhesus macaques, social play for,
    61–62
  size of, 272
  as socializing context, 272–73
  sociocultural factors for, 271
  in Spencer study, 272
  in US, history of play for, 105
  value system variability between, 275
Peer Play Scale, 233–34
Pellegrini, Anthony, 45–46, 83, 92, 112
Penn Interactive Peer Play Scale, 194
physical activity play, autism and, 311.
    See also locomotor play
physical play, 25–27. *See also* locomotor play
  object-mediated, 25
  parent–child, 25–27
  rough play as, 25
  among siblings, 26
Piaget, Jean, 48–56, 301
  conceptualization of play for, 49
  on games, 264–65, 268
  intersubjectivity and, 52–53
  language skills for, 51
  play as sociocultural activity, 51–52
  on pretend play, 284–86, 309
  symbolic play for, 48–56
play, 9–17. *See also* animal models, play
    in; children's play, as social play;
    culture, play and; games; locomotor
    play; nonsocial play; object play;
    observational methods, in play study;
    parent–child play; siblings, play with;
    symbolic play; technology, play and;
    theories, of play; tool use, play and
  ADHD as influence on, 11
  among animals, 10
  antipathies of, 110–14
  with arts, 10
  behavioral patterns of, 15, 17, 70–71
  bullying v., 9
  constructive, 10, 14, 189
  courtship v., 9
  criteria for, 4, 13–16
  cultural context of, 4
  definition of, 3–4, 9–10, 70–71
  developmental theories and, 10
  diversity of, 11–12
  educational policy and, 364–65
  educational theories and, 10
  ethology and, 12–13
  evolution of, 44–46
  exploratory behavior as, 353n1
  as expression of freedom, 101–2
  facial expressions and, 17
  fighting, 9, 15
  as form of plasticity, 45–46
  free, 11
  functional, 189
  games v., 262–64
  as gender role reinforcement, 119
  gestures in, 17
  good v. bad, 111–12

human development and, 83–98
  hunting v., 9
  imitation of adults in, 15
  immaturity and, 364
  language, 10
  large-motor, 10
  during latency period, of
    childhood, 4, 102
  in literature, 13
  litotes and, 70
  make-believe, 10
  mastery, 10, 15
  mental, 17
  motivation for, 277
  as nonfunctional, 111
  non-literality and, 13
  as non-obligatory, 4
  as non-survival based, 13–14
  as nonvoluntary, 111
  positive affect and, 13
  pretend, 15
  process classification for, 16–17
  real behavior v., 42–43
  recognition of, 12–13
  during "relaxed" states, 16
  repetition in, 15–16
  risk-taking, 10
  rough-and-tumble, 10
  rule-based, 10, 15
  in school, 10
  sensory, 10
  similar behaviors in, in definition of, 15
  small-motor, 10
  social, 10–11, 58–65
  as spontaneous, 14
  structural components of, 188–89
  study methodologies for, 4
  symbolic, 10, 189
  temporal limitations of, 14–15
  therapeutic theories and, 10
  as therapy, 12
  tool use and, 158–67
  types of, 10
  in US, history of, 101–8
  with word, 12
Play, Dreams, and Imitation (Piaget), 301
PlayBOT robot system, 333*f*
playdates, 196
play deprivation, 247–48
play ethos, 83, 353n2
play fighting, 245–52. *See also* rough-and-
    tumble play
  during adolescence, among boys, 255
  adult v. juvenile tactics in, 252
  affective states for, 251
  aggression regulation from, 79
  ambiguity in, 247
  in animal models, 247–55
  behavioral patterns in, 245–46
  bias in, 253
  within courtship, 253–55
  defense tactics in, 252
  evasion tactics in, 252

play fighting (*cont.*)
   fairness in, 245–47
   fear responses and, 250
   as form of metacommunication, 298
   in game theory models, 246
   among gelada baboons, 76*f*
   among humans, 255
   during infancy, 251
   joking as, 255
   among lemurs, 77, 79
   marital discord as influence on, for
      children, 251
   movement coordination with, 248
   among nonhuman primates, 72*f*,
      254–55
   in nonsexual contexts, 248
   pain stimuli and, 250
   partner-related modulation of, 253
   reciprocity and, 251
   serious v., 246
   in sexual contexts, 248
   for social advantage, 252–55
   social brain and, 247–52
   social complexity of, 254–55
   social integration as result of, 79
   in social pretend play, 298
   among spider monkeys, 72*f*
   teasing as, 255
playful learning, 343–44
   definition of, 343
playfulness, 20
playground games, in schools, 260–79
   agenda setters in, 274–75
   bullying and, 261–62
   cognitive development and, 269–73
   culture for, 278–79
   among ethnic groups, 270
   friendship and, 269–70
   historical development of, 261
   isolates in, 274
   'kingpins of the playground,' 274
   leadership and, 273–76
   peer groups and, 267, 269–73
   during recess, 261–62, 276–79
   research on, 261–62
   responders in, 274
   social status and, 273–76
   in Spencer study, 274–75
   teachers' views on, 279
   in UK, 261–62, 268–69
   in US, 106, 261–62
   youth violence and, 261
playmates, 102
Play Observation Scheme (POS), 143
play sites
   "pay-for-play," 107–8
   playgrounds, 106
   in US, history of, 102–4
play therapy, 12
POS. *See* Play Observation Scheme
positive affect, play and, 13
Power, Thomas, 83
PPCT model. *See* process-person-context-
      time model

preschool period, play during
   exercise play, 174
   gender segregation and, 216
   social interactions during, 214
   solitude during, 188
   tool use during, 161
Preschool Play Behavior Scale, 194
preteens. *See* bubblegum years, play during
pretend play, 15, 296–305. *See also*
      autism, pretend play in; fantasy play;
      mother–child pretend play; social
      pretend play; symbolic play
   action in, 285
   as affordance, 285
   in autism, 308–18
   as autistic behavior, 284
   children's play and, 234
   complex social, 234, 241
   cooperative social, 234, 241
   coordinated interaction and, 315–16
   criteria for, 284–85
   definition of, 284–85
   development of, 285–88
   functional play v., in autism, 310–11
   metarepresentational nature of, 310–13
   mother–child, 29, 286–93
   onset of, 286
   parent–child, 28–30
   Piaget on, 284–86, 309
   ritualization in, 285
   as secondary representation, 310
   shared, 316
   social context for, 286
   in social play development theory, 240
   symbolism in, 284
   theories of, 309–10
   theory of mind for, 310
   for Vygotsky, 49–50, 313
primary process play, 16
Primate Ethology (Jones), 139
process-person-context-time (PPCT)
      model, 125
public policy, theories of play and, 46
Puerto Ricans, parent–child play for, 22–23

R

racing games, 263
Ransome, Arthur, 90
recess, 276–79
   educational benefits of, 365
   intrinsic value of, 262
   playground games during, 261–62
reciprocal play, 234
   social play development theory and, 241
reciprocity, in children's play, 233
   from games, 277
   play fighting and, 251
repetition, in play, 15–16
representational abuse, 297
responders, 274
reticent behavior, 189–91
   approach-avoidance conflict and, 190
   conceptualization of, 189–90
   correlates of, 190–91

definition of, 189
frequency of, 190
outcomes of, 190–91
Rhesus macaques, social play among, 60–64
   agonistic behaviors, 61
   anxiety levels and, 62–63
   biological outcomes for, 64
   biological systems and, 63
   candidate gene approach to, 64
   care giving and, 62, 65
   deprivation of, 61, 64–65
   early experiences for, 61–62
   environmental stressors for, 62
   fear levels and, 62–63
   genetic influences on, 62–63
   Gene X Environment and, 63–64
   normative development of, 60–61
   among peer groups, 61–62
   prenatal stressors and, 63–64
   social competence from, 60
   stages of, 61
   'therapist monkeys' with, 61
   variations in temperament
      and, 62–63, 65
rhythm, 94–97
   in locomotor play, 174, 176–77, 182
   musicality and, 94–95
risk-taking play, 10
Robbins, Jerome, 95
Roberts, John M., 113
The Role of Play in Human Development
      (Pellegrini), 83
role playing, 301–3
   emotional cognition and, 303
   games, 304
   imaginary companions and, 302
   language skills and, 303
   in social pretend play, 301–2
   theory of mind and, 302
Roopnarine, Jaipaul, 4
rotational play, 10
rough-and-tumble play, 10, 245–55.
      See also play fighting
   autism and, 311
   distinctiveness of, 142
   gender segregation and, 221
   locomotor play and, 173
   observational methods for, 141–42
   as physical play, 25
   play fighting as, 245–52
   in Spencer study, 266
   as spontaneous, 245
rule-based play, 10, 15
   in games, 262–63

S

scaffolding
   during adult play, 91
   autism and, 311
   in children's play, 235
   developmental, 46
   games and, 269–70
   in human development, 86, 97–98
   in locomotor play, 176

in mother–child pretend play, 286–87
in theories of play, 46
schools. *See also* educational policy, play
in schools and; playground games,
in schools
playground activities in, 260–79
play in, 10
Schwartz, David, 5
scripts
intersubjectivity in, 53
with symbolic play, 54
secondary process play, 16
self-constructed play, 102
self-disclosure, from games, 277
self-regulatory skills
free play and, 349–50
guided play and, 350–51
Senegal, play in, 124
sensorimotor play, autism and, 311
sensory play, 10
sex cleavage. *See* gender; gender
segregation
shared pretend play, 316
sheltered-child model, 105
shyness, 196
siblings, play with
among children, 235
in Early America, 103
mother–child pretend play and, 287–88
parent–child pretend play and, 29
physical play among, 26
signaling. *See* social signaling
"similarity-attraction," 221
Simon, Kate, 108
simulation theory, 304–5
Singer, Dorothy, 304
Singer, Jerome, 304
Six Culture study, 31–32
in cultural ecology of play, 120
size matching, 74–75
among gorillas, for social play, 74
skeletal competencies, 155
slavery, play and, in US, 102–3
small-motor play, 10
smart toys, 323–25
smiles, in mother–child pretend
play, 288–89
social referencing, 291
Smith, Peter, 4, 83, 163, 172, 177
Smith, Robert Paul, 107
Smitty Does A Bunk (Sutton-Smith), 90
sociability, children's play and, 239
social brain, play fighting and, 247–52
development of, 249
mPFC development, 249
OFC development, 249
physical damage as influence
on, 248–49
play deprivation and, consequences
of, 247–48
structure of, 249
social bridge hypothesis, 75–79
communicative displays in, 75
grooming in, 75

social cognition, 206–8. *See also* social
competence
aggression and, 207
feedback loops with, 207
from games, skills
development, 275–76, 278
hostile attribution bias and, 207–8
information-processing with, 206
interpretation in, 206
maladaptive cognitive schema
and, 207–8
social competence, 58
children's play and, 233
among nonhuman primates, from social
play, 71–72
among Rhesus macaques, 60
social play and, 58, 233
social groups. *See* peer groups
social integration, from play fighting, 79
social interactions, among children,
214–26. *See also* dyads; peer groups
autism and, 309
emotion regulation and, 223–26
gender and, 215–27
gender segregation and, 215–26
partner selection variability and, 215
during preschool years, 214
rates of, 214–15
research history for, 214
social learning, object play and, 165
emulation in, 165
true imitation and, 165
social play, 10–11, 58–65. *See also*
children's play, as social play; externalizing disorders, social play and;
internalizing disorders, social play
and; nonhuman primates, social play
among; Rhesus macaques, social
play among; social play development,
theory of
ADHD and, 203–4
affective content of, 234–35
among animals, 247
autism and, 311
cognitive development from, 202
conflict resolution from, 59
within cultural community, 231–32
depression and, 204
development of, 58, 60–61
development theory, 231–40
emotion regulation from, 59, 205–6
empathy from, 59
externalizing disorders with, 202–10
as flexible, 58
free play and, 349–50
friendships and, 208–9
gender differences in, 59
genetic factors for, 59–65
Gene X Environment, 59–60
and group formation, 235–36
as intentional, 79
interactive content of, 235
internalizing disorders with, 202–10
locomotor play as, 173

among nonhuman primates, 70–80
Peer Play Scale for, 233–34
physical maturation from, 202
quality of, 58
quantity of, 58
among Rhesus macaques, 60–64
social acceptance and, 208–9
social climate of, 237–39
social cognition from, 206
social competence and, 58, 233
socialization from, 202
structure of, 233–34
social play development, theory
of, 231–40
attachment perspective in, 236–37
childcare programs and, 241
complementary play and, 241
complex social pretend play
and, 241
consequences of, 239–40
continuity in, 239
cooperative social pretend play
and, 241
within cultural community, 231–36
across domains, 240
pretend play in, 240
proto-narratives, 240
reciprocal play and, 241
research on, 240–41
in social policy, 240–41
social pretend play, 296–305
among animals, 297–98
anthropological studies for, 299
community values in, 299
cultural influences on, 298–300
definition of, 296–97
development of, 300–303
after early childhood, 303–4
features of, 297
imagination in, 296–97
intellectual development from, 299
metarepresentational thought
and, 297
during middle childhood, 304
object play and, 296
parental beliefs about, 299–300
play fighting in, 298
properties of, 297
representational abuse in, 297
role play in, 301–2
simulation theory and, 304–5
social development from, 299
theory of mind in, 301–3
social referencing
in mother–child pretend play, 293
smiles, 291
social referencing smiles, 291
social signaling, 72
in evolutionary developmental
psychology, 155
social status, playground games and,
273–76
popularity and, 274
social withdrawal, 187. *See also* solitude

solitary-active play, 191–92
  characteristics of, 191
  conceptualization of, 191–92
  correlates for, 192
  externalizing disorders and, 204
  outcomes for, 192
  social context for, 192
solitary focused play, 204
solitary locomotor play, 10
solitary-passive play, 192–94
  approach-avoidance conflicts
    and, 193
  characteristics of, 193
  conceptualization of, 193
  correlates for, 193–94
  outcomes for, 193–94
  unsociability and, 193
solitary play. *See also* solitary-active play;
    solitary-passive play
  ADHD and, 204
  externalizing disorders and, 204
  mother–child pretend play v., 286–87
  nonsocial play v., 188
solitude, 187–88
  during adolescent period, 188
  benefits of, 187–88
  during preschool period, 188
The Songlines (Chatwin), 93
sound effects, in mother–child pretend
    play, 289
Spalding, Douglas, 45
Spencer, Ethel, 105
Spencer study, 266
  antisocial behaviors in, 266
  peer groups in, 272
  playground games in, 274–75
  rough-and-tumble play in, 266
spider monkeys, play fighting among, 72f
spontaneous play, 14
  autism in, 308–9, 316
  pretend, 14
  rough-and-tumble, 245
Stamps, Judith, 179
Stern, Daniel, 90, 95
strategy games, 113
Surplus Energy Theory, 179
Surplus Resource Theory, 363
  for social play, among nonhuman
    primates, 71
Sutton-Smith, Brian, 11, 84, 90, 111, 173
Swallows and Amazons (Ransome), 90
symbolic play, 10, 48–56, 189, 309
  cultural differences in, 53–55
  definition of, 48–49
  education and, role in, 55
  as intersubjective, 52–53
  among legitimate peripheral partici-
    pants, 54
  long-term outcomes of, 56
  negotiations during, 52
  scripts with, 54
  as social, 52
  social organization and, 54

*Symbolic Play: The Development of Social
    Understanding* (Bretherton), 286
symbolism, in pretend play, 284
symbols, in children's play, 234

T
Tarkington, Booth, 90
Teacher Behavior Rating Scale, 194
teasing, as play fighting, 255
technology, play and, 322–34. *See also*
    educational applications, technology
    and play
  ADHD and, 332
  biofeedback applications of, 332
  children's imagination influenced
    by, 327–29
  content as influence on, 328
  demographic studies on, 323–24
  development of, 323–25
  educational applications of, 325–31
  for elderly, 332–33
  gender as influence on, 324
  health applications for, 331, 332f
  MMOs, 324
  smart toys, 323–25
  for special needs populations, 331–32
  studies of, 333–34
  user-generated content and, 323
  video games, 325
  in workplace, 333
TELD. *See* Test of Early Language
    Development
temperament, social play and. *See also*
    emotion regulation, from social play
  arousability and, 227
  contextual factors for, 227
  among Rhesus macaques, 62–63, 65
  self-regulation and, 227
tertiary process play, 16–17
Test of Early Language Development
    (TELD), 303
Thelen, Esther, 174
theories, of play, 41–46. *See also* Piaget,
    Jean; Vygotsky, Lev
  behavioral biology and, 42–43
  evolution in, 44–46
  of motivation, 42–43
  naming issues in, 41–42
  prevailing conditions in, 43
  projection in, 41–42
  public policy and, 46
  scaffolding in, 46
  utility in, 43–44
theory of human development, 231–33
theory of mind, 301–3
  metarepresentational thought
    in, 310–13
  for pretend play, 310
  role play and, 302
  TELD measurement for, 303
therapeutic theories, play in, 10
'therapist monkeys,' 61
Thurston, Brown, 104

Tools of the Mind program, 352
tool use, play and, 158–67
  action planning in, 160
  affordances and, 159–60
  categorization of, 160
  causal structures in, 159–60
  children's folk psychology and, 167
  children's play and, 163–64, 164t
  "design stance" with, 160
  development of, 158–59
  evolutionary history of, 158–59
  experiential learning for, 165–66
  functional fixedness with, 160
  by gender, 161–64, 164t
  modes of, 164–67
  in nonhuman primates, 162–63
  object play and, 163–64
  observational learning for, 165–66
  perception v. action with, 166–67
  during preschool years, 161
toys. *See also* technology, play and
  aggression and, 217
  for boys, 217
  craze for, 270
  gender segregation and, 216–17
  for girls, 217
  mass production of, 105, 107
  smart, 323–25
  in US, in history of play, 104–5
Toys and Reasons (Erikson), 91
true imitation, 165
Twain, Mark, 102

U
UK. *See* United Kingdom, play in
United Kingdom (UK), play in
  among mixed gender groups, 271–72
  playground games in, 261–62, 268–69
United States, history of play in, 101–8
  during 1800s, 103–6
  Baby Boom as influence on, 107
  birth rates as influence on, 104–6
  for boys, 106
  childhood freedom and, 105–6
  commercialization of, 107–8
  cultural ecology for, 120, 123–24
  death rates as influence on, 102
  in Early America, 102–3
  future directions for, 108
  for girls, 106
  golden age of, 106–7
  as "idling," 103
  labor patterns as influence on, 103–4
  materials for, 102, 103
  among mixed gender groups, 271–72
  observations of children's
    play, 129–33, 130t
  for peer groups, 105
  on playgrounds, 106, 261–62
  "play instinct," 106
  playmates and, 102
  play sites, 102–4
  during Progressive Era, 106

as "rambling," 103
safety policies for, 107
self-constructed v.
   adult-constructed, 102
sex-segregation in, 106
sheltered-child model, 105
with siblings, 103
slavery and, 102–3
in suburban areas, 108
toys, 104–5
unsociability, 193
utility theories, of play, 43–44

V

Van Valen, Leigh, 84
video games, 325, 329–30
   educational applications for, 329–30
   mood management from, 325
   space applications for, 333
   visual perception benefits from, 330

voice pitch, in mother–child pretend
   play, 286–87, 290–91
   CSL measurements, 290–91
   LIWC analysis, 290–91
Vollstedt, Ralph, 172
von Balthasar, Hans-Urs, 95
Vygotsky, Lev, 48–56
   act of representation for, 49–51
   intersubjectivity and, 52–53
   on mother–child pretend
      play, 293–94
   play as sociocultural activity, 51–52
   pretend play for, 49–50, 313
   symbolic play for, 48–56
   on Zone of Proximal
      Development, 49–50, 55

W

Weisner, Tom, 126
Wilson, E.O., 3, 154

word play, 12
   in mother–child pretend play, 289
work, play and, 31–32
   capital theory in, 32
   for children, 31–32
   gender influences on, 32
   integration of, 32
workplace, technology and play in, 333
   Job-related Affective Well-being
      Scale, 333
Wright, Henry, 104
Wundt, Wilhelm, 123

Y

Yeats, William Butler, 94

Z

Zone of Proximal
   Development, 49–50, 55
   mother–child pretend play and, 287